Charles S. Peirce
Logic of the Future Volume 1

Peirceana

Edited by
Francesco Bellucci and Ahti-Veikko Pietarinen

Volume 1

Charles S. Peirce
Logic of the Future

Writings on Existential Graphs
Volume 1: History and Applications

Edited by
Ahti-Veikko Pietarinen

DE GRUYTER

ISBN 978-3-11-077752-9
e-ISBN (PDF) 978-3-11-065140-9
e-ISBN (EPUB) 978-3-11-064962-8
ISSN 2698-7155

Bibliographic information published by the Deutsche Nationalbibliothek
The Deutsche Nationalbibliothek lists this publication in the Deutsche Nationalbibliografie;
detailed bibliographic data are available on the Internet at http://dnb.dnb.de.

© 2021 Walter de Gruyter GmbH, Berlin/Boston
This volume is text- and page-identical with the hardback published in 2020.
Printing and binding: CPI books GmbH, Leck

www.degruyter.com

Acknowledgments

The work on the three volumes of *Logic of the Future* has taken fifteen years to complete. This means a considerable number of people and sources of support have accumulated over the years that are to be acknowledged and deeply thanked for their respective contributions.

An edition on Peirce's graphical logic was conceived during the class I gave at the University of Helsinki on *Peirce's Logic and Philosophy* in autumn 2004. At that time, it became obvious to me that Peirce's logic can never be adequately studied, let alone deeply researched, understood and put into an informed perspective within the history of ideas, when there is a nearly total absence of sources to expose it in full details.

It was the students of that class of 2004 that ignited the work on the present volumes. Its 20-odd students, including Jukka Nikulainen, Henrik Rydenfelt, Lauri Snellman, Lauri Järvilehto, Michael von Boguslawski, Harry Alanen, Peter Schulman and many others, provided initial assistance in manuscript inspection and transcription as part of the course assessment. 'Useless skills', current university management would say; fond of standardised syllabi, rubrics, grading drills and quick flow-through rates, a work that aims at slow editions of old texts is not seen as the world's first priority.

There is one person without whom this edition would not have been possible to be produced at all. My long-term research assistant, Jukka Nikulainen, who has served as a technical editor of these three volumes and has provided the first-ever LaTeX package (EGpeirce) by which one can now typeset any graph, special mark or symbol that ever emanated from Peirce's hand, with ease and uniformity. Jukka also encoded a large majority of the hundreds of complex graphs that appear in these three volumes, improving the package along the way and adding new features to it. We believe that by now everything that Peirce ever designed and wanted to design as a special graph, type, character, mark or sign—a plethora of his typographical eccentricities notwithstanding—have been incorporated into the functionality of the Peirce LaTeX package. And much more is available in it than is in fact needed for the purposes of compiling the present editions. Peirce's ethics of notation dictates that pieces of notation are just as important as the prose overall, and that whenever new notation is introduced, reasons for it are not to be taken lightly. Design and typesetting practices have to follow suit, and indeed Jukka has considerably assisted the production of the CRCs of these volumes for the press, honing the notations and checking many of the transcriptions as I slowly progressed with them. He has also searched and compiled information on many of Peirce's references as well as prepared both the index of names and the index of words. Nikulainen, above all, deserves to be acknowledged as having done an amount of work vastly exceeding anything that is to be expected of a technical editor—probably years rather than months since 2004—in order to bring the edition into its present shape.

Claudia Cristalli also went out of her way in helping to bring the edition into its near-completion. Without her many suggestions and concrete advice on organisation and presentation of the material, the progress on these volumes might have slouched altogether. In particular, she gave valuable proposals on organising the editorial, introductory and survey parts.

Francesco Bellucci deserves an equally immeasurable gratitude for pressing on with finalising these volumes. Not only did he check many of the items and transcriptions but also closely researched their content, coming up with important perspectives concerning their interpretation. The three volumes and their editorial introductions have benefitted enormously from our scholarly collaboration over the last five years.

Marc Champagne and Liu Xinwen have followed the progress of this project over the years. Both have provided a number of comments and corrections on the introductory parts, and deserve a special thanks for having performed such laborious deeds.

An equally special thanks for the reader's drudgery also go to Gary Furhman, Jeffrey Brian Downard and Jon Schmidt, who have checked and proof-read the material in Parts I, II and III, respectively. A number of mistakes has been eliminated thanks to the careful reading of the selections. A number of others that inevitably remain will be of the sole responsibility of the editor.

These editions would probably have not seen the light of day had it not been for the enthusiasm and intellectual support of Nathan Houser, with whom I regularly conversed on the prospects of such a work ever since my stay at the Peirce Edition Project in the autumn of 2005 as a post-doctoral Fulbright grantee. It is thanks to Nathan's vocal accentuation on the importance of bringing about a thematic edition on graphs, and above all the unprecedented scholarship that he represents in the Peirce community, that have kept me going with the work. André De Tienne, Director of the Peirce Edition Project, has been equally supportive of the enterprise from the get-go. Conversations with him have supplied vital links and clues by which one could go about navigating the amazing mazes that the literary output of this American mind puts before us.

Over the years, John Sowa, Matthew Moore and Helmut Pape have all provided experienced advice, John on the topical relevance of Peirce's graphical logic, and Matt and Helmut on the challenges of editing Peirce's papers for a thematic collection. Susan Haack has followed the project with interest, and I do not doubt that any new material that might be found in these texts would only support the conclusions she has already arrived at.

My first graduate class on Peirce was given by Risto Hilpinen, who taught logic and philosophy of science at the University of Turku in early 1990s and who was the first to notice that Peirce had arrived at surprisingly similar semantic and logical ideas as others did much later, in particular the game-theoretical semantics independently discovered by Jaakko Hintikka in the 1960s. I am honoured to have an opportunity of including an Introductory Note from Prof. Hilpinen to the first volume of this edition.

Discussions with the late Jaakko Hintikka in 2000–2015 on Peirce's logic have enabled me to put many of the related contributions into a sharper perspective. "Peirce—miles ahead of Frege in logic and in the philosophy of mathematics", he once told me. The similarities between Hintikka's and Peirce's philosophies are indeed quite striking (Pietarinen 2018), but can be explained by the similarities in the methods of logic and the significance placed on having good logical notations, the relational apparatus of thought, the value placed on proofs, and the semantic (or model-theoretic, semeiotic, notational) outlook on one's philosophical investigations. Both Peirce and Hintikka had put scientific and human inquiry ahead of bare epistemology: both advocated an *action-first* epistemology. That there is reality and truth in such philosophy is reflected in the comment I once received from Jaakko on my presentation that explored connections between the two thinkers. I had suggested that the sheer number of them makes one almost believe in reincarnation, to which he replied: "Yes, but who incarnated whom?"

Discussions with my father, who together with Risto Hilpinen were Hintikka's first doctoral students in philosophy, helped to clarify several conceptions that relate Peirce to philosophical classics, including Spinoza, Kant, Plato and Aristotle. This volume is dedicated to the memory of my parents.

Along the way, Arnold Oostra and Fernando Zalamea provided valuable advice on both the general conception of the edition as well as on the details of Peirce's graphical notation. Zalamea encouraged me to pursue a resolutely comprehensive rather than a critical and limited collation of texts; his answer to my enquiry on what should be included in an edition about Peirce's graphs was, "Everything!" As usual he was right; Peirce's organic gardening is too precious to be cut off at any branch or ligature, as it may be just another verso of his folios that has the mutation needed for the germinal idea to evolve into a substantially new insight.

I have space left only to enlist a number of colleagues and Peirce scholars who have contributed to the edition either by way of advancing the research on Peirce's graphical logic or explicitly concerning the edition: Christina Barés Gomez, Reetu Bhattarchajee, Angelina Bobrova, Daniele Chiffi, Matthieu Fontaine, Juuso-Ville

Gustafsson, Jelena Issajeva, Ma Minghui, Amirouche Moktefi, Marika Proover and Frederik Stjernfelt. They are all to be thanked for having provided important suggestions during our workshops and Peirce Seminars held at the Tallinn University of Technology.

In addition, Jean-Marie Chevalier and Benoit Gaultier have helped with correcting the transcriptions of the letters Peirce wrote in French (LoF 3). Both have provided helpful comments on the edition at various stages of its development.

Over these 15 years, several personal research grants have been instrumental in supporting and sustaining the work on the present edition. They are, in reverse chronological order: Higher School of Economics, HSE University Basic Research Program (*Russian Academic Excellence Project '5-100'*, 2018–2020); Nazarbayev University (*Social Policy Grant*, 2018–2019); Estonian Research Council (*Abduction in the Age of Fundamental Uncertainty*, 2013–2018); Academy of Finland (*Logic and Games*, 2003–2005; *Diagrammatic Mind (DiaMind): Logical and Cognitive Aspects of Iconicity*, 2013–2017); Chinese Academy of Social Sciences (*Peirce's Pragmaticism*, 2006; 2016); Joan Nordell Houghton Library Fellowship of Harvard University (*Peirce's Manuscripts on Logic*, 2011–2012); University of Helsinki Excellence in Research Grant (*Pragmaticism and Its Contemporary Applications*, 2006–2009); Kone Foundation (*Peirce's Scientific and Philosophical Correspondence*, 2008); The Jenny and Antti Wihuri Foundation (*Pragmatic Theories of Meaning*, 2007); ASLA–Fulbright Foundation (*Peirce's Manuscripts on Logic*, 2005), and Finnish Cultural Foundation (*Peirce's Scientific and Philosophical Correspondence*, 2005). These sources of support are gratefully acknowledged. In particular, the staff at Harvard's Houghton Library and curator Leslie Morris are to be thanked for their invaluable assistance during my frequent visits to the library over the years to inspect the Peirce collection.

The publisher's team Christopher Schirmer, Tim Vogel and Jana Habermann have seen through the final preparation of the edition. It is only appropriate that Peirce's late works on logic appear with the same publisher as Peirce's late works on mathematics (*New Elements of Mathematics*, NEM I–IV) did nearly half a century ago.

The title "Logic of the Future" comes from Peirce's 1909 Christmas Day letter to William James. That letter also explains Peirce's bequest to have his work appear in places that will, first and foremost, advance inquiry and not the sham and fake reasoning that he saw plaguing scholarly minds of his time—and surely something that did not disappear from academia during the century that followed. Only then—only in addition to the advancement of inquiry—one may recognise the value of ideas as those that their author has instigated along the way:

> Now when I die, I want proper justice done to my memory as to these things. Not at all that they are any credit to me, but simply that, by being made to appear considerable, they may invite attention and study, when I think they will do considerable good. For logic and exact reasoning are a good deal more important than you are able to see that they are. So I hope that some account of my work may appear in some publication that people will look into, and not solely in the Biographical memoirs of the National Academy of Sciences. (CSP to WJ, December 25, 1909)

Soon after Peirce mentions the "pressing questions of our time" (R 678, 1910). He wanted to resolve them by an application of logic and reasoning. Those questions have not gone away. They can be dispelled only by a collective improvement in the art of reasoning. Everyone involved in advancing the present project has done "considerable good" towards that end.

Abbreviations of Peirce's Works and Archives

Archives:

R = *The Charles S. Peirce Papers, 1787–1951*. Manuscripts in the Houghton Library of Harvard University, as identified by Richard Robin, *Annotated Catalogue of the Papers of Charles S. Peirce*, Amherst: University of Massachusetts Press, 1967, and in "The Peirce Papers: A Supplementary Catalogue", *Transactions of the Charles S. Peirce Society* 7, 1971, pp. 37–57. Peirce's manuscripts and letters are available, in part, in *The Charles S. Peirce Papers, Microfilm Edition*, Thirty Reels with Two Supplementary Reels Later Added. Cambridge: Harvard University Library Photographic Service, 1966.[1]

HUA = *Harvard University Archives*. Pusey Library, Harvard University.

WJP = *The William James Papers*. Houghton Library, Harvard University.

CLF = *Christine Ladd Franklin and Fabian Franklin Papers*. Butler Library, Rare Books and Manuscripts Collection, Columbia University.

VW = *Lady Victoria Alexandrina Maria Louisa Welby fonds*, York University Archives and Special Collections.

Edited Collections:

SiL = *Studies in Logic, by Members of the Johns Hopkins University*. Edited by Charles S. Peirce, Boston: Little, Brown, and Company, 1883. Reissued as a facsimile reprint in *Foundations of Semiotics*, Volume 1, with introductory essays by Achim Eschbach and Max H. Fisch. Amsterdam: John Benjamins, 1983.

DPP = *Dictionary of Philosophy and Psychology*. Three volumes. Edited by James Mark Baldwin, 1901–1902. New York & London: The Macmillan Company.

CLL = *Chance, Love and Logic: Philosophical Essays*. Edited by Morris Cohen, with a supplementary essay on the pragmatism of Peirce by John Dewey. London: Kegan Paul, 1923.

CP = *The Collected Papers of Charles S. Peirce*, 8 volumes. Edited by Charles Hartshorne, Paul Weiss and Arthur W. Burks. Cambridge: Harvard University Press, 1931–1958. Referred to by volume and paragraph number.

---

[1] The microfilm edition is electronically available at https://rs.cms.hu-berlin.de/peircearchive/ Most manuscript and typescript sheets, notebooks and other material from the Harvard Peirce Papers are included in this microfilm edition, but only a minor part of letters and correspondence was included.

PWP = *The Philosophy of Peirce: Selected Writings*. Edited by Justus Buchler. New York: Harcourt, Brace and Company, 1940. Reissued as *Philosophical Writings of Peirce*, Dover, 1955.
CN = *Charles Sanders Peirce: Contributions to The Nation*. Four volumes. Edited by Kenneth Laine Ketner and James Edward Cook. Lubbock, TX: Texas Technological University Press, 1975–1987.
NEM = *The New Elements of Mathematics by Charles S. Peirce*. Four volumes. Edited by Carolyn Eisele. The Hague: Mouton De Gruyter, 1976.
SS = *Semiotic and Significs: The Correspondence between C. S. Peirce and Victoria Lady Welby*. Edited by Charles S. Hardwick with the assistance of James Cook. Bloomington and Indianapolis, IN: Indiana University Press, 1977.
P = *A Comprehensive Bibliography and Index of the Published Works of Charles Sanders Peirce*, with a Bibliography of Secondary Studies. Ketner, Kenneth Laine et al., (eds.). Greenwich: Johnson Associates, 1977. Second edition, *A Comprehensive Bibliography of the Published Works of Charles Sanders Peirce*, Bowling Green, OH: Philosophy Documentation Center, 1986.
W = *Writings of Charles S. Peirce: A Chronological Edition*. Seven volumes. Edited by Max H. Fisch, C. J. W. Kloesel, et al. and the Peirce Edition Project. Bloomington and Indianapolis, IN: Indiana University Press, 1982–2009.
WMS = Manuscripts as cataloged by the Peirce Edition Project, in W.
HP = *Historical Perspectives on Peirce's Logic of Science: A History of Science*. Two volumes. Edited by Carolyn Eisele. Berlin, New York and Amsterdam: Mouton De Gruyter, 1985.
RLT = *Reasoning and the Logic of Things: The Cambridge Conference Lectures of 1898*. Edited by Kenneth Laine Ketner. Cambridge, Mass.: Harvard University Press, 1992.
EP 1 = *The Essential Peirce: Selected Philosophical Writings*. Volume 1 (1867–1893). Edited by Nathan Houser and Christian J. W. Kloesel. Bloomington and Indianapolis, IN: Indiana University Press, 1992.
PPM = *Pragmatism as a Principle and Method of Right Thinking: The 1903 Harvard "Lectures on Pragmatism"*. Edited by Patricia Ann Turrisi. Albany, NY: State University of New York Press, 1997.
EP 2 = *The Essential Peirce: Selected Philosophical Writings*. Volume 2 (1893–1913). Edited by the Peirce Edition Project. Bloomington and Indianapolis, IN: Indiana University Press, 1998.
LoI = *Charles S. Peirce: The Logic of Interdisciplinarity. The Monist Series*. Edited by Elize Bisanz. Berlin: Akademie Verlag, 2009.
PoM = *Philosophy of Mathematics: Selected Writings*. Edited by Matthew E. Moore. Bloomington and Indianapolis, IN: Indiana University Press, 2010.

ILoS = *Illustrations of the Logic of Science, by Charles Sanders Peirce.* Edited by Cornelis de Waal. Chicago: Open Court, 2014.

LoF = *Charles S. Peirce: Logic of the Future. Writings on Existential Graphs.* Edited by Ahti-Veikko Pietarinen. Three volumes. Volume 1: *History and Applications,* 2019. Volume 2: *The 1903 Lowell Lectures,* 2020. Volume 3: *Pragmaticism and Correspondence,* 2020. Berlin and Boston: Mouton De Gruyter.

Introductory Note

Charles S. Peirce was one of the most creative and innovative philosophers of the late 19th and early 20th century. He is known as the founder of American pragmatism, a general philosophical view which he in his later years preferred to call "pragmaticism" to distinguish it from the doctrines propounded by his followers and imitators who, according to Peirce, had "kidnapped" the word 'pragmatism'. He had wide interests, and his pragmaticism permeated his work in many areas of philosophy: logic, semiotics and the philosophy of language, philosophy of science, and metaphysics.

In the 1880s Peirce developed independently of Gottlob Frege a system of quantification theory in which quantifiers were treated as variable binding operators; thus he can be regarded, alongside Frege, as a founder of contemporary formal logic. The standard notation used in contemporary logic is a variant of Peirce's notation rather than that adopted by Frege. As a part of his pragmatic theory of meaning, Peirce developed a game-theoretical interpretation of logical constants, according to which their meaning is explained by means of a semantical zero-sum game between two parties, an utterer and an interpreter. Peirce also studied modal and many-valued logics, and developed the basic ideas of the possible-worlds semantics for modal logic. In his general theory of reasoning Peirce distinguished three main forms of reasoning, namely abduction, deduction, and induction, and revised the traditional account of non-deductive reasoning. In his work in general semiotics (the theory of signs) and the philosophy of language, he analyzed the sign relation as a triadic relation involving a sign, an interpretant (meaning), and an object, and introduced the distinction between types and tokens into linguistics and the philosophy of language. He made a distinction between iconic, indexical, and symbolic signs, and outlined an account of proper names as "directly referential" indexical signs. Peirce developed a complex classification of signs involving several interpretants and objects, and his rich semiotic system provides a useful framework for the comparison of semiotic theories from the Stoics to the present. He anticipated many significant developments in the later 20th century analytic philosophy and logic.

In the 1890s Peirce reformulated quantification theory by expressing it in a language of diagrams which he called *existential graphs*. The switch from the algebraic notation to the language of graphs seems to have been motivated by his belief that the latter was more suitable for the purposes of logical analysis. According to Peirce, a system of logic can be used as a calculus which helps to draw inferences as economically as possible, or it can be developed for the purpose of representing and analyzing deductive processes. Peirce also thought that a graphical notation was more suitable for logical analysis than an algebraic notation because of its higher degree of *iconicity*. An iconic sign can be said to show what it means in the sense that it resembles its objects in some respect, that is, some features of the sign itself determine its interpretation. Peirce himself regarded the theory of existential graphs as one of his most important contributions to logic and philosophy.

Peirce presented his theory of existential graphs in many papers which also discussed various philosophical topics in semiotics and the philosophy of language. Much of this material remained unpublished during his lifetime, and some scholars became acquainted with it by studying his manuscripts. On the other hand, Peirce was able to get some of these works published, for example, his work *A Syllabus of Certain Topics of Logic* was published by Alfred Mudge & Son, Boston, 1903, and the long paper "Prolegomena to an Apology for Pragmaticism" appeared in the philosophical journal *The Monist* in 1906. However, Peirce's contemporaries ignored these works, perhaps because they were not able to see them as significant contributions to logic and philosophy. It might be said that Peirce was ahead of his times; his work on existential graphs began to receive serious attention only in the 1960s.

The three books of the *Logic of the Future* series are the first comprehensive collection of Peirce's writings on existential graphs, especially his previously unpublished writings and unpublished variants of published works. Peirce had the habit of rewriting the same work several times, and the versions often differ from each other in interesting ways. Prof. Ahti-Veikko Pietarinen has performed a valuable service to all students of Peirce's logic and philosophy by making this material easily accessible in book form.

Risto Hilpinen
University of Miami, Coral Gables

Foreword

This is the first volume in the series of three books on Charles Sanders Peirce's writings on Existential Graphs (EGs), the theory which he predicted to be "the Logic of the Future". These editions aim at being both inclusive and resourceful. I have attempted to maximise the amount of alternative versions, incomplete drafts and page fragments that one can gather from Peirce's enormous *Nachlass* of over 100 000 surviving pages, while minimising the reader's effort when following his spawning lines of thought and bursts of brilliant insights. The reader will, just as the editor has, despair over the writings that have frequent break-offs, discontinuities and aberrations; explorations left soberly unfinished and rhizomic, while well aware that so many of the now-lost pages and forgotten thoughts were once around to fill in the blanks. I hope to share with the reader the view that the numerous alternative versions, even when superficially repetitive, idiosyncratic or seemingly superseded by parallel or later attempts, are all too precious to be left out; too "gravid with young truth" to remain forever undisclosed from the eyes of posterity. If they won't appear in the present edition, chances are that much of that material would never find its way to print.

To wit, let us take to the heart the following passage as an example of such a variant:

> We have only to turn our attention for one moment to a relative term to see that the account given in the logic-books of the composition of concepts is entirely inadequate. The present writer showed the true mode of composition in the seventh volume of *The Monist* by means of graphs. But immediately after that publication he discovered another much better system of graphs, making the whole matter perfectly clear. But he has in vain endeavoured to persuade some journal, academy, or institution to print a sufficient account of it. The time will come when the world will be amazed at this; but then Newton's *Principia* would not have been printed yet if Edmund Halley had not been a very different sort of man from those upon whom publication depends in the United States at this day. (R 280, Alt. pp. 19–20, *The Basis of Pragmatism*, late 1904; LoF 3)[2]

The main purpose of the three volumes of the *Logic of the Future* is to facilitate advancement of inquiry on what has remained one of the most neglected topics in the study of Peirce's thought, the logic of graphs and their role in the eventual com-

---

[2] The reference R is to the Charles Sanders Peirce papers deposited at Houghton Library, Harvard University, as listed and catalogued by Richard S. Robin. See "Abbreviations for Peirce's Works and Archives" at the end of the General Introduction for the standard references to the archives, collections and editions of Peirce's work. When the material appears in the present three-part edition of the *Logic of the Future* (LoF for short), a reference to Volumes 1–3 is given.

pletion of his mature logic and philosophy. This oversight shows up in previous editions of his works, which occasionally but quite routinely have left the graphical account out of the picture. Technical limitations are understandable, but the inevitable consequence has been that his favourite method of analysis became unduly suppressed from the perspectives one hopes to gain over the maturation of his later thought, leading to a de-emphasis of the manifold contributions Peirce calculated logical graphs to make towards erecting a fully articulated, architectonic scientific philosophy.

These three volumes on Peirce's logic of graphs should be viewed only as the beginnings of a renewed exposition of the kind of inquiry that a comprehensive access to the largely unpublished late works of this poly-pragmatic American philosopher would facilitate. They do little more than identify the relevant minimal corpus that is not to be neglected in the scholarship on Peirce's method of logical analysis, its history, and its applications to the workings of intellectual cognition. Further editions are needed on Peirce's late writings on the algebra of logic, logic of abduction (retroduction), inductive logic and the logic of science, non-Aristotelian (and non-classical) logics, reasoning, definitions, history of logic, semiotics, methodeutic, modality, continuity, vagueness, imagination and perception; the list goes on with anything that was represented in non-graphical notations (such as Peirce's 1909 work on triadic logics), in order to complete the identification of that minimal logical corpus. Any of these areas, when fully available, will open up new insights on, as well as call for some major revisions to, our current understanding of the logical, philosophical and scientific achievements of this agile mind, and what their proper place in the history of logic will end up being. And although electronic repositories of one's literary remains are certainly useful, and although those, too, will appear before long, they are no substitute for organised, systematic and thematic records of one's profound thoughts.

There are also wider issues that have to do with the kinds of historiographies one gets to write on the development of modern logic, including the virtual histories of what the logic of the later centuries would have looked like had the findings that Peirce produced and presented in various occasions been better and more timely disseminated. Misfortunes happened during Peirce's life all too often—yet on balance, we are also fortunate and privileged as much of his literary estate has been preserved for us to continue its future appreciation and critical scrutiny, however fragmentary or prefatory those surviving segments may appear to be. I hope that the present edition will play its part towards achieving these wider goals.

Ahti-Veikko Pietarinen

Contents

Ahti-Veikko Pietarinen
General Introduction to *Logic of the Future* —— 1

Ahti-Veikko Pietarinen
Introduction to the Theory of Existential Graphs and Volume 1 —— 14

References —— 122

Charles S. Peirce: Writings on Existential Graphs

Part I: Reasoning and Diagrams

1	Essays on Reasoning (R 654, R 680, R 678), 1910 —— 135	
1.1	Essays on Reasoning —— 136	
1.2	The Art of Reasoning Elucidated —— 148	
2	Diversions of Definitions (R 650), 1910 —— 161	
3	[Reasoning, Logic and Action] (R 826, R 616, R 1132, R 838) —— 181	
3.1	Some Reveries of a Dotard (R 826), 1910 —— 181	
3.2	An Appraisal of the Faculty of Reasoning (R 616), c.1906 —— 182	
3.3	[Intention, Resolution, and Determination] (R 1132), 1903 —— 186
4	Of Reasoning in General (R 595), 1895 —— 188	

Part II: Development of Existential Graphs

5   On Logical Graphs (R 482), 1896 —— 211

6   Positive Logical Graphs (R 488), 1896 —— 262

7   On Logical Graphs (Acad. Graphs) (R 480), 1896 —— 268

8   On Logical Graphs [Euler and EGs] (R 481), 1896 —— 282

9   [Memoir on Existential Graphs] (R 483), 1896 —— 292

10   [Six Papers on Existential Graphs], 1897–1898 —— 304
10.1   Existential Graphs (R 497), 1897 —— **304**
10.2   Existential Graphs (R 486), 1897 —— **305**
10.3   The Logic of Relatives (R 438), 1898 —— **309**
10.4   On Existential Graphs (R 485), c.1898 —— **311**
10.5   [Algebra and Existential Graphs] (R 513), 1898 —— **316**
10.6   Logical Graphs (R 495), 1898 —— **327**

11   On Existential Graphs, F4 (R 484), 1898 —— 331

12   Peripatetic Talks (R 502–505), 1898 —— 348

Part III: Theory and Application of Existential Graphs

13   The Principles of Logical Graphics (R 493), c.1899 —— 369

14   On the First Principles of Logical Algebra (R 515), c.1901 —— 385

15   On the Basic Rules of Logical Transformation (R 516), c.1901 —— 399

16   A Proposed Logical Notation (R 530), c.1901 —— 419

17   The Simplest Possible Mathematical System (R 430), 1902 —— 442

18   Multitude and Continuity (R 316a(s)), 1903 —— 470

19   [A System of Existential Graphs] (R 514), 1904 —— 477

20	Reason's Conscience (R 693b, R S-26), 1904 —— 489
21	Topical Geometry (R 145), 1905 —— 506
22	Logical Analysis of some Demonstrations in high Arithmetic (R 253), 1905 —— 517
23	Properties of Positive Integers (R 70(s)), 1906 —— 524
24	A Contribution to the Amazes of Mathematics (R 201), 1907 —— 530
25	Logical Critique of the Creed of Religion (R 855–856), 1911 —— 548
26	Assurance through Reasoning (R 670, R 669), 1911 —— 565
27	[Logical Graphs, from the *Prescott Book*] (R 277), 1907–1910 —— 586
28	[Existential Graphs, from the *Logic Notebook*] (R 339), 1898–1909 —— 595

Bibliography of Peirce's References —— 642

Catalogue of Peirce's Writings —— 652

Name Index —— 655

Keyword Index —— 657

Ahti-Veikko Pietarinen
General Introduction to *Logic of the Future*

Peirce's Logic

Charles Sanders (Santiago) Peirce (1839–1914) was an accomplished scientist, philosopher, and mathematician, who considered himself primarily a logician. His contributions to the development of modern logic at the turn of the 20th century have been colossal, original, and perpetually influential, albeit his overall influence upon the development of modern logic remained ill-understood for a long time (Fisch 1982, Dipert 1995, Hintikka 1996, Putnam 1982).

Formal, or deductive, logic was just one of the branches in which Peirce exercised his logical and analytical talent. His work developed upon George Boole's algebra of logic and Augustus De Morgan's logic of relations. Peirce worked on the algebra of relatives (1870–1885), the theory of quantification (1880–1885), graphical and diagrammatic logic (1896–1913), trivalent logic (1909), as well as higher-order and modal logics (1898–1911).[1] He also contributed significantly to the theory and methodology of induction, and discovered a third kind of reasoning, different from both deduction and induction, which he called abduction or retroduction, and which he identified with the logic of scientific discovery.

Philosophically, logic became for Peirce a broad and open-ended discipline with internal divisions and external architectonic relations to other parts of scientific inquiry. Logic depends upon, or draws its principles from, mathematics, phaneroscopy (phenomenology) and ethics, while metaphysics and psychology depend upon logic. One of the most important characters of Peirce's late logical thought was that logic becomes coextensive with semeiotic (his preferred spelling), namely the theory of signs. Peirce divided logic, conceived as semeiotic, into (i) *speculative grammar*, the preliminary analysis, definition, and classification of signs; (ii) *critical logic*, the study of the validity and justification of each

---

[1] Year ranges are indicative only. The continuous nature of Peirce's explorations and his pluralistic approach to logic routinely challenge pinpointing any definite moment in time when one idea had led to another. For example, higher-order logic was algebraically investigated in his 1885 "On the Algebra of Logic: A Contribution to the Philosophy of Notation" paper but presented in its graphical outfit in 1898. The entire concept of graphical notation for logic is an equally continuous notion and was present in various guises since 1880, as will be explained in Introduction to Volume 1 of *Logic of the Future*.

https://doi.org/10.1515/9783110651409-001

kind of reasoning; and (iii) *methodeutic* or *speculative rhetoric*, the theory of methods and an application of the methods of logical analysis to other fields of science, especially mathematics. Peirce's logical investigations cover all these three areas.

In the early 1880s—roughly at the same time as Gottlob Frege (1848–1925) but entirely independently of him—Peirce discovered a notation of quantifiers and variables for the expression of quantificational logic. Unlike Frege, however, Peirce did not stick to any one formalism. He spent the rest of his logical life experimenting with alternative notations to serve the theory of logic and to advance scientific inquiry. The outcome of his notational researches was a system of logical graphs discovered in 1896, which he termed the system of Existential Graphs (EGs).

Sketchy presentations of EGs appeared in print in 1902 in the *Dictionary of Philosophy and Psychology* (DPP) edited by James Mark Baldwin (entry "Symbolic Logic" in Vol. 2, pp. 640–651; LoF 3), in *A Syllabus of Certain Topics of Logic*, a small pamphlet circulated in less than 100 copies that Peirce wrote to accompany his Lowell Lectures of 1903, and in the 1906 *Monist* article "Prolegomena to an Apology for Pragmaticism". Apart from these, his prolific writings on EGs remained unpublished in his lifetime.[2]

Peirce continued working on the theory of logical graphs for the rest of his life. On Christmas Day of 1909 he wrote to William James (1942–1910) that this graphical method "ought to be the Logic of the Future." The next couple of sections explain the rationale behind this phrase.

Structure of the Edition

Logic of the Future: Writings on Existential Graphs is a three-volume edition providing a comprehensive package of Peirce's late writings on the topic of Existential Graphs (EGs). The first volume, subtitled **History and Applications**, consists of three parts, *Reasoning and Diagrams* (Part I), *Development of Existential Graphs* (Part II), and *Theory and Application of Existential Graphs* (Part III). The aim of Part I is to provide a non-technical introduction, in Peirce's own words, to his method and philosophy of diagrammatic reasoning, especially as conducted and

---

[2] There are only a few references and hints to them in his other published papers from the early 20th century, such as the "Some Amazing Mazes" series (Peirce 1908a,b; Peirce 1909a). The second *Monist* paper "Issues of Pragmaticism" (Peirce 1905b) makes one reference; the first, "What Pragmatism Is", does not (Peirce 1905a). Nor does the published version of the "Neglected Argument for the Reality of God" (Peirce 1908c) refer to EGs.

understood in terms of his theory of logical graphs. Part II tells the story of the discovery of EGs and their relation to what Peirce generally calls the "graphical method of logic"; the discovery that largely happens during his immensely productive year of 1896, followed by two years of significant improvements to that original discovery. Part III, which in many ways comprises the most substantial, detailed and technical set of writings of the entire *Logic of the Future* series, portrays the breath and the depth of the theory of EGs, as well as the impact Peirce took the graphical method to have on the advancement of our understanding of the fundamental nature of reasoning, mathematics, science, mind, and philosophy. This third part covers the period from 1899 until some of his last writings on the topic in 1911.

The second volume, **The 1903 Lowell Lectures**, consists of two parts, *The Logical Tracts* (Part IV) and *Some Topics of Logic Bearing on Questions Now Vexed* (Part VI). *The Logical Tracts* is Peirce's nearly book-length compendium on EGs written while preparing for his upcoming eight lectures in November and December 1903 organised by the Lowell Institute in Boston. The first five of the Lowell Lectures, in turn, contain the most massive body of texts on EGs that Peirce ever undertook to write. Those lectures, their numerous drafts and the accompanying material in the *Syllabus* constitute the centerpiece of Peirce's work on EGs. Chronologically, they mark the half-way point in that dozen or so years during which he produced nearly all of the relevant writings. Content-wise, these lectures portray EGs in their matured form, with the system of conventions fully in place and the sound and complete set of rules of transformation ready to be exposed to the audience.

The most philosophical set of writings is found in the third volume, **Pragmaticism and Correspondence**. In its chapters arranged under Part VI on pragmaticism, Peirce is using EGs to elucidate, and even to prove, his philosophical theory of meaning. Thoughts, signs and minds are extensively discussed, and Peirce sends the graphical method to the service of addressing those difficult and penetrating philosophical questions. Selections from 1904 to 1908 make up this sixth part of the trilogy. The third volume also includes, in Part VII, Peirce's extensive exchange of letters with a number of colleagues, collaborators and friends. Among them is a long letter to William James written on December 25, 1909, in which the allusion to the "Logic of the Future" is made. That final part also presents the dictionary entries and their drafts on EGs that were authored or co-authored by Peirce and which—just as most of the other material in these three volumes—have remained largely unpublished to date.

Each selection begins with a headnote, and introductory essays to each of the three volumes and their individual parts provide further insight into the textual, substantial and editorial encounters that the production of the present collection has involved over the years. In particular, the introductory essays outline the wider context of Peirce's intellectual life and explain the growth and impact of his ideas within that wider context. They also highlight the major novelties and contributions that Peirce is observed to be making in the texts collected in these chapters.

When discussing Peirce's excursions into the theory of EGs and the numerous ventures he had in trying to get his papers published and acknowledged by his peers, I am following the order of the textual selections in their respective chapters. For most if not for each of the texts included in these three volumes, philosophical and technical comments are provided on the content. Those comments aim at being a source of information as much as of inspiration, and have no pretension of exhaustiveness.

Editorial Essay

Text Selection Rationale

The selection of copy-texts and their editorial processing follows a number of general and specific guidelines. As to the general ones, first, the three volumes aim at being *comprehensive* in their coverage of the material Peirce ever wrote on EGs. The number of such manuscript and letter sheets, notebook pages, worksheets, galley proofs, typescripts and published leaves (inclusive of all variant and incomplete draft pages), is nearly 5 000. Virtually all of them have been used as the material for copy-texts of the three volumes of the *Logic of the Future* series. This means that important alternative drafts, variants and fragments have also been included as far as possible. Far from making the text redundant, substantive alternatives often contain information not found anywhere else. Peirce worked incessantly, and routinely did not aim at publishing his findings.[3] Even when he did, his submissions, galleys and offprints can be seen to be superseded by the textual and cognitive context within which they were produced. Variants, alternatives, emendations, parallel and emerging projects, and even substantial rejections, lacunæ and lost pages supply that important context. Although much editorial effort has

---

[3] A pertinent example is the destiny of Peirce's 1885 paper "On the Algebra of Logic: A Contribution to the Philosophy of Notation", which was so ahead of its time that is was understood neither by his peers nor the generations that followed (see Ma & Pietarinen 2018a for a recent study). Two decades later Peirce would still feel that it was the aftermath of that paper that led him to give up publishing efforts on the topic of logic altogether; what he would subsequently produce were "written for my eyes solely, like all my logical papers of the last twenty years" (R 253, 1905; LoF 1).

been expended on identifying, studying, selecting, organising, transcribing and producing the material in its final format, the present series is a *critical edition* only in the sense of having attempted to identify, select and study the thematically relevant material, with much less contemplation whether that material may have accorded with Peirce's intentions and thoughts about the production of final or ultimate versions of any given piece than what is to be expected of critical editions.

Second, the three volumes are *chronological* with respect to their internal thematic organisation. Again, Peirce typically worked simultaneously on many projects, writing assignments, letters, proofs and calculations, producing text and delivering results virtually daily on multiple fronts. (Curiously but understandably, nearly all of the pages included in the present volume were written in the warmth of the months between April and August, 1895–1907; his residence was often too cold during winter to support sustained literary engagements.) *Logic of the Future* aims at preserving thematic unities as far as practicable. This is reflected in the organisation of the material in seven distinct parts. The ordering of writings within those parts is chronological, with a few unavoidable concessions. Peirce's letters are organised in sets of exchanges according to the people involved, and the selections in the first part, *Reasoning and Diagrams*, are presented in a roughly reverse chronological order from 1910 to 1895. The reason for the latter is solely didactic: Peirce's wider perspectives and explanations on the value of the method of EGs find their best formulation in his most mature work deriving from not much earlier than 1910. It is hoped that this retrospective glance helps soften the reader's landing on the more demanding pieces that begin to get off the ground during 1896. Retrospection also aids in placing the superabundant ideas of their inventor into wider philosophical and systematic perspectives.

The methods that have guided the selection of present texts also need an explanation. The leading principle for inclusion is that Peirce writes on, or makes substantial references to, his EGs. The present volumes thus do not cover all of his logic: his pioneering work on the algebra of logic, for example, though in many important ways aiding and abetting the development of EGs and being intimately related to their underlying logical ideas, does not belong to the scope of the present collection. His important other logical, philosophical and semiotic writings that were obviously motivated by the discovery and advancement of the graphical method but do not directly engage with it, have likewise largely been left out.

Often the transitions between algebraic and graphical points of view are without much difference. Sometimes Peirce employs terminology in the logic of the algebra of the copula that may be more familiar from his theory of logical graphs (such as "scriptibility", "sheet of assertion"). For example, in the context of the

Minute Logic (R 430, ms p. 70, 1902), the writing down of a proposition "on some duly validated *sheet of assertions*" makes the proposition so uttered an assertion that "becomes a binding act". This "we will pretend" to be so "[f]or the sake of fixing our ideas" (*ibid.*). The supposition that one takes there to be the "sheet" upon which an utterance or writing down of a proposition makes it an act of assertion is common in Peirce's algebra of logic just as it is in his graphical method. Likewise is the application of the term "to scribe" or "scriptibility": any algebraic or graphical constituent that has a signification by virtue of the fact that it has been asserted as having that signification, is said to be *scriptible* whenever "it is applicable to 𝕍, the *veritas*, in some understood sense" (*ibid.*).

As another example, among Peirce's important writings on logic that are omitted from the present collection is R 501 (c.1901, plus adjacent pages in R 9 and R 11), as these worksheets do not directly employ the notation of logical graphs (and as they are to appear elsewhere).[4] In this treatise, Peirce is seen to present both a general theory of deduction and of the consequence relation, the two cornerstones in the development of modern logic. Its importance thus cannot be overestimated. Peirce is led to these theories by three important generalisations: those of (i) propositions to all signs, (ii) truth to *scriptibility*, i.e. "capable of being written conformably to the purpose" (R 501, late 1901), and (iii) derivation to *transformability*, i.e. "capable of being transformed without changing anything scriptible into anything non-scriptible" (R 430, early 1902). One can also find in R 516 (LoF 1), "On the Basic Rules of Logical Transformation", similar definitions of 'scriptible' and 'transformable' in the context of the graphical method of the logic of existential graphs.

A different set of important texts that regrettably does not have space for inclusion in the present edition consists of Peirce's extensive writings, commentaries and criticism on Alfred Bray Kempe's 1886 publication on mathematical graphical forms (R 708–R 715). Although clearly preceding and influencing Peirce's subsequent studies on logical graphs, these and several other writings of his that antedate the year 1896 have to appear elsewhere.[5] It is ultimately only in connection to everything that Peirce wrote, throughout his life, on mathematics and algebra, both multiple and logical, that we can assess the place of the graphical method

---

[4] Ma & Pietarinen (2019) provide a complete transcription of Peirce's "Dragon Logic" of R 501, with an introduction that relate it to later discoveries in modern logic. In brief, Peirce introduces a new Dragon-Head and Dragon-Tail notation: The Dragon Head, Ω, is the implicational sign, and is used in a dual form which Peirce terms the Dragon-Tail, $\hat{C}$, which is an inverse of the head. (Peirce added the circumflex to $\hat{C}$ because C is a singular sign.)

[5] See Grattan-Guinness (2002, 2007) on the account of Peirce's writings on Kempe's theory and their subsequent influence.

and its genesis in the overall development of these interconnected logical, philosophical, notational and mathematical contributions.

The second criterion for inclusion is that the texts *have not been previously published*. Like the first, this principle has its exceptions, but it is a useful one given how long-lasting the lack of access has been to some of the most important writings dating from Peirce's later years. Duplication of EG-related papers that have long been easily available has been avoided, most prominently that of his 1906 "Prolegomena to an Apology for Pragmatism" paper. There are, however, copious draft versions and leaves pertaining to "Prolegomena" (the galleys have not been recovered) that have not been published before and those are included in LoF 3. Whenever Peirce's writings that have appeared in print before are published in LoF 1–3, the versions that appear are presumed to be more complete versions of their previous publications. The present edition provides not only the alternative and discrete versions and drafts. It also aims to improve upon previous editions by filling in some gaps and omissions. Details are provided in the volume-specific introductions, individual head-notes and annotations.

Editorial Apparatus

The three volumes have aimed at narrating the fairly complex technical and graphical notation in a uniform format. The unique 'language' of graphs and other signs and designs peculiar to Peirce's logic and semiotics obviously presents a number of editorial and interpretative challenges. These challenges have been faced by creating a special LaTeX package that produces any graph of whatever kind in a uniform format which is as close to the authorial hand, intentions and explanations as possible. The package includes commands and designs for all logical signs and symbols that have been encountered in Peirce's *Nachlass*. The design of those signs takes into account both (i) how we find them drawn in the relevant autographic sources, and (ii) what Peirce's detailed—and often unfulfilled—instructions to the typesetters were.[6] Fitting several thousand graphs in three volumes, both inline and as display items, would have been impossible in any other

---

6 For example, in Peirce's algebra of logic the signs similar to sums and products are not the signs of sums Σ and products Π, but those for which "*upright* type should be used without those little finishing-lines the names of which I forget [Sans Serif]. That is *not* $\Sigma\Pi$ but $\Sigma\Pi$ like inscriptions. You will find many examples in the *Mathematische Annalen*. As a general rule of printing formulae, I like all capitals Roman, all l.c. letters Italics. I only use the small alphabet as subscript letters" (CSP to the Open Court, R S-64, draft, 1896; cf. September 2, 1896 CSP to TJMcC [T. J. McCormack, Assistant Editor at the Open Court]; LoF 3).

way than by programming a Peirce-specific LaTeX code, commands and environments that can uniformly produce them all. The next section has more details on editing and typesetting these graphs.

Instead of aiming at a clear-text version, *Logic of the Future* edition follows a quasi-diplomatic protocol. Important changes and alterations have been incorporated into the text, displaying inline Peirce's crossed-out texts, deletions and rejections. The default reading is that any portion of text that is stricken-through or crossed out represents an altered portion of text which Peirce replaced with what immediately follows it in the text. Again, this protocol is fallible as editorial discretion must be exercised on what the most meaningful and significant deletions and alterations are taken to be. The gain is an added insight into the evolution of Peirce's thinking and prose at one glance. Double struck-outs are used when an above-text alteration was itself deleted.

Insignificant changes have been emended silently to improve readability. Accordingly, textual apparatus has been kept to a minimum. The downside is that many of the additions of words, lexical units, phrases and sentences that are found in the manuscripts and papers are non-visibly blended into the flow of the text. Marginalia and corrections from Peirce's galleys, books and offprints have been included whenever available, and collateral and external sources have been resorted to in order to verify details and timings of various episodes as well as to confirm the identity of literary sources.

In short, this is an inclusive, thematic, thematically chronological and quasi-diplomatic edition, which aims at maximising novelty and contribution to the advancement of logic and Peirce's logical philosophy. There is a certain urgency in getting the material to appear in print and to reach audiences beyond the communities of scholars who can work directly with Peirce's manuscripts. The impact of his writings on the development of modern logic and on the improvement of human reason becomes understood only through a widespread access to these complex sources.

The abundance of discrete variant texts that derives from Peirce's later period of life—and especially from his profuse works on logical graphs—has necessitated an inclusive editorial approach that makes room for variant texts and versions that diverge from each other in multiple ways yet pertain to the same authorial project or the line of thought. Often Peirce worked without any expressed authorial purpose of aiming at bringing his thoughts, results and diagrams before the public eye. The present edition aims at maximising the amount of alternative but divergent texts while minimising the amount of effort that the reader needs in order to locate the points in which the variant texts show the beginnings of a divergence. Often this has to be carried out at the expense of sacrificing certain critical editing principles that aim at distilling final authorial intentions from textual masses. But what is gained is the lowering of the risk that significant ideas, terms, definitions or results, which notoriously appear in variants, be left out.

Presenting constantly diverging and evolving sets of texts is hardly possible in a strictly linear format. In the present edition, variant pages and alternative segments have been included in the footnotes or, when they are several pages long, appended to the respective chapters. In both cases it is the vicinity of discrete variants that counts in the final output. The reader can observe where the forking has occurred by following the footnoting and boldfaced references **[Alt. *n*]** prefixed to alternative continuations, where *n* is an index of discrete texts that share the same branching point. Since in many cases there are several substantive alternatives and since at least in some of these cases it is not feasible to venture into guessing whether they represent superseded authorial intentions or whether one or several of them could constitute the final or the maximally authoritative version of the text (or present evidence of the absence of such textual hierarchies), the reader is in such cases presented with options, in hope of furthering the scholarship along the way. It may be that in some cases the alternatives provided in footnotes or appendices in fact represent Peirce's more mature thought, perhaps even those that pertain to some fair copy-text project of his without specific indications. Likewise, substantial deletions and rejections have been retained, either inline or in the footnotes, preceded by editorial tags (**[Del.]**, **[Rej.]**). When in rare cases editorial attempts have been frustrated in deciphering a lexical item or a part of an item that occurs in the original source, [*illeg.*] is used in its stead.

When there is an apparent discontinuity in the text either because of physical reasons such as missing, disordered and torn-out pages, or corrupted sheets due to soiling, fire or ink spills, or because of mental reasons such as interruptions of thought, lapses of focus or concentration, but the two texts otherwise can be judged to be parts of the same writing episode, a non-boldfaced flag '[discont.]' is placed in between the conjecturally discontinuous parts. Short editorial omissions and missing text (words or at most a few sentences) as well as incomplete beginnings of alternative texts are indicated by [...]; longer omissions (typically several paragraphs or pages rather than sentences) by [– – –]. Ellipses are used either in order to avoid or curtail excess and irrelevant material or to indicate missing material and lacunæ of any kind, with explanations added. Frequent abrupt endings of the text are indicated by [end].

All editorial annotations are interspersed within the text or given in footnotes and enclosed in upright brackets. Selection titles supplied by the editor are likewise bracketed. Peirce's inconsistent use of brackets has been emended to parentheses to avoid confusion. Identifiers for textual sources are likewise editorial annotations and are included in the text at the beginning of the respective selections, such as **[R 1601]** or [From R S-30] etc. Page references to manuscript sources are to Peirce's own pagination, and when available, are abbreviated by 'ms p.' or 'ms pp.'. ISP pagination numbers are not used.

The editorial approach is thus conservative both as concerns the selection of texts as well as their collation, annotation and textual apparatus. Authorial revisions are visible in the final output with respect to the most significant alterations. Most of the annotations, clarifications and interpretational issues concerning copy-texts and their compositional stages are incorporated in the introductory surveys or in the chapter-wise head-notes. Textual apparatus itself, including detailed information about copy-texts, alternations, variants and editorial emendations, is largely implicit and retained in the source files but not reproduced in the compiled output. Meta-data such as original pagination, running headers and other information about manuscript pages and their organisation are likewise not included in the final output though preserved in the source file layer. Standard and silent normalisations and alterations apply to minor elements of punctuation, such as adding or toggling between single and double quotation marks, typesetting headings and heading punctuation, italization of book titles, and the like. Peirce's original capitalisation of words is preserved. His Latin, Greek, Hieroglyphic, Hebrew, Arabic and other non-English words, phrases, sentences and quotations are given in full but not translated. The sometimes inappropriate vocabulary has been reproduced as is (e.g., "redskin", "negro", "negress", "Flathead Indians", "lover only of a virgin", "lover of every Pope"). In several cases these appear in Peirce's examples (e.g., "Every Hottentot kills a Hottentot") and as such are made up sentences that are entertained, not asserted.

Editing Graphs

In the present edition, graphs are just as important as the text overall. Special note must therefore be made on the methods, techniques and decisions involved in the editorial process of bringing graphs and similar visually pronounced elements into the appearance they have in these volumes. This is not only because of the sheer number of diagrammatic elements involved, but because the totality of instances of graphs also constitutes an actual corpus of a language. As far as the typesetting of the diagrammatic syntax of such graphical languages is concerned, Peirce would typically scribe graphs inline, and only when they grew relatively large in two dimensions, or when there was need to refer to them with running numbers or figure captions, would he display them as individual items or floated or wrapped figures separated from the body of the text. In all cases it is important to keep in mind that graphs are not pictures. They are formulæ of logic and expressions of a language, just as mathematical, logical and natural languages are composed out of designated constituents and lexical units to express relevant and intended meanings. To scribe a graph on the sheet is to assert it. Graphs that appear on the sheet of paper or on the screen of a computer are to be treated as an integral part of the scholarly prose. This needs to be properly acknowledged and accommodated in one's editorial and textual practices, too.

The way the diagrammatic syntax of the language of EGs has been technically handled in the present edition is in terms of developing a special LaTeX package (EGpeirce.sty) that produces uniform, inline-sized graphs that prevent increase in baseline spacing as much as possible. This implies that their "spots" (the predicate terms) that may appear either in natural language, letters (typically upright capital) or some other special marks or mathematical symbols that Peirce used for that purpose, are regularly typeset in small font. For example, A is a graph scribed on a sheet of assertion, and drawing an oval ("the cut") around it produces Ⓐ. With two ovals the result looks like ⓐ, with three Ⓐ, and so on. When some added spacing becomes unavoidable, the preference is to typeset graphs within the text in that case, too. In this manner, the meaningful units of Peirce's diagrammatic syntax—its graph-instances—can be adequately treated as lexical units and utterances in their own right and without discriminating them against the prose of natural language. In those places in which Peirce did write the graphs as display items and when incorporation of them into the text would have cluttered the result and made the text jarring to read, the copy-text layout has been followed as far as practicable. Often Peirce used figure captions to index displayed graphs; those are always preserved and graphs produced in the location nearest to their original appearance in copy-text, always with the caption and reference number given by the authorial hand. To accord with publisher's house style, graphs and figures that appear wrapped in the manuscripts are unwrapped, however.

As mentioned, examples of logical graphs amount to several thousand in Peirce's vast corpus on EGs, often drawn with tinctures of red, blue, brown and green. While all of them have been inspected and studied in their original form at relevant repositories, there are also pages after pages of doodles, seriously incomplete and repetitive examples, sketches too faint or smudged to read; and countless obscure or meaningless ornaments that obviously need not or cannot be included even in the most comprehensive edition, at least perhaps for no other reason than aesthetics. This said, thousands of graphs have been produced in the three volumes, in uniform and, whenever possible, compressed and space-saving formats, that reduced excess blank space while sacrificing nothing of the readability of graphical texture. (It was a major challenge in Peirce's time to print the graphs, especially the curved lines, at all.) When there are several nests of cuts with only blanks between them, the resulting and sometimes disturbing Moiré effect has been reduced by applying non-symmetric spacing between the cuts.

Caption numbers and their in-text references have been made uniform, standardised and corrected when the occasional slip of the pen has happened. These are all silent emendations and standardisations that pertain to the appearance of graphical forms and change nothing in their meaning.

In all cases, graphs are as close to Peirce's original hand as practicable, and they take into account all meaningful features and information visible in original graphs and their respective explanations. The thickness of the lines as well as the shapes of their loose ends are significant features and need to be accurately reproduced. Likewise, Peirce's occasional use of coloured ink in drawing the graphs is preserved in the electronic edition. Typically, he would draw the thick lines of identity in red and the thin cuts in blue ink, especially in 1903 and later when he had better access to ink palettes. Brown and green ink was also availed of in addition to red and blue by the authorial hand to denote specific logical and notational features, especially in reference to second-order graphs (LoF 2). Peirce also resorted to colours for improved didactic effect when educating his students, audiences and correspondents on the fundamentals of EGs. All colours are preserved in the electronic version of the edition, and its grey-scale rendition is expected to reproduce the contrast between light and dark colours as far as possible.

Several images from Peirce's manuscripts are included, either together with their uniform LaTeX rendition or occasionally as stand-alone illustrations. These are marked with [P.H.] (standing for "Peirce's Hand"). A couple of facsimiles of entire holograph pages from Peirce's collections have also been included to perfect the material.

While nearly every meaningful piece that Peirce ever wrote or scribed on the topic of EGs is presumed to have been included in the three volumes of *Logic of the Future*, this effort is by no means intended to nullify the value of Peirce's original pages, the beauty of which the reader is invited to experience first-hand in the relevant physical and electronic archival locations.

Justification of the Title

It remains to give an explanation of the title chosen to represent the entire edition. On Christmas Day 1909 Peirce wrote to William James that what he had discovered "ought to be the Logic of the Future." What was it that he had discovered? Peirce writes that,

> My triumph in that [algebraic] line, my Existential Graphs, by which all deduction is reduced to insertions and erasures, and in which there are no connecting signs except the writing of terms on the same area enclosed in an oval and heavy lines to express the identity of the

individual objects whose signs are connected by such lines. This ought to be *the Logic of the Future*. (R L 224; LoF 3; added emphasis, capitalisation in the original)

This passage epitomises the most important aspects of that new logic. First, historically, EGs represent a natural continuation, application and expansion of algebraic methods that Peirce had worked on for nearly half a century. We now know that everything that can be graphicalised can also be made to work according to algebraic principles. Second, the method Peirce refers to in this passage shows what deduction consists of: a series of insertions and erasures according to certain specified rules of illative transformations. Third, juxtaposition and enclosure completely characterise propositional logic (termed the "Alpha part" of EGs since 1903). These two signs suffice for a system that agrees with a two-element Boolean algebra. An addition of heavy lines moreover extends an Alpha system to (fragments of) first-order predicate logic with identity (termed the "Beta part" of EGs since 1903). Whatever the graphical systems are—and not necessarily only *existential* graphs—they can now incorporate and exploit these three characteristics in full. It is the realisation of the full generality of the graphical method that Peirce predicts is awaiting us in the future.

It may have been only through the advent of modern-day computers, proof theory, mathematics of continuity, cognitive sciences, and a plethora of diagrammatic and heterogeneous notations invented to aid discovery and development of scientific theories, that have put Peirce's prediction into an interesting albeit perhaps somewhat uneasy perspective. How did a single mind not only manage to predict but also contribute to fields that in reality were far ahead in the future? As is the case with a rare number of brains at any epoch of time, Peirce's mind was an anomaly. Largely devoid of academic context and intellectual stimulation of students, in his later years piles of papers accumulated in the attic of his house "Arisbe" in Milford, Pennsylvania, for apparently nothing else than for the sake of advancing the reasoning of posterity. This incremental and exploratory, often painstakingly slow but persistent effort made him realise that an evolution of altogether new logical theories was taking place. This realisation motivated and guided the investigations of this American brain—not the outside influences or recognition expected of them.

"The time will come when the world will be amazed at this" (R 280).

Ahti-Veikko Pietarinen
Introduction to the Theory of Existential Graphs and Volume 1

Basic Notions

The theory of Existential Graphs (EGs) is a graphical method of logic which Peirce gravitated to in 1896 and for which in the 1903 Lowell Lectures he coined the now-customary terminology that divided the method into the Alpha, Beta, and Gamma parts. The logic of the Alpha part is a propositional (sentential) logic and it agrees with the two-element Boolean algebra. Peirce often began his presentation of EGs with the second, Beta part of the method that corresponds to a fragment of first-order predicate logic with identity. This introduction first provides an informal presentation of the Beta part, followed by a slightly more detailed introduction to the Alpha part. The main ideas of the Gamma part had to do with modal logics, and are presented in the introductory part of the next volume (LoF 2).

Peirce defined the central terms "graph", "graph-replica", "existential graph" and "to scribe" in the 1903 Lowell Lectures as follows:

> Every expression of a proposition in conformity with the conventions of this system is called an *existential graph*, or for brevity, a *graph* (although there are other kinds of graphs). Since it is sometimes awkward to say that a graph is *written* and it is sometimes awkward to say it is *drawn*, I will always say it is *scribed*. A graph scribed on the sheet of assent [the sheet of assertion] is said to be *accepted*. We must distinguish carefully between the *graph* and its different *replicas* [instances]. It is the *graph* which is accepted; and the graph is scribed when a *replica* of it is scribed" (R 450; LoF 2).

The distinction between the graphs as *types* and graphs as *replicas* (or *instances*) is one of the central distinctions. What is scribed on the sheet of assertion (or on the "sheet or assent") is the replica (instance) of a graph. What the graphs are in general, correspond to their types. What is asserted (or "assented" to) are the graphs as types. The same graph could be scribed on different parts of the sheet as different replicas or instances without thus producing different graphs.

The invention of EGs was in part motivated by Peirce's need to respond to the expressive insufficiency and lack of analytic power of the two systems described, first in the "Note B: The Logic of Relatives" of the *Studies in Logic, by Members of the Johns Hopkins University* (SiL, pp. 187–203), which Peirce later termed the algebra of dyadic (dual) relatives, and soon after in the 1885 paper "On the Algebra of Logic: A Contribution to the Philosophy of Notation", which he termed his general (or universal) algebra of logic. The analytic power derives from subsuming algebraic operations under one mode of composition. This composition of concepts is effected in the quantificational, Beta part of the theory of EGs by the device of *ligatures*. A ligature is a complex line, composed of what Peirce terms the *lines of identities*, which connects various parts and areas of the graphs (see e.g. Dipert 2006; Pietarinen 2005a, 2006, 2011, 2015b; Roberts 1973; Shin 2002; Zeman 1964). Here are three examples:

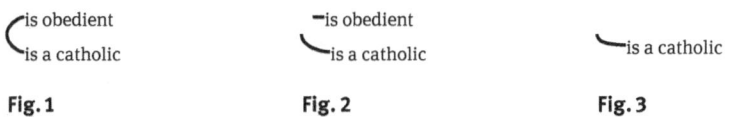

Fig. 1   **Fig. 2**   **Fig. 3**

The meaning of these lines is that two or more descriptions apply to the same thing. For example, in Fig. 2 there is a line attached to the predicate term "is obedient". It means that "something exists which is obedient". There is also another line which connects to the predicate term "is a catholic", and that composition means that "something exists which is a catholic", which is equivalent to the graph-instance given in Fig. 3. Since in Fig. 1 these two lines are in fact connected by one continuous line, the graph-instance in Fig. 1 means that "there exists a catholic which is obedient", that is, "there exists an obedient catholic". Ligatures, representing continuous connections composed of two or more lines of identity, stand for quantification, identity and predication, all in one go.

EGs are drawn on the *sheet of assertion* that represents what the modeller knows or what mutually has been agreed upon to be the case by those who undertake the investigation of logic. The sheet thus represents the universe of discourse. Any graph that is drawn on the sheet puts forth an assertion, true or false, that there is something in the universe to which it applies. This is the reason why Peirce terms these graphs *existential*. Drawing a circle around the graph, or alternatively, shading the area on which the graph-instance rests, means that nothing exists of the sort of description intended. In Fig. 4, the assertion "something is a catholic" is denied by drawing an oval around it and thus severing that assertion from the sheet of assertion:

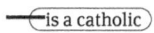

Fig. 4

The graph-instance depicted in Fig. 4 thus means that "something exists that is not catholic".

Peirce aimed at a diagrammatic syntax that would use a minimal number of logical signs but at the same time be maximally expressive and as analytic as possible. His ovals, for instance, have different notational functions: "The first office which the ovals fulfill is that of negation. [...] The second office of the ovals is that of associating the conjunctions of terms. [...] This is the office of parentheses in algebra" (R 430, ms pp. 54–56, 1902; LoF 1). The ovals are thus not only the diagrammatic counterpart to negation but also serve to represent the compositional structure of a graph-formula. Peirce held (see e.g. R 430; R 670, 1911; LoF 1) that a notation that does not separate the sign of truth-function from the representation of its scope is more analytic than a notation, such as that of an ordinary 'symbolic' language, where such a separation is required by the one-dimensional notation. The role of ovals as denials is in fact a derived function from the more primitive considerations of inclusion and implication (Bellucci & Pietarinen 2016; R 300, 1908; LoF 3).

As far as the expressivity of logical languages is concerned, Peirce had already recognised that the notion of *dependent* quantification was essential to the advancement of the theory of logic and that it needed to be captured in any system expressive enough to fully serve the purpose of logical analysis. The nested system of ovals effectuate this in a natural way, much in contrast to algebras that resort to an explicit use of parentheses and other punctuation marks. For example, the graph in Fig. 5 means that "Every Catholic adores some woman". The graph in Fig. 6 means that "Some woman is adored by every Catholic". Peirce notes that the latter asserts more than the former since it states that all Catholics adore the same woman, whereas the former allows different Catholics to adore different women:

Fig. 5 **Fig. 6**

The graph in Fig. 7 means, moreover, that "anything whatever is unloved by something that benefits it", that is, "everything is benefitted by something or other that does not love it":

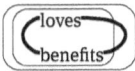

Fig. 7

Graphs can get quite complex, but perhaps still less complex than their natural-language correlates. Peirce occasionally gave examples of some very complicated sentences with intricate quantificational structures, and proposed to model and analyse them with the aid of the graphical method. An example is Fig. 8, which is to be interpreted "in a universe of sentient beings" (R 504, 1898; LoF 1):

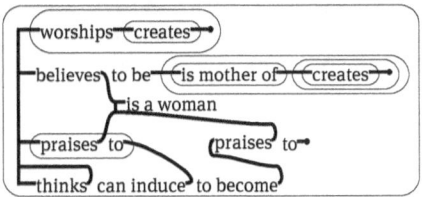 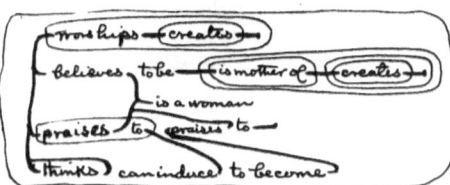

Fig. 8   [P.H.]

The graphical form, Peirce assumes, brings about the meaning of the sentence in a clearer way than what the sentences given in natural language could possibly reveal. For example, the previous graph expresses the following sentence:

> Every being unless he worships some being who does not create all beings either does not believe any being (unless it be not a woman) to be any mother of a creator of all beings or else he praises that woman to every being unless to a person whom he does not think he can induce to become anything unless it be a non-praiser of that woman to every being.

Peirce's example is complicated; the quantificational structure and the dependencies exhibited in the constituents of this sentence are certainly not easily discerned from the linguistic material.

It is on the level of semantics that the power of dependent quantification comes to the fore. Peirce carried his semantics out in terms of defining what today is recognised as two-player zero-sum semantic games that take place between the Graphist/Utterer and the Grapheus/Interpreter.[1] This is explained in a variant

---

[1] Sometimes, and especially in relation to Peirce's *model-building games*, these roles are split so that the Grapheus and the Interpreter are playing separate roles. On this, see Pietarinen (2013).

of "New Elements (Kaina stoicheia)" (R 517, 1901)² as follows. The copulative is *general* and *definite,* as to assert A and B "is to assert a proposition which the interpreter is at liberty to take as meaning A or as meaning B." The disjunctive, on the other hand, is *vague* and thus *individual* in nature, as to assert A or B "is to assert a proposition which gives the utterer the option between defending it by proving A and defending it by proving B" (R 517, ms p. 50). And not only this, Peirce continues that there are strategic advantages according to the order of the choices of selection:

> The asserter of a proposition may be said to [be] *ex officio* a defender of it, or, in the old logical phrase, a respondent for it. The interpreter is, on the other hand, naturally a critic of it and quasi-opponent. Now if a proposition is in one respect vague, so that in that respect the respondent has the choice of an instance, while in another respect it is general, so that in that respect the opponent has the choice of an instance, whichever party makes his choice last has the advantage of being able to adapt his instance to the choice already made by the other. For that reason,
>
> Some woman is loved by all catholics,
>
> where the respondent is obliged to name the woman before the opponent has chosen his catholic, is harder to defend, and less apt to be true, than
>
> Every catholic loves some woman,
>
> where the opponent must instance his catholic, whereupon the respondent can choose his woman accordingly.
>
> It is a curious fact that when there are a number of ~~obvious~~ signified choosings of instances, it is not the later one which has the logical character of an operator upon the one already made, but the reverse. Thus, in the last example [end] (R 517, ms pp. 50–51)³

Peircean semantic games were not limited to interpreting natural-language sentences or graph-instances of the theory of EGs.⁴ He often applied the same idea also to the interpretation of complex quantificational patterns and connectives in his general algebra of logic. In some cases both were considered in unison, as revealed in the following fragment located in R S-64 and probably written sometime in 1893–1894:

Hilpinen (1982) is the first to notice Peirce's logic as having been importantly erected upon the principles of semantic games. On games in logic, see e.g. Pietarinen (2003b); Majer, Pietarinen & Tulenheimo (2011).

2 Internal and external evidence suggests that Peirce wrote "Kaina stoicheia" in 1901 and not in 1904 as has been suggested in the Robin Catalogue and in the publication of that essay in EP 2.

3 Similar textual evidence for the game-theoretic interpretation occurs in numerous places, see e.g. R 238, R S-64 and the references in Pietarinen (2003a).

4 How close Peircean semantic games are to contemporary ones has been explored in Pietarinen (2001, 2003a, 2007, 2013).

It will be found that the algebraic method is the more convenient; but some persons have such a difficulty with algebra that I add the graphical method.

Given a proposition about two things a and b, if you are to select the thing to be represented by a with a view to making the proposition false, and I am to select b with a view to making the proposition true, it may be an advantage to me, and can be no disadvantage to know what your selection is to be, before I ~~determine~~ fix upon mine. Hence, if the proposition be such that it is true even if I make my selection first, much more will it be true if you make the first selection. Accordingly, if a proposition be written either in the algebraic or the graphical system, and that proposition be true, much more will it be true when any letter in a square or affixed to a Π is moved to the left. For a similar reason, of two letters both in circles or in squares, or both attached to Σs or to Πs, it is indifferent which comes first. Thus, to say that every man loves every woman is the same as to say that every woman is loved by every man; and to say that some man loves some woman is the same as to say that some woman is loved by some man; but to say that some man loves every woman is to say much more than that every woman is loved by some man.

[**Alt.:**] There are other interesting system of representing propositions; but it is not necessary to consider them here. The above algebraic system is the most convenient; but I add the graphical for the sake of the many readers who do not take kindly to algebra.

Given a proposition about two subjects, A and B, if *you* are to select the subject A with a view to making the proposition false, if you can,—in which case, plainly, A is universal, for the proposition asserts itself to be true, and hence that you cannot succeed in this,—while *I* am to select B with a view to making the proposition true,—so that B is particular,—then it may be of advantage to me, and can at any rate be no disadvantage, to know what your selection for A is to be, before I fix upon mine for B. That is, if the proposition be true though the particular subject be selected first, much more will it be true if the universal subject be selected first.

The "circles" and "squares" Peirce talks about pertain to the notation of protographs that preceded the discovery of the logical method of EGs (see Introduction to Part II, LoF 1). Importantly, he also emphasises the 'strategic' advantage to those who know what the earlier selections have been, which indeed is a standard property of semantic games (of perfect information) for classical logics.

In another, proof-theoretic sense, it nevertheless speaks to the superiority of EGs over algebraic systems that in it deduction, as follows from Peirce's Johns Hopkins graduate student Oscar Howard Mitchell's (1851–1889) work (Mitchell 1883), is reduced to a minimum number of permissive operations. Peirce termed these operations *illative rules of transformation*, and in effect they consist only of two: *insertions* (that is, permissions to draw a graph-instance on the sheet of assertion) and *erasures* (that is, permissions to erase a graph-instance from the sheet). More precisely, the *oddly-enclosed* areas of graphs (areas within a non-even number of enclosures) permit inserting any graph in that area, while *evenly-enclosed* areas permit erasing any graph from that area. Furthermore, a copy of a graph-instance is permitted to be pasted on that same area or any area deeper within the same nest of enclosures. This is the rule of *iteration*. A copy thus iterated is permitted to be erased by the converse rule termed *deiteration*. An interpretational corollary is that a *double enclosure* with no intervening graphs (other than the blank graph) in the middle area can be inserted and erased at will.

A more detailed exposition of these illative rules of transformation would need to show their application to quantificational expressions, namely applying insertions and erasures to ligatures. A flavor of such transformations is given by a reference to some examples. Regarding the graphs in Figs. 1, 2 and 3, an application of a permissible erasure on the line of identity in Fig. 1 results in the graph-instance in Fig. 2, and that another application of a permissible erasure on the upper part of the graph-instance in Fig. 2 results in the graph-instance as depicted in Fig. 3. Thus what is represented in Fig. 2 is a logical consequence of the graph-instance in Fig. 1, and what is represented in Fig. 3 is a logical consequence of the graph-instance given in Fig. 2.

Roberts (1973) has shown that the transformation rules Peirce had reached by 1903 form a semantically complete system of deduction. Roberts did not mention, however, that Peirce had demonstrated their soundness in 1898 and again in 1903 and that he had argued for their completeness in a couple of places, including unpublished parts of the *Syllabus* that he wrote to accompany his Lowell Lectures delivered in late 1903 (LoF 2).

Facts like these demonstrate that Peirce was a key innovator in the development of modern logic. And there is more. As observed, it is the polarity of the outermost ends or portions of ligatures that determines whether the quantification is *existential* (namely that the outermost end or a portion of the ligature rests on a positive area) or *universal* (if it rests on an odd area). Unlike in the Tarski-type semantics, but much in the fashion of what happens in game-theoretical semantics, the preferred rule of interpretation of the graphs is what Peirce termed "endoporeutic": one looks for the outermost portions of ligatures on the sheet of assertions first, assigns semantic values to that part, and then proceeds inwards into the areas enclosed within ovals. (In non-modal contexts, ligatures are not well-formed graphs because they may cross the enclosures.)

The diagrammatic nature of EGs consists in the relationship between forms of relations exhibited in the diagrams and the real relations in the universe of discourse. Peirce was convinced that, since these graphical systems exploit a *diagrammatic syntax*, they—together with extensions and modifications that would cover modalities, non-declarative expressions, speech acts, and so forth—can express any assertion, however intricate. Guided by the precepts laid out by the diagrammatic forms of expression, and together with the simple illative permissions by which deductive inference proceeds, the conclusions from premises can be "read before one's eyes"; these graphs present what Peirce believed is a "moving picture of the action of the mind in thought" (R 298, 1906; LoF 3):

> If upon one lantern-slide there be shown the premisses of a theorem as expressed in these graphs and then upon other slides the successive results of the different transformations of those graphs; and if these slides in their proper order be successively exhibited, we should have in them a veritable moving picture of the mind in reasoning. (R 905, 1907; LoF 3)

The theory of EGs that uses only the notation of ovals and the spatial notion of juxtaposition of graphs is termed by Peirce the Alpha part of the EGs, and as noted corresponds to propositional logic. The extension of the Alpha part with ligatures and *spots*[5] gives rise to the Beta part, and it corresponds to fragments of first-order predicate calculus. What Peirce in 1903 termed the *Gamma* part consists of a number of developments, including various modalities such as metaphysical, epistemic and temporal modalities, as well as extensions of modal graphs with ligatures. In Peirce's repositories one can in addition find many proposals developing graphical systems for *second-order logic* and *abstraction* in the logic of *potentials*, logics of *collections*, and meta-logical theories using the language of graphs to talk about notions and properties of the graphs in that language. The latter include encoding of permissive rules of transformation in such languages of "graph of graphs". He even proposed this idea also to serve as the method of logical analysis of assertions and meta-assertions. In connection to one of the last writings on EGs (Letter to Risteen, R 500/R L 376, December 1911) Peirce mentions that one would also need to add a "*Delta* part in order to deal with *Modals*":

> The better exposition of 1903 divided the system into three parts, distinguished as the Alpha, the Beta, and the Gamma, parts; a division I shall here adhere to, although I shall now have to add a *Delta* part in order to deal with modals. A cross division of the description which here, as in that of 1903, is given precedence over the other is into the *Conventions*, the *Rules*, and the *working* of the System.

While no evidence remains of the details of what the projected Delta could have been, most likely Peirce thought a new compartment was needed to accommodate the ever-expanding amount of graphical systems that had been mushrooming in the Gamma part. Perhaps he planned the Delta part on quantificational multi-modal logics as can be discerned in his theory of *tinctured graphs* that was fledgling since 1905 (LoF 3).

---

5 The spots are the graphical counterparts to the predicate terms, similar to simple rhemas that do not contain any logical constants (see Bellucci 2019; Pietarinen 2015c).

As will be seen from Peirce's writings collected in Volumes 2 and 3 of LoF, his graphical systems of modal logic included suggestions for defining several types of multi-modal logics in terms of tinctures of areas of graphs. Tinctures enable one to assert, among other things, necessities and metaphysical possibilities, and so call for changes in the nature of how the corresponding logics behave, including the identification of individuals in the presence of multiple universes of discourses. Peirce defined epistemic operators in terms of subjective possibilities which, as in contemporary epistemic logic, are epistemic possibilities defined as the duals of knowledge operators.

Peirce analysed the meaning of identities between actual and possible objects in quantified multi-modal logics. As an example, the two graphs given in Figs. 9 and 10 that he presented in a 1906 draft of the "Prolegomena" paper (R 292a, 1906, LoF 3) illustrate the nature of the interplay between epistemic modalities and quantification:

Fig. 9 **Fig. 10**

The graph in Fig. 9 is read "There is a man who is loved by one woman and loves a woman known by the Graphist to be another." The reason is that in the equivalent graph depicted in Fig. 10, the woman who loves is denoted by the name 'A', and the woman who is loved is denoted by the name 'B'. The shaded area is a tincture (argent, if given in colours) that refers to the modality of subjective possibility. Thus the graph in Fig. 10 means that it is subjectively impossible, by which Peirce means "is contrary to what is known by the Graphist" (i.e., the modeller of the graph), that A should be B. In other words, the woman who loves and the woman who is loved (whom the graph does not assert to be otherwise known to the Graphist) are known by the Graphist not to be the same person.

Peirce's work on such topics and questions highlights the importance of underlying ideas that were rediscovered significantly later, and often in different guises. In Peirce's largely unpublished works one finds topics that later became known as, for example, multi-modal logics and possible-worlds semantics, quantification into modal contexts, cross-world identities (in R 490 he termed these special relations connecting objects in different possible worlds "references", see Pietarinen 2006), and what is termed 'Peirce's Puzzle' (Dekker 2001; Hintikka

2011; Pietarinen 2015a), namely the question of the meaning of indefinites in conditional sentences. Peirce himself proposed to analyse the latter in quantified modal extensions of EGs of his own devising.

Far from only anticipating later findings, Peirce's logical innovations have been applied in a number of areas, including philosophical logic, formal semantics and pragmatics, mathematics, mind and language, AI, cognitive and computing sciences, biology, medical diagnosis and prognosis, astrobiology, physics, cosmology and geology, as much as in economics, game and decision theory, history and philosophy of science, archaeology, anthropology, musicology and art studies.[6]

Introduction to Alpha Graphs

Next, Peirce's Alpha system for classical propositional logic is presented in modern terms. The later volumes will include a presentation of the Beta graphs and those parts of the several systems of Gamma graphs proposed by Peirce that correspond to modal logics. Ma & Pietarinen (2016) define precise algebraic semantics for Alpha and the proof that the Alpha algebras are exactly Boolean algebras. The algebraic completeness of the Alpha system with respect to Alpha algebras justifies the correctness of the system as a completely new one for classical propositional logic.

In order to understand the basic ideas, let us briefly go back to Peirce's famous 1880 paper on the algebra of logic, which presents a calculus for Boolean algebras. Using modern Lindenbaum–Tarski construction, one can prove that his calculus is sound and complete with respect to the class of all Boolean algebras. It is in this way, by improving upon Boole's work, that Peirce came to develop various calculi for classical propositional logic. The main ideas behind Peirce's theory of consequence are presented next.

Leading Principle of Reasoning

In §2 of his 1880 paper, Peirce began with the treatment of illation (deduction). He described the general form of inference as follows:

---

[6] For some further work and applications along the lines Peirce had set out to do see, for example, Bellucci, Pietarinen & Stjernfelt (2014); Brady & Trimble (2000); Lupher & Adajian (2015); Pietarinen (2005b, 2010b, 2012); Pietarinen, Shafiei & Stjernfelt (2019); Sowa (1984, 2006); Zalamea (2012a,b). For details on Peirce's deductive logic, see the collection of Houser et al. (1997). Hilpinen (2004) is a helpful overview on Peirce's logic.

The general type of inference is

$$P$$
$$\therefore C,$$

where $\therefore$ is the sign of illation. (Peirce 1880, p. 17)

Here P is the premiss (or a set of premises), and C is the conclusion obtained by using rules of inference. A general rule of inference as it is represented in the mind of a reasoner is called a "habit" by Peirce. He then introduced the vital *leading principle*:

> A habit of inference may be formulated in a proposition which shall state that every proposition c, related in a given general way to any true proposition p, is true. Such a proposition is called the *leading principle* of the class of inferences whose validity it implies. (*ibid.*)

Peirce then introduced a sign $\prec$ of the copula to express this leading principle. The form $P \therefore C$ expresses an argument, and $P_i \prec C_i$ expresses *the truth of its leading principle*. He presents the meaning of the copula in a modern, model-theoretic fashion:

> The symbol $\prec$ is the copula, and signifies primarily that every state of things in which a proposition of the class P_i is true is a state of things in which the corresponding propositions of the class C_i is true. (Peirce 1880, p. 18)

In 1904, this semantic character of the logical consequence is accentuated in terms of any state of things that connects the consequent and the antecedent:

> *Hypothesis No 2.* In case any two propositions, x and y, should be such that we are entitled to write
>
> $$x \prec y$$
>
> (and we do not here assume that this is the case), this implies that the possible state of things represented by y is in a certain relation to whatever possible state of things there may be to which the state of things represented by x is in that relation. (CSP to Edward V. Huntington, February 14, 1904; LoF 3)

The sign $\prec$ is Peirce's later, cursive notation for $\prec$. From Peirce's interpretation it follows that the copula $\prec$ is the sign that stands for logical consequence. The calculus that he develops is indeed about the copula and its properties.

Peirce emphasises the significance of the leading principle or the copula. He identifies the copula of the form $A \prec B$ with a compound proposition built from A (the premiss) and B (the conclusion) by the sentential operation of material implication. In §3 of the 1880 paper on forms of propositions, he stated the following:

The forms $A \prec B$, or A implies B, and $A \stackrel{\_}{\prec} B$, or A does not imply B, *embrace* both hypothetical and categorial propositions. ... To say, 'if A, then B' is obviously the same as to say that from A, B follows, logically or extralogically. By thus identifying the relation expressed by the copula with that of illation, we identify the proposition with the inference, and the term with the proposition. This identification, by means of which all that is found true of term, proposition, or inference is at once known to be true of all three, is a most important engine of reasoning, which we have gained by beginning with a consideration of the genesis of logic. (Peirce 1880, pp. 21–22, added emphasis)

It has been believed, perhaps ever since Bertrand Russell (1901), that Peirce (and also Ernst Schröder) somehow confused the metalogical consequence relation with the material implication. However, the upshot of Peirce's important identification of the two actually marks a vital discovery in the history of logic. It is this identification that justifies Peirce's calculus as a calculus for Boolean algebras.

The Algebra of the Copula

For the sake of clarity, we separate the two meanings of the copula $\prec$ (or $\stackrel{\_}{\prec}$) by using two signs: (1) the consequence relation (the sign of illation) $\Rightarrow$; and (2) the material implication $\rightarrow$. Peirce introduced the algebra of the copula in §4 of his 1880 paper. His algebra of the copula is a calculus of the consequence relation. An expression of the form $x \Rightarrow y$ is called a *sequent*, according to the standard proof-theoretic terminology.

Definition 2.1. The calculus of the copula consists of the following axiom and rules:
(1) Identity: $\qquad$ (Id) $x \Rightarrow x$
(2) Peirce's Rule:
$$\frac{x \wedge y \Rightarrow z}{x \Rightarrow y \rightarrow z} \text{(PR)}$$

(3) Rule of Transitivity:
$$\frac{x \Rightarrow y \quad y \Rightarrow z}{x \Rightarrow z} \text{(Tr)}$$

The double line in (PR) means that the lower sequent can be derived from the upper sequent and vice versa.

The axiom of identity is easy to understand: every proposition follows from itself. Peirce explained it in terms of the memory (or monotonicity) of belief: what we have hitherto believed we continue to believe, in the absence of any reason to the contrary. The second rule can be named *Peirce's Rule*, because it is probably the first formulation of the *Law of Residuation*: that the material implication is a right residual of conjunction. The nature and significance of Peirce's Rule, as well as its historical discovery, will be noticed below, following a brief presentation of his 1880 calculus.

The meaning of the rule (Tr) is the transitivity of the consequence relation. If y follows from x and z follows from y, then z must follow from x. Peirce mentions that the transitivity of the copula derives from De Morgan's work. He also states that, "the same principle may be algebraically conceived as a rule for the elimination of y from the two propositions $x \prec y$ and $y \prec z$" (Peirce 1880, p. 25). After Gentzen's 1934 work, the rule (Tr) became called a *cut rule* in proof theory. It concerns the elimination of the middle, or the cut term. Later in early 1890s Peirce would return to the topic of the algebra of the copula.

Peirce's Calculus for Boolean Algebras

After the introduction of the algebra of the copula, Peirce continued his 1880 exposition to introduce the logic of non-relative terms. The non-relative terms are constructed from propositions using logical multiplication × and addition +. Here the notation is changed to ∧ for conjunction and to ∨ for disjunction.

First, Peirce commented on the rule (PR) when the negation sign is introduced. For any term x, let $\bar{x}$ be the negation of x. Then the proposition $x \to y$ is equivalent with $\bar{x} \vee y$. Hence by (PR) we can derive:

$$\frac{x \wedge y \Rightarrow z}{x \Rightarrow \bar{y} \vee z}$$

Moreover, Peirce stated the following derived variant of the rule (PR):

$$\frac{x \wedge \bar{y} \Rightarrow z}{x \Rightarrow y \vee z}$$

Two important further variants of (PR) can be stated as follows:

$$\frac{x \Rightarrow y}{\text{(The possible)} \Rightarrow \bar{x} \vee y} \qquad \frac{x \Rightarrow y}{x \wedge \bar{y} \Rightarrow \text{(The impossible)}}$$

Peirce then continued to introduce two notations: 0 for the impossible, and ∞ for the possible. Replacing 0 and ∞ with ⊥ and ⊤, respectively, Peirce gave the following axioms:

$$(\top)\ x \Rightarrow \top \quad (\bot)\ \bot \Rightarrow x$$

Moreover, from the axiom (Id), and using the two variants of (PR), one can easily derive the law of excluded middle and the law of contradiction:

$$\top \Rightarrow x \vee \bar{x} \quad \text{and} \quad \bar{x} \wedge x \Rightarrow \bot.$$

The negation sign can be defined in terms of → and ⊥ as follows:

$$\overline{x} := x \to \bot.$$

Then $\overline{x} \wedge x \Rightarrow \bot$ is obtained from $x \to \bot \Rightarrow x \to \bot$ by (PR).

Peirce proceeds to introduce the rules for conjunction (multiplication) and disjunction (addition). The definition of his calculus is now complete. He proved all the axioms of lattices and stated the distributive laws.

For the convenience of discussion, his 1880 calculus for classical propositional logic can be summarised as follows:

Definition 2.2. Peirce's calculus **PC** consists of the following axioms and rules:
(1) Axioms:
$$\text{(Id) } x \Rightarrow x \quad \text{(T) } x \Rightarrow \top \quad (\bot) \bot \Rightarrow x \quad \text{(Em) } \top \Rightarrow x \vee \overline{x}$$

(2) Rules:
$$\frac{x \wedge y \Rightarrow z}{x \Rightarrow y \to z}\text{(PR)} \qquad \frac{x \Rightarrow y \quad y \Rightarrow z}{x \Rightarrow z}\text{(Tr)}$$

$$\frac{x_1 \Rightarrow z \quad x_2 \Rightarrow z}{x_1 \vee x_2 \Rightarrow z}\text{(}\vee\text{I)} \qquad \frac{z \Rightarrow x_1 \quad z \Rightarrow x_2}{z \Rightarrow x_1 \wedge x_2}\text{(}\wedge\text{I)}$$

$$\frac{x_1 \vee x_2 \Rightarrow z}{x_i \Rightarrow z}\text{(}\vee\text{E)} \qquad \frac{z \Rightarrow x_1 \wedge x_2}{z \Rightarrow x_i}\text{(}\wedge\text{E)}$$

In ($\vee$E) and ($\wedge$E), $i \in \{1, 2\}$. A *derivation* of a sequent $x \Rightarrow y$ in **PC** is a proof tree with the root $x \Rightarrow y$ such that each node is either an axiom or derived by a rule of inference. A sequent $x \Rightarrow y$ is *derivable* in **PC** (notation $\vdash_{\mathbf{PC}} x \Rightarrow y$) if there is a derivation of $x \Rightarrow y$ in **PC**.

The rule (PR) is a formulation of Peirce's leading principle of inference. Leading principles that have a "maximum abstractness" (NEM IV, p. 175, 1898) are *logical* leading principles. The maximal abstractness means that such principles add nothing to the premises of the inference which they govern.

Peirce also introduced the equality sign (=): $x = y$ is a shorthand for "$x \Rightarrow y$ and $y \Rightarrow x$". One can now easily derive the following lattice-theoretic equalities:

(Idempotency)	$x = x \vee x$	$x \wedge x = x$
(Commutativity)	$x \vee y = y \vee x$	$x \wedge y = y \wedge x$
(Associativity)	$x \vee (y \vee z) = (x \vee y) \vee z$	$x \wedge (y \wedge z) = (x \wedge y) \wedge z$
(Absorption)	$x \vee (y \wedge z) = x$	$x \wedge (y \vee z) = x.$

In his 1880 paper, Peirce stated the following distributive laws:

(D1) $(x \vee y) \wedge z = (x \wedge z) \vee (y \wedge z)$; (D2) $(x \wedge y) \vee z = (x \vee z) \wedge (y \vee z)$.

He casually mentions that "they are easily proved ... but the proof is too tedious to give" (Peirce 1880, p. 33; cf. R 516; LoF 1). This passage provoked a challenge from Schröder, who took the distributivity laws to be independent from the lattice axioms. A rejoinder and a lively discussion ensued and Peirce's lost and subsequently recovered proof was finally added to Huntington's 1904 paper.[7]

A proof of (D1) and (D2) is easily given in Peirce's calculus **PC** (see Ma & Pietarinen 2017c). Below it is shown how to prove these laws using the graphical method.

The Diagrammatic Syntax of Alpha Graphs

Let Prop be a denumerable set of propositional variables. The set of all formulæ or terms of classical propositional logic $\mathcal{L}_C$ is defined inductively by the following rule:

$$\mathcal{L}_C \ni x ::= p \mid \top \mid (x \wedge y) \mid \overline{x}$$

where $p \in$ Prop. Define $x \vee y := \overline{\overline{x} \wedge \overline{y}}$ and $x \to y := \overline{x \wedge \overline{y}}$. The set of all formulæ of classical propositional logic is denoted by $\mathcal{L}_C$.

A formula in $\mathcal{L}_C$ is written in the linear order, using the *vinculae* as in Peirce's 1880 algebra. The Alpha graphs are constructed from primitive ones on the *sheet of assertion*,[8] or the *blank*, using a *cut* operation: ◯. The meaning of the cut is the operation of negation.[9] One can double the continuous cut, and get the *double cut* ⊚.

Peirce also has a formal language of Alpha graphs. A simple proposition, that is, a proposition without any occurrence of a propositional connective, can appear in a graph. He did not introduce propositional letters standing for simple propositions, but for the purpose of reconstruction of Peirce's Alpha system, we can fix a denumerable set of propositional letters Prop, the elements of which are primitive

---

[7] Houser (1985, 1991) provides a rich account of the context of Peirce's note and the debates that followed.

[8] In Peirce's terms: "The *sheet*, or *sheet of assertion*, or *actual sheet*, is that surface upon which any graph that may be scribed will be understood to be thereby asserted of the universe. It is so much of the surface originally appropriated to this purpose as remains unoccupied after part of it has been occupied by instances of scribed graphs. The surface originally so appropriated is called the *original sheet*, as opposed to the actual sheet" (R 1589, 1903; LoF 2).

[9] This is not the only meaning of this operation, as it also signifies, among other things, the grouping together of the graphs that it encircles together, as is customarily done by parentheses. Peirce in fact distinguishes altogether five offices of this operation (three for Alpha and two more for Beta, that is, for the first-order logic of quantifiers), only one of which is the negation, and is negation only secondarily, as the primary meaning is that of grouping or linear separation (R 430, 1902; LoF 1; Pietarinen 2015a).

graphs. Moreover, the sheet of assertion, or the blank, is also counted as a graph. The blank is denoted by SA or, when there is no confusion, just by the blank of the sheet and without boundaries: . A *primitive graph P* is a propositional letter or the blank SA. Every Alpha graph is constructed from primitive graphs using operations of juxtaposition and enclosure.

Definition 2.3 (Alpha Graphs)**.** The set $\mathfrak{G}_\alpha$ of all *Alpha graphs* is defined inductively by the following rule:

$$\mathfrak{G}_\alpha \ni G := p \mid \mathsf{SA} \mid G_1 G_2 \mid \overline{G},$$

where p is a propositional letter in Prop. The graph $G_1 G_2$ is obtained from G_1 and G_2 by placing them on the same *area* on the sheet of assertion. By an *area*, we mean a simple continuous region marked on the sheet of assertion by a thin oval line (the cut) and defined by the interior of that oval line. By continuous, we mean uninterrupted by any such cuts. In Peirce's terms:

> The term *cut* shall be applied to a linear separation of a surface, which line of separation returns into itself, so as to enclose a space within which the material of the surface in which the cut is made is replaced by a different material, either by stripping off the original material and disclosing a new surface below, or by putting on a patch fitting into the cut. The new surface of the interior shall be called the *area* of the cut, the outer surface the place of the cut, while the cut and its area, as a single whole, shall be called the hole ~~wound~~ of the cut (R S-28, 1903; LoF 2).

When we say "graphs" we mean "Alpha graphs". To improve readability, one could define abbreviations of compound graphs. For example, given any graphs G and H, one could define graphs $G \mathbin{\varovee} H$, $G \supset H$ and $G \equiv H$:

$$G \mathbin{\varovee} H := \overline{\overline{G}\,\overline{H}}\,; \quad G \supset H := \overline{G\,\overline{H}}\,; \quad G \equiv H := \overline{G\,\overline{H}}\,\overline{\overline{H}\,G}.$$

Here $\mathbin{\varovee}$ and $\Rightarrow$ can be viewed as shorthand operations for compound graphs that can be used to construct new graphs. These abbreviations are not used in what follows; Peirce would occasionally resort to various simplifications in order to "avoid the bewildering number of ovals or other signs of negation" (R 530; LoF 1).

There is an obvious translation from $\mathfrak{G}_\alpha$ to $\mathcal{L}_C$. For any graph $G \in \mathfrak{G}_\alpha$, define its translation $\pi(G)$ inductively as follows:

$$\pi(p) = p \qquad\qquad \pi(\mathsf{SA}) = \top$$
$$\pi(G_1 G_2) = \pi(G_1) \wedge \pi(G_2) \qquad \pi(\overline{G}) = \overline{\pi(G)}$$

Clearly $\pi(\overline{\overline{G}\,\overline{H}}) = \pi(G) \vee \pi(H)$ and $\pi(\overline{G\,\overline{H}}) = \pi(G) \to \pi(H)$.

A graph is constructed from primitive graphs using cuts and juxtapositions. Then a natural notion is a partial graph as a part of a graph.

Peirce mentioned the concept of a partial graph. The *entire graph* is everything that is scribed on the sheet of assertion. A *partial graph* is any graph scribed alone, or in the presence of other graphs (R 450, 1903; LoF 2). He did not present a precise definition of partial graphs, but one can observe Peirce's definition of the *nest* (R 650, 1910; LoF 1), which is a translation of Alpha graphs into a tree structure, as well as his Convention No. 2: "Graphs on different parts of the sheet, called *partial graphs*, shall independently assert what they would severally assert, were each the entire graph" (R 492, 1903; LoF 2). Further, "[a]n *entire graph* is a graph on a sheet otherwise blank. A *partial graph* is a part (possibly the whole) of an entire graph, which part if it were alone upon the sheet would have a meaning as a diagram" (R 491, 1903; LoF 2). In other words, "*[p]artial graphs* are graphs on the sheet of assertion that are not the only ones scribed on the sheet. The *entire graph* is all that is scribed on the sheet. The *total graph* is the entire graph together with the sheet of assertion itself" (R S-27, 1903; LoF 2). This can be defined more precisely by the parsing tree of an Alpha graph.

Definition 2.4. For any graph G, the *parsing tree* of G, denoted by $T(G)$, is defined inductively as follows:
(1) $T(p)$ is a single root node p.
(2) $T(\mathsf{SA})$ is a single root node SA.
(3) $T(G_1\ G_2)$ is a root node $G_1 G_2$ with child nodes $T(G_1)$ and $T(G_2)$.
(4) $T(\overline{G})$ is a root node $\overline{G}$ with one child node $T(G)$.
A *partial graph* of a graph G is a node in $T(G)$.

Definition 2.5. For any graph G, the *history* of a node J in $T(G)$, denoted by $h(J)$, is the unique path from the root to J. We say that J is a positive (negative) node of $T(G)$ if there is an even (odd) number of cuts in $h(J)$.

The notation $G[H]$ stands for that H is a node in $T(G)$. An occurrence of a graph J is *positive* (*negative*) in G, notation $G^+[J]$ ($G^-[J]$), if it is a positive (negative) node in $T(G)$.

Given a graph G with $H \in T(G)$, for any graph J, let $G[H/J]$ be the graph obtained from G by substituting J for H. Note that the substitution is not uniform. It is operated on any node of $T(G)$.

A *position* is a point on the area of a graph (but not on the cut line). Given any graph G, a position in G is *positive* (*negative*) if it is enclosed by an even (odd) number of cuts. A graph can be scribed at a position.

The System α

Peirce's Alpha (α) is a system defined by graph rules. A *graph rule* is of the form
$$\frac{G_1 \ldots G_n}{G_0}$$
where $G_0, \ldots, G_n$ are graphs. The graph $G_1 \ldots G_n$ is called the *premiss*, and G_0 is called the conclusion. Now we can present Peirce's Alpha system.

On the sheet of assertion, the rules of commutativity, associativity and conjunction can be expressed as follows:

$$\frac{G[H_1\ H_2]}{G[H_2\ H_1]}\text{(CM)} \quad \frac{G_1\ (G_2\ G_3)}{(G_1\ G_2)G_3}\text{(AS)} \quad \frac{G \quad H}{G\ H}\text{(Jux)}$$

The commutativity rule (CM) says that the positions of H_1 and H_2 in a partial graph $H_1\ H_2$ of G is immaterial. The associativity is concerned with the order of drawing graphs on the sheet of assertion. The parentheses in (AS) indicate the order of forming the graphs. The rule (AS) says that the order of forming graphs is immaterial. The rule (Jux) says that, if G and H are derived, then the juxtaposition $G\ H$ can be derived. When we have G and H on the sheet of assertion, we obtain $G\ H$.

However, when representing Alpha graphs in their two-dimensional form, the commutativity, associativity and conjunction fall naturally from the properties of the space in which graphs are scribed. They need no independent statement in the graph system. In any proof of a graph, we can identify the graphs obtained by the three rules (CM), (AS) and (Jux).[10] These rules are thus only pseudo-rules.

Definition 2.6. The system α consists of the following axioms and rules:
(1) *Axiom*:
$$SA$$

(2) *Deletion rule*:
$$\frac{G^+[H]}{G^+[SA]}\text{(DR)}$$
Every positive partial graph H in a graph G can be deleted.

---

10 Peirce notes: "Previously to 1880, the associative and commutative principles were regarded as the fundamental characters of copulation, along with a distributive principle. I proved the two first from the above definition; but Rule II shows them in their true light, as mere negations which in no way touch upon the real essence of composition. It is no more necessary to refer to them than it is to state that the graphs can be written in blue ink, if desired" (R 530, c.1901; LoF 1). His Rule II is that "detached graphs may be inserted or erased, as if no others were on the sheet, and that regardless of distance and of direction" (*ibid.*).

(3) *Insertion rule*:
$$\frac{G^-[SA]}{G^-[H]} \text{(IR)}$$
Any graph can be inserted into a negative position in a graph G.

(4) *Double negation rule*:
$$\frac{G[H]}{G[\boxed{(H)}]} \text{(DN)}$$

The double line means that the upper graph can derive the lower graph, and vice versa. (DN) means that any partial graph H of a graph G can be replaced by the double cut of H and any double cut in G can be deleted.

(5) *Iteration/deiteration rule*:
$$\frac{K[G\,H[J]]}{K[G\,H[J/G\,J]]} \text{(IT)} \qquad \frac{K[G\,H[J/G\,J]]}{K[G\,H[J]]} \text{(DIT)}$$

(IT) means that, in any graph $K[G\,H]$, the partial graph G can be iterated at any position in H. (DIT) is the converse of (IT).

A *proof* of a graph G in α is a finite sequence of graphs $G_0, \ldots, G_n$ such that $G_n = G$, and each G_i is either an axiom, or derived from previous graphs by a rule. A graph G is *provable* in α, notation $\vdash_\alpha G$, if it has a derivation in α. A graph rule is *provable* in α if the conclusion is provable whenever the premiss is provable in α.

Remark 2.1. The Alpha system is essentially a *sequent calculus*, because it is a calculus of the consequence relation which is shown in the rules. The axiom SA is not a real axiom of the form in the system **PC**: the blank is nothing but the sheet of assertion. Moreover, the rules in Alpha are stated in terms of the *deep structure* of a graph: the position of a partial graph scribed in an entire graph. This is closely and interestingly related to the Schütte–Brünnler deep sequent calculus for classical propositional logic (Brünnler 2003; Schütte 1977). In deep sequent calculus, derivation starts from SA which stands for the tautology. In Alpha, the derivability of a graph is reduced to the transformations in deep structures by introducing or removing a partial graph and double cuts.

Proposition 2.1. The following graphs and rules are provable in α:
(1) Blank: $(G\,\boxed{SA})$.
(2) Identity: $(G\,\boxed{G})$.
(3) $(G\,\boxed{G\,G})$.
(4) The law of excluded middle: $(\boxed{(G)}\,\boxed{(G)})$.
(5) $(G_1\,G_2\,\boxed{G_i})$ for $i = 1, 2$.

(6) De Morgan rules:

$$\frac{G\,H}{(\!(G)(H)\!)}\;(\text{DM1}) \qquad \frac{(\!(G)(H)\!)}{G\,H}\;(\text{DM2})$$

(7) $G_i(\!(G_1)(G_2)\!)$ for $i = 1, 2$.

(8) Contraposition and Transitivity:

$$\frac{G(H)}{H(G)}\;(\text{CP}) \qquad \frac{G(H)\quad H(J)}{G(J)}\;(\text{TR})$$

(9) Prefixing and Modus Ponens:

$$\frac{G}{H(G)}\;(\text{PF}) \qquad \frac{G\;\;G(H)}{H}\;(\text{MP})$$

Proof. (1) is obtained from **SA** by (DN) and (IN). (2) is obtained by adding the step (IT) to (1). (3) is obtained from (2) by (IT). (4) is obtained from (2) by (DN). De Morgan rules and (CP) are straightforward by (DN). (7) is obtained by (DN), (IN), (IT), (DN) and (IN) rules, in that order. The proofs of (2), (5) and (TR) are given below, respectively:

$$\frac{\mathbf{SA}}{\dfrac{(\;)}{\dfrac{G(\;)}{G(G)}\;(\text{IT})}\;(\text{IN})}\;(\text{DN}) \qquad \frac{\mathbf{SA}}{\dfrac{(\;)}{\dfrac{G_1\,G_2(\;)}{G_1\,G_2(G_i)}\;(\text{IT})}\;(\text{IN})}\;(\text{DN})$$

$$\frac{G(H)\quad H(J)}{\dfrac{G(H(H(J)\!)\!)\quad H(J)}{\dfrac{G(H(H(J)\!)\!)}{\dfrac{G(H(J)\!)}{\dfrac{G(J)}{G(J)}\;(\text{DN})}\;(\text{DR})}\;(\text{DIT})}\;(\text{DR})}\;(\text{IT})$$

As to (9), (PF) and (MP) are shown as follows:

$$\frac{G}{\dfrac{(\!(G)\!)}{H(G)}\;(\text{IN})}\;(\text{DN}) \qquad \frac{G\;\;G(H)}{\dfrac{G\;(H)}{\dfrac{(\!(H)\!)}{H}\;(\text{DN})}\;(\text{DR})}\;(\text{DIT})$$

This completes the proof. □

Remark 2.2. In R 417 (1893) Peirce reproduces the Modus Ponens rule (MP) in the algebra of the copula using iteration and deletion in the following fashion:

from t and $\bar{t} \curlyvee n$, compound first the premises: $t \cdot (\bar{t} \curlyvee n)$. Then infer (by iteration and deletion) $t \cdot \bar{t} \curlyvee n$, which is the same as $0 \curlyvee n$, and which now gives n. (The sign $\curlyvee$ stands for logical aggregation, that is, logical disjunction.)

Proposition 2.2. The following transformation rules are derivable in α ($i = 1, 2$):

$$\frac{G_i\,(H)}{G_1\,G_2\,(H)}\;(\&\mathrm{L}) \qquad \frac{G\,(H)\quad G\,(J)}{G\,(H\,J)}\;(\&\mathrm{R})$$

$$\frac{G\,(J)\quad H\,(J)}{((G\,H)\,(J))}\;(\varovee\mathrm{L}) \qquad \frac{G\,(H_i)}{G\,((H_1)\,(H_2))}\;(\varovee\mathrm{L})$$

$$\frac{G\,(H\,(J))}{(H)\,G\,(J)}\;(\mathrm{NL}) \qquad \frac{G\,H\,(J)}{H\,((G)\,(J))}\;(\mathrm{NR})$$

Proof. The rule (&L) is obtained by (IN) directly. The proofs of (&R) and (NL) are as follows:

$$\frac{G\,(H)\quad G\,(J)}{G\,(H)\quad G\,(J\,(G\,H))}\;(\mathrm{IT})$$
$$\frac{}{G\,(J\,(G\,H))}\;(\mathrm{DR})$$
$$\frac{}{G\,(J\,(G\,(H\,J)))}\;(\mathrm{IT})$$
$$\frac{}{G\,((G\,H\,J))}\;(\mathrm{DR})$$
$$\frac{}{G\,G\,(H\,J)}\;(\mathrm{DN})$$
$$\frac{}{G\,(H\,J)}\;(\mathrm{DIT})$$

$$\frac{G\,(H\,(J))}{G\,(H\,(H\,(J)))}\;(\mathrm{IR})$$
$$\frac{}{G\,(H\,(J))}\;(\mathrm{DIT})$$

The remaining rules can be derived easily. $\square$

Corollary 2.1. The following rules are provable in α:

$$\frac{G\,(H)\quad J\,(K)}{G\,J\,(H\,K)}\;(\&) \qquad \frac{G\,(H)\quad J\,(K)}{(G\,(J))\,(H\,(K))}\;(\varovee)$$

Proposition 2.3. The following *distributivity rules* are provable in α:

$$\frac{G\,(H\,(J))}{(G\,H)\,(G\,J)}\;(\mathrm{D1}) \qquad \frac{G\,(H\,J)}{(G\,(H))\,(G\,(J))}\;(\mathrm{D2})$$

Proof. For (D1), we have the following proofs:

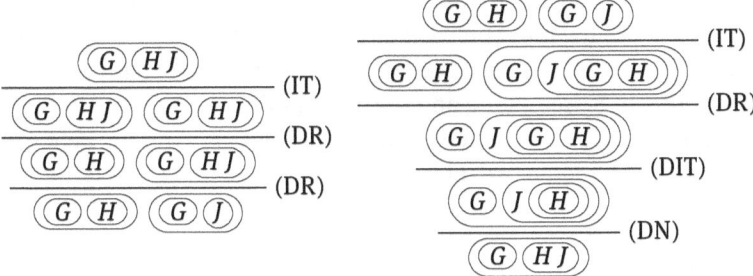

For (D2), we have the following proofs:

□

Remark 2.3. The proof of distributivity in the α-calculus is short. In the proofs from (GH)(GJ) to G(H)(J) (D1), and from (G)(HJ) to (GH)(GJ) (D2), the premises are first cloned by iteration. Peirce had noted in R 418 how this 'non-syllogistic' operation of reusing the premise on the same area of the sheet which he had discovered in 1893 can be eminently useful:

> The same premise may be written in more than once …the student of exclusively non-relative logic is quite unaware that anything can be gained by bringing in again a premise already used. Ordinary syllogistic gives no hint of such a thing; nay seems rather opposed to it. (R 418)

The proof of (D1) in system α is exactly the graphical version of his 1893 proof of distribution as given in Chapter XII (R 418, "The Algebra of Relatives") which he wrote for his projected book *How to Reason*. In his previous Chapter XI of the same work (R 417, "The Boolian Calculus"), Peirce had produced a nearly equivalent proof of (D1), which does use the rule of iteration but without the initial cloning step. There he stated that the proof was what he always intended his demonstration of distributivity to be. He must also have meant his 1880 statement of the proof, namely the "easy but tedious" one. (In the 1880 system he does not yet have the rule of iteration at work, which may cast some doubt on the credibility of the claimed universality of his 1893 demonstration.)

Proposition 2.4. The following rules are provable in α:

$$\dfrac{\;(G\,H\,(J))\;}{\;(G\,((H\,(J))))\;}\text{ (RG1)} \qquad \dfrac{\;(G\,((H\,(J))))\;}{\;(G\,H\,(J))\;}\text{ (RG2)}$$

Proof. (RG1) is straightforwardly obtained from (DN) by adding a double cut. (RG2) is equally straightforwardly obtained from (DN) by eliminating a double cut. □

The rules (RG1) and (RG2) are the graphical correlates to Peirce's logical leading principle (Peirce's Rule). In the Alpha system, Peirce's leading principle becomes provable. For (RG1), the proof only needs one application of (DN) that introduces a double cut. For (RG2), the proof needs one application of (DN) to delete a double cut. The validity of Peirce's Rule and thus the residuation laws are in the system of Alpha graphs matters of immediate observation. This leads, as Peirce notices, to the justification of deductive inference.

Conclusions

Contemporary logical studies have started to observe Peirce's contributions belatedly, sometimes only after a century has passed. A comprehensive list of recent studies would be too long to be provided here; in brief summary, the issues and topics that have been covered in the secondary literature include various modal and non-classical modifications, extensions, deviations and restrictions of the basic systems (Bellucci, Chiffi & Pietarinen 2017; Chiffi & Pietarinen 2019; Ma 2018, Ma & Pietarinen 2017a,b; 2018b,c; Pietarinen 2004, 2008), proof analysis provided by the graphical method (Ma & Pietarinen 2016), the origins of sequent calculus, deep inference and the logical consequence relation (Ma & Pietarinen 2017c, 2018a, 2019), as well as the contribution graphs make to the philosophy of notation, the field that started off with Peirce's 1885 paper (Bellucci 2018; Bellucci, Moktefi & Pietarinen 2017; Chiffi & Pietarinen 2018; Liu 2005, Bellucci & Pietarinen 2016, 2017c). The encyclopædia article on Peirce's Logic (Bellucci & Pietarinen 2015) provides further details and perspectives on Peirce's general theory of logic.

In the next two volumes of the *Logic of the Future* series, an introduction to the Beta and Gamma parts of Peirce's theory of existential graphs is included.

Introduction to Volume 1: History and Applications

The first volume of the *Logic of the Future* series has its textual material organised in 28 chapters and three parts: *Reasoning and Diagrams* (Part I), *Development of Existential Graphs* (Part II) and *Theory and Application of Existential Graphs* (Part III). An account of these parts, their theoretical background and a descrip-tion of the texts selected in individual chapters is provided next.

Part I: Reasoning and Diagrams

This section contains an introduction to the themes of the first part, followed by a survey of its four individual selections. The selections are organised in a roughly reverse chronological order, starting from the late writings of 1910 and ending at 1895.

Introduction to Part I:
Peirce's Late Philosophy of Diagrammatic Reasoning

Two tenets characterise Peirce's philosophy of logic and reasoning. One is that all reasoning is diagrammatic, and another that every diagram is at bottom a logical diagram.[1] What does Peirce mean by diagrams, and what is his notion of reasoning? In the texts gathered under the heading of "Reasoning and Diagrams", Peirce proposes several such accounts, seen from the mature perspective of his late writings on the topic.

In some of his latest writings on the topic, Peirce maintained that diagrams belong to those "quite other systems of signs into which [mathematicians and logicians] are accustomed to translate words and forms of words" (R 654, 1910; LoF 1),

---

[1] These tenets include reasoning other than deduction, that is, abduction and induction as well. While the evidence that Peirce thought abduction and induction to be diagrammatic as well is rather meagre (see Pietarinen 2019), he certainly thought both to be logical (Bellucci & Pietarinen 2019). LoF 2 includes examples of graphs from the 1903 Lowell Lectures that may be his sole examples of abduction in logical diagrams.

https://doi.org/10.1515/9783110651409-003

namely systems of signs other than those natural language has at its disposal. The logical theory of diagrams, which the system of existential graphs (EGs) is the most advanced form is, in contrast, "the simplest possible system that is capable of expressing with exactitude every possible assertion" (*ibid.*). In this system of diagrams, Peirce writes,

> there are none of the ordinary parts of speech. [...] its expressions are diagrams upon a surface, and indeed must be regarded as only a projection upon that surface of a sign extended in three dimensions. (*ibid.*)

He then proceeds to present one of the central tenets of logical diagrams to make it a superior method for the analysis of the meaning of assertions:

> Three dimensions are necessary and sufficient for the expression of all assertions; so that, if man's reason was originally limited to the line of speech (which I do not affirm), it has now outgrown the limitation. (*ibid.*)

Peirce clarifies the meaning of the term 'diagram' to refer to imaginary activities and mental constructs, intending that term to be "used in the peculiar sense of a concrete but possibly changing mental image of such a thing as it represents." "A drawing or model", he remarks, "may be employed to aid the imagination; but the essential thing to be performed is the act of imagining" (R 616, LoF 1). One definition of a diagram is found in R S-64 (c.1893–1894, entitled "Logic", a piece which may be related to his planned chapter on "Graphs and Graphical Diagrams", see introduction to Part II, LoF 1):

Definition 1. A mathematical *hypothesis* is an imaginary state of things proposed for study.
Definition 2. Any imaginary state of things is mathematically *possible* for which the hypothesis leaves room.
Definition 3. A *diagram* is a drawing whose parts are related like the elements of a hypothesis sufficiently to assist the study of it.

Examples of such diagrams follow these definitions. Many other relevant writings that pertain to the topic of reasoning and diagrams derive from Peirce's later years of 1904–1908, which he produced in connection to his mature philosophy of pragmaticism. They are collected in Part VI of Volume 3 of *Logic of the Future* under the heading of "Pragmaticism". An unpublished manuscript entitled "PAP" (R 293; LoF 3, an acronym of his 1906 "Prolegomena to an Apology for Pragmaticism" but written afterwards in late 1906 or early 1907) shows Peirce's concern to be the connection between phenomenological reflections and the logical theory of graphs:

> To begin with, then, a Diagram is an Icon of a set of rationally related objects. By *rationally related*, I mean that there is between them, not merely one of those relations which we know

by experience, but know not how to comprehend, but one of those relations which anybody who reasons at all must have an inward acquaintance with. This is not a sufficient definition, but just now I will go no further, except that I will say that the Diagram not only represents the related correlates, but also, and much more definitely represents the relations between them, as so many objects of the Icon. (R 293)

Peirce takes a diagram to be an "Icon of a set of rationally related objects." What are the objects that are rationally related to one another? What is an icon, anyway, and what does it mean that a relation is rational? To see Peirce's preferred meanings of these terms, let us observe another, related thought from an alternative and likewise unpublished version of the relevant paragraphs of PAP:

But we do not make a diagram simply to represent the relation of killer to killed, though it would not be impossible to represent this relation in a Graph-Instance; and the reason we do not is that there is little or nothing in that relation that is rationally comprehensible. It is known as a fact, and that is all. I believe I may venture to affirm that an intelligible relation, that is, a relation of thought, is created only by the act of representing it. I do not mean to say that if we should some day find out the metaphysical nature of the relation of killing, that intelligible relation would thereby be created. For if such be the nature of killing, such it always was, from the date of a certain "difficulty" and consurrection in a harvest-field. No; for the intelligible relation has been signified, though not read by man, since the first killing was done, if not long before. (R 293)

It is the "act of representing" that creates rational, intelligible relations. The nature of rational relations is a matter of logical analysis, not metaphysics. The objects of a diagram, as an icon, are representations that represent the relations between the correlates involved in a relation, such as the relation of killing in the proposition involved in the sentence "Cain killed Abel".

Thinking is not at bottom a matter of psychological operations that bring imaginary objects under the inspection of the 'Mind's Eye', either. Peirce calls such thinking "a fabled 'operation of the mind' by which an imaginary object is brought before one's gaze" (R 293). Some such objects may be thoughts, such as signs "upon which an argument may turn" (R 293). Thinking as a logical operation is not a description of what goes on in our minds but the matter of logical analysis that translates a thought into another thought: "Assuming that we know that thinking is 'talking' with oneself", he notices in R 678 (LoF 1), "we see at once that our knowledge of how we think is no mere *description* of it, as a knowledge of how the brain, or any other physical machine, works would be, but, so far as it is correct, amounts positively to a *translation* of it, or in some cases to a 'grammatical', a 'syntactical', analysis of thought." In logic, this translation is called reasoning according to the leading or guiding principle of reasoning. Peirce had expressed the principle since 1880 as the rule of residuation (the rule of the copula of inclusion, or 'Peirce's Rule'), which articulates an important relation between conjunctions and implications and provides an algebraic basis for an analysis of logical consequence as the copula and its properties.

This latter passage comes from Peirce's late writings in 1910 on the nature of reasoning. It constitutes a crucial piece of the puzzle: why a mechanical arrangement of data, such as when we produce a photograph to represent an object, cannot be considered thinking? Taking evidence from what a camera produces would be a psychological event just as taking evidence for what happens in reasoning from the processes in the physiology of the brain would be. Peirce makes the point in his 1906 address to the National Academy of Sciences when describing how logic itself has nothing to do with the process of thinking:

> [Logic] only compares the premisses with the conclusions and it therefore has no concern with any character of the mind that might not be shared by unconscious machines or by external signs. (R 490; LoF 3)

In other words, a "'syntactical' analysis of thought" as an analysis of thought that one would get by investigating the workings of the brain is just as mistaken an approach as taking grammatical analysis of language to be its graphology, or notational analysis to concern typography of signs, or to take language use to be a sociological phenomenon.

In contrast, a "thinking proper", as proposed in the same paper, "takes the form of a dialogue":

> If we agree to apply the word "talk" to all [the] ways of expressing sensations, actions, and ideas in signs of any kinds and also to all [the] ways of interpreting signs, and if we apply this word "signs" to everything recognizable whether to our outward sense or to our inward feeling and imagination, provided only it calls upon some feeling, effort, or thought, then every reader will be able by experiments and observations of his own [...] reasonably to satisfy himself that all meditation, consideration, and thought consists or is embodied in *talk with oneself*. (R 678)

On such "inner dialogue" characterisation of thinking Peirce is following in Plato's footsteps, so much so that he once wrote in the margins of his copy of Lutosławski's *Plato's Logic* (1897) that "this was Plato's greatest contribution to thought" (p. 376).[2] Not dependent on any peculiarities of the human mind but merely acting according to the affordances that the theory of reasoning can take,

---

[2] Peirce's marginal note refers to Lutosławski's account of Plato's explanation of thought as a conversation of the soul with itself, leading to a choice between affirmation and negation, which is judgment: "Thought as moving between affirmation and negation, according to the law of contradiction" (Lutosławski 1897, p. 376).

the dialogical approach springs from the theory of reasoning, as he explains in a draft of his 1906 "Prolegomena" paper:

> A subpoena upon psychology to testify that deliberate reflexion takes the form of a dialogue, whether with or without the spicery of chat about the two sides of the brain, would, on the part of one who understood the matter, be nothing less than charlatanry. For it is not the question how man does think, but what is the essential nature of thought. Those whom we hear all-confidently asserting that anything like reasoning is a phenomenon peculiar to human consciousness or to the specific type of consciousness to which the human variety appertains, have not sufficiently considered the subject, and in particular fail to recognize that the question is not what happens to be extant but what the essential nature of reasoning allow. (R 292a; LoF 3)

The point can also be put into semiotic terms just as it can be explained in logical terms. The action of signs upon the mind, perhaps intended as its transcendental element—the possibility of reasoning as such—is independent of physical, physiological and intentional constraints. Compared by Peirce to the action by which a row of bricks aligned upwards on the floor falls when a first brick falls upon its neighbour, explicit references to the characteristics of a singular or human mind is not needed when erecting such theories:

> A line of bricks stand on end upon a floor, each facing the next one of the line. An end one is tilted so as to fall over upon the next; and so they all successively fall. The mechanical statement of the phenomenon is that a portion of the sum of the energy of motion that each brick had at the instant its centre of gravity was directly over its supporting edge, added to the energy of its fall is transformed into an energy of motion of the near brick. Now I assert no more than this, but less, since I do not say whether it was mechanical energy, or what it was that was communicated, when, applying my definition of a Sign, I assert (as I do), that each brick is a Sign (namely, an Index), to the succeeding bricks of the line, of the original effect produced on the first brick. [...] Until you see this, you do not grasp the meaning that I attach to the word 'Sign'. (R 293)

These remarks cover only a small fragment of some of the chief features of Peirce's semiotic approach to thinking, reasoning and diagrams, but in a summary fashion assist us in seeing why he thought that it is the logical theory of graphs that is the best method to represent such dialogues and to perform the needed logical analyses of intellectual thought.

This is not to claim that the relevant studies would have nothing to do with experimental issues. Peirce was an experimental scientist himself, and among the pioneers of setting up blinded, randomised and controlled experiments in psychology and related fields. Indeed diagrams are ubiquitous in science, including experimental science, and not restricted to analysing intellectual thought or inferential processes. What is it then that experimental scientists are experimenting upon? Let us examine the chemistry quote that was also central in the earlier discussion:

> [A]fter the experiment is made, the particular sample he operated upon could very well be thrown away, as having no further interest. For it was not the particular sample that the chemist was investigating; it was the molecular structure. [...] you slipped in implying that it is otherwise with experiments made upon diagrams. For what is there the Object of Investigation? It is the *form of a relation*. (Peirce 1906, p. 494)

What does Peirce mean that the objects of scientists' investigation are "forms of relations"? The answer that he sees the objects of interest in chemistry, as much as in other fields of science, too, to be structures of whatever kind is only half of the reason, and as such is not enough of an explanation to what Peirce is after. The reason is that Peirce sees the purpose of an experimental scientist to be not in observing experimental phenomena in atomistic fashion, that is to say, in the sense of the experimenter aiming at gaining information about some particular cases whenever an experiment or measurement is completed. Experiments aim at answering questions that the formulation of research hypotheses allows the experimenter to put forth. The experimenters ultimately want to have their information states updated concerning general phenomena and general laws as answers to a question, in the sense that whenever the same sort of an experiment is made, the same sort of result would follow. But general laws are not directly available in experiments. They have to be inferred from observational phenomena. Forms of relations concern such *inferred generalities of the structures*. Their nature has to be inferred from the representations of those structures by certain peculiar means of reasoning best fitted to the task at hand.[3]

An alternative version of the above quotation from its draft version is equally revealing in supporting this interpretation:

> The object of the chemist's investigation, that which he experiments upon, that to which his question put to Nature relates, is the molecular structure; and this has, in all samples, as complete an identity as it belongs to molecular structure to possess. Accordingly, he does, as you say, experiment upon the very object under investigation. But if you stop [for] a moment to consider it, you will see that you tripped in saying that it is otherwise with experiments made upon diagrams. For what is here the object of investigation? It is the *form of a relation*.

---

3 Pietarinen (2009, 2010c) argues, against Hookway (2012), that Peirce is not a 'structuralist' in any ordinary sense of that term in philosophy of science or in philosophy of mathematics. Nor, of course, is he a structuralist in the quite different sense inherited from Ferdinand De Saussure. One would need to take into account Peirce's scotistic, scholastic theory of real possibilities, and to modify the modal-realist account of hypotheticals to suit the purpose of mathematical practice. The latter line of thought is developed in Pietarinen (2014).

> Now this form of relation is the very form of the relation between the two corresponding parts of the diagram. (R 292a)

Here Peirce tells us that, in the case of the chemist, it is the molecular structure that possesses the identity of "the very object under investigation." The object under investigation is not assumed to be an individual that exists, nor does it need to coincide with a particular observation. Molecular structures are inferred from observations that chemists perform in the course of the investigation. Their experimentation upon actual elements—instances of that general structure—provides information on what general form that structure may possess. The real object *is* the form of the structure.

Importantly, diagrams are not only icons but also symbols, because they are general signs that have general objects. They do not reproduce particular structures of the objects under investigation, but the general form of that structure which the investigator purports to produce in the course of experimenting upon the relations concerned in the diagrams. These relationships may be concrete and actual, but if the diagram represented only concrete and actual relationships it would cease to be a diagram proper. Peirce's "pure diagram" is a pattern of activities that can "represent" and "render intelligible" the forms of those relations, and nothing else. Diagrams thus concern intelligible, rational relations, and they have a generality that is brought out only by diagrams that are of the nature of symbols.

> A Diagram, in my sense, is in the first place a Token, or singular object used as a Sign; for it is essential that it should be capable of being perceived and observed. It is, however, what is called a General sign; that is, it denotes a general Object. It is, indeed, constructed with that intention, and thus represents the Object of that intention. Now the Object of an intention, purpose, or desire is always General. The Diagram represents a definite Form of Relation. This Relation is usually one which actually exists, as in a map, or is intended to exist, as in a Plan. But this is far from being essential to the Diagram as such, that if details are added to represent existential or experiential peculiarities, such additions are distinctly of an undiagrammatic nature. The pure Diagram is designed to represent and to render intelligible the Form of Relation merely. Consequently, Diagrams are restricted to the representation of a certain class of relations; namely, those that are intelligible. (R 293)

Diagrams become symbols capable of representing the generality of forms of relations by abstraction. Ideal forms that diagrams put before us are what Peirce would in the 1903 *Lowell Lectures* logically analyse as the "substantive possibilities" in the Gamma part of the logic of existential graphs (R 467, R 459, R 464; LoF 2): they instruct scientists on how things might be. They concern the reality of the results of experiments, not their actuality. These ideals occupy the realm of potentiality, entertained by scientists as vital parts of their attempt at the construction of successful scientific theories.[4]

Besides symbols, diagrams are also icons, as already confirmed by the earlier passage where Peirce had explained the meaning of rational and intelligible relations. An important additional explanation of how diagrams represent general forms of relations as icons of those forms is provided by the following passage:

> No such doubt bedims our perception that it is as an Icon that the Diagram represents the definite Form of intelligible relation which constitutes its Object, that is, that it represents that Form by a more or less vague resemblance to thereto. There is not usually much vagueness, but I use that word because the Diagram does not itself define just how far the likeness extends, and in some characteristic cases such definition would be impossible, although the Form of Relation is in itself Definite, since it is General. (R 293)

Icons provide information about their objects by their relational structures, including structures and patterns that are creations of the mind. Icons are products of rational considerations as created by the mind. They need not resemble their objects by virtue of appearance or by perceptually, let alone visually, induced associations. It is by reasoning and information mediated by signs that we can find out what the relationships in the objects are, which in the case of iconic signs means to preserve or map their essential structure in those skeleton signs that represent the structures of rationally related objects into other structures. And since "it is icons only that rationally determine any true representation of the object" (R 292a), what lies at the core of such icons belongs to the theory of icons as logical representations.

But it would be misleading to claim that logical graphs are visual any more than sentences of language or formulæ of mathematics are. For one, there are also other types of logical diagrams than those that can be drawn or visually perceived.[5]

> We form in the imagination some sort of diagrammatic, that is, iconic, representation of the facts, as skeletonized as possible. The impression of the present writer is that with *ordinary*

---

[4] What is often in the contemporary literature proposed as 'idealisation' would in Peirce's view be generality of objects of diagrams rather than intentionally modified models that are in some ways indefinite. As symbols, models that interpret results of scientific experimentation are perfectly definite.

[5] See Pietarinen (2010a) and Champagne (2015) on such possibilities in the domain of auditory diagrams of logic. On the related criticism of the 'visual', see Bellucci & Pietarinen (2017b), and on a further but still related problem of taking static images to be arguments, Champagne & Pietarinen (2019).

persons this is always a visual image, or *mixed visual and muscular*; but this is an opinion not founded on any systematic examination. (CP 2.778, 1901, added emphasis)

Peirce nevertheless believed that mental imagery could be analysed in logical precision by the method of EGs, given that its graphs "furnish a moving picture of the intellect" (R 298, ms p. 10) and a "system for diagrammatizing intellectual cognition" (R 292, ms p. 41). In doing so, EGs analyse the reasoning process into its smallest parts, yet into such parts that are continuously connected with one other.

As far as general properties of diagrams are concerned, Peirce intended diagrams to be precise and non-vague snapshots of particular thoughts of the mind. As a representation of the mind, logical diagrams give a "rough and generalized diagram of the Mind", but in any case a better one "than could be conveyed by any abstract account of it" (R 490). Depicting the mind well calls for the use of logic to capture the meaning of general and indefinite propositions. Depicting the thoughts produced by minds, on the other hand, hinges upon the depiction of the properties of definite and determinate diagrams. The mind, according to Peirce, is really nothing much else than the factory of signs whose engine is powered by reasoning (R 318, 1907). Being definite means lacking vagueness and being determinate means that these diagrams are not general. Definite and determinate diagrams can represent assertions in iconic forms.

The significance of diagrams thus lies in great measure in their capacity to render the content of thoughts transparent and rigorous. How they accomplish this relies on the fact that the universe of discourse they communicate about is determinate and part of the mutually agreed upon and known common ground of the agents who undertake to discourse upon it. This idea of the universe, or the plurality of the universes of discourse, was indeed a vitally important development in the dawning of modern logic during the latter half of the 19th century. In Peirce's theory of logic, universes of discourse occupy a central place.

Thoughts, on the other hand, are not regimented in the same way as their contents are, and so in thoughts there is room for vagueness and generality. To mitigate vagueness and generality, reasoning upon diagrams is called for:

The Diagram sufficiently partakes of the percussivity of a Percept to determine, as its Dynamic, or Middle, Interpretant, a state [of] activity in the Interpreter, mingled with curiosity. As usual, this mixture leads to Experimentation. It is the normal logical effect; that is to say, it not only happens in the cortex of the human brain, but must plainly happen in every Quasi-mind in which Signs of all kinds have a vitality of their own. (R 293)

Whenever one forms a diagram that represents thoughts, it is reasoning as its inevitable effect that is called to action. We find the clarification of the meaning of what initially remained vague not in the diagrams as such but in the effects of experimenting on the relationships exhibited in diagrams.

As diagrams are not perfect pictures of the mind, they aim at preserving its essential structure. Here Peirce's doctrine of *hypostatic abstraction* is called for,[6] just as such abstractions are needed in scientific experimentation and theory formulation. Preserving the essential structure or feature of something is much the same phenomenon as what happens in, say, topology where one aims at preserving some essential property of the object, such as the 'nearness of two points on a surface'. You never need to pinpoint exactly where those points are. The facts that these notions express are partly imaginary and partly real.

What else is essential in Peirce's notion of a diagram? The presence of rationally related objects in icons makes the general notion of diagram a logical one. What the exact structure of the set of rational relations that the diagrammatic representations presuppose is, or what the rational relations between objects of icons are, are not questions that empirical investigation could ultimately resolve. For Peirce, rational relations are matters of second intentions. They are non-elementary but representable in higher-order logic. And it is only such rational relations that are really representable. A logic which is of higher-order is thus needed to analyse rational relations involved in icons. Since the presence of those relations is presupposed by any feasibly general notion of a diagram, the possibility of a general but non-logical notion of a diagram is excluded. Indeed the theory of second-order (second-intentional) diagrams would arise in Peirce's 1903 Lowell Lectures from the material he had developed and presented already in his 1885 "Algebra of Logic" paper, in the 1896 investigation of logical graphs (R 482), and elsewhere.

In the opening paragraph of the "Prolegomena" paper and its drafts Peirce presents an imagined dialogue between the military General who wishes to draw the map of the land for the purposes of his campaign, and Peirce the author who argues that the point of having such a map at one's disposal is that it becomes a diagram of thought in reasoning. The purpose of the dialogue is to make us realise how diagrams guide the General's thought by allowing him to make "exact experiments upon diagrams, and look out for unintended changes thereby brought about in the relations of different parts of the diagram to one another." These operations of reasoning "take the place of the experiments upon real things" (R 292a). Peirce makes here the point that the General, who wants to use pins on the map to experiment with various military strategies that are needed in order to prepare the

---

[6] Writings dating from Peirce's *annus mirabilis* of 1903 provide some of the best logical accounts of hypostatic abstractions (LoF 2; cf. Stjernfelt 2007).

troops for unexpected events, is reasoning about possible future behaviour just as the truths of logic have to do with general strategies of what is logically possible and conceivable. Both kinds of strategies, the military and the logical, thus have to do with general forms of relations that may obtain in the models and which, if indeed such a model exists, makes the theory consistent and the sentences in it true.

Every topological or topographical map therefore is, when it is used to reason about general courses of events, at bottom representable as a system of relations and the properties of those relations. Every map is therefore also representable as a logical statement.

Armed with the logical conception of diagrams as icons of rationally related objects, it takes little further effort to undo the dichotomies that maintain a segregation between empirical and formal, or synthetic and analytic, as such dichotomies do precious little work in Peirce's logic. It may be one of the chief lessons that we hope to learn from his later philosophy of pragmaticism and from the kind of methodological pluralism which he exercised in his logic, that one ought not to fix in advance what it is that may in the future be considered to fall within the purview of logical studies.

What is needed for analysing signs that can represent and analyse various systems of relations is a consistent, simple and easily intelligible system of representation. In *The Logical Tracts* (R 492; LoF 2), Peirce describes such a system, beginning with a semiotic chracterisation of diagrams:

> A Diagram is a representamen which is predominantly an icon of relations and is aided to be so by conventions. Indices are also more or less used. It should be carried out upon a perfectly consistent system of representation, one founded upon a simple and easily intelligible basic idea. (R 492)

A "perfectly consistent system of representation" is of course nothing else than logic. Indeed, from these considerations of what a diagram is—as well as what it is not—Peirce moves on to present his *chef d'œuvre*, the method of EGs. It is this theory which would clear up the issues of imprecise logical representation and reasoning, facilitate mathematical discovery by analysing its methods of reasoning, and making the meaning of one's language free from ambiguities and polysemy. This latter point derives from Peirce's own experiences as he saw diagrams as the means to elevate analysis of meaning of assertions to new heights, undisturbed by attempts to contemplate those meanings by the language itself:

> I do not think I ever *reflect* in words: I employ visual diagrams, firstly, because this way of thinking is my natural language of self-communion, and secondly, because I am convinced that it is the best system for the purpose [of logical analysis]. (R 619, 1910)

To sum up, the essential properties required of a general diagram concept are its iconically representative character, its definiteness and determinateness, having universes of discourse and presupposing the common ground, plus moderate non-psychologism about reasoning, together with notational simplicity and consistency of its systems of representation and transformation. We can observe that the development of a logical theory of diagrams, one that may also to be studied in semeiotic terms, is imminent. Understanding the nature of diagrams calls for a theory of diagrams as an important part of the theory of signs. Every diagram is an icon of sets of rationally related objects and hence at bottom a logical diagram, and every logical diagram is expressible as a statement in systems of various logics which EGs bring out at our disposal.

Survey of Part I: Selections 1–4

This section contains extended head-notes of the items included in the first part of the present volume, organised in a roughly reverse chronological order, from 1910 to 1895.

Selection 1: Essays on Reasoning (R 654, R 680, R 678), 1910

Our first selection in this part of Peirce's late writings on reasoning and diagrams collates two connected sets of manuscripts, both of which he supplied with a preface and an introduction. The first section, "Essays on Reasoning", which is also chosen as the title of this selection, consists of a preface (R 654) written in August 17–19, 1910, and an introductory section (R 680). Peirce began R 654 by noting that "This may serve [as] a 'Preface', the long piece already written under this title figuring as the 'Introduction' ." The undated R 680 may be one of the intended introductory sections of his planned 1910 book *Essays on Reasoning*. There are also other such introductions, but R 680 fits the purpose of the present collection of his essays best. This introduction bears the title "Analysis of the Trustworthiness of the Different Kinds of Reasonings". The Robin Catalogue gives it a later date of 1913. The book or essay as a whole was never written. Beginning in 1910 Peirce was much occupied in compiling and revising his *Illustrations of the Logic of Science* papers for publication with the Open Court. The book finally appeared in 2014 edited by Cornelis de Waal (ILoS).

For further interest, some superseded pages of alternative drafts of his 1913 "Essay toward Improving Our Reasoning in Security and in Uberty" (R 683) are appended to the introduction. His take on then-recent interpretations of famous scientific experiments as well as on the possibility of imaging the logic of relations in a "moving stereoscopic view" are certainly worthy of notice, and should be appreciated in conjunction with his remarks on stereoscopy that he elsewhere makes, especially in a June 22, 1911 letter draft to James H. Kehler: "At great pains, I learned to think in diagrams, which is a much superior method to [thinking in algebraic symbols]. I am convinced that there is a far better one, capable of wonders; but the great cost of the apparatus forbids me learning it. It consists in thinking in stereoscopic moving pictures" (R L 231, NEM III, p. 191; cf. CD II: 1589, CD IV: 4763).[7]

The second section is Peirce's "The Art of Reasoning Elucidated" (R 678), which he wrote sometime in late 1910. This section comes with its own preface and introduction. An alternative draft of the latter is provided in the appendix. Peirce's blanket dismissal of faith-based beliefs from homeopathy to the "Christian Scientists"; his method of reason by which we distinguish truth from falsehood; his analysis of the love of truth, love of knowledge, and love of scientific economy; and his classification of "passions for knowledge" into wide, deep and accurate, make this piece an eloquent testimony of what he saw as the looming decay of reason by the increasing love of dogma. Peirce's planned table of contents for the late redux of *The Art of Reasoning* (R 686(s))[8] reveals further that these topics would have comprised its Book I, with the chapters "Of Human and Other Activities" and "Of Science and Its Classification and Its Terminology". Existential Graphs would have been treated in Book II, Chapter II, right after the chapter on mathematics, and to be followed by chapters on numbers, matrices, fractions, limits, infinitesimals, dimensions, vector analysis, among other things. Book III was to be on Phaneroscopy, Book IV on Normative Science (Esthetic, Ethics, Logic), and Book V on Logic (Stechic, Critic, Methodeutic). What is interesting is of course that existential graphs are classified according to this late division into Book II on mathematics (here called "The Juice of Mathematics"), and neither to Book IV on Normative Science and its planned third chapter on logic nor to Book V on the division of logic into its three parts of study of speculative grammar (stechic), logical critic (critic) and speculative rhetoric (methodeutic).

These late papers on reasoning are chosen as the opening selection of the entire collection for three main reasons. First, they provide Peirce's most developed, mature and perennial views of logic. Second, they are those among his later writ-

---

7 Since a significant portion of this letter has been published in NEM III, it is not reproduced in full in the present series. Peirce's long letter is nevertheless an important testimony to his work and one of the most explicit late attempts at his architectonic philosophy, with several examples and reflections on EGs some of which were left out from the publication of the letter in NEM III. These relevant and unpublished parts of R L 231 (and R 514) are included in LoF 3.
8 This late plan comes along with a weighty subtitle: *Reflexions of Reasonings, especially with reference to their foundations, to right and wrong method and to the mysteries of human existence.*

ings on reasoning that are congenial to the topic of existential graphs and make explicit references to it. In the first preface, for example, Peirce tells how EGs are "the simplest possible system that is capable of expressing with exactitude every possible assertion." We should keep in mind that this is Peirce's conclusion from a lifelong study of logic and philosophy. What follows is equally resounding: "Three dimensions are necessary and sufficient for the expression of all assertions; so that, if man's reason was originally limited to the line of speech (which I do not affirm), it has now outgrown the limitation." Third, the two prefaces and introductory sections to the *Essays on Reasoning* and *The Art of Reasoning* serve as possibly the best and the most accessible initiation from Peirce's vast but scattered corpus. They put the entire selection of texts that is to follow in the wider context of reasoning in general, the theory of signs, and mature philosophical perspectives.

Selection 2: Diversions of Definitions (R 650), 1910

Written in July 20–23, 1910, the relevance of including in the present collection the full transcription of Peirce's unpublished "Diversions of Definitions"—one among many of his late writings concerning the nature of definitions—lies in its section "Brief Exposition of the System of Existential Graphs". In that exposition, Peirce is motivated by what he notes in R 654 as well, namely the system's capacity of diagramming any fact however complicated. He also manages to explain the basic features of the Alpha part of the system in an admirably accessible fashion. His exposition is also one of the rare instances in which the key concept of the *nest of graphs* is defined (namely that Alpha graphs form a tree structure), as well as the eminently important *endoporeutic* principle, that is, the outside-in interpretation of EGs, according to which "a nest sucks the meaning from without inwards unto its center, as a sponge absorbs water."

Other remarks of note include Peirce's testimony that his notion of the *scroll* (conditional) preceded the notion of the *cut*, an observation that has important ramifications to the philosophy and development of logical notations, as it is now clear that it is from the sign of illation that other logical constants, including negation, will germinate. Peirce repeatedly returns to this order of priority of the scroll over negation, the idea which in the graphical context of logic had emerged in "On Logical Graphs" (R 481; LoF 1) and which dates back to Peirce's development of the algebra of logic in the 1880s.

In R 650 Peirce also purports to explain how in sound reasoning, over and above what occurs in degenerate and dialogical models of communication, the *triadic form* is ever-present. Triadic forms show up both in the semantics of the system and in applying the inferential rules of transformation in graphical systems of proofs. Even more importantly, they show up as soon as one performs the analysis of the key diagrammatic elements involved in reasoning. It is those otherwise hidden elements in reasoning that the analysis conducted by the graphical method can bring to view. Peirce then seeks for a chemical analogy to an occurrence of the triadic form from the bonding known as *double decomposition*, and poignantly pens how his "heart is breaking for the raw-material for my exposition of sound reasoning. The world hates sound reasoning as a child hates medicine"— a comment that a century later has not lost its edge.

Selection 3: [Reasoning, Logic and Action] (R 826, R 616, R 1132, R 838)

The following three short pieces from three Robin folders at the Harvard Peirce Papers elucidate Peirce's ideas on the nature of reasoning and its relation to logic, diagrammatic thought and action.

The first, "Some Reveries of a Dotard" (R 826), was written in late 1910. The reader will notice the semantic consequence relation being mentioned in the first paragraph in terms of the "obvious character of all mathematical reasoning", where "the state of things" has to remain the same in the passage from premisses to the conclusion. This of course is the method that Peirce had frequently used since his 1880 "The Algebra of Logic" paper. How the logical consequence relation is to be defined is perhaps nowhere else more pronounced than in what Peirce wrote in a draft letter to Kehler the following year (CSP to Kehler, R L 231, April 22, 1911; LoF 3), connecting consequence to the derivability relation as given by the permissions of the system of existential graphs:

> [A] consequence follows necessarily only in case it asserts no state of facts that has not been already asserted in the premisses from which it is supposed necessarily to follow. [...] My three Permissions state the truth more explicitly:
>
> – Whatever cannot be produced by manipulating the premisses by those three permissions does not follow logically from the premisses.
>
> These permissions, in order to have that character must pick the reasoning to pieces into as many steps as possible, and therefore they are intentionally made to reach the conclusion as slowly as possible.

In the second paragraph of R 826, Peirce is led to summarise what philosophically speaking is the key question of logic. The reader finds him taking up the interconnected themes familiar from the problems of leading principles, justification of deduction, Bradley's regress, and the 'paradox' of deduction made famous by Lewis Carroll (1895), the solution of which he would outline in the 1903 Lowell Lectures (LoF 2).

In the second piece, "An Appraisal of the Faculty of Reasoning" (R 616), estimated to have been written around 1906, Peirce talks about a diagram as a "concrete but possibly changing mental image of such a thing as it represents." He emphasises the "act of imagining", which instead of "drawing a diagram" or building a "model" is in fact the "essential thing to be performed." The model-building process, which he mentions at the end of the selection R 654 of the previous chapter, follows the imaginary activity. The third step is the process of evaluation, in modern terms the determination of the truth-conditions of the graph instances thus constructed.

The third segment ("[Intention, Resolution, and Determination]") is a constellation of three short pieces (R 1132 and two selections from R 838). First, we have a two-page draft from late 1903. In mentioning how the resolution to act is of the nature of a plan, and that such plans now come close to what Peirce means by a diagram, R 1132 puts a new twist on his notion of a diagram. This snippet is part of an early draft of Lecture 1 entitled "What Makes a Reasoning Sound?" of his 1903 Lowell Lectures, the series of eight lectures Peirce delivered in Boston in November and December (LoF 2). Second, a brief record of Peirce's later remarks on closely similar topics is included (R 838). Third, there is a presentation of an example of Peirce's repeated late attempts to proceed with his treatise on three kinds of reasoning, likewise drawn from R 838.

The early parts of the second selection (R 616) have been published in Carolyn Eisele's NEM IV, pages 217–219. The transcription of the first lecture of the Lowell Lectures, which is the one Peirce actually delivered, was published in EP 2, pages 242–257.

Selection 4: Of Reasoning in General (R 595), 1895

Moving back in time in our selection of Peirce's writings on reasoning and diagrams, the manuscript R 595, written in summer 1895 was the first and only chapter Peirce ever wrote for the book project entitled *Short Logic*. It is placed at the end of this reversely chronological Part I simply because it lands us on the time that immediately precedes the emergence of logical graphs, while also setting much of the philosophical and semiotic ground for the later cultivation of the graphical method whose fruits Peirce would then harvest for nearly two decades. In this piece, Peirce sets out to establish the "philosophical trivium", which is the study of logic and its sign-theoretic context in three parts or areas of study, namely speculative grammar, critic and speculative rhetoric.

"Of Reasoning in General" is a complete version of the text which has been known to scholars through its fragmented publications in the *Collected Papers of Charles S. Peirce* (CP) and in Justus Buchler's *Philosophical Writings of Peirce* in 1940 (PWP). However, less than half of the relevant material was published in those places, with omissions and errors so numerous that one could hardly speak of a coherent piece. R 595 was later published in the second volume of *Essential Peirce* (Chapter 3, pages 11–26), with only one larger omission concerning features of many languages, including Egyptian hieroglyphs. In the text below, this omitted passage is the segment from "That different races…" until "There are too many types of speech.…" The variants and the last three paragraphs were likewise omitted from the publication of R 595 in EP 2.

In this chapter, Peirce makes a number of observations on logic, language, semiotics and notation. One finds not only a fresh application of his three-fold division of signs but also a real improvement of his 1885 indexical interpretation of quantification, now fleshed out in terms of iconic features of quantifiers. Some generalised types of quantification, much ahead of his time, are also proposed. Of particular interest is Peirce's remark towards the end (EP 2 omits those last three paragraphs) which states that, "If there are two selective indices one universal, the other particular, and the latter selection is made last, the order of the selections can be reversed. But all these changes in the indices are justified only by considering icons." That expressivity depends on notational resources to represent dependent quantification, and that the "laws of the indices" depend on the iconic or predicative component of the sentence, were Peirce's discoveries which, hardly much more than a year later, would blossom in the theory of existential graphs. By 1902 (R 430; LoF 1) he would realise the full potential and import of what such orders of selections have to the development of logical theories of quantification.

Soon after having completed this masterful semeiotic overture Peirce would be fully immersed in writing another massive treatise on logic, now exclusively on logical graphs. This manuscript, or rather what is left of it in R 482 and reconstructed in the next selection, deserves to be known as the mother of all his subsequent papers on the topic. The year 1896 saw Peirce's work being erected to symphonic heights, and, as he would soon signal to others, he took that period to represent his *chef d'œuvre* in logic. But these endeavours might not have fully succeeded without Peirce having first been in the prepossession of the kind of philosophical trivium that guided the cultivation of his logical studies.

Part II: Development of Existential Graphs

The pieces chosen for this second part consist only of those writings that can be judged to be directly relevant to the discovery and immediate development of Peirce's theory of Existential Graphs (EGs). They span the period from summer

1896 until August 1898. There are several other, pre-1896 writings on graphs in the vast repository of Harvard Peirce Papers. Especially his explorations in logical algebra are in many ways essential to the later development. The inclusion of those writings would have made the already extensive selection of texts far too long, and after all many of them are expected to appear in the chronological edition of the *Writings of Charles S. Peirce* (W) before long.

Both a general introduction to the history of existential graphs and a chapter-by-chapter breakdown of the selections included in Part II are provided next.

Introduction to Part II: History of Existential Graphs

This section provides some explanations on the methodology followed in the study of the history of logical graphs in Peirce's overall works, followed by a brief account of the development in Peirce's studies in logic since 1880 that led to the emergence of logical graphs in 1896.

Historical Methodology

Several pre-1896 writings in Peirce's *Nachlass* reveal his experimentation on graphical and diagrammatic logical notations, including mathematical, formal and logico-chemical studies on graphs. Especially prominent is his critique of the formal theory of graphs that Alfred Bray Kempe (1849–1922) had proposed in his theory of mathematical forms, of which Peirce wrote several accounts (R 708–715, plus Peirce's detailed marginal notes on the offprint of Kempe's paper deposited in R 1600, Box 2). Peirce's work on logical graphs was also inspired by the resemblance with chemical graphs and by his colleague and friend William Kingdon Clifford's (1845–1879) and his Johns Hopkins colleague James Joseph Sylvester's (1814–1897) studies that described algebraic invariants in chemical bonding models.

Peirce was initially, and still in early 1896, fascinated by the analogy of a chemical atom to a relative term "in having a definite number of loose ends or 'unsaturated bonds', corresponding to the blanks of the relative" (CP 3.469, 1897). It is certainly true that the idea of bonds and valencies proved useful in the initial stages of these explorations. Rhemata as spots, with hooks on their peripheries to which lines are connected, are an essential sign type in the system of logical graphs. But the continual search for better and better notations for the overall purposes of logical analysis would also reveal the reasons why Peirce had to overcome this analogy between logic and chemistry. At some point, the analogy becomes restrictive and is bound to break down. What initially was an appealing analogy in fact became one of the major reasons that prevented Peirce from constructing logical graphs earlier than he did. For those systems to do real work in logical analysis, they would need to be as analytic as possible and, in particular, to be able to model quantification in the right way. Peirce recounted the limitations involved in the analogue in hindsight as follows:

> Now what does Existential Graphs represent the structure of the Phaneron to be like? I can answer this best if you will indulge me with a little flight of fancy. Not a doctrine. An innocent and helpful figure of speech whose comparison is like a chemical compound.
> True there are the *cuts*. There is nothing like them in chemistry. No, not yet. But we have not yet got to the bottom of the constitution of the Proteins; and with their 15 000 atoms to a molecule, is it not *quite possible*,—possibility is all I contend for, and not even physical possibility; logical possibility will do—is it not possible that some division of areas of the graph of the great molecules of the protoplasm may be called for yet? It certainly is. But I will not insist upon it. I only affirm that the constitution of thought is like that of a chemical molecule in being composed of atoms each with a definite valency. (R 499s, "Z, Monist 1907 Scheme", 1906; LoF 3)

Graphs that draw their logical form from the analogy to chemical compounds would at the end have to be radically modified. That modification is done by the nested system of cuts. But such a modification deforms the continuity of space and the chemical analogy loses its appeal. Can there be any physical analogue to the absence of elements in the enclosures marked by the cuts? Gradually Peirce is seen to depart from the analogy, leaving us only with a hope in the possibility that the concepts such as that of an absence of something physical may turn out to have some correlate at the molecular level—something which only the future discoveries in chemistry or physics could tell.

Several examples of various proto-graphs had appeared in Peirce's writings in several outfits since the early 1880s. Especially his frequent explorations in logical algebra are in many ways essential building blocks for the later development of the graphical systems. The inclusion of those pre-1896 writings would nevertheless have multiplied the already fairly extensive selection of texts in this first volume. The cap on the inclusion of material is around mid-1896, the time immediately preceding the discovery of EGs, with R 595 as the sole exception.

This said, the genesis of EGs, the method of logical graphs in general, and the philosophy of diagrammatic reasoning in logic, science and mathematics in particular is a story that can be told in the preset volume only in part. Bellucci & Pietarinen (2016) is an exploration of the pre-history of them in Peirce's pre-1896 writings. A number of articles on existential graphs have appeared in recent years, but only Don D. Roberts's *The Existential Graphs of Charles S. Peirce* (Roberts 1973) is dedicated to the factual aspects of existential graphs and their development as found in the manuscripts, including a brief chapter on their history. As Roberts' book is mainly an exposition of Peirce's final systems, the present introduction places these final systems in a deeper historical and systematic perspective.

What were the main ideas that led Peirce to develop the theory of logical graphs? To outline what the factual account of Peirce's theory and method of logical graphs should contain, one needs to go back to his early investigations in two-dimensional notations for the logic of relatives in the early 1880s, and trace the numerous incremental ideas, elements and crucial missing links up to the emergence of the full-blown systems of Alpha, Beta and Gamma graphs in 1896 and in the later years, perfected during the first decade of the twentieth century.

Now, precisely which steps and lines of philosophical, logical and semiotic thinking did Peirce follow in order to arrive at the theory of logical graphs? What were the textual and theoretical details and insights of his notational innovations that we encounter during the 1880s and 1890s and what, if any, prevented him from constructing a graphical theory of logic, quantification and modalities already in the early 1880s? Peirce would later claim that EGs were the best instrument of logical analysis hitherto invented. Why did he think so, and in what sense are logical graphs more analytic than the algebraic logic of relatives? These questions can be fully answered only by a precise genetic reconstruction of Peirce's thirty years of research into logical graphs. The present edition is calculated to shed light upon the latter half of this period from the point of view of the theory of existential graphs and its development.

It has been a common method of Peirce exegetes to look at his early writings to support interpretations of his later writings. This has also been taken to apply to his logical *œuvre* as a whole, as well as to his work on logical systems and notations in particular. There is an alternative method that one could follow, however. Rather than describing the preliminary stages of the theory by means of the concepts intrinsic to the later stages of the genesis of the theory of logical graphs, one can conduct a study of the reverse, namely describe the developed theory in terms of the early theory, that is, in terms of those systematic logical problems and questions that Peirce recognised while working on his early theory of graphs, quantification and other logical notions but which he could not solve well in that earlier context.

Several benefits can be reaped from this approach. One is that we can understand the systematic development of Peirce's logical notations throughout his life while uncovering the underlying reasons behind his numerous notational experimentations and the trials, errors and solutions he came to propose along the way. This historical method also gives us a better chance of determining the scope and breadth of other and related ideas and theories that are connected to his work on the logical graphs. An obvious example concerns iconicity of logic and the diagrammatic nature of deduction as two important consequences of the theory of existential graphs, along the lines which commentators have typically taken Peirce to have attested them. But a closer look reveals that such claims appear in Peirce's writings much earlier than 1896, thus significantly predating EGs. Obviously there is meaning to the claim that deductive logic is iconic already much before 1896. Adopting this methodology, then, we are in a better position to explain the various other contributions Peirce took logical graphs to make to the analysis of logic, language and mathematics.

Early 1880s

Peirce explored alternative (non-Aristotelian) logical theories and notations for as long as he studied logic. Characteristic in those explorations is his motivation to look for non-linear forms of logical languages. Since the 1880s, he had already proposed some such non-linear notations for logical languages. Possibly the earliest instance is a marginal note to his "Lecture Copy" of the 1880 offprint of his "On the Algebra of Relatives" paper (R 1600, Box 2), a copy of the paper with abundant marginalia which he had lectured from in his elementary and advanced logic classes at the Johns Hopkins University in the early 1880s.[9] On page 23, Peirce invents new notations to describe Augustus De Morgan's eight propositional forms that used $\prec$ and a combination of $\prec$ with the vinculum, $\overline{\prec}$. The first column is the well-known *spiculæ* notation of De Morgan, the second a code symmetric in vertical dimension and explored later in the paper, while the third proposes an implication $A \prec B$ to be written as $^a b$, that is, with the antecedent, a, lifted up from the baseline along the second dimension as well as made somewhat smaller than the consequent, looking like a superscript prefixed to the main letter. "Some A is not B", that is, $A \overline{\prec} B$, adds the vinculum, $\overline{^a b}$, and so on, until the seventh and eighth, namely that "A includes all B" ($\overline{A} \prec \overline{B}$) and that "$A$ does not include all B" ($\overline{A} \overline{\prec} \overline{B}$), are inscribed as a^b and $\overline{a^b}$, respectively. The year 1880 might thus have been the first instance in which we see the idea of a logical 'graph' or 'diagram' to emerge in representing logical notions—if by graphs or diagrams we mean anything like "languages written in more than one, or linear dimension".

---

9 Listed on the cover of that offprint are the names of his students: elementary class lists "[Henry A.] Short, [Willian H.] Howell, [Gustav] Biss[ing]" as enrolled; advanced class seems to have included "[Fabian] Franklin, [Christine] Ladd[-Franklin]; [Allan] Marquand, Biss[ing], [Oscar Howard] Mitchell, [Benjamin Ives] Gilman, Core?, and [Robert W.] Prentiss." These lists suggest that the advanced logic class in question was one of Peirce's four advanced logic classes he held in the academic year 1880–1881 (see Pietarinen & Chevalier 2015), and the elementary logic class was that of spring 1880 (Henry A. Short took Peirce's elementary logic class only in 1879–1880).

The added second direction serves as a scope-denoting device that now distinguishes between antecedents and consequents of the conditional.

That Peirce was exploring not only algebras but also logical graphs during his appointments as an instructor of logic at Johns Hopkins University in 1880–1883 is indeed confirmed by what he tells Paul Carus in December 29, 1896: "That there were two principal logical systems of graphs, I used to teach as long ago as my Johns Hopkins lectures" (R L 77; LoF 3). Not only two principal systems of logical algebras, but two systems of graphs, according to this testimony.

Soon after, in 1882, Peirce would propose, in a letter to his Johns Hopkins graduate student and colleague Oscar Howard Mitchell, some further proto-graphical ideas to express logic of relatives and quantification. In a fragment written in fall-winter 1882 (WMS 427 = R 747, W4, pp. 391–393) and in a letter to Mitchell dated December 21, 1882 (R L 294, W4, pp. 394–399), Peirce explores and regiments a two-dimensional notation capable of expressing relatives and quantification. Roberts wrote that the 1882 notation was "the first attempt by anyone to apply diagrams to the logic of relatives in general" (Roberts 1973, p. 18). The notation, as Roberts suggested, is in a very important sense an anticipation of the system of EGs invented fourteen years later, and it introduces quantification, just as in the Beta part of the EGs, by lines of identity. What these early graphical notations lack, however, is the sign that characteristically denotes negation. In these early experiments on alternative logical notations, in order to denote negations Peirce uses a short cross-bar, much like a vinculum at large, that is supposed to fulfill the office of the negation when abutting the lines.

However, in order to have these proto-graphs of 1882 represent logic in the similar sense in which EGs do would mean that the former adopt the characteristic forms by which EGs express negation. These are the lightly drawn, simple closed curves, variously called by Peirce "ovals", "cuts" and "seps" (from "separation-lines"). Now taking the two-dimensional substructure of 1882 and straightforwardly substituting the 1882 cross-bar line for negation with the 1896 device of negation as ovals might suggest that the system tantamount to that of EGs would now have been created without further ado. But Peirce's 1882 notation does not lack a device to express negation, nor would that device, if straightforwardly changed into the 1896 device for negation, yield the system of EGs. The reason is that the ovals are not simply, and not even primarily, signs of negation. They are signs of scope, and create order on the two-dimensional sheet on which these graphs are written. This is the reason why, though adding the ovals to the 1882 substructure does yield EGs, using the ovals as mere substitutes for the 1882 device for negation does not. This puts the development of Peirce's graphs into a new perspective that highlights the systematic and gradual nature of the evolution of graphical logics into the full-blown systems of the Alpha, Beta and Gamma parts of the theory.

To fully overcome the defects and to fill in the missing parts of that early notation takes Peirce another 14 years to complete. The details of the story have been accounted in Bellucci & Pietarinen (2017) and Ma & Pietarinen (2018a). Even in 1896, we occasionally meet Peirce experimenting with what is clearly an inadequate notation for negation in terms of the cross-bars drawn over the lines (R 488; LoF 1), or even over the spots and rhemas (R 494; LoF 1).

Much of Peirce's explorations during these intermediate years is fuelled by his studies on the algebra of the copula of inclusion and on the sign of consequence, both of which were instrumental in paving the way towards the 1896 graphical systems of logic.

The 1891 Algebra of the Copula

After having completed writing his paper on the algebra of logic and philosophy of notation in the summer of 1884, in the paper that was published the next year in the *American Journal of Mathematics*, Peirce wanted to push his pursuits on these topics still further. Unfortunately prospects were not rosy as his lifelong nemesis Simon Newcomb was eager to see such publication plans to scupper, under the pretense that Peirce's papers were not suitable for a mathematical journal. A few years later, Peirce nevertheless resumes his interest in the algebra of the copula of inclusion and begins to reformulate new algebraic rules of reasoning. In spring 1891, he had drafted two versions. In Version 1 (Peirce 1891a; W8, pp. 210–211), he introduced five algebraic rules. Rules 1–4 are quite thoughtful while the fifth one is rather intangible. The first four rules are cited here (Peirce 1891a, pp. 201–211):

Rule 1. The order of antecedents is immaterial.
Rule 2. Any antecedent may be inserted under an even number of parentheses, or none, and omitted under an odd number.
Rule 3. The insertion of an antecedent of a proposition a second time as antecedent of the proposition or of a clause of it has no effect.
Rule 4. The insertion of a clause having an antecedent identical with the consequent of the proposition has no effect; and a proposition having an antecedent identical with its consequent is identically true.

Rule 1 is familiar: from $a \prec (b \prec c)$ we can infer $b \prec (a \prec c)$. This has the same effect as his second icon (I2) of 1885. Rules 2–4 concern insertion and deletion of antecedents in a formula. Peirce's example of Rule 2 is that from $(a \prec b) \prec c$ we can infer $(d \prec (a \prec b)) \prec c$ and $b \prec c$. One can also observe that from $a \prec (a \prec b)$ we can infer $a \prec b$ because the second occurrence of a is within the odd number of parentheses. Peirce explains Rules 3 and 4 with similar examples. As we will see, in some five year's time this emerging idea of insertions and deletions will become central in the form of graphical transformation rules in systems of EGs.

The second version of the algebra of the copula is more detailed. Peirce first rewrote the three basic rules (α, β, γ) to define the copula of consequence (Peirce 1891b, p. 212):

α. If b is true, then $a \prec b$ is true.
β. Either a or $a \prec b$ is true.
γ. If $a \prec b$ and a are true, b is true.[10]

In contemporary terms, the rules α and γ are the rules of Weakening and Modus Ponens, and we find them already in Peirce's 1885 icon system. The rules α and β are obtained by the meaning of $\prec$. Peirce then introduces seven algebraic rules, which are easier to understand than the rules of Version 1.

The first rule is the *principle of commutation*, namely that the order of the different antecedents of a proposition is indifferent. This rule is the same as Rule 1 in the first version. We can express it more visibly as follows:

$$\frac{a \prec (b \prec c)}{b \prec (a \prec c)} \text{ (R1)}$$

The double-line means that the upper and lower formulæ can be inferred from each other. The rule (R1) corresponds to the icon (I1) of the 1885 paper.

The second rule is the *principle of contraposition*: "If a is an antecedent, c is the consequent of any proposition, then in place of a and c respectively we may put $c \prec x$ and $a \prec x$, whatever expression x may be" (Peirce 1891b, p. 213). This rule can be expressed more visibly as follows:

$$\frac{a \prec c}{(c \prec x) \prec (a \prec x)} \text{(R2)}$$

This is exactly the icon (I3) of 1885.

---

10 In the earlier draft, he had spoken of "scriptibility" instead of truth values: α. "If b is scriptible, then $a \prec b$ is scriptible", etc. The difference is not only a terminological one, as it is here in the latter draft that the philosophy of notation becomes increasingly pronounced. Later he defined *scriptibility* as that which is "capable of being written conformably to the purpose" (R 501, c.1901). This semantic characterisation suggests that Peirce was thinking about a generalisation of truth-values to other values besides truth and falsity, which he then goes on to examine in detail in R 501. As early as 1886, Peirce had used modal notions when referring to "the sheet of conceivable states of things" (W5, pp. 331–332). The allied notion to scriptibility is *transformability*, which concerns graphs or formulæ that are "capable of being transformed without changing anything scriptible into anything non-scriptible" (R 516, c.1901; LoF 1).

The third rule is the *principle of insertions and omissions*: "any antecedent may be inserted under an even number of parentheses (or none) or dropped under an odd number" (Peirce 1891b, p. 213). The crucial example can be expressed as follows:

$$\frac{b}{a \prec b} (R3)$$

Peirce is now explicit about the rules of insertion and omission.

The fourth rule is the *principle of repetition*: "If an expression occurs twice as antecedent, and one of these times under no parenthesis which does not enclose the second occurrence, then this second has no effect and may be inserted or dropped" (Peirce 1891b, p. 213). Formally, we can express this rule as follows:

$$\frac{a \prec (a \prec c)}{a \prec c} (R4)$$

Here we can observe a new rule being born. The principle of repetition corresponds to that of the rule of iteration ("may be inserted") and deiteration ("may be dropped") in the Alpha system.

After having formulated (R3) and (R4), Peirce derives some new rules. One important rule is the fifth one (R5). It is the *principle of breaking parentheses*. This rule is for any copula within an even number of parentheses (Peirce 1891b, p. 215):

Rule 5.1 Bring the beginnings of the two innermost parentheses forward to the beginning of that copula.

Rule 5.2 Repeat all to the left of the innermost parenthesis from the beginning of the next innermost parenthesis follows by one of the antecedents to the left of the break in the innermost parenthesis. This is to be done for each of these antecedents.

His proof of (R5) is again a semantic one. By the basic rule β, we know that $a \vee (a \prec b)$ is true. If $(a \prec b) \prec$ is true, in each case, we get that a is true.

What makes this fifth rule peculiar is that it proposes applying inferential rules to parentheses, that is, to what may be considered as punctuation marks (the "Klammern"). Having delved deeper into the philosophy and ethics of notation, Peirce explains: "The Klammern, which are commonly spoken of in the elementary algebra-books as mere subsidiary signs, are in reality the very heart of algebraic notation" (R 530, c.1901; LoF 1).

Rule 6. The sixth rule is the *principle of identity*:

$$(R6)\ a \prec a.$$

Rule 7. The seventh rule is the *principle of double consequent*. This rule is about a proposition of the form $(a \prec b) \prec b$. Three basic rules for it are given in the draft (Peirce 1891b):

$$\frac{a}{(a \prec b) \prec b} \text{(R7.1)} \quad \frac{b}{(a \prec b) \prec b} \text{(R7.2)} \quad \frac{(a \prec b) \prec b}{a \vee b} \text{(R7.3)}$$

How close to the heart of algebraic notation these notions are is shown by the next phase in the development of his logical calculi, namely the *qualitative logic*, which introduces a novel sign of consequence presented below. That new notation accomplishes an assimilation of the notations for the scope of the operators and their truth-conditional import. Apparently Rule 5 is no longer needed in such systems, and with the presence of Rule 4, they come to be replaced by the paste-and-copy rule (the rule of iteration/deiteration).

Summarising, it is the philosophy of notation that is Peirce's guideline in these developments. His reformulation of algebraic rules considers positions that antecedents have in a formula. The really interesting rules are the insertions and omissions of antecedents (Rule 3), the repetition (Rule 4), as well as the fifth rule of breaking the parentheses (Rule 5). They are all germane to his next major revision of his algebra, as they would soon give rise to the invention of an entirely different-looking system of logical graphs. But before that, there is another intermediate development that needs to be exposed as well.

Qualitative Logic and the Sign of Consequence

A further step in this indirect journey towards graphical systems of logic was taken in *Qualitative Logic* (NEM IV, pp. 101–115; R 736; W5). This treatise was at first written for students of logic in 1886. The material was retained and later revised for Peirce's projected long treatise on logic entitled *How to Reason: A Critick of Arguments* (later known also as the "Grand Logic"), on which he worked incessantly in 1894.[11]

Qualitative logic introduces a new notation for the sign of illation: x̄ or x̄⊹. The latter sign consists of ⊹ (an aggregate, a special variant of the plus sign), with a connected "streamer" or vinculum covering the antecedent of the conditional, producing ⊹. Again, Peirce's treatment of this new connective is well-nigh semantic: "To say that N follows from M, is to say that every possible state of things in which M is true is a state of things in which N is true" (R 411, 1893). In the proofs of this system Peirce attaches a truth value to all propositions.[12]

---

[11] This work was never published but it is projected to appear as Volume 11 of the critical chronological edition, the *Writings of Charles S. Peirce* (W).

[12] Possibility can be understood either in logical or informational (material) senses. Peirce gravitated towards the substantial sense in which "there is but a single possible state of things, namely that which is actual" (R 411). He takes the actual state of things to be "represented by a single

Peirce's "purpose for selecting the special sign" was that it does something that "would not be accomplished by any of the signs that have been proposed hitherto" (R 411).[13] This new sign of consequence can also denote, without any additional signs such as parentheses, the scope of the antecedent. Indeed, the reason Peirce provides for the introduction of this new sign is that his "excuse is that this is not a mere sign of inclusion" (R 580).

With the new sign of illation at his disposal, Peirce regains confidence in his algebra of the copula. One can now express "the most complicated relations without the slightest ambiguity" (NEM IV, p. 107; R 736). The new sign in fact makes all other logical constants, as well as parentheses, superfluous. It can be noticed that *falsum* is represented by the right-hand side of this sign being empty: ⊸ ; thus the negation of x is represented as $\overline{x}$⊸ .

One of the simplified systems of codes Peirce proposes as the set of formal rules of translation of this language consists of the following three rules (R 737, 1897?):

(1) $\overline{x}$⊸ x.
(2) If from x and y, follows z, then if x, $\overline{y}$⊸ z and *conversely*.
(3) Hence $\overline{x}$⊸ $\overline{y}$⊸ z = $\overline{y}$⊸ $\overline{x}$⊸ z.

The rule (1) is the law of identity (cf. (R6) above). The clause (2) expresses Peirce's Rule (PR), which is the logical leading principle. Axiom (3) is the principle of commutation (Peirce's second icon I2 of 1885). It follows from the other two rules. The law of excluded middle is also immediate from the identity law. Because of the special nature of this new notation, the validity of the rule of transposition also follows virtually immediately, which is not the case in notations that use parentheses. It is clear that this parenthesis-free calculus of qualitative logic forms a complete system that agrees with a two-element Boolean algebra.

As usual, Peirce exercises with many different systems and sets of formal codes. Among them is the following, which he calls substitution:

---

point in the field of possibility" (R 737). The conditional involved in this sign is thus the material conditional. That a is false is written as $\overline{a}$⊸ , that is, with a blank space occupying the place of the antecedent of the copula (the formula above it is mistakenly produced in NEM IV, p. 106; the second streamer should extend over a).

13 Among the earlier suggestions he lists Giuseppe Peano's reversed-C or ⊃, Ernst Schröder's subsumption ⋹, Hugh MacColl's colon :, mathematicians' ≦, Augustus De Morgan's), William R. Hamilton's cuneiform line ⊢ , as well as Peirce's own previous signs for illation, ⤙ and its cursive form ⫏ (see R 580, c.1892).

The general rule of substitution is that if $\overline{m} \mathrel{\text{⊸}} n$, then n may be substituted for m under an even number of streamers (or under none), while under an odd number m may be substituted for n. (R 736)

This rule is also valid. One can see that this rule is essentially that of (R3) dating from 1891 and that it also expresses what would soon became the two rules of insertion and erasure in the system of graphical logic: first for the *entitative* system and then, by duality, for the positive system of *existential* graphs.

The upshot of introducing the sign of consequence $\mathrel{\text{⊸}}$ and the revised rules for the system of qualitative logic is that we need not wait until "The Logic of Relatives" materialised in summer 1896 in order to see that the transition from the algebra of logic to graphical logic—or what somewhat ill-advisedly has been termed the transition from symbolic logical languages to iconic ones—had already taken place before.[14] In fact the rules of an equivalent and complete calculus were established by 1894. It was only the notation that underwent some further modifications from the algebra of copula to the sign of consequence and then, finally, to the notation that Peirce proposed to employ in the language of logical graphs. As seen above, the germs of this account were present even much earlier, in Peirce's writings, lectures and letters ever since the early 1880s.

The Graphs of 1894

One final step that Peirce needed remains to be explained. The $\mathrel{\text{⊸}}$ -notation for copula was further explored in Peirce's *Art of Reasoning* project of 1893–1894. After that, when graphical logic was, in a few short years, up and running, the old sign disappears. However, in Peirce's transitional work the rules became reformulated in important ways.

In September 1894 Peirce provides an outline of his long manuscript *The Art of Reasoning*, an account of which he had presented to Edward C. Hegeler of the Open Court in July 11, 1894, in the hopes of getting a major book published; Hegeler acknowledged the reception of the material but ultimately decided against publishing. In its projected Chapter 11, the book proposed to deal with "Graphs and Graphical Diagrams". In a letter addressed to his friend Judge Francis C. Russell, who Peirce hopes would recommend the prospectus to Carus and Hegeler, Peirce writes that this chapter was estimated to show "the value and

---

14 Dipert (2006, p. 293) takes the 1897 Logic of Relatives and the Entitative Graphs as the "transitional work between the Algebraic and the Diagrammatic periods". But all important aspects of his transitional period were accomplished by 1894.

limitations of the geometrical way of thinking" (CSP to FCR, September 6, 1894; R L 387).

On the algebra of the copula Peirce's outline stated that "this difficult subject is here perfectly cleared up and systematized for the first time, and made to lead directly to the Boolian algebra." Moreover, he went on to claim that he could now "show that the rules of the non-relative Algebra may be immensely simplified by dropping all connection with arithmetic", thus fulfilling "our *hope* that the question which happens to occupy our minds is capable of final decision" (*ibid.*).

What entitled such confidence in his logic? The answer is that at this stage of the development of the algebra of the copula, Peirce already had the complete system of rules including, as the last finding of the system, the rule of iteration/deiteration. This rule permits taking a copy of a proposition that has already been inscribed and asserted on the sheet deeper inside the formula. Iteration can also be usefully applied by re-using the premise. As noted above, the application of this copy-paste rule of iteration gives a short graphical proof of the law of distributivity. Iteration completes the rule of which the direction of deiteration (R4) was already present in 1891. Together with the rules of deletion, insertion, and the double negation, Peirce has accomplished a complete calculus, just as he would for his graphical system five years later.

Before arriving at the definite idea of combining the 1882 graphs with the sign of consequence or the ovals, Peirce experimented with yet another alternative system in which an important further step was taken. In some fragments contained in R 553, which might belong to his 1894 *How to Reason* or to the planning of a chapter "Graphs and Graphical Diagrams" for *The Art of Reasoning*, he presents a sketch of a notation for the logic of relatives in which the bonds are, as in the 1896 graphs, of one kind only, and not of two different kinds as in the 1882 graphs:

> It is one thing to say that there is a woman for whom every man has some kind of love, and quite another to say that there is a kind of love that every man has for some woman. Either of these propositions might be true, though the other were false. But this is a little puzzling. Let us find a method of stating, or ~~symbolizing~~ otherwise representing, such facts, which shall free us from all puzzles of this sort. The method I prefer is to begin by indicating the order in which the different individual things we are talking about are supposed to be ~~selected~~ settled upon, and whether each is to be chosen to suit the speaker and make the assertion true, or by some external agency, no matter how.
>
> Thus, the proposition that there is a woman for whom every man has some kind of love would be formally stated as follows: Let me select a woman, *w*, then you cannot select a man, M, but I will then select a kind of love, *l*, so that M shall have the sentiment, *l*, for *w*. But the proposition that there is a kind of love that every man has for some woman may be formally stated as follows: Let me select a kind of love, *l*, then you cannot select a man, M, but I will then select a woman, *w*, such that M has the sentiment, *l*, for *w*. The difference between the two lies in the order of selection. I am accustomed to use a sort of algebra in

which Σ means a suitable choice and Π taking no matter what one. With this convention, I should write the first proposition thus,

$$\Sigma_w \Pi_m \Sigma_l (mlw);$$

and the second thus,

$$\Sigma_l \Pi_m \Sigma_w (mlw).$$

In such a formula, the Σs and Πs with their affixed letters are collectively called the quantifier.[15]

Another method would be to make a diagram like this.

Here the order of the letters from left to right is that of the selection; a circle round the letter shows that a suitable choice is to be made, a square that any one can be taken, and the relation, l, is joined by a line above to its subject and by a lone below to its object. The above diagram represents the first proposition. The second is shown by the diagram below.

(R 553, c.1894; diagrams in Peirce's hand)

In these graphs the lines function exactly as in the 1896 graphs Peirce is soon to expose: they connect the "hooks" of the "spots", and m and w are monadic spots or rhemas (and thus there is only one line departing from them) while l is a dyadic spot (and thus there are two lines departing from it). Peirce also suggests that in the case of dyadic spots, one needs to distinguish the relate from the correlate (or the first correlate from the second). Such convention is needed as the graphs are now formulæ written in two dimensions. To represent the order of the correlates a vertical order is used: the line departing from the top of the spot denotes the first correlate and the line departing from the bottom denotes the second correlate.

Since the lines are of the same kind, Peirce is obliged to distinguish existential from universal quantification by some other means than the nature of the line. Universal quantification is represented by a square that encloses the quantified term, while existential quantification is represented by a circle. That certain quantificational lines are functionally dependent on some others is here represented by the linear or horizontal ordering in which the terms occur, and accordingly the

---

15 [The text has an upright capital M although the letter appears as a lowercase italics m in the formulæ]

graphs are read from left-to-right: a quantifier occurring to the right of another is read to be in the scope of that other one.

This notation is however only sketched in these drafts and assorted pages. Unlike in 1882, here Peirce gives no indication of how to represent negation, for example. In order to represent dependent quantification, Peirce is forced to resort to some additional conventions, namely the sequential arrangement of lines. Moreover, since the order of correlates is represented in one dimension, such notation cannot express triadic relatives without employing some further sign (such as numerical indices) to indicate the position of the third correlate in the sequence. This interim notation is nevertheless important because it contains one more step towards logical graphs proper: that there is just one kind of bond (a simple line).

In a three-page fragment (R 915), which might pertain to the same writing project as *The Art of Reasoning*, Peirce arrives at the notation of the line as a quantifier through the consideration of the three relational categories and the two parts of the irreducibility thesis. Here is a reproduction of that entire fragment:

> Three ideas are basic: those of *something, other*, and *third* or middle. For suppose anything, and there is at once the idea of something. But this something cannot have any distinct property, unless it be opposed to something else. Nor can this opposition exist without the opposites are [sic.] connected through some *medium*.
>
> In this mathematical proposition (for such it is shown to be), you have all logic and all metaphysics in a nut-shell.
>
> The idea of third cannot be reduced to that of second. For, attempting such reduction, you find the third defined as that which is *at once* second to the first and second. Now this idea of being in one act in two different relations, which is the idea of synthesis, contains more than the idea of otherness.
>
> On the other hand, the idea of four, or any higher number, is but a complication of that of three (which of course involves those of two and one). Thus, no combination of bivalent atoms can make a trivalent radicle; but with trivalent atoms radicles of every degree of valency and complication can be constructed.*
>
> All this is objective logic,—a self-evolution of ideas. Now the notion of an objective logic is, very rightly, met with such a degree of scepticism, that brief and slight as this outline sketch is intended to be, I must dwell upon it a moment. For according to this, general ideas are not dead counters, as our nominalistic friends would have it (and when I call them *friends*, I do not mean it personally, but in recognition of the healthfulness and usefulness of their spirit), nor even *coins*, as the trimmers among them will admit, but, as it were, capital, which breeds interest. In short, to admit what has just been brought to the bar of the reader's judgment is to admit that ideas are alive. Let us avail ourselves, here, of the method of graphs, of which Williamson[16] raised the first seedling in chemistry, which Sylvester imported into mathematics, which Clifford further developed, and which Kempe has converted into an engine of philosophy. By this method, a system of dots and lines is made analogous to

---

16 [Alexander William Williamson (1824–1904), an English chemist.]

any system of relationship about which reasoning is to be performed. Let us by this method represent *something*. Then, we must set down a dot; for unless we set down something we represent nothing. But having set down a dot, what have we done? We have simply divided the plane of the paper into two parts, one white and the other black, for the size and shape of the dot is of no consequence. Thus, to represent *one* we are forced to use the idea of *two*. Not that *one* logically involves *two* as a part of its conception; but that to realize *one* (even in thought), some *second* must be used. Let us now explicitly represent *two* by the method of graphs. For this purpose we set down two dots connected by a line. To omit the line would leave it to be supplied by the mind, which must think the dots together to construct the idea of two. Besides, in the method of graphs every pair of dots is to be conceived as connected by one kind of line or another; for to leave a pair unjoined is to represent them as joined in another way. So *two* cannot be represented without the ~~medium~~ *middle* between them. But here this sequence closes. To represent three explicitly, we make three dots connected by three lines. There is nothing new here, unless it be the idea of two lines branching out from one dot. But this is only the three-idea, the same in form as the two dots connected with one line, which was used to represent *two*.

The ideas of one, two, three are thus shown to be inseparably connected; and this having been shown once for all, it will [end]

---

* Professor Sylvester seems very proud of having first enunciated this axiom; but I gave it in the *Memoirs of the American Academy of Arts and Sciences, New Series*, Vol. 14, p. 374 (p. 38 of my memoir) [Peirce 1870; "my memoir" refers to the separate publication by Welch, Bigelow, and Company for Harvard University, 1870]. This was read and printed early in 1870. Of course, Hegel preceded us both, but he was not exact enough.

Apparently the planned chapter "Graphs and Graphical Diagrams" (of which we do not know whether the above fragment is part) was never fully written. Instead, by the end of summer 1896 Peirce had already drafted a long paper (R 482) on logical graphs, which, in the hopes of its publication, he had submitted to *The Monist* in August that year and in revised and expanded form resubmitted early next year. That paper never got published either, but what we find in it would pave the way to a new and explicitly graphical and topological approach to logic, in Peirce's terms a "diagrammatic syntax". This episode and its consequences call for our attention next.

Survey of Part II, Selections 5–12

The final selection of Part I, "Of Reasoning in General" (R 595), which was written in the wake of *The Art of Reasoning*, landed us in the immediate vicinity of Peirce's renewed formulation of the fundamental ideas of logical graphs and diagrams. The first selection of Part II is, in turn, a long paper that Peirce described as "the first of very great study and labor", claiming that it "would be quite below the truth to say it cost me two years over and above anything spent in work already published" (CSP to Carus, August 13, 1896; LoF 3).

Selection 5: On Logical Graphs (R 482), 1896

Most of the material directly relevant to the discovery of EGs is found in R 482, a long and spawning collection of segmented attempts at something like a fair copy-text, the majority of which Peirce apparently wrote between summer 1896 and March 1897. In so far as the above remark to Carus can be relied upon, research on it would have started even considerably earlier, perhaps soon after Peirce's exile in New York City in late 1895, and probably largely contemporaneously with the drafting of "The Regenerated Logic" written in spring 1896 and certainly to an even larger degree parallel to the writing of "The Logic of Relatives" which he submitted to Carus in July 1896.

Consistently entitled "On Logical Graphs", these surviving pages and segments deserve, despite being severely incomplete and fragmentary, to be called the mother of all of Peirce's papers on logical graphs. For here we find the birthplace of existential graphs, and the first completed and submitted manuscript version also presents the antedating entitative system of graphs in greater detail and depth than anywhere else. Peirce retrospectively described this piece (the final version of which is apparently lost) as the "perfect Calumet mine" for his own later endeavours. In the later sections which Peirce added to the main sequence we can literally experience how the system that is to become existential graphs undergoes the stages of improvement necessary for its healthy delivery.

Yet among the 221 pages that remain in the folder, plus a dozen or so related draft sheets located in R 839, we most likely do not have the ultimate version of the paper Peirce had submitted to Carus sometime in early 1897 and no later than March. What has been preserved in R 482 is the first, 30-page submission from August 31, with ten sections and 94 examples of graphs; soon after the paper underwent substantial revisions that could have made it at least twice as long: the highest page number count among the surviving fragments is 66, and the figure captions run up to 159.

It is that first, August 1896 submission that is transcribed here as the first, continuous sequence identified in R 482 constituting the main body of the text (Sections § 1–§ 10). Section § 11 was added to it later, apparently sometime during the fall when Carus had returned the first submission back to Peirce.

The amount of parallel, rejected, overlapping—and the most likely missing pages—is formidable, and it is beyond possibility to reconstruct a definite linear sequence that could reflect Peirce's actual final version or even his ultimate intention in producing one in anything but a modest and approximate degree. A number of superseded and rejected pages and sequences supply crucial pieces to his overall early conception of EGs. The total of 94 manuscript pages has been chosen to serve as copy-text for the current selection, which makes roughly half of the relevant sheets that we find in R 482 and in related folders among the Harvard Peirce Papers. The folder also contains pages that pertain to his "The Logic of Relatives" paper and are related to the pages 169–183 of that article published in *The Monist* in January 1897. Those pages, not provided here, present his earlier 1894 notation for logical diagrams that used the sign of the universal and which derives its meaning from his earlier writings and commentaries on Kempe's formal and mathematical theory of graphs.

Peirce shortly abandons this notation in the early stages of composing the first main sequence of R 482. The earliest draft versions of what was to become the major article on logical graphs do use similar rectangular and not the oval forms, but their meaning is neither a cut (negation) nor a universal quantification. At this point Peirce realises that the chemical analogue of logical graphs has to go, as those are nothing more than mere "illustrations". The problem with the analogy is that chemical graphs are not naturally "polar" and that they cannot be "unbalanced", which however are the properties that graphs that are to be logical need to possess.

Ketner (1987) has argued that R 482 is what Peirce had in mind when he much later in a letter to the historian Frederick Adams Woods (CSP to FAW, November 6, 1913, R L 477) makes reference to his "most lucid and interesting paper":

> But the purpose of the Logical graphs is to express assertions analytically; and since an assertion is the analytical representation of a state of things as Real, i.e. as independent of any representation, it follows that *every* logical term must be regarded as linked, or bound, to *one real universe*, unless it is *denied*; that is unless its negation is so bound. And the denial of denial being precisely the affirmation denied in the latter denial.
>
> It was 17 years ago, lacking between two and three calendar months, that it first forcibly struck me that herein was the key to the true formal (i.e. deductive) logic, and that my paper of January 1897—of course written some months previous—required considerable modification. Not that I had said anything false but that I had failed to state the matter in the simplest and best form. Thereupon, I wrote the most lucid and interesting paper I have ever written; but I had no way of publishing it. The editor to whom I sent it refused it on the ground that he was afraid I should soon make some further discovery; so he preferred the old mumpsimus to my sumpsimus.
>
> Nine years later, having found that system of expressing assertions that I had given my rejected article to have been a perfect Calumet mine in my own work.

Ketner's identification of R 482 as that most lucid paper is certainly on the right track. The matter is clarified by noticing that Peirce submitted the paper to Carus twice, first on August 31 and later sometime between January and March 1897, and that in the meantime he continually reworked its sections and added a wealth of new material to the original version. Possibly he rewrote the original version from the ground up (also the graphs appearing early in the later draft have thick lines of identity). At any event, it is that final, and lost, version of "On Logical Graphs" which Peirce presumably had in mind when referring to his most lucid and interesting production.

What is it that had "forcibly struck" Peirce sometime in autumn or late summer of 1896, after which ("thereupon" in the previous quotation) he would write his account of existential graphs? The preceding quotation reveals that it is the recognition of the natural duality of the system: that there must be another system besides entitative graphs: one that is received by changing the polarities by once encircling all the subgraphs. But the duality does not mean that the two systems would, conceptually speaking, be at an equal footing. What one gets from encircling the subgraphs (and then removing the double cuts) is a *simplification* of the system in which everything that is scribed upon the sheet is asserted, that is, is bound to the real universe by an indexical connection. Today we would take such binding to refer to the model-theoretic idea of an assignment of values to logical constants.

If Peirce's recollection of the dating of these events is accurate, then the idea of simplifying entitative graphs occurred to him sometime as early as in August 1896, that is, right around the time when he was finalising or had just submitted the first sequence of his paper to Carus on August 31. Now on August 13 he writes that "I have the graphical method all written out in a formal, scientific statement." The following day he promises Carus to "send you a more formal statement of the graphical method." A few days earlier he had written to Russell to have "a more formal and exact statement of all the properties of the graphical method, if Carus prefers such a statement" (LoF 3). In his submission letter on August 31 Peirce nevertheless holds his paper far "too dry" for *The Monist*, yet having "much more matter on this subject." At this point, Peirce's strategy is to have "On Logical Graphs" substituted for the earlier and not yet published "The Logic of Relatives", insofar as its sections on logical graphs were concerned. Rather than to be considered as a separate or new submission, Peirce represented the former as an improvement on his logic of relatives paper. Carus hesitates to undertake such major changes to an already accepted paper that is on its way to print, however, and sometime before October 21, Peirce requests the original "On Logical Graphs" manuscript to be returned, stating that he wanted to "read the paper" at the upcoming National Academy of Sciences meeting which was to take place in New York City on November 17–18.

Earlier in the month Peirce was in great despair, starving and probably ill, even threatening to end his life (CSP to FCR, October 4, 1896; LoF 3). It is worthy of thought that what "forcibly struck him" was to become the system of EGs and seems to have coincided with what was one of the worst periods of Peirce's life. The 1911 letter to Risteen confirms that it was indeed a paper on the system of existential graphs (not yet named as such) that he read in the November meeting. Indeed that paper that appears to come closest to his presentation is R 480 (LoF 1), which he was likely to be preparing while waiting for the long manuscript to be returned from the Open Court.

At some point between late October and well before December 29, the initial submission is returned to Peirce. At most three months later the paper is back in Carus's hands, now considerably revised and extended, and submitted under the delusion that Carus had paid $250 for it and for that reason would already have made a commitment to accept it for publication, in addition to "The Logic of Relatives" accepted earlier. Perhaps realising that Carus might not publish Peirce's "long and dry" paper after all, Peirce pitches it as "unquestionably the strongest of all my logical papers. In it I mention the other system of graphs [the positive/existential graph] and briefly describe it [...] [it is] the *chef d'œuvre* of my logical life" (December 29, 1896). Here we find Peirce's first use of the phrase, but by *chef d'œuvre* he does not quite mean EGs as such but the work what went into the preparation of the manuscript which he now is resolutely finalising for publication.

Still in April 1, 1897, Peirce pleads Carus to "take the article on Logical Graphs (with suppression of the 2 or 3 pages based on misapprehension)", and agrees that if Carus desires "the form changed, so as to be less stiff and technical, to that I have no objection. I could, if desired, add to what is there, another article explaining and illustrating the method of working with the diagrams in the most expeditious and simple way." Another article could be R 488 or R 481. But neither this nor the subsequent correspondence succeeds in persuading Carus to publish what Peirce saw as his major accomplishment.

Much of the most interesting material in R 482 is thus found in the appendix of the proposed reconstruction. There the reversed rules of interpretation (§ 9) follow immediately after the simplification of the system, which clearly is a later draft of both § 8 and of another version of § 9. The rules of simplified graphs, which now effectively mean existential graphs, are presented in § 11. That section might be the final addition (or a draft of the final version of § 11) to the paper, with running page numbers from 59 to 66. Whether § 11 was written later than August 1896 may not be altogether obvious; what certainly did happen was that there were multiple revisions and additions to the final version, including a lost "appendix" which created controversy with Carus: "I do not know what to think about the return of your MS on 'Logical Graphs', and your appendix of MS pages 54–57 is based on a misconception of the situation" (Carus to CSP, March 29, 1897; LoF 3).

Peirce probably wrote the earliest parts of his manuscript on logical graphs and his published paper on the logic of relatives roughly contemporaneously over the summer. There is a related important typographical evolution in the notation of graphs worth pointing out and which is preserved in the present edition. In the main sequence of R 482, the unenclosed lines (later to be termed the "lines of identity") are at first just as thin as the closed curves, termed here the "ovals" and later the "cuts". Peirce first draws the lines of identity thin, and gappy when crossing the ovals, in order to prevent misreading and in order to emphasise their discontinuity with the lines that make the ovals. Likewise, in the beginning of the first draft, Peirce represents graphs and chemical formulæ in the same fashion. In the later drafts (§ 10, beginning with the graph in Fig. 86, ms p. 28 onwards), his notation for the lines of identity changes to thick lines. It is a notational convention that would become the standard in all of his subsequent writings.

Two of the later drafts, which are omitted from this selection, present "five simplifications" and "rules of simplified ideographs". Figs. 83–, which are transcribed in the appendix, antedate § 11 in which EGs make their first appearance. Apparently Peirce is rewriting much of the later parts of the first sequence when he had the better, EG notation in view. The first sequence may have been written as early as in late June and July, and was continued with two later sequences (ms pp. 23–30) worked out in August and still more throughout the month or later during the fall. By the turn of the year, the piles of sheets on this pet project of his on logical graphs must have been outtopping everything else on his desktop.

In R 280 (late 1904; LoF 3) Peirce recounts how the "ink was hardly dry on the sheets" when he discovered that EGs "are merely entitative graphs turned inside out, and sent the gracious Editor a paper on the subject that could have been squeezed into a simple number by simply excluding everything else." Dry on what sheets? The submission of "The Logic of Relatives" on August 10 is too early, and in another occasion a year before he recollects those having been printed sheets. Any galley in January or later in the next year would come in too late, however, so he might have meant the galley proof sheets of "The Logic of Relatives" that were returned to him from the Open Court perhaps in late October.

The matter is explained in R 479 (ms p. 2, 1903; LoF 3) in terms of Peirce referring to his paper that he saw "in type":

> Similar diagrams [to Clifford and Sylvester], though not called graphs, were employed by Kempe in his remarkable memoir on Mathematical Form to represent relationships of all kinds between individuals. I subsequently proposed (*Monist* Vol. VII, pp. 161–217) a system capable of representing all facts of relation between classes as well as between individuals; but this was no sooner seen by me in type than I perceived that it was one of a pair of twin systems of which the other was to be preferred, and I wrote at once an elaborate paper on the subject to which I vainly endeavoured to find an asylum. At that time, I drew up an elaborate

definition of a graph, contemplating all sorts of possible generalizations; but I have since bestowed a great deal of study upon the matter both in its details and in its general aspects, and have been led to prefer a very much simpler definition which includes diagrams already in general use among logicians,—being one of the few things which all schools unite in finding valuable, and this catholic confession would seem to be an argument in favor of that intuitional theory of reasoning which was so forcibly defended by Friedrich Albert Lange.

The earlier remark that EGs "are merely entitative graphs turned inside out", should now also be compared with what we observe happening in R 481 a few chapters later. The improvement Peirce presents there on Euler graphs is to turn them inside out: the negative terms are denoted by classes that face the concave side. It is the shape of the curve, and not the label of the class, that determines whether the term is negative or positive. Peirce is thus introducing a natural duality to the theory of Euler diagrams, too. Interestingly, in R 481 this innovation is at once followed, without further ado, by an analysis of the circle in a system of logical graphs, which of course is very different from that of Euler's, together with several instructive examples of EGs.

Peirce recounts much later in 1911 that EGs were "suggested to me in reading the proof sheets of an article by me that was published in *The Monist* of January 1897; and I at once wrote a full account of it for the same journal. But Dr. Carus would not print it. I gave an oral account of it, soon after, to the National Academy of Sciences" (CSP to Risteen, December 6, 1911, R L 376; LoF 3). Therefore this full account must have been ready by mid-November when Peirce presented his paper on "A Graphical Method of Logic" to the Academy. That full account was also likely to have been the version that now had §11 added to it, as that was clearly written later than the original paper that Carus returned to Peirce during the fall. Maybe Peirce received the original set back from Carus together with the galleys of the other article. The description of this "full account", as he reports to Risteen, "fills 55 pages", and was in retrospect deemed vastly more successful than what the published "Prolegomena" paper ever managed to accomplish.

Sometime in early 1897 these 55 pages became the final version that contained, or was appended with as its last unidentified pages (pages 54–57 according to Carus), a statement of "some of the circumstances, in order that in the future my not carrying forward the development may in some measure be understood" (CSP to Carus, March 1897). Following Carus's complaint Peirce agreed that statement to be purged if Carus was to so insist. On April 13 Carus telegrams "Your MS will be returned to you" but there is no further confirmation or acknowledgment either of its reception earlier that year or its safe return to the author. Only some incomplete and discontinuous runs of that full 55-odd page account, which could have been Peirce's final and near fair copy-text of "On Logical Graphs", have been preserved among the sheets in the folder R 482, including fragments in R 839 and in R S-34. Moreover, according to Peirce's later recollection, the full account "defines over a hundred technical terms applying to it. The necessity for these was chiefly due to the lines called 'cuts' which simply appear in the present [1911] description as the boundaries of *shadings*, or shaded parts of the sheet" (CSP to Risteen, December 6, 1911, R L 376). No such pages that would define anything like a hundred technical terms are to be found among the surviving ones, not even if we were to put together all the definitions from his writings on logical graphs from the next couple of years. The cuts and the precise conventions and definitions for the essential terms and notations of the system certainly necessitate lots of technical vocabulary, but those do not appear in R 482 or in related manuscripts of that era. Defining a hundred technical terms is rather the undertaking, six years later, of his *Logical Tracts* and the 1903 Lowell Lectures (LoF 2).

Hence the final version of Peirce's seminal paper on existential graphs can never be fully reconstructed on the basis of the material that remains at our disposal. The missing, orphan and out-of-sequence pages are far too many. For instance, pages with figure captions 132–156 are nowhere to be seen. The surviving pages consist of over a dozen different attempts by Peirce to write up the paper, and none of them comes near what is to be expected of the appearance of the final submission he had made in early 1897. A few singular pages (e.g., R S-34, ms p. 34) are what most likely survive from one of the later drafts or from the near-fair copy of that final account—with Figures 78–81 it is somewhere halfway towards what we would expect Peirce's full account to have accomplished. Indeed a version longer than the 55–57 page account was likely to have been prepared as well (the highest figure numbers 157–159 appear on a manuscript page 61, and the highest manuscript page count in R 482 is 66).

Be this as it may, the above events and reports support the conclusion that the final version that reached Carus in early 1897 was still a very different, enlarged and polished-up version than anything that is reconstructed here as "On Logical Graphs", or indeed anything that can be reconstructed on the basis of the surviving pages—and that it is that lost version, if any, that could deserve the honor of the "most lucid and interesting paper" on logical graphs.

Selection 6: Positive Logical Graphs (PLG) (R 488), 1896

The system of "positive logical graphs" (PLG) that Peirce presents in R 488 dates from late 1896 and presents the dual of the system of entitative graphs which was presented and published in January 1897 in *The Monist* as "The Logic of Relatives". What Peirce terms as positive graphs are virtually those of existential graphs. The present manuscript does not yet propose the name "existential" but the meaning with the "positive" is practically the same. That term had already occurred in some alternative draft sequences of R 482 (see Alt. § 10), which were later additions after Peirce's initial submission of the paper for *The Monist* in August 1896. It is not clear whether the pages of § 10 were included in the manuscript that Peirce and Carus tossed during the autumn months of 1896, but R 488, for which Kloesel's annotation on the Robin catalogue gives an unlikely date of 1898, was probably composed soon after the first, submitted version of R 482 was completed but before Peirce wrote R 484 and before he had renamed the system as "existential". That is, the timing falls somewhere before the end of December but no earlier than October. Since it is in October that Peirce learns that his logic of relatives paper is going to appear in the January issue, from that point on he was able to refer to its date of publication.

The timing that falls between October and December makes it possible that PLG was Peirce's presentation copy in November's Academy meeting, under the published title "A Graphical Method of Logic". On the other hand, the content of PLG makes it unsuitable for oral delivery, and the next selection is more likely to be the one Peirce perused for that occasion. PLG is nonetheless important as it is one of the very first complete sequences in which the system that is to become that of existential graphs is presented. Peirce's exposition is largely carried out with a large number of examples: to illustrate the workings of the six conventions he scribes 75 graphs with their English equivalents, all neatly laid to fit four large manuscript sheets. A presentation of all those graphs to a live audience would have been highly inconvenient, but on paper, their progression brings out a systematic combinatorial exploration of what can be represented with this system, up to three verbs and relations with up to three arguments. These graphs also testify for Peirce's power of spontaneously improvising inferential relations and equivalences between graphs, like Bach improvising four-part fugues.[17] That this paper is still an early exposition of the system of such graphs is attested to by the fact that some of the claimed logical equivalences, which the reader is invited to identify, are in fact logical consequences.

There are several noteworthy points that Peirce makes in this paper. They include the realisations (i) that quantifiers need not be assumed to come with existential presuppositions, (ii) that the "characters", which Peirce would later term "spots" (or "terms" or "rhemas") in the theory of EGs are, according to the first convention, surrounded by parts corresponding to the blanks of the verb, and (iv)

---

[17] Recall Peirce's coincidental words, "The intelligent listening to a fugue of Bach is certainly more like reading a piece of higher mathematics than the lesson of the schoolboy in elementary geometry is like the higher geometry" (R 748).

that they will have a definite order of interpretation that begins at a designated blank, and (iv) that it is mostly what he would later name the "scrolls", namely the continuous, self-returning and once-intersecting lines that designate nested ovals, that appear as the primitive signs of conditionals in these positive logical graphs.

The first point, that quantifiers need not have existential presuppositions, is Peirce's common assumption which he made, often tacitly, when designing the theory of quantification for logical graphs. It is found articulated elsewhere in his later writings in more detail.[18] The point (ii), which Peirce phrases slightly differently in the alternative draft version, is not in fact repeated in so many words in his later writings on EGs. The importance of it is nevertheless clear as the properties of the relations exhibited in the system should not be limited to symmetric ones, which they would have to be unless a convention is given that dictates the order in which one is to read and interpret the attachments of lines to the parts on the circumference of characters. The absence of this convention, quite conspicuous in Peirce's later writings, would mean that systems of logical graphs (such as the Beta part of EGs) are, strictly speaking, fragments of full systems (such as those of first-order logic with identity) in which non-symmetric and asymmetric relations are not expressible.

Some further details concerning Peirce's unusual choices in the notational design of these graphs are worth pointing out. One can observe that in addition to the point (iii) of using intersecting loops in many of his examples, some of the scrolls actually have more than one inloop, the practice of which is virtually non-existent in Peirce's later expositions. The benefit of (iii) may be that it enables one to draw the loop structures, that is, to model the conditional relations which in principle could be of indefinite complexity, without lifting the pen. The problem is that unless there were other specific and separately given conventions, having more than one inloop in one scroll destroys the recursive structure of the formation of the language of graphs and makes it impossible to unambiguously represent the relation of illation that is of paramount importance to Peirce's philosophy of logic. It is the recognition of this defect that would soon cause Peirce to avoid using such complex designs to express the conditional in subsequent writings.

A few supplementary observations are in order. Figure 41 might come as a surprise, as indeed might the last four graphs appearing in Figures from 72 to 75. The graph in Figure 41 must of course be read, not as composed out of two overlapping ovals in the manner of what the Euler–Venn diagrams may do, but as having

---

[18] See e.g. R 493 and the distinction between lines that have a loop or a swelling at their loose ends and those that do not; LoF 1, cf. R 513.

two inloops of the scroll that have been merged with each other. In contrast, however, graphs in Figures 72–75 do not at the first sight appear to conform to the later, standardised notation for EGs at all and thus do not seem to be examples of well-formed positive logical graphs. For if there is a gap (a "meaningless" blank) in the line of identity, it would not, contrary to what Peirce states in PLG and in his later accounts, be used to assert the co-existence of two existing things. The gap marks a discontinuity of the line, thus making the graphs in Figures 71 and 72 logically equivalent. Here, however, the graph in Figure 73 is the denial of the "meaningless" blank, which according to Peirce is "self-contradictory" and would turn the graph in Figure 73 into an expression of absurdity. The "bond" that is omitted from Figure 73 in order to result in the graph depicted in Figure 74 is the line, which means that the graph of Figure 74 is something that the diagrammatic syntax of his later theory of EGs does not allow to be scribed, namely one in which the thin line of the denial would somehow be attached to the verbs or spots. The graph in Figure 75 is likewise fairly non-standard and seems to connect two denials and the verbs, though in the text he is proposing to read it as a conditional. Although this graph resembles some of those we find in R 482 too, it is unclear what the intended notational idea and the meaning of this last graph is. In general, it remains unclear what the status of Peirce's proposed Convention 6 here amounts to.

In the transcription of PLG, the direction of the scrolls has been preserved, that is, the openings of the loops are, just as in Peirce's original drawings, mostly diagonal in orientation. With the exception of the last three graphs whose meaning is unclear, the manuscript R 488 is among the firsts in which Peirce consistently preserves the difference in the thickness of the line: lightly drawn closed lines denote "precise denials" while the thick ones stand for identity, quantification and predication.

Selection 7: On Logical Graphs (Acad. Graphs) (R 480), 1896. The Academy of Science presentation

On November 18, Peirce presented a paper titled "A Graphical Method of Logic" at the National Academy of Sciences meeting that gathered at Columbia College, New York City.[19] In that meeting, with 36 members in attendance,[20] the last two papers were by Peirce who presented the paper number 13, "A Graphical Method

---

[19] The presentation is catalogued in Peirce's published works (P) as P 00632: Fiche 114, "A Graphical Method of Logic", 17–18 November 1896 and is cited in *Report of the National Academy of Sciences for the Year 1896*, Senate Document No. 50, 54th Congress, 2nd Session, Washington: Government Printing Office, 1897, p. 11; it is filmed in the catalogue of Peirce's publications at P 00631.
[20] *Science* 27, November 1896, p. 769.

of Logic", followed by his second and the last paper of the session, "Mathematical Infinity". Peirce's numerous writings, catalogued at R 14–17, are from autumn 1896 and they bear on quantitative logic and address the topic of mathematical infinities that constantly occupied him just as the logical graphs did. The occasion was reported as follows: "The meeting concluded with two papers by C. S. Pierce [sic.] of Pike county, Pa., on the Graphical Method of Logic and Mathematical Infinity. Mr. Pierce put forth some new views as to the infinities, which Prof. Roland [sic., Rowland] of John [sic.] Hopkins did not endorse. A warm discussion followed in which several delegates participated."[21]

Although clearly related to the previous as well as to the next two selections, this 19-page draft from late 1896 is also closely related in content to the later segments of R 482 and for that reason makes itself a perfect candidate for the paper that Peirce read to the Academy. What speaks in favour of this conclusion is naturally the header "Acad. Graphs" in Peirce's hand on the top left corner of each sheet. On the other hand, this paper has an inconvenient count of 68 examples of logical graphs, which makes one wonder how he would have managed to present them all and what was the point of including that many examples in the actual delivery.

Presented or not, R 480 is unique in a number of respects. First, Peirce draws a distinction which is not made anywhere else in precisely the same terms, namely that between *logical* and *semi-logical* (arithmetical) verbs (spots, rhemas). The difference in modern terms is that neither the truth-value (satisfaction) nor the falsity-value of logical verbs is affected by the values of the assignment function, while as concerns the latter, semi-logical verbs, having the same assignment functions would make such verbs equisatisfiable. It is only logical truths and logical falsehoods that pertain to the provenance of the former. Propositions that consist of logical verbs are thus *closed* formulæ or *sentences*. The ensuing semi-logical triads which Peirce calls those of "severalty", "duality", "oddness", "triality" and "non-triality", also present terminology not found anywhere else in his writings on logical graphs.

Second, Peirce formulates a precise rule for interpreting the graphs (Article 10), which he later terms the "Endoporeutic Rule" or method of interpreting existential graphs. This is what we find rediscovered much later in the late 20th-century as the dialogue or game-theoretical semantics. In R 480 Peirce indeed explains that it is the "deliverer of the graph" who is to choose the objects from the universe of discourse for what the bonds denote, in order to suit her "intention" as the "supporter of the graph". The deliverer is thus the *verifier* of the graph.

---

[21] *Los Angeles Herald* 26(59), November 19, 1896.

Proceeding from the endoporeutic, outside-in direction, which is completely provided by the nested structure of ovals, it is then the "interpreter" who is the "opponent of the truth of the assertion of the graph", and who is freely to select the objects "as he pleases" in order to "attempt the refutation of the assertion." The endoporeutic rule of interpretation continues in the manuscript by Peirce's presentation of how to arrange the subgraphs, in a numerical fashion, into what effectively amounts to a tree structure resulting from the assignments that the deliverer and the interpreter had proposed in their interaction. It is this interactive process that analyses the meanings contained in graph-instances.

The endoporeutic rule of interpretation implies that the logical graphs in the present paper are those that Peirce would soon label as the "existential". If, as it is likely, it indeed was this paper that was presented to the Academy on that late afternoon, that occasion should be regarded as the first public appearance of not only the system that agrees with existential graphs but also the semantical ideas anticipating later logical theories. Certainly Peirce made an effort to publicise his ideas and to leave a permanent trace of them in the records and in the minds of the listeners. We even know who participated the meeting and were likely to be sitting in the audience, including Peirce's Johns Hopkins colleagues Ira Remsen and Henry A. Rowland and, as might be expected, Simon Newcomb, too.

The Academy paper is also likely to have been composed slightly later than R 488. The latter presents no such interpretational rule, and its presentation of the illative transformations in Articles 13–21 is not quite as refined as what we find in R 480. Article 21 is seen to coincide with what Peirce later added to the expanded version of R 482 (its § 11), in which the rules of segmentation and fusion are presented as derived illative transformations. A peculiarity here is the graph of Figure 67, with its sharp enclosures facing one another. This would be, Peirce might have thought, what the result of a split or segmentation of the ovals would concretely look like immediately following an application of that rule.

It can be concluded that R 480 was written in late October or in the very least well before the Academy session. Further support for this (and for the fact that R 480 is the graphical method of logic Peirce had in mind for the meeting) comes from the relation, both circumstantial and substantial, it has to the manuscripts R 13–17, the drafts most closely related to the presentation of his second paper on mathematical infinity. For example, the title of both R 14 and R 15 is "On Quantity, with special reference to Collectional and Mathematical Infinity."[22]

---

[22] See NEM III, pp. 39–63. What is referred to as MS 14 in NEM is in fact R 15, a later draft of R 14. It summarises the research questions that Peirce probably wanted to tackle in his second paper (see NEM III, p. 40).

Several textual, terminological and technical facts confirm the inextricable relation in the ideas and approaches of R 480 and R 14–17. First, the latter were written before R 480, probably even before the first draft of R 482 was completed. For instance, R 16 is the only place strictly outside his writings on logical graphs which refers to the "deliverer" and the "interpreter", namely the two theoretical puppets that Peirce had introduced in order to explain his semantical theory; agents that purport coming to an agreement on the meanings of words with the aid of icons that expressions evoke in their minds given the mutual and common experience in the mathematical domain. In a very concrete sense it is the "Graphical Method" which is the ultimate logical method by which diagrams are to be drawn such that they can exhibit relations that precise statements given in mathematical definitions suggest are to be drawn. In order to understand what the nature of those systems of relations is, and what deductive reasoning ultimately consists of, Peirce is led to claim that it is the nature of that logical method that must first be learned well.[23] Hence he is led to present a novel exposition of that method in R 480, followed by the delivery of his paper on the same fundamental questions but now with a renewed mathematical perspective and content. In the National Academy of Sciences April 1896 meeting, Peirce had read "On the Logic of Quantity" (R 19–R 21) on the nature of infinities, and so he indeed had begun writing on the related topics several months earlier. That earlier paper presents exact definitions with logical content, and in order to analyse it further Peirce would now summon the graphical method he had planned for the autumn meeting. After all, the fundamental question that characterises much of his work both in mathematics, logic and philosophy was to address "what the logical nature of mathematical infinity is" (R 13).

---

23 Notice, indeed, what Peirce writes in R 14: "It is very useful in tracing effects of compounding relations to be provided with a lettered diagram of all possible combinations of the relations dealt with. Such a diagram is of course merely to have blanks or places for the related objects and is not to take note of the accidental character of the relations, but only of any essential peculiarities of their modes of combination. It is to show every possible compound of the relations concerned; and therefore every part of it will be precisely like every other part, unless the relation is of such a kind that after certain compoundings, the character of the compoundings changes. An ordered arrangement of dots, everywhere uniform, and therefore unlimited, would, for example, answer the purpose. But the dots must be lettered, or otherwise designated, in order that it may serve any use, for the same reason that indices, or signs of individual objects, have to be made use of in all deductive reasoning, as the logic of relatives clearly shows.

Such a diagram is a schema of the scale of quantity. Thus a *quantity* is nothing but one of the hecceties in the system of possible forms of combination of certain relations, whose characters except in regard to their forms of combination do not concern the scale of quantity."

Moreover, the verb is defined as a valental concept in the same manner both in R 480 and in R 15, and in the latter there are likewise seven rules of inference, namely omission, insertion, iteration, combination, contradiction, excluded middle, and commutation, plus the derived ones. The only difference is that R 15 formulates these definitions and rules of inference not by graphical but algebraic vocabulary and notation. But this is a distinction without difference, since as Peirce would have seen by now everything that can be expressed in the language of graphs can also be made algebraical.

The influence of Peirce's parallel work in mathematics can be observed from Article 8, where he introduces the distinction between "logical" and "semi-logical or arithmetical" verbs. While logical verbs are verified by proper names, namely names whose objects are common to the experience of both the utterer and the interpreter, semi-logical or arithmetical verbs are verified according to whether their structure reflects their numerical properties. Peirce declares at the end of Article 8 that the logic of semi-logical relations is the foundation of arithmetic itself, but postpones a full account of the claim. Article 9 deals with first and second-intentional verbs; Article 10 aims at giving "a precise rule for the interpretation of the graphs above described", namely instructions on how to read the graphs, which he later terms the "Endoporeutic Rule" or the method of interpreting existential graphs. Articles 1–6 present the basic definitions (verb, particular proposition, ideograph, oval, continuous line, assertion), Article 7 gives the basic examples, and Articles 11–21 help identifying the account with Peirce's later additions to R 482 and to his attempts at simplifying the transformation rules of this new system, making the text of R 480 a perfect synopsis of his autumnal cornucopia.

Selection 8: On Logical Graphs [Euler and EGs] (R 481), 1896

This neat 10-page manuscript could in principle also contain the essential material Peirce drafted in anticipation of the Academy's November meeting. The finished style and the concise and controlled nature of its prose suggests that the manuscript was written with a scientific audience in mind. Although R 480 is the most likely actual presentation, R 481 could well have been a superior choice.

Yet this unique piece has gone unnoticed in the subsequent scholarship. Peirce presents in it thoughts on graphs that are found nowhere else. The following ten discoveries stand out. (i) Peirce presents novel forms of Euler graphs with convex edges (the only other surviving place for them is the draft entry on "Logical Graphs", R 1147, written in 1901 for James Mark Baldwin's *Dictionary of Philosophy and Psychology* DPP; LoF 3). (ii) He then suggests representing disjunctions as dots placed on the lines of the ovals. (iii) Arguments for the unsuitability of Euler diagrams for the purposes of logical analysis are given. (iv) Peirce notices the importance of dependent quantifiers and scope reversals when studying logical forms of natural language. (v) The distinction between two kinds of quantifiers is marked in terms of oddly- and evenly-enclosed heavy lines. (iv) A close progression from Euler circles to the birth of EGs is demonstrated in terms of the progression from extensional to intensional representation ("the spread of the sheet represents the logical depth", which is in contradistinction to the theory of Euler diagrams in which the sheet represents "the logical breadth"). (vii) Peirce shows how the development of logical graphs is slated for the rise of the Beta part, here yet unnamed as such. (viii) A surprising notation for the scrolls is suggested in which the inloops are saw-edged. (ix) A comparative analysis of ovals is performed both in the context of the Euler-like theory of the circles and in the context of EGs. (x) Peirce then realises that the concept of the negation is not primitive and has to be derived from the illative sign of the scroll ("we have virtually analyzed the conception of negation"). Hence the introduction of negation by the "fourth iconic device", equivalent to that by which he had introduced negation in his 1885 "Algebra of Logic" paper.

The tenth point is certainly consequential, so a few additional remarks on it are in order. Why Peirce decided to use the rather salient saw-edge lines to mark the interior boundaries of scrolls is unclear, as that notation is not much explained and as he never resorted to that notation again. He merely states that its effect is "to restore us to the spread of assertion", where the spread is not exactly that of the original one of "absolute assertion", which one would expect from how the double cut behaves in the standard theory of EGs whenever the antecedent place is unoccupied by anything else other than the blank. The spread is one that is located within the antecedent context of that outer oval. Peirce mentions that since the two ovals (see Fig. 27) have "opposite effects", it is this opposition, much like the convex curves in his proposed new extension of Euler diagrams (see e.g. Fig. 29 in Peirce's hand), which brings to view that the innermost area of the scroll is the logical extension of the spread, while the outer area is, in contrast, its intension.

Peirce also articulates, without using the term here, the *endoporeutic* (from outside-in) interpretation of the scrolls as well as the lines. The saw-cut loops may thus be considered as those evenly-enclosed curves that undo the effects of the oddly-enclosed ovals. As their sharp edges point outwards, they may for that reason be regarded as sufficiently powerful iconic reminders of the fact that, when one is endoporeutically interpreting these graphs, one should suppose the truth of all of those elements that lie on their outer, intensional or convex-side, areas.

What is the dating of R 481? In late December Peirce begins writing the "Memoir" for the Academy yearbook (see the follow-up selection R 483 and Peirce's December 21 and 29, 1896 letters to Carus in LoF 3), which he unfortunately never managed to complete and submit for publication in that proceedings. Though it is difficult to put an exact stamp on the present paper, R 481 should perhaps be dated in the near vicinity of that "Memoir".

On December 29 Peirce wrote to Carus to be "engaged in writing another paper in which I apply the system of graphs developed in the paper I return to you, in order by its means to set finally at rest one of the most vexed of questions. This it must do to the mind of anybody who applies himself to understand the paper." What was that vexed question that occupied him at that moment? What was that "another paper"? Apparently he means a paper other than the "Memoir" which he had already outlined to Carus, and it is not R 484 or R 488 either, since the former is clearly a later one and the latter does not contain anything like a conclusion or attempt to set some major topics at rest. But R 481 fits the description well, not least because it is written on the same type of paper as the "Memoir", while different from that on which manuscripts in the folders R 482, R 488 and R 484 are written.

One can only conjecture what those most vexed questions of logic were for Peirce at that time. First, as he would later explain, *the* "most vexed question of logic" is to understand the essential nature of propositions:

> Another trichotomy of representamens is into ~~primi~~ single signs, substitutes, or *sumisigns*; double signs, ~~or quasi propositions~~ informational signs, or *dicisigns*, and triple signs, ~~monstrasigns~~ *suadisigns*, or *arguments*. Of these three classes the one whose nature is most easily understood is, by all odds, the second, that is, the quasi-proposition, notwithstanding the fact that the essential nature of propositions is today the most vexed question of logic. (R 478, *Syllabus*, p. 43, October 1903)

From the context set up by the 1903 Lowell Lectures, the kinds of questions of logic that he at that time regarded as the most vexed ones, the following three can be identified: (i) the soundness of reasoning, (ii) finding the best method for performing logical analysis, and (iii) finding logical forms of thought under which one could also subsume qualities and laws.

But there were also other, more specific vexing questions. One was how to distinguish between "Some woman is adored by every catholic" and "Every catholic adores some woman." This is vexing, according to the account we have in R 481, as one has to come up with an appropriate graphical representation of the logic of relatives first. The difficulty is to accomplish in the logic of relatives the same for the meanings of complex linguistic forms as what Euler circles do for syllogisms. Thus the most vexed of questions of 1896 was to find how to graphically represent, not merely quantification as such, but the *dependent* form of quantification, indeed a problem Peirce had recognised ever since his proposals of 'proto-graphs' and their variants in the early 1880s and 1890s. But now he can finally put that question to rest with existential graphs. If this indeed was the main puzzle, then the paper Peirce mentions to Carus must indeed be R 481. And then the most vexed of questions of logic is resolutely answered by the graphs in which ovals and lines of identities are each other's transversals on the sheet of assertion.

Further support for the conjecture that R 481 is already at Peirce's desk by the time of the composition of the "Memoir" comes from a remark in "Prolegomena" (1906, p. 534). There the scroll is characterised not as a "haphazard" device but as the result of experiments that brought him to see how conditionals are to be expressed. "This form once obtained", he explains, "the logically inevitable development brought me speedily to the System of Existential Graphs." R 481 seems to be the earliest paper in which the scroll is indeed recognised as the primitive logical sign to be used, thus capturing the relation of illation better than any other sign would. Also realised for the very first time is the fact that negation, on the other hand, is not a primitive sign of logic, and that in the course of the logical development of reason, one in fact derives the idea of the negation from the idea of the scroll.

Peirce repeatedly mentions that his second system (that is, the system of existential graphs), which he was able merely to sketch in the last paragraphs of R 482, is "less philosophical" than the first (that is, the system of entitative graphs), because the former starts with negation and conjunction as primitive instead of staring with the conditional form. Indeed Peirce bases algebraic formulations of logic strictly on the conditional footing, and the task that really remained to be done was only how to combine the conditional form with quantification. He had already acknowledged in print in his Schröder reviews that the logical development begins with the "paradisiacal" state of innocence and freedom (Peirce 1897, p. 184), and that there should thus exist a philosophical reason for preferring EGs as one could define negation by the primitive sign of the conditional while the converse does not hold. The realisation of this fact could also explain why Peirce at this point proposes to draw the inner loop of the scroll initially as saw-edged in R 481 but not in his coeval manuscripts: the inner loop is always present although it can disappear from sight. In later writings on reasoning he again takes up this topic of the two nested ovals being not exactly of the same form and quality, with notational, logical and terminological distinctions between them, such as by calling the outer loop "the Wall" and the inner loop "the Fence" (R 292, R 295, R S-30).

If this is right, then it is the recovery of such philosophical foundations that was missing in Peirce's earlier expositions of the graphs, prematurely leading him to regard entitative graphs as the more philosophical of the two. But as he is now busy with bringing a reader-friendly exposition of EGs into completion, the development of such philosophical aspects of the method had to be postponed. It is the follow-up papers such as R 497, R 485 and the Cambridge Conference Lectures (R 438) that would take up that task, including the question of the nature of assertions. The later manuscripts such as R 484 (F4) will also afford plenty of further room for such thoughts and details.

In sum, the present manuscript, together with the two preceding chapters, are among the very few early papers that study the system of EGs proper, making R 481 one of the earliest unambiguous presentations of that system. It furthermore does so within the unique context set up by his innovative proposal of dualising the earlier account of Euler diagrams. What he would later call lines of identity are in R 482 drawn as thick lines, and hence the earlier parts of R 482 were certainly written before R 481. It is R 481 that has a more accessible and expository style of the two, almost lucid, thus providing a unique window both into the development of EGs, its major difference to Euler diagrams, and its relevance to some of the most central issues in the philosophy of logic. Peirce even hinted at his intention to offer another paper, which might have been R 481, for consideration in *The Monist*. Sadly he did not, as this paper might have stood some real chances of appearing in print and making an impact, but instead it remained unacknowledged for over a century.

Selection 9: [Memoir for the National Academy of Sciences] (R 483), 1896

Following his November presentation Peirce was invited to submit the paper for the Academy's proceedings, with the deadline set to be on January 1st. Written between 21 and 29 December 1896, and seriously ill-dated in the Robin catalogue as c.1901, the pages of R 483 represent that attempt. R 483 is also the very first exposition—together with the roughly parallel additions Peirce made to R 482 along the way—of the system of Existential Graphs in which the system is also named as such.

On December 29 Peirce writes Carus having started working on the memoirs which he needed to finish right away, and tries to get Carus to publish it with the Open Court. Carus replies that Peirce should go ahead with the Academy and not to mind *The Monist*. Why Peirce finally did not complete and submit his "Memoir" is unknown, given that the presentation is fairly balanced and well thought-out, avoiding excess and complex examples, and outlining the important basic conventions. For these reasons it would have made a more successful contribution than the megalomanic R 482 or even that of R 488. Did he receive comments from the conference delegates and colleagues to write up a paper with less graphs and more explanations than his presentation had, and hence was led to avoid "as much as possible the philosophy of logic"? Or had the reasons for the non-delivery to do with his by-now mounting frustrations with Carus and the fading prospects of getting his most lucid and interesting paper to appear?

Be this as it may, the "Memoir" is the first and almost complete text to take up what Peirce had previously termed the positive logical graphs and what in the later additions to R 482 was baptised as the existential system. Some specifics are worth pointing out. One peculiarity is Convention 3, according to which it is a graph "having a line drawn across it" and not an oval encircling the graph that "shall have its signification reversed", such as receiving a reading as "being other than." It quickly occurs to Peirce, however, that having mere crossings of the lines of identity would fail to carry out the task ovals do, namely the denotation of scope of quantificational lines and logical connectives. In the alternative drafts he actually does speak about "lightly drawn endless lines" around regions of the sheet: such endless lines would have the same effect as "parenthesis in algebra" or "quotation marks" in language. Interestingly, he proposes that such endless lines could also be used to single out universes that subsist outside of the universe of existence.

Peirce is seen to arrive at such thoughts when contemplating the nature of assertions. For example, he realises a problem that one cannot assert that some properties are attributed to someone, although one could well *represent* assertions to do so. He is led to this dilemma on the nature of assertions by his thoughts on "widening the universe of discourse" and by certain experiments he made on graphs in which special spots or rhemas are added to the language of graphs that signify meanings such as "___ asserts the truth of ___" and "___ is true". These meta-graphical elements will resurface in the 1903 Lowell Lectures in relation to the logic of potentials and in the theory of graph of graphs.

The important and new parts of the "Memoir" thus have to do with the basic conventions and the role of the universe of discourse in logic. His opening purports to avoid the philosophy of logic, but in reality the manuscript is vastly focussed on philosophical topics, including remarks on philosophy of language that make it of interest also in contemporary research on assertions and pragmatics that study the nature of meta-assertions. A little later Peirce would (such as in the 1898 Cambridge Conference Lectures, see RLT and R 438) use the method of encircling graphs by ovals not to express denials but as a meta-assertoric device to draw relevant distinctions, such as those between making and representing assertions.

In the variant of "Illustrations of the Effects of the above Conventions" (Appendix A) we also find a new explanation of the line as the "continuum of verbs" that guarantees that the existential identity holds between objects marked by the extremities of the line. This may be an anticipation of what he would consider to pertain to "continuous predicates" in the later stages of the development of the graphical method.

Selection 10: [Six Papers on Existential Graphs], 1897–1898. The formative years

The months following Carus's definite and final refusal to publish Peirce's papers on logical graphs appear to have him turn to a low-battery mode. There are nonetheless several writings of considerable importance that improve upon the first batch in the period until around the time of his permanent return to Arisbe in summer 1898. The last three chapters of the present volume collate this output produced during those 18 months that followed Peirce's ultimately failed battles with the publication of R 482, in these precious little segments of texts that have survived in the Peirce Papers at the Harvard Houghton Library.

R 497. In summer 1897, Peirce writes in a small notebook he had received from his friend Francis Augustus Lathrop (1849–1909), an artist and literary agent, some refinements to one of the basic rules, namely the cutting or erasure of a portion of a line of identity on positive areas in the graphs that express quantification and identity (R 497, June 15, 1897, first selection).

In the next summer, Peirce writes back to Lathrop (CSP to Lathrop on July 24, 1898, R L 245; LoF 3) concerning the system of rules of EGs. His letter reveals that he had discovered these basic rules and studied them "since last summer". The rules as given in R 497 are still somewhat imprecise and incomplete, but Peirce's records in the *Logic Notebook* (LoF 1) confirm that it is during the summer months of 1898 when back home in Arisbe that he succeeded in completing the presentation of the basic formal rules of transformation for what he would later distinguish as the Alpha and Beta parts of EGs. Those rules are sound and now they also form a semantically complete set of formal rules, and so in that sense, by the end of summer 1898, his work was done.

R 486. Peirce shares his comments and corrections on the presentation of those rules which Lathrop had written and sent to Peirce in the previous summer (this R 486, second selection), apparently in order to receive Peirce's comments. These rules, albeit written in Lathrop's hand, were derived from one of Peirce's syllabi on logic that he had sent to Lathrop in 1897, which may be identical to those we find in R 497. After the recovery of Lathrop's 1897 letter Peirce would, in July 1898, check the material, add some explanations to its rules, and send this amanuensis back to Lathrop.

R 438. "The Logic of Relatives" (third selection) was written in February 1898 and it forms part of the first draft of the third lecture on the logic of graphs Peirce planned for the Cambridge Conference Lectures which he delivered in February and March that year. This earlier draft was probably ready by January or even in late 1897 as Peirce sent it to William James, who had arranged those lectures, for comment. The paper focusses on the question of the nature of assertions. Interestingly, Peirce does not interpret the oval drawn around a graph as a denial, but as an attentional device one interpretation of which is that of negation. There are other interpretations, too, and the oval in the syntactic sense is thus an operator the interpretation of which can be made to vary according to the purposes of the notation.

The final draft of R 438 is what Peirce may have delivered at that Brattle Street gathering, and it has adequately been published in *Reasoning and the Logic of Things* (RLT). However, only a few and disorderly snippets from the present draft were included in the *Collected Papers* (CP), and a word of warning is therefore in order. CP published only two paragraphs from this draft version, ending the first (CP 4.4) right where our selection begins, with the editors' comment that "Peirce here gives a number of elementary graphs to illustrate the logic of relatives. The papers in book II of this volume cover the same ground." They do not, as the graphs in the present selection are not all elementary: two of them are meta-logical graphs, that is, make assertions about the graphs themselves. CP then resumes, with its second paragraph taken from this lecture draft (CP 4.5) right where our selection below on those graphs ends. After that it fast forwards to 1906 for the next few paragraphs.

R 485. Entitled simply "On Existential Graphs" (fourth selection), this text also belongs to the same bumper crop as the previous couple of selections. While it also emerged in the wake of Peirce having had to put R 482 to rest, we can feel this renewed attempt breathing with some fresh energy and novel ideas.

Three points call for our attention. First, what is distinctive in R 485 is that Peirce takes up the topic he introduced in the "Memoir", namely the scribing of the graph-instances on a sheet of paper as an act of making assertions. This would grow in his later expositions into a prominent feature that distinguishes Peirce's approach to logic and its philosophy so markedly from those of his contemporaries. Here Peirce introduces the term "diagrammatic syntax" in order to describe the special character of the language of graphs. The phrase itself will recur only much later in his writings during 1911, but indeed it is the diagrammatic nature of this new syntax that characterises the language of graphs and its well-formed (or, as one should say, 'well-scribed') expressions.

Another facet of the question "What assertion is" is the modality Peirce mentions, namely that of "being destined to be experienced". The reference to 'being destined' is noteworthy in two respects: it marks a departure from the fundamental relation that characterised entitative graphs and their mode of being in which it "involves necessarily the truth of the description." This is not, as Peirce can now observe, well suited to representing conditional propositions. The idea of the modality of 'being destined' would reappear only much later in 1906 in *tinctured* EGs and in reference to what Peirce takes to consist of the universe of tendencies (LoF 3).

Second, as Peirce already had done in his 1885 "Algebra of Logic" paper here, too, he presents the triad of icon, index and symbol as the essential first movement (speculative grammar) to the logical suite that is to follow. The triad aids the development of a perfect, that is, maximally analytic system of logical notation unfolding from earlier algebraic logics and their notational explorations. The sign triads are not the building blocks of any theory on their own; rather they offer promissory notes to orient the development of proper logical theories, here of the diagrammatic syntax that must be involved in order for EGs to succeed in analysing the nature of deductive reasoning in its ultimate elements.

In R 485, third, Peirce emphasises what we may call the strategic and non-mechanical nature of inference, including deductive inference (cf. e.g. R 201, R 669; LoF 1). What he has to say about inference is that inferential reasoning concerns habits of reasoning as "expressed by the premise." The nature of reasoning, namely the connection between the premises and the conclusions was—as we saw in the texts included in Part I of the present volume—Peirce's lifelong quest. What makes inference good (or valid) cannot, even in deductive reasoning, be exhaustively reduced into mechanical steps. Something has to establish the connection. Interestingly, the present manuscript suggests that these connections are given by "definite icons": the premises (or signs of conclusions) are connected to their conclusions (or their objects) by virtue of a possibility of resemblance between them. But what is it that gives rise to such icons? There must be something else that shapes the formation of icons as such inferential possibilities. According to Peirce, premises and conclusions express habits of reasoning. There are habits, he writes, that are "unstable and be destroyed", as well as those that "will ultimately prove stable and endure." If the habits that the premises express are unstable, then the inferential steps fail to lead to preferred outcomes and such reasoning is no good. If the habits that the conclusions express are stable, then the reasoning is assured to take the right course. The way Peirce explains the nature of reasoning is the way of game-theoretical semantics: the stability of strategies is ascertained by the indexical connection between definite icons and objects of the universe of discourse, that is, by the payoffs assigned to terminal nodes. The illative transformation from premises to conclusions is an effective transformation of indices into icons.[24] Peirce is seen to provide effective methods

---

[24] The process of transformation may call to mind some much more modern ideas such as evolutionarily stable strategies that can serve as solution concepts familiar from evolutionary versions of game theory.

for such transformations in his fledgling theory of EGs. Habits are the *would-bes*—the strategy profiles in the game-theoretical sense—that assertions are intended to inculcate in the mind of the reasoner. It is then pragmaticism that is later to become the official name for Peirce's general doctrine of meaning of assertions, defined in terms of 'conceivable conditional resolutions to act on them', the topic to which Volume 3 of the *Logic of the Future* is devoted.

R 513. The fifth selection (R 513, [May 1898?]) collects what remains in Chapter XI of a long piece of writing entitled simply FL (Formal Logic?). This slightly longer piece may have been related to Peirce's plans to write a book on logic and its principles. Peirce explores in this chapter the relationship between algebra and existential graphs. The longer piece was planned to have at least fourteen individual chapters, of which only a disappointing 132 manuscript sheets have been preserved in the archives. As far as can be told, the purpose of FL was to compare algebraic and graphical logics. Peirce weighs on the advantages and disadvantages of the notation, signification and, in particular, the means of representing relations according to these various systems. The main question of the full manuscript—though seriously incomplete and with a great number of lost, misplaced and early draft sheets—seems to have studied the expressivity of the general algebra of logic and how well it would fare with representing and reasoning about complex relations that call for an increase in the complexity of quantifier strings.

This is the problem that haunts Peirce for years to come. The question is finally resolved in his February 26, 1909 letter to William James (R L 224; LoF 3), where a comparison between three approaches, the general algebra of logic, the algebra of dyadic relatives, and the logic of existential graphs, is carried out by paying close attention to how quantifier scopes get expressed in these systems.

In the present selection, the first part of a version of the chapter that predominantly deals with these matters is represented in terms of the recently developed logic of EGs. Due to the abundance of lost pages, it is impossible to know for sure what the various topics concerning the graphical method in this chapter had been, let alone what the motivations and plans for this chapter were in the wider context of comparing algebraic and graphical methods and notations. The large number of missing pages also makes it impossible to ascertain whether Peirce by this date, presumably in late spring 1898, had the definite set of illative rules for quantified EGs at his disposal. He does remark, importantly, that "All such rules are reducible to *permits to draw* and *permits to erase*."

What survives from Chapter XI are fifteen manuscript sheets that fall between manuscript pages 52–78. The running figure captions suggest that this very chapter alone contained at least 122 examples of graphs, of which 33 have been preserved in the folders and are all produced in this selection. Of note is the large image towards the end, taken from the next Chapter XII (ms p. 91), which shows the significant increase in complexity when expressing distributions across collections in a graphical form.

R 495. The sixth and final selection in this chapter is a text written in a notebook in August 1898. The text is closely related to Peirce's summer 1898 notes in the *Logic Notebook* (R 339) and to the other selections of this chapter. It is a recap of the essentials of the system of EGs, now concisely presented in the form and shape that effectively has found its final and definite expression. This study encompasses constitutive conventions, basic formal rules, and reflections on the index-icon relation in the context of graphs: "Every graph is in so far an index in that it asserts something of the actual universe, which *exists* (or rather is the sum of existence) and *is an individual* in as much as of it every proposition is either true or false." In closing, Peirce notes that the process through which a *quality* comes to be regarded as an *individual*, or rather as a quality individuated as a predicate that can be so quantified in our universe of discourse, is a process of *abstraction*.

Shortly after having completed the presentation of the system and what now is the complete set of rules, Peirce would fall seriously ill and any further attempt at significant developments had to wait for his *annus mirabilis* of 1903. But for the time being, his job was done.

Selection 11: On Existential Graphs, F4 (R 484), 1898. Graphs in proofs

In summer 1898 Peirce also composes a slightly longer text that deserves a separate chapter. R 484, entitled "On Existential Graphs, F4" dates from late summer 1898 and is closely related to the previous texts, especially that of R 495. The date of August 2, 1898 marked on the last two pages of R 484 corroborates the dating of his several other and roughly coeval writings. This manuscript is eye-catching, if only for the reason that Peirce marshals an array of proofs using the graphs, thus creating not only eloquent deductions but also aesthetical experiences of what proofs with graphs look like. Peirce's purpose is to establish the set of basic rules of illative transformations and a systematic method of deducing other rules from the set of basic rules. He also aims at proving soundness of many of them. A record number of twenty-eight rules are presented and the correctness of most of them is argued for. Inspection of these rules leaves Peirce ultimately with seven basic rules of transformation, a conclusion consistent with what he had stated in the *Logic Notebook* on August 4, 1898 (R 339; LoF 1).

F4 (it is not known what this acronym means) could well have been published in a mathematical journal. Peirce reaffirms several points made in the preceding couple of selections. Negation is a derived property of a thin closed line surrounding propositions ("Hence, on the whole the oval denies that which is within") and primarily is to be taken as a description of "what is intended." Peirce even proposes a topological possibility that a double cut is a coarsened form of one continuous line infolded within itself "so as to produce cells and cells within cells." Graphical logical forms of many natural-language sentences are given in the section that entitles those "equivalences." Peirce then suggests a systematic way to graphically represent numerical propositions, such as "there are at least X individuals in the universe." The illative relation is interpreted in the deductions of elementary rules from the basic rules as "is transformable into." The analytic virtues of the existential system are demonstrated by applying it to the analysis of the workings of the syllogism Darii into its smallest details.

Selection 12: The Peripatetic Talks (R 502–505), 1898

Four pieces of this rather mysterious "Peripatetic Talks" series have survived: numbers 2, 4, 6 and 7, and a likely addition (R 489) that develops upon the fourth talk and is presented in the appendix. There is no information that Peirce delivered or was even planning to deliver what he here decided to call 'talks'; the Aristotelian term suggests an authorship forced to an isolation and without right to permanent residence or property in which to conduct work with students of logic.

Indeed that was Peirce's situation. His writing of these talks can be dated to August 1898, the summer that falls between his permanent return to Milford in May from the intermittent exile in New York City since late 1895, and September when he fell seriously ill, incapacitated from work until well into the next spring. That might have been typhoid contracted from the outbreak that had taken place near Milford; together with the brain fever and the raging neuralgia we have enough to explain why Peirce's explorations on EGs came to a sudden halt from September. The interval from June to August is also when his notices on EGs were jotted down in the *Logic Notebook*. During these summer months Peirce reworked the illative transformation rules and it is in the notes of the *Logic Notebook* as well as in the material we find in the previous two chapters that we see Peirce finally converging on what has come to be their standard account in the secondary literature. From August 1898 also sprouts his abstractive extension of EGs (R 339; LoF 1) that proposes the 'moustache' notation to express higher-order concepts in the logic of graphs, the topic which he is able to take up again in his correspondence with Ladd-Franklin in 1900 (LoF 3).

But the "Peripatetic Talks" describe neither this notation nor the rules; rather they are occupied with the semantical and interpretational side of the new logic and with the question of how EGs can effectively be used to analyse meanings. With the exception of **Talk 2 (R 502)**, which outlines his philosophy of logic and categories in general, the other three surviving talks present detailed analyses of complex meanings.

Maybe in the anticipation of students of logic arriving in Arisbe, **Talk 4 (R 503)**, together with R 489 appended to the chapter, read as diligently crafted instruction that could well have served as an introductory lecture on EGs. The system's constitutive conventions and permissive rules are now finally seen to be cleared from mist, making them worthy of communicating in public. Peirce further explains how logical equivalence of propositions is characterised and how such equivalence is ascertained in the system. The emphasis is on meanings, with an abundance of natural-language examples and analyses of meanings of various illustrative propositions. The selection principles that he needs for the semantics to work are presented in a beautiful fashion that makes it clear that the two agents, here aptly termed the "speaker" and the "listener", act according to the specific purposes of verification and falsification of assertions, respectively, as they indeed ought to according to the dialogical and game-theoretic semantics.

The undated paper R 489 from another folder is an exercise that sprouted from the fourth "Peripatetic Talk". In it, Peirce undertakes a meticulous analysis of what might seem to be a simple meaning of a proposition (It thunders). He concludes its logical equivalence with "either it thunders or ○ is true."

Talk 6 (R 504) has another surprise. Peirce analyses scope differences that the graphical analysis of propositions reveals in the logical form of natural-language sentences involving multiple quantifiers. He then notices a "grave defect" in his system of Beta graphs. He claims that the Beta system is not fit to represent the logical form of his complex clergyman example. What Peirce effectively discovers is cumulative quantification, which nearly a century later has indeed been shown to refer to meanings that are not first-order but rather refer to their special cases and extensions of first-order quantification such as branching quantification. The proposed "makeshift" contrivance was to resort to an altogether different type of rhema "___ is a character possessed by the individual___ ", which he needed to track the unexpected invariant property involved in such cumulative readings (cf. R 513 of the previous selection). But using that rhema would at once introduce further complications that would result from an unrestricted use of higher-order notions and would take the analysis out of the tidy domain of first-order logic. Indeed Peirce is not entirely content with his own proposed patchwork. But the fact that the investigation of language had led him to see not only the necessity of introducing some such generalised types of quantifiers but also that a graphical analysis of complex forms of assertions calls for non-standard types of quantification that refer to the "world of ideas" in addition to the "world of existence", has to be recognised as a considerably novel finding.

Talk 7 (R 505) may be the first instance where Peirce comes up with another noteworthy idea: a meta-logical representation of fundamental illative transformations in the language of graphs themselves. It is here that the idea of the 'graph of graphs' is germinated, something which he would return to and develop further in the 1903 Lowell Lectures, namely how the language of graphs can be used to talk about or represent properties of logic of that very language. Three properties of illative transformations are represented here in such a manner: the transitivity of the relation of illation, its inductive or Euclidean property, and its hypothetical character.

Whatever the purpose of this "Peripatetic Talks" series might have been, it is clear that any actual presentation or publication would have made not only an enthralling and challenging summer course for students of logic but also an important contribution to the future of logical research.

Part III: Theory and Application of Existential Graphs

This section introduces the selections chosen for the third part of this volume, an assortment of Peirce's writings on EGs between 1899 and 1911.

Introduction to Part III: Diagrams in the Logical Analysis of Mathematical Reasoning

Over the years, Peirce would improve and extend his systems of graphs and seek motivating them by applications to a host of issues in mathematics, philosophy, linguistics and other special sciences. Among the most important of such applications was to have graphs perform the logical analysis of mathematical reasoning. Peirce firmly believed that the graphical method provided by EGs or one of its appropriate extensions is the right tool to be exploited for that purpose, and at one point took speculative rhetoric (methodeutic) to comprise a study of "applications of logic to mathematics" (R 339, LN [145r], September 29, 1898). All mathematical reasoning, in his own words a few years later, "relates to some schema of the nature of a diagram, that is, a sign having parts related similarly to the objects denoted, and having letters or other indices to distinguish those parts" (R 87, c.1905). Moreover, in the items collected in Volume 2 of the *Logic of the Future* we will see that the entire project of his 1903 Lowell Lectures was predicated on the success of understanding the nature of mathematics and science from philosophical and logical points of views. Peirce proposed to carry this out by analysing the types of reasoning and arguments involved in scientific practice and in drawing mathematical conclusions with the plurality of methods brought out by logical graphs.

One way of looking at Part III of the present volume is to see it as a diverse collection of all those writings on EGs that do not pertain to any other thematic part of the trilogy: history and development, the Lowell Lectures, philosophy of pragmaticism, or Peirce's correspondence. Covering writings from c.1899 until 1911, the third part is at the same time the most diffuse and perhaps also the most consequential of all the seven parts in this three-volume edition. Here we find Peirce carrying out extensive studies on topics such as philosophy and ethics of notation, proposals for variant and non-standard syntax of EGs and their rules of transformation, systematic graphical analyses of natural-language statements, epistemological investigation on topics such as an analysis of practical knowledge, mathematical work on topology, axioms of natural numbers and collections, as well as studies on abduction and the theory of signs, all receiving their respective and often considerably sustained expositions. These theoretical studies, just as the predicted application of graphs to other and new areas of inquiry were, in turn, calculated to contribute to the development of the method of logical analysis itself, which as Peirce hoped would rise into a colossal doctrine by which one could ultimately reach a deep and much improved understanding of meanings as they occur in our language, mind, thought, mathematics and science.

A brief account of the selections that appear in this third and final part of Volume 1 of *Logic of the Future* is given next.

Survey of Part III: Selections 13–28

The arrangement of the altogether seventeen individual chapters in Part III is nearly chronological. A number of inclusions from the *Prescott Book* (Selection 27) 1907–1910 and the *Logic Notebook* 1898–1909 (Selection 28) span several years and are for that reason placed at the end. Selections 15–17 (undated but likely from 1901) delve into the ethics and philosophy of notation, as does the selection (R 253) from 1905. The former three papers are likely to have been written around the same time and are for that reason grouped together and before the selections from the *Minute Logic* written in early 1902.

Selection 13: The Principles of Logical Graphics (R 493), c.1899

With its staggering systematic presentation of 126 examples of graphs with only one 0, 1, 2 or 3-ary verb, plus another three dozen more complicated ones, the text that appears in this small red leather notebook is one of the rare pieces of Peirce's writings on EGs that fall between the first batch that ended with the "Peripatetic Talks" of summer 1898 and his resolute return to the study of logic with the enormous "Minute Logic" of early 1902. Peirce recollects his "makeshift contrivance" he introduced in the sixth talk of the previous selection, namely using a special rhema of "possesses as a character" to represent meanings difficult to capture otherwise. The justification falls from the "axiom", not too distant from the unrestricted axiom of comprehension, that every set of individuals has some unique property. The dots that we find Peirce carefully scribing at the loose ends of the ligatures are used elsewhere in his writings around these times as well though they would soon disappear from subsequent studies. As the principles, definitions and the terminology overall are not yet fully matured while also somewhat different from what we have encountered before, we can tentatively date his notebook to the intermitted period of c.1899.

Three further points need to be highlighted. A remark follows his first 126 examples: "Besides these forms there should be others not easily represented expressing such assertions as the following." This remark stands out because Peirce found no Beta graph to capture the assertions that follow in natural language. This leads one to suspect that he has hit upon some examples—not unlike those few others he had discovered a year back in the "Peripatetic Talks", and also resembling those that he would soon propose in the *Minute Logic* excerpts (R 430; LoF 1) as well as in his 1906 National Academy of Sciences address (R 490; LoF 3)—which involve meanings that are not first-order representable yet are devoid of any overt intensional or modal concepts which he could deal with in the Gamma part of the theory (R 464; LoF 2). A careful logical analysis of his example may lead to non-standard quantifier structures such as branching quantification, indeed minimally above the first-order level but below the full second-order apparatus. The example certainly involves strings of first-order quantifiers whose dependence relations on each other are both complex, exceptional, and "not easily represented" in the language of graphs currently at his disposal.

Another unique point made in R 493 concerns the nature of assertions. Principle 5 states that a lack of a "head or finish" in the line of identity deprives it from being of the nature of an assertion. A line is usually an assertion, but it needs "an indefinite index" at its end which must be separately denoted by a "swelling, or button." The notation that Peirce proposes accentuates the fact that the loose end of the line of identity actually hits upon (by the button) or lassoes (by the swelling) *some* individual on the sheet of assertion. The swelling, as depicted in Fig. 12 in Peirce's hand, is a *hapax legomenon* in his writings. The button, a small dot placed at the loose ends or outermost extremities of the line appears once in a while in other and mostly coeval writing although that notation, too, is soon to be dropped.

Apparently Peirce assumed Principle 5 implicitly in his further works; one could interpret the principle making explicit that individuals are well-defined whenever there is such a loop or swelling (which can atrophy to a dot), as the self-returning line of identity represents self-identity. Thus the notation of a loop at the line's extremity is an insightful conceptual innovation—after all, topologically a complete classification of manifolds in zero dimensions is a loop.

Third, Peirce's dissection of the illative rules of transformation is also exceptional. The rules are given according to which rules are permitted to be applied, on the one hand, within even enclosures, namely on the areas that have positive polarity, and, which rules of transformation are permitted to be applied, on the other hand, within odd enclosures, namely on the areas that have negative polarity. A cross-section of the rules presented delivers the familiar rules of erasure from positive areas, insertion in negative areas, and the reversible iteration/deiteration rules, but the way Peirce itemises them is not the one we standardly meet.

Selection 14: On the First Principles of Logical Algebra (R 515), c.1901

The next three chapters (plus R 253 from 1905) comprise an interconnected bouquet of writings which Peirce produced on general notational aspects of logic. These papers present his new thoughts on the ethics and philosophy of notation. Much less known than his writings on the ethics of terminology from the *Syllabus* of the 1903 Lowell Lectures, Peirce now formulates the principle of the ethics of notation, and urges this maxim to be followed in the sciences whenever new notations are about to be introduced. These writings thus add the significant notational side to his ethics of terminology. They also add to the theory of logical graphs important comparisons with his algebraic systems. Indeed these writings confirm that graphs are kinds of algebras.

The first paper on this sub-theme of the ethics of notation, "On the First Principles of Logical Algebra", may have been written in 1901 or in the early months of 1902, in order to expand his *Minute Logic* project (and not least because his friend Francis Lathrop had promised to pay $150 for each chapter). It could also be something that Peirce wanted to become Part 3 of his later *Logical Tracts* project (LoF 2), which was largely composed during summer–fall 1903, the first part of which was "On Existential Graphs" (R 492) and the second on "Euler's Diagrams" (R 479). The third part, which does not survive in any obvious form, was projected to be composed under the title "Logical Algebra".

In "On the First Principles of Logical Algebra", Peirce presents rules of transformations for his general algebra of logic equivalent to those of the rules for EGs. Comparison between general algebra and existential graphs reveals that there is no significant difference between either using the vinculum or drawing ovals to stand for negation, or indeed that of having the sign of aggregation or encircling ovals around juxtaposed propositions enclosed within ovals to stand for the sign of disjunction. Accordingly, Peirce argues that using either the dot or juxtaposition for the sign of logical conjunction is essentially of the same significance, too.

Comparisons between algebraical and graphical notations for quantification are also presented. Here, as indeed already was the case in Peirce's 1885 "Algebra of Logic", it is observed that Σ—and notice that also the design of this sign is not exactly that of the sign of the arithmetical sum $\sum$ or the Greek Sigma letter Σ—does not strictly speaking represent a logical sum but that it merely "simulates" it, since the domains may be uncountable (that is, are not "capable of linear arrangement"). Peirce also considers the constraints under which new terms may be introduced in the course of proofs, and investigates whether the treatment of indefinite individuals and singular terms coincides. Notably, both are quite modern perspectives on the study of logic.

Equally noteworthy is Peirce's observation how in algebraic notation the *obelus* designates, just as the lines that abut ovals in graphical systems, the binding scope of quantified variables, without any need for parentheses as punctuation marks. His last comment suggests reserving the name "Hopkinsian"—and not the "Peircian" or the "Quantifying part" as he had earlier proposed—for the entire string of ordered quantifiers that are placed in front of the "Boolian" expression. The comment on the prenex normal form is preceded by the presentation of scope differences between some–all and every–some in graphical logic—one of the "most vexed questions of logic" as he earlier had described the issue (cf. R 481). Peirce's reflection thus exemplifies his own maxim on the ethics of terminology at work in this phase of the development of fundamental conceptions of modern logic.

Selection 15: On the Basic Rules of Logical Transformation (R 516), c.1901

This second paper on the philosophy and ethics of notation is another and slightly more matured development of the previous chapter. It demonstrates how both the logic of relatives and the graphical method of logic are built up from Peirce's earlier work on Boolean algebra, and how those earlier principles are to be conserved to the fullest degree. The focus is on two notions, scriptibility and transformability, and the soundness and validity of the latter, which at once show the generality of the basic principles of the philosophy of notation: such basic rules are not meant to advance the philosophy of logic in particular but are the very principles for setting up such philosophy in the first place. Again, it is conceivable that this chapter or its still later versions could have become one of the first sections of the second chapter of Part 3 of the *Logical Tracts*, given that the proposed full version of the *Tracts* was to include the section "Basic Principles", in which Peirce planned to explain the principles of illative transformations in its first part concerning existential graphs (LoF 2). As can be learned from coeval writings, Peirce is led to these notions by making three important generalisations to fundamental theoretical notions of logic: that of (i) propositions to all signs, that of (ii) truth to scriptibility, namely "capable of being written conformably to the purpose" (R 501, late 1901), and that of (iii) derivation to transformability, namely "capable of being transformed without changing anything scriptible into anything non-scriptible" (R 430, early 1902). Important observations then follow these advancements of the theory of logic and the emerging analytic method of graphs, such as the statement of the deduction theorem, according to which $(A(B))$ "is scriptible, if, and only if, A, if written as an entire graph, would be transformable into B."

Selection 16: A Proposed Logical Notation (R 530), c.1901

Peirce continues redrafting his contributions to the philosophy and ethics of notation with the present piece, which proceeds from where he had left off with previous attempts. A total of 62 running manuscript pages from R 530 are published here plus the most significant variants; some 75 additional pages of alternative runs remain dormant in the folder, including long sections on the "terminology of the mathematico-logical relations" with extensive passages on the history of logic. Even so, this third paper unanimously belongs to those hitherto unpublished treasures that bear the potential of opening up entirely new fields, or at least paths less frequently travelled, on the ethics and philosophy of logical notations.

A couple of additional points are worth making concerning the enterprise that is now well underway. In the pages below (Peirce's pagination of ms pp. 27–28) Peirce lists the sixteen binary connectives. Fisch (1986) had coined the term "Box-X" notation, and the system itself has been studied in Clark (1997) and Zellweger (1997). Peirce's own presentation of the system of sixteen binary connectives has remained unpublished to date, however. Aside from the present piece, these connectives appear in his writings from the early 1902 on the *Minute Logic*, while their idea dates back to Peirce's earlier investigations in the algebra of logic and his correspondence with Christine Ladd-Franklin. Peirce also gives credit to another gifted student of his, Oscar Howard Mitchell; among Mitchell's landmark insights that were proven right much later in contemporary algebraic logic and in the study of adjunctions, was that "copulas are nothing but conjunctions."

Let us at this point recapitulate on the editorial note of the General Introduction that explained the essential typographical and design features of graphical notations. Peirce has by now made the maxim of the ethics of notation explicit. The abundance and sophistication of the special notations clearly poses an ethical issue of their accurate reproduction. Many of the special characters, icons and operators are not readily available even in the most comprehensive repertoires and mathematical typesetting packages. To match the standards of Peirce's unforgiving design, no approximation or substitution is acceptable, however. Whenever the required symbols are not standardly available, special types have to be designed that take into account not only what they look like in Peirce's hand or in his papers but also how he conceived and described their proper composition, typesetting and printing. As noted, special LaTeX commands have been designed in order to accurately reproduce those special characters with relative ease. The Box-X notation of the present selection is a fairly simple example, but there is now much else besides and some of the more uncommon ones, such as the cursive forms, require close attention. The cursive versions of the Box-X notation are representative cases. It is not only the form and the shape of the notation but also the relative size that may differ from commonplace character designs. Peirce's preferred signs may be slightly larger, taller, narrower or thicker than the usual ones, the thickness of the lines might vary, or they may have to be offset from the baseline. For instance, despite appearances, the cursive sign of equivalence ⧜ is not to be represented by an approximate sign of infinity, ∞. For one thing, the connective would then be confused with the actual sign of infinity that occurs earlier in the same manuscript. It is also the process of how these icons are formed that must not be overlooked: the cursive form of the sign of equivalence is flat, and as such is the *result* of applying uniform pressure on the sixth box notation (the sign of equivalence ⋈) at the same time both from the top and the bottom, until it is flattened into the cursive character ⧜ that we see Peirce using here and elsewhere. (It is an operation that makes an elastic shape with a positive Poisson ratio bulge out.) The effect is even more pronounced when the rounded convex-concave variants of the Box-notation signs are evoked (see R 91, c.1902, "A Treatise on the Calculus of Differences"). Likewise, ⪤ is the cursive form obtained from the Box-notated sign of consequence, ⋈. Moreover, the *order* in which the lines of these characters are scribed is also material. Chinese calligraphy serves as an example of such time-honoured writing system, which Peirce occasionally alluded to when, for instance, he instructed editors on the design of the cursive sign of consequence standing for transformability (⪤) and in which the order of strokes is part and parcel of the meaning of logograms.

Variations on the scorpio tails such as ʓ, ʓ, ʓ, ʓ —another challenge for the type designer—appear both in Peirce's general algebra of logic and in his algebra of dyadic relations. In the long alternative continuation of the text we see Peirce comparing the effect of these signs with the algebra of logic that uses quantifiers. The scorpio-tail types have been designed by relying on Peirce's most characteristic and recurrent examples and explanations as the prototype. Also, in order to fulfill the notational ethical standards Peirce set for logic, we have modified standard astronomical signs such as ♈ into ⚭, as the former would only approximate what Peirce's preferred sign for that purpose was designed and instructed to be.

Such considerations suggest that notations are vital parts of the operation of our cognitive systems of perception and reasoning. Intellectual cognition surely avails itself of well-crafted notations in order to empower its own faculties of observation and reason. None of these notational considerations should thus be treated as superfluity or pedantry but are, just as Peirce argues, indispensable features in the meaning and signification of the notations in question. It is a much greater modification that the introduction of parentheses to a language prescribes than just dispensing them for the sake of something else, such as graphical or diagrammatic two-dimensional notations. For what is the office of parentheses in logical algebra? Obviously, they denote scope, but what is scope? It can mean binding of variables, but it also means the order of selection and hence quantifier dependence. In the text, Peirce remarks how "the order in which the selections of instances are to be made" becomes an indispensable property that needs to be reflected in logical notation. What the graphical notation does is that it proposes a single sign to denote scope in both of these two senses of binding and selection. Such issues were subsequently overlooked in what became the standard notation in modern logic.

Summarising, the maxim of the ethics of notation dictates that notational considerations must nowhere be overlooked. The maxim must thus be kept in mind at all times when reproducing Peirce's manuscripts in a printed form. R 530 stands out both in its compelling arguments for the necessity of such ethics of notation as well as in providing vital examples by which to test that maxim at work both in logical and scientific work as much as in one's textual and editorial practices.

Selection 17: The Simplest Possible Mathematical System (R 430, 431a), 1902

Peirce's gargantuan undertaking to write a detailed account of his theory of logic and analysis of reasoning resulted in four long unpublished chapters and the infamous Carnegie Institute application (R L 75), brutally rejected upon Simon Newcomb's recommendation, despite strong endorsements from an army of prominent scientists and decision makers.[25] Peirce's book, *Minute Logic*, is preserved in

---

25 Those who wrote letters of support to Daniel Coit Gilman, the President of the Carnegie Institution, included Richard Clarke Cabot, Andrew Carnegie, James E. Creighton, John Dewey, Benjamin Ives Gilman, G. Stanley Hall, William James, Senator Henry Cabot Lodge, Allan Marquand, Henry Rutgers Marshall, Dickinson S. Miller (aka R. E. Hobart), William Pepperell Montague, E. H.

four large chapters; several others were planned to follow.[26] The selection below that concerns EGs is from Chapter III ("Mathematics. Section 1") written between January and March 1902.

By summer 1902, and within a period of only a few short months, Peirce had amassed over 2 500 manuscript pages solely for this projected book. Lathrop had many of the pages typeset and Peirce wrote dozens of letters and over 500 pages of related plans for the Carnegie Institute (R 75; NEM IV, pp. 13–73) in order to secure the book's completion and publication. The shocking results of the failed application were communicated in late 1902, and the appeals soon made by various parties were of no avail. In the spring and summer he would have to turn his energies—the little that was left of them—to the upcoming Harvard and Lowell Lectures. Since those lectures would be written for a live audience rather than for the purposes of a scientific monograph, the exploration of some of his most marvellous and complex ideas concerning logic, mathematics and their philosophy that he had recorded in the chapters for the *Minute Logic* were discontinued.

Our selection consists of two alternative and unpublished sections from Chapter III: "The Essence of Mathematics" and "Specimens of Mathematical Reasoning". The first and the only subsection Peirce wrote of the latter, "A. The Simplest Possible Mathematical Systems", is also the only place where Peirce explored the logic of EGs in the context of this project.

In these two sections Peirce applies EGs to the analysis of mathematical reasoning and logical problem-solving. He gives the most minute analysis of the meanings of the basic signs of the system, namely the cuts (ovals) and the lines of identity, indeed more detailed than anything so far during the five-year history of EGs.

Peirce distinguishes five "offices" of the ovals, only one of which is negation. What were these offices and why was the notation of ovals chosen as the best notation in the EG schematism? Peirce argues that "even when there are no lines

---

Moore, Edward C. Pickering, President Theodore Roosevelt, Josiah Royce, Benjamin E. Smith and William E. Story. Many members of the institute, including Elihu Root (cf. R 514; LoF 1), also supported Peirce's application.

26 The preserved chapters and their sections are as follows. Chapter I (R 425, 176 ms pages): Intended Characters of this Treatise. § 1. Logic's Promises. § 2. Of Minute Accuracy. § 3. Different Methods in Logic. § 4. Synopsis of Contents of this Book; Chapter II: Prelogical Notions. § 1. Classification of the Sciences (R 426–427, 291 ms pages), § 2. Why Study Logic? (R 428, 128 ms pages); Chapter III. § 1. The Essence of Mathematics (R 431, 200 ms pages), § 2. Division of Pure Mathematics (R 430, 108 ms pages) / Specimens of Mathematical Reasoning (R 430, 68 ms pages); Chapter IV: Ethics (R 432–434, 234 ms pages). According to the plan and its revisions ("List of Proposed Memoirs on Minute Logic", R 1574), at least 33 chapters were to be accomplished in total, together with a lucrative paycheck, at least according to Peirce's calculations in the margins.

of identity", the ovals "fulfill three distinct offices, and that in introducing these lines we have imposed upon them two more." The graphs "fulfill all five with success", he states, though he notes that, importantly, "in performing the last [sic., the fourth] they slightly hamper that freedom of manipulation which mathematics requires;—for, in the course of this chapter, the reader will perceive more and more clearly that all mathematical inquiry advances by means of experimenting upon schemata."

The first office which the ovals fulfill is indeed that of negation. But an argument is needed why. The ovals fulfill this by distinguishing between affirmative and negative assertions. For if in substituting a term with a coexistent one the resulting assertion must be true when the original assertion is true, then the term is affirmative. If the original assertion must be true when the result of the substitution is true, then the term is a negative one. Peirce does not take the primary effect of linear separation to be that of negation. The primary effect is polarity, namely whether there is an odd or an even number of enclosures. Even in light of this first office, then, to take cuts or ovals as denials and therefore to exhaust the meaning of the separation line would be inadequate.

Next, the second function is "that of associating the conjunctions of terms." Peirce explains this by likening association to the role parentheses have in algebra. He then proceeds to present a detailed argument of how associativity functions in the Alpha part. The third office of the ovals is "to distinguish the modes of conjunction of the parts of propositions." This is explained by the six Alpha graphs that follow. If the ovals would just serve the first role of being signs of negation, these six modes of conjunction would be indistinguishable.

In the system of Beta graphs, namely in the graphs endowed with quantificational lines of identity, the fourth office of the ovals is "to indicate the order of succession of the identifications." The fifth office, which Peirce does not mention in R 430 (the relevant segment breaks off after the fourth) is that the ovals represent non-identity of the extremities of the identifications. We can also add to Peirce's list of five a sixth role, which emerges as soon as ovals are combined with ligatures. Namely, they show the binding scope of quantified variables. For according to the endoporeutic interpretation of the graphs, the direction of interpretation is from the outermost ends of the ligatures towards the innermost ends thus covering the extent to which the lines bind values across the ovals. The ovals thus serve as punctuation marks in the same sense in which parentheses in formulæ serve as punctuation marks for quantifier binding and logical priority of connectives.

It is in connection to this fourth function that Peirce discovers something of further significance. He is led to investigate what the graph means that represents "whatever man there may be is born of some woman." What one needs to capture is, according to Peirce, the meaning of "Any man there may be is born of something, X; and any man there may be is coexistent with a woman who is that X." He then asserts that "our schematic affords no means of expressing these." He appears to be on the right track in this hunch. The reason is that the logic of the sentence above, and thus of those graphs that assert the meaning of that what is expressed in natural language as that sentence, might not be a first-order one. For the selection of the values for "a woman who is that X" in the lower sub-graph must not depend on the selection of the values for the first "Any man there may be" that occurs in the upper sub-graph juxtaposed with the lower one. Since there are two universally and two existentially quantified ligatures, and since the latter of the existential ligatures may not co-vary with the first universal one, what we have is an example of complex quantifiers structures that might require extensions of first-order structures, such as branching quantifiers. The reader may contrast these possibilities with what Peirce already had proposed as potentially non-first-orderisable concepts in R 493 and in R 504.

The reason why the standard first-order quantification as a model for Beta graphs in their general sense fails to represent the requisite meanings is due to the significant geometrical limitations of the two-dimensionality of the sheet of assertion. Peirce notices such limitations well, and the rest of the section indeed presents several potential modifications, five in total, to overcome those geometrical limitations, either by changing or extending the notational part of the language of graphs in various ways unique to the present piece. Whether successful or not, such discoveries are relevant to modern discussions in logical semantics that try to deal with complex donkey-type anaphora and cross-over pronominalisation in natural language.

Moreover, Peirce desires to proceed analysing novel mathematical concepts that he presumes are likewise non-first-orderisable, in his remark connected to the above on the order of succession of selections:

> [T]he ovals were chosen for negation because they would at the same time show the order of connection. They answer the two purposes well in all cases where there is no identification. But when there is identification, a third office is imposed upon the ovals, that of determining the order of the lines of identity. Even this they will always do fairly well; but there are a few cases in which they do not give us the *freedom of manipulation which is desirable in mathematics*. (R 430, added emphasis)

There is a certain natural freedom in forming mathematical ideas which ought not to be straight-jacketed by the notations, especially by those of the ordinary, linear arrangement of logical connectives and quantifiers. However, that may have happened in the wake of the Frege–Russell notation, which do not fully permit the kinds of analyses mathematical freedom of expression would call for. Peirce does not explicate here what these exceptional mathematical propositions are, but for example in the *Logic Notebook* we find notes from the same months that suggest that they concern second intentions, collections and multitudes, as well as definition of pairings, the impossibility of defining the character of characters, and the difficulty of representing properties such as being "at least as small in multitude as" as examples of such "freedom of manipulation". Indeed these are examples that are non-elementarily definable.

In any event, "The Simplest Possible Mathematical System" marks Peirce's return to the theme of EGs after the hiatus between August 1898 and late 1901. It also deserves a place not only as a chapter in the history of modern logic but also in its future development. Some of its issues took nearly a century to re-emerge and their exploration has begun only quite recently.

Selection 18: Multitude and Continuity (R 316a(s), R S-36, R 1584), 1903

Entitled "Multitude and Continuity", with the subtitle "A Lecture to students of Philosophy to be delivered in Harvard University 1903 May 15 (by Charles S(antiago?) Peirce)", the draft in R 316a(s) represents Peirce's sketchy plan for the additional eighth lecture he gave to the Division of Mathematics at Harvard University. It supplemented the seven lectures on "Pragmatism as a Principle and Method of Right Thinking" that were arranged for him by Harvard's Department of Philosophy. What survives from that eighth lecture is a fragmentary set of notes, with an autobiographical tone, on Georg Cantor, Richard Dedekind, and Peirce's own system of existential graphs.[27]

Not much may have been delivered on the announced topics of multitude and continuity, a proper treatment of which would in any case have had to presuppose knowledge of Peirce's system of logical graphs. Additional pages from the related writings and notes in R S-36 and in R 1584 suggest that Peirce rather attempted in this lecture, or at least in its first part, to draw a connection between EGs (about which he had just begun to think anew in light of the Lowell Lectures scheduled for the next winter) and pragmatism, which he proposes is the philosophy present

---

27 *The Harvard Crimson* announced the lecture on May 11 and 14 as follows: "MORE LECTURES BY MR. PEIRCE. Mr. Charles S. Peirce '59 has decided to give a supplementary lecture to his recent series under the auspices of the Department of Philosophy on 'Pragmatism as a Principle and Method of Right Thinking'. The lecture will take place next Thursday in Sever 11 at 8 o'clock and will be open to the public. Mr. Peirce will give a summary of his previous lectures and will put in clearer light the relation of the views maintained to the general doctrine of pragmatism.

By invitation of the Division of Mathematics Mr. Peirce will speak in Sever 8 next Friday at 8 o'clock on 'Multitude and Continuity'. The lecture will deal with 'Number' and 'Continuous Quantity', and reference will be made to Cantor and other writers on these subjects. This lecture is specially intended for students in philosophy and mathematics, but will also be open to the public."

in the basic principles by which to set up and conceive the graphical system. This topic, namely the conventions of EGs that were much elaborated later on during the year, as well as the arguments to establish their philosophical and pragmatistic kernels, would grow into colossal proportions during the next several years in connection to his *Monist* papers (both published and unpublished) on the maxim of pragmaticism and its proof (LoF 3). Since this supplementary lecture was presented to an audience that consisted of students of mathematics (albeit Peirce cleverly addresses them as "students of philosophy"), he might have also wanted to speak further on the basic illative rules of insertions and omissions. Whether any time was left for the treatment of multitude and continuity cannot be definitely determined. In his next lecture series six months later he would again struggle but fail to reach that topic that was to follow the presentation of the theory of EGs (LoF 2).

This 'eighth' lecture was not included in the 1997 publication of Peirce's 1903 Harvard Lectures, but it has been published in NEM III(1) (pp. 128–131), with omissions. The present selection includes material from R S-36 and a notebook R 1584 circumstantially and conjecturally related to the presentation or its plans and drafts. An interesting tidbit occurs on the titlepage of this Harvard Cooperative Society notebook: Peirce's early change of his middle name to Santiago, perhaps as some have suggested in order to honour James's continuing financial, emotional and intellectual support.

From June until the end of 1903 Peirce's writings on EGs concern the Lowell Lectures and are provides as a separate volume (LoF 2). Following his failed attempt to get the lectures published in a book form, the next selection may be his next effort to take up the topic of EGs afresh.

Selection 19: [A System of Existential Graphs] (R 514), 1904

Among a confusing set of assorted pages and segments in the Robin folder R 514 there remain 28 fragmentary leaves of a sequence (of which the first four pages are lost and which might have been a continuous run of some draft paper), which appear as the only text on EGs in which Peirce prefers to use the term "the Sheet of Truth" in place of the standard "Sheet of Assertion", in order to describe one of the most important notions of his later logic. Indeed truth-values take the central stage of this treatise which is about the fundamentals of the Alpha and Beta parts of EGs. An important observation is made on what is commonly thought to be among the basic rules of the Alpha system, namely the insertion of a double cut around any graph, which is not a primitive rule of proofs but a consequence of three more fundamental permissions: (i) the rule of 'soundness', namely that any rule that "can never change a true graph into a false one" is permissible, (ii) that any graph "that we know to be true" is permitted to be scribed on the sheet of truth, and (iii) the rule of "truism" (tautology), namely the blank on any area is a graph "regarded as meaning anything that is too obvious to take the trouble to say." To draw a light circle around a blank graph twice is not primarily a double negation of a blank, either, but an implication from an obvious truth, truism or tautology, to an equally obvious truth. Peirce then stresses the importance of having a representation for an absurdity, or a denial of a truism (elsewhere termed the empty cut or the pseudograph) in the system, in order to signal "absurd alternatives" or those of "unmeaning supplements." Indeed to be able to perform a systematic and effective search for contradictions in one's logical system is an important and often a desirable property of one's inferential system.

Peirce's maturing three-fold classification of sentences into 'inquiry-making' interrogations, those involving perlocutionary acts such as commands and imperatives, and those of propositions that have a force in influencing the 'conduct of thought', suggests that this piece was written in tandem with his revisions of the classification of signs that began in 1904, as it is those revisions that came to accommodate various forms of such speech acts.

Selection 20: Reason's Conscience. A Practical Treatise on the Theory of Discovery; considered as Semeiotic (R 693b, R S-26), 1904

Inspired by Kant's *Critique of Practical Reason*, Peirce's next big project *Practical Treatise on the Theory of Reasoning*, written to fill up six Harvard Cooperative notebook volumes, was meant to become a new book on reasoning. The general title for the text that altogether comprises some 280 autograph pages in these notebooks was "Reason's Conscience: A Practical Treatise on the Theory of Discovery; considered as Semeiotic".

In this aptly named "practical treatise", Peirce argues that logic ought to depend on the three sciences of mathematics, phenomenology and ethics. The plan was to devote a chapter on each of these sciences before moving on to the topic of logic. He manages to address mathematics, and to some extent phenomenology and ethics, after which the part on logic, largely unwritten, was supposed to follow.

The first and the main variant below is from Volume 4 of the treatise. Peirce wrote four sections for it (§ 23–§ 26), and they provide a convenient introduction to the topic of existential graphs. This fourth volume follows his preceding analysis of mathematical aspects of *pons asinorum*, namely Euclid's fifth proposition. He indicates that the variant he had written is to be replaced by what is included in Appendix A of the present selection as the second variant and which is on the analysis of the nature of mathematical reasoning. The first variant differs from the version in the appendix in introducing the logic of existential graphs and it is previously unpublished.

Peirce's introduction is important in a number of respects. For example, it serves as an accessible glossary of the main technical terms. It also presents the syntax of graphs first, and instructs how to scribe the scroll in the right way. The introduction then details what is meant by "nests" and "oppleted graphs", and outlines the six fundamental permissions. Probably Peirce meant to keep the first variant for later uses in the book in case that material was needed, although he never carried the project further beyond these six notebook volumes.

The version given in Appendix A is Volume 5 of the *Practical Treatise*. It was published, with minor omissions, in NEM IV (pp. 185–216). Volume 5 wrestles with the nature of mathematical reasoning, especially the question of mathematical practice that draws inferences that are corollarial. This question—familiar from the 1903 Lowell Lectures and from many other places of his work—is how to tackle a mathematical problem that is altogether novel, a problem that is never seen or thought of before. This question occupied Peirce throughout his life, and *Reason's Conscience* may be taken to be a contribution towards certain resolutions of that question.

Appendix B is an alternative version of § 24 from R S-26, entitled "The Alpha Part of Existential Graphs". It is written on the same notebook type as R 693b, here numbered § 24–§ 25 and located in the supplementary catalogue folder R S-26 as § 25–§ 26. In it, Peirce presents a complete glossary of key terms of the Alpha part of the theory. Another such list was prepared for the *Logical Tracts* dating from the previous year; together the two may now be taken to accomplish what Peirce wanted to write already for his 1896 seminal paper on logical graphs (R 482), namely a glossary of "some hundred terms". The abundance of such terms can be explained by the need to precisely define the notation and the workings of the ovals.

Much of what is contained in the sixth volume, and which presumably was to be followed by a revised chapter on the logic of existential graphs, deals with various aspects of "applicable knowledge". This epistemological theme was suggested to Peirce when thinking about how to prove theorems of geometry. It is such applicable knowledge that justifies his choice of the general title: it is to be a practical treatise on aspects of reasoning and logic. It is both fascinating as much as disappointing to notice that he planned but did not carry out in any length the preliminary idea of how to put the logic of existential graphs to use in analysing that sort of practical knowledge.

Selection 21: Topical Geometry (R 145, R 145(s)), 1905

On November 16, 1904, Peirce read a paper entitled "On Topical Geometry" at the National Academy of Sciences meeting in New York City, with 28 members of the Academy in attendance.[28] R 95 is the folder closest to that presentation, with 34 pages of notes preserved, and as those notes address "Mr. President" it may well have been the actual presentation. But as R 95 does not mention EGs, it is not the text that is produced here. Notebooks R 145 and R 145(s), on the other hand, together with a number of loose and alternative pages collated from several other folders (R 507, R 839, R 1575, R S-31), portray his slightly later attempt to write up a fuller account. This fuller account, written in April–May 1905, now takes the graphs on board.

Five years earlier, Peirce had worked on three papers for the Academy's autumn meeting: "The Definition of Continuity", "Topical Geometry" and "The Map-Coloring Problem", of which the first two were read by title. Now this much later occasion would finally give Peirce a chance to present his work on the interconnected topics of geometrical topics, hypostatic (or "subjectal") abstraction and map coloring, and now even encompassing existential graphs. He might have wanted to venture into an application of the graphical method of logic to the so-far unsolved four-color problem, but the presentation did not allocate time for such further explorations. His subsequent attempts on a longer version—though written with a potential publication in mind and advancing yet another and unfulfilled prospectus to evolve into a book-length treatise—represent a relatively hurried hand and the result is an uncompleted and sketchy version of the presentation from the previous autumn. Yet it is not without considerable new ideas; in one of the variants found in a supplementary folder (R 145(s)) Peirce for instance proposes representing hypostatical abstraction in graphs by a purple line that blends the colours of the spots (red and blue) connected by the abstracted line of identity, together with a reference to the map-coloring problem. His remarks on properties of space detail the definition of graphical notations that later in R 683 he would take to concern spatial arrangements of whatever is scriptible. In another and roughly coeval piece entitled "Properties of Space" (R S-10, only the first page is extant), the topological notion of 'ambient space' is implicit in his definition of the properties of space:

§ 1. *Definition*. Anything that anything is situated in is called a *Place*.
§ 2. The geometrical properties of the relation of being situated in a place are two, as follows:

---

[28] That presentation, which was one out of the four mathematical papers presented in the Academy's annual meeting, is cited in the *Report of the National Academy of Sciences for the Year 1904*, Senate Doc. No. 178, Washington: Government Printing Office, 1905, p. 16.

a. Every place is situated in itself.
b. If anything, A, is situated in a place B, while B is situated in a place C, then A is situated in C.

§ 3. *First Property of Space.* Every place is in Space.

Space, says Dr. Fr. E. Abbot, is the Receptacle of Things.

Selection 22: Logical Analysis of some Demonstrations in high Arithmetic (R 253), 1905

This attempt to produce a paper on the philosophy and ethics of notation could be considered as Peirce's belated continuation of the series that began with the three previous pieces R 515, R 516 and R 530 in 1901. R 253 derives from summer 1905, the time of new hope and prospects for Peirce to make a final return to the philosophical matters of logic. While struggling to contain his and Juliette's failing health issues, including frequent domestic injuries resulting from falls, Peirce was busy again preparing his papers on pragmaticism for his third *Monist* series which he had just negotiated with Paul Carus of Open Court.

This summer he mentions to William James his work on arithmetic (CSP to WJ, July 23; LoF 3), and in the same month proposes to Victoria Welby a new schema to serve as the logic of abduction (CSP to VW, July 16; LoF 3). Both of these letters were unsent drafts. The present selection is mostly concerned with notational prerequisites for his general algebra of logic as well as for EGs, with a view of applying them to the discovery of logical forms of mathematical proofs, such as Fermat's and Wilson's famous theorems. It never proceeds as far as actually presenting such application, and like other logical papers "of the last twenty years" was no longer intended for publication but "written for my eyes solely." This does not make the piece any less interesting, however, as it is not just a strict continuation of his philosophy of notation project which had started two decades earlier with the 1885 publication of "On the Algebra of Logic: A Contribution to the Philosophy of Notation" in the *American Journal of Mathematics*. What we find Peirce doing in R 253 is a comparison of algebraic and graphical notations which he would soon develop into further treatises to help tackle that "most vexed of questions of logic", namely the analysis of the meaning of propositions that come equipped with the "Peircians", that is, with complex strings of first-order quantifiers. The paper could also have been projected to fill in the slot in the *Logical Tracts* (LoF 3)—a book-length draft written two years previously and which he still might have hoped to complete and whose prospective third chapter of the first part concerning existential graphs was named "Logical Analysis".

Selection 23: A New Deduction of the Properties of Positive Integers (R 70(s)), 1906

This study from August 1906 contains a definition of properties of positive integers by what are better known as the Peano's axioms of natural numbers. The way Peirce presents them is, first, to define the two-place successor function: each positive integer N has a successor S(N). Then, that successor is defined to be unique, and zero is defined to be not a successor of any positive integer. Third, the principle of finite induction is provided. Peirce then derives further axioms such as that being a successor of two positive integers implies the identity of those integers, and the property that 0 is the only integer (natural number) that is not a successor of any integer, among other things. He struggles to uncover fundamental reasons for the property that no integer is a successor to two different integers. (Frequent interruptions and health issues obviously prevented Peirce from completing this text.) The matter is returned to in the next summer and in the studies related to the publication of his "Amazing Mazes" series in 1908–1909. What is distinctive about the present piece is of course the definition of Peano's axioms and the derived properties expressed here in the language of Beta graphs. (See W4, pp. 575–576; Moore 2010 (PoM), Shields 1981 and the references cited in those works on the question of the discovery of Peano's axioms and Peirce's earlier studies on number theory.)

Selection 24: A Contribution to the Amazes of Mathematics (R 201), 1907

The three-part publication of "Amazing Mazes", which appeared in 1908–1909 in *The Monist*, is Peirce's testimony to his career as a publishing academic, as well as an unfulfilled and somewhat derailed finale to his ambitious *Monist* series during the unforgiving years of 1904–1908. The "Amazing Mazes" papers arose from some 750 draft sheets he worked on during summer 1907, probably soon after his return to Arisbe from the lodging at Prescott Hall, Cambridge, in July. Much of the "Amazing Mazes" related papers and worksheets have since been published in NEM III(1) (pp. 555–622) and some in the *Collected Papers*. The selection from R 201 complements the material included in NEM and in Peirce's original publications of the "Amazing Mazes" series.

The major quest for Peirce during that year was to solve the puzzle of continuity. His famous argument aimed at showing that the Cantor–Dedekind approach captures only the imperfect or pseudo-continuum, not the true continuum that he had been hunting for much of his life.[29]

The present selection, which comes from the draft of the published articles that carries the working title of "A Contribution to the Amazes of Mathematics", is intended to bring forth a few additional glimpses into that quest. Those include the role of non-mechanical, or as Peirce's choice of the word goes, *theoric inferences* (misspelled in NEM p. 622 as "*theoretic* inference"; in the papers published in *The Monist* the choice of term is the "theoric *step*") that take place amidst mathematical reasoning and mathematical proofs. Peirce assures the reader that what is meant by the "theoric" is a real mode of inference and not a singular creative step, element or moment encountered in the course of proofs, and that an account of those inferences is best exposed in the language of the graphical logic of EGs, as it is such logic that represents and analyses higher-order relations and mathematical concepts in graphico-logical terms in the fashion expected of theoric inferences.

Paul Carus, the editor of these papers at the Open Court, had asked Francis C. Russell to explain the general idea and significance of these rather convoluted papers to the readers (Russell 1908). Russell's digest explains, among other things, that

> one of the cardinal points of the method championed by Mr. Peirce that in so far as the same is possibly attainable, reasoning, indeed all serious thought, should be *iconized* (the word is mine but the idea is his), [...] that the idea dealt with should so far as is possible be represented by a sign or sign-complex, fit by its constitution to display in detail to the intellect all the essential features of the said idea, and especially all the various interrelations that subsist between the constituent elements thereof; in other words, that the plan, so to speak of the said idea should be as concretely expressed as possible. To this very end Mr. Peirce has invented two schemes of logical algebra and two systems of logical graphs. Now in the present case the cards used in the card tricks fulfil an iconic office. They fulfil it in some respects in a superior way. They are not only concrete but are also corporeal. (Russell 1908, pp. 406–407)

---

[29] An addendum to the published paper, dated May 26, 1908, tells how Peirce had reworked the issue since the present drafts: "In going over the proofs of this paper, written nearly a year ago, I can announce that I have, in the interval, taken a considerable stride toward the solution of the question of continuity, having at length clearly and minutely analyzed my own conception of a *perfect continuum* as well as that of an *imperfect continuum*, that is, a continuum having *topical singularities*, or places of lower dimensionality where it is interrupted or divides. These labors are worth recording in a separate paper, if I ever get leisure to write it" (Peirce 1908b, p. 463). What follows in his addendum is a synopsis of those later efforts.

Russell then proceeds to a synopsis of existential graphs, as they are Peirce's language for the "definitional statements" of the mathematics of these card tricks. Russell concludes that "Peirce in this part [Peirce 1908b, pp. 433–440] has not only illuminated several very dark corners of the field of inquiry but has also indicated foundations and principles that sooner or later will win general acceptance" (*ibid.*, p. 415). The part Russell refers to concerns precisely the "quasi-mechanical" nature of logical reasoning, and the prospects for logical machines given the importance that theoric inference has in creative logical and mathematical discovery. Some complexity considerations occupy the later part of the draft, and Peirce observes that as the members of the cyclic system grow in number, so does the size of the class of relations over those members. But the growth is enormous, factorial growth, which suggests that problems concerning cyclic systems are in the class of NP-complete problems and have the complexity equal to that of the travelling salesman problem. Logical reasoning is only quasi-mechanical, as mathematical proofs involve theoric inferences and as problems like those involving finding Hamiltonian cycles are fundamentally intractable (reasonably assuming $P \neq NP$), no matter how fast the logical machines may become in the future.

Selection 25: Logical Critique of the Creed of Religion (R 855–856, R 846), 1911

"Logical Critique of the Creed of Religion" is another of Peirce's late attempts to bring his ideas on logic and its applications to a book-length fruition (R 846–856, April–May 1911). His plan was to write the "Critique" in two parts: one on the theory of logical critic, which concerns the justification and validity of different types of reasoning, and the second part on the application of critic to metaphysical questions concerning religion and faith.

In this previously unpublished selection, Peirce explains at length the abductive mode of reasoning, which since 1898 had often gone by the name of retroduction. An important part of the task of logical critic is to exhibit a theory of the degree and quality of assurance provided by the three different but interconnected modes, or stages, of reasoning: abduction, deduction and induction, and now it is the time to explore in depth what the first of these is about. Peirce has some pertinent remarks to be made on how reasoning by retroduction guides us to the grasping of the possibility (or as one should rather say, plausibility) of another kind of state of things which facts of the matter alone do not reveal, rendering those surprising facts that we are confronted with "comprehensible", "likely", or "comparatively simple and natural." The multiple attempts (on this see also R 846) at formulating an evidential argument that there is no fourth kind of reasoning—which he had announced as early as 1868 and claims to have had "prominently in mind" since 1860—leave something to be desired, however, as the strength of such argumentation is based on not much more than the fact that no one had as yet discovered there to be reasoning of any other kind. These alternative and somewhat compulsive attempts to demonstrate the non-existence of modes of reasoning beyond these three variants are collected in the appendix.

Our justification for the inclusion of the present piece in this volume is found in one of the trailblazing accounts of those attempts and the allied argument for the justification of deductive reasoning, which had lead Peirce to the domain of EGs. In this context, he takes EGs to be the best possible demonstration of the highest level of security provided by the mode of reasoning which is deduction, namely inference in which the certainty of the conclusion cannot overcome the certainty of its premises. In addition, R 846 refers to EGs as providing that "language of self-communion" that he had alluded to in an autobiographical sketch meant to serve as the opening words of yet another of his planned books, *Studies in Meaning*:

> I may here mention that I am naturally deficient in aptitude for language. When a new bit of slang comes into vogue, I am about the last person who discovers what it means, and when I come to do so, it is by requesting somebody to explain it to me. I am very frequently in such doubt about the shade of meaning of some common word, such as "lovely", that I am obliged to hunt it up in concordances and in the poems to which they relate, and scarcely a day passes that I do not resort, once or twice, to the quotations in the Oxford Dictionary. Unfortunately for me, that work does not seem to have been designed for such defectives as I am, and familiar quotations, which have oft-times had decisive influence upon the shades of meaning, the associations of words are distinctly avoided there. I do not think I ever *reflect* in words: I employ visual diagrams, firstly because this way of thinking is my natural language of self-communion, and secondly, because I am convinced that it is the best system for the purpose. But there is nothing fanciful about my diagrams. I do not, for example, see numbers with colors attached to them and placed upon some curve; and it perfectly astounds me to find how useful some persons are able to make such strange constructions. When I am in health I am not aware of having any dreams, unless perhaps of a problem in algebra where no real significations are attached to the letters, or something equally abstract. My "Existential Graphs" have a remarkable likeness to my thoughts about any topic of philosophy. (R 616, March 27, 1909, ms pp. 7–9)

Obviously Peirce denies being synesthetic; it is just that when the graphs are vividly serving one as the icons of philosophical thoughts that new truths may come to light, which would not happen if those thoughts would have to be mediated by natural languages.

Ultimately, then, perhaps the most important lesson from R 846 is nevertheless its reminder that the logical consequence relation concerns reasoning under general states of affairs, not relations between singular events. Consequently, experimental science does not claim demonstration from single experiments, as it rather is—as emphasised in Introduction to Part I—the general form of relations that scientists are on the lookout for in designing, conducting and interpreting results of their experiments.

Selection 26: Assurance through Reasoning (R 670, R 669), 1911

This selection of texts reproduces two manuscripts of the same title, R 670 written on June 7–17, 1911, and its earlier but independently significant discrete variant R 669 written from May 25 to June 2, 1911. These two manuscripts may have been drafts of the paper Peirce planned to deliver in the upcoming autumn meeting of the National Academy of Sciences, where he was invited to give two presentations. Manuscripts 669 and 670 are his last (namely the ninth and the tenth) attempt to complete the series of papers on the grounds and rationale of reasoning he had worked on since the summer of 1910, in view of publishing a collection of his essays on reasoning. They might also be the ones that were to be his contributions to the *Festschrift* in honour of Victoria Welby (1837–1912). The relevant manuscripts are R 651–670, and were entitled "Assurance" since November 1910 (R 661–670).

Perhaps only days before the November meeting, Peirce trod on papers lying on a waxed floor at his home Arisbe, causing a serious injury which made him unable to attend the Academy session. Consequently, the announced paper, "The Reasons of Reasoning, or Grounds of Inferring", together with his "A Method of Computation", were read by title on November 22, 1911. It was not until much later in 1913, though now terminally ill from colorectal cancer, that he recovered some strength to continue working on these topics.[30]

While the content of the latter presentation, "A Method of Computation", has not been preserved, it is likely that Peirce wanted his former paper to communicate ideas that survive in the following pages. The two manuscripts "Assurance through Reasoning" present what may be one of his most successful attempts to explain the logic of existential graphs and the philosophy concerning the notation of diagrammatic syntax. The notions of identity, teridentity, composition of graphs, plurality, conditional, scroll, and the derivation of the idea of negation as a consequence of the scroll, all get their fair shares of exposition. Peirce then makes the important observation in R 670 that in the diagrammatic syntax, logical constants ought to be such that can serve both the roles of (i) *collectional signs* capable of expressing their own scope, and (ii) the *truth function* that those constants have in the context of making assertions. He then notes that "there is no

---

[30] Peirce writes to F. A. Woods on October 14, 1913, recounting his accident to have happened "23 months ago", that is, sometime in November (LoF 3). In the August 28, 1913 letter to Paul Carus he dates the accident to December 13, 1911 but could have been at variance for about a month.

reason why a single sign", "as it is seen by the mind's eye", "should not perfectly fulfill both these purposes." Moreover, tinctures are reintroduced to enable logic to assert, among other things, modalities such as necessities and metaphysical possibilities, that call for changes in the nature of the universes of discourse.

There are two further and noteworthy observations that Peirce draws in the final paragraph of R 669. First, his transformation rules are semantically complete: as he notes they "will suffice to enable any valid deduction to be performed." Second, even in the presence of such a relatively simple set of rules of transformation, any attempt at an automated or mechanised theorem-proving that is unaided by a "living intelligence" would fall short of completing the performance of deductive inferential tasks.

On August 10 Welby writes to George F. Stout that Peirce is still planning to submit his paper, which he originally conceived to be "an abstract" of his "entire system of logic", to the *Essays on Significs* which Stout and John W. Slaughter were in the process of editing in Welby's honour. The project was abandoned in 1912 following her death in late March. Peirce had just recently written to Welby that for health reasons he now has to limit his chapter to "*Logical Critics*; that is, to the quality of grade of assurance that the three classes of reasoning afford." Remarks on his diary suggest that the last communication was sent to Welby in February 1, 1912 (R 1626) on Juliette's behalf, probably lamenting their ill state of health. Welby's daughter-in-law, Maria Welby, acknowledges the letter to the Peirces on February 25th and implicates Victoria Welby's desire for *exitus*. Between these days Peirce had managed to scribble a short piece, titled "Notes Preparatory to Criticism of Bernard Russell's *Principles of Mathematics*" of which fragments remain in R 12. Perhaps Peirce wanted to tell about his intentions of writing a criticism of Welby's old acquaintance to cheer her up. Peirce's accident in late 1911 and the mounting abdominal pain would mean that the completion or the submission of any longer pieces were put on hold indefinitely. The material that we find in these two last versions of Peirce's attempt to complete the studies under the title of "Assurance through Reasoning" remains, as he rightly predicted to Welby on May 20, 1911, "my last unless by good luck we should sell this estate [Arisbe]. It would fetch with patience near forty thousand dollars, and it is ridiculous for us to live in such a place." Nor was he able to present any of his later works before the Academy or anywhere else any longer; his April 1907 lectures at Harvard University's Emerson Hall remained Peirce's last public appearance.

As neither the Academy presentation, nor the *Logical Critics* or indeed none of the planned later publications on the assurance of reasoning or planned criticism of Russell's second volume eventually materialised, one is led to wonder what the subsequent course in the 20th century logic and its philosophy might have been had the fortunes been even slightly more favourable towards an early dissemination of Peirce's results.

Selection 27: [Logical Graphs, from the *Prescott Book*] (R 277), 1907–1910

This paginated notebook of 171 pages consists of elaborate notes mostly on mathematics, topical geometry, logic of graphs, theory of signs and pragmatism. Peirce named it the "Prescott Book" as he began writing it while lodging in Prescott Hall next to the Harvard campus from December 1906, until his return to Arisbe, Milford, the following July. During that time he was meant to give private tutoring to one of his admirers. During his boarding at Cambridge he also delivered his last lectures, which were on the topic of "Logical Methodeutic" (the theory of inquiry and scientific thought), given before the Harvard Philosophy Club on April 8 and 12, 1907.[31] It was during this period of Peirce's stay at Harvard that James, fearing that Peirce could not survive on his own, rescued him from starvation and despair by the resolute establishment of the Peirce Funds.

The selection below provides nine excerpts from the *Prescott Book* that concern the logic of graphs and related topics. A few additional entries from it that concern the theory of signs are interpolated to the end of the selections from the *Logic Notebook* in the next chapter.

Selection 28: [Logical Graphs, from the *Logic Notebook*] (R 339), 1898–1909

Peirce's entries on EGs in his *Logic Notebook* (LN) are numerous and mostly from 102r–128r of the LN pagination. Between the Novembers of 1865 and 1909, he kept detailed notes on his ideas and the progress of his studies of logic and semeiotic. This notebook, of which 340 non-blank pages survive, is a treasury of insights on how to advance logical inquiry (see W1, p. 555 for a description of its compositional history). Over the years, the notebook became unbound and its sheets loose and displaced, and many of its pages appear to have been lost. The

---

[31] "Philosophical Club. Logical Methodeutic. I. Retroduction, or the Framing of Hypotheses. Mr. C. S. Peirce. Emerson B, 8pm", *The Harvard Crimson*, April 6, 1907; "Philosophical Club. Logical Methodeutic. II. Induction, or the Experimental Method. Mr. C. S. Peirce. Emerson B, 8pm", *The Harvard Crimson*, April 12, 1907. Max H. Fisch (1982) mentions that Peirce delivered three lectures of which the second was on deduction, but there is no record of announcement of that lecture in *The Harvard Crimson*. Its draft is in R 754, "Second Talk to the Philosophy Club. DEDUCTION." The draft of the lecture on induction designates it as the "third lecture on methodeutic" (R 773), which Peirce struggled to deliver, if at all, having "been really very ill for 24 hours previously and had had no sleep" (*ibid.*).

copy-text of the present selection consists of sixty manuscript pages, and they date from the most intensive periods of Peirce drafting his notes.

A living testimony to how a creative mind forms conceptions of logic that are altogether novel, LN reveals that there were four salient periods which Peirce devoted to the development of EGs. Those are altogether not much more than 12 months in duration: the summers of 1898 and 1903, from late 1905 until early March 1906, and from late 1908 until early 1909. The first period covers the setting up of the constitutive conventions and his revisions to earlier permissive rules of transformation. (Peirce did not carry the notebook with him during his stays in New York City and there are no entries from the first, 1896–1897 phase of the development of the theory.) The second period, which falls between the Harvard and the Lowell Lectures and which is preceded by a five-year hiatus of virtually no record of EGs in LN whatsoever, portrays Peirce's preliminary studies in view of bringing the theory into full fruition. These notes helped him compose a detailed account of his logical architectonic in the style that can be found in the *Logical Tracts* and in the Lowell Lecture drafts (LoF 2). The surprising "Studies of the eight systems of existential graphs", which comes from a separate note (R 1483), derives from the time of the initial planning of his 1903 Lowell Lectures. The third period consists of the study notes as he prepared for the series of papers on pragmaticism to appear in *The Monist*. It is here that Peirce is struck by his realisation of how to express necessity in graphs; his coveted "special sign" is no more and no less than the verso of the sheet of assertion.

As LN is also instructive in showing the reciprocal influence of algebra and graphs; some holograph pages are included to that effect ("A New Logical Algebra", December 11, 1900 [178r, 179r]). They depict Peirce's draft systems of algebra that include the scroll ◯ as the top element (proposition that is "always true" or "is to be (always) accepted"). His drafting of those systems follows a reply to the letter from Christine Ladd-Franklin, who had told Peirce that she was anxious to try the graphical method. "You ask whether Logical Graphs have any bearing on Non-Relative logic", Peirce replies. "Not *much*, *except* in one highly important particular, that they supply an entirely new system of fundamental assumptions to logical algebra" (CSP to Ladd-Franklin, November 9, 1900; LoF 3; see also Ma & Pietarinen 2018c and R 481, LoF 1).

Peirce's last logical notes from September 1908 to February 1909 are written in the somber mood of finally realising that plans for bringing his later logic before the public in any book-length form had to be forfeited. These notes portray an assortment of modifications, proposals and beginnings of new kinds of graphs and types of graph, and their potential applications. Among them one can mention explanations of "Peirce's Puzzle" ([319r, 320r]); plans for a new book *Logic* and its planned preface on assertions, followed by a proposal for a graphical analysis of assertions ([329v–332r]); a non-trivial definition of the property of 'next after' ([335r]); proposals to extend the interpretation of the line to the quantification over situations and time ("is true under some circumstances'; "is true some times", etc., [340r]); and, in particular, three further stand-alone excerpts which are interpolated from non-LN sources but coincide with the LN entries both topically and chronologically. The first is from the *Family Record* (R 1601), the second, "The Calculus of Existential Graphs", is interleaved from R 124 (February 7, 1909), and the third, "The System of Existential Graphs applied to the Examination of Itself" is taken from the Harvard sketchbook that derives from 1903 but was written in mid-February 1909 (R S-3).

The first addition, with the editorial title of "[Collections]", comes from the pages of another notebook named "Family Record" that Peirce began writing as early as in June 1864. It is an unusual late study of the logic of collections, higher-order logic, and some modalities (alethic, epistemic, presumptive, temporal), with the shading of areas instead of encircling them by cuts. The dating of the relevant pages of the notebook is uncertain, but topically it fits well within these closely related topics in LN and in R 124 from early 1909. The *Family Record* may indeed have been Peirce's preferred place to continue recording some entries on logic after they ended in LN in early 1909. The second (R 124) deals with matters that are both preceded by the LN sketches on modal and temporal logic of events as well as followed by [343r] on "Geometrical Topics" and the part-whole considerations, among other things. The third is a belated follow-up on the 'graph of graphs' theory Peirce had fleshed out in the Lowell Lectures drafts which he fell short of actually presenting to the audience. Instead, in that occasion he had announced that he would send material on it to anyone interested (LoF 2). This attempt in R S-3 is too sketchy to make a communicable presentation, but at least two new things stand out: graph types that represent the assertion that "something *justifies* some other thing", and the idea of the "Logic of Time" that "involves more than one state of things." The next day, February 16, 1909, Peirce would embark on the development of three-valued (triadic) logics, first under the heading "Studies of Modal, Temporal, and Other Logical Forms which relate to Special Universes" [341r], followed by an additional couple of pages later in the month. Since those studies on three-valued logics are presented in non-graphical notation, they are not included in the present collection (see Fisch & Turquette 1966 for the original study of Peirce's triadic logic).

The closing sentence of the entire *Logic Notebook* concludes Peirce's final, semiotic entries from the late 1909: "Let it be admitted then that no act of thinking can involve thinking about that very act of thinking." This can be read as a perfect epitome of Peirce's lifetime of accomplishments: in one way or another his graphical method of logic was intended to tackle those "vexed questions of logic", by now fully conceived as semiotic (semeiotic) questions, including the maxim of pragmaticism, logic of abstraction and scientific reasoning, relationship of signs to minds, meta-logical theory of graphs, and the analysis of assertions and propositions, all emerging from the plurality of systems developed within the framework of the method of EGs.

Conclusions

The amount of logical and semiotic ideas Peirce produced not only throughout his life but in particular those that burgeoned from his later years is notable. Regarding logical graphs in particular, several and hitherto unacknowledged innovations are still to be unearthed in his notebooks from 1909, as seen from the selections and interpolations included towards the end of the last chapter (Selection 28, LoF 1). Those proposals and sketches constitute largely the final record of his logical developments, only to be soon followed by his largely final attempt to bring the general theory of signs to some kind of closure. These proposals also bring us back to where the present volume had its beginning, the year 1910 when Peirce would reflect on the import of these achievements, striving to put them into a mature philosophical and systematic perspective.

The three parts and altogether 30 chapters of this Volume 1 of the *Logic of the Future* series provide comprehensive textual evidence on the essential history, discovery, development and maturation of the graphical method of logic. They also encompass practically all the major applications, as well as philosophical, notational and logical reflections, that Peirce took his later theory of logic to imbue.

In the next two volumes of *Logic of the Future*, the story of EGs continues along two trajectories: First, we see how Peirce wanted the world to receive that theory, and what his sustained effort to communicate the fullest possible account of it to his peers and listeners looked like (Volume 2: *The 1903 Lowell Lectures*). Second, we see Peirce applying EGs to his philosophical thought, proposing graphs to deliver their yet another and final service, the proof of his philosophical theory of meaning (Volume 3: *Pragmaticism and Correspondence*). The title letter to William James from Christmas Day 1909 is an exposition of some of his most important achievements in logic, as were several other exchanges dating from the last years of his life. These and many other important letters, letter drafts and communications between his friends, colleagues, collaborators and editors are arranged in the third and final volume of the series.

References

Only those of Peirce's manuscripts are included in the reference list below which do not appear in the *Logic of the Future* editions. Titles are those given in the Robin Catalogue. The copy-text content of Volume 1 is listed in the separate "Catalogue of Peirce's Manuscripts", and Peirce's own references are listed in "Bibliography of Peirce's References" appended at the end of the present volume.

Bellucci, Francesco 2018. *Peirce's Speculative Grammar: Logic as Semiotics*. New York: Routledge.
Bellucci, Francesco 2019. Analysis and Decomposition in Peirce. *Synthese*. In press.
Bellucci, Francesco and Pietarinen, Ahti-Veikko 2015. Charles Sanders Peirce: Logic. *The Internet Encyclopedia of Philosophy*. http://www.iep.utm.edu/
Bellucci, Francesco and Pietarinen, Ahti-Veikko 2016. Existential Graphs as an Instrument for Logical Analysis. Part 1: Alpha. *The Review of Symbolic Logic* 9(2), pp. 209–237.
Bellucci, Francesco and Pietarinen, Ahti-Veikko 2017a. Two Dogmas of Diagrammatic Reasoning: A View from Existential Graphs. In K. Hull & R. K. Atkins (eds.). *Peirce on Perception and Reasoning: From Icons to Logic*. New York: Routledge, pp. 174–195.
Bellucci, Francesco and Pietarinen, Ahti-Veikko 2017b. From Mitchell to Carus: 14 Years of Logical Graphs in the Making. *Transactions of the Charles S. Peirce Society* 52(4), pp. 539–575.
Bellucci, Francesco and Pietarinen, Ahti-Veikko 2017c. Assertion and Denial: A Contribution from Logical Notation. *Journal of Applied Logics* 24, pp. 1–22.
Bellucci, Francesco and Pietarinen, Ahti-Veikko 2019. Icons, Interrogations, and Graphs: On Peirce's Integrated Notion of Abduction. *Transactions of the Charles S. Peirce Society*. In press.
Bellucci, Francesco, Chiffi, Daniele and Pietarinen, Ahti-Veikko 2017. Assertive Graphs. *Journal of Applied Non-Classical Logics* 28(1), pp. 72–91.
Bellucci, Francesco, Moktefi, Amirouche and Pietarinen, Ahti-Veikko 2017. *Simplex sigillum veri*: Peano, Frege, and Peirce on the Primitives of Logic. *History and Philosophy of Logic* 39(1), pp. 80–95.
Bellucci, Francesco, Pietarinen, Ahti-Veikko and Stjernfelt, Frederik (eds.) 2014. *Peirce: 5 Questions*. Copenhagen: VIP/Automatic Press.
Brady, Geraldine and Trimble, Todd H. 2000. A Categorical Interpretation of C. S. Peirce's Propositional Logic Alpha. *Journal of Pure and Applied Algebra* 149, pp. 213–239.

Brünnler, Kai 2003. *Deep Inference and Symmetry in Classical Proof*. PhD thesis. Technische Universität Dresden.
Carroll, Lewis 1895. What the Tortoise said to Achilles. *Mind* 4, pp. 278–280.
Champagne, Marc 2015. Sound Reasoning (Literally): Prospects and Challenges of Current Acoustic Logics. *Logica Universalis* (9)3, pp. 331–343.
Champagne, Marc and Pietarinen, Ahti-Veikko 2019. Why Images Cannot be Arguments, But Moving Ones Might. *Argumentation*. In press.
Chiffi, Daniele and Pietarinen, Ahti-Veikko 2018. Assertive and Existential Graphs: A Comparison. In: Chapman P., Stapleton G., Moktefi A., Perez-Kriz S., Bellucci F. (eds.). *Diagrammatic Representation and Inference. Diagrams 2018. Lecture Notes in Computer Science* 10871. Springer.
Chiffi, Daniele and Pietarinen, Ahti-Veikko 2019. On the Logical Philosophy of Assertive Graphs. *Journal of Logic, Language and Information*. In press.
Clark, Glenn 1997. New Light on Peirce's Iconic Notation for the Sixteen Binary Connectives. In Houser, N., Roberts, D., Van Evra, J. (eds.). *Studies in the Logic of Charles S. Peirce*. Bloomington and Indianapolis, IN: Indiana University Press, pp. 304–333.
Dekker, Paul 2001. Dynamics and Pragmatics of 'Peirce's Puzzle'. *Journal of Semantics* 18, pp. 211–241.
Dipert, Randall 1995. Peirce's Underestimated Place in the History of Logic: A Response to Quine. In Ketner, K. L. (ed.), *Peirce and Contemporary Thought*. New York: Fordham University Press, pp. 32–58.
Dipert, Randall 2006. Peirce's Deductive Logic: Its Development, Influence, and Philosophical Significance. In Misak, C. (ed.). *The Cambridge Companion to Peirce*. Cambridge, Mass.: Cambridge University Press, pp. 257–286.
Fisch, Max H. 1982. Peirce's Place in American Life. *Historica Mathematica* 9, pp. 265–287.
Fisch, Max H. 1986. *Peirce, Semeiotic, and Pragmatism: Essays by Max H. Fisch*. K. L. Ketner and C. J. W. Kloesel (eds.). Bloomington and Indianapolis, IN: Indiana University Press.
Fisch, Max H. and Turquette, Atwell 1966. Peirce's Triadic Logic. *Transactions of the Charles S. Peirce Society* 2(2), pp. 71–85. Reprinted in Fisch, M., *Peirce, Semeiotic, and Pragmatism: Essays by Max H. Fisch*. K. L. Ketner and C. J. W. Kloesel (eds.). Bloomington and Indianapolis, IN: Indiana University Press, pp. 171–183.
Frege, Gottlob 1879. *Begriffsschrift: eine der arithmetischen nachgebildete Formelsprache des reinen Denkens*. Halle: Louis Nebert.
Gentzen, Gerhard Karl Erich 1934. Untersuchungen über das logische Schließen. I. *Mathematische Zeitschrift* 39(2), pp. 76–210.

Grattan-Guinness, Ivor 2002. Re-Interpreting 'Λ': Kempe on Multisets and Peirce on Graphs, 1886–1905. *Transactions of the Charles S. Peirce Society* 38(3), pp. 327–350.

Grattan-Guinness, Ivor 2007. From A. B. Kempe to Josiah Royce via C. S. Peirce: Addenda to a recent paper by Pratt. *History and Philosophy of Logic* 28(3), pp. 265–266.

Hilpinen, Risto 1982. On C. S. Peirce's Theory of the Proposition: Peirce as a Precursor of Game-Theoretical Semantics. *The Monist* 65(2), pp. 182–188.

Hilpinen, Risto 2004. Peirce's Logic. In Gabbay, D. M. and J. Woods (eds.). *Handbook of the History of Logic. Vol. 3: The Rise of Modern Logic From Leibniz to Frege*. Amsterdam: Elsevier, pp. 611–658.

Hintikka, Jaakko 1996. The Place of C. S. Peirce in the History of Logical Theory. In Brunning, J. and Forster, P. (eds.). *The Rule of Reason: The Philosophy of Charles Sanders Peirce*. Toronto: University of Toronto Press, pp. 13–33.

Hintikka, Jaakko 2011. What the Bald Man Can Tell Us. In Biletzky, A. (ed.). *Hues of Philosophy: Essays in Memory of Ruth Manor*. London: College Publications.

Hookway, Christopher 2012. *The Pragmatic Maxim: Essays on Peirce and Pragmatism*. Oxford: Oxford University Press.

Houser, Nathan 1985. *Peirce's Algebra of Logic and the Law of Distribution*. Dissertation. University of Waterloo, Ontario.

Houser, Nathan 1991. Peirce and the Law of Distribution. In: Drucker, T. (ed.). *Perspectives on the History of Mathematical Logic*. Boston: Birkhäuser, pp. 10–32.

Houser, Nathan, Roberts, Don D., Van Evra, J. (eds.) 1997. *Studies in the Logic of Charles S. Peirce*. Bloomington and Indianapolis, IN: Indiana University Press.

Huntington, Edward V. 1904. Sets of Independent Postulates for the Algebra of Logic. *Transactions of the American Mathematical Society* 5, pp. 288–309.

Kempe, Alfred Bray 1886. A Memoir on the Theory of Mathematical Form. *Philosophical Transactions of the Royal Society of London* 177, pp. 1–70.

Ketner, Kenneth 1987. Identifying Peirce's "Most Lucid and Interesting Paper". *Transactions of the Charles S. Peirce Society* 23(4), pp. 539–555.

Liu, Xinwen 2005. An Axiomatic System for Peirce's Alpha Graphs. In F. Dau, M.-L. Mugnier, & G. Stumme (eds.). *Common Semantics for Sharing Knowledge: Contributions to ICCS 2005*, Kassel: Kassel University Press, pp. 122–131.

Lupher, Tracy and Adajian, Thomas (eds.) 2015. *Philosophy of Logic: 5 Questions*. Copenhagen: VIP/Automatic Press.

Ma, Minghui 2018. Peirce's Logical Graphs for Boolean Algebras and Distributive Lattices. *Transactions of the Charles S. Peirce Society* 54(3), pp. 320–340.

Ma, Minghui and Pietarinen, Ahti-Veikko 2016. Proof Analysis of Peirce's Alpha System of Graphs. *Studia Logica* 105(3), pp. 625–647.
Ma, Minghui and Pietarinen, Ahti-Veikko 2017a. Graphical Sequent Calculi for Modal Logics. *Electronic Proceedings in Theoretical Computer Science* 243, pp. 91–103.
Ma, Minghui and Pietarinen, Ahti-Veikko 2017b. Gamma Graph Calculi for Modal Logics. *Synthese* 195(8), pp. 3621–3650.
Ma, Minghui and Pietarinen, Ahti-Veikko 2017c. Peirce's Sequent Proofs of Distributivity. *Logic and Its Applications: 7th Indian Conference, Lecture Notes in Computer Science* 10119, Springer, pp. 168–182.
Ma, Minghui and Pietarinen, Ahti-Veikko 2018a. Peirce's Calculi for Classical Propositional Logic. *Review of Symbolic Logic*. In press.
Ma, Minghui and Pietarinen, Ahti-Veikko 2018b. A Graphical Deep Inference System for Intuitionistic Logic. *Logique & Analyse* 245, pp. 73–114.
Ma, Minghui and Pietarinen, Ahti-Veikko 2018c. A Weakening of Alpha Graphs: Quasi-Boolean Algebras. In Chapman P., Stapleton G., Moktefi A., Perez-Kriz S., Bellucci, F. (eds.). *Diagrammatic Representation and Inference. Diagrams 2018. Lecture Notes in Computer Science* 10871. Springer, Cham.
Ma, Minghui and Pietarinen, Ahti-Veikko 2019. Peirce's Logic of Dragon Head (R 501). Preprint.
Majer, Ondrej, Pietarinen, Ahti-Veikko and Tulenheimo, Tero 2009. Introduction to Logic and Games. In O. Majer, A.-V. Pietarinen and T. Tulenheimo (eds.). *Games: Unifying Logic, Language, and Philosophy*. Dordrecht: Springer, pp. ix–xxiii.
Mitchell, Oscar Howard 1883. On a New Algebra of Logic. In: C. S. Peirce (ed.). *Studies in Logic, by Members of the Johns Hopkins University*. Boston: Little, Brown & Company, pp. 72–106.
Moore, Matthew (ed.), 2010. *New Essays on Peirce's Mathematical Philosophy*. Chicago: Open Court.
Peirce, Charles S. 1867a. On an Improvement in Boole's Calculus of Logic. *Proceedings of the American Academy of Arts and Sciences* 7, pp. 250–261. (Presented March 12, 1867. Reprinted in W2, pp. 12–23; CP 3.1–19.)
Peirce, Charles S. 1867b. On the Natural Classification of Arguments. *Proceedings of the American Academy of Arts and Science* 7, pp. 261–287. (Presented April 9, 1867. Reprinted in W2, pp. 23–49; CP 2.461–516.)
Peirce, Charles S. 1867c. Upon the Logic of Mathematics. *Proceedings of the American Academy of Arts and Science* 7, pp. 402–412. (Presented September 10, 1867. Reprinted in W2, pp. 59–69; CP 3.20–44.)
Peirce, Charles S. 1870/1873. Description of a Notation for the Logic of Relatives, Resulting from an Amplification of the Conceptions of Boole's Cal-

culus of Logic. *Memoirs of the American Academy of Arts and Sciences* 9, pp. 317–378. (Communicated on January 26, 1870; a separate publication by Welch, Bigelow, and Company for Harvard University, 1870. Reprinted in W2, pp. 359–429; CP 3.45–149.)

Peirce, Charles S. 1880. On the Algebra of Logic. *American Journal of Mathematics* 3(1), pp. 15–57, 1880. (Reprinted in W4, pp. 163–209; CP 3.154–251.)

Peirce, Charles S. 1881. On the Logic of Number. *American Journal of Mathematics* 4, pp. 85–95. (Reprinted in W4, pp. 299–309.)

Peirce, Charles S. c.1882. [Fragments on Logic] (R 747). Houghton Library.

Peirce, Charles S. 1882. Letter (draft) to Oscar Howard Mitchell, December 21, 1882 (R L 294). Houghton Library.

Peirce, Charles S. 1883a. A Communication from Mr. Peirce (P 245). *Johns Hopkins University Circulars* 2(22) (April 1883), pp. 86–88. (Reprinted in W4, p. 470.)

Peirce, Charles S. 1883b. Note B: The Logic of Relatives. In Peirce, C. S. (ed.). *Studies in Logic*, pp. 187–203. (Reprinted in W4, pp. 453–466; CP 3.328–358.)

Peirce, Charles S. (ed.) 1883c. *Studies in Logic by Members of the Johns Hopkins University*. Boston: Little, Brown, and Company. (SiL)

Peirce, Charles S. 1885. On the Algebra of Logic: A Contribution to the Philosophy of Notation. *American Journal of Mathematics* 7(2), pp. 180–196. (Reprinted in W5, pp. 162–190; CP 3.359–403.)

Peirce, Charles S. c.1886. Qualitative Logic (R 736). Houghton Library.

Peirce, Charles S. 1889a. Notes on Kempe's Paper on Mathematical Forms (R 714). Houghton Library.

Peirce, Charles S. 1889b. Kempe Translated into English (R 715). Houghton Library.

Peirce, Charles S. 1891a. Algebra of the Copula [Version 1]. In *Writings of Charles S. Peirce* Vol. 8 (1890–1892), pp. 210–211. Bloomington and Indianapolis, IN: Indiana University Press, 2010.

Peirce, Charles S. 1891b. Algebra of the Copula [Version 2]. In *Writings of Charles S. Peirce* Vol. 8 (1890–1892), pp. 212–216. Bloomington and Indianapolis, IN: Indiana University Press, 2010.

Peirce, Charles S. 1893a. *How to Reason: A Critick of Arguments*. Division I. Stecheology. Part I. Non Relative. Chapter VIII. The Algebra of the Copula. (R 411). Houghton Library.

Peirce, Charles S. 1893b. *How to Reason: A Critick of Arguments*. Chapter XI. The Boolian Calculus. (R 417). Houghton Library.

Peirce, Charles S. 1893c. *How to Reason: A Critick of Arguments*. Book II. Division I. Part 2. Logic of Relatives. Chapter XII. The Algebra of Relatives. (R 418). Houghton Library.

Peirce, Charles S. c.1894a. [On the Algebra of Relatives] (R 553). Houghton Library.

Peirce, Charles S. c.1894b. [The Three Categories and the Reduction of Fourthness] (R 915). Houghton Library.
Peirce, Charles S. c.1894c. [Logic: Fragments] (R S-64). Houghton Library.
Peirce, Charles S. 1894. Letter to Francis C. Russell, September 6, 1894 (R L 387). Houghton Library.
Peirce, Charles S. 1896. The Regenerated Logic. *The Monist* 7(1) (October), pp. 19–40. (Reprinted in CP 3.425–455; LoI, pp. 170–185.)
Peirce, Charles S. c.1897. Memoir § 4. Algebra of Copula (R 737). Houghton Library.
Peirce, Charles S. 1897. The Logic of Relatives. *The Monist* 7(2) (January), pp. 161–217. (Reprinted in CP 3.456–552; LoI, pp. 186–229.)
Peirce, Charles S. 1898. Reply to Mr. Kempe (K) (R 708). Houghton Library.
Peirce, Charles S. 1901a. New Elements (Kaina stoicheia) (R 517). Houghton Library. (Reprinted in NEM IV, pp. 235–263; EP 2, pp. 300–324.)
Peirce, Charles S. 1901b. [The Logic of Dragon Head] (R 501, R 9, R 11). Houghton Library.
Peirce, Charles S. c.1902. A Treatise on the Calculus of Differences (R 91). Houghton Library.
Peirce, Charles S. 1902. Logic, Regarded As Semeiotic (The Carnegie Application of 1902), Version 1: An Integrated Reconstruction. Joseph Ransdell (ed.), *Arisbe*, preprint. (R L 75), Houghton Library.
Peirce, Charles S. 1903. *A Syllabus of Certain Topics of Logic*. Boston: Alfred Mudge & Son.
Peirce, Charles S. 1905a. What Pragmatism Is. *The Monist* 15(2) (April), pp. 161–181. (Reprinted in CP 5.411–437; LoI, pp. 230–244.)
Peirce, Charles S. 1905b. Issues of Pragmaticism. *The Monist* 15(4) (October), pp. 481–499. (Reprinted CP 5.438–463; LoI, pp. 245–258.)
Peirce, Charles S. 1905c. Rough Sketch of Suggested Prolegomena to your [James Mills Peirce's] First Course in Quaternions (R 87). Houghton Library.
Peirce, Charles S. 1906. Prolegomena to an Apology for Pragmaticism. *The Monist* 16(4) (October), pp. 492–546. Errata: *The Monist* 17(1) (January), 1907, p. 160. (Reprinted in CP 4.530–572; LoI, pp. 307–342.)
Peirce, Charles S. 1907. Second Talk to the Philosophical Club and Second Talk. On Deduction. April 12, 1907 (R 754). Houghton Library.
Peirce, Charles S. 1908a. Some Amazing Mazes. *The Monist* 28(2), pp. 227–241. (Reprinted in CP 4.585–593; LoI, pp. 394–403.)
Peirce, Charles S. 1908b. Some Amazing Mazes (Conclusion). Explanation of Curiosity the First. *The Monist* 28(3), pp. 416–464. (Reprinted in CP 4.594–642; LoI, pp. 404–445.)
Peirce, Charles S. 1908c. A Neglected Argument for the Reality of God. *Hibbert Journal* 7, pp. 90–112. (Reprinted in CP 6.452–485; EP 2, pp. 434–450.)

Peirce, Charles S. 1909a. Some Amazing Mazes, A Second Curiosity. *The Monist* 29(1), pp. 36–45. (Reprinted CP 4.643–646; LoI, pp. 446–451.)
Peirce, Charles S. 1909b. Studies in Meaning. March 25–28, 1909 (R 619). Houghton Library.
Peirce, Charles S. 1911. A Letter (draft) to James H. Kehler, June 22, 1911 (R L 231). Houghton Library.
Peirce, Charles S. n.d. Note on Kempe's Paper in Vol. XXI of the *Proceedings of the London Mathematical Society* (R 709); Notes on Kempe's Paper (R 710); Notes on Kempe's Paper (R 711); (Kempe) (R 712); (Kempe (R 713). Houghton Library.
Peirce, Charles S. n.d. [Peirce's Reprints and Books from his Library; Editor's Materials and Preliminary Catalogues of the Collection]. (R 1600), 14 Boxes. Houghton Library.
Pietarinen, Ahti-Veikko 2001. Most Even Budged Yet: Some Cases for Game-Theoretic Semantics in Natural Language. *Theoretical Linguistics* 27(1), 20–54.
Pietarinen, Ahti-Veikko 2003a. Peirce's Game-Theoretic Ideas in Logic. *Semiotica* 144(14), pp. 33–47.
Pietarinen, Ahti-Veikko 2003b. Games as Formal Tools versus Games as Explanations in Logic and Science. *Foundations of Science* 8(1), pp. 317–364.
Pietarinen, Ahti-Veikko 2004. Peirce's Diagrammatic Logic in IF Perspective. *Lecture Notes in Artificial Intelligence* 2980, Berlin: Springer-Verlag, pp. 97–111.
Pietarinen, Ahti-Veikko 2005a. Compositionality, Relevance and Peirce's Logic of Existential Graphs. *Axiomathes* 15(1), pp. 513–540.
Pietarinen, Ahti-Veikko 2005b. Cultivating Habits of Reason: Peirce and the *Logica Utens* versus *Logica Docens* Distinction. *History of Philosophy Quarterly* 22, pp. 357–372.
Pietarinen, Ahti-Veikko 2006. *Signs of Logic: Peircean Themes on the Philosophy of Language, Games, and Communication* (Synthese Library 329). Dordrecht: Springer.
Pietarinen, Ahti-Veikko 2007. *Game Theory and Linguistic Meaning*. (Current Research in the Semantics/Pragmatics Interface 18). Oxford: Elsevier Science.
Pietarinen, Ahti-Veikko 2008. Diagrammatic Logic of Existential Graphs: A Case Study of Commands. In G. Stapleton, J. Howse, & J. Lee (eds.). *Diagrammatic Representation and Inference, Lecture Notes in Computer Science* 5223, Heidelberg: Springer, pp. 404–407.
Pietarinen, Ahti-Veikko 2009. Pragmaticism as an Anti-Foundationalist Philosophy of Mathematics. In B. Van Kerkhove, R. Desmet & J. P. Van Bendegem (eds.). *Philosophical Perspectives on Mathematical Practices*. London: College Publications, pp. 305–333.

Pietarinen, Ahti-Veikko 2010a. Is Non-Visual Diagrammatic Logic Possible? In A. Gerner (ed.). *Diagrammatology and Diagram Praxis*. London: College Publications, pp. 73–85.
Pietarinen, Ahti-Veikko 2010b. Peirce's Pragmatic Theory of Proper Names. *Transactions of the Charles S. Peirce Society* 46(3), pp. 341–363.
Pietarinen, Ahti-Veikko 2010c. Which Philosophy of Mathematics is Pragmaticism? In M. Moore (ed.). *New Essays on Peirce's Mathematical Philosophy*. Chicago, IL: Open Court, pp. 59–79.
Pietarinen, Ahti-Veikko 2011. Existential Graphs: What the Diagrammatic Logic of Cognition Might Look Like. *History and Philosophy of Logic* 32(3), pp. 265–281.
Pietarinen, Ahti-Veikko 2012. Peirce and the Logic of Image. *Semiotica* 2012(192), pp. 251–261.
Pietarinen, Ahti-Veikko 2013. Logical and Linguistic Games from Peirce to Grice to Hintikka. *Teorema* 33(2), pp. 121–136.
Pietarinen, Ahti-Veikko 2014. A Scholastic-Realist Modal-Structuralism. *Philosophia Scientiae* 18(3), pp. 127–138.
Pietarinen, Ahti-Veikko 2015a. Two Papers on Existential Graphs by Charles S. Peirce: 1. Recent Developments of Existential Graphs and their Consequences for Logic (R 498, R 499, R 490, S-36; 1906), 2. Assurance through Reasoning (R 669, R 670; 1911). *Synthese* 192, pp. 881–922.
Pietarinen, Ahti-Veikko 2015b. Exploring the Beta Quadrant. *Synthese* 192, pp. 941–970.
Pietarinen, Ahti-Veikko 2015c. Signs Systematically Studied: Invitation to Peirce's Theory. *Sign Systems Studies* 43(4), pp. 372–398; Recent Studies on Signs: Commentary and Perspectives, pp. 616–650; [Division of Signs, by Charles Peirce], pp. 651–662.
Pietarinen, Ahti-Veikko 2018. To Peirce Hintikka's Thoughts. *Logica Universalis* 13(2), pp. 241–262.
Pietarinen, Ahti-Veikko 2019. Abduction and Diagrams. *Logic Journal of the IGPL*. In press.
Pietarinen, Ahti-Veikko and Chevalier, Jean-Marie 2015. The Second Metaphysical Club and Its Impact to the Development of the Sciences in the US. *Commens Working Papers no. 2*. Commens: Digital Companion to C. S. Peirce.
Pietarinen, Ahti-Veikko, Shafiei, Mohammad and Stjernfelt, Frederik 2019. Mutual Insights on Peirce and Husserl. In Pietarinen, A.-V. and M. Shafiei (eds.). *Peirce and Husserl: Mutual Insights on Logic, Mathematics and Cognition*. Dordrecht: Springer. In press.
Putnam, Hilary 1982. Peirce the Logician. *Historia Mathematica* 9, pp. 290–301.

Roberts, Don D. 1973. *The Existential Graphs of Charles S. Peirce*. The Hague: Mouton.

Russell, Bertrand 1901. Sur la logique des relations avec des applications á la théorie des séries. *Revue de mathématiques/Rivista di Matematiche* 7, pp. 115–148.

Russell, Francis C. 1908. Hints for the Elucidation of Mr. Peirce's Logical Work. *The Monist* 28(3) (July 1908), pp. 406–415.

Schröder, Ernst 1890. *Vorlesungen über die Algebra der Logik*. Volume 1, Leipzig: Teubner.

Schütte, Kurt 1977. *Proof Theory*. Berlin: Springer-Verlag.

Shields, Paul 1981/2012. *Charles S. Peirce on the Logic of Number*. 2nd ed. Boston: Docent Press.

Shin, Sun-Joo 2002. *The Iconic Logic of Peirce's Graphs*. Cambridge, Mass.: MIT Press.

Sowa, John 1984. *Conceptual Structures: Information Processing in Mind and Machine*. Addison-Wesley.

Sowa, John 2006. Peirce's Contributions to the 21st Century. *Proceedings of the 14th International Conference on Conceptual Structures*. Lecture Notes in Computer Science 4068, pp. 54–69.

Stjernfelt, Frederik 2007. *Diagrammatology: An Investigation on the Borderlines of Phenomenology, Ontology, and Semiotics*. Dordrecht: Springer.

Sylvester, James Joseph 1878. On an Application of the New Atomic Theory to the Graphical Representation of the Invariants and Covariants of Binary Quantics. *American Journal of Mathematics* 1, pp. 64–104.

Zalamea, Fernando 2012a. *Synthetic Philosophy of Contemporary Mathematics*. Urbanomic.

Zalamea, Fernando 2012b. *Peirce's Logic of Continuity: A Mathematical and Conceptual Approach*. New York: Docent Press.

Zellweger, Shea 1997. Untapped Potential in Peirce's Iconic Notation for the Sixteen Binary Connectives. In Houser, N. et al. (eds.). *Studies in the Logic of Charles S. Peirce*. Bloomington and Indianapolis, IN: Indiana University Press, pp. 334–386.

Zeman, Jay 1964. *The Graphical Logic of Charles S. Peirce*. Ph.D. dissertation, University of Chicago.

Charles S. Peirce:
Writings on Existential Graphs

Part I: **Reasoning and Diagrams**

1 Essays on Reasoning

R 654, R 680, R 683, R 678, 1910. Houghton Library. This chapter is articulated into two sections. The first section groups together the first three manuscripts, while the second is constituted by the last one and an alternative version of a part of it.

R 654, August 17–19, 1910. Houghton Library. This manuscript is the preface written for the planned book *Essays on Reasoning*. Peirce defines reasoning as thinking in signs. Signs are anything that is capable of a sensible form, applicable to something other than itself, and interpretable. The sensible form which is made available for the study of reasoning is the system of Existential Graphs.

R 680, undated, c.1910. Houghton Library. This late manuscript may have been conceived as the introduction for *Essays on Reasoning*, titled "Analysis of the Trustworthiness of the Different Kinds of Reasoning". Its interest lies in its detailed analysis of awareness, which constitutes an example of a non-psychologistic use of psychological investigations. First, a "state of awareness" is defined as including actual consciousness as well as all that could become conscious if attention were to be directed towards it. Thus awareness is not limited by actuality as it includes potentiality. Peirce's analysis then distinguishes three elements which compose awareness: *sensation* (with its limit case, feeling), *perception of difference* (of contrast or of change), and *intentional attention*. All forms of awareness have elements of activity, although it is probably the third which most clearly exhibits them. Moreover, beyond pure sensation, all awareness involves the *perception of a relation*. A discontinuity appears in the manuscript; in the latter part Peirce introduces another triad, distinguishing between an *actual* fact, one that *may be*, and one that *would be* "under conditions." Logical principles are not to be mistaken with "laws of thought": actual facts and extant things are subject to the principle of contradiction and the principle of excluded middle not in virtue of their actual presence in the mind but in virtue of their being *determinate*. The "real" is defined as to include *can-be*s and *would-be*s. Two varieties of *would be*s are then distinguished: dispositions and habits.

R 683, 1913. Houghton Library. This manuscript contains a two-page alternative draft of the 1913 manuscript "Essay Towards Improving Our Reasoning in Security and in Uberty". We find a definition of "graphical" as "capable of being written or drawn, so as to be spatially arranged." Peirce's ultimate view is that the spatial dimension of graphs is their great advantage over traditional ways of representing and analysing thoughts.

R 678, late 1910. Houghton Library. Peirce gave this manuscript the title "The Art of Reasoning Elucidated". The topics that he wanted to cover in this extensive projected work are (1) irreducibility of different types of reasoning; (2) artificiality of the methods, namely that each type of reasoning can be carried out in different ways, but the more "instinctive" or "natural" way is not necessarily the best one; (3) structure of reasoning, that every reasoning has premises and conclusions; (4) soundness; (5) faults of reasoning; (6) good practice in reasoning; and finally (7) application of the art of reasoning to some "pressing questions of our time." A draft of "Introduction" is included, in which Peirce analyses the first pre-requisite for being able to reason well: the love of truth. Appendix presents an alternative version of this "Introduction", in which Peirce argues that the answer to the question of "how we think" cannot be found in a psychological or physiological description of the mind, but rather has to be sought for in the syntactical, grammatical and structural analysis of thought.

1.1 Essays on Reasoning

Preface

[R 654, 1910] The most celebrated of all modern treatises on logic, *L'Art de Penser*, of Arnauld and Nicole, commonly called the Port Royal Logic, which, as may well be inferred from its celebrity is more distinguished by good sense and by literary excellence than by really penetrating far into its subject or by laying bare the true nature of reasoning, begins with two charming paragraphs which tell how it was undertaken with the conviction that all that is of any genuine value in the doctrine of reasoning can easily be developed in a few hours. The present writer quite agrees that when a person has once found out what reasoning really consists in,[1] —a task for which he should allot a time varying from five seconds to fifty years, proportionally to two factors. By far the more variable of these will be the degree of distinctness of conception that will satisfy him. But the natural aptitude of the person for this kind of study should also be taken into account, since with this aptitude the number of difficulties he perceives will be increased, and the time needed will be increased. Once this part of the work is done, the recording of the result will be mere child's play comparatively. Its place in the scale of difficulty of different kinds of writing will not be far from that of the composition of technically faultless sonnets. When one has gone so far as to frame a definition of what the word reasoning ought to mean in its broadest sense, without allowing one's conception to be in any degree trammelled by the usages of speech, the next step should be to distinguish the different types of reasoning.

Every reasoning consists in interpreting a sign. For whenever we think, we think in signs. Every action of thought is either the formation, or the application, or the interpretation of a sign, or else it is some other kind of action upon a sign or

---

1 [Alt.:] [...] consists in,—to do which will require from five seconds to fifty years or more, according to one aptitude for the subject and according to the degree of distinctness of conception aimed at,—it will be comparative child's play to set down the result, although he does not hesitate to say that it is the slowest kind of prose-writing there is, every paragraph, in many places every sentence, being an undertaking comparable to the composition of a sonnet. That comparatively very few words are required, however, to enunciate a truth of logic is certainly quite true, although those words must be understood in such precise senses, that the distinct apprehension of them always requires deliberate and close attention.

For instance, if I were required to condense the science of logic into a single paragraph, I should, with my present lights, write something like the following:

- Logic is the business of that social group who devote themselves to ascertaining the principles upon which the attainment of one's purposes in thinking depends.

signs, this other kind of action being rather psychological, or say, physiological, than rational. Those psycholo[gicians] who tell us that thought needs language and could not have taken place before men possessed language are so far right that speech is man's instinctive vehicle of thought, even from himself to the self of a subsequent moment, and that we know as yet little or nothing of how this faculty originated. But every mathematician and every logician will tell the linguists that they are in possession of quite other systems of signs into which they are accustomed to translate words and forms of words and so to render them more intelligible.

One such system, equivalent to a syntax, and of great utility for logic is briefly described in this volume. It is called the system of Existential Graphs. It is the simplest possible system that is capable of expressing with exactitude every possible assertion. In this system, there are none of the ordinary parts of speech; for the indivisible elements are, one and all, complete assertions. It may be that this is the case in some existing language: grammarians have, until very recently, had such an inveterate habit in their accounts of all languages of stretching them all alike upon the Procrustes Bed of Greek–Latin grammar that we cannot tell. But in one respect at any rate Existential Graphs is essentially different from language. Namely, instead of being merely protracted in time, its expressions are diagrams upon a surface, and indeed must be regarded as only a ~~picture~~ projection upon that surface of a sign extended in three dimensions. Three dimensions are necessary and sufficient for the expression of all assertions; so that, if man's reason was originally limited to the line of speech (which I do not affirm), it has now outgrown the limitation.

By a Sign I mean anything whatever, real or fictile, which is capable of a sensible form, is applicable to something other than itself that is already known, and that is capable of being so interpreted in another sign which I call its Interpretant as to communicate something that may not have been previously known about its Object. There is thus a triadic relation between any Sign, an Object, and an Interpretant.

Analysis of the Trustworthiness of the Different Kinds of Reasonings. I.

[R 680, c.1910] This first chapter of the present essay must absolutely be devoted to explaining my purpose in writing the whole, to showing that it is an intelligent purpose, and to declaring for what class of readers it is intended.

It is meant most especially for the small class of thoughtful boys, of ages, say, from 12 to 18; because it is they to whom it can be most serviceable in settling and in furthering their purposes: there are a few of them to whom the author is confident of being able to become a valuable assistant; and he will have them uppermost in his mind as he writes. At the same time, there are no persons, — not even the most eminent philosophers, — who have thought so deeply or read so much about reasoning that they can cast [the] book aside and be really sure that there can be nothing here that can be of any value to them. It will be quite valueless only to those who are past the age of reasoning or otherwise do not care for it.

The writer is an aged man so near the tomb that it is quite out of the question that he should gain any substantial good from anything that he might write, no matter how forcibly; and he never was a skilled writer. But all his life long he has [been] pondering one question that concerns every rational being of each kind; and whatever else has at any time temporarily engaged his ~~energy~~ attention has been for him merely a help, — whether as a stepping stone or as a strengthening exercise[2] — toward reaching a satisfactory solution of the problem. Now the result of the study has been to assure the writer of certain truths of practical importance for every one whenever he has occasion to reason; and for that reason it seems worth while to publish the proofs of them although they cannot be presented under any attractions of literary style. It is to the very young that they will be particularly addressed, since among these are those whose habits of reasoning are not yet fixed, and who are destined to become the reasoners of a more advanced generation.

The usual belief that every human being that has drawn its first breath, if not every animal, is composed of two parts, a body and a mind, or soul, seems to be, in some sense, indisputably true. Yet the boundary between "body" and "mind" may be drawn in different ways, since different pairs of meanings may be attached to these two words, though to each pair meanings may be so matched that in each case the "body" and the "mind" together shall make up the entire person. For present purposes the distinction shall be defined as follows: all that essentially depends upon the animal's being "aware", or "conscious", of anything, so that otherwise it absolutely could not be, under any conditions, real or imaginary, shall be called *psychical*, or *mental*; and all that might conceivably be or happen even though the animals were as utterly unconscious as any automaton, machine, or other thing seems to be, shall be called "bodily", and either "physiological" or "physical", according as it is supposed to be due to its anatomical organization or to the combined effects of its chemical structure and composition together with those general laws of nature to which all unorganized matter and electricity conform; while, since there are many human and animal phenomena that do not come under either of these two heads, but concern relations between the con-

---

[2] Summaries of half a dozen such exercises shall be appended to this essay, for the benefit of any reader who may deem such information pertinent. [No exercises were appended.]

scious and the unconscious, this third class of appearances or things, shall be called (as the celebrated Gustave Theodor Fechner) called them, *psychophysical*.

The subject into which this essay is to inquire has nothing to do, directly and essentially, with matters physiological or physical. It barely touches even the psychophysical. The things about which it is concerned are almost exclusively psychical. It is not, however, with the whole of any of these phenomena that it concerns itself. In order, therefore, to explain what it is occupied with, it becomes necessary to begin by stating that in a psychical phenomenon we discern three kinds of elements of awareness as intimately mingled as in *sal ammoniac* are the chlorine, the nitrogen, and the hydrogen;—three different gases making up a familiar solid which can hardly be volatilized without more or less decomposition. The reader must be informed that not all psychologists, or students of psychical phenomena, hold it to be nearly certain that all that is psychical may properly be regarded as composed of no other than the three elements mentioned, though a large proportion of them do so. Perhaps it is only a way of considering the phenomena. It does not seem to matter much, as far as the substantial truth of this essay is concerned, how these three elements come to be discerned in awareness. They are important in any case.

Before going on to describe the three elements which seem to the writer to be all there is in psychical phenomena, it is requisite that he should say what he will mean when he speaks of a *state of awareness*, and that the reader should hold the definition in mind. He will mean indifferently by this either all that a person is aware of during some short time, or any part of that whole which seems as if it might at some other time constitute the whole of his awareness under some conceivable circumstances at some other time. Suppose, for example, that the reader while in the deepest sleep, were in the night, without warning, to be carried into a strange chamber strikingly unlike any that he ever was in—a new beautiful room,—and there were to be left in a luxurious bed; and suppose that in the bright morning he were suddenly to wake up with open eyes. What he would be aware of at the very first, before he had had time at all to collect himself would constitute in itself a state of awareness. In addition to the optical impression, the warmth and other skin-sensations, would modify his awareness, though he would not be attending to them at the time; and since it is conceivable that on another similar occasion the skin-nerves should be entirely paralyzed, not only would there be the actual state of awareness, but this *minus* the skin-sensations would be a *state of awareness*, which though not his actual state would be a part of it. So there might be present, though not attended to, a faint agreeable odour, which would modify the total actual awareness.

Let us now go on to explain the three kinds of ingredients which the author finds in states of awareness. These ingredients have no separate existence; yet it is very important to distinguish between them. The first is the dominant quality of a single state of awareness (as above defined) apart from any other and therefore without change. This will, throughout the essay, be called ~~Feeling~~ *Sensation*; and this word will be used in no other sense. Strictly speaking, then, a sensation must be single and not compound. Yellow, for example is a sensation, or a generalization of sensations. It results it is true, from the effect upon the eye of throwing a red light and a green light upon the same part of the retina of the eye,—i.e. upon the so-called "net-work" (Latin, *retina*) that form the screen at the back of the eye upon which visual images are projected. But that fact is psychophysical, and as such does not concern us. That a certain red, a certain green, and a certain violet-blue (appearing to be fully violet when diluted or weakened) are "fundamental", in the sense of not being producible in their fullest chroma (or color-character) by any mixture of other colors, is another psychophysical fact. Sensations might, of course, be distinguished as being either visceral or internal or external; but this would be a psychophysical distinction to which it will be needless, for the present, to pay any heed. A sensation which communicates a tinge to other elements of consciousness present with it, and that in a matter that partly escapes consciousness, may be called a *Feeling*.

The second kind of ingredient of ~~consciousness~~ awareness is the perception of a relation between different sensations in one consciousness. This kind embraces several varieties which call for separate mention; but all the varieties alike agree in regarding what is before the mind as an *object*; and the doing of that involves some consciousness of the mind itself as that over against which the object appears. Suppose a person to be aware of two sensations at once, say for example of a color and a sound. Then, although he *need* not in every case, yet he *can be*, or may be, conscious of their being two different sensations. This will be, however, a reflection quite distinct from the sensations themselves; and as such it will require, not perhaps an *effort*, but at least an exertion, or activity. The objectification of sensations always involves exertion, and it is, presumably, the awareness of that activity that supplies the idea of self and thus of an object, over against sense. Consciousness of contrast is the first variety of this second kind of ingredient of awareness; and although the reader may be quite unpracticed in internal self-observation, he can soon master his first lesson in this needed art so far as to be able to assure himself that the sort of activity here spoken of consists purely in awareness, and involves no psychophysical ingredient, whether it be accompanied by a fact of that nature or not. For the word "psychophysical" involves, in the very meaning of it, the notion of a real object quite outside of the awareness of the person to whom the psychophysical phenomenon appears, and so outside of any phenomenon or appearance itself. To say that one *knows* a fact to be psychophysical is to assert that one knows that there is a real object that is quite independent of any awareness; and to *suppose* a fact to be psychophysical is to assert that one supposes such an object to exist. But the active awareness that two simultaneous sensations are different is of the same general sort as the activity of excited *attention*, and is an activity of awareness, merely. One can recognize two colors that are only dreamed of as being contrasted. It may be that some physical change takes place in the brain when one does so; but in merely recognizing the contrast, one does not necessarily know, or suppose, or in any way recognize that any such psychical change takes place, and therefore the perception of the contrast is in itself merely an affair of awareness, or purely psychical fact; and indeed, whatever our own opinion may be, the person who recognizes the contrast need not have the slightest suspicion that any change in his brain takes place.

Two different simultaneous sensations may differ in their quality, or they may merely differ in their intensity, or, agreeing in both these respects, they may differ in being due to excitations of different parts of the body. For certainly the sensation of a prick of the leg differs from that due to a prick of the arm. All these, and perhaps such differences as those between what is remembered and what is anticipated may be reckoned as alike cases of the first variety of a perception of a difference of simultaneous sensations. But when what is perceived is a change in one sensation gradually taking place it seems proper to distinguish this difference coming to in time from the perception of a difference of simultaneous sensations. The perception of change going on is certainly no less distinguishable from a simple sensation than is the perception of a contrast between simultaneous sensations. It is, on the contrary, rather more so. It is decidedly more apt to excite attention; so that there seems to be more of the active element in it. Let this, then, be reckoned as the second variety of the perception of difference. This temporal contract may fairly be called "experience", — a word hardly applicable to the mere perception of a difference between simultaneous sensations.

The third variety is still more active and still more emphatically sets the object over against the awareness. This occurs when a person exerts his will to produce a change. Of course, if the effort is muscular, there will be a consciousness of a psychophysical fact, which will complicate the case, and introduce circumstances foreign to the present inquiry. But the effort may be considerable without any muscular or other psychophysical contamination. Imagine, for example, a person trying hard to follow a mathematical demonstration while a second person is talking to him, and perhaps plying him with questions: his effort may very well be equal to that[3] of carrying a barrel of flour; but it will be but a purely psychi-

---

3 [Alt.:] [...] of carrying a barrel of flour. Still the ~~effort~~ awareness of attention will be a purely psychical experience: that is to say, it will not, in every case, involve the idea of an object that is

cal effort of attention, not necessarily involving any apparent consciousness of an

independent of one's awareness of it. It is one thing to make a deliberate, intentional effort to fix one's thoughts on a problem, and another thing to be betrayed into noticing a novel and interesting object which unexpectedly presents itself; yet, after all, *this* difference lies entirely in the preparation for the exertion, and not in the act of attention itself. In order, however, completely and definitively to satisfy himself whether or not any such utter unlikeness as that between a simple sensation and the perception of the nature of the relation between two sensations does or does not exist between the kind of awareness in attention and that in the perception of a contrast, the reader will probably have to go through a considerable course of experiments, each followed by a most careful consideration of its teaching.

One or two points need to be well considered in advance of any experimentation. The chief of these is that when any character is recognized in a sensation, the latter ceases to be a mere sensation and becomes the perception of a relation between the sensation and the remembered or otherwise known character; for all recognition is perception of a relation. Another point to be considered is that an effort to attend is not the same thing as attention itself, which appears in its purer forms in what some writers call "involuntary" attention, which phrase, whatever signification they may think they attach to it, they really employ words in an unintelligible way. This shows that they are mere formulae without real meaning, that, taken together, make up a definition of what it is to deny. If it is true, as indeed it seems to be, that a man cannot think without using some signs, and so conversing with himself, then it may be admitted that these principles hold good for thinking, though not concerning the substance of what is really thought, but only as rules of the syntax of the signs used in thinking. In this respect, if they were not so obtrusively obvious, they might even be of service to those who use language without having any meaning to express, as well as to those who acknowledge themselves bound to all the opinions they ever expressed, without bearing in mind exactly what opinions they were. But even so, there are other relations besides negation they have bound themselves to support. concerning which analogous rules hold good. [discont.] the two properties of negation after we have determined exactly what they are.

Still it may be well to explain comment one fact inference that has been already implied though not directly the reader has perhaps been entitled to draw from what has been stated; namely that the principles of contradiction and of excluded third were not distinguished until modern times. In the first place, this is not quite true, though it is true that they were not *generally* distinguished until Christian Wolff in 1710 pointed out the distinction in a German tract entitled *Vernünftige Gedanken von den Kräften des menschlichen Verstanden*. This may seem surprising considering how much more attention was paid to the minutiae of reasoning in the middle ages than has been paid to them by any of the leading philosophers of modern days, and the more surprising, seeing that independence of the two principles was perfectly apprehended by Aristotle, whom the earlier scholastics used to call "The prince of philosophers". But in the first place, it must be noticed that in medieval times, every educated boy was taught that of two "contradictories", that is, of two assertions flatly contradicting one another, and no more, one or other must be true, which is about as accurate satisfactory a statement of the *substance*, of the principle of excluded third, though without characterizing it as a *principle*; as the usual formula of today, "A is either B or not B". In the second place, one could not possibly be more completely off the track of the truth than in supposing that the minds of the middle ages were much given to the consideration of the broader principles of logic. Their attitude was too purely passively receptive, and

object [present in] awareness itself, which is what we mean by a purely psychical. There is a good deal of difference between an exertion of attention that is deliberate and intentional, and one into which one is betrayed ~~unintentionally~~ by the unexpected appearance of a novel and interesting object: yet, after all, this difference lies entirely in the preparation for the exertion, not in the act of attention itself. In order to completely satisfy herself whether or not any such utter unlikeness between simple sensation and a perception of a contrast, the reader will have to make a good many experiments and closely observe the results of them.

But now let the reader ponder upon the difference between the following two states of awareness: the one being the unintentional attention that he might bestow upon a strange and curious insect, and the other the contemplation of a moving picture while the machinery was working very slowly. Let him ask himself whether there is any material difference between the ~~modes~~ natures of those two states of mind except that in the latter case he would be comparing objects successively perceived, while in the former case he would be comparing an object he was perceiving with objects he remembered. If this be the main difference, there is no world-wide foreignness between purely psychical volition and mental perception: they are no more than two of the three varieties of contrast-awareness.

---

their intelligence too destitute of original vim, for that. If they read the simpler of the logical ~~tracts~~ papers of Aristotle, it was simply because, at first, those were the only writings they possessed from which they could hope to receive any intellectual enlightenment. The topics of their logical studies which excited the chief interest of the brightest of them ~~were not points~~ lay, in strictness, quite outside the domain of logic. They were such metaphysical questions, as that of the intension and remission of forms. If the reader does not know what these things are, any true friend of his must hope that he will not waste any portion of such a precious inheritance as life-time is in trying to find out what they are, unless, indeed, his genius has taken a very odd and obstinate bent. about the beginning of the thirteenth century more than very noticeable change seems to have come over the minds of the Western Europe in widely separated departments of activity; and when one runs down the chronological table in search of a possible cause of this mental revolution, one is arrested at A.D. 1204 when the crusaders captured Constantinople in that stage of degeneration from a mental condition never healthy, which at the time of the capture bordered on universal idiocy. One minute's reflection should suffice to satisfy those who know human nature that from such a source nothing vitalizing nor energetic, nothing like experimental research, nothing like the ogival, or "Gothic" architecture with its numerous now effective and elevating features, could have been imported. But manuscripts of old Alexandrian and classical Greek were probably brought, and some of them by more highly refined men than the Western folks remembered having seen before, and these men would be capable of teaching Greek ~~a few other useful~~ very likely some minor accomplishments and arts.[4] In the third place, Aristotle never emphasized the distinction in his logical writings, but only in his *metaphysics*, (Book Δ) with which the Latin world did not become acquainted until considerably later than   [year left blank]; and when this work did come to be studied, its doctrines were found to be quite unacceptable to catholics; and it never attracted the attention of logicians until the nineteenth century.

There have been, in the past, thinkers truly more than eminent, men really great, who have opined the two broad classes of awareness that have been mentioned,—sensation and contrast-consciousness—to include all of which the human mind is capable; and although just at present, this doctrine is laid to rest, it would be strange, considering what empty absurdities are making themselves disciples, if this one alone were never more revived. The reader will do prudently, therefore, to consider attentively the evidence of its falsity, and to store it up in his mind for some possible future application.

It will be aid to the appreciation by the reader of the evidence on this subject if his attention is first drawn to a very characteristic triadic distinction between, firstly, an *actual* fact, secondly, one that merely *may* be, and one that, under conditions, *would be*.

Actual facts and existing things are subject to two principles which modern logicians have distinguished under the names of "the principle of contradiction" and "the principle of excluded middle, or of excluded third". Many writers inadvisedly call them "laws of thought" for no better reason than that, as long as we think distinctly, we cannot conceive of their being violated. This very circumstance, however, shows that they form no part of the science of psychology as the phrase "laws of thought" would seem to imply, and also that they are not "laws" at all, in the modern sense of that now sovereignly important word, are truths that need or have needed to be proved. Self evident propositions of importance are properly called principles. Nor does psychology,—any more than any other real science,—as opposed to acquaintance with the received language of a science—include anything that everybody will know to be true as soon as he apprehends its meaning. Of course, the teachers of any science whatever, when he first takes up a new topic, has to explain the terminology of that topic, and the disciple will, in paying attention to these explanations, learn to draw certain distinctions accurately without which the real truths of the science could not be apprehended, although they are not themselves any part of the real science.[5]

---

5 [Alt.:] The words "subject" and "predicate" shall here be used, the one for that which the grammatical subject designates (or, to use the proper term of logic, *denotes*,—not meaning, however), by this an *outward* object, but the mental object, the *idea*, that the grammatical subject summons memory to yield up to recollection, or else bids fancy to build up out of such materials as experience has accumulated, and the other word—"predicate"—for that which the grammatical predicate *signifies*, i.e. supplies as an additional detail, or rather as the special feature required to render the hearer's or reader's idea, already produced by the grammatical subject, adequately representative of the speaker's or writer's idea of the fact he asserts. For be it explained that throughout this essay the word "assertion" will be used to mean a certain kind of *communication*, and so to denote a performance requiring the cöoperation of two parties (though not necessarily

Using the words "subject" and "predicate" for that which the grammatical subject names—not meaning by this the outward object, but the mental idea, the object of which one is directly aware,— and other that which the grammatical predicate signifies, or calls up, the principle of contradiction is that of a *definite* subject no predicate can truly be both affirmed and denied; where by a "definite" subject is meant either a mentally identified object or else something which if multiple or general, at least remains indistinguishable in respect to the predicate. Thus, it is not supposable that whatever lives is at once certain to die and *not* certain to die; and again, *some person* is young and *some person* is not young; but this is because the expression "some person" at different times refers to persons distinguishable in respect to being young or not. A person who seriously informs another of a fact about "some person" must, if he well knows that what he asserts is true, must also know or have known of its being true of a definite individual, although, for some reason, he refrains from mentioning, it is this want of circumstantiality that the epithet "indefinite" is intended to signify. The principle of excluded middle is

---

two different persons, since one person, for example, may write a memorandum for his own future information); one of these parties, which shall be called the *utterer*, by an exertion of will renders that other party, who shall be called the *interpreter*, sensible of certain signs by which he must recognize the fact that the utterer has willed to assert; and in the great majority of cases he will regard it as a *real* fact. The signs of which the interpreter becomes sensible may be indirect; that is, signs of signs, which means ever so complex an assertion may be made in a single sign through a "code". But if all the signs are direct, at least two will be required; the one to denote the subject, the other to signify the predicate. If the assertion is not *complex*, that is, if it neither affirms nor denies a relation between two facts, whether as a relation actually existing or as one that might be or that would be, then the predicate might be [two ms pages missing] facts are.

It is to be observed that the mere denial of a fact about a single object is the affirmation of an opposite fact, which however is *indefinite*, not in the way in which this term has been employed above, which is called by the logicians the *quantitatively indefinite* (because they call the difference between "Every" [Gr. πᾶς] and "Some" [Gr. τις] a difference in "Quantity") and which consists in the term's being applied sometimes to one object and sometimes to another, but in that kind of indefiniteness which consists in a word or phrase *meaning*, i.e. *signifying*, or implying at one time one character and at another time another, as the English word *fast* is noted for doing. The horse ran so fast that he ran into a quicksand and there stuck fast. This kind of indefiniteness may with the greatest propriety be called qualitative; and it is all the more appropriate in particular so to call the indefiniteness of denials, since the usage of logicians of applying the word "quality" as a technical term for the difference between affirmations and denials began we can never know when, since the Alexandrian library is destroyed: it must have been before the time of Nero, or say roughly, in millennia ago; and it is now found in all the logic-books. The nonexistence of an actual fact is itself an actual fact, though a qualitatively indefinite one; but the unreality of a definite *may-be* is a qualitatively indefinite *would-be*; and the unreality of a definite *would-be* is a qualitatively indefinite *may-be*. For to deny that every line would everywhere have a definite direction (as most mathematicians [end]

that of any *determinate* subject the affirmation and the denial of the same predicate cannot both at once be false. The truth must be with one or other since there is no third possibility. It is not supposable that, even in fairy-land, it should at once be false that some person is ill-tempered and equally false that some person is *not* ill-tempered; and although it might at once be false that whatever lives is destined to die and equally false that whatever lives will live forever, this is only supposable because the idea of "whatever is a living being" remains *indeterminate* in respect to subsequent death, that is, it is neither limited to living beings that are mortal, nor is it limited to beings that are immortal. The idea of "some person" is, on the other hand, quite determinate, because, being in the singular number, it denotes an *individual* object, that is to say, one not *divided* into parts of which some predicate is truth and others of which it is false.

We call that *real* concerning which whatever is true will forever have been true, no matter what may at any time in any way be thought about it, using the word thought in the widest sense. Thus, the opinions of Malebranche were *real* opinions, since he opined as he did, whatever we may think he opined. The substance of a dream is not real, because whatever is true of it is so in that so the dreamer dreamed; and dreaming is only a particular kind of thinking. But the fact of the dream, if it actually took place, is a real fact, because it will always remain true that so and so was dreamed, whether the dreamer remembers it or not. Taking the word "real" in this sense, which has been its proper sense ever since Duns Scotus coined the word late in the thirteenth century,[6] it must be admitted that not only actual facts and existing things, but also innumerable *can-be*s and *would-be*s are real.

There is one class of *would-be*s whose reality it would seem that no reflecting man could well doubt, considering how onerous we all sometimes find them, though incomparably oftener how indispensable others of them daily and almost every moment show themselves to be. The older psychologists, who in great part fixed this department of our language, used to call those of them that were naturally developed with our physical development, or that we possess from birth, by the name of *dispositions*; while those that are formed as consequences of the

---

[6] There is another word "real", preserved in the phrase "real property"; and this is an older, by centuries, than the one that has become so much commoner; but although this older word appears in medieval Latin as *realis*, I cannot help suspecting that its original form was *regalis*, since the *g* would inevitably have been dropped, both in French and in Latin, and because I can understand why *regalis* should in those days have been applied to real property, which was then supposed to have been originally the gift of the king, while I fail to discover any very convincing reason for its being called *realis*. Of course if my suspicion is correct it must be supposed that the Latin word was taken from the French or the Spanish.

repetition of certain actions they termed *habits*. But since for the purposes of this essay the distinction between these two varieties of *would-be*s has little or no significance, all shall alike here be included under the designation *habits*.

II.i. Explanation of Terms, to be used in Special Senses[7]

It is always a great convenience to a reader to find any writing not very short and calling for considerable thought to have been broken up into brief sections, so that he can readily turn back to any previous passage. Locke's celebrated *Essay concerning Humane Understanding*, is a particularly convenient work in that respect. Of its greater merits I need not speak. It is divided into Books, Chapters, and Sections, each of the last, with few exceptions mostly in the concluding *Book IV*, consisting of a single ~~ordinary~~ paragraph of no exorbitant length and often of half a dozen lines. But to chop up the present essay so fine as that would[8] be objectionable as not marking sufficiently the concatenation of ideas.

---

7 [From an alternative draft of R 683, 1913, "An Essay toward Improving Reasoning in Security and in Uberty".]

8 [Alt.:] [...] be objectionable as not sufficiently marking the concatenation of the thoughts.

No science can be conveniently discussed without a provision of *technical terms*; that is to say, words or phrases having much more precise meanings than it would be at all convenient to restrict ordinary words to. For if we were to be confined to precisely defined terms, we never could express any though or feeling or other state of mind that was not composed of such as were sufficiently familiar to all the world to have had a common word assigned to it.

Logic, a word which I shall employ as a technical term for the science of the security and uberty of reasonings, is like all the other sciences in having a practical need of technical terms; and it further resembles the others in that a good deal of the labour of developing the sciences has to go to the work of forming a suitable *"terminology"*, or system of technical terms with their *definitions*, or precise explanations of their meanings; and as in many of the other sciences, these definitions can, many of them, only come to be understood in their precision by the learner's familiarizing himself with the particular kind of observation that each express. Success in the study, depends, for one of its conditions upon the learner's diligence in the formation of that habit which such "familiarization" signifies. I shall give my definition in batches, each comprising more or less similar notions, each batch preceding as closely as other considerations will allow, the passages in which there will first arise a need for using some of the terms defined.

[Alt.:] Mathematics is the only science which still professes to confine itself to necessary reasoning, and in the proper place it will be here shown (so far as is possible without going to any great depth into its abstruser parts) to what an astonishing extent its greatest advances in modern, and even in ancient, times have been due to mathematicians' lack of the peculiar subtlety required to keep their reasoning strictly of the necessary kind at important junctures. No great originality is claimed for this part of the essay: something of the same sort was said by John Stuart Mill in the first edition of his *System of Logic, Ratiocinative and Inductive*, published in March, 1843, but in that writer's mind older by a dozen years.

I shall show the reader, when the proper time comes, how much reasoning is dependent upon Graphical Signs. By "graphical" I mean capable of being written or drawn, so as to be spatially arranged. It is true that one can argue *viva voce*; but I do not believe one can go very deeply into any important and considerably large subject of discussion with calling up in the minds of one's hearer's mental images of objects arranged in ways in which *time*, without *space*, is incapable of serving as the field of representation, since in time of two quite distinct objects one must be antecedent and the other subsequent. Of course, the one temporal relation can be spatially imaged in various ways. But the combined field of space and time seems to be adequate to the imaging of Lorentz's explanation of the famed experiment of Morley and Michaelson; and although mathematicians talk of a space of any number of dimensions, I do not think it has been shown that they render any relations logically consistent (without breaches of continuity), that ~~cannot~~ could not be imaged in a moving stereoscopic view.

1.2 The Art of Reasoning Elucidated

Preface

[R 678, 1910] The writer's endeavor and aim in this essay will be to make the following points as plain and evident as philosophemes that are doubted or denied can very well be rendered:

First, that [there] are certain radically different ways of reasoning, no one of which can properly be represented as any mere variation of another nor as a combination of others; that each of these "*types*" of reasoning (as they shall here be called), can be defined so clearly that there need be no hesitation in determining to which of them any particular reasoning that one may have occasion to examine belongs or, if it be composite to which its several parts belong. These differences of type constitute the most important distinctions there are between different modes of homogeneous inference, and that from a practical, as well as from a theoretical, point of view, since each type supplies its own peculiar *kind* and, in a rough and general way, its own *degree* of ~~approximation to~~ surety.

In reasonings of different types of the principles of inference, the reasons why the reasoner is justified in believing his conclusion true, if his premises were so, are of utterly disparate natures; their surety does not have the same meaning. But hardly any writers have ever fully appreciated how radically unlike they are. In modern times a variety of theories have been put forth, which if they were correct would obliterate the radical differences between the different types of reasoning, although in many cases the authors of these have themselves failed to remark that such would [be] the legitimate effect of their teachings.

The author of this essay, in comparing himself with other men, has often remarked that his very exceptional interest in reasonings is quite unaccompanied [by] any unusual natural sagacity; and the few proofs of difficult theorems that he has been the first to discover have been the fruit of long studies, and do not compare in ~~lucidity~~ simplicity with the subsequent demonstrations of some of them that other men have produced; and he has found so many examples of obtuseness in the literature of logic that he has often asked himself whether more men have not been drawn to the study of reasoning because their instinctive power in that direction was somewhat insufficient than because, like Leibniz and Euler, reasoning was their *forte*.

It is surprising that among students of reasoning there should still be found some who incline to think that the processes of mathematics suffice to explain all sound inferences and who even assert positively that it is so. To be sure, if these gentlemen are mathematicians themselves, their opinion is comprehensible enough and quite in accordance with common opinion of mathematicians. But should they not belong to that class, one wonders how the easily observed predominant character of the non-mathematical views of mathematicians can have failed to cause them to examine the different types of reasoning more closely before pronouncing an opinion of so mathematical a flavor. In the section of this essay that deals with types of reasoning will be found a very simple argument which seems to the writer to be quite decisive of this question; but since there are many minds who are never satisfied with simple resolutions of questions on which they have labored, for their benefit a number of other reasons shall be presented, and they might readily be multiplied so as to conform to the views (not entirely unfounded) of those who think that the discussion of a momentous subject should occupy a great length of time. For example, no proposition is more momentous than that twice two makes four; and, in the aggregate, no doubt a great deal of time has been devoted to it, perhaps more than to the squaring of the circle.

Second, of each type of reasoning there is one form that is more natural, or instinctive, than any other; but for each type there are certain more or less artificial conceptions by means of which one can immensely economize thought, such for example, as that of ordinal numbers, that of abstract nouns, that of numerical probability, with many inventions of amasses of mathematicians, [*illeg.*, a word cut out] imaginary, and infinitesimal quantities, exponents and logarithms, etc. reach conclusion each of which is equivalent to an indefinite amount of reasoning of the natural variety. Then, by grouping together such of those artificial conceptions as we usually require to employ together, we attain the idea of a more or less artificial "general method" of reasoning of the same type; and accordingly we have to study, besides, the natural general method of each type, several artificial methods of the same type; and there is enormous advantage, as well as the satisfaction of a great need to be gained from a careful examination of each of these general methods from its superficial aspect down to its very bottom.

Third, in any reasoning, the assumed facts from which it sets out, or rather the mental assertion of those facts (if any difference can be detected between the meanings of the two descriptions), are termed the *premisses*; while the mental assertion which the reasoning causes the reasoned to accept with more or less confidence is throughout this essay to be termed its *conclusion*, being nearly, if not quite, the same thing as the state of fact which the reasoning tends to make him believe is a real fact.

Now he may have so chosen his premisses that something is true of them which, although, taken by itself alone, it has no bearing whatever upon the conclusion, and though the taking of it into account leaves the conclusion, and therefore the "general method", as above defined, quite the same, yet will complicate the reasoning very advantageously, either by heightening the degree of confidence that ought to be placed in the conclusion, or by making the precise meaning of this conclusion plainer, or by otherwise improving the reasoning materially. In such a way, there may be, connected with one and the same general method of reasoning, several different modes of improving it without essentially altering it; and the different divisions of one general method so resulting may very well be termed so many different "*orders*" of reasoning, since zoölogists seem to apply this term to sections of any one class which result from *complications* of the essential character of the class that render that character, or the accomplishment of its quasi-purpose, more perfect; and the term shall be adopted throughout this essay. But it must not be supposed that there is any intimate relationship between our classifications of animals and those of reasonings, since the former must represent, in great measure, the accidental point of view, since we cannot know nor make any considerable approach to knowing, precisely why any group of animals have in common just those characters they have and why they differ from one another just as they do; while it is to be hoped that, after an attentive and thoughtful perusal of this essay, the reader will be convinced that there is nothing at all mysterious in reasoning itself, since it is of the very substance of understanding, however mysterious it may be how man ever came to be endowed with the faculty, how this congeries of bits of amido acids and albuminoids (or whatever the name and description of them may be by the time this sentence falls under the reader's eye and understanding) come to have that *inside*, that inner side, that we call awareness of any kind. Yet perhaps even this may sooner be solved than the zoological conundrum. Only the solation of the latter may be approached gradually; while that of the former may be recognizable as probably true as soon as it is clearly stated. Only a few of the "orders" of reasoning will here be noticed.

Fourth, the reasons why the different types of reasoning yield true conclusions oftener than false ones, and how we know that they will do so, having been proved, there will be no difficulty in stating the conditions under which each kind of reasoning is sound; and these statements will be made and proved.

Fifth, faults of reasoning will be studied in four classes. The first will embrace all the fallacies recognized by Aristotle. The second will include only such others as inexperienced reasoners are particularly apt to fall into; the third embraces those in whom bad habits of thinking have become ingrained; the fourth are such as the ablest reasoners of our time are apt to fall into.

Sixth, the habits which a seeker of truth ought especially to cultivate will be considered, and the general rules for conducting investigations of certain kinds. These will be illustrated by accounts of several inquiries.

Seventh, finally, guided by the principles of investigation herein defended, the author will apply them to the discussion of some of the most pressing questions of our time.

But before attacking any of these seven points, it will be necessary, in an introduction to bring to the reader's attention certain considerations based upon observations which the latter will be easily able to verify for himself. Nothing would be gained by giving a list of these reflexions beforehand. They relate, in part to certain habits of thinking which it would be prudent for the reader to cultivate, and to one or two that [he] ought to fight against as being manifestly fatal to the purpose of thinking, which is to form such habits as will lead us so to act as will secure to us the most satisfaction; and in part they relate to processes of thought and effort which are not themselves reasonings but are indispensable to reasoning, and with which it is desirable that we should be well acquainted in order that we may understand reasoning, and know what is needful in order to perform it well. Although he will thus be called upon to think and to reason before he has learned how to avoid the pitfalls that occur in this business, yet not only will his own reasoning instinct emphatically concur in the recommendations, but he will find that there is none among them that has not been warmly approved by all the great thinkers. Nothing prevents bad ways of reasoning from irreconcilable conflict, while methods that even *tend* toward the truth will, on the whole, agree better and better the further they ~~are continued~~ go.

Introduction

I. The most indispensable prerequisite, by far, for reasoning well is a lively love of truth, which is of slow growth and cannot exist alone, since in the course of acquiring it, one always gains considerable experience in reasoning, and learns many of the risks in it, and something of the ways of meeting them. Many people do not so much as know what the love of truth is, but confound it with a love of *dogma*, where this word is used for whatever statements there may be assent to which on their parts has been inculcated either before they could really apprehend their meaning,—even if they have any meaning, or at any rate in a way that could afford no reasonable assurance of their truth. Such people wear an armor almost impenetrable by any correct notion of the love of truth, or even of truth itself, while the inculcated formulae themselves, whether catholic, or calvinistic, or spiritualistic, or "christian-scientistic", or pseudo-pragmatistic, or "positivistic", or homeopathic, or what not, are almost always of a nature to undermine and wreck the reason that is natural to man but which their victims have been taught to regard as not merely fallible but thoroughly evil. What do we mean by "human reason"? It is the name for such power as men have, by the exercise of their energies, and from such information as their senses and feelings can furnish, of ascertaining the truth. Therefore, by the very meaning of the expression, what human reason cannot, men cannot find out at all; and when the inculcators of dogma talk, as they so commonly do, of the ~~radical falseness~~ inevitable error of human reason, they simply betray their secret purpose of inducing their disciples not to use the only means in man's power of distinguishing truth from falsehood. They wish to induce him unreasonably to constrain himself if to do as they tell him, by exercising over him a sort of hypnotic power that they gained while he was too childish to resist. At a later day they will unblushingly deny that they ever did this; just as the homeopathists continue stoutly to maintain that Hahnemann was in the right, and conveniently forget that his doctrine was, first, that all diseases are varieties of the itch; second, that it is idle to inquire whether yellow fever, for example, is caused by the bite of mosquitoes or the plague by those of fleas, etc., and third, that all that is necessary is to give a medicine which will produce in a healthy subject and in a large dose symptoms "similar" (all things being more or less similar) to those of the patient, remembering however, fourth, that the power of medicines is greater the more they are diluted and the more their solutions are shaken; so that the effect of one drop of sea water taken out of New York harbor after one drop of a medicine had been put into the harbor of Melbourne or Sydney (time being allowed for its diffusion) would hardly be perceptible, *owing to the medicine not being sufficiently diluted*. But it must be confessed that the doctrines of the homeopatheists are no more contrary to human reason than those of the

"Christian Scientists", nor than various others inculcated by several churches; to the absurdities of which some men think it wise to pretend to shut their eyes.

The pretension, then, that is often made by lovers of this or that system of dogmas to be ardent lovers of truth is utterly unfounded. We may also dismiss such a claim in so far as it may be founded upon an interest in any particular branch of knowledge since nobody acquainted with the use of the phrase would allow that a philatelist, or a philologist, or a philogynist, or any other such specialist has any better claim to be considered as *ipso facto* a lover of truth more than his neighbour.

Then, what does the phrase mean? Is there any difference between a lover of truth and a lover of knowledge? Perhaps it will be wisest for the writer, avoiding all assumption of more authority upon how words ought to be used than the nature of his studies would naturally entail, to confine himself to stating how he will aim to use them in the present essay.

There seem to be three distinct passions for knowledge; that for wide knowledge, that for deep knowledge, and that for accurate knowledge. The first is the passion of the explorer in any field, whether he be an ordinary passer through it, or whether he be [a] Stanley, or whether he be a Humboldt. Such a man wisely recognizes that a little acquaintance with many things that had previously belonged to the unknown Vast is generally speaking more profitable than an equal addition of new details concerning things with which we were already acquainted. Mankind in general show that they think so by the greater interest they take in discoveries of things quite novel than they do in much closer and more minute knowledge of what was known before; and they are quite right, since it is found that, on the whole it requires more labor to make a given amount of increase in our knowledge of any subject the greater the previous knowledge was, while the utility of a given increase of a knowledge becomes, in the long run less and less the more one knows about the matter already. The reader cannot reasonably expect that these two propositions should here be treated at such length as would be required to prove them, considering what a very moderate part they play in this introduction; but their truth may be illustrated in an example, that the more the general subject is studied [it] will be found to be the more typical for the usual situation. Suppose then, that one has occasion to make a voyage from one part to another along the same pretty straight coast. If the intervening waters have never been sounded, the prudent navigator will wisely make a considerable detour, so as to get into deep water for as much of his passage as possible; and this will cost considerable time at least. But let a single more adventurous mariner make the same passage along a straighter course, while diligently heaving the lead all along; and if he finds the soundings decidedly more uniform than might have been expected, he will have obtained valuable information, without having added materially to his own labour nor to that of his crew. This will encourage the first shipper to shorten his next voyage, at a reduced cost, the passage being more direct and shorter; and after a number of such voyages, he will get better terms from the underwriters. Subsequently, the government will feel called upon to order a regular survey of those waters at great expense. This may develop some hitherto unknown dangers, and ought to reduce the insurance very sensibly, but it cannot shorten the passage by more than a mere trifle. Thus, both principles are illustrated. The government survey has not more than doubled the knowledge obtained from the first shorter voyage, though it has cost enormously more; and as for the saving the first short voyage was decidedly more effective than the government's survey. Although individual instances show wide departures from his generalizations the writer is led by long attention to the subject to believe that they express the mean or usual facts.

The passion of the explorer, then, is justified by the fact that wide knowledge pays best at first; and this becomes strikingly true in the case of one who brings to his task the peculiar virtues of a great explorer. But very few minds, and those more peculiar than eminent, can be much interested in merely making the acquaintance of many hundreds of different objects, whether whose objects be individuals, or classes, or characters. It becomes more profitable to know much about a selection of them. As long as only four of the asteroids, or minor planets, were known, educated people generally knew at least the names of the four; but now that seven hundred, more or less, are known, not even astronomers in general take any interest in any of them unless they have some specially interesting character. The same shifting of interest has taken place in natural history and chemistry, and must come about in every science. Deep knowledge becomes more profitable than wide knowledge, and every science must in time split up into several. The passion for collecting masses of facts concerning single objects, without any narrowly defined ulterior purpose will throughout this essay [have] the meaning to be attached to the phrase "love of learning", whether the objects or objects to which the facts refer are individual and the facts are their histories or descriptions, or whether the objects are kinds or classes of things, the facts relating to where and how they are to be obtained, or their properties, anatomies, etc., or whether the objects are characters or properties and the facts collected about them be different degrees in which they are possessed by different kinds of substances or things, or whatever else may be the natures of the objects and of the facts that the person affected by this passion loves to accumulate.

But those who talk of the passion here called "love of knowledge", and in a measure even those who speak of "love of learning", are, for the moment, thinking of *knowing* any given proposition as if it were as definite a state as that of having any given sum to one's credit on the books of a bank, supposing these to be perfectly kept, though they must know very well that it is far from being so. For instance every chemist who "knew" his atomic weights said in 1904 that that of tantalum was 183; but in 1909 he called it 181, and toward the end of 1910 he made it about $182\frac{1}{2}$, though nobody dreamed of there having been any change meantime. In the more exact of the physical sciences, it is now usual to affix to every determination of a value the sign ± followed by an estimate (commonly recognized as too small), of the "probable error" of the determination. It is open to doubt whether there be any single sentence whatever of whose truth any man can be absolutely certain. If there be any such, it is probably something like the following "We cannot be sure that any exact statement of actual fact is absolutely free from error". Thus, we are not quite sure that a body moving uninfluenced by any force would continue to describe (or pass over) equal distances in equal times, unless we measure time by the distances which that body describes, in which case the statement is not one of fact, but is merely an inverted definition of what we mean by "equal times". But this whole question will come up for consideration in due time. What is pertinent in the present connection is to call attention to the fact that we are already rapidly approaching the time where most of our knowledge of *physics*, at least, can be stated in the form "such and such a quantity (defining it accurately) seems probably not to be larger than one given value nor to be smaller than another given value"; and we can conceive that the other natural sciences, even those which relate to language, history, etc. should ultimately be brought to somewhat similar conditions, so that we should no longer look for unexpected additions to our knowledge so much as to narrowing the limits between which it seems likely that each truth will ultimately be found to lie.

When we once reach that point we can calculate what it will probably cost (in the efforts of men of different rarities) to narrow those limits by any given amount, and also what the practical gain of that limitation will be; and these two quantities being calculated for all our problems, the quotients of the probable gains divided by their probable costs will represent the urgencies of the different inquiries at the time, which of course we shall strive to equalize, and thus put into practice a wise scientific economy. The mere prospect of such a future already animates the wiser of the men of science with an ardent desire to reduce the urgencies of the different problems to equality; and this passion shall here be designated by the name of *the love of scientific economy*. It seems to be the highest form that the love of knowledge has been able, as yet, to assume.

Appendix (Variant, R 678)

Introduction[9]

I. If one wishes to rent his house, and an elegant stranger appears at the door and expresses a desire to look it over, common sense will stimulate the owner to explain all the conveniences of the dwelling that need any explanation, and to display its chief elegances, without concealing any trifling faults that it may have; since it will be a contented tenant that he seeks, and not an incessant fault-finder. If there be serious objections, he must have known them and ought to have remedied them before he posted his notice that the premises were to let. Just so, supposing that he who is casting his eye over these lines has just taken up the volume from a book-seller's counter to see what it may contain, the writer is eager to explain what benefit he may gain from the perusal of it, as well as what he must not expect from it. But if it is not a *he*, but a *she*, that is inspecting this poor little essay, the writer hardly dares hope that she will hold it longer, albeit he knows well the ability of women to penetrate to the truth of things. For it is only men's way of finding out the truth, the method of reason,—strong but slow,—too slow, apparently, for most women, and perhaps they feel their genius lies in another quarter,—that this book can pretend to teach.

The kind of readers whom the writer would most welcome, because it is them for whom he could be of most service, just as the owner of a vacant house would most rejoice over such tenants as the house would suit best, are the fellows who are just beginning to enjoy thinking, having either not yet reached the stupid age, or just recovered from it. Only their minds must not be crammed and incommoded with a lot of stuff that they have not learned how to put to useful service.

When the writer was a child, Brattle Street, where the old royalist families had lived when the Revolution came, still retained something of its old gentility and dignity, and was bordered by the grandest and most gracious elms. Ward by the ancient mansion, known as "the   House", where the children went to school, was a shoemaker's (for it need hardly be said that shoes were made by hand seventy years ago, except that they were imported for ladies, with "gauche" and "droit" *written* on their white kid linings) where that old sage would sit at work on his low bench, muttering to himself meantime somewhat thus: "Why aint I in Heaven? uq." This "uq" stands for a sound consisting of a grunt made deep down in the throat and unmodified by the mouth but with the nasal passage left open, and terminating with a violent contraction of the bronchial tubes, syllable which began with a grunt made deep down in the throat but was quite unmodified by tongue or other mouth-parts, while the vocal chords were vibrating and the nasal passages open, and which ended by a consonant sound more like that our *ng* than anything else but produced by a violent contraction of the bronchial tubes aided by the muscles of the abdomen. This interjection escaped the old man every time he pulled on his threads. "Because Man is created, uq!"—"And so is under the rule of Time, uq."—"And so he can't be nothing and something at once, uq."—"Improving is the best that can happen to us, uq"—"We can grow happier if we try in the right way, uq."—"But we can't try in the best way, uq"—"Because we don't know the best way, uq"—"We can only learn more and more about it, uq."—"It was lucky for me, uq"—"That I didn't know how to get what I used to long for, uq."—"I should have been a badly disappointed man by this time, uq."—

---

[9] [Alternative version of "Introduction" (R 678).]

Now it is pretty clear that this talk must be much more an illusion that has grown up in the writer's imagination rather than a correct recollection; since at that tender age he could not have comprehended an old man's reflections. But calling it a dream, it is nevertheless very true that every human being's likings, and energies, and reason grow much more than his body does, and in this process of development undergoes transformations about as great as that of a caterpillar into a butterfly; and that, on this account, what a boy ought first to acquire are those powers which are sure to be needed by every kind of man.

Still, it is very important that long before the young man comes to choose his line of life, so far as any choice is open to him, he should have compared himself, very soberly, with his different companions, so as to get a true idea of what general kind of man he is going to turn out to be. His guardian should be studying the same question; but in *some* respects the youth is in a better position to find out the real truth than even the most impartial outward observer can be; and few parents or guardians are able to be quite impartial, however carefully they may have recorded and digested his observations. Therefore, the individual himself should not fail to take special note of every fact that indicates an inferiority of his to any other person, whether in delicacy and liveliness of feeling, in control over the wills of others or of oneself, or in quickly acquiring ways of doing things of using language, and of reasoning.

A man probably attains his greatest native powers of feeling, action, and reason at about 35 to 40 years of age; but his greatest mental efficiency in the three lines only comes much later, because his forces need to be exercised and disciplined; and of course the whole work of education has to be performed by the man himself,—and woe be to him if he does not do it well: his teachers can only guide him and furnish him with some information which is *comparatively* of small consequence.

The writer, in his long life has found out for himself, what had often been told him while he was under tutelage, but which he then never could sufficiently realize, that the chances are large that any given young boy will become a miserably unhappy man,—however he may try to lie to himself for consolation,—because he had not worked hard enough in his youth upon the work of his own self-development and self-government. That is the reason that so many successful and happy men have had the lowest origins. For they could not help seeing from the first that that must be true of them which is really true of the highest born, as well, namely, that their education and training must be their own work being due to their own nice observation, their own strenuous attention and other endeavors, and their own cultivation of useful habits.

II. If we agree to apply the word "talk" to all ways of expressing sensations, actions, and ideas in signs of any kinds and also to all ways of interpreting signs, and if we apply this word "sign" to everything recognizable whether to our outward senses or to our inward feeling and imagination, provided only it calls up some feeling, effort, or thought, then every reader will be able by experiments and observations of his own,—though in order to satisfy himself sufficiently of the fact may take a good deal of time,—reasonably to satisfy himself that all meditation, consideration, and thought consists or is embodied in *talk with oneself*. To say this is only to speak of what passes in the mind, or perhaps, in part, only virtually engages our consciousness: it does not in the least involve any theory of what passes in the brain or other part of the body. The writer may, however, allow himself, in response to possible curiosity, to mention that he does not believe the "talk" in question takes place between the two halves of the brain. He does not intend, in this introduction, and still less in the body of this essay to touch upon any point of psychology (except to illustrate the ways of reasonings of psychologists) unless it be such as the reader can readily verify for himself.

Assuming that we know that thinking is "talking" with oneself, we see at once that our knowledge of how we think is no mere *description* of it, as a knowledge of how the brain, or any other physical machine, works would be, but, so far as it is correct, amounts positively to a *translation* of it, or in some cases to a "grammatical" a "syntactical", analysis of thought. For the "signs" in which we think, whatever they may be in any particular case (and it will not concern us to determine of what sort they actually are), must be subject to rules more or less analogous to the rules of syntax.

For example, if we take a piece of blank paper, and form the resolve to write upon it some part of what we think *about some real or imaginary condition of things*, then, that resolve being made, and the whole sheet[10] having been devoted to that purpose exclusively, by the common understanding called of the *graphist* (as the person who makes assertions by "scribing",—that is, by writing, drawing, or otherwise putting—on the sheet so devoted is to be called), and the *interpreter* (i.e. the person to whose understanding the graphist addresses the assertions that he scribes on the sheet), the graphist is at liberty to scribe any assertion on the sheet that he may be disposed to assert. Now assertions differ in *modality*,—a term which must be explained at once. It refers to the different relations there may be between the *affirmation* of the state of things asserted and the *denial* of it, these different relations distinguishing three different "modes" of assertion. If a man says "It may rain tomorrow", his assertion is in "the mode of possibility", because it may be true that possibly it will rain tomorrow and, at the same time, be true that possibly it will not rain tomorrow. Any assertion is said to be made in the mode of possibility if, and only if, it is conceivable that the affirmation and the denial of that which it so asserts should be both at once *true*. Observe carefully that to deny that *it is possible that it will rain tomorrow*, is much more than a denial of all that is asserted in saying that it is possible that it will rain tomorrow. On the other hand, an assertion is said to be made in "the mode of necessity", if, and only if, the affirmation and the denial of that which is so asserted could conceivably be both alike *false*. Thus if a person says "it will *certainly* rain tomorrow", it may be alike false that it is certain to rain and that it is certain not to rain.

That precisely the same state of things cannot at once, both be, and not be, is called by modern logicians, since 1828 or the somewhat earlier, "the principle of contradiction".[11] It does not apply to mere *may be*s or mere *can be*s or other mere possibilities.

That every precisely defined state of things must either be or not be is called in the same terminology "the principle of excluded third", or "of excluded middle", there being no third state of things besides, nor half-way between, being and not being. It does not apply to a pair of opposite assertions of *certainties* or *necessities*.

---

10 [Alt.:] [...] and the whole paper having been devoted to that purpose exclusively, and we then happen to think of rainy weather, though we need write nothing, since we have not resolved to write *everything* we think, yet we are at liberty to write

It is rainy

or anything else that we assume to be true. If we write two assertions, we assert the truth of both.

An assertion always consists of two parts, the *subjects* and the *predicates*. But first, of names (or virtual names) of one or more objects that the interpreter (or person addressed) must already be more of less familiar with, or else he will not know what the assertion refers to; and these object are called by the writer the *subjects* of the assertion [end]

11 [Carl Friedrich Bachmann, *System der Logik*, Leibzig: Brockhaus, 1828.]

Any assertion is said to be "in the mode of actuality", or to be "without modality", if, any only if, both the principle of contradiction, and the principle of excluded third equally apply to it. If two persons, neither of them saying anything about *possibility*, nor about *certainty*, asserts, one of them that it does, did, or will, rain at a stated time, and the other, that it does not, did not, or will not rain within that same time, then plainly one or other of them must be right and his opponent wrong; and they may be said to have spoken "in the mode of actuality", or "without modality".

Strictly speaking, however, and carrying the precision of our speech to a degree that no man could long maintain, there would be a difference between making an assertion "without modality" or "without modification", and making it "in the mode of actuality". The former would mean speaking only of the state of facts; the latter would mean that the speaker sought to convey the impression that he had considered the questions of whether he would have a right to say he was *sure* of speaking the truth, and of whether he ought not, on the other hand, to intimate the possibility of his being in error, and that his decision had been that he ought not to express himself in either way, but simply to indicate that he had come to the belief he expressed under a due sense of his responsibility.

In the cases of two of *Modes*, or determinations of Modality, that is, Possibility and Necessity, we have to distinguish Modes of *Reality* from Modes of ~~Evidence~~ *Reason*. That which there is little reason for believing to be true nor too much for believing to be false is *Rationally Possible*; we say in English that it "may be" so. This is, or seems to be, a radically different thing from the *real* possibility, for example, of amber's becoming electrified by slight friction against hair, which we say "can" be, thought perhaps only when the actual occurrence depends upon voluntary effort. Would you say that a circle or eclipse "can" cut an even number of times a nest of concentric spherical shells, or would you prefer to say that it *may* do so? Would, or would not, the "can" express a real, and the "may" a cognitive possibility? In the case of necessity we likewise have two different auxiliary verbs, *must* and *shall*, and it would seem desirable that the use of "shall" should be restricted to the expression of *Compulsion*, or Real Necessity, while "must" were confined to expressing the highest degree of Rational Evidence, or Ratiocinative Certainty. The overwhelming majority of languages are unprovided with any regular way of expressing the distinction between Real and Ratiocinative modality, immensely important as the distinction is. The cause of the confusion however, is obvious enough: when a man recognizes that a proposition rationally *must* be true, he finds he compulsively *shall* believe it; and consequently as soon as he finds he *can* doubt it, this sufficiently shows that the fact *may* be otherwise; and this constant association of a recognized outward "must" with his inwardly felt "shall", and of an inward "can" with an outward "may" allows primitive men, who are continually mistaking inward dreams for outward perceptions, to overlook entirely the momentous difference, just as they are continually liable to mistake fancies for facts.

The third kind of Modality, which many philosophers with much reason regard as the mere abstinence from any modification of an assertion, which, when spoken of as a variety of reality, is called *Actuality*, or in the case of thing, *Existence*. It is simply that character of an assertion which it must take when its utterer does not react at all upon, nor pay any attention to, his reasons for believing it. His mind being wholly occupied with the fact and the reality of it,—that is, with its being as he describes it, no matter what people may think,—he is not, for the moment, attending to his reasons for his belief in it, and nothing of the sort being in his mind at the moment, he naturally cannot express any ratiocinative modality at all. The result of course, is to concentrate all the force of his assertion upon the *real* modality of it. Now, in this respect, a simply assertory proposition differs just half as much from the assertion of a Possibility, or that of a Necessity, as these two differ from each other. For, as we have seen above, that which characterizes and defines an assertion of possibility is its emancipation from the Principle of Contradiction, while it remains subject to the Principle of Excluded Third; while that which characterizes and defines an assertion of Necessity is that it remains subject to the Principle of Contradiction, but throws off the yoke of the Principle of Excluded Third; and what characterizes and defines an assertion of Actuality, or simple Existence, is that it acknowledges allegiance to both formulae, and is thus just midway between the two rational "Modals", as the modified forms are called by all the old logicians.

On the other hand, the purely assertory proposition makes usually no reference either to compulsion or to power. Those old logicians, therefore, were right in denying that it involves any logical ~~modality~~ modification at all. For compulsion and power are matters of fact, like any others, and appear to belong to the substance of what is asserted and not at all to the profession of assurance, which is the question of logic, as the science of reasoning. Yet, on the other hand, the acknowledgement of subjection to the principles both of Contradiction and of Excluded Third would seem to have a great deal of importance in relation to reasoning.

2 Diversions of Definitions

R 650, July 20–23, 1910. Houghton Library. The relevance of including in the present collection the full transcription of Peirce's unpublished "Diversions of Definitions"—one among many of his late writings concerning the nature of definitions—lies in its section "Brief Exposition of the System of Existential Graphs." In that exposition, Peirce is motivated by what he notes in R 654 of the previous selection as well, namely the system's capacity of diagramming any fact however complicated. He also manages to explain the basic features of the Alpha part of the system in an admirably accessible and didactic fashion. His exposition is also one of the rare instances in which the key concept of the *nest of graphs* is defined (namely that Alpha graphs form a tree structure, see Introduction to LoF 1), as well as the eminently important *endoporeutic*, the outside-in interpretation of EGs, according to which "a nest sucks the meaning from without inwards unto its center, as a sponge absorbs water."

Other remarks of note include Peirce's testimony that his notion of the *scroll* preceded the notion of the *cut*, an observation that has important ramifications to the philosophy and development of logical notations, as it is now clear that other logical constants, including negation, will germinate from the sign of illation, represented by the scroll. Peirce repeatedly returns to this order of priority of the scroll over negation, the idea which in the graphical context of logic had emerged in "On Logical Graphs" (R 481; LoF 1) and which dates back to Peirce's development of the algebra of logic in the 1880s.

Peirce also purports to explain how in sound reasoning, over and above what is the case in degenerate and dialogical models of communication, the *triadic form* is ever-present. Triadic forms show up both in the semantics of the system and in applying the inferential rules of transformation in graphical systems of proofs. Even more importantly, they show up as soon as one performs analysis of the key diagrammatic elements involved in reasoning. It is those otherwise hidden elements in reasoning that the analysis conducted by the graphical method can bring to view. Peirce then seeks for a chemical analogy to an occurrence of the triadic form from the bonding known as *double decomposition*, and poignantly pens how "[t]he world hates sound reasoning as a child hates medicine"—a comment that a century later has not lost its edge.

No. 1. Of Number

'First', 'second', 'third' and other adjectives one of which is applied to a single member, or term, of a sequence, to express thereby the relative position of that member in the sequence, are universally called *ordinal* numbers; and certainly no exception can be taken to the adjective *ordinal*. Whether the noun it qualifies would better be 'number' or 'numeral' seems not to be an important question. Any of the adjectives 'two', 'three', 'four' etc. limiting a plural substantive, and signifying the multitude, or maniness, of the collection, or plural, that that substantive, in view of the context, denotes are very often called *cardinal numbers*; but I question the propriety of that designation. The adjective *cardinalis*, from *cardo*, a 'hinge', makes its appearance in Latin about the end of the IVth century. It is said in the Latin-English dictionaries to mean *chief, principal*; but it seems to me that its meaning is somewhat narrower and more definite. For instance, the learned Isidorus Hispalensis, who died early in April, A.D. 636, says in his great work usually called his *Origines* (lib.XIII, cap.xi.tertus 2) that there are four "principal" winds which blow from, the north, the south, the east, and the west.[1] Yet only a few lines lower he says there are only two "cardinal" winds, the north wind and the south wind.[2] Whether or no there be anything in the meteorology of Seville, the see of Isidorus, to suggest the notion I do not know. But the notion itself seems to be that the other winds may be regarded as resulting from shiftings, or turnings of these two somewhat as a door turns on its hinges. So it is with other uses of the word. Anybody who should, in the middle ages, have taught that the cardinal virtues, prudence, justice, temperance, and fortitude, are the most important of virtues, would I think have found himself in a pickle, since it is the theological virtues, faith, hope and charity, that St. Paul recommends as such. But St. Thomas Aquinas tells us that the four Aristotelian virtues are so-called because all others are varieties, or variations, of them. The expression "cardinal numbers" first appears in Priscian's grammar. He is thinking of the *words* only, and makes them to be *unus* (I feel sure he includes this, although I have not his book at hand with which to refresh my memory), *duo, tres, quattuor*, etc. I wish I had the book to make me quite sure that he includes *unus* among the cardinal numbers, since nobody but a mathematician, which he was not, would say that this is an adjective signifying a *multitude*; and therefore unless my memory fails me as to Priscian's marking it a cardinal number, it is certainly an inaccuracy to say that the cardinal numbers of Priscian are such adjectives. But I wish to point out that there is another use of these numbers, in which they may very well be regarded as the most "cardinal" of all numbers. The use of numbers begins with *counting*, which is the operation with which all books on arithmetic begin, always have begun, and always will begin. But in what precisely does this operation consist when it is performed with the utmost fullness and formality? Suppose, for our logical purpose, which has nothing to do with the improbability of the imaginary case, that there was a question of peace or a war which must involve all civilized nations for a generation, and that the only chance of avoiding it was to count certain things,—say certain ballots that had been deposited in the form of balls,—and to count them before a solemn congress of the nations. The supposition costs us nothing and is important as making the counting as solemn an affair as possible; and suppose it was you who had to do it. After the box containing the balls had been taken

---

[1] Ventorum quatuor principales spiritus sunt. Quorum primus ab Oriente *subsolanus*, a Meridie *Auster*, ab Occidente *Favonius*, a Septemtrione ejusdem nominis, ventus aspirat, habentes geminos hinc in de ventorum spiritus.
[2] Ex omnibus autem ventis duo cardinales sunt: *Septemtrio*, et *Auster*.

out of the safe where it had been under a separate lock for each nation, and the balls had been poured into one of two bowls on the table before you, how would you proceed? Suppose you would begin by holding up the second bowl with its inside turned toward the delegates so that they could see it was empty, and having set it down, would with a slender pair of tongs so formed as to grip a bell firmly without hiding it, take a ball out of the first bowl and putting it in the second one, would call out "One!" You would then transfer another ball in the same way and call "Two!" You surely would not say, "This transfer makes two balls in the receiving-bowl", because so many needless words would tend to derange your count. Then, supposing that after you had called out "Fifty-nine" you were to find that the first bowl was empty, you would hold it up so that its emptiness could be seen, and would say, "Gentlemen, fifty-nine is the number. Is it your pleasure that the count should be repeated?" The numbers that you would thus pronounce in counting, would be, according to my notion, primitive, or *cardinal*, numbers. They are not "parts of speech" of any recognized kind, unless it be that of interjections, which the grammarians of the middle ages, those ages when men were attentive to points of logic, never would recognize as *parts* of speech, because they are *entire* speeches; not *partes orationis*, but *orationes integrae*, characterizing the situation which calls them forth; and so are these numbers. I do not wish to look upon them from a linguistic point of view; but since counting is an experiment made to ascertain something, I wish if I can to make out exactly what the calling out of the numbers do toward that end. Now if you want to tell another person what you find out by any operation of counting, of course, you and he must possess a language in common, just as you must in order to tell him anything else. But if you only wish to use the result in your own private inquiries, any series of sounds with which you are perfectly familiar will do as well. Suppose, for example, you wish to know which of two series is numerically the longer, you can just as well go over first one and then the other, pronouncing for each number, as you go, the successive feet of any piece of poetry that is sufficiently long, such as

'Tis sweet | to view | from half | past five | to six
Our long | wax can- | dles with | short cot- | ton wicks
Touched by | the lamp- | lighter's | Prome- | thean art
Start in- | to light | and make | the light | er start
etc. etc. etc.[3]

---

3 [The verse appears in *Rejected Addresses: or, The new theatrum poetarum* by James Smith and Horace Smith, London: John Murray, 1879, p. 89.]

Now, Reader, convince yourself that you are a sane human being, into whom God has breathed His Breath of Reason, by forthwith, starting from what has been shown you, and drawing up a full statement, without any superfluous admixture, of just what it is that the numbers I call cardinal are good for! If you don't, you will carry about with you the consciousness of being, as yet, a sham, or, at least, a half-made member of the race of men.—But hold one moment! I will present you with a valuable tool, to help you to work with the necessary precision. It is a sort of simplified grammar, or more precisely, it is an apparatus which performs the same office that grammatical syntax does, but which instead of appealing to the mind through the ear, appeals to it by that more intellectual organ, the Eye. For there is no other way of representing complicated facts that begins to be so expressive as the way a *diagram* represents it. Compare for example all one could possibly carry away from a half-hour's oral description of a tract of country with the idea one could gain of it from three minutes study of a good map,—supposing of course, that one is habituated to the use of maps. The latter idea would far surpass the former; and yet it would not nearly so much surpass the description as the knowledge one would gain from a half-hour's study of the map would surpass that which could be gained from a five hours' oral account;—to say nothing of the relative fatigue. Well, what I propose to put you into possession of is a way of making a diagram of any fact you please, and to this I shall add a way of writing a description of a fact somewhat resembling an algebraical expression. The diagrammatic method I call the ~~system~~ method of *Existential Graphs*; the other I call my *Universal Algebra of Logic.*

Brief Exposition of the System of Existential Graphs

I mean to make this statement as simple and intelligible as I can, without aiming to make it absolutely accurate. I prefer to correct any minute inaccuracies in a second more formal statement.

You are to take a piece of paper and call one side of it "the sheet of assertion", for that is the name by which I shall call it. Perhaps I should have done better to call it the sheet of *affirmation*, since whatever state of things you represent on this page, you will be understood to affirm as existing somewhere, or, at least, consistently to make believe to affirm. You may use any shapes that can be drawn or written or partly drawn and partly written, provided they be not among those to which fixed meanings are attached in this exposition, and may give them such significations as you like. I would suggest the astronomical signs for your use, since they are easily written and will not have any fixed meanings in the system. I mean such as these ♈ ♉ ♊ ♋ ♌ ♍ ♎ ♏ ♐ ♑ ♓ ☾ ☿ ♀ ☉ ♂ ♃ ♄ ≈ □ △ ☍ ☌ ☊ ☋. Egyptian hieratic and Chinese signs will afford a rich plenty. Any shape or combination of shapes that put on the Sheet of Assertion would be an assertion, I term a *graph*, and your act of putting it on any surface by writing or drawing or a mixture of the two I express by saying that you *scribe* that sign on that *area*; and the result of doing so, that is any single one among the inexhaustible multitude of possible embodiments of the graph, I call a graph-instance. To illustrate the utility of this distinction, I call your attention to the fact that we ~~usually~~ most commonly use the word "word" with a meaning analogous to that of "graph",—for we say that hounds, beagles, curs, mastiffs, spaniels, terriers, poodles, and an incredible variety of other stocks are alike included under the *single word*, dog. Yet when an editor asks me to write him ~~an article~~ a paragraph of a hundred words on some subject, he means to count every occurrence of "the" as a separate word. He does not mean *words*, but *word-instances*; but in this case the value of brevity outweighs that of accuracy. In the case of graphs and graph-instances, it is quite the other way. Suppose you were to take ⊙ to mean that the sun shines and ↷ to mean it is cold. Then if you scribe both on the Sheet of Assertion, you will assert both. For separate graphs are quite independent of one another, and your scribing both does not commit you to the sun shining and its being cold *at the same time*. You are always at liberty to erase a graph scribed on the sheet of assertion. (I use the expression "erase a graph" meaning that I undo the act of scribing it; for the expression cannot possibly mean anything else.)

I now pass to a second feature of the system. Any line that you may draw, that shall be *fine*, not thick, and that simply returns into itself so as to have no extremity, in short, an oval, and having a graph or graphs enclosed within it, is called a *Cut*, and is neither said to be "scribed" nor is regarded as lying on the surface, but as being cut *through* the sheet, and the area within (in defiance, very likely, of geometrical impossibility) is considered as belonging to the *reverse face* of the sheet, and as forming no part of the sheet of assertion, although *the whole*, i.e. the cut and its "area" or enclosed surface with whatever is scribed thereon, which whole is called an "enclosure", is regarded as being on the sheet of assertion, and *as asserting that the graph on its area is not entirely true unless that area itself contains another enclosure the graph on whose area is true, which may be the case, such enclosure having the same signification as if it were on the sheet of assertion except that it declares false all that in the latter situation it would declare true*. I will presently give an example or two to make this rule perfectly clear. But I must add that any area may contain cut, and enclosure, and that the interpretation is in all cases the same. The area on which[4] a cut or enclosure is, is called the *place*, as

---

4 [Alt.:] [...] a cut or enclosure is, is called the *place*, as contradistinguished from the *area*, of that cut or enclosure. For the cut or enclosure is *in* its place, but *encloses* its area.

contradistinguished from the *area* of it, which is within. The cut or enclosure is *in* its *place*, while its *area* is within it.

Fig. 1   Fig. 2

Let ♃ mean it thunders, ♀ it has lightened, ♅ it is cloudy. The graph of Fig. 1 asserts that it does not thunder, and if this is true so also must be the graph of Fig. 2, which declares that it does not both thunder and lighten. It at once suggests itself that any graph may be inserted into the area of a cut whose place is the sheet of assertions. And this can be demonstrated as follows. The first step is that you are at liberty without danger of error to erase everything on the field of assertion. For this is as much as to cease saying anything. Now to assert anything is a positive act. To keep silence, and cease asserting anything involves no falsity. For to utter falsity is positive act. Next two disconnected graph-instances are independent; and therefore whatever transformation you would be free to make in one of them if it were alone on the sheet, you are free to make when the other is there with it. The third step is that if it will result in no falsity to change a given graph scribed on the sheet of assertion into a given second graph, then if the second graph is scribed in the area of a cut whose place is the sheet of assertion, it will result in no falsity to change it into the first graph. For the former of these changes might produce a falsity unless every possible state of things in which the first graph would be true were a state of things in which the second would be true, or, in other words, unless in every state of things either in the first state of things were false or else the latter were true. Consequently, that first change not involving any falsity if the second state of things is not true the first cannot be true. Which is as much as to say that since a graph scribed on the area of a cut whose place is the sheet of assertion is thereby declared to be false, it follows that in such area the second graph can be changed into the first. Now we may regard a blank place as a graph

---

To say that a proposition is false, means precisely that if it is true everything is true. For if everything is true there is no limitative truth in what is called truth, but every thing is mere ~~appearance~~ seeming without reality which is as much as to say, that nothing is true, the very idea of truth being that it distinguishes some mere seeming from reality. Therefore to deny that a proposition is true is the same as to say, and one means by it that to call that proposition true amounts in view of what *is* true, to fail to admit that every truth forbids us to call its ~~denial~~ contradictory true, when were it not for that there would be no distinction between seeming and real being. This is not very clearly put, I must admit, [end]

expressing a truism or matter of course. Therefore because every graph on the sheet of assertions can be altered into such a null graph, or blank, it follows that on the area of a cut whose place is the sheet of assertion, any graph whatever may be inserted without introducing any falsity.

In order to take the next step, I must introduce a new bit of terminology. I call every graph that is on the area of a cut whose place is the sheet of assertion a graph *once enclosed*, and every graph that is on the area of a cut whose place is once enclosed (that is which place is the area of a cut whose place is the sheet of assertion) a graph *twice* enclosed; and in general whatever positive whole number n may be, I will call a graph that is on the area of a cut that is n times enclosed, a graph $1+n$ (or, more than n) times enclosed. Furthermore, I will call a graph that is enclosed any even number of times an *evenly enclosed* graph, and a graph that is enclosed any odd number of times an *oddly enclosed* graph. Now, then, armed with this aid to thought and engine of expression, you can easily demonstrate that any graph-instance that is evenly enclosed and that is physically capable of removal may be erased by you without prejudice to your veracity while in any oddly enclosed area you may as surely permit yourself to scribe what graph you will.

And now I am going to point out in your hands a right more efficient that those I have mentioned, though of course you never, without further information, either from observation or from memory, must add any assertion that is not expressed upon the sheet already. But I am going to show you another way of repeating what has been substantially asserted already. In order to do this, it will be convenient, though quite unnecessary, and perhaps you will mind needless, to make another addition to our glossary of technical terms. Namely, if there be a collection, i.e. a definite, individual plural of cuts, of which one is placed in the sheet of assertion, and another encloses no cut at all, while every other cut of the series has the area of another cut of this collection for its place, and has its area for the place of still a third cut of this collection, then I call that collection a *nest*, and the areas of its different cuts *its successive areas*, and I number them ordinally from the sheet of assertions as the *origin*, or zero, with an increase of unity for each passage across a cut of the nest inwards that one can imagine a moving point to make some insect to make if it never passes out of an area that it has once entered.

For example, in Fig. 3 there are five nests as follows:

1. One of 5 areas or 4 cuts A–B–C–E–F,
2. ⎫
3. ⎬ Three of 4 areas or 3 cuts, each: ⎰ A–B–C–D, A–B–H–I, A–B–H–J,
4. ⎭
5. One of 3 areas, or 2 cuts, A–B–G.

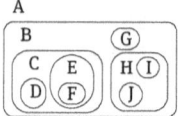

Fig. 3

Now the liberty which I wish to point out, leaving you to demonstrate it for yourself (though you might postpone doing this until the Existential Graphs are as fully explained as I propose here to explain them, when you may demonstrate this, as you may any other demonstrable proposition by their machinery), is this: *If you have a right to scribe a graph on the place of a cut, you have a right to scribe it on its area*; whence it follows that any graph that is scribed on any area may be *iterated*, or repeated, on any higher-numbered area of the same nest, and may equally be "de-iterated", as my term is, from any higher-numbered area of the nest; that is to say, if a graph is scribed on two areas of the same nest (with similar *ligatures*, a feature of the system I have not yet described), the instance that is on the more inward area of the nest may be erased. This right may be expressed by saying that the interpretation of existential graphs is *endoporeutic*, that is proceeds inwardly; so that a nest sucks the meaning from without inwards unto its center, as a sponge absorbs water. Yet I must not leave this simile standing on my page without remarking that it has absolutely no element of truth in it except the mere endoporeusis, or inward-going. For instead of proceeding in one uniform flow, as the soaking of the water does, it is much liken a march to a band of music, where every other step only is regulated by the arsis or beat of the music, while the alternate steps go on of themselves. For it is only the iteration into an evenly-enclosed area that depends upon the outer occurrence of the iterated graph, the iteration into an oddly-enclosed area being justified by your right to insert whatever graph you please into such an area, without being strengthened or confirmed in the least by the previous occurrence of the graph on an evenly-enclosed area. So the analogy to a march is pretty close. But if anybody were to find fault with the system for expressing truth endoporeutically,—as if we opened a closet to whisper it in, instead of speaking out and ever further out, I should be disposed to admit that is a poetical fault. But I had difficult enough conditions ~~in seeking to construct~~ to fulfil in constructing the system, without considering purely esthetical points in its essential features. If anybody will construct a system which does all this does with rules of permissible changes as simple as the rules of this system, and with its other merits, and can give his system, besides all that, any merit whatever that this system has not, he will find me the very earliest of all men to proclaim its superiority over my own, if he will only make me acquainted with it in time to have that privilege.

I am now going to introduce another bit of nomenclature. Before I had the concept of a cut, I had that of two cuts, which I drew at one continuous movement as shown in Fig. 4.

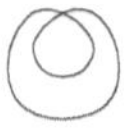

Fig. 4

This I called a *scroll*, and the areas of the outer and inner cuts respectively I called the *outer* and *inner close*.

I shall use these two expressions in enunciating another permission to modify graphs.

Namely, it is permitted to you to draw a scroll on any evenly-enclosed area, without it having any graph in either close. It is not permissible to draw a single cut on such an area, unless a false graph be at once enclosed in it, or else one be at once inserted in it by iteration according to the rule. You will be able to see for yourself why an empty scroll can be drawn while an empty cut must not. It follows, of course, from this permission that from an oddly-enclosed area any scroll whose inner close is vacant can be removed.

I am now about to bring to your notice the last but one of those features of the system that are Cardinal. It is [the] last one that will ordinarily be required; and I shall not set forth here the very last but quite slightly, since I really do not think I am a complete master of it myself. There will remain some little features which I shall expound because they are indispensable, although, being but modifications of the Cardinal features, the briefest statements of them will be sufficient.

But first of all, in order that you may more readily comprehend the penultimate feature, for though you will laugh when you find how simple it is, you would hardly at once discover all there is in the system without this little introduction, I must tell you what I have aimed to do, in constructing it. For of course, one can comprehend no apparatus until one fully comprehends its purpose.

Its purpose is to aid one in talking to himself. Have you ever read either of two little books by Max Müller published by the Open Court Co. at a quarter each[?] That is to say, that is the price in thick paper covers; but they are worth binding. What most struck me in reading them,—their principal point is stated in each; but it is the one on the nature of language which is the best of the two, though both are richly worth reading. Though their doctrine is little more than half true,—what chiefly struck me, I say, was the singular ignorance they betray Müller, like a good many men who begin by swallowing whole the philosophy of their teachers without sticking to it afterwards as if they were glued to it, was pretty well along in life before he found out that the medieval scholastics went deeper into the nature of thought and things than he had supposed. Nearly the same thing happened to me. Like Müller, I was soaked through and through with Kant, and knew the *Critik der reinen Vernuft* almost by heart in both editions, when something in Kant led me to a study which opened up almost exactly what Müller found too; and a more famous man than he made the same discovery. I mean Leibniz, who, beginning, if not as a disciple of Hobbes, at any rate at about Hobbes's stand-point, gradually as his studies deepened, approached nearer and nearer to being a Scholastic Realist as I am. Had he known all that has since been brought to demonstration, he certainly must either have come to where I stand now, or passed beyond my position to one whose truths are hidden from me. But what I was about to say was that as soon as I found out that the scholastics were deeper than I had supposed, I devoted all the time I could spare to the study of their tomes, with interruptions due to the difficulty of obtaining those books. But really not many days of serious study would be required to save a ~~student~~ writer from such wild statements as Müller makes about medieval doctrines. He also falls into great errors of psychology, but they are mostly of the nature of exaggerations. The kernel of his doctrine is more than half true, or a mighty good half, at any rate, is both true and of the highest importance. He has done as well as a man could do who should undertake to solve one of the great problems of linguistic with absolutely no other training in the subject than was involved in learning to talk the simplest vernacular dialect of his mother-tongue. To say then, that the little books I speak of are worth reading is high praise.

When I was a young man, I often used to meet with the statement that there are three "parts of the soul", or three departments, or elements, of thought; and this is substantially true, although the lines were never accurately drawn between the three. Since then, certain "Profs", who pull long faces and frown, put on airs of authority and use other mountebank tricks to cow the judgment of the public, seem to have been bitten by some rabies for attacking Form in philosophy, generally; and in particular, the number three, which enters quite frequently into the forms of logic and of almost every branch of pure mathematics seems to have a virtue almost mystical in moving their rage.

The simplest form of consciousness is Feeling. Apparently, we are always, except perhaps in deep sleep, in a state of feeling, which is as much as to say that we have a Feeling. Every Feeling is, in itself, absolutely simple. To say that it is compound means that it is or could be, produced by concurrent circumstances, each of which would produce a Feeling. We may learn to recognize a feeling as thus a resultant of other feelings. But, in itself, as we can equally learn to recognize, the immediate consciousness is absolutely simple. I sometimes ask myself whether feeling is not the only form of consciousness. For though we have other forms of mental life, and know that we have them, it sometimes seems to me that without feeling, we should not know them. However, this question is merely a psychological one, and I desire to keep clear of psychology. For logic must not rest on psychology since psychology rests more directly upon logic than does any other science. Of course, phenomena and even inferences which antecede all science and are part of the absolutely indubitable common-sense of all men do not form any part of science of any kind. No research has ever been made into their truth and never will be.

So then, since it may be a question whether we have any directly and primitively relational form of consciousness, I will content myself with pointing out that we have relational elements of mental life; and in the first place there are some of them in which the relation is of that simplest kind that subsists between two correlates, like the relation signified by ordinary transitive verbs, such as *strike*. Of these I will first mention acts of muscular exertion. I used twice a week to lift a thousand pounds several times for my health; and as I never, I suppose, was a man up to the average of strength, it was a marked experience; and I may mention by the way that I found it not only highly beneficial in the long run, but remarkably exhilarating. There was first the exact adjustment of my person, then a relatively long time,—I do not know how many seconds,—of gathering my strength. Then, I would, as it were, give the word and the weight was lifted while I felt the pressure coming upon almost every part of my body. But I never could make out clearly any sense of lifting, apart from the phenomena I have mentioned. It was, however, plainly a mental act, though I suppose there is no precise scientific distinction between a mental phenomenon and a phenomenon of the nervous system. Of course, I knew I performed the act; but how can I tell whether I should have known but by my sensations. I once, by the way, saw a boy all whose nerves of sensation (and they alone) were paralyzed on one side of his face, while on the other all the nerves of motion were paralyzed but none of those of sensation. He made apparently any motion on the former side that one chose to ask him.

I say that an action of a man on something independent of him, if such there be and we believe there is, and cannot help believing it, is distinct from a Feeling. For a Man's having a Feeling is not in itself, inconsistent with his being the only actually and independently existing thing in the universe, since the Feeling is not independent of him, and nothing else is involved in Feeling, and besides a Feeling is not an individual object but only a *Kind*, a *May-be*. There is the special capacity for that special feeling; but this again is only a May-be or Can-be. But an action takes place between two distinct Existents. But you may ask, what if a man acts on himself? If you mean inhibits his own action, that is, reduces the energy of it (for if he were utterly to prevent any modification of it from coming into the world [of] actualities, there would be no action at all), I admit that that is something, but it is not an *action* in the sense I am now using that word (namely, as something which involves two independent existents only, since the man must have created a somewhat independent entity, when he made that which it costs him *effort* to inhibit. Now let us postpone implicating our discourse with plural phenomena, until we have done with dual phenomena. If not all of man's actions upon himself, at least, a great part of them, I think you will yourself, Reader, pronounce to be *plural* and not dual, when we shall have reviewed the characteristics of such actions; and yet I do not venture to say that a man never acts dually upon himself. That I should think extremely rash. A man goes to bed a little later than usual, and drowsy in the extreme. But he bethinks him that he has no alarm, mechanical or human, to waken him for the early train he has to take in the morning; and he *says to himself* "you have *got* to be awake at exactly half past five: mind you do it, or there will be the very devil to pay! You must! You know it, yourself!" and, sure enough, at 5:25 he awakes with a start, and pulls his watch from under his pillow with alarm. Or a man who in the heat of conversation is apt to let fall tactless remarks that his better judgment condemns, one night as he is reviewing the events of the day, recalls with shame a certain speech he made and says to himself, "You fool, how often must I tell you not to say such things. Now tomorrow you are to have an interview in which you will be sure to do the same thing again. Just think carefully over the reasons for not talking so. A parrot would know better. Think over now what you *will* say. Go through it thrice, for a good habit can just as well [sic.] in imagination as in actual experience; or rather as well in the experience of imagination as in the experience of *outward* action". He does as he is told on the spot, and behaves as he really wishes the next day, and thus begins a reformation of his habit. Now without referring to the habit-forming, the giving oneself a "talking-to", in such wise as to influence one's conduct on a foreseen occasion is exactly—as far as I can see, at least, and in as sound a psychology as one needs for the purpose of reasoning right, in general,—analogous to the self-influence to wake up at a given hour. I make no pretence to knowing anything about what is hypnotism and what not, I only say that in both cases alike the man exerts himself to overcome a resistance, and acts upon himself: just as he would upon a son or a pupil. Still he acts upon a second person. If he talks in words, he probably addresses himself in the grammatical second person, and even if he does not, *he means it*, just the same. That is to say, he intends to act upon himself,—upon his *other* self, the self of the morrow, the self of the next minute or two, the self who meekly takes the rating that the self of the first person administers. We are conscious of their being two. I used to think they were the two sides of the brain; but only reflexion, it seems to me that that hypothesis is uncalled for. It suffices for me that they are two attitudes of mind, and two persons within one soul. I often use the expression *brute will*, in speaking of this "part of the soul", or department of our mentality; and I had better state just why I select that phrase. I use the word *will* in order to express my general agreement with those who regard Volition as one of the most general categories of our life, although if it were not for expressing that general assent, I should like the word Action better; and I use the adjective *Brute* to show that I do not include the having a *purpose* as belonging to this department of mentality, inasmuch as I think that purpose implies a third reference; and I think that the fundamental differences between the three departments lie in their differences of Form, and that these differences of Form consist in this, that in the first place the element of Feeling has but one reference, namely the Quality of the Feeling, all else that is predicated of it such as its Intensity, its Composition, the Likeness or Unlikeness between one Feeling and another belonging not to Feeling itself but to the thoughts which have about Feeling which spring up when two are compared, these thoughts being quite veracious, but attributed to the wrong subject; that in the second place Action, or Brute will, has two references, that which exerts it and that which resists it, exertion and resistance being the same phenomenon, just as striking and getting struck are, only their references or subjects are transposed; and finally that Habit of Thought, which is mental habit, involves three references as I shall now proceed to show you.

Search me out the very most ruinously thoughtless of boys, who as he approaches the age of sixty will have lost the last spark of his boyhood, without having gained the first fibre of man-hood,—you will most probably find him among those lads whose native powers of thought had been the most vigorous,—and even he must be able to see that the faculty which has served to elevate man above all the rest of the fauna of our globe is the power of self-control. Let us try then,—as if we were chemists of the mind,—to analyze that power and isolate its basic element. Max Müller's theory, hasty and crude though it certainly is,—the theory that we first speak, and then clothe in speech the meaning of what we had at first spoken without thought, will perhaps help our gropings.

The most striking ingredient of self-control, and certainly an indispensable one, is that giving of a command to, and obedient fulfillment by, a future self, that I have already noticed. But a logical microscope is required to detect in such an act anything more than dyadic action; while Reasoning, to which appeal is usually made in an endeavor for self-control, is manifestly a triadic phenomenon, as I shall show you. Meanwhile let it suffice to note that a syllogism is a relation between two premisses and a conclusion. The simplest form of syllogism is the *modus ponens* by which from a consequence and its antecedent we infer its consequent. It can do no harm to show how such an inference is performed by Existential Graphs. Let ♀, as before affirm that it lightens, and ♃ that it will thunder. Then our premisses are thus shown together: 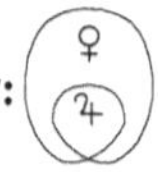 ♀. We first deiterate ♀ getting 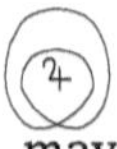 ♀. But the scroll, or double cut, with nothing to fill out its outer close, always may be made to collapse and disappear, when we have, ♃ ♀, and then erasing the evenly enclosed ♀ which is beside our purpose, we get ♃, or it will thunder. Thus the inference is analyzed into three distinct steps, of which the first is plainly triadic, requiring two distinct conditions, namely that a graph-instance should be in an area, and that a second instance of the same graph should be outside that area not enclosed in any cut not enclosing the other, whereupon we are permitted to erase an oddly enclosed graph-instance. The *modus tollens*, by which from a consequence and the falsity of its consequent we infer the falsity of its antecedent appears in Existential Graphs as involving precisely the same triadic step and otherwise as being even simpler than the *modus ponens*. Thus from 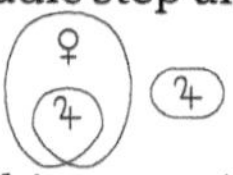 we infer by the same first step as in the other case 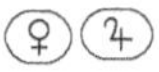. But now nothing remains but to take the third step, without any occasion to take the second. But then it must be remembered that necessary reasoning never does really advance our knowledge. For as Kant said, the only ground for the acceptance of any of its conclusions is that we have already asserted that very thing already; so that it is too late to be cautious about it now. To lock the barn door when the occasion when the horse may have been stolen is past, is a reprehensible futility.

I will give an instance of a reasoning one degree more complex than the last. In addition to the two characters, or incomplex graphs that we have already used, let us employ ☿ to assert "The sky is clear"; and let us affirm the following:

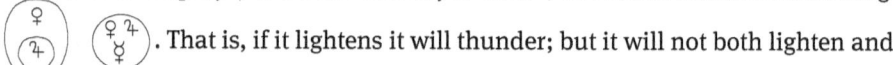

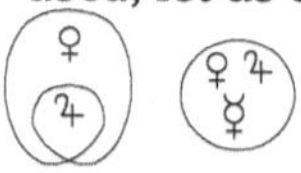 . That is, if it lightens it will thunder; but it will not both lighten and thunder with a clear sky. Now by the rule of iteration, we have right to scribe the following:

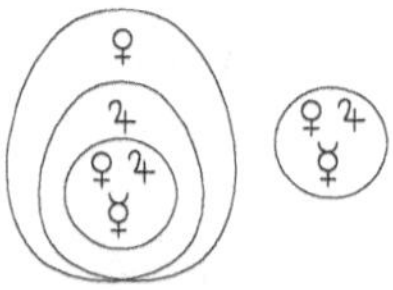 Whence, by deiteration, we obtain, first [5] 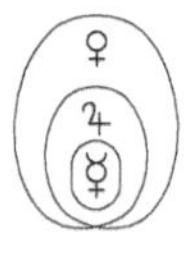 and then, by the same rule [6] 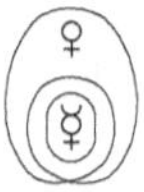

and finally, by the collapse of the double cut, , or, it will not lighten with a clear sky.

5 [The rule of erasure is also applied.]
6 ["By the same rule" Peirce means erasure implicit in the previous transformation.]

One often says, "I put two and two together", meaning that he draws a simple inference, which might, however, have been missed if he had considered the second fact as a part of the first. The expression is inaccurate and would better apply to an operation such as the chemists call "double decomposition". This consists in the interchange of two analogous constituents of two substances when the two residual constituents are also analogous.

The simplest example I can give in illustration of this proposition will necessarily involve a fictitious, or arbitrary hypothetical element, since I know of no true double decomposition between binary compounds. Moreover, I may as well confess at this my first occasion for doing so, that my scientific information, besides being limited in scope, as everybody's must be, more or less, is for the most part about twenty years behind the times, owing to my having been, during that time, too poor to get any books at all or to mingle with men of science. It is true that for strictly logical purposes, a fictitious example is sometimes as good as a real one; but it is a deathly regret, a killing regret to me, that I am entirely unable to render my writings as useful as it would be, if the givers of libraries cared as much to enable a teacher of right reason to get books as they do to enable the shop-boys and shop-girls, whose lighter needs I suppose are more like what their own once were, to procure "reading matter". I do not need "reading-matter". I find it more plentiful than fraud is, if that be possible. But my heart is breaking for the raw-material for my exposition of sound reasoning. The world hates sound reasoning as a child hates medicine.

In order to illustrate double decomposition, I wish to suppose a mixed solution of the iodide of lithium, LI, and fluoride of potassium (kalium), KI. But unfortunately I am not well acquainted with any solution of either of the salts. To be sure, I know well enough what are called aqueous solutions of them; but as every chemist knows, there is little of either salt in such solutions. If they are dilute, the one contains little but "ions" of L and I, together with electrons, and the other little put ions of K and of F with electrons. When this statement was first broached, it was scouted by many chemists, because they misunderstood it to mean that the solution of LI contained little but metallic lithium and iodine, and that of KF little but metallic potassium and free fluorine gas; and they were quite right in thinking *that* to be as wild a fable as any that the alchemist had ever imagined. For in those early days when Buchanan's administration was just beginning, when the Indian Mutiny had just broken out, when people were hardly yet puzzling their heads over Buckle's astounding assertion that just about so many people commit suicide every year, almost with the regularity of a physical law, and when physical science was in an even more benighted condition than it is today, very few people realized that the doctrine of ions was not a hypothesis, but that Clausius, in enunciating it, had accompanied it with a proof as nearly demonstrative as a physical proof is susceptible of being made. People then took it for granted that the metallic properties of pure Lithium and pure Potassium belonged essentially to those kinds of matter instead of being due to the electrostriction of the great cloud of electrons with which they were pressed down. It was not until fourteen years later that the word *electron* was invented and although Helmholtz had remarked that Faraday's experiments with voltameter and other electrolysis in the circuit together proved that there was such a thing as an atom of electricity. I do not think that physicists regarded it as proved, if atom were understood in anything like a literal sense; and I cannot think it was, myself. It was not until the Zeemann effect was discovered in 1896, and developed and discussed, that its agreement with the theory of electrons as worked out by Lorentz in 1880, convinced everybody.

It would be quite irrelevant to our subject to consider further the nature of ionization. I have said too much about it already. I will simply suppose that we have a liquid which dissolves both LI and KF without decomposing them. No doubt there are such liquids.

Those two kinds of molecules flying about in vast numbers will, no doubt, often encounter, one of them one of those of that the iodine of a molecule of LI will exchange its lithium for the potassium of some molecules of KF.[7] How often that will occur will depend upon many circumstances, such, for example, as the temperature, which means the speed with which the molecules rush about, and especially how fast the molecules of the two kinds of salts wander among those of the solvent as well as the speed with which the two atoms of the same molecule move relatively to each other. But for our purpose we have to separate all the influential circumstances into two classes, those which alter during the progress of the reaction and those which do not. The latter can all be lumped as determining one constant factor of the speed with which the reaction speeds. The other class of circumstances are the only ones which can give any trouble; and fortunately the mixing of two solutions of salts which only react by double decomposition does

---

[7] **[Alt.:]** [...] that the iodine of the LI will exchange its lithium for the potassium of the KF. How often that will happen will depend upon any circumstances and among them upon the temperature (that is, upon the velocities with which the two kinds of salt-molecules rush about among the solvent-molecules, and the velocities of the two atoms with instances relating to any pair of such molecules). In addition to that it will happen with a frequency proportional to the number of molecules of LI per centimetre cube of the solution and also with a frequency proportional to the number of molecules of KF per centimetre cube of the solution. The frequency of the event on the whole will be equal to the product of these three factors. The action for each pair of molecules that do act will consist in the conversion of $\genfrac{(}{)}{0pt}{}{L\ I}{F\ K}$ into $\genfrac{}{}{0pt}{}{L+I}{F+K}$.

If there were nothing to counteract the tendency this would go on, although more and more slowly, in consequence of two of the four influential circumstances that do change during the reaction; namely the concentrations of the mixed solution in LI, in KF, in LF, and KI. [end]

not occasion any sensible change of temperature, supposing the two solutions are of the same temperature before being mixed. This happy fact leaves but three factors of the frequency of the single actions depending on the quantities of the two substances on which the action depends. Let q and p be the quantities of the Ll and the KF respectively. Then if k is the third factor which is constant, and t is the time, we shall have

$$D_t q = D_t p = -kpq.$$

The quantities are of course to be reckoned in chemical equivalents as their units. Supposing then that p and q are not equal, let a be the excess of the KF over the Ll; and this excess must remain throughout the action. We have, then, the equation

$$D_t p = -kp(a + p).$$

the integral of which is

$$e^{ak(t-t_0)} = \frac{(1 + \frac{a}{p})}{(1 + \frac{a}{p_0})} = \frac{q}{p} \div \frac{q_0}{p_0}.$$

As the reader cannot be supposed to be so familiar with numbers as to see, at a glance, what sort of relation is here expressed, I will take an example. I will suppose that in the first one hundredth of a second after the solutions are mixed, one *per cent* of the Ll is used up, and that there is at first 101 equivalents of KF to every 100 of Ll. Then the following table shows in what times given *per centages* of the original salts would be used up, *if there were no reversed* action.

Appendix

Exposition of the System of Existential Graphs[8]

Although this system is, I believe, the very simplest of all possible ways of expressing every assertion, yet, owing to the extreme exactitude that will be requisite in this Exposition, I find it convenient to employ in it nearly two hundred abridged expressions; and though each of these will be clearly explained on its first occurrence, yet I am sure that an alphabetical glossary of them will be welcomed. Indeed, I myself sometimes refer to it, to remind me of the microscopically exact meaning of some expression, although I have constantly been employing the system for nearly fourteen years (i.e. since January 1897).

However, there are reasons why I should be confused when another person would have no such difficulty, for I remember debating in my mind whether I would give an expression one meaning or another, and still oftener whether I would use one name or another for a given feature of the system. The glossary will be found at the end of the essay. I should recommend cutting it out, so as always to have it in sight.

The whole system may be stated in a nutshell as follows.

First, you begin by selecting a surface of paper to contain what I call the *Sheet of Assertion*, because the truth of the diagram which you will proceed to place upon this sheet you will assert or, more usually, make believe that you assert to whomsoever understandingly interprets it. This diagram will be *either written, or drawn, or partly written and partly drawn*; and in order to avoid the incessant repetition of these ten italized words, I shall adopt, as TT2 (i.e. technical term No. 2),[9] the verb *scribe* to signify after the manner of a verb the same action that the phrase of ten italicized words expresses participially. But hold: with all my talk about exactitude, I have wrongly defined the word scribe, since I shall not use this verb as to say that I scribe the very

---

8 [R 650, an earlier version of the first four manuscript pages of "Brief Exposition of the System of Existential Graphs", plus variants.]

9 [**Alt.:**] [...] I shall adopt, as TT2 (i.e. technical term, No. 2) the verb *scribe* to signify verb-wise that which these ten words express participially. But hold: with all my high talk about exactitude, I have blundered already, though all would have been right, instead of "This diagram will be *either written, or drawn*", etc., I had written: The design of this diagram will be *either*, etc. I might have made the correction without mentioning it; but I do not want to commit a blunder without your profiting by it. All such words as write, draw, speak, etc. have two different meanings or constructions. In the one use, that which is written, etc. is created thereby; in the other it is the cause, or model, of the production. Now that which I shall say is *scribed* is the model and not the product of that performance.

And while I am about it, I will take the opportunity of noting the eminently useful truth that Reality, or Real Being, has three Modes, or, as a grammarian might say, three Moods. There is, in the first place, the Mode of Actuality or Existence, which words differ only as the former is only applied to facts or their predicates, while the latter is confined to the subjects of facts (including the grammatical objects of actions). But a much better definition is that this Mode of Reality belongs exclusively to that which individual; that is, to that to which both the Principle of Contradiction applies and also the Principle of Excluded Middle, apply them how you will. The Principle of Contradiction is that of no real subject [is] both a predicate and its negative true. The Principle of Excluded Middle is that of no real subject is both a predicate and [its] negative false.

lines that appear on the paper. On the contrary, what I scribe is the meaning together with the form of the lines in so far as my way of expressing that meaning determines that form; so that if I were to repeat what I had scribed, I should not say that I had scribed two things but that I had scribed the same thing twice; and if the second time I were to shape my lines differently, but the difference were not one of which the rules of the system took any cognizance, I should still say I had scribed the same thing twice. If, however, the difference was one that must be taken account of in the interpretation by the rules, I should say that [I] had scribed two things which had the same meaning. I shall be able to state this more clearly when I have given some of the rules.

Essays
DEFINITION
9
1910 July 23
P.M. 1:45

Brief Exposition of the System of Existential Graphs.
I mean to make this statement as simple and intelligible as I can, without aiming to make it absolutely accurate. I prefer to correct any minute inaccuracies in a second more formal statement.

You are to take a piece of paper and call one side of it "the sheet of assertion"; for that is the name by which I shall call it. Perhaps I should have done better to call it the sheet of affirmation, since whatever state of things you represent on this page, you will be understood to affirm as existing somewhere, or at least, consistently to make believe to affirm. You may use any shapes that can be drawn or written or partly drawn and partly written, provided they be not among those to which fixed meanings are attached in this exposition, and may give them such significations as you like. I would suggest the astronomical signs for your use, since they are easily written and will not have any fixed meanings in the system. I mean such as these ♀ ☿ ♄ ♃ ♁ ♍

Essays
DEFINITION
10
1910 July 23
P.M. 2:15

♆ ♏ ♐ ♑ ♒ ♓ ⚹ ⚺ ☉ ☽ ♂ ♀ ♄ ⚶ * □ △ ⚸ ⚹ ⚵
Egyptian hieratic and Chinese signs will afford a rich plenty. Any shape or combination of shapes that put on the Sheet of Assertion would be an assertion, I term a graph, and the act of putting it on any surface by writing or drawing or a mixture of the two I express by saying that you scribe that sign on that area; and the result of doing so, that is any single one among the inexhaustible multitude of possible embodiments of the graph, I call a graph-instance. To illustrate the utility of this distinction, I call your attention to the fact that we most commonly use the word "word" with a meaning analogous to that of "graph", for we say that hounds, beagles, curs, mastiffs, spaniels, terriers, poodles, and an incredible variety of other stocks are alike included under the single word, dog. Yet when an editor asks me to write him an article paragraph of a hundred words on some subject, he means to count every occurrence of "the" as a separate word. He does not mean words

Two holograph pages (Harvard Peirce Papers, R 650).

3 [Reasoning, Logic and Action]

The following three short pieces gathered here preview Peirce's ideas on the nature of reasoning and its relation to logic, diagrammatic thought and action.

R 826, late 1910. Houghton Library. The first manuscript, titled "Some Reveries of a Dotard", reflects on the consequence relation between premises and conclusion of a reasoning. The notion of consequence is the model-theoretic one mentioned in the first paragraph as the "obvious character of all mathematical reasoning" where "the state of things" has to remain the same in the passage from the premises to the conclusion. This of course is the method that Peirce had frequently used since his 1880 "The Algebra of Logic" paper. In the second paragraph, he is led to summarise what philosophically speaking is the key question of logic. The reader finds him taking up the interconnected themes familiar from logical leading principles, justification of deduction, Bradley's regress, and the 'paradox' of deduction made famous by Lewis Carroll.

R 616, c.1906. Houghton Library. The second item, "An Appraisal of the Faculty of Reasoning", is estimated to have been written around 1906. Peirce talks about a diagram as a "concrete but possibly changing mental image of such a thing as it represents." He emphasises the "act of imagining", which instead of "drawing a diagram" or building a "model" is in fact the "essential thing to be performed." The model-building process, which he mentions at the end of R 654 of the previous chapter, follows the imaginary activity. The third step is the process of evaluation, in modern terms the determination of the truth-conditions of the graph-instances thus constructed.

R 1132, 1903; R 838, April 10, 1911, February 22, 1913. Houghton Library. The third segment ("[Intention, Resolution, and Determination]") is a constellation of three short pieces (R 1132 and two selections from R 838). First, we have a two-page draft from late 1903. In mentioning how the resolution to act is of the nature of a plan, and how such plans now come close to what Peirce means by a diagram, R 1132 puts a new twist on his notion of a diagram. This snippet is part of an early draft of Lecture 1, entitled "What Makes a Reasoning Sound?" of his 1903 *Lowell Lectures*, the series of eight lectures Peirce delivered in Boston in November and December (LoF 2). Second, a brief record of some of his late remarks on closely similar topics is included (R 838). Third, there is an example of Peirce's repeated late attempts to proceed with his treatise on three kinds of reasoning, likewise from R 838.

The early parts of the second selection (R 616) have been published in Carolyn Eisele's NEM IV, pages 217–219. The transcription of the first lecture of the *Lowell Lectures*, which is the one Peirce actually delivered, was published in EP 2, pages 242–257.

3.1 Some Reveries of a Dotard

[R 826] I have long ago abjured psychophysical psychology, by which I mean that study of the mind which is founded on psychophysics, or the scientific comparison of outward and inward experiences. My reason for abjuring it has, by no means, been due to any distrust of it. On the contrary, I most warmly approve of it, and admire it. My reason for abjuring it has been that my special study has been Logic. How has this circumstance so influenced me? I will explain. Logic is the science which aims to distinguish bad or weak reasoning from sound and assured reasoning. Now by reasoning I mean the passage of the mind from telling oneself that an assertion is true, to thinking that, because of that, and regardless of what else may be true, one ought, or almost ought, to tell oneself that another assertion is true; and by Logic I mean the science which endeavours to discover what ones of such judgments one ought to tell oneself because of telling oneself that another assertion is true are themselves really true. If the reader should ask, as he naturally might, why I did not more simply define reasoning as the passage from judging one state of things to be real to judging another state of things to be real, I should reply that,—to mention only one of reasons,—such simpler form of statement would overlook an obvious character of all mathematical reasoning. For in mathematical reasoning, at least the mind does not pass from the contemplation of one state of things to the contemplation of a different state of things. The state of things in which $(a + b)x = y$ is *itself* a state of things in which $ax + bx = y$; and indeed, it may be said that no kind of reasoning concludes that anything ought to be accepted as true in one state of things merely because something is admitted to be true in ~~an entirely~~ a quite different state of things.

Moreover, the simpler form in question does not so inevitably draw attention to the "ought", the sense of obligation, in reasoning,—not at all a moral obligation, but an obligation in reason,—which is present in reasoning, and is the very point upon which the curiosity of the logician has to be focussed. Why does one truth follow, whether certainly or with more or less approach to certainty, from another? There must be some reason, since everything does not follow. But if this reason states any truth not already stated in the original premisses, X, then the conclusion, Y, did not really follow from X taken alone. On the other hand, if the reason does not involve such a pertinent truth, it does not answer the question why Y follows from X. Besides, if there is any reason why Y follows from X, there must equally be a reason why Y should follow from X *with* this reason, any more than from X without the reason, and there must equally be a reason for this, and so on endlessly. Therefore, since we are unable to examine critically every one of an endless series of reasons, the only result of not being content with anything short of absolute certainty as to whether one thing follows from another, can only be the everlasting dissatisfaction, with which we have to put up as cheerfully as our dispositions allow.

3.2 An Appraisal of the Faculty of Reasoning

[R 616] A query lately appeared in these columns that seems worthy of being followed out. It was whether, in case a given planet were known to be the habitation of a race of high psychical development, and that in the direction of knowledge, it would be safely presumable that that race was able to reason as Man does.

Next after the laws of inanimate nature and after sense-perception, nothing works so uniformly and smoothly as the Instinct of the lower animals. A downright blunder on the part of Instinct is extremely rare, to say the least, while our reasoning goes entirely wrong and reaches conclusions quite contrary to the truth and unwarranted by its premises with such distressing frequency that an incessant watch has to be maintained against these lapses. As for small divergences from strict logic, they are to be found in the majority of human inferences. We may as well acknowledge that Man's self-flattery about his "reason", though we all indulge in it, is prodigiously exaggerated. Reason itself winks satirically in its boasting, and broadly hints at its own mendacity; and yet were some divinity to offer to exchange any man's logical faculty for that "Intuition" that is usually attributed to women,—the Intuition premised reaching, however, the same pitch of perfection as the Instinct of bees and seals, or ever so much higher, how many, think ye, would close with the offer? Hastily to conclude that such an exchange would result in making its subject appear as a fool would be simply to furnish a new example of Reason's blundering. Far from that, it would surely enhance the transformed individual's reputation for sound judgment. If one had it in his power to collect a numerous sample of the men that are today known and honored for their intellect throughout the better informed classes of Europe and American,— only taking care not to draw too many from the ranks of exact science,—and, having withal authority to test their reasoning powers, were to set to each of them the task of reasonably proving or disproving a given promising scientific hypothesis, one would certainly find that a notable percentage of these justly respected minds would not know at all how to go to work. Not a few of them, for example, would begin, as we have many a time seen just such men begin, by studying with promiscuous assiduity the facts upon which the hypothesis had been based, instead of beginning, as they ought, with the study not of the facts, but of the hypothesis, in order to ascertain what observable consequences of the truth of the hypothesis, in case it were true, would contrast with the consequences of its falsity, in case it were false; and only thereafter turning to the facts, to examine them, not in a promiscuous way, but only in these pertinent respects. When one's purpose is to produce a reasonable hypothesis, it is right to begin by immersing oneself in the study of the facts until the mind is soaked through and through with the spirit of their interrelations; but when one has to estimate the ascertainable truth in a hypothesis already presented, it is the hypothesis that should take precedence in one's inquiry. The experiment supposed would not, however, be an altogether satisfactory test of a man's reasoning power, partly because the task set is too special and peculiar, and partly because a man who had been trained in testing hypotheses would at once set to work in the right way even though he merely followed a rule of thumb, without at all knowing why that way should be the right way, and perhaps not even knowing there was any other; while the best reasoner in the world, if the problem were novel to him, might halt and stumble in his procedure owing to the very circumstance that he was taking his steps in the constraint and tight boots of too much reasoning instead of in the old slippers of habit.

A better test is the ability to follow a simple mathematical demonstration; because mathematical conceptions are all conceptions of visible objects, and involve no other difficulty than the extreme complexity of most of them, which, however, does not affect the simple demonstration; and because there is no element of mathematical reasoning which is not found in all reasoning unless forming a conjecture be called reasoning. Nevertheless, it is well-known that among those who have never been able to cross the *pons asinorum*, i.e. Euclid's demonstration that the angles at the base of an isosceles triangle are equal, there are men who are so far from being asses that their heads touch the very heavens of human intelligence, jurist's whose opinions are authoritative the world over, diplomats renowned from their skill in unravelling the most tangled of human snarls, naturalists of the first order, and minds who shake the senate of philosophy. It is, no doubt, true that elementary mathematics is so abominably taught that a pretty bright mind may quite fail to apprehend the thought. He may, for example, suppose that mathematics deals with questions of fact, instead of with questions of whether the truth of an arbitrary hypothesis would involve the truth of another proposition or not. It is further true that the elliptical style of writing which mathematicians have inherited from the Greeks tends to veil the connexions between the different steps. But examples can be framed which are not open to these objections. At the end of this article will be found a little mathematical discussion which has been carefully designed to serve as a test of capacity from such mathematics as is not very intricate. The beginning of it is excessively easy; but the last part of it is not so; and who clearly sees the cogency of the whole may rest assured that he labors under no mental defect in respect to mathematical reasoning.

The writer of this would hold himself deeply obliged, in the interests of psychology, of logic, and of the pedagogy of mathematics, if those persons who are reputed to be of superior intelligence, but who have believed their minds to be mathematically defective, would report to him whether or not they can follow the whole reasoning of the appended example; and if not, how far they do follow it, and what appears to them to be the hindrance to going further.

The difficulties of different minds may be different, so that it is desirable to enumerate the different kinds of mental processes that enter into mathematical discussions. In the ancient style, which is still much followed,¹ a mathematical demonstration is prefaced by a statement of the proposition to be proved, expressed in the abstract terms of ordinary speech;—a form of expression relatively difficult of apprehension to the mathematical mind.

Calling this the first step, the second will consist in translating the words which denote that which the proposition supposes, or takes for granted, into diagram language. Thus, if the proposition was that the sum of the angles of a spherical triangle is greater than two right angles, the diagram should show a spherical triangle and two right angles. The word diagram is here used in the peculiar sense of a concrete but possibly changing mental image of such a thing as it represents. A drawing or model may be employed to aid the imagination; but the essential thing to be performed is the act of imagining. Mathematical diagrams are of two kinds; first, the geometrical, which are composed of lines (for even the image of a body having a curved surface without edges, what is mainly seen with the mind's eye as it is turned about, is its generating lines, such as its varying outline); and second, the algebraical, which are arrays of letters and other characters whose interrelations are represented partly by their arrangement and partly by repetitions of them. If these change, it is by instantaneous metamorphoses.

The diagram-language into which a proposition in mathematics is translated cannot possibly consist in nothing but a diagram, since no diagram, even if it be a changing one can present more than a single object, while the verbal expression of the proposition to be proved is necessarily general. To revert to our example, a proposition about any spherical triangle whatsoever, relates to something that no single image of a spherical triangle can cover. Accordingly, every diagram must be supplemented by certain general understandings or explicit rules, which shall warrant the substitution for one diagram of any other conforming to certain rules. These will be rules of permissible substitution, partly limited to the special proposition, partly extending to an entire class of diagrams to which this one belongs.

---

1 [Rej.:] [...] is still much followed, a mathematical demonstration is prefaced by a statement of the proposition to be proved, expressed in the abstract terms of ordinary speech; and to the only semi-mathematical mind of the writer this is often the part the most difficult of apprehension. Indeed, he cannot understand it at all until he has made the translation into algebraic or geometrical terms which traditionally immediately follows. This translation takes the form of a diagram, a word here used in an extended sense. Mathematical diagrams are of two kinds; first, the geometrical, composed of lines (for even in the model of a curved surface, what we mainly see, as we turn it about, are its generating lines); and second, the algebraical, which are arrays of letters and other characters, the relations between which are expressed partly by their arrangement, and partly by repetitions of them.

3.3 [Intention, Resolution, and Determination]

[R 1132] **P 11.** In the first place, then, every ~~reflecting~~ man has certain ~~general~~ ideals of the general description of conduct that is fitting to a man in his position. There will generally be very little in these ideas that is original or personal to him: they are the ideas of the circle to which he belongs. He imbibed them in childhood. Reflecting upon these ideals, he is led to *intend* to make his own conduct conform to a whole or to a part of them, that part of them in which he most thoroughly believes; and to strengthen his intentions he adopts certain rigid rules of conduct. Being in this condition, he foresees that a special occasion is going to arise; and these rules, together with his natural dispositions and his habits cause him to form a *resolution* as to how he will act on that occasion. This resolution is of the nature of a plan. One might almost call it a *diagram*. It is a mental formulation always more or less general. Being nothing but an *idea*, it does not necessarily influence his conduct. But now he sits down and goes through with a process similar to that of impressing a lesson upon his memory. The result of this process is that the *resolution*, or ~~mere idea~~ mental formula, is converted into a *determination*, by which I mean a really efficient agency, such that if one knows what its special character is one can *forecast* the man's conduct on the anticipated occasion. You cannot make *forecasts* that will come true in the majority of the ~~experiments~~ trials, by means of any figment. It must be by means of something true and real. We do not know by what machinery the conversion of a resolution into a determination is accomplished. Several hypotheses have been proposed; but they do not much concern us now. Suffice it to say that the determination, or efficient agency, is something hidden in the depths of our nature. There is, I think, a peculiar quality of feeling that accompanies a real impression upon our dispositions; although, in me, it is a very dim feeling. But afterwards we have no consciousness of our determination. ~~Next, the anticipated occasion arises.~~ We may become aware of it, especially if it is pent up. In that case, we shall recognize it by a feeling of *need*, of *desire*. Next, the anticipated occasion arises.

[R 838, April 10, 1911] Reasoning to be sound must be an exceedingly long and laborious process, — as is shown most strikingly by the centuries of hard thinking that have been required to bring mathematics, the very easiest of all subjects to reason about to the degree of conclusiveness that it has so far attained (and this is far from perfection). For that reason, every ~~operation~~ work of even a little complexity that a man can foresee a future likelihood of his having to perform ought to be made the subject of close consideration for years before the time for action shall come; and in particular any situation in which he is in danger of finding himself in which impulses, persons, temptation will gain a force in a contrary direction to that which sufficient meditation would bring about. For it is a remarkable fact that not only do repeated rehearsals facilitate any performance, but even repetitions of it in the imagination have the same effect that rehearsals of either kind, the physical and the imaginary, are capable of being marvellously fortified in their effects on subsequent conduct by a certain mental act which might be called a command to oneself (since the meaning of the word "self-command" has been limited to prohibitions mentally addressed to oneself and strengthened by habitual repetition). However, in the nomenclature that I shall employ, such a command to oneself (whose effect will be increased by an energetic reiteration of it), shall be called a *Resolution*, while the effect that this will produce on future voluntary conduct but which may equally be otherwise produced, I shall term, regardlessly of how it comes about a *Determination* (*statical*, of conduct).

[R 838, February 22, 1913] **Notes for Essay on the Justification of Reasoning.** The purpose of this Essay is to state and prove exactly how every kind of reasoning is justified, and utterly to disprove all the theories which have hitherto been advanced on the subject.

It will be shown in the course of the essay that there are three distinct kinds of reasoning; provided we understand by reasoning the acceptance of one assertion as true because on holds such acceptance to be rationally justified by the fact that we have accepted certain other assertion or assertions as true. By acceptance here I do not mean to imply any definite degree of belief in the assertions accepted, nor to imply that the conclusion is necessarily as confidently accepted as the premises.

I shall prove that there are three essential distinct kinds of reasoning that are justified in three different ways and in three different degrees.[2]

---

[2] That I announced in 1868, but it was not till much later that I got a definite conception of the third kind of reasoning.

4 Of Reasoning in General

R 595, summer 1895. Houghton Library. Moving back in time in our selection of Peirce's writings on reasoning and diagrams, the manuscript R 595, written in summer 1895 was the first and only chapter Peirce ever wrote for the book project entitled *Short Logic*. It is placed at the end of this reversely chronological Part I simply because it lands us on the immediate neighbourhood of the emergence of logical graphs, while also setting much of the required philosophical ground for the cultivation of the graphical method whose fruits Peirce would then harvest for nearly two decades. In this piece, Peirce sets out to establish the "philosophical trivium", which is the study of logic and its sign-theoretic context in three parts or areas of study, namely speculative grammar, critic and speculative rhetoric.

"Of Reasoning in General" is a complete version of the text which has been known to scholars through its fragmented publications in the *Collected Papers of Charles S. Peirce* (CP, 1933) and in Justus Buchler's *Philosophical Writings of Peirce* (1940, PWP). However, less than half of the relevant material was published in those places, with omissions and errors so numerous that one could hardly speak of a coherent piece. R 595 was later published in the *Essential Peirce* 2 (Chapter 3, pages 11–26), with only one larger omission concerning features of many languages, including Egyptian hieroglyphs. In the text below, this omitted passage is the segment from "That different races ...." until "There are too many types of speech ...." The variants and the last three paragraphs were likewise omitted from the publication in EP 2.

In this chapter, Peirce makes a number of observations on logic, language, semiotics and notation. One finds not only a fresh application of his three-fold division of signs but also an improvement on his 1885 indexical interpretation of quantification, now fleshed out in terms of iconic features of quantifiers. Of particular interest is his remark towards the end: "If there are two selective indices one universal, the other particular, and the latter selection is made last, the order of the selections can be reversed. But all these changes in the indices are justified only by considering icons." That expressivity depends on representing dependent quantifiers, and that the "laws of the indices" depend on the iconic or predicative component of the sentence, were Peirce's discoveries which, hardly much more than a year later, would blossom in the theory of existential graphs.

Only about a year after having completed this semeiotic overture Peirce would be fully immersed in writing another massive treatise on logic, now exclusively on logical graphs. This manuscript, or rather its remnants reconstructed in the next chapter, deserves to be known as the mother of all his subsequent writings on the topic. The year 1896 saw Peirce's work being erected to symphonic heights, and, as he would soon signal to others, he took that period to represent his *chef d'œuvre* in logic. But these endeavours might not have fully succeeded without Peirce having first been in the prepossession of the kind of philosophical trivium that guided the cultivation of his logical investigations.

Short Logic. Chapter I. Of Reasoning in General

Article 1. *Logic* is the art of reasoning. The old times saw endless disputes as to whether logic was an *art* or a *science*. It is not worth while even to explain what those words were taken to mean. The present definition, respectable in its antiquity and superficiality, is intended merely to afford a rough preliminary notion of what this treatise is about. This chapter shall tell something more; but the student cannot expect to attain a real comprehension of the nature of logic till after he has gone through the book.

The facts upon which logic is based come mostly within ordinary knowledge; though many escape ordinary notice. The science is largely, not wholly, one of rearrangement.

Article 2. *Reasoning* is the process by which we attain a belief which we regard as the result of previous knowledge.

Some beliefs are results of other knowledge without the believer suspecting it. After a sojourn among young people exclusively, an acquaintance met may seem to have aged more than he really has. This is a case of error. But not all such results are erroneous. A stranger with whom I am dealing may make an impression of being dishonest owing to indications too slight for me to know what they are. Yet the impression may be well-founded. Such results are usually set down to "intuition". Though inferential in their nature, they are not exactly *inferences*.

Again, a given belief may be regarded as the effect of another given belief, without our seeming to see clearly why or how. Such a process is usually called an *inference*; but it aught not to be called a *rational* inference, or *reasoning*. A blind force constrains us. Thus, Descartes declares himself obliged to believe that he exists because he remarks that he thinks. Yet he seems to doubt (in that stage of his inquiry) whether everything that thinks exists.

The word *illation* signifies a process of inference. Reasoning, in general, is sometimes called *ratiocination*. *Argumentation* is the expression of a reasoning. *Argument* may be mental or expressed. The belief to which an inference leads is called the *conclusion*, the beliefs from which it sets out are called the *premises* (sometimes written *premisses*). The fact that the premises necessitate the truth of the conclusion is called the *consequence*, or *following* of the conclusion from the premises.

Article 3. A *Belief* is a state of mind of the nature of a habit, of which the person is aware, and which, if he acts deliberately on a ~~certain~~ suitable occasion, would induce him to act in a way different from what he might act in the absence of such habit.

Thus, if a man *believes* a straight line to be the shortest distance between two points, then in case he wishes to proceed by the shortest way from one point to another, and thinks he can move in a straight line, he will endeavour to do so. If a man really believes that alcohol is injurious to him, and does not choose to injure himself, but still drinks for the sake of the momentary satisfaction, then he is not acting deliberately. But a habit of which we are not aware, or with which we are not deliberately satisfied, is not a belief.

An act of consciousness in which a person thinks he recognizes a belief is called a *judgment*. The expression of a judgment is called in logic a *proposition*.

Article 4. "The unit of speech is the sentence", says one of the most illustrious of living linguists, the Rev. A. H. Sayce, in the article *Grammar* in the *Encyclopaedia Brittanica*. (1st Ed. VI. 43.b.) Modern logicians have come to a conclusion analogous to that of modern linguists in holding that the unit of thought is the judgment.

Still, it is as necessary in logic to dissect judgments as it is in grammar to analyze sentences.

Our grammars teach that a perfect sentence consists of a *subject* and *predicate*. There is some truth in that; yet it rather forces the facts to bring all sentences even in the European languages to that form. But Indo-European languages are to all languages what phanerogams are to plants as a whole or vertebrates to animals as a whole, a smallish part though the highest type. Grammarians are children of Procrustes and will make our grammar fit all languages against the protests of those to whom they are vernacular. In the Eskimo tongue what we call the subject is generally put in the genitive case, and in many languages, except for proper names, words that are distinctly and decidedly nouns are quite exceptional. Still, there is something like a subject and a predicate in most languages; and something of the sort must exist in every logical proposition. In order to be able to understand precisely how this is we must turn our attention to signs.

Article 5. A *sign* is a thing which serves to convey knowledge of some other thing, which it is said to *stand for* or *represent*. This thing is called the *object* of the sign; the idea in the mind that the sign excites, which is a mental sign of the same object, is called an *interpretant* of the sign.

Signs are of three classes, namely, *Icons* (or images), *Indices*, and *Symbols*.

Article 6. An *icon* is a sign which stands for its object because as a thing perceived it excites an idea naturally allied to the idea that object would excite. Most icons, if not all, are *likenesses* of their objects. A photograph is an icon, usually conveying a flood of information. A piece of mimicry may be an auditory icon. A diagram is a kind of icon particularly useful, because it suppresses a quantity of details, and so allows the mind more easily to think of the important features. The figures of geometry are if accurately drawn such close likenesses of their objects that they are almost instances of them; but every student of geometry knows that it is not all necessary, nor even useful to draw them so nicely, since if roughly drawn they still sufficiently resemble their objects in the particulars to which attention has to be drawn. Many diagrams resemble their objects not at all in looks; it is only in respect to the relations of their parts that their likeness consists. Thus, we may show the relation between the different kinds of signs by brace, thus:

$$\text{Signs:} \begin{cases} \text{Icons,} \\ \text{Indices,} \\ \text{Symbols.} \end{cases}$$

This is an icon. But the only respect in which it resembles its objects is that the brace shows the classes of *icons*, *indices*, and *symbols* to be related to one another and to the general class of signs, as they really are, in a general way. When, in algebra, we write equations under one another in a regular array, especially when we put resembling letters for corresponding coefficients, the array is an icon. Here is an example;

$$a_1 x + b_1 y = n_1,$$
$$a_1 x + b_2 y = n_2.$$

This is an icon, in that it makes quantities look alike which are in analogous relations to the problem. In fact, every algebraical equation is an icon, in so far as it *exhibits*, by means of the algebraic signs (which are not themselves icons), the relations of the quantities concerned.

It may be questioned whether all icons are likenesses or not. For example, if a drunken man is exhibited in order to show by contrast, the excellence of temperance, this is certainly an *icon*, but whether it is a likeness or not may be doubted. The question seems somewhat trivial.

Article 7. An *index* stands for its object by virtue of a real connection with it, or because it forces the mind to attend to that object. Thus, we say a low barometer with a moist air is an *indication* of rain; that is we suppose that the forces of nature ~~may~~ establish a probable connection between the low barometer with moist air and coming rain. A weather-cock is an *indication*, or *index*, of the direction of the wind; because in the first place it really takes the self-same direction as the wind, so that there is a real connection between them, and in the second place we are so constituted that when we see a weather-cock pointing in a certain direction it draws our attention to that direction, and when we see the weather-cock veering with the wind, we are forced by the law of mind to think that direction is connected with the wind. The pole star is an *index*, or pointing finger, to show us which way is north. A spirit-loyal, or a plumb-bob, is an ~~indication of which~~ *index* of the vertical direction. A yard-stick might seem, at first sight, to be an icon of a yard; and so it would be, if it were merely intended to show a yard as near as it can be seen and estimated to be a yard. But the very purpose of a yard-stick is to ~~furnish~~ show a yard nearer than it can be estimated by its appearance. This it does in consequence of an accurate mechanical comparison made with the bar in London called the Yard, either the yardstick used, or some one from which it has been copied, having been transported from the Westminster Palace. Thus, it is a real connection which gives the yard-stick its value as a representamen; and thus it is an *index*, not a mere *icon*. When a driver to attract the attention of a foot-passenger and cause him to save himself, calls out "Hi!" so far as this is a significant word, it is, as will be seen below, something more than an index; but so far as it is simply intended to act upon the hearer's nervous system and to rouse him to get out of the way, it is an index, because it is meant to put him in real connection with the object, which is his situation relative to the approaching horse. Suppose two men meet upon a country road and one of them says to the other, "The chimney of that house is on fire". The other looks about him and descries a house with green blinds and a verandah having a smoking chimney. He walks on a few miles and meets a second traveller. Like a Simple Simon he says, "The chimney of that house is on fire". "What house?" asks the other. "Oh, a house with green blinds and a verandah", replies the simpleton. "Where is the house?" asks the stranger. He desires some *index* which shall connect his apprehension with the house meant. Words alone cannot do this. The demonstrative pronouns, "this" and "that", are indices. For they call upon the hearer to use his powers of observation, and so establish a real connection between his mind and the object; and if the demonstrative pronoun does that,—without which its meaning is not understood,—it goes to establish such a connection; and so is an *index*. The relative pronouns, *who* and *which*, demand observational activity in much the same way, only with them the observation has to be directed to the words that have gone before. Lawyers use A, B, C, practically as very effective relative pronouns. To show how effective they are, we may note that Messrs. Allen and Greenough, in their admirable (though in the edition of 1877 too small) Latin Grammar, declare that no conceivable syntax could wholly remove the ambiguity of the following sentence, "A replied to B that he thought C (his brother) more unjust to himself than to his own friend". Now, any lawyer would state that with perfect clearness, by using A, B, C, as relatives, thus: A replied to B that he, $\left\{\begin{smallmatrix}A,\\B,\end{smallmatrix}\right.$ thought C (his, $\left\{\begin{smallmatrix}A's,\\B's\end{smallmatrix}\right.$ brother) more unjust to himself, $\left\{\begin{smallmatrix}A,\\B,\\C,\end{smallmatrix}\right.$ than to his, $\left\{\begin{smallmatrix}A's,\\B's,\\C's\end{smallmatrix}\right.$ own friend.[1] ~~All the pronouns are indices, or involve indices.~~ The terminations which in any inflected language are attached to words "governed" by other words, and which serve to show which the governing word is, by repeating what is elsewhere expressed in the same form, are likewise *indices* of the same relative-pronoun character. Any bit of Latin poetry illustrates this, such as the twelve-line sentence beginning, "Iam satis terris". Both in these terminations and in the A, B, C, a likeness is relied upon to carry the attention to the right object. But this does not make them icons, in any important way; for it is of no consequence how the letters A, B, C, are shaped or what the terminations are. It is not merely that one occurrence of an A is like a previous occurrence that is the important circumstance, but that *there is an understanding that like letters shall stand for the same thing*, and this acts as a force carrying the attention from one occurrence of A to the previous one. A possessive pronoun is two ways an index: first it indicates the possessor, and, second, it has a modification which syntactically carries the attention to the word denoting the thing possessed.

Some indices are more or less detailed directions for what the hearer is to do in order to place himself in direct experiential or other connection with the thing meant. Thus, the Coast Survey issues "Notices to Mariners", giving the latitude and longitude, four or five bearings of prominent objects, etc., and saying *there* is a rock, or shoal, or buoy, or light-ship. Although there will be other elements in such directions, yet in the main they are indices.

Along with such indexical directions of what to do to find the object meant, ought to be classed those pronouns which should be entitled *selective* pronouns, because they inform the hearer how he is to pick out one of the objects intended, but which grammarians call by the very indefinite designation of *indefinite* pronouns. Two varieties of these are particularly important in logic, the *universal selectives*, such as *quivis, quilibet, quisquam, ullus, nullus, nemo, quisque, uterque*, and in English, *any, every, all, no, none, whatever, whoever, everybody, anybody, nobody*. These mean that the hearer is at liberty to select any instance he likes within limits expressed or understood, and the assertion is intended to apply to that one. The other logically important variety consists of the *particular selectives*,

---

1 Modern grammars define a pronoun as a word used in place of a noun. That is an ancient doctrine which, exploded early in the thirteenth century, disappeared from the grammars for several hundred years. But the substitute employed was not very clear; and when a barbarous rage against medieval thought broke out, it was swept away. Some recent grammars, as *Allen and Greenough's*, set the matter right again. There is no reason for saying that *I, thou, that, this*, stand in place of nouns; they indicate things in the directest possible way. It is impossible to express what an assertion refers to except by means of an index. A pronoun is an index. A noun, on the other hand, does not *indicate* the object it denotes; and when a noun is used to show what one is talking about, the experience of the hearer is relied upon to make up for the incapacity of the noun for doing what the pronoun does at once. Thus, a noun is an imperfect substitute for a pronoun. Nouns also serve to help out verbs. A pronoun ought to be defined as *a word which may indicate anything to which the first and second persons have suitable real connections, by calling the attention of the second person to it*. Allen and Greenough say "pronouns indicate some person or thing without either naming or describing" This is correct,—refreshingly correct; only it seems better to say what they *do*, and not merely what they *don't*.

quis, quispiam, nescio quis, aliquius, quidam, and in English, *some, something, somebody, a, a certain, some or other, a suitable, one*.

Allied to the above pronouns are such expressions as *all but one, one or two, a few, nearly all, every other one*, etc. Along with pronouns are to be classed adverbs of place and time, etc.

Not very unlike these are, *the first, the last, the seventh, two-thirds of, thousands of*, etc.

Other indexical words are prepositions, and prepositional phrases, such as, *on the right (or left) of*. Right and left cannot be distinguished by any general description. Other prepositions signify relations which *may*, perhaps, be described; but when they refer, as they do oftener than would be supposed, to a situation relative to the observed, or assumed to be experientially known, place and attitude of the speaker relatively to that of the hearer, then the indexical element is the dominant element.[2]

Article 8. Icons and indices assert nothing. If an icon could be interpreted by a sentence, that sentence must be in a "potential mood", that is, it would merely say, "Suppose a figure has three sides", etc. Were an index so interpreted, the mood must be imperative, or exclamatory, as "See there!" or "Look out!" But the kind of signs which we are now coming to consider are, by nature, in the "indicative", or, as it should be called, the *declarative* mood.[3] Of course, they can go to the

---

[2] If a logician had to construct a language *de novo*,—which he actually has almost to do,—he would naturally say, I shall need prepositions to express the temporal relations of *before, after*, and *at the same time with*, I shall need prepositions to express the spatial relations of *adjoining, containing, touching*, of *in range with*, of *near to, far from*, of *to the right of, to the left of, above, below, before, behind*, and I shall need prepositions to express motions into and out of these situations. For the rest, I can manage with metaphors. Only if my language is intended for use by people ~~surrounded by~~ having some great geographical feature related the same way to all of them, as a mountain range, the sea, a great River, it will be desirable to have prepositions signifying ~~relations~~ situations relatively to that, as *across, seaward*, etc. But when we examine actual languages, it would seem as though they had supplied the place of many of these distinctions by gestures. The Egyptians had no preposition nor demonstrative having any apparent reference to the Nile. Only the Esquimos are so wrapped up in their bearskins that they have demonstratives distinguishing landward, seaward, north, south, east, and west. But examining the cases or prepositions of any actual language we find them a haphazard lot.

[3] The nomenclature of grammar, like that of logic, is derived chiefly from a late Latin, the words being transferred from the Greek, the Latin prefix translating the Greek prefix, and the Latin stem the Greek stem. But while the logical words were chosen with fastidious care, the grammarians were excessively careless, and none more so than Priscian. The word *indicative* is one of Priscian's creations. It was evidently intended to translate Aristotle's ἀποφαντική. But this is precisely equivalent to *declarative* both in signification and according to the rules of transference, *de*, tak-

expression of any other mood, since we may declare assertions to be doubtful, or mere interrogations, or imperatively requisite.

A *Symbol* is a sign naturally fit to declare that the set of objects which is denoted by whatever set of indices may be in certain ways attached to it is represented by an icon associated with it. To show what this complicated ~~description~~ definition means, let us take as an example of a symbol the word "loveth". Associated with this word is an idea, which is the mental icon of one person loving another. Now we are to understand that "loveth" occurs in a sentence; for what it may mean by itself, if it means anything, is not the question. Let the sentence, then, be "Ezekiel loveth Huldah". Ezekiel and Huldah must, then, be or contain indices; for without indices it is impossible to designate what one is talking about. Any mere description would ~~make~~ leave it uncertain whether they were not mere characters in a ballad; but whether they be so or not, indices can designate them. Now the effect of the word "loveth" is that the pair of objects denoted by the pair of indices Ezekiel and Huldah is represented by the icon, or the image we have in our minds of a lover and his beloved.

The same thing is equally true of every verb in the declarative mood; and indeed of every verb, for the other moods are merely declarations of a fact somewhat different from that expressed by the declarative mood.

As for a noun, considering the meaning which it has in the sentence, and not as standing by itself, it is most conveniently regarded as a portion of a symbol. Thus, the sentence "every man loves a woman" is equivalent to "whatever is a man loves something that is a woman". Here "whatever" is a universal selective index, "is a man" is a symbol, "loves" is a symbol, "something that" is a particular selective index, and "is a woman" is a symbol.

An important remark has to be made at this point.[4] Namely, that it is of little or no consequence in logic to analyze a judgment precisely as it is thought. For logical purposes two judgments which assert the same fact are precisely equivalent. Whatever can be inferred from the one can equally be inferred from the other, and when one can be concluded, so can the other. They are necessarily true and false together. Hence, in logic, we put a judgment into some standard, or canonical form, which is chosen for its adaption to logical purposes.

---

ing the place of ἀπο, as is usual in these artificial formations (demonstration for ἀπόδειξις, etc.), and *clarare* representing φαινειν, to make clear. Perhaps the reason Priscian did not choose the word *declarativus* was that Apuleius, a great authority on words, had used this in a somewhat different sense.

4 [This paragraph is crossed out by Peirce and was not published in EP 2.]

Article 9. The astonishing variety which exists in the syntax of different languages shows that different men think the same fact in vary different ways. There is no respect in which the constructions of languages differ more than in regard to the noun. Our Aryan languages are quite peculiar in the distinctness with which nouns are marked off from verbs. When we speak of a noun, we do not think of what its effect in a sentence may be, but we think of it as standing alone. Now a common noun as "man", standing alone, is certainly an index, but not of the object it denotes. It is an index of the mental object which it calls up. It is the index of an icon; for it denotes whatever there may be which is like that image.

That different races regard nouns in sentences in quite different lights admits of no doubt; though we may not find it easy to express with precision the manner in which we ourselves think. Many languages have no "verb substantive".[5]

The Old Egyptian often has, in place of *is* a relative pronoun. To our way of thinking this seems very unapt. But the Egyptian had a pictorial mind; and when he saw a hieroglyphic ideograph of a man, what it said to him was, "what we are thinking of is a man". Hence, the sentence "Aahmes is a man" would be thought by him under the form "What we are thinking of is Aahmes *which* what we are thinking of is a man".

The pronoun in question is ◻︎ 𓅮 *pu*, primarily a "demonstrative". But demonstratives are used as relatives in almost all languages, if not in every one. The following is an actual example of this common construction:

| dm'k | pw | Bχτn | Hnwk | pw | rθf. |

The hand corresponds to Hebrew *Daleth*, and is by Brugsch transliterated *d*. The lute is *m'*, that is Mem-Aleph, and the bowl is *k* (Kaph). The signs of a tongue and a plan of cross-roads are ideographs, the latter suggests a town, the former speaking, and both are often used together for an ordinary town. Without these ideographs which show us that the word *dema'k* means "thy town", it might mean "thy purse". In *dema'k*, *dm'* is the stem, *k* the sign of the second person masculine; for nouns have persons in Egyptian. Second word: Package = *p* (Pe), chick = w

---

[5] That is, *to be*, so-called by Priscian, translating ῥῆμα ὑπαρκτικόν. The Greek means the verb of happening or inherence, as in "man *is* an animal", "a griffin *is* an animal breathing fire". Priscian committed a common error, that of supposing ὑπαρκτικόν here to mean *existential*, because existence is one of the meanings of ὕπαρξις. He probably chose *substantiuum* to represent the adjective because the *sub* corresponds to ὑπό, without considering that nothing could be less alike than the main stems ἄρϊεις, to begin, and *stare*, to stay.

(vau). *Puw*, "that", used for "is". Third word: leg = *b* (Beth), sieve = x (Cheth), drill-head, *t* (without semitic equivalent), water = *n* (Nun). The hills is an ideograph suggesting ~~region~~ country. *Bechten* is the name of the town. Fourth word: Lotus = H*n* (Cheth-Nun), the man is an ideograph suggesting man, the woman is an ideograph suggesting woman, three marks ideograph of plurality (pronounced *w*); bowl *k*. *Henunk* means 'thy slaves'. *Hn* means majesty, *w* plural, *k* second person masculine. Fifth word: *puw*, "that". Sixth word: mouth = *r* (Resh), tongs = θ (Tau?), man and woman forms an ideograph, serpent flat = *f*.(without Semitic equivalent). *Rethef* means "its people", *re*, mankind, *f.* third person masculine.

The Samoyedes when they have to ~~express~~ assert anything by a transitive verb with a direct object put the subject into the possessive case, and so do the Eskimo, whose language ~~bears some~~ has other resemblances to the Samoyedic languages. This is certainly a peculiar way of thinking. Instead of saying and thinking "Maurice eats bacon", they say and no doubt think, "The eating of bacon is Maurice's"; for Castrén, a grammarian of those languages says, "the nouns coincide in many respects with verbs".[6]

The language of the natives in the neighborhood of Adelaide is remarkably rudimentary, and hence instructive. It belongs to the Malay tribe of languages, having disyllabic roots with monosyllabic particles agglutinated to them. Among other curious features, the subject or agent of an active transitive verb is put in the ablative. For instance, they say, "*ngai ningka palta ngaityo tokutyurlo*". *Ngai* is me, *ningka* almost, *palta* throw, *ngaityo* my = *ngai* (I) + *yo* ('s), *tokutyurlo* by little = *tokytyu* (little) + *rlo* (by). That is, "my little one has almost thrown me". This is very different from our way of thinking.

Tibetan is a language of the monosyllabic family, allied to Chinese, though not so thoroughly monosyllabic. It is, therefore, of a radically different type from the Adelaide language. Nevertheless, whether by accident or otherwise, the Tibetan has a number of points of resemblance with that tongue. In Adelaide the verb has not a very marked verbal character; in Tibetan Mr. Csoma de Körös says that what is called a verb is nothing but a participle. Both languages make great use of the reduplication of roots to express intensified and modified ideas. A surprising number of *forms* are somewhat alike, though one cannot see how that can be anything but accident. In Adelaide the genitive is in *-ko* and the ablative in *-lo*; in Tibetan, the genitive is in *-kyi* and the ablative in *-la*. In Adelaide, "I" is *ngai*, in Tibetan *nga*; in Adelaide self is *ndi*, in Tibetan *nyid*, etc. Finally, Tibetan resem-

---

6 [Castrén (1854). Matias Aleksanteri (Matthias Alexander) Castrén (1813–1852), a Finnish ethnolinguist and a pioneer in the research of Uralic languages and cultures, including Samoyed (Nenets).]

bles Adelaide in that the subject of a transitive verb is put in the instrumental case, as *rgyalpos gsungngo*, the king commands, where *rgyalpos* is "with king", = *rgyal*, king, + *pos*, with; and *gsungngo*, commands, = *gsung*, commanding + *ngo*, reduplication of last consonant with *o* to show that an *assertion* is intended. Thus, in Tibetan we find nearly the same strange syntax as in Adelaide, a language of a structure far less like its own than Latin is like English.[7]

The Basque tongue is a stranger among languange. It is the relic of the occupation of Europe by some forgotten people long before the Celts. It is agglutinative speech; but it belongs to no family of languages otherwise known. It is a cultivated speech. Here again the subject of a transitive verb is put in the ablative. Thus, *Nik ezagutsen dudan emaste bertutusena da* means "she is the most virtuous woman I know". *Nik* by me = *Ni* me + *k* by, *ezagutsen* at to know = *ezazu* know + *tse* to (sign of infinitive) + *n* at, *dudan* that I have = *d* it + *u* have + *d* I + *an* which, *emaste* woman, *bertutusena* the most virtuous = *bertutus* virtuous + *en* -est + *a* the, *da* she is = *d* it + *a* is.

The language of our Flathead Indians is a very savage tongue. It is spoken slowly with great prolongations and emphases. There are no cases. But a *t* is put before a noun which follows the passive of a transitive verb as agent, and also before the subject of the same verb in the active voice. Thus, *tnesehaz shiskagaei* means "I tie the horse by the feet", *tnesehaz* I tie = *t* agent + *n* I + *es* present time + *ch* on + *az* bind, *shiskagaei* foot horse = *shi* foot + *skagae* horse + *i* so no more at present. Again, *polls askusi tpiel* means "Peter struck your son" *polls* struck = *poll* strike + *s* third person singular perfect, *askusi* your son = *a* your + *skusi* son, *tpiel* Peter = *t* agent + *Piel* Peter.[8]

There are too many types of speech to allow the insertion here of illustrations of all the different ways in which one and the same fact is thought by different peoples. Sufficient has been said to show the danger of assuming that because a certain way of thinking is natural to us Aryans, therefore, in the absence of any more positive evidence than that no other way occurs to *us*, it is a law of the human mind that man must think in that way. Still more presumptuous would it be assume on those grounds that a given form of thought belongs to every intelligent being.

Article 10. Thinking a fact in a different way will not alter its value as a premise or as a conclusion. Whether from the judgment, A, it is proper to infer the judg-

---

[7] To be inserted: That in the Irish language the subject (which usually comes after the verb) is generally put in the genitive.

[8] Most of the above information about languages has been drawn from [James] Byrne's *[General Principles of the] Structure of Language*. [See Byrne (1885).]

ment, C, depends upon whether or not the fact which A expresses could possibly take place without the fact which C expresses going along with it. On this connection of *facts* mere thinking can have no effect.

But it is now time to draw attention to three different tasks that are set before teacher and learner of the art of reasoning.

The principal business of logic is to ascertain whether given reasonings are good or bad, strong or weak. In this regard, whether we think our propositions in one form or in another is of no more consequence than whether we express them in English or in German, whether we write them or enunciate them, whether we drawl or gabble. In the eye of logic, two propositions expressing the same fact are *equivalent,* or virtually (at least) identical.

Accordingly, the practice of logicians has always been to adopt certain *canonical forms* in which they require that judgments should be expressed, before the reasonings which involve them are brought before them for examination. In choosing these forms, logicians need not be biased by the usage of any languages nor by the ways in which Aryans, or all the races of this little planet, may employ in their thinking. They will do best to take the forms which are the most convenient for their own purpose of tracing the relationship of dependence between one *fact* and another.

To say whether a given way of thinking is correct or not, it is requisite to consider what facts the thought expresses. To this, then, those who occupy themselves with the art of reasoning must attend. The logician cannot be asked to teach the tongues: it is the business of the philologist to do that. Syntax must explain what facts different forms of expression signify; and the forms of expression undoubtedly follow in the main the ways of thinking. Comparative syntax is a recognized branch of philology; and this must survey the whole ground of different ways of thinking the same fact, so far as they betray themselves in speech. Thus, a very important part of the labor of the art of reasoning is undertaken by the grammarian, and may be severed from logic, proper. Every form of thinking must betray itself in some form of expression or go undiscovered. There are undoubtedly numerous other ways of making assertions besides verbal expressions; such as, algebra, arithmetical figures, emblems, gesture-language, manners, uniforms, monuments, to mention only *intentional* modes of declaration. Some of these are of the highest importance for reasoning. Philologists have not deemed those sorts of language interesting to them. So, cultivators of the art of reasoning found themselves long ago obliged to institute a *speculative grammar* which should study *modes of signifying*, in general.⁹ It is best regarded as separate from logic proper; for one of these days philologists may take it in hand, for which logicians will thank them.

An art of thinking ought also to recommend such forms of thinking as will most economically serve the purpose of Reason. The doing of this in a well-reasoned way involves a great theory. We shall get some glimpse of this in another chapter. Logicians have done little in this line of study. Yet a number of books, not called logics (for the most part), have made unsystematic explorations into this science. Since this is the general foundations of the art of putting propositions into effective forms, it has been called *speculative rhetoric*.¹⁰

The sciences of speculative grammar, logic, and speculative rhetoric may be called the *philosophical trivium*.¹¹

Article 11. We shall now be able more fully to explain the nature of a proposition. We have seen that a judgment is an act of consciousness in which we recognize a belief, and a belief is an intelligent habit upon which we shall act when occasion presents itself. Of what nature is that recognition? It may come very near action. The muscles may twitch and we may restrain ourselves only by considering that the proper occasion has not arisen. But in general, we *virtually resolve* upon a certain occasion to act as if certain imagined circumstances were perceived. This act which amounts to such a resolve, is a peculiar act of the will whereby we cause an image, or *icon*, to be ~~stamped~~ associated, in a peculiarly strenuous way, ~~upon~~ with an object represented to us by an *index*. This act itself is represented in the proposition by a *symbol*, and the consciousness of it fulfills the function of a symbol in the judgment. Suppose, for example, I detect a person with whom I have to deal in an act of dishonesty. I have in my mind something like a "composite photograph" of all the persons that I have known and read of that have had that

---

9 The *Tractatus de modis significandi sive Grammatica Speculativa* has been regarded by all those who have carefully examined the question, as a genuine work of Duns Scotus. A minute comparison with the works of Siger of Brabant and Michael of Marbais, together with undisputed works of Duns, leaves no reasonable doubt of this. The conjecture that it was written by Albert of Saxony is utterly untenable. It would seem to have been written in 1299 or 1300. Though it clearly sets forth some Scotistic opinions, its greatest merit is the idea of the sciences embodied in the title.
10 *Proceedings of the American Academy of Arts and Sciences*, May 14, 1867. Vol. VII. p. 295.
11 The seven Liberal Arts of the Roman Schools of the fourth and fifth centuries (see Davidson's *Aristotle and Ancient Educational Ideals*, App.) were Grammar, Logic, Rhetoric, making up the "Trivium", Geometry, Arithmetic, Astronomy, Music, making up the "Quadrivium". *Quadrivium* means cross-wards, *trivium* a form in a road, hence, a public place. The fanciful application to the arts was in familiar use. The word *trivial* in its Latin form, was used meaning commonplace long before the application to arts was heard of; but in modern languages the adjective does not occur until after the rage against scholasticism must have influenced the associations of the word.

character, and at the instant I make the discovery concerning that person, who is distinguished from others for me by certain indications, upon that index at that moment down goes the stamp of RASCAL, to remain indefinitely.

A proposition *asserts* something. That assertion is performed by the symbol which stands for the act of consciousness. That which accounts for *assertion* seeming so different from other sorts of signification is its *volitional* character.

Every assertion is an assertion that two different signs have the same object. If we ask why it should have that *dual* character, the answer is that volition involves an action and reaction. The consequences of this duality are found not only in the analysis of propositions, but also in their classification.

It is impossible to find a proposition so simple as not to have reference to two signs. Take, for instance, "it rains". Here the icon is the mental composite photograph of all the rainy days the thinker has experienced. The index, is ~~his present experience~~ all whereby he distinguishes *that day*, as it is placed in his experience. The symbol is the mental act whereby he stamps that day as rainy.

The traditional logic divided propositions into the *categorical*, or incomplex, and the *hypothetical*, or complex. Very many logics of this century, in place of the hypothetical in the sense of complex, put the *conditional* (now often called the *hypothetical*) and the *disjunctive*, throwing out other kinds of complex propositions for no good reason, probably because of a fancy for triads. The categorical proposition, according to the usual variety of the traditional doctrine, is made up of two names called its *terms*, namely its *subject* and *predicate*, as principal parts; in addition to which it has a *copula*, the verb *is*. The doctrine of subject, predicate, and copula is so far true that it may be retained, with corrections, and so far false that it is doubtful whether it is expedient to retain the phraseology. It cannot be disputed that a proposition *can* be so analyzed, and with certain modifications, it is the most convenient analysis for the purposes of logic. The categorical proposition of traditional logic follows the Aryan syntax and is like this: "man is mortal". The grammatical subject is the logical *subject*. The grammatical predicate is replaced by *is* followed by a name, which is the logical *predicate*. The subject contains the whole or a part of the *index*, which gives it its peculiar thing-like character as subject, while the predicate involves the *icon*, which gives it its peculiar ideal character as predicate. The *copula* is the *symbol*.

The traditional analysis answers its purpose well enough in the simplest kind of reasonings, which alone the traditional logic considers. But in order properly to exhibit the relation between premises and conclusion of mathematical reasonings, it is necessary to recognize that in most cases the *subject-index* is compound, and consists of a *set* of indices. Thus, in the proposition, "A sells B to C for the price D", A, B, C, D form a set of four indices. The symbol "___ sells ___ to ___ for the price ___ " refers to a mental icon, or idea of the act of sale, and declares that this image represents the *set* A, B, C, D, considered as ~~distributed to its~~ attached to that icon, A as seller, C as buyer, B as object sold, and D as price. If we call A, B, C, D four *subjects* of the proposition and "___ sells ___ to ___ for the price ___" a *predicate*, we represent the logical relation well enough, but we abandon the Aryan syntax.

It may be asked, Why may not an assertion identify the objects of any two signs whatever, as two indices? Why should it be limited to declaring the object of an *index* to be represented by an *icon*? The answer is that an assertion *may* identify the objects of any two signs whatever; yet that in every case this will amount to declaring that an *index*, or set of indices, is represented by an *icon*. For instance, let the proposition be, that William *Lamare*, the author of the book "Correctorium fratris Thomae" is really the William *Ware* who was the teacher of Duns Scotus. Here the objects of two indices are identified. But this is logically equivalent to the assertion that the icon of identity, that is, the mental composite image of two aspects of one and the same thing, represents the objects of the set of indices William *Mare* and William *Ware*.[12] We are not, indeed, absolutely forced to regard one of the signs as an *icon* in any case; but this is a very convenient way of taking account of certain properties of inferences. It happens, too, to have some secondary advantages, such as that of agreeing with our natural metaphysics, and with our feeling in regard to subject and predicate.

As the index may be complex, so also may the icon. For instance, taking the universal selective index, *everything*, we may have an icon which is composed alternatively of two, a sort of composite of two icons, in the same way that any image is a "composite photograph" of innumerable particulars. Even what is called an "instantaneous photograph", taken with a camera, is a composite of the effects of intervals of exposure more numerous by far than the sands of the sea. Take an absolute instant during the exposure and the composite represents *this* among other conditions. Now, the two alternative icons are combined like that. We have an icon of this alternation, a composite of all the alternative cases we have thought of. The symbol asserts that one or other of those icons represents the universally selected index. Let one of the alternative icons be the idea of what is not a man, the other the idea of what is mortal. Then, the proposition will be: "Take anything you please, and it will either not be a man or will be mortal". Two signs so conjoined are said to be *aggregated*, or *disjunctively* ~~combined~~ *connected*, or *alternatively conjoined*. Take another example. Let the index be particularly selective. Let

---

[12] That *Marra* and *Warra* were really the same cannot be positively asserted; but the hypothesis suits the known facts remarkably well, except for the difference of names, which is perhaps not an insuperable obstacle.

an icon be so compounded of two icons that in each variation of it both these icons are conjoined. For instance, let one be an *icon* of a Chinese, the other of a woman. Then, the combined *icon* will be an icon of a Chinese woman. Thus, the proposition will be, Something can be so selected as to be at once a Chinese and a woman. Two signs so conjoined are said to be *combined*, or *conjunctively connected*, or *simultaneously conjoined*. The matter of compound icons will have to be more fully considered in another chapter.

Article 12. It is now time to examine more carefully the nature of *inference*, or the conscious and controlled adoption of a belief as a consequence of other knowledge. The first step of inference usually consists in bringing together certain propositions which we believe to be true, but which, supposing the inference to be a new one, we have hitherto not considered together, or not as united in the same way. This step is called *colligation*. The compound assertion resulting from colligation is a *conjunctive proposition*, that is, it is a proposition with a composite icon, as well as usually with a composite index. Colligation is a very important part of reasoning, calling for genius perhaps more than any other part of the process. Many logicians refuse the name of reasoning to an inferential act of which colligation forms no part. Such an inferential act they call an *immediate inference*. This term may be accepted; but although colligation certainly gives a higher intellectuality to inference, yet its importance is exaggerated when it is represented to be of more account than the conscious control of the operation. The latter ought to determine the title of *reasoning*.

An inference, then, may have but a single premise, or several premises may be united by colligation. In the latter case, they form, when colligated, one ~~composite~~ conjunctive proposition. But even if there be but one premise, the icon of that proposition is always more or less complex. The next step of inference to be considered consists in the contemplation of that complex icon, the fixation of the attention upon a certain feature of it, and the obliteration of the rest of it, so as to produce a new icon.

If the question is asked in what the processes of contemplation and of fixation of the attention consist, this question being psychological, it is necessary, before answering it, to describe some phenomena of the mind.[13] Be it known, then, that

---

13 **[Alt.:]** [...] of the mind. Since these facts belong to psychology, and not to logic, they will be briefly stated here, without explaining how they have been ascertained. Suffice it to say on that head that they are not hastily adopted; but result from the logical and mathematical discussion of elaborate experiments. The word *feeling* will here, and throughout this book, be used to denote that which is supposed to be immediately, and in one moment, present to the consciousness. "Supposed to be", because we cannot directly observe what is directly present to consciousness.

consciousness, or feeling, has been ascertained by careful observations mathematically discussed to have the properties now to be stated. Feeling, by which is here meant that of which we are supposed to be immediately conscious, is subject to degrees. That is to say, besides the *objective intensity* which distinguishes a loud sound from a faint sound, there is a *subjective intensity* which distinguishes a lively consciousness of a sound, from a dull consciousness of it. Though the two kinds of intensity are apt to go together, yet it is possible for a person at the same time to recall the tick of a watch and the sound of a neighboring cannon, and to have a livelier consciousness of the former than of the latter, without however remembering the latter is a fainter sound than the former. Feelings of slight subjective intensity act upon one another, undergo transformations, and affect the emotions and the voluntary actions; although they do all this less decisively than they would do if they were more intense. They are also, *other things being equal*, much less under control than more subjectively intense feelings. This remark needs explanation. A feeling may be forced upon the mind through the senses, or by experience, directly or indirectly, and bear down the power of the will; and those feelings are the most subjectively intense we have. Why they should be so, will soon be explained. But when a feeling is *not* thus forced upon us our being conscious of it sufficiently to attract attention makes it act more upon us, and at the same time enables us to affect its transformations, more than if it were scarcely perceptible. Now there are certain combinations of feelings which are specially interesting. These are those which tend toward a reaction between mind and body, whether in sense, in the action of the glands, in contractions of involuntary muscles, in coordinated voluntary deeds, or, finally, in discharges of an extraordinary kind of one part of the nerves upon another. Interesting combinations of ideas are in every way more active than others, both in the way of suggestion, and in the way of subjective intensity. The action of thought is all the time going on, not merely in that part of consciousness which thrusts itself on the attention, and which is the most under discipline, but also in its deeply shaded parts, of which we are in some measure conscious but not sufficiently so to be strongly affected by what is there. But when in the uncontrolled play of that part of thought, an interesting combina-

---

Before we can focus attention upon what passes in the mind, that state is long passed, and the idea has undergone transformations which have to be allowed for conjecturally.

There is an illustration of the impossibility of directing thought upon itself, which may appropriately be mentioned in a logical treatise. There are certain logical puzzles,—non-sensical in themselves but interesting from a logical point of view,—which the medieval logicians called the *Insolubilia*.

tion occurs, its subjective intensity increases for a short time with great rapidity.[14] This is what constitutes the fixation of the attention. Contemplation consists in using our self-control to remove us from the forcible intrusion of other thoughts,[15]

---

[14] It may be remarked that this is a very temporary condition, and shortly after the interesting idea will be found to have a lower subjective intensity than it would have had if it had not been interesting.

[15] **[Alt.:]** [...] to seclude us from the forcible intrusion of other thoughts and in dwelling upon the interesting bearings of what may lie hidden in the icon, with a view of causing its subjective intensity to increase.

Thus, then, it is that the complex icon suggests another that is a feature of it. Whenever one thing suggests another, both are together in the mind for an instant. In the present case, this conjunction is specially interesting, and in its turn suggests that the one necessarily involves the other. A few mental experiments,—or even a single one, so expert do we become at this kind of experimental inquiry,—satisfies the mind that the one icon would at all times involve the other, that is, suggest it in a special way, into which we shall soon inquire. Hence, the mind is not only led from believing the premise to judge the conclusion true, but it further attaches to this judgment another that *every* proposition *like* the premise, that is having an icon like it, *would* involve, and compel acceptance, of a proposition related to it as the conclusion then drawn is related to that premise. Thus we see, what is most important, that every inference is thought, at the time of drawing it, as one of a possible class of inferences. In the case of a rational inference, we *see*, in an icon which represents the dependence of the icon of the conclusion upon the icon of the premise, about what that class of inferences is, although as the outlines of icons are always more or less vague, there is always more or less of vagueness in our conception of that class of inferences.

There is no other element of inference essentially different from those which have been mentioned. It is true that changes generally take place in the indices as well as in the icon of the premise. Some indices may be dropped out. Some may be identified. The order of selections may sometimes be changed. But these all take place substantially in the same manner in which a feature of the icon attracts attention and must be justified in the inference by experiments upon icons.

It thus appears that all knowledge comes to us by observation. A part is forced upon us from without and seems to result from Nature's mind; a part comes from the depths of the mind as seen from within, which by an egotistical anacoluthon we call *our* mind.

The three essential elements of inference are, then, colligation, observation, and the judgment that what we observe in the colligated data follows a rule.

Article 13. There is a great distinction between reasoning which depends upon the laws of the inner world and reasoning which depends upon the laws of the outer world.

We observe the outer world and seem to catch the idea of a given line of phenomena. In this way, we have so well detected the nature of the regularity in the motions of the stars that we can make very accurate predictions about them. This we certainly never could do even approximately if there were not an affinity between our mind and nature's. But even granting that affinity, since it is only here and there that we catch an idea, and that, doubtless, only imperfectly, we never can be *sure* that our predictions will be verified. In fact, we are so very far from sure, that the imperfection of our knowledge attracts our attention markedly.

Unscientific people have a very imperfect sense of the grades of assurance that attach to scientific propositions. The first inferences a scientific man makes are very uncertain. Not infrequently, if their value were to be rated simply on the basis of the chances in favour of then being strictly true, they would be worth much less than nothing; for they are much more likely to prove false than true. But knowledge must begin somewhere as well as it can. Those inferences are not valueless, because scientific inquiry does not rest upon them, but goes forward until it refutes them; and in refuting them gains indications of what theory it is that ought to be tried next. Thus, suppose a quantity of inscriptions to be found in a wholly unknown mode of writing and in an unknown tongue. To find out what that writing means, we have to begin with some guess. We should naturally make the most likely guess we possibly could; and that is an inference. Yet it is considerably more likely to be wrong than right. Still, it has to be *tried*. By the time it is satisfactorily refuted, we shall be perhaps in condition to make another guess. But no matter how far science goes, those inferences which are uppermost in the mind of the investigator are very uncertain. They are on probation. They must have a fair trial and not be condemned till proved false beyond all reasonable doubt; and the moment that proof is reached, the investigator must be ready to abandon them without the slightest tenderness toward them. Thus, the scientific inquirer has to be always ready at a moment to abandon summarily all the theories to the establishment study of which he has been devoting perhaps his whole life many years. Take, for example, the case of those who have made the study of telepathy the business of their lives. Notwithstanding all that there is to be said in favor of the theory, those men must, if they were coldly logical, have foreseen when they staked their fortunes upon that hypothesis that the chances were that it would prove to be unfounded. Nevertheless, on they marched, a forlorn hope attacking a terrible problem; and if they are good scientific men, they must be ready any day to come forward and declare that the evidence now is, the whole thing is a delusion. A degree of heroism is required to maintain that attitude which is all the more sublime that the mass of mankind, instead of praising such recantation, will look upon it as utterly contemptible.

But reasoning based upon the laws of the inner world is not thus uncertain. It is called *demonstrative reasoning*, or *demonstration*. For instance, if you add up a column of five hundred figures, you get the sum total by mathematical reasoning. It is said to be absolutely certain that your result will be correct. This is an exaggeration. We have seen that it depends upon observation; and observation is always subject to error. But experimentation is so handy upon creations of our own imagination. The trials can so quickly and at so little cost be repeated; and doing it very frequently we get to be so extremely expert at it, that the probability of error is reduced to a point at which those people who only make dual distinctions, and who class propositions questions into those of which we *positively know* the answers and those of which we *guess* the answers, prefer to class our knowledge of such inferences as positive certainty. In truth, positive certainty is unattainable by man. Are you *sure* twice two are four? Not at all. A certain *per centage* of the human race are insane and subject to illusions. It may be you are one of them, and that your idea that twice two is four is a lunatic notion, and your seeming recollection that other people think so, the baseless fabric of a vision. Or twice two may ordinarily be *five*, but when anybody counts it up, that may have the affect of temporarily reducing it to *four*.

Nevertheless, there is undoubtedly a great distinction between inferences resting on merely inward observation, which a moderate amount of attention can put beyond all reasonable doubt, and inferences based upon our attempts to catch the regularities of Nature, essays in which we

and in considering the interesting bearings of what may lie hidden in the icon, so as to cause the subjective intensity of it to increase.

The observation of the icon may be ordinary direct observation, or it may be scientific observation aided by the apparatus of logical algebra and other technical means.

A third step in ~~reasoning~~ inference is performed upon the indices. Thus, an index may be dropped from consideration. If there are two selective indices one universal, the other particular, and the latter selection is made last, the order of the selections can be reversed. But all these changes in the indices are justified only by considering icons. We may, therefore, say that excepting the colligation of different beliefs the whole of inference consists in *observation*, namely in the observation of icons. Even the colligations well up from the depths of consciousness in precisely the same manner as that in which the special features of icons are remarked.

Thus, all knowledge comes to us by observation, part of it forced upon us from without from Nature's mind and part coming from the depths of that inward aspect of mind, which we egotistically call *ours*; though in truth it is we who float upon its surface and belong to it more than it belongs to us. Nor can we affirm that the inwardly seen mind is altogether independent of the outward mind which is its Creator.

---

can never hope to attain more than a somewhat close approach to the truth, and whose surmised regularities we can hardly be much surprised to find are only quite exceptionally even at all near the ~~truth~~ veritable law. This is the great distinction of *demonstrative* and *experimential* reasoning. Of these two kinds of reasoning the demonstrative, depending upon inward observation and inward regularities, has to be studied first.

The remark that reasoning consists in the observation of an icon will be found equally important in the theory and the practice of reasoning.

Part II: **Development of Existential Graphs**

5 On Logical Graphs

R 482, summer 1896–March 1897. Houghton Library. Produced below are 94 manuscript pages out of 221 sheets that occupy folder R 482, including a dozen or so draft sheets located in R 839 and R S-34. Entitled "On Logical Graphs", the manuscript presents the *entitative* system of graphs, the first system of logical graphs that Peirce elaborated, in greater detail and depth than anywhere else in his work. Later revisions of the manuscript constitute the birthplace of the *existential* system of graphs (EGs), which will at once replace entitative graphs. See Introduction to Part II on Peirce's transition to EGs.

R 482 opens *in medias res* with a description of the parts that compose a graph (§ 1); graphs are connected to Listing's theory of space and thus appearing from the very beginning as topological, multi-dimensional objects. According to the number of *bonds* that graphs may have, they are assigned a *valency*; the valency will be used to designate both graphs and parts of graphs (§ 2). Other than the influence of Listing's topology, the inspiration comes from chemistry (§ 3), even though this analogy will not hold its ground in the long run, as logical graphs need to express different properties than chemical diagrams, in particular asymmetrical relations and negations.

Graphs represent either a complete assertion, i.e. a verb referring to some extant object via a subject or an object, or a relative, that is, a verb without a subject or an object, or without indexical connections (§ 4; Appendix; see also Peirce's "The Logic of Relatives", 1897, p. 163). "In order to interpret a logical graph", Peirce states, "it is first requisite to *indicate the individuals* denoted by its loose ends" (§ 4; emphasis added). This means that these graphs will not talk about the "general range of possibility" but about individuated cases. An important consequence is that the logical meaning of a graph is that of a conditional *de inesse*: "either the antecedent is not true or the consequent is true" (§ 4). § 5–§ 6 then give a graphical illustration to this description. § 6 touches upon the relation of inclusion. The graphical representation is still attached to the conventions of the entitative graphs; nonetheless, Peirce does have a clear idea of where the value of his system of notation lies (§ 7), namely in its analyticity. In § 8, the notion of "second intention" is introduced: "characters of *second intention* are characters which are brought to our knowledge [. . .] by observation of logical forms." Accordingly, characters which do not belong to the objects but to the logical graphs themselves, such as their valency, are characters of second intention. In § 9 Peirce shows how the permissive rules of the previously introduced graphs can be simplified. § 10 introduces and explains several and by no means the final versions of the transformation rules, with plenty of examples. § 11, which is Peirce's later addition, now presents the existential graphs, as the result of reflections on simplifications of rules of transformation.

Appendix reports several alternative drafts in which Peirce returns to and reworks these definitions and rules of transformation just seen. There the shift from entitative to the *positive*, or existential system is present in the "reversed" rules of interpretation. Fragments on the philosophical significance of relations for conduct and alternative formulations of graphs are included at the end of the appendix. Relations are connected with the "maxim of clearness" familiar from Peirce's "How to Make Our Ideas Clear" of his 1878 *Illustrations* series (EP 1, pp. 124–141; W3, pp. 257–276) and the maxim itself becomes further clarified: the meaning of something resides in the "practical difference" that it may cause; feelings are not meaningful *per se*, but insofar as they amount to a change in conduct.

These papers, consistently entitled "On Logical Graphs", thus deserve without any doubt to be called the mother of all of Peirce's papers on logical graphs. Peirce himself retrospectively called this piece the "perfect Calumet mine" for his own later endeavours, and it is his 1896 work that marks the culmination of achievements so much so that he in the letter to Carus boasts it as his *chef d'œuvre* (CSP to Paul Carus, December 29, 1896; LoF 3). Yet among the many pages of R 482 and relevant fragments we most likely do not have the ultimate version of the paper Peirce had submitted to Carus in early 1897 and which he later described as his "most lucid and interesting paper." What has been preserved is the first, 30-page submission from August 31; soon after the paper underwent substantial revisions and additions that could have made it at least twice as long (the highest page number count is 66, and the figure captions run up to 159). It is that first submission which is transcribed here as the first continuous sequence in the main body of the text (§ 1–§ 10), with § 11 and several variants considered as slightly later additions.

§ 1. A *graph*, in its most general sense, would be a diagram composed, first, of *spots*, or parts treated as points, though they have distinguishable sides and are differentiated by simple visible qualities called their *colors*; second, of *bonds*, or parts treated as lines, thought they too may have sides and colors; third, of *faces*, or parts treated as surfaces; and so on to higher dimensions. A graph of the lowest dimensionality has no faces nor higher parts. A *simple-bonded* graph is a graph of lowest dimensionality in which every bond is a simple line with two ends, one of which, at least, is attached to a spot, while the other may either be so attached or may be a *loose end*.

The *Listing numbers* of a graph may be defined as follows. Let a particle have space within the colored parts of the graph to expand in $\mathcal{M} - 1$ dimensions, so as to form an *unlimited* (but not generally infinite) $\mathcal{M}$-dimensional continuum (like a ring or a closed surface), which, once formed, can by no motion within those colored parts of the graph without rupture collapse. Then, the number of such continua each of which occupies some point into which none of the others can be gradually moved within the graph without rupture is the $\mathcal{M}^{\text{th}}$ Listing number. The first Listing number, which may be called the *chorisis*, is the number of separate pieces. The second is the *cyclosis*, or number of independent rings. A graph of chorisis 1 may be called a *connected whole*. A graph of cyclosis 0 may be called *non-cyclic*.

Listing's census-theorem, applied to a simple-bonded graph of the lowest dimensionality is, that the chorisis of a graph *minus* its cyclosis equals the number of spots less the number of *connecting* bonds (bonds with loose ends not being counted).

§ 2. A *valental* graph is a graph of which every spot, by virtue of its color, or inherent quality, has a determinate number of bonds attached to it on determinate sides of it. An attachment to one side of a spot will be different in kind from an attachment to another side. For example, the two graphs of Figs. 1 and 2 will have different diagrammatic meanings, since in the one the pointed sides of the spots are connected, while in the other the pointed sides are connected with the round sides. The places of attachment will be called the *ends* of the spot; and the ends of the spots of a graph which are not attached to a graph by bonds to other spots of the graph or to other ends of the same spot will be called the *ends of the graph*.

Fig. 1   Fig. 2

The graphs of chemistry are valental graphs, although (so far as they are as yet conceived) by a special property the different sides of all the spots are alike. But it must be acknowledged that distinctions between the different bonds of a carbon atom (for instance) may in future be made out. The number of ends of a graph, or of a part of a graph, is its *valency*. Every spot has *in itself* ends, although the whole graph of which it forms a part there may have no ends. There is nothing in the essential nature of a graph to prevent one end of a spot from being attached to another end of the same spot.

Valental graphs (and parts of graphs) receive designations expressive of their valencies, as follows:

Valency	Name of the graph.
0	Medad.
1	Monad.
2	Dyad.
3, etc.	Triad, etc.
> 2	Polyad.
$2N$	Artiad.
$2N + 1$	Perissid.

Besides the Listing theorem, the following second census-proposition holds of valental graphs. *The valency of a graph equals the sum of the valencies of its spots less twice the number of connecting bonds.* It follows, as a corollary, that no perissid can be composed exclusively of artiads; and this constitutes a fundamental distinction between artiads and perissids.

Between Listing's theorem and this second census-proposition the number of connecting bonds may be eliminated. Let a graph be composed of n_0 medads, n_1 monads, n_2 dyads, n_3 triads, etc.; and let k_0 be the sum of the cycloses of the medads, k_1, that of the monads, etc.; and let V, N, K denote respectively the valency, chorisis, and cyclosis of the graph. Then we have the equation

$$V - 2N + 2K = \sum_{0 \le v \le \infty} vn_v - 2n_v + 2k_v.$$

There are evidently still other topical conditions. We may (as the equation shows) conceive of a tetrad spot as composed of two triads, of a pentad spot as composed of three triads, etc. In a connected whole graph, that is, in a graph where $N = 1$, $2 + n_3 - n_1$ may be any number from zero up, while K may be any number whose double does not exceed $2 + n_3 - n_1$. But as long as $N = 1$, $n_0 = 0$, unless $n_0 = 1$ with all other n's equal to zero. We may, therefore, write, for the connected whole graph,

$$V + 2K = 2 + n_3 - n_1 = 2 + \sum_{0 \le v \le \infty} (v - 2)n_v.$$

Thus, the medad spot if it enters into such a graph has the paramount effect upon $V + 2K$, the dyad has none at all, while the monad and the triad act in opposite ways. These four kinds of spots are thus strikingly different in their properties. As for spots of higher valencies, they may naturally be conceived to be composed of triads, and then effects upon $V + 2K$ may be deduced accordingly.[1]

---

1 [Alt.1:]

Description of a Graphical Method of Representing Relations

A *graph* is a diagram composed of *spots* and *bonds*. The spots have qualitative distinctions. The bonds are simple lines, each ending one way at least at a spot while the other way it may either have a *loose end*, or unattached termination, or may end at a spot.

A *valental* graph is a graph of which each spot has a *valency*, or inherent character belonging to every spot of the same quality by virtue of which a ~~definite~~ determinate number of bonds proceed from it, and each from a determinate part of it. (But in the valental graphs of chemistry the different parts of the spots (which represent atoms) have not hitherto been considered as making differences between the bonds.)

Valental graphs and parts of graphs are divisible, according to the number of their loose ends, into

medads whose loose ends are 0,
monads whose loose ends are 1,
dyads whose loose ends are 2,
triads whose loose ends are 3, etc.

A *polyad* has more than 2 loose ends, an *artiad* an even number, a *perissid* an odd number.

Two census-propositions concerning valental graphs are important. The first is, that the valency of the graph equals twice the number of connnecting bonds *minus* the sum of the valencies of the spots. It follows that no combination of artiads can make a perissid; and thus is established a fundamental distinction between artiads and perissids.

The second proposition is that the *chorisis*, or a number of separate pieces comprising the graph, *minus* the *cyclosis*, or number of cuts through bonds and through spots so as to return to its starting-point; equals the number of spots *minus* the number of connecting bonds. It follows that graphs of all valencies can be composed of triads but not all exclusively of graphs of lower valency.

By the combination of these two propositions, we find that the addition to a graph of an α-ad will increase its valency by $\alpha - 2$ *plus* twice the increase of the chorisis *minus* twice the increase of the cyclosis. The addition of a piece cannot increase the chorisis by more than 1; and if it does that, it cannot affect the cyclosis. If one only of the bonds of the added graph is connected, neither chorisis nor cyclosis is affected. If N bonds are connected, the cyclosis minus the chorisis is increased by N. Consequently, the α-ad may either add α to the valency or subtract α from the valency, or add or subtract every alternate number between $+\alpha$ and $-\alpha$. But when we consider only *non-cyclic combinations*, it is the monads only which reduce the valency, while the dyads can be inserted anywhere without affecting the valency. Hence, in chemistry most compounds contain either monads or dyads with parallel bonds like monads; while dyads, such as O and S, are remarkable for multiple proportions in which they combine, as K–O–Cl, K–O–O–Cl, K–O–O–O–Cl, K–O–O–O–O–Cl.

[Alt.2] [From R S-35]

Description of the Graphical Method of Representing Relations

A *graph* is a diagram consisting of *spots* and *bonds*, or simple lines each having one end, at least, at a spot, while the other end is either loose or is connected with a spot.

A *valental* graph is a graph each spot of which has a *valency*, or inherent character by virtue of which a definite number of bonds proceeds from it, and that from definite parts of it.

Valental graphs are divisible, according to the number of their loose ends into *medads* (which have no loose ends), *monads* (which have one), *dyads* (which have two), *triads, tetrads, pentads, hexads*, etc., *polyads* (which have more than two), *artiads* (which have some even number), *perissids* (which have some odd number), etc.

It is obvious that in a valental graph the sum of the valencies of the spots equals twice the number connecting bonds plus the number of loose ends. Hence no combination of artiads can make a perissid, which establishes a fundamental difference between artiads and perissids.

It is obvious, that the graph will consist of a number of pieces equal to the number of spots minus the connecting bonds *plus* the cyclosis, or number of ~~rings formed~~ cuts that can be made without ~~severing~~ increasing the number of pieces. Hence, it follows that the *triad* is the lowest order of graph out of the combinations of which all other orders can be formed.

A *polar* graph is a graph which, if it has more spots than one, has its spots divided into two parts, a *positive* and a *negative*, the negative being encircled by an oval, and the positive not encircled, and the parts of these parts being similarly related, so that the negative part of the negative part is twice enclosed, etc. And a bond is considered as encircled, if both extremities are within the same oval.

A logical graph is a polar valental graph. Its spots represent *relations* and its lines *hecceities*, or objects having positive identities and diversities but, in themselves, no qualities. It signifies that, the denotation of its loose ends being determined, whatever hecceities its unenclosed bonds may denote, if they have the relations signified by the negative part, then they have the relations signified by the positive part.

The following census-propositions concern valental graphs.

§ 3. A *polar* graph is a valental graph which is not simple-bonded, but in which each bond connects a pair of antithetical graphs into a combined graph which has for its ends all the ends of the two antithetical graphs except those by which those antithetical graphs are connected together.[2] Each bond has its two ends unlike, the one being *positive* and the other *negative*; and the two antithetical graphs

---

I. The valency of a graph equals the sum of the valencies of its spots *minus* twice the number of connecting bonds.
   Corollary. No combination of artiads can make a perissid. Hence, the distinction between artiads and perissids is important.
II. The chorisis of a graph minus its cyclosis equals the number of spots minus the number of connecting bonds.
   Corollary. A [end]

2 **[Alt.1:]** By a *polar* graph, I mean a graph which is compound [and] consists of two parts, the one a *negatived*, or reversed polar graph, and the other a polar graph together with the bond between this and the negatived part. This polar graph and the bond make up the *positive* part of the polar graph. The negative part if compound consists again of a negatived polar graph, which, being thus twice negatived, has a positive character on the whole, another polar graph not again negatived and therefore retaining its negative character, and the bond between them which likewise has a negative character. The negative part of a polar graph is marked by being encircled in an oval line, which is not a bond.

The logical graphs are polar valental simple-bonded graphs of the first dimension. Their spots signify relations; then bonds denote the correlates of those relations. An unencircled bond, that is, a bond whose two extremities are not encircled in one oval, mean that any objects of the universe may be taken in the place of those bonds; and the signification of the graph is that if the relation in the negative part is true of those objects then the relation in the positive part is so. In other words, either the relation in the negative part is *not* true or the relation in the positive part is true. A graph must be a medad in order to constitute a complete proposition.

The following are examples of medads of two spots. Let $w-$ mean "___ is wise", $v-$ "___ is virtuous", $-l-$ "___ loves___ ", $-b-$ "___ benefits___ ", $-g_|-$ "___ gives$_|$ to___ ", $-\beta_|-$ "betrays$_|$ to___ ".

[Alt.2:] Chemical formulae are here used as illustrations. It is not unlikely [that] the true chemical graphs are ~~really~~ polar, although it is hardly conceivable they should be unbalanced.

The graphs of logic are unbalanced, polar, valental graphs. The spots represent characters; the bonds their subjects. To interpret a graph, the denotation of the loose ends must first be fixed. Then, the unencircled connecting bonds represent each anything in the universe; and the signification is that if the negative constituent is true of the subjects denoted by its bonds then the positive constituent is true of the subjects connected by its bonds. This is the same as to say that either the negative constituent is not true of its bonds or the positive constituent is true of its bonds. This is the same as to say that either the negative constituent is not true of its bonds or the positive constituent is true of its bonds. This, if w means "___ is wise", v "___ is virtuous", u "___ is intelligent", l "___ loves___ ", b "___ benefits___ ", s "___ is servant of___ ", g "___ gives$_|$ to___ ", t "___ takes$_|$ from___ ", Fig. 5 means "if anything is wise it is virtuous", Fig. 6 means "if anything benefits anything, the latter loves the former"; Fig. 7 means "anything

are the positive and the negative constituent of the combined graph which they compose. Of course, in a polar graph no two ends of the same graph can be directly connected.

An *imbalanced* polar graph is a polar graph in every part of which the negative constituent has a reversed character, so that the negative constituent of the negative constituent has a positive character. The bond or bonds connecting the two constituents of a combined graph of this kind are best drawn so as to encircle the negative constituent, while they are merely attached to the positive constituent.

The following figures illustrate unbalanced polar medads. In order to give them some conceivable meaning, the spots are lettered as chemical atoms, although there is no reason to suppose that chemical compounds, even if they can

---

whatever is given only by a person from whom it is taken by every person to whom it is given", etc. Fig. 8 illustrates the effect of double reversal of the negative constituents of the negative constituent of a medad. It means "take any two persons X and Y; then if X is so related to Y that taking any person, Z, if X is a servant of Z then Z is a lover of Y it follows that X is a benefactor [end]

[Alt.3:] The graphs of logic are unbalanced, polar, valental graphs. Each spot stands for a character and has a number of loose ends equal to the number of subjects required by that character for its embodiment. The bonds stand for the subjects. To interpret a graph it is first necessary to determine the subjects which its loose ends denote. Then, the unencircled connecting bonds represent each anything in the universe; and the signification is that if the negative, encircled constituent graph, which is called the *antecedent*, is true of the subjects denoted by its bonds, then the positive, unencircled constituent graph, which is called the *consequent*, is true of the subjects denoted by its bonds. Since before this assertion can be enunciated, the individuals denoted by the bonds must be selected, this statement that if the antecedent is true, the consequent is true, is equivalent to the assertion that either the antecedent is not true or the consequent is true. A complete proposition is represented by a medad. This must either be a medad spot, unanalyzed, which would be useless for logical purposes, or it must consist of an antecedent and a consequent, having the same number of loose ends. These loose ends are connected and denote any things in the universe which the reader of the graph may choose. The consequent, if compound, again consists of an antecedent and a consequent; and the bonds connecting them also denote any things which the reader may choose. The antecedent, if compound, also consists of an antecedent and a consequent; but the connecting bonds being here encircled, are reversed in their representative function and the choice of the individuals they denote is transferred to the writer of the graph, who is supposed to choose them suitably so as to render the assertion true. Moreover, the antecedent of the antecedent, being twice encircled is twice negatived, and thus becomes affirmative. Thus, bonds and spots encircled odd times are negative on the whole. Negative spots represent characters denied. Negative bonds represent subjects which the writer suitably selects. But bonds and spots encircled even times (including no time) are positive. The characters represented by such spots are affirmed. The subjects represented by such bonds are to be selected at the pleasure of the reader. The subjects denoted by unencircled bonds are to be first selected; then those denoted by bonds once encircled; then those denoted by bonds twice encircled, and so on.

be correctly represented by polar graphs, can be so represented by *unbalanced* polar graphs. Fig. 3 represents a medad composed of two monads. Fig. 4 is a medad composed of two dyads. Fig. 5 is a medad composed of two triads. Fig. 6

Fig. 3   Fig. 4   Fig. 5   Fig. 6

is a medad composed of two monads. Namely, the positive part is a monad, CN, composed of the tetrad, C, as its negative part and the triad, N, as its positive part; while the negative constituent of the whole medad is a monad, PH_4, composed of the monad, H, as its negative part and the dyad, PH_3, as its positive part; and this dyad, again, is composed of the monad, H, as its positive part, and the triad, PH_2, as its positive part; and this triad is composed of the monad, H, as its negative part and the tetrad, PH, as its positive part, and this tetrad is composed of the monad H as its negative part and the pentad, P, as its positive part.

§ 4. The graphs of logic are of the kind just described. Each spot stands for a character, and has a number of hands equal to the number of subjects requisite for the embodiment of that character. Thus, the character of giving ___ to ___ supposes a giver, a "donee", and a gift; but the character of giving something to ___ only supposes a giver and a receiver, since in this character the gift is generalized, and its embodiment already determined. The nexes of logical graphs stand for the subjects of the characters. A logical graph is either a complete assertion or a *relative*. A *relative*, or *complete relative*, precisely defined, is an incomplete assertion, requiring only certain subjects to be determined to make it complete. These missing subjects are indicated by the hands of the graph. A logical medad expresses a complete assertion. In order to interpret a logical graph, it is first requisite to indicate the individuals denoted by its loose ends. Then, the bonds by which the encircled, or negative, constituent graph, which is called the *antecedent*, is joined to the unencircled, or positive constituent graph, which is called the *consequent*, denote any things which the reader of the graph may choose; and the meaning is that if the antecedent is true of the subjects denoted by its hands, then the consequent is true of the subjects denoted by its hands. This hypothetical proposition is a *consequentia de inesse*, because everything having been already precisely specified, it refers to no general range of possibility. Hence, it merely means that either the antecedent is not true or the consequent is true. If antecedent and consequent are each compound, each is composed of an antecedent and a consequent. The consequent being taken positively, its mode of composition is precisely like that of the whole graph; but the antecedent being negative, its mode of composition is reversed. The assertion that it is not true means that, the subjects denoted by its hands being determined, the *writer* of the graph (not the *reader*) is to choose the subjects denoted by the bonds connecting its antecedent and consequent, and that these can be so chosen that the antecedent of the antecedent shall be true of the subjects denoted by its loose ends, while the consequent of the antecedent shall not be true of the subjects denoted by its loose ends.

§ 5. I proceed to illustrate these general statements by examples. Let the universe be the totality of men. Let $u-$ mean "___ is ugly", $v-$ "___ is virtuous", $w-$ "___ is wise", $-l-$ "___ loves ___", $-b-$ "___ benefits ___", $-s-$ "___ serves ___", $-\dot{g}-$ "___ gives^l to ___", $-\dot{t}-$ "___ takes^l from ___", $-\dot{\beta}-$ "___ betrays^l to ___", $-\dot{p}-$ "___ praises^l to ___". Then, Figs. 7, 8, 9 show how antecedent and consequent can be connected by any number of bonds. Fig. 7 means "any man, X, being chosen at pleasure by the reader, either X is not wise or X is virtuous", that is, "every wise man is virtuous". Fig. 8 means, "any men, X and Y (the same or

Fig. 7   Fig. 8   Fig. 9   Fig. 10

different) being taken at pleasure, either X does not love Y or X benefits Y", that is, whoever loves anybody benefits that person. Fig. 9 means, "any men, X, Y, Z, being taken at pleasure, either X does not give Y to Z or Z takes Y from X"; that is, whoever is given by a man to a man is taken by the latter from the former.

Figs. 10, 11, 12 illustrate compound antecedents and consequents. In Fig. 10, the antecedent is the part containing w and l, the latter being the antecedent of the antecedent. The consequent is the part containing b and v, the former being the antecedent of the consequent. The meaning is, "any man, Y, being taken at

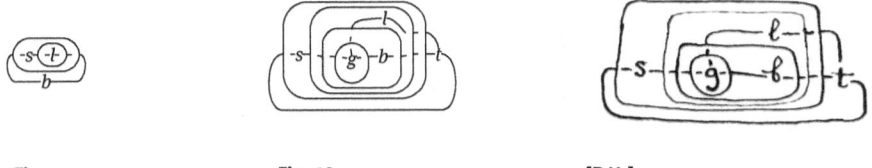

Fig. 11   Fig. 12   [P.H.]

pleasure, and any man, Z, being taken at pleasure, a man, A, can be so chosen, that either A is not wise but loves Y or Y does not benefit Z, or Z is virtuous"; that is, whoever is loved only by the wise benefits only the virtuous. In Fig. 11, the antecedent is "___ is a servant of every lover of ___", the consequent is "___ benefits ___". The medad means, "any two men, X and Y, being taken at pleasure, a man, A, can be so chosen that either X is not a servant of A but A loves Y or else X benefits Y"; that is, any servant of all lovers of a person benefits that person. In Fig. 12, t is the consequent, s is the consequent of the antecedent, l is the consequent of the antecedent's antecedent, b is the consequent of the antecedent's antecedent's antecedent, and g is the antecedent of the antecedent's antecedent's antecedent. The assertion is "any three persons, Z, X, Y, being taken at pleasure, a person A can be found such that taking any person, W, at pleasure, a person B can be found such that Z takes Y from X if X serves A in case W loves Y provided that supposing A gives W to B, B benefits Z"; that is, every servant of every giver only to benefactors of anything, X, the gift being only of lovers of anybody Y, is a person from whom X takes Y. In the last case, a relation is accurately expressed in a form useful for logical purposes, although it is too complicated for the facile apprehension by an ordinary mind.

§ 6. Another way of expressing in words the meaning of a medad may now be explained. The rule is somewhat varied according to the cyclosis of the unenclosed bonds considered as continued through the spots and encircled graphs. First, in case the cyclosis of the unencircled bonds is 1, as in Figs. 2 and 5, we begin at any unencircled bond, and calling it "everything", proceed round the ring in either direction, asserting of it the relations represented. In passing from a bond, X, through an encircled graph, μ, then through a bond and through an unencircled spot, v, to a bond, Y, we read "X is μ, if of anything at all, only of a v of Y". If μ is an unencircled spot and v is an encircled graph, we read, "X is μ of whatever v of Y there may be". If both μ and v are encircled graphs we read, "X has to Y the relation of a μ to some of it". Thus, Fig. 2 may be read by this rule in four ways as follows:

1. Beginning at the left and proceeding clockwise, "everybody loves only what is benefitted by himself";
2. Beginning at the left and proceeding counterclockwise, "everybody is benefitted by whoever is loved by him";
3. Beginning at the right and proceeding clockwise, "everybody is benefitted by whoever loves him";
4. Beginning at the right and proceeding counterclockwise, "everybody is loved only by benefactors of him".

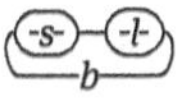

Fig. 13

Fig. 13 may be read as follows:

- "Any person stands only to persons benefitted by him, in the relation of serving lovers of them";
- "Anybody is a lover only of persons benefitted by every servant of his";
- "Everybody is benefitted by every servant of a lover of him";
- "Everybody benefits everybody loved by a person served by him";
- "Anybody stands only to his benefactors in the relation of being loved by their masters";
- "Everybody is served only by benefactors of everybody loved by him".

By the same rule, Fig. 11 may be read as follows:

- "Everybody stands only to persons benefitted by himself in the relation of servant to whoever may love them";
- "Everybody benefits everybody who stands to him in the relation of being loved only by persons served by him";
- "Everybody stands only to his benefactors in the relation of being loved only by persons served by them";
- "Everybody is benefitted by everybody who stands to him in the relation of serving every lover of his".

Second, in case the cyclosis of the unencircled bonds is 0, we begin at any such bond and read separately the two parts between that bond and the extremities of the line of unencircled bonds, not as assertions, but as descriptions of that bond. The assertion then is, supposing C be the part containing the unencircled spot, and A is the other part, either "The things that are C embrace whatever there may be that is A" or "The things that are A, if they exist at all, embrace only things that are C".

Thus Fig. 10 may be read in the following ways:

- "The persons that are loved only by the wise include only benefactors only of the virtuous";
- "The persons that benefit only the virtuous include whatever there may be that is loved only by the wise";

- "The virtuous include whatever there may be that is benefitted by a person who is loved only by the wise";
- "The persons benefitted by persons that are loved only by the wise include only virtuous persons".

Third, in case the cyclosis of the unencircled bonds exceeds 1, it seems most in harmony with this style of reading to read round the rings as far as possible and then join them by separate statements. Thus, Fig. 14 may be read (among many such ways) as follows:

Fig. 14

- "A person stands to two persons in relation of being benefitted by a lover of a giver of him to a taker of one of those persons from the other only if the former serves the latter";
- "A person stands to two persons in the relation of benefactor of a person given by a person loved by him to a taker of one of those persons from the other etc.";
- "One person stands to another in the relation of being taken from that other by a person to whom is given a person benefitted by a lover of the given only if the former is a servant of the latter".

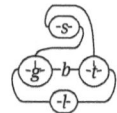

Fig. 15

Fig. 15 may be read,

- "Everybody is a benefactor of every taker of a slave of a person given to him by a lover of the person from which the person he benefits takes the slave".

§ 7. The rule that a logical graph consists of two parts differently connected the one to the other, and that the circle is an intrinsic part of the bond, is not an arbitrary convention. For we are bound in logic to restrict ourselves to one kind of sign where one will suffice. This is not from a blind instinct to economy. Its reason is that if two signs are used where one will suffice, each of these signs is capable of expression as some complication or specific determination of one sign. But we are bound to carry our logical analysis to the furthest point, when the analysis of thought is the very business we have in hand. Hence, if one sign can be expressed as a complication or special determination of another, we are bound so to express it in logical analysis. Now an unsymmetrical relation can never be expressed as a complex or special case of a symmetrical relation; but a symmetrical relation may be expressible by means of an unsymmetrical relation. Moreover, a combination other than in pairs can be expressed by means of combinations by pairs. The method adopted is believed to be the only method by which all connections of relatives can be expressed by a single sign. Besides, the mode of connection here used must be recognized by the logician as the fundamental mode of logical connection, since it is that mode in which the premise of reasoning is connected with its conclusion. For to say that C follows logically from A, is the same as to say that, taking any logical possibility at pleasure, that is either a case of the falsity of A or it is a case of the truth of C.

§ 8. Characters of *second intention* are characters which are brought to our knowledge, not by observation of their subjects, but by observation of logical forms. Relatives of second intention are of high importance in logic, as might be anticipated. Especially so are those which express the numbers of collections. All such arithmetical relatives are expressible in terms of three fundamental arithmetical relatives, a monad, a dyad, and a triad.

Without these the most elementary requisites of logic cannot be fulfilled. For instance, a medad asserts alternatively, or disjunctively, either the falsity of its antecedent or the truth of its consequent. Another medad may, perhaps, owing to the relations between the meanings of the relatives involved, precisely deny the first medad. But for the purposes of logic we wish so to express this denial that it may be shown by the inspection of the logical forms that it is a precise denial of the first. For this purpose, the form must show that it copulatively, or simultaneously, asserts two things: For the denial of an alternative assertion of one or other of two things is a copulative assertion of two things. Now the form of the medad does not permit us to make a formally copulative assertion without alternative. It is true that if the antecedent is compound, the truth of the antecedent of the antecedent and the falsity of the consequent of the antecedent are copulatively asserted, but this assertion is conditional upon the falsity of the consequent of the medad. The only way to express a copulative proposition, is to make the falsity of this consequent formally apparent. The consequent must be such that its truth is self-contradictory. It must directly assert its own falsity. For this purpose, a monad is required which shall mean "___ is not anything".

So much is evident. It is not yet proved that this monad must be an unanalyzed one, that is, a spot; but we may provisionally represent it by a dot with a small tail to show that it is a monad, as in Fig. 16. It is already plain that the monad of nullity must be expressed by an unencircled graph. By means of this relative, we can express such copulative assertions as "nobody loves every virtuous man", as shown in Fig. 17, and "nobody loves only the virtuous", as shown in Fig. 18. These are cop-

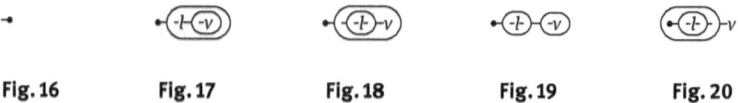

Fig. 16   Fig. 17   Fig. 18   Fig. 19   Fig. 20

ulative; for the former asserts that anybody, M, being taken at pleasure, somebody, N, can be found such that M does not love N and N is virtuous; while the latter asserts that M loves N and N is not virtuous.

The form of the medad requires every direct combination to consist of an affirmative and a negative assertion. It is true that any number of negatives can practically be directly connected; but an affirmative must always accompany them. This is partly remedied by the monad of nullity. Thus, the medad of Fig. 19 means "Taking any two men, M and N, at pleasure, either M does not love N or N is not virtuous". So, Fig. 20 means, "Taking any man N at pleasure, a man, M, can be found such that either M loves N or N is virtuous". But this does not help us in case the relatives to be combined are both monads. Thus, we have as yet no means of expressing, "every man is either wise or virtuous", nor "every man is either not wise or not virtuous", that is, no wise man is virtuous. We can, indeed, do so by taking a monad which shall signify "___ is not wise"; but it is requisite for the purposes of logic that the relation between such a proposition and "every wise man is ugly" should be exhibited, and therefore that the monad "___ is wise" should be used. It is plain that the reason the monad of nullity fails to answer the purpose in such cases is that it is a monad. In order to express "no wise man is virtuous", we require a dyad, like the spot of Fig. 21,

Fig. 21   Fig. 22

having such a meaning that the assertion, "Taking any two men, M and N, at pleasure, either M is not wise or N is not virtuous or M has the relation signified by the spot to N" shall be equivalent to the assertion, "Taking any man, M, at pleasure, either M is not wise or N is not virtuous". That is to say, the dyad represented by the spot must be "___ is not one and the same individual as ___". Then, Fig. 22 means "Taking any man, N, at pleasure, either N is virtuous, or there is a man, M, who is one and the same individual as N, who is wise", that is, every man is either wise or virtuous. It is evident that such propositions could not be expressed without such a graph, whether it be a spot or not. It is further plain that this dyad of negation much be expressed by an unencircled graph.

The form of the medad still limits us to two assertions about any individual. This may, at first glance, seem to be an arbitrary convention. It may be asked why we should not use Fig. 23 to express the proposition "Everybody is either not ugly, or not virtuous, or not wise". The answer is that there is every reason why we should do so; only we must not overlook the fact that the node joining the three bonds is here a relative meaning "___, and ___, and ___ are not one individual". So Fig. 24 means "Everybody is either both ugly and virtuous or is wise". This triad of diversity is very important. In writing it, it is best to put a dot at the node.

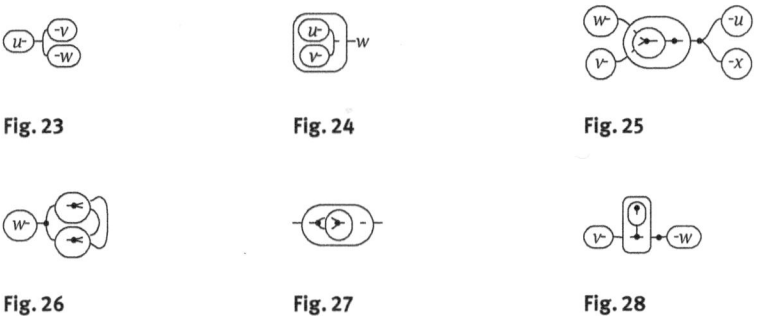

Fig. 23   Fig. 24   Fig. 25

Fig. 26   Fig. 27   Fig. 28

These three relatives all signify non-unity. No fourth is required; for Fig. 25 expresses that anybody is either not ugly, or not virtuous, or not wise, or not extravagant. Nor can any of the three relatives of non-unity be expressed by means of the other two. It is true that Fig. 26 would usually amount to saying that nobody is wise; but strictly, it expresses that if anything is wise, that is the only individual that exists. The dyad of Fig. 27 expresses that "___ is not ___"; but it only does so as an encircled graph and, therefore, does not answer the purpose.

We must now notice an important arithmetical dyad expressible by means of the three relatives of non-unity. It is shown in Fig. 28 the medad of which means "Either no man is virtuous or no man is wise". The dyad which is here interposed between *v* and *w* asserts that its correlates are neither two nor one, but are none. In short, it signifies the relation of non-coexistence. It may be called the *dyad of nullity*. By means of this relative we can formally and precisely deny the assertion of any medad. Thus, Fig. 29 precisely denies Fig. 7.

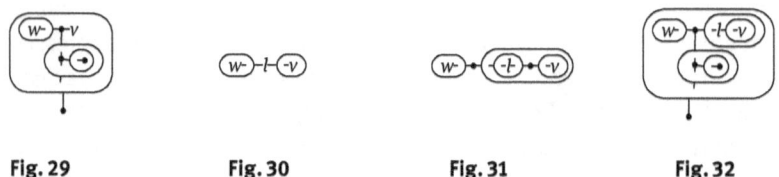

Fig. 29 **Fig. 30** **Fig. 31** **Fig. 32**

We are now in condition to express every possible proposition. A few examples will be useful. Fig. 30 means "Every wise man loves every virtuous man". Fig. 31 means, "Every wise man loves some virtuous man". Fig. 32 means, "Some

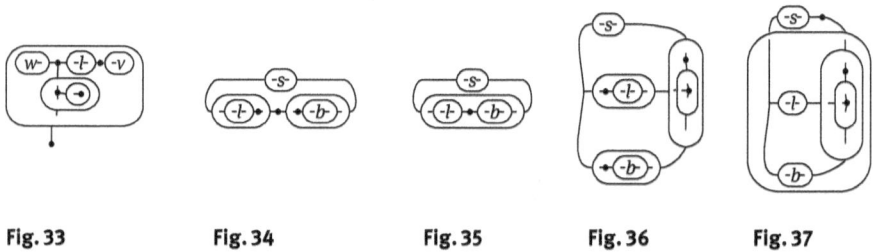

Fig. 33 **Fig. 34** **Fig. 35** **Fig. 36** **Fig. 37**

wise man loves every virtuous man". Fig. 33 means, "Some wise man loves some virtuous man". Fig. 34 means, "Every servant of a man is a lover of everybody except benefactors of that man", or, what is the same, "Every servant of a man is a

Fig. 38 **Fig. 39**

non-lover only of benefactors of that man". Fig. 35 means, "Every servant of a man is a lover of a benefactor of that man". Fig. 36 means, "Every servant of a man is either a lover or a benefactor of that man". Fig. 37 means, "Every servant of a man is both a lover and a benefactor of that man". Fig. 38 means, "Either every wise man is virtuous or every lover of a man is a benefactor of the man". Fig. 39 means, "Some wise man is not virtuous and some lover of a man is not a benefactor of that man".

These examples will suffice to show the expressive power of our single sign of the connection of relatives when it is aided by the three fundamental arithmetical relatives. At the same time, they leave vast fields of its powers unexplored, in some respects the most important.

§ 9. Although for the reasons partially stated in §7 and partly in §8, the above statement of the theory of the logical graphs is correct, yet there are certain simplifications which are more than permissible abbreviations. They positively ought

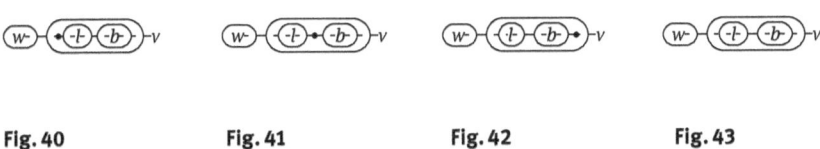

Fig. 40 Fig. 41 Fig. 42 Fig. 43

to be used in order to exhibit the full truth about graphs. In the first place, the dyad of negation ought to be omitted. For it may be inserted at any point in the bonds within the same enclosure in which it is placed. For instance, Figs. 40, 41, and 42 mean the same thing, namely, "Every wise man stands to every man except the virtuous in the relation of lover of some benefactor of his". Writing Fig. 43, it is evident that, in order to give a consequent to the antecedent of the consequent of the medad, the dyad must be inserted somewhere in the circle enclosing *l* and *b*; and it is all the same thing where it is inserted. Of course, when the dyad of negation is enclosed by itself in a circle, this circle must by no means be omitted; and in such case, it is material where the dyad is to be inserted. For it is only the bonds within one circle which are indifferent in respect to the placing of the dyad of negation. Thus, Fig. 44 means, "Nobody is wise or everybody is a lover only of the virtuous, except for one individual who may be the only wise man and the only lover of somebody not virtuous". But Fig. 45 has a different meaning, namely, "Every wise man is a lover of nobody and everybody

 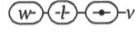

Fig. 44 Fig. 45

is virtuous except for one individual who may be at once the only wise man who loves anybody and the only man not virtuous".

In the second place, the loose ends of the dyad of nullity ought not to be shown; and a triad of diversity directly connected with a dyad of nullity ought to be omitted. The reason is, that whatever indeterminacy in the completed graph such omission occasions can have no effect upon the meaning. Thus, Figs. 46 and 47 have precisely the same meaning, namely, "Either nobody loves anybody or everybody benefits everybody"; and therefore Fig. 48 ought to replace them both. Again, Figs. 33 and 49 have the same meaning. For to say that some wise man loves some virtuous man is the same as to say that some virtuous man is loved by some wise man. Hence, both should be replaced by Fig. 50, where the attachment to the outer

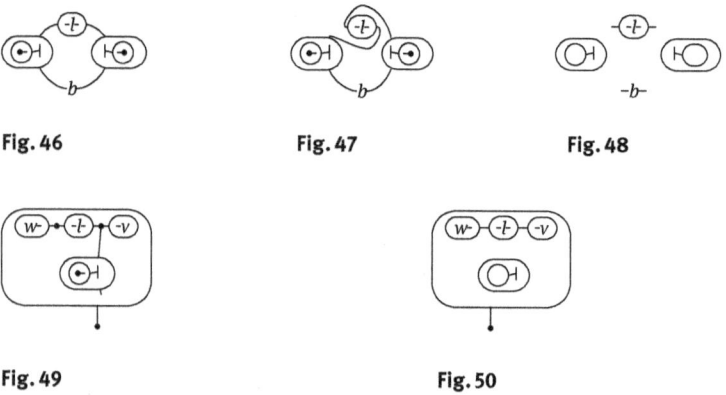

Fig. 46 Fig. 47 Fig. 48

Fig. 49 Fig. 50

circle must be due to one of the loose ends of the dyads of nullity. So, Figs. 51, 52, and 53 have the same meaning, and should be replaced by Fig. 54.

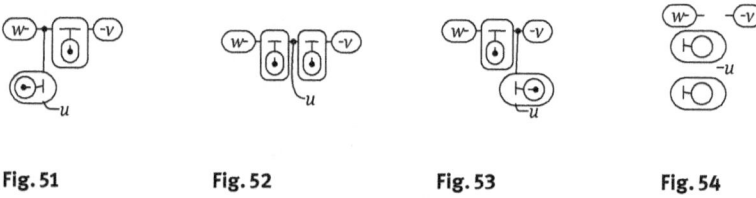

Fig. 51 Fig. 52 Fig. 53 Fig. 54

In the third place, when, in consequence of omissions, a graph appears within two circles, the one immediately enclosing the other and nothing else, both ought to be dropped, as annulling each other. For in such a case, there are always two graphs either of which may be so doubly enclosed, without any difference in the meaning. For instance, Figs. 55 and 56 have the same meaning, that "All but the virtuous are loved by all the wise". Hence, they should be replaced by Fig. 57, which does not make meaningless distinctions, and thus avoids complications, and shows the real similarity in the modes of connection of *l* and *v*. On the same principle, Fig. 34 is to be replaced by Fig. 58; Fig. 36 by Fig. 59; and Fig. 38 by Fig. 60.

Fig. 55 **Fig. 56** **Fig. 57** **Fig. 58** **Fig. 59** **Fig. 60**

These simplifications consist in omitting features which diversify graphs without any corresponding diversification of meaning. The more diagrammatically perfect a system of representation, the less room it affords for different ways of expressing the same fact. Still further to carry out this idea, we ought, in the fourth place, when two triads of diversity are directly connected to shorten the bond of

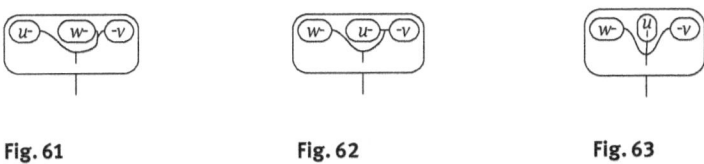

Fig. 61 **Fig. 62** **Fig. 63**

connection to nothing. Thus, Figs. 61 and 62, which mean that "Every man is ugly, or every man is wise, or every man is virtuous", are to the replaced by Fig. 63.

Upon the same principle we ought, in the fifth place, to cut off any loose end of a triad of diversity which is attached merely to a monad of nullity. Thus, Fig. 64 will

Fig. 64 **Fig. 65** **Fig. 66** **Fig. 67** **Fig. 68** **Fig. 69** **Fig. 70**

be replaced by Fig. 7; and by the same principle Fig. 65 will be reduced to Fig. 66 which will then show one circle directly outside another and will therefore be replaced by Fig. 67. The meaning is, "No man is wise". Upon the same principle,

Fig. 68 will reduce to Fig. 69, where the circle has no loose end. The meaning is, "Some man is not wise"; while with a loose end, as in Fig. 67, the denial is universal. Thus, the tailless circle becomes the sign of precise denial. In the same manner Fig. 63 is replaced by Fig. 70.

In Fig. 70, the u, v, w are all positive and the double enclosure ought for simplicity to be dispensed with. That which prevents this being done is that the bonds are only once enclosed. But there is no reason why we should not have enclosed bonds connecting unenclosed spots, that is bonds enclosed an odd number of times connecting spots enclosed an even number of times. That is, in fact, the description of Fig. 70. We do not depart from the essential idea of the method in selecting the lowest odd and even numbers convenient. Since we have represented an evenly enclosed bond by a single line (though we now see that it would have been more logical to use two parallel lines), an oddly enclosed bond ought to be represented by any even number of parallel lines; and the most convenient even number to use is zero. Hence, Fig. 70 may properly be replaced by Fig. 11, where

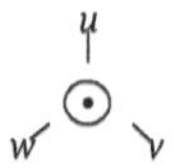

Fig. 71

Fig. 72

nothing but a dot remains of the polyad of diversity. This being encircled may be represented by a blank; and we thus finally reach Fig. 72, where the copulation of the propositions, "Every man is wise, and every man is virtuous, and every man is ugly", is represented by simply writing them down together. Notwithstanding these six rules of simplification, the graphical method uses but a fundamental single sign, over and above the spots. But abbreviations are resorted to in six cases in which the complications of the fundamental sign become meaningless.

§ 10. The ratiocinative transformations of graphs appear to be of ~~six~~ seven kinds, corresponding to steps which I have independently recognized in inference. Enumerating them in the order of difficulty, they are: First, Copulation (or colligation) and Disjunction (or enumeration); second, Omission and Insertion; third, Duplication and Unification; fourth, Identification and Diversification; fifth, Reassociation, ~~consisting of Extraction and Intraction~~ depending upon Involution and Evolution; sixth, the Introduction, Transformation, and Elimination of the three fundamental arithmetical relatives, seventh, Abstraction and Generation.[3]

All illative processes are subject to the apagogical principle, or principle of contraposition, which, as applied to graphs, is as follows: *If any illative process is valid within an even number of enclosures, its reverse is valid within an odd number, and vice versa.*

Copulation consists in uniting a number of premises into one proposition. Thus, given the two premises, All men are mortal and Enoch was a man, we immediately infer the single proposition, All men are mortal and Enoch was a man. This is effected by simply writing the different graphs together, as in Fig. 72.

Disjunction is the separation of the different elements of a condition for the purpose of tracing their separate consequences.

Omission is the dropping out of irrelevant parts of a statement: *Insertion* is the ~~apagogical modification of omission~~ attachment of an unnecessary alternative. The rule of these processes, as applied to graphs, is as follows: *Within odd enclosures any part of a medad may be struck out and within even enclosures any arbitrary attachment may be made, so long as the connections of parts that are neither omitted nor inserted remain undisturbed. But with negatived bond between the permanent and transient parts, this rule is reversed.* The omission or insertion of a triad of diversity does not disturb the connections of the permanent parts. An example or two may be given. By Insertion, from the medad of Fig. 67, meaning "Nobody is wise" may be inferred that of Fig. 7, meaning "Whatever is wise is virtuous", or, less paradoxically stated, "Nobody but the virtuous is wise". From this again

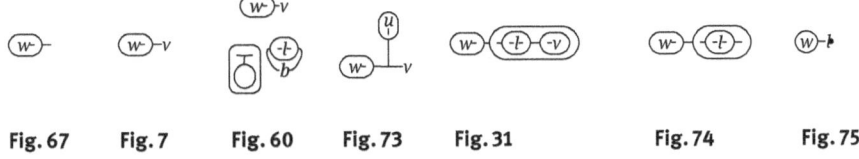

Fig. 67   Fig. 7   Fig. 60   Fig. 73   Fig. 31   Fig. 74   Fig. 75

can be inferred the medad of Fig. 60, meaning, "Either every wise man is virtuous or every man is benefitted by every lover of his". Or, from the medad of Fig. 7 that of Fig. 73 can be inferred, meaning, "Whoever is both wise and ugly is virtuous". By Omission, from the medad of Fig. 31, meaning, "Every wise man loves some virtuous man", that of Fig. 74 can be inferred, meaning, "Every wise man loves

---

[3] [Alt.:] § 9. The chief illative transformations of graphs may be termed Copulation, or obligation, and Disjunction, or enumeration, Omission and Insertion, Identification and Diversification, Involution and Evolution, and manipulation of second intentions.

somebody". This may be written as in Fig. 75, where the dot is connected with the *l* by a negatived bond. Again from Fig. 24, meaning, "Everybody is either wise or both virtuous and ugly", is obtained by omission Fig. 76, which by striking out the mutually annulling circles becomes Fig. 77, meaning, "Everybody is either wise or virtuous". So from Fig. 28, meaning, "Either there is no virtuous man or there is no wise man", can be inferred the medad of Fig. 78, meaning, "There are not more than one man who are either wise or virtuous, if there be any wise man and any virtuous man". If it be desired to omit a dyad oddly enclosed, this can be done by putting in place of it the dyad of nullity; and so in place of an evenly enclosed dyad of nullity any dyad may be inserted. Thus, from the medad of Fig. 31 may be inferred that of Fig. 79 meaning, "If there is any wise man, there is a virtuous man". So from the medad of Fig. 28 may be inferred that of Fig. 30, meaning, "Every wise man loves every virtuous man". It is to be observed that universal propositions are throughout this paper taken in the Philonian sense, that is, are understood not to assert the existence of their subject.

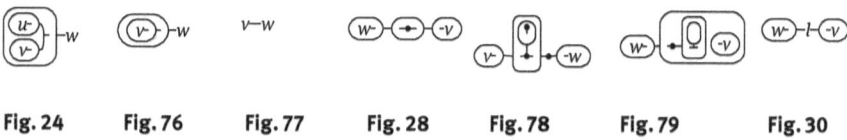

Fig. 24   Fig. 76   Fig. 77   Fig. 28   Fig. 78   Fig. 79   Fig. 30

Duplication, or immediate iteration, is the reassertion of a part of the premiss, just as the hypotheses of mathematics are used over and over again in the course of the reasoning. *Unification* ~~Condensation~~ is the removal of tautology from a condition. Duplication differs from insertion in being permissible when omission, but not insertion, is permissible; and in like manner unification may take place when insertion, but not omission, is permissible. The rule, as applied to graphs, is as follows: *A graph forming a part of a medad may be duplicated by placing a triad of diversity upon each of its bonds and connecting these in their proper order with a repetition of that graph; and such a duplication of a part of a medad may be removed.* Nothing is said in the rule about the enclosures because the duplication when not permissible by *Insertion* is permitted by its special rule, and the removal when not permissible by Omission is so by Unification. Thus from the medad of Fig. 8, may be inferred by Insertion that of Fig. 80, and by Duplication that of Fig. 81; and from the former the medad of Fig. 8 can be reinferred by Unification, as it can from that of Fig. 81 by Omission.

Fig. 8   **Fig. 80**   **Fig. 81**

Identification is the inferential step whereby the number of objects chosen at the will of the hearer is reduced. *Diversification* is the apagogical modification of identification whereby the number of objects chosen at the will of the speaker is increased. The rule, as applied to graphs is as follows: *Any oddly enclosed bond can be severed in its midst and any evenly enclosed bond can be severed at its junction with a circle, so as to leave one new end outside and the other inside that circle; and any two evenly enclosed bonds can be joined by placing a triad of diversity in the midst of each and joining these two triads by a new bond, and an evenly enclosed bond can in the same manner be joined to an oddly enclosed bond, provided the new bond cannot be severed by this rule.* When a bond is spoken of as oddly or evenly enclosed, it must be conceived as ending at any circle which it reaches and as ending before it reaches any circle within which any part of it lies. Thus, the whole of the bond is plainly enclosed in the same circles. As an example of the severance of a bond in its midst, from the medad of Fig. 11, meaning,

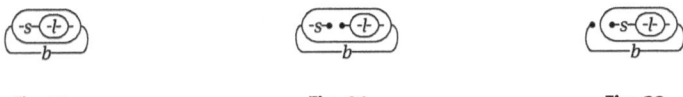

Fig. 11   **Fig. 82**   **Fig. 83**

"Every servant of every lover of a person is a benefactor of that person", can be inferred that of Fig. 82, meaning, "Taking any two persons, X and Y, if X serves everybody or Y is loved by nobody, then X benefits Y". As an example of the severance of an evenly enclosed bond from the same medad of Fig. 8 can be inferred that of Fig. 83, which means, "Whoever is loved only by persons served by all men is benefitted by all men". As an example of the first kind of identification, from the medad of Fig. 84 can be inferred that of Fig. 85. That is, from "Whoever is praised to whoever benefits everybody that serves only virtuous men by everybody loved only by wise men is ugly", is inferred, "Anybody, X, is ugly or else persons, A and B, can be found such that A praises X to B, while taking any person, Y, whoever he may be, if he loves A he is wise and if he is a servant only of virtuous persons, he is benefitted by B". As an example of the second kind of identification, from the same medad of Fig. 84 can be inferred that of Fig. 86, which means, "Anybody, X, is ugly unless two persons, A and B, exist one of whom, A praises X to the other B, and taking any person, Y, a person, C, can be found who is either wise or does not love A, and unless Y is benefitted by B, Y is a servant of C and C is not virtuous". As a simpler example, from the medad of Fig. 87, meaning, "Every wise man stands to every virtuous man in the relation of lover of some benefactor of his", can be inferred the medad of Fig. 88, meaning, "Every man both wise and virtuous both loves and is benefitted by somebody". By the second mode of identification from the same medad of Fig. 87 can be inferred that of Fig. 89, which means, "If there is any wise man, then every virtuous man is benefitted by somebody; and that benefactor, if he be wise, loves himself".

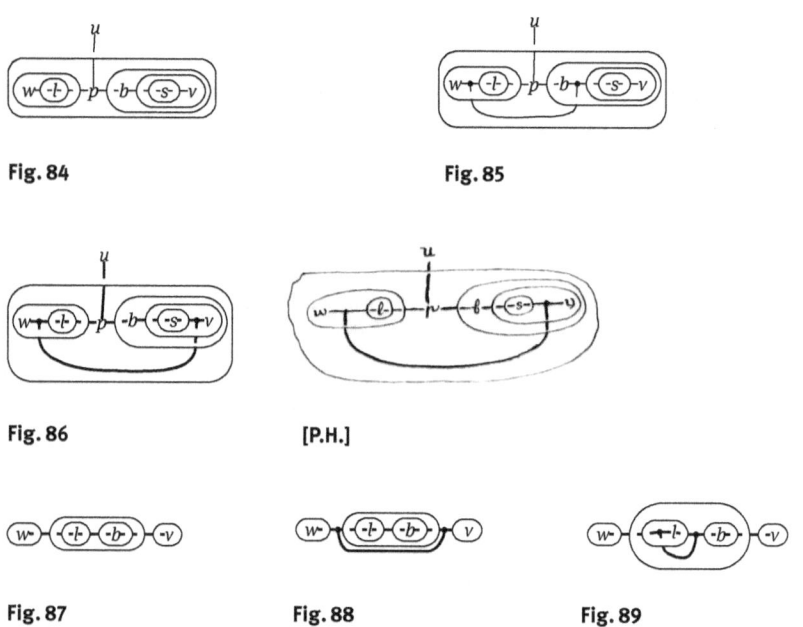

Fig. 84

Fig. 85

Fig. 86

[P.H.]

Fig. 87

Fig. 88

Fig. 89

Reassociation is the inferential step whereby the groupings of terms are changed without change in the order of their connection. Thus, in algebra, from $x = (a + b) + c$ we pass illatively to $x = a + (b + c)$. But this is a complex operation, consisting, first, in inserting something in one group and second, in removing it from the other. In the algebraic example, from $x = (a + b) + c$, we pass, first to $x + b = (a + b) + (b + c)$ and then to $x = a + (b + c)$. Algebraists usually make the associative and commutative processes distinct, but if an operation is thoroughly commutative (so that, for example, if a term is added to a polynomial, it may be inserted at any part of the polynomial), it is necessarily associative; and associative property is a mere corollary from its commutative property. Even if an associative operation is not commutative in the ordinary sense, its associative property is a modified commutative property. Thus, in quaternions, where $(uv)w = u(vw)$, although $uv \neq vu$, let Π'_u signify the operation of multiplying *by u*, so that *u* shall be the active factor, and let Π''_w signify the operation of multiplying *into w*, so that *w* shall be the passive factor. Then, the statement of the associative property will be $\Pi'_u \Pi''_w = \Pi''_w \Pi'_u$, which amounts to saying that Π'_u and Π''_w are commutative relatively to one another. Now, commutation, or the reversal of the order of two things, is a complex operation, consisting of first taking away from one place and second putting back in another place. It does not necessarily follow that a rule of commutation can be analyzed into two rules; but it does point out a way in which such analysis ought to be looked for. In logic, illative reassociation consists of two distinct illative steps. That which is peculiar in it is a kind of indirect iteration and its apagogical reversal. These may be called Involution and Evolution. They include Duplication and Unification as special cases, although the peculiar relation of the latter to Insertion and Omission makes it desirable to consider them separately. A graph may be said to be *iterated* when it is joined to another precisely like it, by every one of its ends being joined to the corresponding end of the other with the interposition of a triad of diversity and nothing else. Thus, Figs. 90, 91, 92 show an iterated monad, dyad, and triad. The iteration is said to be *direct*, or to be *duplication*, when, as in these figures, the two graphs are within the same enclosure. But they may still be said to be iterated when, as in Figs. 93 and 94, one is in enclosures which the other is outside of.

Elimination is substantially the illative dropping of a relative according to the principle of contradiction. *Distribution* is substantially the illative introduction of a relative according to the principle of excluded middle.

Fig. 90　　　　**Fig. 91**　　　　**Fig. 92**　　　　**Fig. 93**　　　　**Fig. 94**

The rule is as follows: *Any unencircled conjugation may be introduced under even enclosures and dropped under odd enclosures; and any encircled graph may be dropped under even enclosures and introduced under odd enclosures.*

The rules of the illative processes are the same in the two systems except that references to odd enclosures are to be changed to references to even enclosures and *vice versa*.

Rule I. *Of Entitative and Existential Graphs.*

1. A *relative* is an incomplete assertion which requires only to have certain blanks in it filled up with signs of objects experientially known to the person who is to understand the assertion, in order to complete it.
2. By a *logical graph* is meant a diagram composed of lines and of spots of various colors which is intended so to exhibit the composition of an assertion or relative that its logical relations can be studies.
3. By a *simplified logical graph* is meant a logical graph composed only of *letters* of various qualities, of *circles* all of one Kind, and of *nexes* all of one Kind.
4. Every part of a simplified logical graph which can be separated from the rest by merely cutting nexes and taking it out of a circle (if either or both these operations be necessary) is itself a *graph*.
5. According to the interpretation which a simplified logical graph is intended to bear it is either an *Entitative* or and *Existential Graph*. These interpretations will be given in these rules; and where two different statements are put one over the other and connected by braces, the upper refers to entitative, the lower to existential graphs.

Rule II. *Of Letters.*

1. By a ~~atom~~ *letter*, in the special sense here intended, is meant a graph which is indivisible, except for dots, called *hands*, on certain sides of it.
2. Each letter signifies either a complete assertion or a materially significant relative. In the former case, it has no hand:
3. Each *hand* of a letter represents a determinate blank of the relative which the letter signifies.
4. By a *hand of a graph* is meant a hand of a letter contained in that graph, which hand is not connected by a nex with another hand of a letter contained in that graph.
5. A graph without a hand is called a medad and means a complete assertion. A graph with a hand or hands signifies a relative and is termed a *monad*, *dyad*, *triad* etc., according to the number of its hands.

Rule III. *Of Circles.*

1. By a ~~oval~~ *circle* is meant a lightly-drawn closed line of any shape, intersecting no other such line, together with any hands it may possess. It may be called a *circumference* when the single boundary alone is referred to.

2. The whole of the contents of a circle is said to be *encircled* by it; and the parts are said to be *enclosed* in it, but not encircled by it. By an *encircled graph* is meant the graph composed of a graph together with a circle round it alone.
3. Anything unenclosed, or enclosed within an even number of circles is said to be *evenly enclosed*; but if the number of circles is odd everything enclosed in them is said to be *oddly enclosed*. The circles may be collectively termed *an even enclosure* or *an odd enclosure*.
4. Graphs which, together with their nexes, make up the entire contents of a circle are said to be *encircled together*.
5. Every encircling circle has a hand for every hand of the graph it encircles; and it has no others.
6. Every circle either encircles a graph, or is void, or encircles a headed-line, a plain line, or a furcation, as shown in Figs. 157, 158, and 159. These four may be called *semi-significant* graphs.

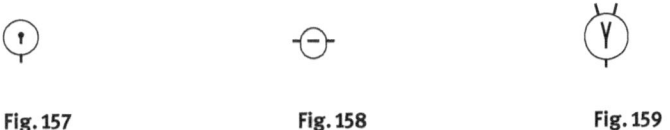

Fig. 157 **Fig. 158** **Fig. 159**

7. A void circle may have any number of hands, including zero. A medad void circle means { "something exists." / "nothing exist." }. A monad void circle signifies { A void circle with more hands than one signifies
8. A circle encircling a headed line is a monad and signifies { " ___ exists." / " ___ does not exist." }.
9. A circle encircling a dash is a dyad and signifies { " ___ is ___ ." / " ___ is not ___ ." }
10. A circle encircling a three-way line is a triad and signifies { " ___ and ___ and ___ are one and the same." / " ___ and ___ and ___ are not all the same." }
11. An encircled graph precisely denies the relative signified by the graph that is encircled.
12. The effect of writing down a number of graphs together in the same enclosures, is to assert their { disjunctive / copulative } conjunction, that is that { some one / every one } is true. It is the office of the circle, not merely to deny, but also to group together, the graphs which it encircles together.

Rule IV. *Of Nexes.*

1. A *nex* is a { heavily-drawn / dotted } line, of which neither the whole nor any part returns into itself, but which is interrupted for a brief space close to and on the inside of any circumference it may cross, having each end of it either

loose $\{$ or headed with a spot $\}$ or at a semi-significant graph, or at a letter, and not in two places extending out from the same circumference.

2. A *simple nex* is one which does not branch.
3. A *nex-branch* is a part of a branching nex extending from an end to a node or from node to node.
4. The *bond* of a nex is that uninterrupted portion of it which is not enclosed in any circle that encloses any other portion of it.
5. Every nex is conceived to be *enclosed* in all the circles in which its bond is enclosed and in no other; and one nex is said to be *outer* relatively to another, said to be *inner*, when the former is not enclosed in some circle which encloses the latter, while the latter is enclosed in every circle which encloses the former.
6. The significance of an assertion lies in its representing that a given description applies to an individual or set of individuals that are or may become known to the experience of him who understands it. This individual or individuals are not usually named by their proper names; but the assertion virtually contains directions for taking them out of a collection. In regard to each, it is either asserted that the description will apply whatever individual be taken, or that it will apply if a suitable individual be taken. If of one individual of the set of individuals referred to it is asserted that it makes no difference what it be, while another is required to be suitably selected, then the assertion will be vague, unless there is a virtual direction as to which is to be take first. By the *universe of discourse* is meant the whole collection of existing individuals which in the collection of all the assertions entertained at one time we alone had in mind.
7. Every nex asserts that the blanks which the hands it connects represent are to be filled with designations of the same individual taken from among the individuals existing in the universe of discourse.
8. If a nex be $\{$ evenly / oddly $\}$ enclosed, it indicates that the blanks corresponding to the hands it connects, can be filled with designations of any one individual existing in the universe of discourse; but if it be $\{$ oddly / evenly $\}$ enclosed, it indicates that one suitable individual is to be chosen.
9. The individuals whose designations are to fill the blanks corresponding to the hands connected by different nexes are to be taken one after another. Of the individuals denoted by two nexes, the one outer and the inner relatively to each other, that denoted by the former is to be taken first.
10. Of two individuals denoted by nexes of which neither is inner nor outer relatively to the other, either may be taken first, provided that the order chosen is consistent with other similar orders of succession in view of 9.

Part B. Theorems

Rule V. *Theorems necessary for Delineation.*

1. A node in a nex may be placed at any point of that nex, regardless of the quality of the enclosure, as to being even or odd, provided the last clause of Rule IV.1 be observed.
2. A branch of a nex not attached to any graph nor joining two nexes has no effect unless it contains the bond of the nex, and in any other case may be introduced or suppressed at pleasure.
3. If two branches of a nex begin and end at the same points, the inner one is of no effect, and may be introduced or suppressed at pleasure. If neither is inner or outer relatively to the other, either may be introduced or suppressed, as long as the other remains.
4. If the inmost nex of two graphs have its enclosure of different quality, as to being even or odd from the graphs themselves, it is of no effect, and may be introduced or suppressed at pleasure.

Rule VI. *Fundamental Illative Transformations.*

1. *Double Encirclement and Mutual Annulment.* If a circle encircles a circle, the two circles are of no effect, and may be drawn or erased at pleasure.
2. *Insertion and Omission.* Under $\left\{ \begin{smallmatrix} \text{even} \\ \text{odd} \end{smallmatrix} \right\}$ enclosures, any graph may be illatively inserted; and under $\left\{ \begin{smallmatrix} \text{odd} \\ \text{even} \end{smallmatrix} \right\}$ enclosures, any graph may be illatively omitted.
3. *Protraction and Retraction.* Any $\left\{ \begin{smallmatrix} \text{evenly} \\ \text{oddly} \end{smallmatrix} \right\}$ enclosed nex may be illatively carried outward through any number of circumferences or inward through any odd number; and any $\left\{ \begin{smallmatrix} \text{oddly} \\ \text{evenly} \end{smallmatrix} \right\}$ enclosed nex may be illatively carried inward through any even number of circumferences.
4. *Junction and Severance.* Under the same $\left\{ \begin{smallmatrix} \text{even} \\ \text{odd} \end{smallmatrix} \right\}$ enclosures, two nexes may be joined; and under $\left\{ \begin{smallmatrix} \text{odd} \\ \text{even} \end{smallmatrix} \right\}$ enclosures, any nex may be severed { the two new ends being headed. } Junction and protraction together are termed by the writer, *Identification*; Severance and retraction together, *Diversification*.
5. Several single graphs precisely alike are termed different *embodiments* of the same species of graph. If any graph have all its hands connected by nexes with another embodiment of the same species of graph, it is said to be *iterated*. If of the two embodiments of an iterated graph one is not outside of any circle which the other is within, the former is of no effect, and may be drawn and erased, at pleasure. But no new circle must be drawn and no change of the enclosures of nexes must take place (not justified by 3.).

6. A *conjugation* is a medad, composed of two graphs of the same species; one encircled and the other not so, the two joined by all their corresponding hands. An encircled conjugation is of no effect and may be drawn or erased at pleasure.

Rule VII. *Derived Illative Transformations.*

1. *Contraposition.* If any transformation is illatively valid under even enclosures, the reverse transformation is valid under odd enclosures, and *vice versa*.
2. *Reassociation.* Under $\{ \substack{\text{even} \\ \text{odd}} \}$ enclosures, any graph can be extracted from within double enclosure; and under $\{ \substack{\text{odd} \\ \text{even}} \}$ enclosures, any graph can be introtracted into a double enclosure.
3. *Segmentation and Fusion.* Under $\{ \substack{\text{even} \\ \text{odd}} \}$ enclosures, two circles one within another may be each twice severed, and each part of each extended so as to close it and form two double enclosures; and under $\{ \substack{\text{odd} \\ \text{even}} \}$ enclosures, two pairs of circles, one circle of each pair enclosed in the other, may be severed and reclosed so as to form one such pair of circles.

Appendix (Variants)

The above simplifications have wrought such metamorphosis of the graphs that their rules require restatements, as follows:[4]

1. A logical graph is a diagram standing either for an assertion or for a relative, i.e. an incomplete assertion wanting only subjects to make it complete. A *logical ideograph* is a logical graph constructed and intended to be interpreted as above described. A *simplified ideograph* is a graph constructed and understood according to these present rules.
2. A simplified ideograph consists of *letters*, *nexes*, and *circles*.
3. By a *letter*, in the special sense in which the word is here used, is meant an incomplex logical ideograph with a heavy dash attached to it at an appropriate side of it for each wanting subject of the relative for which it stands. A letter ought to be a conventional picture, like the ideographs of the Egyptian hieroglyphics, but it is more convenient to use initial letters of the alphabet.
4. By a *circle* is here meant a lightly drawn closed line of any convenient shape, but without cusps or nodes. No two circles intersect or touch one another, and none runs through a letter. Every circle has an inner and an outer side. Everything upon the inner side is said to

---

4 [See §9 in the main body of the text for an earlier version of those simplifications. Peirce appeared to have written several versions of variable length of which only the first, his original submission, is, and can be, fully transcribed. In light of these simplifications and their variations he was led to rewrite the rules for simplified ideographs several times. It is the outcome of those revisions that leads Peirce to the reversed interpretation of logical graphs and, in turn, to existential graphs.]

be *enclosed* in the circle. The whole of what is enclosed except the heavy dashes running up nearly to the circle, is said to be *encircled*. Several parts of the graph which, except for such dashes and for heavy lines running from one to another of them, make up all that is within a circle are said to be *encircled together*. Anything enclosed within an even number of circles, or not enclosed at all, is said to be *evenly enclosed*; if the number is odd, it is said to be *oddly enclosed*. Parts of the graph which are encircled together are said to be *evenly enclosed*, if, counting the encircling circle and all which enclose it, but not those interior to it, those parts are evenly enclosed, and are said to be *oddly encircled* in the contrary case. Two circles, the one encircled by the other, annul each other.

5. By a *nex* is meant a heavily drawn line which may have interruptions in the course of its length, and may have a single point of branching, but can have no cyclosis, i.e. cannot form of itself a ring in any part of it. A *branch* of a nex is a part of it running from one end to another through a furcation without itself dividing. A nex can run up to and be continuous with a dash attached to a letter, but it cannot run up to a letter except by continuity with the dash; and a nex which runs up to a letter ends there. A nex can run up to the outside of a circle but cannot touch a circle on its inside. The only interruptions a nex can have are at circles up to the outside of which it runs and, after an interruption, continues in the inside. A nex cannot twice enter the same circle nor twice run out from the same circle, whether in the same or in different [discont.] A nex can run up to and be continuous with a dash belonging to a letter, and will end there. It cannot otherwise run to a letter.

The end of a nex which is not at a letter can have a *head*, that is, can be bulbous.

The end of a nex which is neither at a letter nor has a head must be loose, or attached to anything, and unenclosed.

A nex can run up to and touch the outside of a circle; and if so it will continue on the inside and have a short interruption, so as not to touch the circle on the inside. But the nex is not considered to have ends at such an interruption.

By a *branch* of a nex is meant a part of it running from end to end through the point of branching, but not itself branching. But if the nex has no point of branching the whole of it is its only *branch*. By a *bond* is meant a part or the whole of a branch of a nex which runs, without interruption, from one end or from the outside of a circle to an end or to the outside of a circle. Every branch of a nex has one bond and but one.

6. If one circle encircles another, both are to be removed.
7. If a headed end of a nex is in all the same enclosures as the point of branching, the head and the part of the nex from the head to the point of branching are to be removed. And if a bond ends at two heads it is to be removed.
8. If a nex runs into two circles, one within the other, and then passes out of the two, it should be altered so as to go round them. And if a nex enters two circles, one within the other, and ends at a head there, it should be cut off before entering the circles, and a head be placed at the new end.
9. A nex should not be allowed to pass twice in or out of the same circle; but parallel parts should be made to coalesce until they reach the space within which one of them ends; and if this process turns a bight of the nex into an end, this end should receive a head.
10. Any part of a graph which can be excised from a graph by merely cutting bonds is itself a graph. If a branching-point of a nex is within two circles and the graphs it connects are not otherwise connected, the circles may be separated into as many parts as those graphs, by closing in each part separately.

11. If two graphs enclosed together evenly have the bond of the inmost nex between them oddly enclosed, or if two graphs oddly enclosed together have the bond of the inmost nex between them evenly enclosed, that bond should be severed, and heads put upon the new ends so made.

Article II. *Of the Interpretation of Simplified Ideographs.*

12. Every letter of a logical graph signifies a relative; every nex denotes an individual subject to be chosen either suitably or no matter how.
13. Nexes having loose ends without heads represent the blanks of the relative. The subjects denoted by nexes running into a circle are to be chosen before those which are enclosed by the circle.
14. Every nex whose bonds are evenly enclosed denotes a subject to be taken, no matter how; every nex whose bonds are oddly enclosed denotes a subject which is to be suitably chosen.
15. Graphs evenly encircled together signify relatives which are to be combined disjunctively. Graphs oddly encircled together signify relatives which are to be combined copulatively.
16. The blanks of the relative signified by each partial graph are to be filled by the subjects denoted by the nexes which end at the sides of the graph appropriated to those blanks.
17. Every circle denies the relative it encircles.
18. A head at the end of a graph signifies the relative "___ is nothing".
19. An empty circle, if a medad, means the assertion, There is something. If a relative, it signifies that its hands coexist.

§ 9. The fundamental illative transformations of graphs seem to be six pairs of opposite processes which may be named as follows:

- First Pair: Contraposition, consisting Double Encircling and Mutual Annulment;
- Second Pair: Insertion and Omission of graphs;
- Third Pair: Identification and Diversification of subjects, by Joining and Severing graphs;
- Fourth Pair: Reassociation; composed of Involution and Evolution;
- Fifth Pair: Fusion and Segmentation of circles;
- Sixth Pair: Development and Elimination.

It is possible some of these processes can be shown to be derivative.

(A) B

Fig. 99

(A) (B)

Fig. 100

Double encircling is substantially a double negation, by the principle of contradiction; *Mutual annulment* is substantially the dropping of such double negation by the principle of excluded middle. The rule is as follows:

Any graph may be illatively twice encircled; and if one circle encircles another, the two circles may illatively annul one another, and be removed.

From this, follows an important corollary. Namely, suppose one medad, A, can be illatively transformed into another, B. This fact is expressed in the medad of Fig. 100. Let B, in this medad, be doubly encircled according to the rule. Then, we infer Fig. 100, which means that encircled B can be illatively transformed into encircled A, so that we infer,

If any transformation is illatively valid under even enclosures, its reverse is illatively valid under odd enclosures, and vice versa.

Omission is substantially the deletion of irrelevant assertions, *Insertion* the attachment of unnecessary conditions and alternatives. The rule is as follows:

Under even enclosures, any graph may be inserted, under odd omitted.

Hardly ever will anything but a medad be so inserted or omitted. The rule is seen to be correct, because graphs evenly encircled together are disjunctively combined and graphs oddly encircled together are copulatively combined. After insertion a junction of bonds is usually desired; before omission a severance of bonds is usually requisite. The next pair of process do these.

Diversification is substantially the inference from an assertion concerning a designate subject to the same assertion concerning *some*thing. *Identification* is substantially the inference from an assertion concerning *every*thing to the same assertion concerning a designate subject. The rule is as follows:

Any nex may be illatively joined by a new branch to any evenly enclosed nex not outside of it; and any nex may be illatively erased, beginning at any oddly enclosed point and erasing outwards as far as desired, but without passing a node; and if loose ends are thus left, they are to be headed with monads of nullity;

And the courses of nexes may be illatively changed (by adding or subtracting branches ending in monads of nullity, or otherwise), so that an evenly enclosed nex is carried outward, relatively to any other, or made oddly enclosed, or so that an oddly enclosed new is carried inwards relatively to any other; but the reverse changes are not illatively valid.

And if any nex be within another which is within a third, the first must be considered to be within the third.

The first clause of this rule permits any two evenly enclosed nexes to be joined. Since each denotes any individual, no matter what, they may be taken so as to be identical, which is what their junction indicates. The same clause permits an evenly enclosed nex to be identified with an oddly enclosed nex not outside of it. A subject which can be any individual whatever may be identified with any other already designated; though not with any which can be thereafter designated. Though every man has a father, it does not follow that anybody is his own father. If the oddly enclosed nex and the evenly enclosed nex are neither in the enclosure of the other, there is nothing to prevent the former from being designated before the latter; and they may be identified, subject to a restriction to be mentioned soon. In every such case, it will be necessary to run out branches ending in monads of nullity in order to preserve the order of selection. Thus, the medad of Fig. 101 means, Every wise man is ugly and every extravagant man loves a virtuous man. The oddly enclosed nex between the *l* and *v* and the evenly enclosed nex between the encircled *w* and the *u* are neither within the other. They may, therefore, be connected; and as they fortunately happen to be oddly enclosed together, the nex has the right quality, but it is now outside of the nex of the *x*, which it has no right to be. Hence, a branch has to be sent out from the latter nex, as shown in Fig. 102. This means, There is a man who is not wise or there is a man who is ugly, and if there is any extravagant man in the universe, he loves a virtuous man who either is not wise or is ugly. There is here no effectual bond between the encircled *w* and the *v*; so that a transformation is possible. Such will generally be the result of identifications of evenly and oddly enclosed nexes.

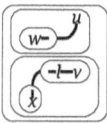

Fig. 101

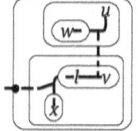

Fig. 102

The second clause of the rule permits the erasure of any part of a branch of a nex beginning at any oddly enclosed point erasing outwards. In order to comprehend the rationale of this, it must be remarked that if a branch of a nex is delineated according to the rules given, a point moving along upon it from its termination at a latter to the node, if there be one, or to the other end if there be no node, may pass out of one series of circles and into another but cannot pass inward and then outward. Consequently, where the nex is severed at any oddly enclosed point, the inner part, if either part be enclosed in an enclosure within the enclosure of the other, since the enclosure of a nex is determined by that of its outermost part, is always oddly enclosed. The separation, then, has this effect, that of two hands which had been are [sic.] identified, the one which is first designated, after the severance, is designated as before, while the other is to be suitably chosen. Being suitably chosen, it can, if need be, be the same that it was before; and therefore the assertion of the medad is as true as it was before the severance. The erasure only proceeds as far as the node, for the sake of simplicity; but after that, the remaining nex, now generally simple, may be subjected to the same process of erasure.

The second paragraph of the rule declares that an evenly enclosed nex may be carried outward or an oddly enclosed nex may be carried inward, through an even number of circumferences. Let i and j be the subjects denoted by two nexes, and let the assertion made be that i is in the relation R to j, or is R to j. This relation may be any sort of assertion, no matter what. If, then, the i and j are represented by two evenly enclosed nexes, each may be any individual whatever. In that case, the order of their designation is immaterial; for the fact represented by asserting, No matter what individual i may be, i is R to j whatever individual j may be, is the same as the fact represented by asserting, No matter what individual j may be, i is R to j, whatever individual i may be. So, if the two nexes be oddly enclosed, the order of designation of their subjects is immaterial. For the same fact is represented by the assertion, If i is suitably chosen, and if j is then suitably chosen i is R to j, and by the assertion, If j is suitably chosen, and i is then suitably chosen, i is R to j. If, however, one nex, say i, be evenly enclosed and the other, j, be oddly enclosed, the order of selection is material. For the subject i may then be any individual whatever, while j has to be suitably chosen. Now, if i has been already determined, the proper choice of j can be adjusted accordingly; and there is a better opportunity for the verification of the assertion than if j has to be chosen first, without reference to i. Thus, when the selection of the suitably chosen individual is reserved to the last, the proposition will be quite as true and perhaps truer. Hence, the inference is valid from a suitably chosen individual, j is R to i, no matter what i may be, to, No matter what i may be, something j may be found such that i is R to j. Thus, the change in the relative positions of two nexes which makes an oddly enclosed nex which had been exterior to an evenly enclosed nex, now come to be interior, is illatively valid.

This paragraph of the rule also declares that an evenly enclosed nex may be changed to being oddly enclosed. That is to say, the inference is valid from, Everything is R, to, Something is R. It is assumed in this, that there is some individual in the universe.

The meaning of the third paragraph is this. Suppose there be two series of circles, as in Fig. 103, and let the nex, i, be within the nex, j, and the nex, l within the nex, k. If, now, j and k be evenly enclosed and i and l be oddly enclosed, nothing prevents the identification either of k with i or of j with l. But let k be identified with i. Then, j can no longer be identified with l. For l is within k and i which is identical with k, is within j. Consequently, according to the rule l is within j. Now l is oddly enclosed and j is evenly enclosed; so that, their identification is forbidden. The reason is that, at first, there is no reason why either the subject, i should not be selected before the subject k, or the subject k before the subject j. But either of these successions being fixed, the other becomes impossible according to the rule that the subjects of outer nexes are to be designated before those of inner ones.

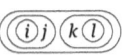

Fig. 103

Fig. 104

The use of branches headed by monads of nullity will be frequent in illative operations with this system of graphs, that is examples of this class of processes. But they usually involve complications requiring the use of other illative steps not yet considered. In order to avoid these, it will be best to consider the pentad spot of Fig. 104, meaning, A elevates B in rank at least as high as C, whom he had been below, for rescuing D from E. Then, the medad of Fig. 105,[5] where, for perspicuity's sake, oddly enclosed spaces are shaded, means, Everybody elevates somebody in rank as high as anybody (when he had been below everybody) for rescuing somebody from all men. That is, the person elevated was *brought* to a rank at least as high as each man, so that he had been lower than anybody (this is self-contradictory, but that may be overlooked); but different persons may raise the rank of different men, so that it is not asserted that anybody is raised by *all* men; and the person elevated may have received one elevation for rescuing one man and another elevation for raising the rank of another man, so that he need not have been carried from the lowest to the highest rank for rescuing any one person. Now, the second nex, which denotes the person elevated, being oddly enclosed, may be carried inward, so long as it still remains oddly enclosed. Thus is inferred the medad of Fig. 106. But the outermost circle here encircles the next circle, and they annul each other, giving the medad of Fig. 107, which means, Everybody raises at least as high as each man somebody for rescuing somebody from all men. This asserts less than the medad of Fig. 105 inasmuch as it does not assert that anybody is raised from the lowest to the highest rank.

Or, the third nex of the medad of Fig. 105, which denotes the person outranked, being evenly enclosed, may be carried outwards, while remaining evenly enclosed, as in Fig. 108. But now the second circle encircles the third; and they annul each other, again giving the medad of Fig. 107.

Or, the fifth nex of the medad of Fig. 105, which denotes the person rescued, being evenly enclosed, may be carried outwards, while remaining evenly enclosed, as in Figs. 109 and 110. The medad of Fig. 109 means, Everybody raises the rank of somebody at least as high as any man for

---

5 [Marginal note:] I recommend that the shading be done by stippling. [R 839 contains some more drafts of these figures, some of them drawn with non-concentric circles.]

rescuing from every man somebody. This does not say that any one person is rescued from all men. The medad of Fig. 110 means, Everybody raises some rescuer from each man, as high in rank as anybody, while Fig. 109 asserts that the person raised in rank was a rescuer from all men (though the same man was not necessarily rescued from all), Fig. 110 does not even assert that any one man was a rescuer from all men. Next, the third nex of the medad of Fig. 105, which denotes the person outranked, being evenly enclosed, may be carried outwards so as to be oddly enclosed, as in Fig. 111. That done, the second circle encircles the third; and they annul one another, giving Fig. 112, whose medad means, Everybody rises somebody up to the rank of somebody for rescuing somebody from all men.

Next, the first nex of the medad of Fig. 105, which denotes the raiser in rank may be carried in while changed to an odd enclosure, as in Fig. 113. If then, the third nex is carried out two circles, the second and third circles annul one another, and the medad of Fig. 114 is inferred, meaning, Everybody is outranked by somebody by the act of somebody for rescuing somebody from all men.

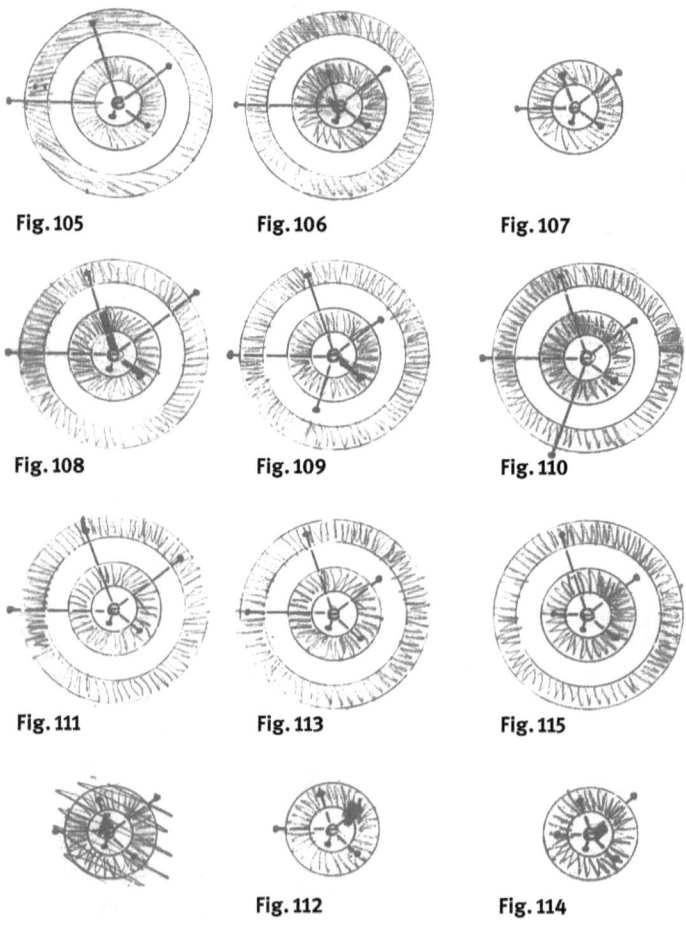

Fig. 105　　　Fig. 106　　　Fig. 107

Fig. 108　　　Fig. 109　　　Fig. 110

Fig. 111　　　Fig. 113　　　Fig. 115

Fig. 112　　　Fig. 114

Next, the first nex of the medad of Fig. 105 may be carried in three circles giving Fig. 115, which means, Somebody is raised in rank as high as anybody by somebody for rescuing somebody from all men.

In short, any such headed branch if evenly enclosed may be carried outward through any number of circles or inward through any odd number of circles; but if oddly enclosed can only be carried inward through some even number of circles.

Reassociation is substantially that illative step by which the grouping of relatives is changed, as in the inference from Some wise man loves all virtuous men to Every virtuous men is loved by a wise man. It will be remarked that some identifications and diversifications, if not all, are reassociations; but it is not pretended that the analysis here given of the illative processes is perfect. Reassociation may be conceived to consist of two steps, that of repeating a relative in the same or another group, which has been called by the present writer *Involution*, and that of removing one of the repetitions of a repeated relative, which may be called *Evolution*.

When a graph is written twice, and the two individual like graphs, which may be called different *embodiments* of the same species of graph-quality idea nature, have all their corresponding hands connected, the species of graph-nature may be said to be iterated. If the two embodiments are in precisely the same enclosures, the species of graph-idea-quality may be said to be *directly iterated*. If one of two embodiments of the same species of graph-idea-quality is encircled, and the encircled embodiment and the unencircled embodiment have all their corresponding hands joined, and are in the same enclosures, the pair may be said to constitute a *conjugation* of that species of graph-quality. If all the hands are joined but one, two, etc., it may be called a *once-broken*, *twice-broken*, etc. conjugation. A conjugation contains an iteration; but it is not an iteration, since the drawing of a circle is no part of any iteration.

The rule of Involution and Evolution is as follows:[6]

---

6 [Alt.:] The rule of Involution and Evolution is as follows:
Any graph may be iterated, a triad of diversity being interpolated into each of its nexes, and the new iteration being placed anywhere within all the circles that the old one was within, provided that no new circle is created; and any iterated graph may be dropped, and its nexes cut at the omitted graph, and headed, if the remaining iteration is outside of all circles that the one dropped was outside. Of course other cases of iteration are permissible by the rule of Insertion and Omission. The present rule cannot fail on account of any transposition of the order of selection of the subjects, because in the involution, the new nexes pass inward and therefore, because of the rule that a nex is not to pass out of a circle and return again, the order of selection will not be changed, and in the evolution the nexes remain in place. Hence, the rule is correct if it is correct when the iterated graph is a medad. Now, if any medad can be directly iterated in the space where it is, and also within one circle which is in that space, then it can be iterated within any number of such circles. It will therefore be sufficient to show that this is true, first of an oddly-enclosed medad, and secondly of an evenly-enclosed medad.

Fig. 91   Fig. 92   Fig. 93   Fig. 94   Fig. 95

[...]⁷ rule also holds good when the iterated graph is oddly enclosed; and in short, it is always correct.

An example may be given to show the operation of involution and evolution in effecting reassociation. The medad of Fig. 122 means whoever is benefitted by everybody who is loved

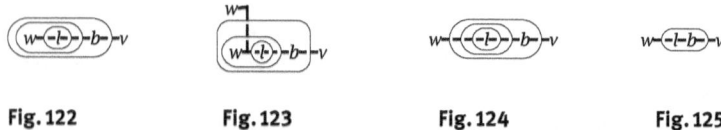

Fig. 122   Fig. 123   Fig. 124   Fig. 125

only by the wise is virtuous. By insertion, w→ can be added outside of this. By Identification, the medad of Fig. 123 is inferred. By evolution, the interior w is omitted giving the medad of Fig. 124. Finally, by Mutual Annulment the medad of Fig. 125 is reached, meaning who ever stands only to the wise in the relation of being benefitted by some lovers of them is virtuous.

An example may be given to show that the process called in algebra distribution and appearing in graphs as segmentation and fusion is merely an effect of involution and evolution.⁸ The medad of Fig. 126 means, A is false and either B or C is true. Involution gives Fig. 127. Double encircling gives Fig. 128. Involution gives Fig. 129. Omission gives Fig. 130. Mutual annulment gives Fig. 131, meaning, Either A is false while B is true or A is false while C is true.

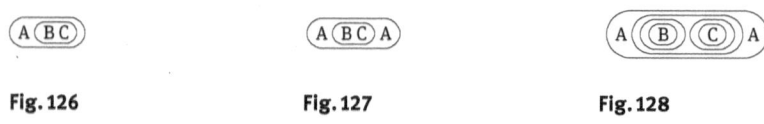

Fig. 126   Fig. 127   Fig. 128

Let A and B in Fig. 91 be any medads. Then, the medad of that figure means, B is true and A is false. Let A be directly iterated, as in Fig. 92; and the effect is merely to repeat that A is false. It is evident then that any oddly-enclosed medad can be directly iterated. Next, let A be iterated within the circle enclosing B, as in Fig. 93, and the resulting medad will mean, Either A or B is true, but A is false. This is the same as to say that A is false and B is true. Nor would the case be different, if another medad, C, were with A, but not iterated, as in Fig. 94, so as to give Fig. 95 after the iteration; for this would only add to both assertions the denial of the truth of C. Thus, an oddly enclosed medad can be iterated where it is or within one circle, without any change of meaning. Since there is no change of meaning, the inferences might be made from the iterated graph to the omission of the inner iteration. Hence by the rule of contraposition, an evenly enclosed graph can be iterated where it is or within one circle. Hence, the rule holds good for Involution, and by an obvious application of contraposition it holds good for Evolution, and is thus entirely correct.

7 [One manuscript page (p. 52) with seven graphs is not extant.]

8 [Alt.:] *Segmentation* is substantially the illative passage from denying a copulative or disjunctive combination of propositions to asserting the ~~contrary~~ opposite combination of the denials of those propositions, while *Fusion* is the illative passage from treating them severally to treating them in combination.

Fig. 129   Fig. 130   Fig. 131

Elimination is substantially the illative dropping of a relative according to the principle of contradiction. *Distribution* is substantially the illative introduction of a relative according to the principle of excluded middle. The rule is as follows:

Any unencircled conjugation may be introduced under even enclosures and dropped under odd enclosures; and any encircled graph may be dropped under even enclosures and introduced under odd enclosures.

The rules of the illative processes are the same in the two systems except that references to odd enclosures are to be changed to references to even enclosures and vice versa.

§ 10. Evidently, all forms of graphs might, with perfect consistency, be understood to precisely deny those propositions which they have hitherto been interpreted as asserting; and furthermore, the meanings of all letters might be reversed. Thus arises a second system of interpretation according to which each graph means what upon the first system it would mean if two changes were made to it, namely, if, first, a circle were drawn round each letter, and if, second, a circle were drawn round the whole graph. This second system of interpretation may be called the *existential*, that hitherto considered the ~~ideal~~ *entitative*, system of interpretation.[9]

---

9 [Alt.:] § 10. Evidently, all forms of graphs could with perfect consistency be understood to deny those propositions which they have hitherto been interpreted as asserting, and furthermore the meanings of all the letters could be reversed. Thus, another system of interpretation arises in which each graph has the meaning which it would have in the system above described if a circle were drawn round each letter and another round the whole graph. To avoid confusion it would be well to introduce some inessential peculiarities into the delineation. It might be agreed that in such case the circle should always have a node or cusp; and one circle with another enclosing it might be drawn as one continuous line. This is suggested by the circumstance that an ordinary universal proposition would have to be enclosed in a circle, a complexity so much at variance with the philosophy of logic as to constitute perhaps the greatest objection to this system of interpretation. Nexes, too, on this system might be distinguished by consisting of an even number of parallel lines, with a preference for zero for that number. Different numbers might be used to aid grouping. A dotted line might represent a zero number of parallel lines.

This system of interpretation might be called the *existential* system, and the system above described might be called the *ideal* system. The following would be the rules of interpretation, the rules of delineation remaining essentially unchanged.

1. Graphs written together are copulatively combined.
2. A circle denies its contents. Hence when graphs are oddly enclosed their negatives are disjunctively combined. No two circles intersect.
3. Nexes denote subjects and identify the graph-hands they join. The individual subjects [are] to be designated according to the enclosure of their nexes. The individual denoted by an evenly enclosed new is to be suitably selected; but the individual denoted by an oddly enclosed nex can be any individual of the universe of discourse. The enclosure of a nex is that of its outermost part. If the enclosure of one nex is outside that of another its subject is to

Among the advantages of the existential system may be mentioned first, that in it no heads need be affixed to unattached nex-branches, since it comports with the genius of this system to

---

be designated before that of the latter. If the enclosures of two series of nexes are external to one another, the two series of subjects may be designated in any order, consistently with the rule. If the inmost nex between two graphs has its enclosure of opposite quality, as to being even or odd, from the graphs themselves, it is of no effect; and such a nex may be added or removed. No nex-branch, or part of a nex from an extremity or to an extremity or node, must enter a circle and leave it.

4. The end of a nex (no head is needed) signifies, "___ is one individual of the universe of discourse"; the dyad point signifies, "___ and___ are one individual", the triad node signifies "___ and___ and___ are one individual", and so for higher nodes. An unencircled node may be slipped along its nex and cross circles; but it cannot have two nex-branches running outwards.
5. A double circle, or circle encircling a circle, may anywhere be introduced or removed.
6. Under even enclosures any graph may be omitted; under odd enclosures any graph may be inserted.
7. Any evenly enclosed nex may be carried inward through any even number of enclosures. Any oddly enclosed nex may be carried inward through any odd number of enclosures, or outward through any number whatever.
8. Any nex may be joined to an oddly enclosed nex not outside of it; and any nex-branch may be erased from any enclosed point outwards, so long as a node is not passed. But in applying this rule if any nex is within another which is itself, before or after the junction, within a third, the first must be treated as within the third.
9. Any graph may be iterated, its nexes remaining unbroken, provided the new embodiment is not outside the old one, and that no new circle is drawn; and if a graph is iterated, one embodiment may be struck out, with its nex branches to the nodes, provided the embodiment remaining is not within the one struck out. But no change in the enclosures of the nexes must be made, unless it is permitted by Rule 7. Any nex may be repeated not outside its first appearance, and the inner of two nex branches between nodes on one nex may be erased.
10. Any encircled conjugation may be introduced under even enclosures or erased under odd enclosures.

[Alt.:] The rules of graphs as thus simplified may be stated as follows. An enclosure or a spot may be called a *piece*. Unenclosed pieces or evenly enclosed pieces in the same enclosure are conjoined disjunctively; oddly enclosed pieces in the same enclosure are conjoined copulatively. Bonds and *branching bonds* (that is, bonds with polyads of diversity interpolated) identify subjects, and when evenly enclosed show that those subjects may be taken in any way, no matter how, but when oddly enclosed show that they must be suitably chosen. Oddly enclosed graphs are negatived. A void circle, if a medad, means "Something exists". If not a medad it means that its hands coexist.

But these rules merely result from simplification. The real constitution of graphs is as set forth in former sections.

§ 9. The rules of interpretation might be reversed, as follows: Evenly-enclosed pieces to be understood as conjoined copulatively, oddly-enclosed pieces disjunctively. Evenly-enclosed bonds to

neglect the distinction between "___ is of a given nature", and "something is of that nature"; and second, that propositions written together are thereby all asserted. Among the disadvantages of the system may be mentioned that all universal propositions require circles round them, contrary to their natural simplicity.

When the existential system is employed, it will be advisable to introduce some inessential peculiarities of delineation, so that a continual reminder may be present of which system is in use. ~~It may be a rule that every circle should have a node or an angular point; and one circle enclosing another may commonly be drawn in one continuous line with the latter, which will simply [be] the delineation of universal medads. Nexes, too, may be distinguished by being drawn as dotted lines.~~

By a logical graph is meant a diagram consisting of spots of various quality and of lines intended to represent an assertion or *relative* that its logical relations can be studied.

show that the subjects are to be suitably chosen; oddly-enclosed bonds to show that the subjects may be taken no matter how. Oddly-enclosed graphs are negative.

In this case, the monad spot would signify "___ is". The encircled monad spot would be absurd. The dyad spot would signify "___ and ___ are one and the same individual". The node, or triad spot, would signify "___ and ___ and ___ are one and the same individual".

This system would have two advantages. First, it would give, as nearly as possible, the right interpretation to a graph not a medad. Thus, Fig. 67 would mean "Somebody loves somebody". Secondly, the mere writing together of propositions would assert them all. It would have the disadvantage of giving too complicated an expression to a simple hypothetical; but "If A is true then C is true" could be written as in Fig. 68, where C is twice enclosed and "All wise men are virtuous as in Fig. 69. "All wise men love all but virtuous men" is shown in Fig. 70.

Fig. 67    **Fig. 68**    **Fig. 69 [P.H.]** 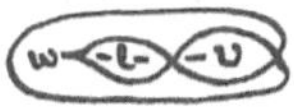   **Fig. 70 [P.H.]**

The rules of inference given in the next section would be merely reversed.

§ 10. There are three rules for the illative transformations of graphs; that of Insertion and Omission, that of Involution and Evolution, and that of Development and elimination. Involution and Development are special kinds of insertion, evolution and elimination special kinds of omission.

In this section only the first, or negative, system of graphs will be referred to; but everything that is said will apply with a simple change to the second, or positive system. For the rule of contraposition holds in both, to wit: *If any substitution is illatively valid under an even number of enclosures, its reverse is valid under an odd number, and* vice versa. Now the same forms of graphs in the two systems signify denials, each meaning of what the other would be after reversing the meaning of every letter. Hence, whatever is illatively permissible under even enclosures in either system is so under odd enclosures in the other, and *vice versa*.

[R S-34, ms p. 54]¹⁰ It will be sufficient for this purpose to carry the nexes continuously through the enclosures.

The conventions of the existential system may be ~~conveniently~~ stated with remarkable simplicity as follows:

1. Every unanalyzed relative, or verb, is to be represented by a special character; and to each blank of the relative is to be appropriated a special side of that character, so that anything denoting an individual being written close to the character on that side of it fills that blank.
2. A blank space, considered as a relative, is meaningless, that is, is necessarily true of any subjects whatever.¹¹
3. The end of a heavy line is to denote some individual object suitably chosen from among those existing in the universe of discourse.
4. The unbroken continuity of a line, whether simple or branching, signifies the identity of its extremities.
5. The writing down of a proposition unenclosed is to be understood as asserting it, and the writing down of two or more asserts them all.
6. The encircling of a proposition by a lightly drawn endless line is to be understood as transmuting it into its denial.

These conventions are certainly remarkably natural, and may be said to have their roots in human nature. Nevertheless, in considering the most difficult questions requiring the analysis of reasoning to be carried to its furthest point,—as, for example, in applying graphs to the study of the nature of quantity and of the reason of its importance in thought,—the entitative system of interpretation is distinctly superior. [End of R S-34]

Rules of Existential Graphs

Rule 1. *Of Entitative and Existential Graphs.* An *existential graph* is a simplified logical graph intended to be interpreted in a particular way. A simplified *logical graph* is a diagram composed of *letters*, *circles*, and *nexes*; and every such graph which can be separated from the rest by merely cutting nexes, and taking it out of a circle (if either operation be necessary), is itself a graph.

---

10 [Page number is illegible and 4 in 54 is conjectural.]
11 [Alt.:]
2. A blank, considered as a relative, is to be understood as meaningless, that is, as necessarily true of any subjects whatsoever.
3. The end of a line is to denote some individual object existing in the universe of discourse.
4. The unbroken continuity of a heavy line signifies the identity of its extremities, whether it branches or not.
5. The writing down of a proposition is to be understood as asserting it, and the writing down of two or more propositions asserts them all.
6. The encircling of a proposition by a lightly drawn endless line is to be understood as transmuting it into its denial.

These conventions are certainly remarkably natural. They may be said to be rooted in human nature. Never[theless] [end]

Rule 2. *Of Letters.* By a *letter*, in the special sense here intended, is meant a graph of a special kind, namely a character which is indivisible, except for dots, called *hands*, on certain sides of it.

A letter signifies, or stands, either for a complete assertion or for a materially significant *relative*, i.e. an assertion which is (taken by itself) incomplete, but which requires only to have certain blanks filled up with signs of objects experientially known to the person who is to understand the assertion, in order to make up a complete assertion. Each *hand* of a letter represents a determinate blank of the relative which it signifies.

By a *hand of a graph* is meant a hand of a letter contained in that graph which hand is not connected by a nex with another hand of a letter contained in that graph.

A graph without hands is called a *medad* and represents a complete assertion. A graph with hands signifies a relative, and is called a monad, dyad, triad, etc. according to the number of its hands.

Rule 3. *Of Circles.* By a circle is meant a lengthy drawn closed line, of any shape, intersecting no other such line. The whole of its contents is said to be *encircled* by it; and the parts are said to be *enclosed* by it. Anything unenclosed or enclosed within an even number of circles is said to be *evenly enclosed*; but if that number is odd, it is said to be *oddly enclosed*. Graphs which, together with their nexes make up the entire contents of a circle are said to be *encircled together*.

A void circle means ⓐ ⊖ ⌠⌡.

Rule 4. *Of Nexes.* A nex is a { heavily drawn / dotted } line of which neither the whole nor a part returning into itself, but interrupted for a brief space on the inside of any circle it may cross, having every end of it either loose or { headed with a spot, called the monad of nullity } or at a letter, and not extending twice out from the same circle. A *simple nex* is one which does not branch. A *nex-branch* is a part of a branching nex [end]

§ 7.[12] Characters of *second intention* are brought to our knowledge by observation of logical forms, not of things.[13] Three relatives of second intention are of special importance. Namely, they are the

---

12 These pages, though abrogated, are interesting. [An alternative continuation of § 6 above.]

13 **[Alt.:]** Those relatives of second intention, that is, relatives signifying relations brought to our knowledge by observation of logical forms, not of things, are of special importance. Namely, they are those which signify that their correlates are not one thing. The monad of non-unity is "___ is not anything", the dyad of non-unity is "___ is not the same as ___". The triad of non-unity is "___ and ___ and ___ are not one and the same". I designate them by dots with one, two, and three tails.

The monad of non-unity is in itself absurd. Hence, then negatived it is empty, and consequently when encircled by itself is of little use. But when not encircled by itself, its effect is to leave its antecedent absolutely negatived. Thus, as the consequent of a medad, its effect is to assert the non-existence of the antecedent in any subject. Fig. 1 signifies "nothing is wise". As the

monad, the dyad, and the triad which signify that their subjects are not one thing. They may be termed the relatives of *non-unity*, and may be drawn as dots, or small round black spots.

The monad of non-unity, which signifies "___ is not anything", is in itself absurd; so that its negative is empty. Consequently, this relative when encircled by itself as an ultimate antecedent (an antecedent by itself of some partial graph) is of little use. When it is an ultimate consequent, the partial graph of which it is consequent asserts that nothing has the character signified by its antecedent.

consequent of the antecedent of a medad, the monad of non-unity signifies that the negative of the consequent of the consequent of the medad has universally the relation signified by the antecedent of the antecedent to some thing. Thus, Fig. 2 signifies "whatever is not wise is loved by something". If the monad of non-unity appears also as the consequent of the medad, the latter means that everything is in the relation expressed by the antecedent of the antecedent to some thing. Thus Fig. 3 signifies "everything loves something". If it appears both as the consequent of a medad and is the consequent of the antecedent of the antecedent, it signifies that everything has to everything the negative of the relation expressed by the consequent of the antecedent to something which has the negative of the relation expressed by the antecedent of the antecedent of the antecedent to the second thing. Thus Fig. 4 signifies "everything is to everything a non-benefactor of some thing that does not love it".

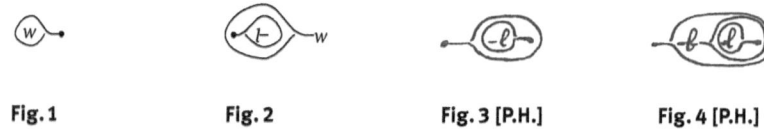

Fig. 1   Fig. 2   Fig. 3 [P.H.]   Fig. 4 [P.H.]

The monad of non-unity encircled by itself has the effect of depriving everything else within the next outer circle of all distinctive force, so that that latter circle might itself as well be the monad of non-unity, except that the rules of forming graphs would then require its consequent to be an antecedent. Thus, Fig. 5 has no meaning. Fig. 6 means "everything is wise", just as Fig. 1 means "nothing is wise".

The dyad of non-unity, which is a mere knot in the bond of connection has, when not encircled and an encircled graph can alone be directly combined. Thus, Fig. 7 means "everything is either not wise or not virtuous". Fig. 8 means "everything is either wise or virtuous". Fig. 9 means "nothing loves itself".

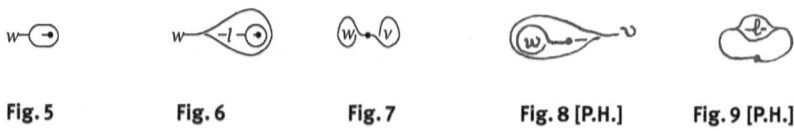

Fig. 5   Fig. 6   Fig. 7   Fig. 8 [P.H.]   Fig. 9 [P.H.]

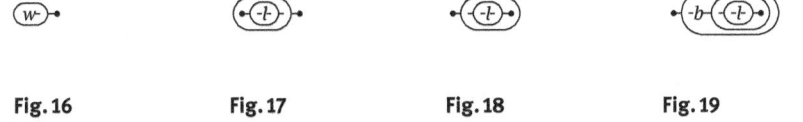

Fig. 16   Fig. 17   Fig. 18   Fig. 19

Thus, the medad Fig. 16 means "nobody is wise"; that of Fig. 17, "everybody is either virtuous or is loved by somebody"; that of Fig. 18, "everybody loves somebody"; that of Fig. 19 "nobody benefits all those who love nobody".

The monad of non-unity as an ultimate antecedent has the effect of depriving every other relative within the next outer circle of all distinctive force, so that this circle might as well be the monad of non-unity except for the rule requiring an unencircled graph to be joined only to an encircled one. Thus, Fig. 20 has no meaning. Fig. 21, which is to be composed with Fig. 16, means "everything is wise".

Fig. 20   Fig. 21

The dyad of non-unity, "___ is not one and the same as ___", which is a mere knot in a connecting bond, has, when it is not an ultimate antecedent, no other effect than that of evading the rule that an unencircled and an encircled graph can alone be directly combined. Thus, Fig. 22 means "nobody is both wise and virtuous"; Fig. 23 means "everybody is either virtuous or wise"; Fig. 24 means "nobody loves himself"; Fig. 25 means "every wise man loves some virtuous man".

Fig. 22   Fig. 23   Fig. 24   Fig. 25

The dyad of non-unity, as an ultimate antecedent, though less useful, has familiar applications. Thus, Fig. 26 means, "everything loves everything but itself". Fig. 27 means, "everything is other than somebody not wise"; that is, "there are at least, two men not wise".

Fig. 26   Fig. 27

The triad of non-unity, "___ and ___ and ___ are not one and the same", when not an ultimate antecedent, has for its chief effect the evasion of the rule that a relative can have each loose end connected with but one other relative. Thus, Fig. 28 means "Taking any men, X, Y, Z, at pleasure, if X is intelligent, and Y is virtuous, and Z is wise, then X, Y, and Z are not all the same individual";

that is, "every intelligent man is either not wise or not virtuous", or, "nobody is at once wise, intelligent, and virtuous". Fig. 29 means "everybody is either wise or both intelligent and virtuous". Fig. 30 means "whoever is virtuous but not wise is intelligent". Fig. 31 means "in case whoever there may be that is virtuous is wise, then whoever there may be who is not wise is unintelligent". This, at least, is as near the assertion as I can find any simple form of words to express it. A twice encircled triad of non-unity is not easily expressed.

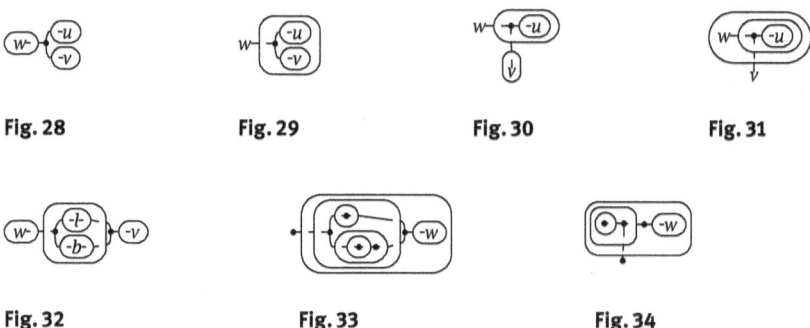

Fig. 28   **Fig. 29**   **Fig. 30**   **Fig. 31**

Fig. 32   **Fig. 33**   **Fig. 34**

Triads of non-unity are particularly useful in pairs. Fig. 32 means "every wise man is both lover and benefactor of every virtuous man". Fig. 33 means "some man is wise". Fig. 34 is a simpler expression of the same thing.

Those propositions which contain relatives of non-unity as ultimate antecedents belong to a class of propositions a large part of which were called by De Morgan spurious propositions. They might also be called arithmetical propositions, since every assertion that a collection contains at least a certain number is a "spurious" proposition, and every assertion that a collection contains at most a certain number is an "antispurious" proposition.[14]

§ 8. Characters of *second intention* are characters brought to our knowledge, not by ordinary observation of things, but by observation of logical forms. Relatives of second intention are of high importance in logic; but the most important of them is the triad which signifies that "___ and ___ and ___ are not one and the same individual". This may be called the triad of diversity. It may be noticed, at once, that to say that A is different either from B or from C is precisely the same as to say that B is different either from C or from A.

It has been insisted above that every relative has a definite number of loose ends each of which can be joined only to a single loose end of another relative. This may seem to be an arbitrary convention. Why should we not draw the graph of Fig. 16 to signify "taking anybody whatever, he is either not wise, or not intelligent, or not virtuous"?

The answer is that there is no objection to our doing so; but there is an objection to our failing to recognize a true logical generalization. We must not fail to observe that the node of junction of the bonds from $u-$, $v-$, and $w-$ is itself a relative. It is simply the triad of diversity. For if we say

---

14 [This sequence continues with another version of § 8; omitted are six ms pages and Figures 35–60. § 8 below is from another, earlier segment of which the previous sections, including the first 15 graphs, have not been preserved.]

"taking any three men X, Y, Z, at pleasure, if X is wise, Y intelligent and Z virtuous, then X, Y, Z are not one and the same individual", we make the same assertion as the above, namely, that no wise man is, at once, intelligent and virtuous. The rule is, therefore, not arbitrary, but only involves the recognition of an important generalization.

Fig. 16

It is necessary carefully to study the triad of diversity in order to learn how to express by logical graphs all forms of propositions. There are eight different forms of medads consisting of two triad and three monads. The first is that of Fig. 16. The others are shown in Figs. 17–23.

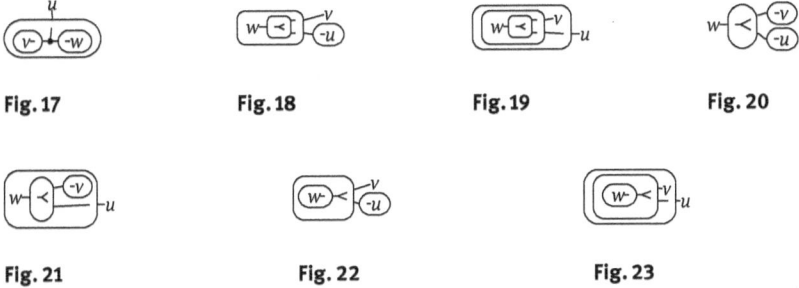

Fig. 17   Fig. 18   Fig. 19   Fig. 20

Fig. 21   Fig. 22   Fig. 23

Fig. 17 means "everybody is either uncommon or is both virtuous and wise", Fig. 18 means "whoever is both uncommon and wise is virtuous"; Fig. 19 means "Everybody is uncommon unless somebody is not virtuous who alone (if anybody) is not wise"; Fig. 20 means, "If there be anybody that is uncommon, and anybody that is virtuous, and anybody that is not wise, they are the same sole person, nobody else having any of these characters"; Fig. 21 means, "Everybody is uncommon unless there are two different persons one virtuous and the other not wise", Fig. 22 means, "If there be anybody uncommon and anybody not virtuous, they are the same person and he is wise"; Fig. 23 means, "If a man is the only vicious man and is wise, he is uncommon".

The triad of diversity is particularly in combination with itself. Thus, Fig. 24 [end]

[Fragments][15]

[A.] [...] conduct is essentially complex and not simple. If there were a certain word which when it was uttered had the simple effect of causing the listener to contract a certain muscle, say his

---

15 [Several discontinuous fragmentary pages, drafts and segments exist in folder R 482. These discrete fragments are enumerated here as A–G. Some are related to Peirce's other and roughly coeval writings, such as drafts of his 1897 "The Logic of Relatives" paper.]

left biceps, we should say this has a peculiar physiological effect. We should not call such a convulsion "conduct", nor the effect a mental effect. Conduct is action shaped toward some result. The significance of the word consists in that. In essence lies in its relations to other things. The old logicians left all relations except the relations of similarity and dissimilarity out of account. My logic shows that relation is everything in logic. When you analyze relations of things, you do not ultimately reach anything simple and without relation; the components are as far from being simple as the compound.

It is in relations that the intellectual significance of any object consists.

As to our maxim of clearness, it is proper to notice that though the significance of a word lies in its relation to conduct, yet when we can define it in terms of *sensible* relations, or relations of everyday *experience*, it will not usually be needful for us to proceed further, and consider what practical difference those sensible, everyday relations can make to us. It is evident that every sensible difference may become a practical difference. The significance of it lies in that, and not in the peculiar feelings excited. Thus, to define *yellow*, it is sufficient to say that it is the color resulting from a mixture of red and green. This is a practical definition; for it shows how the color can be produced. It is not usually necessary to define *red* and *green* further than to say that they are two of the three fundamental colors. That brings them down to ground where there is no fear of meaningless distinctions. Still, if definition is required, we mean by red that color which in dilution is seen in the less refrangible of the hydrogen-rays, etc.

The purpose of this maxim is not, however, so much to aid us in defining ordinary words so much as it is in aiding us to get clear ideas of the real significance of philosophical terms, such as *reality*, *necessity*, *belief*, *cause*, the *self*, in which there is great danger of our using words without attaching any significations at all to them.

[B.]

Rule I. *The principle of identity.* A medad whose positive and negative parts are exactly alike with bonds uniting all like blanks is necessarily true.

Thus, the medad of Fig. 14 is necessarily true.

Fig. 14

Rule II. Given two medads, if an unencircled bond of each be broken, and the broken ends of the one be joined to those of the other, the veritability of the result will be as high as one or other of the given medads.

Thus, if the medads of Fig. 15 be both true, so is that of Fig. 16.

Fig. 15 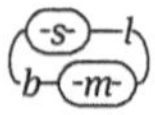   **Fig. 16**

Rule III. *The syllogistic principle.* If the negative part of one medad occurs in affirmative quality in another, then the medad formed by substituting the affirmative part of the former and the relative in affirmative quality in the latter will have a veritability as high as one or other of the two first.

Thus, if the medads of Fig. 17 are both true, so is that of Fig. 18.

Fig. 17   **Fig. 18**

So, if the medads of Fig. 19 are both true, so is that of Fig. 20.

Fig. 19   **Fig. 20**

[C.] The second proposition going to define "being smaller than" is,

   Nothing is smaller than itself.

It will be remarked that nothing in the formal definition of "smaller than" distinguishes it from "greater than". But the second proposition excludes the possibility of a thing being at once greater than and smaller than itself. In short "smaller than" cannot be distinguished by a definition alone, but it needs an *index* to distinguish it, just as right and best do.[16]

The third proposition completing the formal definition of "being smaller than" is (in a universe of *magnitudes*)

 Take any two magnitudes, then either one is smaller than the other or they are one identical magnitude.

I now proceed to define the series of whole numbers. The universe is supposed to be a universe of whole numbers.

1st No number is smaller than the number *zero*.

2nd Every number has a number greater than it, but not greater than any third number intermediate between them. That is, there is a number *next* greater than any given number.

---

16 [This paragraph is from a loose leaf of R 813(s).]

3rd 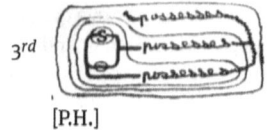 The jagged line refers to the universe of characters. Every character that is possessed by a number is possessed by some number that is identical with or greater than every number that possesses that character.
[P.H.]

"___ is smaller than ___". -s-   (1) ◯   (2) ◯   (3)

If there is something larger than any A, there is an A larger than any other A.

[D.] Thus, dichotomy rules the ideal world; whence Plato for whom that world alone was real held dichotomy to be the only true mode of division. There are thus but two forms of results of ideal experimentation. If either proves that $\Sigma_i m_i$; or it proves that $\Pi_i m_i$, that a proposition is *possible* (and its contradictory consequently *impossible*) or that a proposition is *impossible* (and its contradictory consequently *possible*).

Every result of an ideal induction clothes itself in the form of a contradiction. Hence, in the absence of contradiction, every *particular* proposition, that is, every proposition of the form $\Sigma_i m_i$ is true and every *universal* proposition, that is, every one of the form $\Pi_i m_i$ is false. But the effect of contradiction,—or, to speak causally, the inductive conclusion which clothes itself as a contradiction, is to reverse this and make a proposition of the form $\Pi_i m_i$ true and to make its contradictory $\Sigma_i \overline{m}_i$ false. If there are several quantifiers, it is the *last* of these which determines the character of the proposition as universal or particular.[17]

[E.] I now come to a point of doubt. Suppose a collection of boys and a collection of girls, both ~~abnumeral~~ infinite. Suppose that for every way of distributing the boys in two houses there is a way of distributing the girls in two houses. Does it not follow that for every boy there is a girl? It would seem so; yet I have not succeeded as yet in proving it. If not, it is possible for a collection of children, each with one wish, to wish for all possible ways of their being placed in two houses. Thus some one child must be entirely satisfied with every arrangement. Yet every child might be placed in the house where he did not wish to be.

[F.] Such a branch must always project outwards; for since its whole significance is to change the order of selection of subjects, and since outer subjects are chosen before inner ones, a branch ending at a monad of nullity and extending inward can have no effect whatever. There is no reason but the convenience of writing why the graphs should be constructed upon a surface rather than have three dimensions. This limitation is not founded in their nature. In three dimensions, any number of regions can all touch one another, and any two graphs could be directly connected, without extending beyond their common enclosure, however complicated might be the connections of the different graphs. But owing to the graphs being drawn in two dimensions, from this utterly extrinsic circumstance arises an [end]

---

[17] Herein, I correct my former view which denominated a proposition *particular* which stated the existence of something, thus making the *first* quantifier the determining one. It now seems to one better to say that the first quantifier if a Σ makes the proposition *affirmative* and if a Π makes it *negative*. According to this, "Some woman is adored by whatever catholics there may be" is universal affirmative, "whatever catholic there may be adores some woman" is particular negative.

[G.] [Some autograph sketches of graphs found on verso pages of R 482 manuscript leaves.][18]

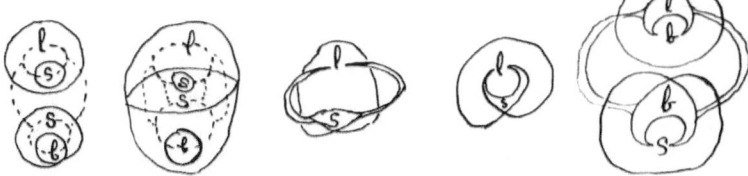

---

18 [In R 482 and elsewhere Peirce is seen to experiment with numerous non-standard or ill-formed forms of graphs that are nevertheless helpful in illustrating what went into his thought processes and experimentations when struggling to produce the right, sound and complete set of permissions for the system while simplifying the transformations. In the first two examples, for instance, one might see a preliminary but an incomplete idea of iteration (or involution) taking shape, in an attempt to force two implicational graphs to weld into each other, by having them overlap rather than placing one entirely inside another as would be proper. There are also dashed lines and other pieces of notation that are hardly anywhere else appealed to. The other four examples also remain somewhat puzzling, with unusual shapes for the scroll which Peirce did not explain in the preserved leaves.]

6 Positive Logical Graphs (PLG)

R 488, late 1896. Houghton Library. The system of positive logical graphs (PLG) presented in the text below is "essentially the same" as the one published in Peirce's "The Logic of Relatives", "except that the interpretation is nearly reversed." Since the system exposed in *The Monist* 1897 paper was that of entitative graphs, Peirce is now referring to his newly developed system of existential graphs (EGs). Instead of "existential", R 488 employs the term "positive" (as the sheet on which these graphs is scribed is that of the sheet of truth [cf. R 514], representing algebraically the top element), but the meaning of the two is practically the same. The term "positive" had occurred in some alternative sequences of R 482 added to it (see Alt. § 11 in the previous chapter). R 488 was probably composed soon after the first, submitted version of R 482 was completed, sometime before the end of December 1896 but no earlier than October 1896, being instrumental to the proposed revisions of R 482 in order to turn the latter to his "most lucid and interesting paper".

PLG is short but important as it is one of the first complete sequences in which the system that is to become the method of existential graphs is presented. Peirce's exposition is largely carried out with a large number of examples: 75 graphs with their English equivalents illustrate the workings of the six fundamental conventions. This manuscript is also the first (together with the later revisions to the first draft segments of R 482) in which Peirce consistently preserves the difference in the thickness of the line: the lightly drawn closed line denotes "precise denials" while the thick ones are lines for the identity and quantification.

The other noteworthy points made in this paper include (i) that quantifiers are not assumed to come with existential presuppositions, (ii) that the "characters", which Peirce later will term "spots" (or "terms", "rhemas") in the theory of EGs are, according to the first convention, surrounded by parts corresponding to the blanks of the verb, (iii) that characters have a definite order of interpretation beginning at a designated blank and continuing clockwise, and (iv) that it is the "scrolls" (the continuous self-returning lines that designate two or more nested ovals; the term which shall be introduced later on) that appear as the primary sign of conditional in the system of positive logical graphs. (See the survey of selections in the introduction to Part II for details.) The transcription below preserves the unusual orientation of such scrolls: the openings of the loops are here mostly diagonal.

The system of logical graphs here described is essentially the same as that which was sketched by me in a paper in *The Monist* for January 1897, except that the interpretation is nearly reversed. I shall distinguish the present system as positive, since it proceeds upon the principle that writing a proposition down asserts it.

I shall in this paper use three unusual dictions which all depend upon the same principle. Namely, when I use a noun in the plural, and speak for example of "men, A and B", I do not mean to imply that the men are necessarily different. They may be the same man. Also when I use the word "every", I mean "every, if there are any". Thus, if I say "M adores every angel", I mean whatever angels may exist, without asserting that any *do* exist. So when I use the word "only", I mean "only, if at all". Thus if I say "M adores only angels", I mean he adores nothing but angels; I do not assert that he adores anything.

Logical Definitions

- A *proposition* is a sign which is true or false.
- A *proper name* is the sign ~~signifying~~ denoting by association by contiguity something common to the experience of the deliverer and interpreter of the proposition of which it is a part, and that which it denotes has an identity consisting in continuity of existence.
- A *verb* is a fragment of a possible proposition having certain blanks which being filled by proper names make the verb a proposition.
- An *individual subject* of a verb is that which is named by the proper name filling any one of the blanks of the verb.

Conventions concerning Graphs

1. Each unanalyzed verb shall be represented by a special character, and to each blank of the verb is to be appropriated a special side of that character, so that anything denoting an individual being written close to the character on that side fills that blank of the verb. The circumference of the character being divided into as many equal parts as there are blanks to the verb, beginning at the left hand side, the blanks may be appropriated to successive divisions proceeding clockwise.[1]

---

1 [Alt.:] Conventions about Graphs
1. Each unanalyzed verb is to be represented by an initial letter or other character (including a point and a blank) with heavy lines projecting from it to stand for its subjects, a determinate side of the character representing the verb being appropriated to each blank.
2. Unbroken continuity between two lines is to be understood as imposing upon the things they denote the condition of being identical.
3. The writing down of anything which can be constructed as a proposition is to be understood as asserting it; and the writing of two or more propositions together is to be understood as asserting them all.
4. The encircling of a proposition by a lightly drawn closed line is to be understood as denying it.
5. A blank is to be understood as meaningless when considered as a proposition, that is, as implied in every proposition by logical necessity. "~~This proposition~~ What I am telling you is true" is the type of a meaningless proposition. Every proposition true by logical necessity

2. The end of a line shall denote some individual thing existing in the universe of discourse.
3. The unbroken continuity of a heavy line is to be understood as imposing upon its ends the condition of being identical.
4. The encircling of a proposition by a lightly drawn endless line is to be understood as transmuting that proposition into its precise denial.
5. The writing down of anything which can be construed as a proposition shall be understood as asserting it; and the writing down together of two or more propositions shall be understood as asserting them all.
6. A blank, when considered as a proposition, is to be understood as meaningless, that is, as something the analogue of which is implied in every proposition. Thus, "What I tell you is true" is a meaningless proposition. And every proposition which, in case a second proposition is true, is true by logical necessity, will be considered to be implied in that second proposition. For example, "every man is either green or not green" is implied in every proposition, because this proposition is in any case true by logical necessity.

Examples illustrating the above Conventions

If w signifies "___ is wise", then Fig. 1 means, in a universe of men, "Some man is wise", Fig. 2, "No man is wise"; Fig. 3, "Some man is not wise"; Fig. 4, "Every man is wise". If v signifies "___ is virtuous", then Fig. 5 means, "Some wise man is virtuous"; Fig. 7 "Some besides the wise are virtuous"; Fig. 8, "Some wise man is not virtuous"; Fig. 9, "Some beside the wise are not virtuous"; Fig. 10, "Some man is either not wise or not virtuous"; which is the same as Fig. 11, "Either some man is not wise or some man is not virtuous", that is, "Some man is not wise if every man is virtuous"; Fig. 15 means, "Some man is wise if virtuous", which is the same as Fig. 19 and Fig. 22 "Some man is wise if every man is virtuous"; Fig. 16 means "Some man if he be wise is virtuous", which is equivalent to Fig. 20 and Fig. 23 "If every man is wise, some man is virtuous"; Fig. 17 means, "Some man is either wise or virtuous", which is equivalent to Fig. 21 and Fig. 24, "Either some man is wise or some man is virtuous"; Fig. 6 means "No wise man is virtuous"; Fig. 12, "Every man is wise if virtuous", or "Only the wise are virtuous"; Fig. 13, "If any man is wise he is virtuous"; Fig. 14 means, "Every man is either wise or virtuous"; ~~which is equivalent to Fig. 25, "Of any men, A and B, either A is wise or B is virtuous"~~. Fig. 18, "Every man is both wise and virtuous", which is equivalent to Fig. 26, "Of

---

in every case in which a second proposition is true, will be considered as implied in that second proposition.

any men, A and B, it is true that A is wise and B is virtuous"; Fig. 27 means, "Every man is virtuous without being wise", which is equivalent to Fig. 28, "Every man is virtuous and no man is wise", which is also expressed by Fig. 32; Fig. 29 means, "Every man is wise without being virtuous", which is equivalent to Fig. 30, "Every man is wise and no man is virtuous"; Fig. 31 means, "Any man is not wise and not virtuous", which is equivalent to Fig. 33, "No man is wise and no man is virtuous".

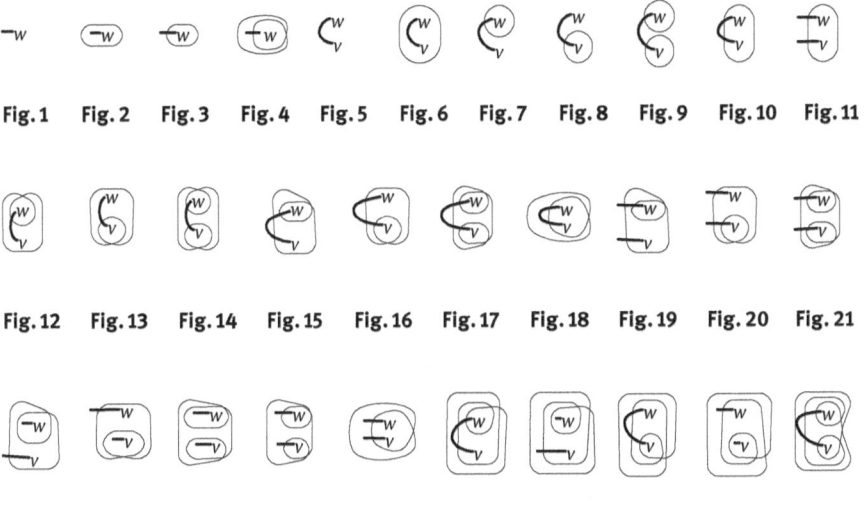

If *l* signifies "___ loves ___", then Fig. 34 means "Some man loves some man"; Fig. 35, "Some man does not love some man"; Fig. 36, "Some man loves no man"; Fig. 37, "Some man loves every man"; Fig. 38, "Some man is loved by no man"; Fig. 39, "Some man is loved by every man"; Fig. 40, "No man loves any man"; Fig. 41, "Every man loves every man"; Fig. 42. "Every man loves some man"; Fig. 43, "No man loves every man"; Fig. 44, "Every man is loved by some man"; Fig. 45, "No man is loved by every man"; Fig. 46, "Some wise man loves some virtuous man"; Fig. 47, "Some wise man loves all virtuous men"; Fig. 48, "Some wise man loves only virtuous men"; Fig. 49, "No virtuous man is loved by all wise men"; Fig. 50, "No virtuous man is loved only by wise men"; Fig. 51, Every wise man loves every virtuous man"; Fig 52, "All but the wise love only the virtuous"; Fig. 53, "Some man, A, loves some man, B, and either A is not wise or B is not virtuous", which is equivalent to Fig. 54, "Either somebody is loved by somebody beside the wise, or somebody beside the virtuous is loved by somebody". If *s* signifies "___ serves ___", and *b* signifies "___ benefits ___", then Fig. 55 means,

"Some man, A, serves some man, B, who is benefitted by some man, B, who is loved by A". Fig. 56 means, "Whoever loves any benefactor of any man serves that man", or "Every lover of any man serves everybody benefitted by that man", or "Any benefactor of any man is loved only by servants of that man". Fig. 57 means, "Whoever serves any man loves everybody but the benefactors of that man", or "Any man benefits every man served only by lovers of him".

Fig. 32 Fig. 33 Fig. 34 Fig. 35 Fig. 36 Fig. 37 Fig. 38 Fig. 39 Fig. 40 Fig. 41 Fig. 42

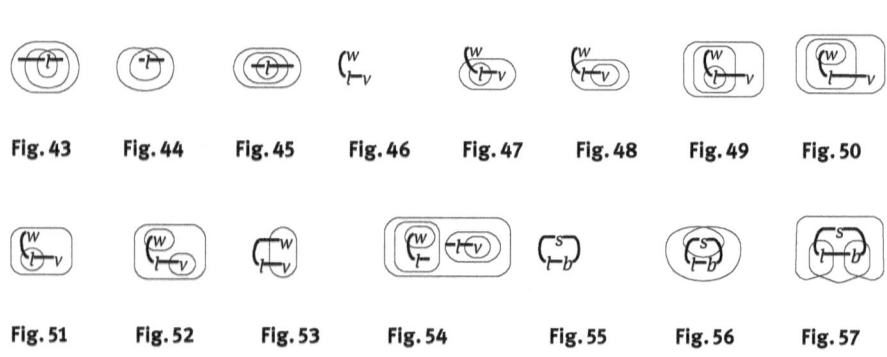

Fig. 43 Fig. 44 Fig. 45 Fig. 46 Fig. 47 Fig. 48 Fig. 49 Fig. 50

Fig. 51 Fig. 52 Fig. 53 Fig. 54 Fig. 55 Fig. 56 Fig. 57

If g signifies "___ gives ___ to ___" and t signifies "___ takes ___ from ___", then Fig. 58 means, "There are men, A, B, C, such that A gives B to C and C takes B from A". Fig. 59 means "There is a man, A, such that whoever man B may be, there is a man, C, such that A gives B to C and C takes B from A". If h signifies "___ is happy", k "___ is a king", r "___ is rich", then Fig. 60 means, "Some wise man is happy and some virtuous man is a king"; Fig. 61 "No wise man is happy but some virtuous man is a king"; Fig. 62, "Either no wise man is happy or some virtuous man is a king"; Fig. 63, "Either some wise man is happy or some virtuous man is a king"; Fig. 64, "There are men, A and B, such that A is wise, and B is virtuous, and either A is not happy or B is not a king". Fig. 65 means, "Some man is, at once, wise, happy, and a king"; Fig. 66, "There is a wise man, A, a happy man, B, and a king, C, and A, B, and C are not all the same man"; Fig. 67, "There is a wise man, A, and a wise man, B, and A and B are not the same man"; that is, there are, at least, two wise men.

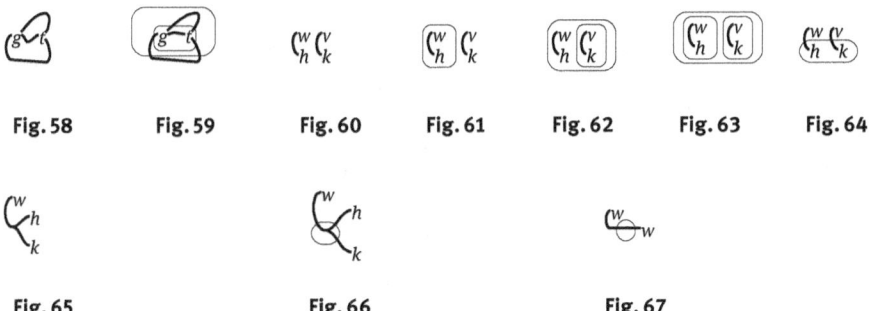

Fig. 58 **Fig. 59** **Fig. 60** **Fig. 61** **Fig. 62** **Fig. 63** **Fig. 64**

Fig. 65 **Fig. 66** **Fig. 67**

Fig. 68 means, "There are men, A, B, C, L, M, N, P, Q, R, such that A is wise and is identical with L and P, B is wise and is identical with M and Q, C is wise and is identical with N and R, L is not identical with Q, M is not identical with R, and N is not identical with P"; that is, "There are, at least, three wise men". Fig. 69 means, "There is only one wise man". Fig. 70 means, "There are two wise men, but there are not three".

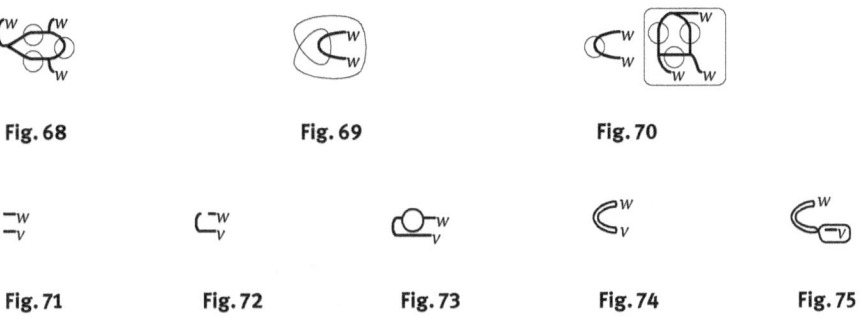

Fig. 68 **Fig. 69** **Fig. 70**

Fig. 71 **Fig. 72** **Fig. 73** **Fig. 74** **Fig. 75**

Fig. 71 means, of course, "There is a wise man and there is a virtuous man". In Fig. 72, the two bonds are brought together, with a blank between them. A blank is, by convention, meaningless. All meaningless propositions are logically equivalent. It is a meaningless proposition to assert that existing things are coexistent. Hence, Fig. 72 may be read, "Some wise man is coexistent with some virtuous man". The negative of a meaningless proposition is self-contradictory. Hence, Fig. 73 is absurd. But if the bonds be omitted, as in Fig. 74, the meaning is "Whatever is a wise man is not coexistent with whatever is a virtuous man", that is, either no man is wise or no man is virtuous. On the same principle, Fig. 75 means, "Either no man is wise or some man is virtuous", that is, if there is a wise man there is a virtuous man.

7 On Logical Graphs (Acad. Graphs)

R 480, October 1896. Houghton Library. It can be argued that it was this 19-page manuscript—or a paper very close to this one—that Peirce presented at the National Academy of Sciences meeting on November 18, 1896 as "A Graphical Method of Logic", together with another paper on mathematical infinity. (For a discussion of R 480 and its relations to R 14–17 on mathematical infinity, see Introduction to Part II, LoF 1.) The influence of Peirce's parallel work in mathematics can be observed for instance in Article 8, where he introduces the distinction between "logical" and "semi-logical or arithmetical" verbs. While logical verbs are verified by proper names, namely names whose objects are common to the experience of both the utterer and the interpreter, semi-logical or arithmetical verbs are verified according to whether their structure reflects their numerical properties. Peirce declares at the end of Article 8 that the logic of semi-logical relations is the foundation of arithmetic itself, but postpones a full account of the claim. Article 9 deals with first and second-intentional verbs; Article 10 aims at giving "a precise rule for the interpretation of the graphs above described", namely instructions on how to read the graphs, which he later terms the "Endoporeutic Rule" or method of interpreting existential graphs. Articles 1–6 present the basic definitions (verb, particular proposition, ideograph, oval, continuous line, assertion), Article 7 gives the basic examples, and Articles 11–21 help identifying the account with Peirce's later additions to R 482 and to his attempts at simplifying the transformation rules of this new system, making the text of R 480 a perfect synopsis of his autumnal cornucopia.

§ 1. Article 1. By a verb, I mean either a complete proposition or a fragment of a proposition which would be rendered complete by filling up certain blanks belonging to it with proper names.[1] Thus, "___ sells ___ to ___ at the price of ___" is a verb.

A verb having no blanks, that is, a complete proposition, I call a *medadic verb*, or *medad*: a verb having a single blank I call a *monadic verb*, or *monad*: a verb having two blanks, a *dyadic verb*, or *dyad*, a verb having three blanks a *triadic verb*, or *triad*; etc. The number of blanks of a verb I call its adicity.

Article 2. The assertion that there are real things whose proper names filling the blanks of a verb give a true proposition, as "something sells something to something at some price", I call a thoroughly particular proposition. Such a proposition may be called medadic, monadic, dyadic, triadic, etc.

---

1 [Alt.:] **§ 1. Article 1.** By a *verbal relative*, a phrase which in this memoir I shall shorten to *relative*, I mean a fragment of a proposition which would become a complete proposition if certain blanks were filled up with proper names. Thus, "___ sells ___ to ___ for the price ___" is a *verbal relative*.

A relative, properly speaking, has at least two blanks; but it will be convenient to include under the term *verbs*, or fragments of propositions which would become [end]

Article 3. I propose to represent a verb by an ideograph, or sign of the like of some ~~thing or fact~~ state of things,—usually, if the verb is not analyzed, by an initial letter,—with the ends of lines attached to it at definite places to indicate its several blanks. Thus, Fig. 1 shall mean "___ sells ___ to ___ at the price of ___ " where the four blanks in their order are indicated respectively by the lines at the left, at the right, below, and above the letter. If these lines are drawn heavy the corresponding thoroughly particular proposition shall be meant.

Fig. 1

Article 4. A lightly drawn oval encircling the ideograph of a verb shall be understood to deny it. The ~~encircled~~ verb with the circle round it is the *negative* of the verb that is encircled. The negative of a verb has a blank for each blank of the verb. Hence, lines must project from the oval corresponding to the several lines which project from the graph it contains. Thus, Fig. 2 will mean "Something does not sell something to something for some price".

Fig. 2

Article 5. If two heavy lines run into and become continuous with one another, the meaning is that there is one real object whose proper name can truly fill both blanks. If the light lines of a verb run into one another the meaning is that it is conceived that the two blanks are filled by the same proper name of a real object. Thus, Fig. 3 is not a tetrad but a dyad, meaning "___ sells something, A, to itself at the price of ___ ".

Fig. 3

Article 6. If a proposition is written down, it is to be understood as asserted. If several propositions are written down, they are all asserted.

Article 7. The following examples show how this apparatus suffices for the expression of ~~all~~ a great variety of propositions. The medad of Fig. 4 asserts the truth of both A and B. For the denials of A and B are written together, and their aggregate

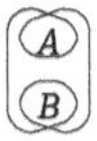

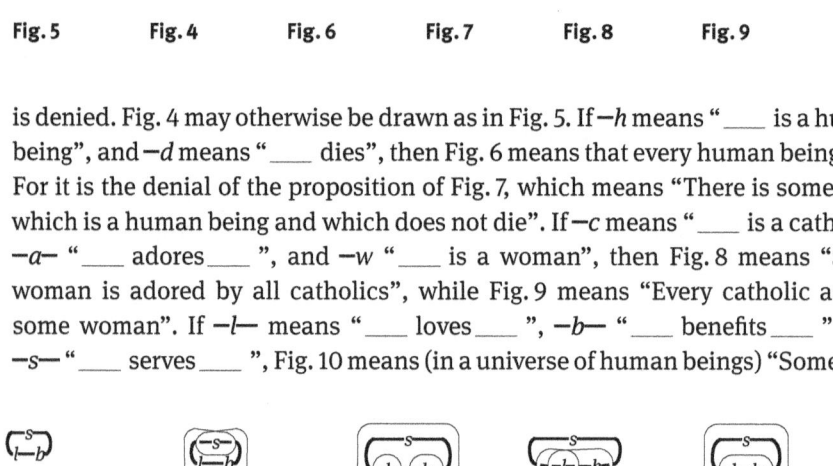

Fig. 5 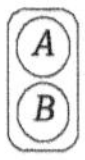   Fig. 4 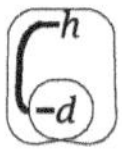   Fig. 6 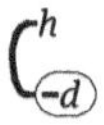   Fig. 7 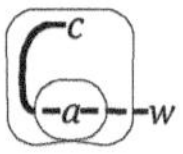   Fig. 8 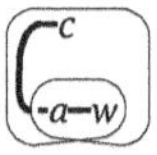   Fig. 9

is denied. Fig. 4 may otherwise be drawn as in Fig. 5. If —*h* means "___ is a human being", and —*d* means "___ dies", then Fig. 6 means that every human being dies. For it is the denial of the proposition of Fig. 7, which means "There is something which is a human being and which does not die". If —*c* means "___ is a catholic", —*a*— "___ adores ___", and —*w* "___ is a woman", then Fig. 8 means "Some woman is adored by all catholics", while Fig. 9 means "Every catholic adores some woman". If —*l*— means "___ loves ___", —*b*— "___ benefits ___", and —*s*— "___ serves ___", Fig. 10 means (in a universe of human beings) "Somebody

Fig. 10   Fig. 11   Fig. 12   Fig. 13 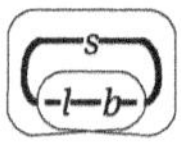   Fig. 14

serves somebody benefitted by somebody loved by him", or "Somebody loves some benefactor of somebody whom he serves", or "Somebody is benefitted by somebody loved by a servant of him", or "Somebody is served by a lover of a benefactor of him", or "Somebody is loved by a servant of somebody whom he benefits", or "Somebody benefits somebody served by a lover of him".

Fig. 11 means:

- "Anybody stands only to persons whom he serves (if to anybody) in the relation of lover of a benefactor of them", or
- "Anybody is a servant of whoever is benefitted by anybody whom he loves", or
- "Anybody is served by every lover there may be of a benefactor of him", or
- "Anybody stands only to his servants (if to anybody) in the relation of being benefitted by persons loved by them", or

- "Anybody benefits (if at all) only persons served by whatever lover he may have", or
- "Anybody is loved (if at all) only by servants of whoever may be benefitted by him".

Fig. 12 means:

- "Anybody stands to all but lovers of him in the relation of benefitting whoever may be served by them", or
- "Anybody stands only to persons benefitted by him in the relation of being loved by whatever servants they may have", or
- "Anybody is served (if at all) only by lovers of everybody but benefactors of him", or
- "Anybody stands to whatever servants of him there may be in the relation of being benefitted by all but those loved by them", or
- "Anybody serves (if at all) only persons benefitted by all but persons loved by them", or
- "Anybody stands to whoever he may serve in the relation of loving everybody but benefactors of them".

Fig. 13 means:

- "Somebody is a servant of a person benefitted only by persons loved by him", or
- "Somebody stands to somebody whom he serves in the relation of loving whoever may benefit that person", etc.

Fig. 14 means: "Nobody is a servant of anybody but a person benefitted by a person whom he loves", etc.
Fig. 15 means: "Somebody sells a person to that person at the price of himself".

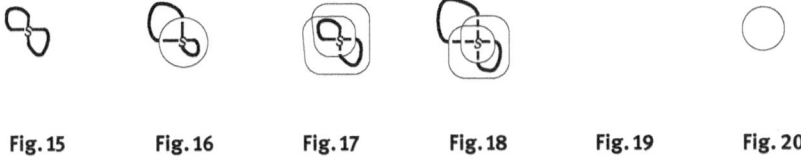

Fig. 15   Fig. 16   Fig. 17   Fig. 18   Fig. 19   Fig. 20

Fig. 16 means: "Somebody sells for the ownership of himself every person to that person".

Fig. 17 means: "Somebody sells, taking in payment himself, every man to himself".

Article 8. In order to express certain classes of propositions, it is necessary to take account of *logical* and *semi-logical,* or *arithmetical* verbs. By a *logical verb*, I mean a verb which, no matter with what proper names its blanks are filled, always gives results of the same verity. By saying that two propositions are of the *same verity* I mean that both are true or both false. By a *semi-logical* or *arithmetical verb*, I mean a verb which, when its system of blanks are filled with similar systems of proper names, always yields propositions of the same verity.

—   ○

Fig. 21   Fig. 22

There are just two logical verbs of each degree of adicity, one giving necessarily true propositions and the other necessarily false propositions. A true logical verb is most suitably imaged by The most suitable ideograph of a true logical verb is a blank space; that of a false logical proposition is an empty oval. Thus, Fig. 19, which is a simple blank is the true logical medad, which is *meaningless*. "I tell you the truth", is an expression of it. Fig. 20 is the false logical medad, which is *self-contradictory*. "This very proposition is false" is the purest expression of it. The true logical monad is shown in Fig. 21. It is expressed by the words "___ is something". The false logical monad is shown in Fig. 22. It is expressed by the words "___ is nothing". Propositions in which these occur are exemplified in Figs. 23, 24, and 25. Fig. 23 means "Something is a human being". This is not necessarily true. But if we substitute a proper name for *h*, as in Fig. 24, where A is Alexander, the proposition is necessarily true, because by proper names

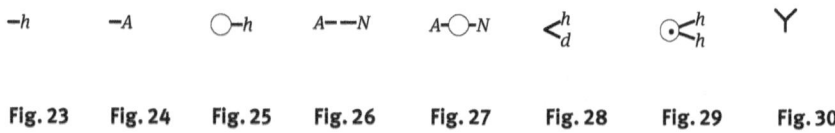

Fig. 23   Fig. 24   Fig. 25   Fig. 26   Fig. 27   Fig. 28   Fig. 29   Fig. 30

in Logic are meant names of individual objects of the common experience of the deliverer of the graph proposition and of its interpreter. Fig. 25 means "Some human being is nothing", which is absurd; for "some" implies existence in the universe of discourse. The true logical dyad means *coexistent with*, that is "___ and ___ are together in the universe of discourse". It is exemplified in

Fig. 26, which means "Alexander is coexistent with Napoleon", that is, is in the same universe of discourse. The false logical dyad means "___ is *incompatible with* ___", that is, is not in the universe of discourse along with it. It is shown in Fig. 27.

There is no semi-logical medad; and the semi-logical monads are the same as the logical monads. Conceived as semi-logical, they may be called the *monad of unity* and the *monad of nullity*. The chief semi-logical dyads are two. The first is the *dyad of unity*, which forms a true proposition whenever the two *bonds*, or projecting lines, run into one another. Expressed in words it is "___ and ___ are one individual". Its proper ideograph is a point, and the whole line is a continuum of dyads of unity. The dyad of unity is exemplified in Fig. 28, which means "Some human being is *identical with* something that dies. The other chief logical dyad is the *dyad of duality*, which forms a false proposition whenever its two bonds run into one another. It is exemplified in Fig. 29 which means "Some man is not some man", or "There are at least two human beings". The chief semi-logical triads are six, of which two are fundamental. The first of the latter is the affirmative *triad of unity*, which forms a true proposition whenever its three bonds run together. It means "___ and ___ and ___ are one individual". Its proper ideograph is a point of branching on a line, as in Fig. 30. Its use is illustrated in Fig. 31, which means, "Every Catholic both adores and loves some woman". Fig. 32 means "Something either does not love or does not benefit something without being a servant of that thing".

The affirmative triad of unity is evidently required for the expression of copulative and disjunctive propositions. The negative of the triad of unity, which is that triad which gives a false proposition whenever its bonds all run together, may be called the *triad of severalty*. It means "___ and ___ and ___ are more than one individual". It is exemplified in Fig. 33 which means, in a universe of human beings, "Somebody has a servant and is loved by somebody and benefitted by somebody and is either loved or benefitted by somebody else than one servant".

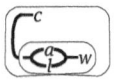
Fig. 31

Fig. 31

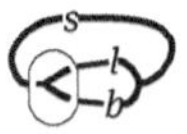

Fig. 33

The next semi-logical triad is the affirmative *triad of duality*, which forms a true proposition in some way in which two of its bonds run together, but a false proposition if all run together. It means "___ and ___ and ___ are two individuals". It needs no proper ideograph since it may be formed of seven triads of unity and three dyads of unity as shown in Fig. 34, where the bonds are numbered to facilitate the tracing out of the interpretation. It means, "A is identical with something, 1, and something, 7, B is identical with something, 2, and something, 8, C is identical with something, 3, and something, 9, and 1, 2, and 3 are not all identical, and taking any six things, 7, 8, 9, 10, 11, 12 either 4, 10, and 11 are not identical, or 5, 7, and 12 are not all identical, or 6, 8, and 9 are not identical or 7 is identical with 8, or 9 is identical with 10, or 11 is identical with 12. The negative of the triad of duality is the *triad of oddness*, which either forms a true proposition if all its bonds run together or else a false proposition if any two of them run together. It means "___ and ___ and ___ are all related to one another in the same way in respect to identity and diversity".

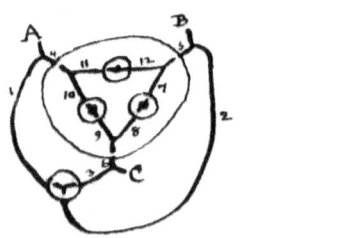 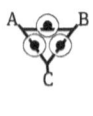

Fig. 34 [P.H.] **Fig. 35**

The next semi-logical triad is the *triad of triality*, which forms a false proposition if any two of its bonds run together. It means "___ and ___ and ___ are all different". It is shown in Fig. 35, which means "A, B, and C are three". Its negative is the *triad of non-triality*.

A further account of the logic of semi-logical relations, upon which arithmetic is founded must be postponed.

Article 9. Another class of verbs requiring special study in logic are *verbs of second intention*. When we first begin the study of any department of experiential science, we form classes and systems of objects of experience and these give the ordinary verbs, or *verbs of first intention*. But when we come to observe the signs themselves which we have so created, we make classes and systems based on the characters of the signs, and these are verbs of second intention. We especially remark the dyad of second intention, which is "___ has the character (or is a subject of the monad) ___ " and the triad of second intention which is "___ and ___ are subjects which can truly fill respectively the first and second blanks of the dyad ___ ".

Article 10. It is now necessary to give a precise rule for the interpretation of the graphs above described. This can only consist in a rule for the expression of the meaning of a graph in ordinary language. But ordinary language is very ill-fitted to express at once precisely and comprehensibly the complicated relations which graphs are well-adapted to express. No student can have any mastery of the method of graphs until he learns to think in their language, any more than he could have any mastery of algebra as long as he had to translate every equation into words. The only kind of linguistic syntax which does not utterly break down in dealing with complex triadic relations is that which the lawyers have developed and which simply consists in using letters of the alphabet as relative pronouns. Though this is not very familiar, it has the merit of precision and therefore the rule for interpretation shall consist in showing how to express the meaning of a graph in that syntax. The bonds of a logical graph of the above description denote individual objects of the universe of discourse. They are the *subjects* of discourse, or, in the language of grammar, the subjects and objects. The spots, or letters, of the graph signify ideas. They are the *verbs*.

The first step in interpreting a logical graph is to assign letters to denote the individuals denoted by the bonds. We are to begin with the bonds any parts of which are unencircled. To each of these one of the first letters of the alphabet is to be assigned. These objects are to be suitably chosen, to suit the intention of the deliverer of the graph, that is, the supporter of its truth. The word "some" implies such choice.

Next letters from the latter part of the alphabet are to be assigned to bonds of which the outermost parts are once enclosed. These denote objects which the interpreter, or the opponent of the truth of the assertion of the graph, is free to select as he pleases. The word "any" expresses such a freedom of selection.

Next letters from the fore part of the alphabet are to be assigned to bonds of which the outermost parts are twice enclosed; and these denote objects which must be suitably chosen to support the truth of the assertion of the graph. So the assignment goes on, bonds whose outermost parts are less enclosed being taken before those whose outermost parts are more enclosed, and those whose outermost parts are within even number of enclosures denote individuals which must be selected suitably to support the assertion, which those whose outermost parts are within odd numbers of enclosures denote individuals which may be freely chosen so as to attempt the refutation of the assertion.

After the individuals denoted by the bonds have all been so lettered, the next step consists in analyzing the assertion of the graph. The interpreter begins by picking out all the unenclosed letters. These, or rather the verbs they signify, are all ~~asserted~~ affirmed, each of the individuals denoted by its bonds. Next the unenclosed enclosures are to be taken. These are so many simultaneous denials. They will best be numbered, and be copulatively denied while their significations are only distinguished by the numbers so affixed to them. Next are to be taken up the letters and enclosures within each of the numbered enclosures. These are all disjunctively, or alternatively, denied. Within each numbered enclosed the letters will best be taken first and their significations substituted for them with their blanks filled by the bonds, and then the enclosures can be numbered, each by a second number following the first. Thus, the enclosures within enclosure 1 will be numbered 11, 12, 13, etc.; those within enclosure 2, will be numbered 21, 22, 23, etc. Next will be taken up all the letters and enclosures within each of the once enclosed enclosures. These are all simultaneously, or copulatively, affirmed, the letters by their significations (with the blanks fitted up by the letters attached to the bonds) and the enclosures by numbers on the same system. That is, the enclosures within enclosure 21 will be numbered 211, 212, 213, etc. The rule is that letters and enclosures evenly enclosed are copulatively affirmed, while those which are oddly enclosed are disjunctively denied.

For example, the interpretation of Fig. 8 according to this rule will be as follows: There is a thing, A, such that no matter what thing, Z, may be, A is a woman, and it is either not true that Z is a catholic or else proposition 1 is not true. Proposition 1 is that it is not true that Z adores A. The interpretation of Fig. 9 is as follows: Anything whatever, Z, having been chosen, a thing A can be found such that either Z is not a catholic or else Z adores A and A is a woman.

The interpretation of Fig. 13 is as follows: There are things, A and B, such that anything, Z, no matter what, being taken, A is a servant of B, and either A loves Z or else Z does not benefit B.

Different branches of bonds separated only by an unenclosed triad of unity need not receive separate letters. Thus, Fig. 34 may be interpreted thus: A, B, and C are not all identical, and further either it is not true that A is not B, or it is not true that B is not C, or it is not true that C is not A.

§ 2. Illative transformations of the above graphs

Article 11. The dyad of duality means "___ is not___ ". Now this is precisely the meaning of an enclosure. Suppose, then, we attempt to express the medad of Fig. 36, "Some human being does not die", by introducing the dyad of duality. We[re] we to write Fig. 37, we should only have expressed that "Some human being is different from something which dies". We wish to express, "Some human being differs from *everything* that dies". Fig. 38 signifies, "There is something, A, such that whatever thing, Z, be taken, A is a human being and either A loves Z or Z does not die", that is, some human being loves everything that dies. Accordingly, we have only to replace the *l* by the dyad of duality, and we have the mode of expression sought. It is delineated in Fig. 39. We have thus reached the theorem that

Fig. 36   Fig. 37   Fig. 38   Fig. 39

every graph like Fig. 39 is equivalent to the corresponding graph like Fig. 36. By such reasoning a formal demonstration would soon be reached that two circles, the one immediately enclosing the other, annul one another's effect. Hence two such circles can anywhere be introduced or, if they exist, be erased.

Article 12. It is a theorem that that effectual bond between two parts of a graph whose outermost part is as much enclosed as that of any other bond between those parts must agree with those parts in being oddly or evenly enclosed. Thus, the interpretation of Fig. 40 is, "Taking any man Z, there is some man, A, that both loves and benefits Z". But the interpretation of Fig. 41 is "There is a man, A, such that taking any man, Z, whatever, A both loves and benefits Z". This has precisely the same meaning as Fig. 42, of which the interpretation is, "There is a man, A,

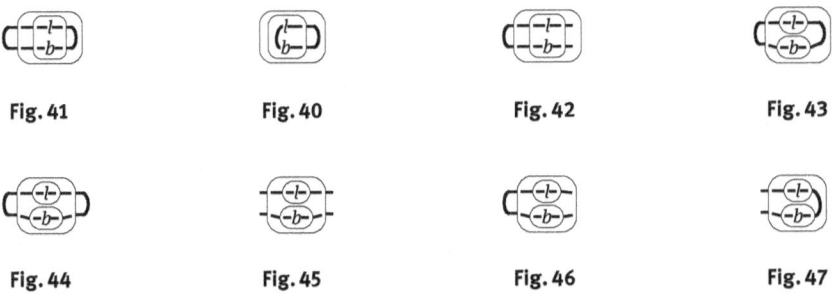

Fig. 41   Fig. 40   Fig. 42   Fig. 43

Fig. 44   Fig. 45   Fig. 46   Fig. 47

such that, any men, Y and Z being taken, A loves Y and benefits Z". For if a man both loves and benefits every man, he both loves and benefits both of any pair of men; and consequently he loves either and benefits the other. But it does not follow that because of every man has a double relation to some man that every two men are in the parts of this relation to the same man. Again, the interpretation of Fig. 43 is, "There is a man, A, such that, any man, Z, being taken, A either loves or benefits that man". This does not imply the truth of Fig. 46, that "There is a man, A, such that, any men, Y and Z, being taken, A either loves Y or benefits Z". For it may be that A benefits Y without loving him and loves Z without benefitting him. Moreover, the truth of the assertion of Fig. 43 is not implied in that of Fig. 47, namely that, there are men, A and B, such that, any man, Z, begin taken, either A loves Z or B benefits Z. For it may be that there are some men whom A loves but whom B neither loves nor benefits, while there are others whom B benefits but whom A neither benefits nor loves. But consider the assertion of Fig. 44, "There are men, A and B, such that A either loves or benefits B". This is equivalent to the assertion of Fig. 45, namely: "There are men, A, B, C, D, such that either A loves B or C benefits D". The theorem can be strictly proved by considering that *some* is in itself disjunctive, meaning either one or another individual of the universe, and disjunction is an associative operation; and so *any* is in itself copulative, meaning both one and another individual of the universe, and copulation is an associative operation.

From this theorem follows the rule of illation that a bond which is ineffectual from the circumstances above described can either be inserted when it does not exist or when it does exist can be ~~broken~~ sundered at its outermost part.

Article 13. The triad of identity has the peculiarity that it may be pushed into or out of an envelope without affecting the meaning, so long as two bonds from the triad do not proceed out through the envelope in which it is. That this is not the

Fig. 48 **Fig. 49** **Fig. 50** **Fig. 51**

case with an ordinary triad may be shown by an example. Let *w—* mean "___ is wise", *–p–* "praises'to ___", *–v* "___ is virtuous". Then, Fig. 48 means "There is a man, A, such that whatever man, Z, be taken, there is a man, B, such that both B is wise and B praises A to Z, or else Z does not love A", that is, some virtuous man is praised to every man who loves him by some wise man. Now if the triad *p* is moved out of the inner oval, Fig. 49 results; and the interpretation of this is, "There is a man, A, such that whatever men, Y and Z may be, either Y is wise or else Y does not praise A to Z, or else Z does not love A", that is, some virtuous man is praised to lovers of him only by wise men (if at all). Thus, a great change of meaning results. If, on the contrary the triad of identity be pushed into the outer envelope we get Fig. 50; and Figs. 48 and 50 are equivalent. For the fuller interpretation of Fig. 48 is, "There are men, A, B, C, such that whatever man, Z, be taken, there is a man D such that both D is wise and D praises C to Z, or else Z does not love B; and in every case, A, B, and C are identical and A is virtuous". The full interpretation of Fig. 50 is "There is a man, A, such that whatever men X, Y, and Z may be, there is a man, D, such that both D is wise and D praises X to Z, or else Z does not love Y or else A, X, and Y are not the same man but in any case A is virtuous". It is evident that these two assertions are equivalent.

If, however, the triad of identity is so far drawn in that two of its bonds stretch out from the enclosure in which it is, as in Fig. 51, the meaning is modified. For the interpretation of Fig. 51 is as follows: "There is a man, A, such that, whatever men Z and Y may be, there are two men C and D such that both D is wise and D praises C to Z and C, A, and Y are identical, or else Z loves Y; and in any case A is virtuous", that is, there is a virtuous man who alone of all men is not loved by all men and who is loved by all men except those to whom he is praised by wise men. But all propositions in which two but not three of the bonds of a triad of identity pass out beyond the enclosure in which that triad is can be written so as to avoid that protrusion of two bonds of the triad of identity. Thus, Fig. 52 is equivalent to Fig. 51.

Article 14. If any transformation of a graph, say from a form A to a form B, is illatively valid under an even (or odd) number of enclosures, then the reverse transformation, from B to A, is illatively valid under an odd (or even) number of enclosures. This is merely the logical principle of contraposition.

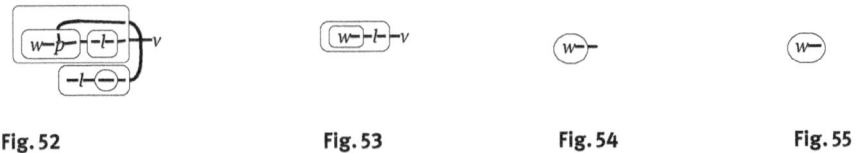

Fig. 52   **Fig. 53**   **Fig. 54**   **Fig. 55**

Article 15. Under even enclosures, any graph may be illatively omitted; under odd enclosures any graph may be illatively inserted. Thus, from the assertion of Fig. 48 may be inferred the assertion of Fig. 53, by omission of p. For Fig. 53 is interpreted as follows: "There is a man, A, such that whatever man Z may be, there is a man, D, such that A is virtuous, and either Z does not love A or D is wise", that is, Some virtuous man is not loved by anybody unless some man is wise.

Article 16. Any bond of a graph can be illatively protracted, or stretched so as to reach out from an enclosure which it had been wholly within and can be illatively retracted, or made to shrink so as not to extend out from an enclosure from which it had extended, provided that such protraction or retraction does not result, first, in a bond whose outermost parts had been evenly enclosed becoming oddly enclosed, nor second, in a bond which had stretched out beyond an evenly enclosed bond coming to be oddly enclosed while not stretching out so far as that other.

For example, from the assertion of Fig. 54, that some man is not wise, cannot be inferred by retraction that of Fig. 55, that no man is wise. Again the interpretation of Fig. 56 is: "Take any two men, X and Y. Then there is man A such that X does not praise Y to A". From this we may infer, by protraction, Fig. 57, that there is a man, B, such that whatever man Y may be, there is a man, A, such that B does not praise Y to A. Or, by retraction, from Fig. 56 may be inferred Fig. 58, that is, Any man whatever is praised by some man to some man. But if the left hand bond of Fig. 56 which extends out beyond the evenly enclosed right hand bond be retracted, as in Fig. 59, so as not to extend out so far as the right hand bond the rule is violated. Thus Fig. 59 means, Every man is praised to some man by all men.

Fig. 56 **Fig. 57** **Fig. 58** **Fig. 59**

Article 17. Any bond may be illatively severed at any evenly enclosed point of it; and any two bonds may under odd enclosures be joined by putting a triad of identity upon each and making the two new bonds thus formed run into one another. This is evident since the severance causes the assertion to be that there are things which fulfill certain conditions which before the severance were asserted to be fulfilled by one thing; while after the junction the assertion is that everything has one or other of two characters which before the junction it was asserted were such that either all things have the one or all things have the other.

Article 18. A verb may be said to be *iterated* when it is written down again and each bond of the new writing is joined to the corresponding bond of the first. Any verb may be illatively iterated, provided the new writing of it is not placed outside of any enclosure which the first writing was within. And if, after the iteration, one writing is within all the enclosures of the other, the former may be illatively removed, together with its bonds: but no such operation must change the order of designation of the subjects in a way not permitted by the rule of Article 16.

Article 19. If a verb is written twice, and one of the writings is enclosed in an oval, but the other not, and if every bond of the one writing is joined to the corresponding bond of the other, the result may be termed a *conjugation*. Thus, Fig. 60 is an *encircled conjugation*. It means, whatever things, X and Y may be, either X loves Y or X does not love Y. An encircled conjugation is thus a meaningless proposition, while an unencircled conjugation is a self-contradictory proposition. Consequently, an unencircled conjugation inserted ~~under even enclosures~~ anywhere has the effect of rendering everything else within the same enclosure nugatory, so that all that residue may as well be erased. But an encircled conjugation is itself nugatory and may be inserted or erased at will.

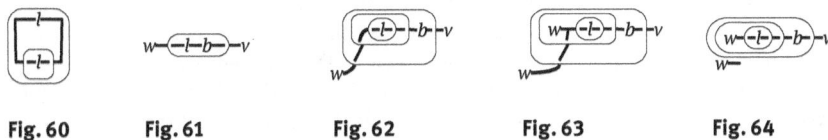

Fig. 60   Fig. 61   Fig. 62   Fig. 63   Fig. 64

Article 20. It follows from the above rules that if an evenly enclosed verb can by the shortening of its bonds be carried into two enclosures, this is a valid illation; while if by the lengthening of its bonds an oddly enclosed verb can be brought out from two enclosures, this is a valid illation. Suppose, for example, that the assertion of Fig. 61 be accepted, that some wise man stands to some virtuous man in the relation of loving only persons who do not benefit him. Then, by twice encircling the *l*, we get Fig. 62. Then, by iteration of the *w*, we get Fig. 63. Then, by severing the bond of the lower *w* inside two enclosures, we get Fig. 64. Finally, by omission of the outer *w* we get Fig. 65, which differs from Fig. 62 by *w* having been carried into two enclosures. This process and its reverse may be called *reassociation*.

Article 21. The same principles may give rise to the *segmentation* and *fusion* of two enclosures, one within another. Thus, from Fig. 66 may be inferred Fig. 68 by reassociation. But, by double circles, Fig. 66 and Fig. 67 are equivalent. Now, Fig. 68 is derivable from Fig. 67 by fusion of double enclosures. Under even enclosures fusion, and under odd enclosures segmentation, of double enclosures may be made.

Fig. 65   Fig. 66   Fig. 67   Fig. 68

8 On Logical Graphs [Euler and EGs]

R 481, late 1896. Houghton Library. This neat 10-page manuscript could also in principle contain the essential material Peirce drafted in anticipation of the National Academy of Sciences meeting in November. The finished style and the concise and controlled nature of its prose suggests that the manuscript was written with a scientific audience in mind. Although the purpose of this item remains unclear, it is not a mere recapitulation of preceding expositions. At least the following ten discoveries stand out: (i) Novel forms of Euler graphs with convex edges, which reappear in the 1901 draft entry on "Logical Graphs" (R 1147) written for Baldwin's *Dictionary of Philosophy and Psychology* (DPP; LoF 3). (ii) Disjunctions as dots placed on the lines of the ovals. (iii) Unsuitability of Euler diagrams for the purposes of logical analysis. (iv) Dependent quantifiers and scope reversals for logical forms of natural language. (v) Distinction between the two kinds of quantifiers (oddly- and evenly-enclosed heavy lines). (iv) The progression from Euler circles to EGs as that from extensional to intensional representation ("the spread of the sheet represents the logical depth", in contradistinction to Euler diagrams in which the sheet represents "the logical breadth"). (vii) The development of logical graphs towards the Beta part, here yet unnamed as such. (viii) Scrolls whose inloops are saw-edged. (ix) A comparative analysis of the ovals both in the context of Euler-like circles and in the context of EGs. (x) The realisation that the concept of the negation is to be derived from the illative sign of the scroll ("we have virtually analyzed the conception of negation") and recognised as the primitive notation for conditionals *de inesse*. (On these discoveries, their philosophical implications and the place of R 481 in the context of Peirce's early writings on logical graphs, see Introduction to Part II.)

On Logical Graphs

The so-called "Euler's Diagrams" can be improved by drawing some of the enclosures with curves convex inwards, the positive, or affirmative, term being supposed to have its logical extension always on the side toward which the curves of the periphery are concave. Thus, Fig. 1 expresses "Any man there may be is mortal", Fig. 2. "No man is a quadruped", Fig. 3, "Everything is either just or wicked".

These figures ought not to be considered as asserting the existence of anything, but only as asserting the non-existence of the class for which no room is left, in Fig. 1 non-mortal man, in Fig. 2 quadruped man, in Fig. 3, non-wicked injustice.

Fig. 1

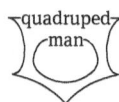

Fig. 2

Fig. 3

In order to assert existence a large dot may be used. Thus Fig. 4 asserts that there is a soul; Fig. 5, that there is something besides money:

Fig. 4   Fig. 5

Then the universal syllogisms are shown in Figs. 6, 7, 8, 9:

Fig. 6   Fig. 7   Fig. 8   Fig. 9

The particular syllogisms are shown in Figs. 10–17. M is the middle term in all cases.

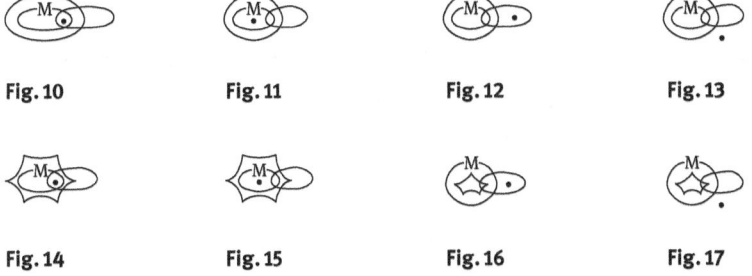

Fig. 10   Fig. 11   Fig. 12   Fig. 13

Fig. 14   Fig. 15   Fig. 16   Fig. 17

In order to represent spurious syllogisms, we may make the dot upon the line of an oval to represent uncertainty whether the existing individual spoken of lies within or without the class that oval represents. Figs. 18–21 represent the spurious syllogisms. These figures seem to me useful in teaching. They show that in all cases one extreme (or the part of it spoken of) is outside, the other inside the middle term; and therein lies the force of the reasoning. The objection to Euler's diagrams that they are almost impracticable in complicated problems seems to me trifling; first, because their purpose is to show the nature of the syllogism, not to solve problems; and secondly, because any complicated problem is very readily broken up into a succession of problems with four terms each, or fewer.

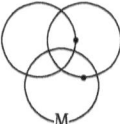 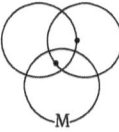 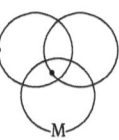

Fig. 18   Fig. 19   Fig. 20   Fig. 21

The difficulty of representing the logic of relatives graphically, lies entirely in the circumstance that it is necessary to distinguish between

Some woman is adored by every catholic.

and

Every catholic adores some woman.

1. Let us take a sheet of paper, or blackboard, and say that anything we write upon it, unless we cut it off from the rest of the sheet by drawing an oval lightly around it, shall be considered to be affirmed by us, and therefore to be true.
2. If two propositions are written unenclosed on the sheet, both are affirmed.
3. We connect by a heavy line individuals whose identity we assert. Thus, Fig. 22, says "John adores Susan":

John—adores—Susan

Fig. 22

but Fig. 23 only says "John exists, and somebody adores Susan", for it differs from Fig. 22 only in not asserting the identity of John and the adorer of Susan.

John— —adores—Susan

Fig. 23

Hence, Fig. 24, asserts "Somebody adores somebody",

—adores—

Fig. 24

and Fig. 25 "Somebody adores himself"

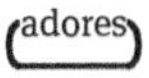

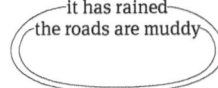

Fig. 25

4. We now must introduce a fourth iconic device, which requires careful consideration. It will be observed that the second principle already adopted is equivalent to making the ~~extension~~ spread of the sheet represent the logical depth, not, as with Euler's diagrams, the logical breadth. The logical breadth of a proposition is the aggregate of the possible states of things in which the proposition is, or is asserted to be, true,—the breadth being thus of two kinds *true* and *asserted*. But it is seldom necessary to discriminate between these; or rather, it is the *true* breadth that is usually referred to. For the contradictory of a proposition, say S is P, is S is not P, and not 'S is not asserted to be P'. The logical depth is the composite of everything which is, or is asserted to be, true of the states of things that make up the breadth. Now when we write two propositions side by side to ~~show~~ assert that both are true, we mark the nature of two elements of logical depth of the state of things spoken of. The places on the sheet where those propositions are written stand for those elements of logical depth. Thus, the ~~extension~~ spread of the sheet represents the spread of logical depth. Accordingly, in order to represent the assertion that 'if the roads are muddy, it has rained', we must not use Fig. 26, which is the Eulerian diagram, but Fig. 27.

Fig. 26 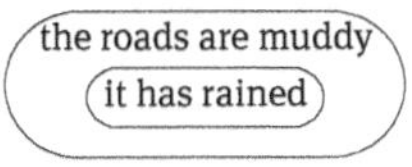   **Fig. 27**

(There is no Fig. 28)

We must carefully analyze what each of those ovals means. To begin with, I do not assert that the roads are muddy; and that is the reason an oval must be drawn round this proposition. (Do not pass over this analysis as if it were unimportant, as relating merely to a particular device. On the contrary, it is a particularly valuable analysis of the proposition, precisely because it looks upon the matter from a point of view to which we are not accustomed.) The effect of the outer oval is to cut off the logical depth within from the asserted depth. That the roads are muddy I do not assert; but now, supposing they are muddy, then I *do* assert, that it has rained. Thus the effect of the inner oval is to restore us to the spread of assertion; but not now of absolute assertion, only of assertion, supposing it is true that the roads are muddy. Since the two ovals have opposite effects it might be as well to use Fig. 29. Of course, any number of ovals may be

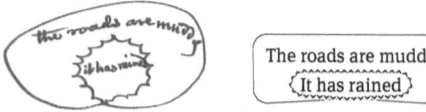

Fig. 29 [P.H.]

contained one within another, the odd ones, counting from the outside, having an effect which the even ones undo. But starting from the outside and proceeding inward, each new space contains elements *posterior to*, i.e. supposing the truth of, those outside.

It will be observed that Fig. 30 asserts absolutely that it has rained.

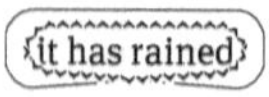

{it has rained}

Fig. 30

Thus the less there is *odd*-ly *enclosed*, that is within an odd number of enclosing ovals, the more the proposition asserts. That is as it should be, since the less is excluded from the spread of depth, the greater the depth.

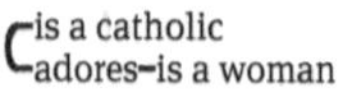

C⎰is a catholic
 ⎱adores–is a woman

Fig. 31

Now, the promised analysis of the proposition still hanging in the air, let us consider relative propositions. Fig. 31 asserts that there is something that is a catholic, and there is something that is a woman, and the former adores the latter. Fig. 32 asserts that if anything is a catholic there is something that adores a woman. Fig. 33 asserts that if anything is a catholic, that same individual adores a woman;

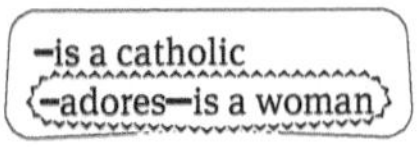

Fig. 32 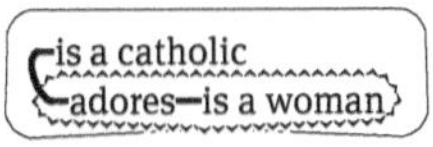   **Fig. 33**

that is, that every catholic adores a woman.[1] On the same principle, Fig. 34 asserts that if anything is, it is a catholic, or everything is a catholic. Fig. 35 asserts that there is a certain woman and if anything is a catholic it adores *her*, or some woman is such that every catholic adores her.

Fig. 34   **Fig. 35 [P.H.]**

We see then that, interpreting these propositions in the exemplar "trope" (to revive an old Greek term of logic), that is, understanding that each speaks only of as many individuals as it contains of disconnected heavy lines, we are to determine these individuals, by beginning at the outside and going inward, and in that progress every heavy line we meet with evenly enclosed, refers to a *suitably chosen* individual, while every line which in its outermost part is oddly enclosed, refers to *any individual taken at pleasure*.

It is obvious that anything unenclosed, or evenly enclosed can be erased. Thus from Fig. 36, some catholic is obedient, we can infer Fig. 37 'something

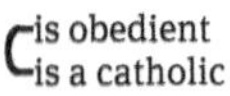

⌐is obedient   ⌐-is obedient
⌊is a catholic   ⌊is a catholic   ⌊is a catholic

Fig. 36 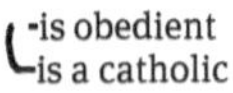   **Fig. 37** 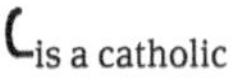   **Fig. 38**

---

1 [Marginal note:] Insert Note at end.

is a catholic and something is obedient' and thence again Fig. 38, 'something is a catholic'.

In like matter, anything oddly enclosed can be inserted. Thus from Fig. 35 we can infer Fig. 39, some woman is adored by all obedient catholics. This shows us

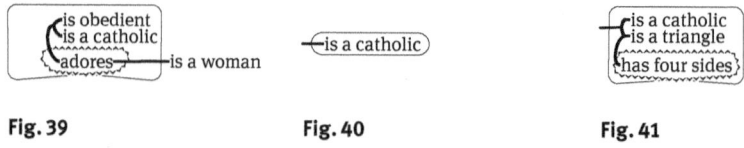

Fig. 39   **Fig. 40**   **Fig. 41**

what Fig. 40 must mean. For Fig. 41 follows from it. Namely, 'There is something which if it is a catholic and is a triangle has four sides'. That is, it is absurd to suppose that this thing is a catholic and has any character whatever. In fact we can always iterate anything with the same connections. Thus if we have Fig. 42 we can attach to it, the same thing and make Fig. 43, some ghost is a ghost. So likewise then

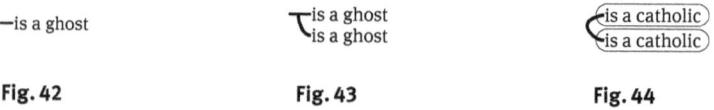

Fig. 42   **Fig. 43**   **Fig. 44**

given Fig. 40 we can attach to it itself and get Fig. 44. Now then, since anything can be inserted under odd enclosures, we can further transform Fig. 44 to Fig. 45, that is if something has the character implied in Fig. 40, that same thing if it is a catholic is not a catholic. Hence when a thing has the character implied in Fig. 40, it is absurd to suppose it to be a catholic. Hence Fig. 40 implies that something is not a catholic.

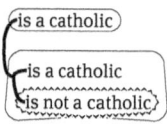

Fig. 45

It will be observed that we did not assume that any sign represented negation, but we have proved that certain signs having certain significations, otherwise defined, must express negation. In other words, we have virtually analyzed the conception of negation.

We now have an apparatus capable of analytically expressing every proposition which can be analytically expressed by the "general algebra of logic", so-called, and it thus involves a virtual analysis of the proposition which I will not lengthen this paper by explicitly developing; for I hope that others will think the matter out for themselves.

I will however call attention to the fact that this system is far more perfect than logical algebra in being more analytical, and *analysis* is the chief thing in logic. It also supplies a far more fundamental list of rules for logical algebra than has ever been given before. This system is also more perfect than any algebra of logic yet devised in that it is not encumbered with a mass of formal theorems which have no meaning except the equivalence of two ways of writing the same thing.

The Rules are as follows:

I. Any unenclosed part of a graph can be erased.
(Of course a singly enclosed part, *together with its enclosing oval*, is unenclosed.)
II. Two graphs severally scriptible are scriptible together, without contact.
III. Two indices joined by a heavy line which in the part connecting them is unenclosed and uncrossed by the line of an oval would be, in all cases, mutually transformable.
IV. Any two mutually transformable indices may be joined by a heavy line, provided that this, if it pass out of one oval into another, shall pass so far out as to be unenclosed.
V. Any part of a heavy line may be excised, provided all the loose ends so left are joined to mutually transformable indefinite indices (write I and I, for example) under the same enclosures as those ends. (This does not permit
VI. If any graph is juxtaposed, without contact, to an oval containing nothing but the same graph wholly enclosed in it, then any graph taken at pleasure may be juxtaposed to the others (which is absurd).

If to two graphs juxtaposed without contact could (if they were written) be juxtaposed any or every graph, at pleasure, then, if, in fact, one of these graphs *is* written, to it may be juxtaposed, without contact, an oval containing only the other.

The equivalent algebraic rules are easily made out.

If anybody cares to learn how extremely analytic this system is, let him start with every man is an animal, and all animals are mortal, and work with the above seven rules to every man is mortal, and see into how many distinct inferential steps the syllogism is analyzed.

Also note that by this system every proposition is either hypothetical, categorical, or relative, according to the number of heavy lines necessary to express its form.

N.B. It may be objected that Fig. 33 asserts more than Fig. 32 although it only differs from the latter by adding an oddly enclosed bit of line. But in fact it also adds an evenly enclosed bit of line. Fig. 46 would differ from Fig. 33 in erasing an oddly enclosed bit of line, and thus means 'If anything is a catholic *everything* adores a woman':

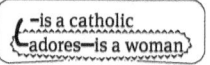

Fig. 46

On Logical Graphs

We see then that, interpreting these propositions in the exemplar "trope" (to revive an old Greek term of logic), that is, understanding that each speaks only of as many individuals as it contains of disconnected heavy lines, we are to determine these individuals, by beginning at the outside and going inward, and in that progress every heavy line we meet with evenly enclosed, refers to a *suitably chosen individual*, while every line which in its outermost part is oddly enclosed, refers to *any* individual taken at pleasure.

It is obvious that anything unenclosed, or evenly enclosed can be erased. Thus from Fig. 36, some catholic is obedient,

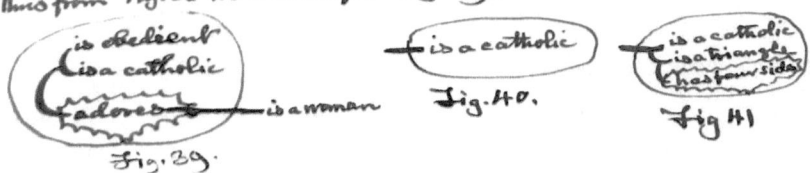

We can infer Fig. 37, "something is a catholic and something is obedient," and thence again Fig. 38, "something is a catholic."

In like manner, anything oddly enclosed can be inserted. Thus from Fig. 35 we can infer Fig. 39, some woman is adored by all obedient catholics. This shows us what Fig. 40 must mean. For it follows from it. Namely "There is something which if it is a catholic and is a triangle has four sides. That is, it is absurd to suppose that this thing is a catholic and has any character whatever. In fact we can always repeat anything.

A holograph page, ms page 7 (Harvard Peirce Papers, R 481).

9 [Memoir for the National Academy of Sciences on Existential Graphs]

R 483, December 21–29, 1896, Houghton Library. Peirce refers to this text as his "Memoir" for the *Memoirs of the National Academy of Sciences* ("the present memoir"). Seriously ill-dated in the Robin Catalogue for c.1901, R 483 is Peirce's final though incomplete attempt of about 20 manuscript pages to have his 'Academy Graphs' project appear in print. The "Memoir" begins by contextualising the exposition within Peirce's research into entitative and existential graphs. A list of "Logical Definitions" follows, together with an exposition of the "Basic Conventions of Existential Graphs" and some "Illustrations" of the conventions. The final part of the "Illustrations" and the footnoted variants present a noteworthy analysis of assertion, beginning with "some facts of common observation": the necessity of a *mind* as the interpreter of the assertion; the relation between the *meaning* of the subjects of the assertion and the *experience* of the mind; the relation between *vagueness* and *truth*, and the requirement that the determination of vague parts of an assertion be made in accordance with the *aim* of the deliverer, that is, whenever possible, the determination of an assertion should show the assertion to be true. Peirce also tackles the problem of the determination of an assertion of an assertion, to which he would return in the 1903 Lowell Lectures (LoF 2). If there is some vagueness in indirect speech, priority shall be given to determining the quoted proposition. In the variant of "Illustrations of the Effects of the above Conventions" (Appendix A), Peirce gives a new explanation of the line as a "continuum of verbs" that guarantees the existential identity between objects marked by its extremities.

Terminology of Logical Graphs

A *graph of lowest dimensionality* is a diagram, or part of a diagram, composed of at least one *spot*, and perhaps also of *bonds* and *circles*. A graph need not be all connected into one piece.

A *spot* is a part of a diagram treated as a point, yet having distinguishable *sides* and also a *quality* which makes it like or unlike any other spot. But no relations between the qualities other than that of being alike or unlike are imaged in the graph.

A *bond* is a simple line collecting two spots and thus having two ends and no more, and no furcations or branchings. A *circle* is an endless line enclosing a graph. An *enclosure* is a circle with its contents. A graph is said to be *encircled* by a given circle when it alone is contained in that circle; it is said to be *enclosed* in the circle when it is contained within that circle.

An *element* of a graph is a spot, bond, or circle forming part of the graph.

A *node* is a spot or enclosure not itself enclosed. We may consider the nodes of the graph and the nodes of each enclosure. The *second nodes* of a graph are the nodes of its nodes, etc. The number thus distinguishing a node is the *order of its nodality*.

A graph is said to be *oddly* or *evenly* enclosed according as it is enclosed in an odd or even number of circles. The number of circles enclosing a part of graph is its *degree of enclosure*.

The *chorisis* of a graph is the number of separate pieces, each enclosure being considered as one piece or part of a piece.

The *cyclosis* of a graph is the number of bonds which need to be cut to prevent their forming any ring, continuity being assumed through each node, and each enclosure being treated as a point.

A *valental system of graphs* is one in which all spots of any given quality have a determinate number of sides at which bonds are or may be attached.

A *blank* of a spot is a side at which bonds are attached.

The *adicity* (from αδα) the accusative termination of μόναδα, δύαδα, etc.) of a graph is the number of blanks of spots in it to which no bonds *that are parts of this graph* are attached. It is to be explained that though an entire graph may have its adicity zero, yet certain parts of it may have high adicities, because the attached bonds do not belong to these parts.

According to the adicity of a graph is 0, 1, 2, 3, etc. it is to be termed a *medad*, *monad*, *dyad*, *triad*, etc.

On Existential Graphs

By C. S. Peirce.[1] In the *Monist* for January, 1897, I have sketched a system of graphs to serve the purposes of a logical calculus; and in another paper, which will probably be published before the present memoir, I have shown that these graphs may be ~~interpreted~~ understood according to two systems of interpretation, the Entitative and the Existential and have given a philosophical development of the former system. My ~~present~~ purpose now is to explain the existential system by itself so as to exhibit its remarkable simplicity, avoiding as much as possible the philosophy of logic. To read this paper no knowledge of modern exact logic will be requisite, but only a slight smattering of the traditional formal logic.

I shall throughout this memoir employ certain unusual dictions, all of which depend upon this principle, that in logical writings the author ought not to be obliged to resort to circumlocutions in order to avoid making two distinct assertions at once. For example, he ought to be allowed to say that one straight line is "as long as" another, without being forced to add "or longer than" if merely to avoid being understood to mean that the former is as long as, but not longer than

---

[1] [The "Memoir" begins here. The preceding "Terminology of Logical Graphs" is a summary of what Peirce drafted for the segments in R 482.]

the other. For the conception expressed by "as long as or longer than" is simpler than the conception expressed by "as long as but not longer than". This might be formally demonstrated, but it will here be sufficient to point out that in order to show that one straight line, a, is as long as or longer than another straight line, b, it is only necessary to show that if b can cover at once ~~certain~~ any division on the scale of measurement, it follows that a can likewise cover them, while to show that a is as long as but not longer than b, it is necessary to show, in addition, that if a can cover at once any divisions on the scale, it follows that b can likewise cover them. On this principle, when in this memoir I speak of "objects, A and B", I must not be understood to imply that A and B are necessarily *different* objects, but only that an object, A, is to be taken, and that an object, B, is to be taken. Again, when I use the word "every", I shall mean "every, if any there be"; as, for example, if I say, "M adores every saint", I am not to be understood as implying that there are any saints, but only that M adores every angel there may be. So when I use the word "only", I shall mean "only if at all"; as, for example, if I say, "M adores only saints" I am not to be understood as implying that M adores anything, but only that he adores, if anything at all, only saints.

Logical Definitions

That is *false* which conflicts with the real state of things. That is *true* which is not false.

A *proposition* is anything considered as being false or true.

A *proper name* is a sign denoting something having an identity consisting in continuity of existence and common to the experience of the deliverer and interpreter of the proposition of which it forms a part.

A *verb* is a fragment of a possible proposition having blanks which being filled with proper names make the verb a proposition.

An *individual subject* of a verb is that which is named by the proper name filling any one of the blanks of the verb.

Two propositions are *logically equivalent* if neither can possibly be false while the other is true. Two parts of propositions are logically equivalent if when all the other parts of the two propositions are precisely alike the two propositions are necessarily logically equivalent.

Basic Conventions of the System of Existential Graphs

1. Each unanalyzed verb [Alts. 1–5, Appendix B] shall be signified by an ideograph,[2] a suitable point of which shall denote each blank, or wholly indeterminate subject, of the verb.[3]
2. A blank space, as an ideograph, shall be a verb void of meaning.
3. An ideograph having a line drawn across it shall have its signification reversed.
4. A point or black dot shall denote an individual object actually existing in the universe of discourse.
5. The writing down of a proposition without quotation mark or disavowal shall be construed as asserting it, anything vague in the statement being understood or designated so as to be favorable to the veraciousness of the proposition.
6. A lightly drawn endless line encircling a proposition or verb shall be a quotation mark; and whatever is vague in the encircled proposition shall be understood and designated (after the similar determination of everything vague in the parts of the graph outside the quotation mark has been declared), in such a way as to be favorable to the veracity of its author. And an undesignated author of a quoted proposition shall be understood to be the *advocatus diaboli*, or hypothetical indefinitely clever opponent of the assertion of the graph.

Illustrations of the Effects of the above Conventions

Taking mankind as the universe of our discourse, let w signify "___ is wise". What, then, does Fig. 1 mean? If two ideographs are in juxtaposition, their com-

Fig. 1   Fig. 2   Fig. 3   Fig. 4    Fig. 5 [P.H.]   Fig. 6   Fig. 7

---

[2] A *direct* ideograph is one directly suggestive of the idea; an *indirect* one is an ideograph suggestive of the *word* that expresses that idea. Such, for example, is an initial letter.

[3] In particular, if the four right angles about the centre of the ideograph are divided into as many equal parts as the verb has blanks, then the successive divisions between those parts going round clockwise, beginning at the left-hand horizontal side may denote the blanks of the verb in the order of statement used in the definition of the ideograph.

mon point, as a side of each ideograph, denotes, by Convention 1, the corresponding subject of its verb, while as a point it denotes, by Convention 4, an individual object existing in the universe of discourse. Thus, juxtaposition necessarily signifies existential identity. Hence, every point of a continuous black line signifies the existential identity of the contiguous point on the two sides of it. Thus, the whole line is a continuum of verbs, "___ is identical with something that is identical with something that is identical, etc. with ___ " In short, a black line generated by a black dot signifies the identity of its extremities as one individual object existing in the universe of discourse. In Figure 1, one of these extremities is the subject of the verb "___ is wise", while the other is left vague except that it is an existing man. By Convention 5, the graph asserts the truth of the proposition after the indeterminacy has been removed in the way most favorable to the truth of the graph. That is, the indesignate man must be taken as a wise man (if there be one), so that Fig. 1 asserts "Some man is wise".

So if v signifies "___ is virtuous", Fig. 2 will assert, Some wise man is virtuous.

The blank space of Fig. 3 is, by Convention 2, void of meaning. A meaningless verb is true of all subjects, since it cannot conflict with fact. Moreover, all meaningless verbs are logically equivalent, since none can be false while another is true. To say that individuals existing in the universe of discourse coexist is a form of assertion void of matter, a mere tautology. Hence, any blank considered as a verb may be interpreted, "___ is coexistent with ___ ". Thus, Fig. 3 asserts, Some wise man is coexistent with some virtuous man. Fig. 4 is the same thing with the blank space larger, but it more naturally suggests wording the interpretation thus: Some man is wise and some man is virtuous. This is a graph in two pieces; and it is evident that, by Convention 5, writing down several propositions side by side asserts them all.

If l signifies "___ loves ___ ", Fig. 5 asserts, Some wise man loves some virtuous man. Since, as just shown, every point of a black line signifies "___ is identical with ___ ", it follows by Convention 3 that a point on a black line where that line is traversed by another line signifies "___ is other than ___ ". Hence, Fig. 6 asserts, Some wise man is other than some virtuous man. So Fig. 7 asserts, Some wise man is other than some wise man, or in other words, There are more wise men than one.

Fig. 8   Fig. 9   Fig. 10

If u signifies "___ is ugly", and if c signifies "___ converts ___ into ___ ", then Fig. 8 asserts, Some ugly man converts some wise man into a virtuous man. So Fig. 9 asserts, Some ugly man is at once wise and virtuous. Fig. 10 asserts, There are at least three wise men.

Let us now consider this problem:[4] Required to construct an existential graph, G, which shall assert that a given individual proposition, P, implies that some man is wise. G does not assert that P is in any relation whatever to a wise man; for to do so would be to assert that a wise man exists; whereas G only asserts that P asserts this. It is necessary to distinguish between the assertion that there exists some individual to whom definitely P whom P designates and to whom it attributes wisdom, and the assertion that P asserts that there is some individual whom it may not designate to whom it attributes wisdom. Let us, in the first instance, suppose that G only makes the latter assertion.

---

4 **[Alt.1:]** Let us now consider how it is possible with this system of graphs to assert of an individual proposition that it asserts a given hypothesis to be true, say that it asserts that there is a wise man. The [end]

[Alt.2:] Let us now consider this problem: Required to find an existential graph, G, which shall assert that a given individual proposition, P asserts that a given hypothesis is true, say that some man is wise. When G asserts that P asserts that some man is wise, G does not assert that P is in any relation to a wise man; for to do so would be to assert that a wise man exists, which G asserts that P asserts, without itself asserting it. Let us compare this with the assertion that P *causes* a man to be wise. Here G deals with the proposition, P, with some man, and also with a quality, which G asserts that P imparts to that man. If this assertion of G be true, there is some individual man existing among mankind of whom it is true that P imparts wisdom to that man. But when G asserts that P *attributes* wisdom to some man, this may mean that there is some individual man to whom P attributes wisdom, or it may merely mean that P *represents* that there is some man to whom it attributes wisdom. It is evident that we have to consider image not only the real universe of mankind but also the universe of things supposed asserted or allowed by P to exist. It is further requisite that we should be able to represent something asserted by P to exist as either agreeing or not agreeing with something in the real universe, that is in the universe asserted or allowed by G to exist. Can this agreement, from the nature of things, consist in existential identity? When one person conveys any information to another, it must concern some object element of their common experience. When a man tells me something, he *forces* my attention to something which I am already acquainted with or which he then brings before my vision or other field of experience for the first time. It is the real active force which bears down my will which is the basis of my conviction that the object he has in mind and the object I have in mind are existentially identical.

If a force can really act from P upon G, then an object in the universe of things admitted by P may be existentially identical with an object in the universe of things admitted by G; but otherwise it is not so. In the former case the object belongs to the universe of G and P is in some kind of real relation to it; so that the object does not belong to any universe peculiar to P. In the latter case, although existential identity cannot be affirmable, it may be deniable, but only by its having some character which discriminates it from *every* object in the universe of G.

It will be necessary here to consider some facts of common observation about assertions. In order that an assertion should be consummated, it is requisite that it should have not merely a deliverer, or assertor, but also an interpreter, or ~~person~~ mind addressed. Thus, when a man consults an old diary of his own, the lapse of memory has somewhat impaired his personal identity, so that he is not precisely the same mind. Yet the assertion would convey nothing if it did not relate to some object or objects in the common experience of deliverer and interpreter. Thus, one man may inform another that if he pursues a certain road over which he has never travelled, and if he takes certain turns, he will come to a house concerning which he tells some story. But though the interpreter has never yet seen the house nor the road, yet the beginning of the road is there before the eyes of both parties. Without that or something analogous to it, the whole narrative would be a mere romance conveying no information. Moreover, as the interpreter travels over the road, the assertion acquires more and more meaning to him. The object of ~~common~~ shared experience to which the proposition ~~relates~~ refers, however complex it may be, is an *individual* object,[5] in this sense, that it possesses existential identity, consist-

---

Now a black dot denotes an individual object existing in the universe of G. If we are to consider a universe outside of the universe of G, we must fence it off, by drawing lightly an endless line around a region of the paper which is to be appropriated to such objects. A black dot inside that boundary will represent an object in a universe excluded from the universe of G. If we attempt to connect that dot with a dot outside the boundary by means of a heavy line, that line must cross the boundary. Now a heavy line traversed by a line signifies "not"; and therefore the existential identity of an object represented by a dot outside and of an object represented by a dot inside the boundary cannot be asserted in the graphical form, just as it cannot be asserted in fact. But non-identity may be asserted, or it may be left uncertain.

5 **[Alt.:]** [...] objects, in this sense, that it possesses an existential identity, consisting in a continuity of existence. The only assurance that the interpreter can have that the deliverer referred to the very thing he has in his own experience consists in a real force which he feels overbears his will and compels him to attend to that object.

When a proposition refers to something designated by its proper name, as Spain, or Hannibal, or Desdemona's handkerchief, its assertion is only consummated when that object is directly or indirectly connected by continuity of existence with the interpreter's experience. When the subject of the proposition is designated by a general name, reference is made to a universe of discourse, or department of experience shared by the two parties, which universe, though it is a collection of possible objects, at the same time, the individual object referred to. An experiment is then in all cases described. Either any object whatever is to be taken in that universe, and the verb of the proposition is said to be true of it, or an object is to be suitably chosen from among the objects of that universe, and the assertion is that it can be so chosen that the verb shall be true of it.

Let us now return to the case in which G asserts that P asserts something. Here, the universe of discourse of P is different from that of G, and in general nothing in the former can be identified with anything in the latter. But if G acknowledges a force which identifies subject of P with

ing in a continuity of existence. The only assurance that the interpreter can have that he understands the proposition,—without which to him nothing would be asserted,—lies in his sense that he is compelled, apart from any will of his own, to attend to that object.

When a proposition refers to something designated by its proper name, as Thibet, or Hermolaus Barbarus, or Desdemona's handkerchief, its assertion is only consummated when that object is directly or indirectly connected by continuity of existence with that which experience, or the course of life, has irresistibly impressed upon the interpreter's own mental map of the world. The assertion has more import to him the more direct that connection is. When the subject of the proposition is only designated in a general way, as "some a country", "some a writer", "something in the world of Shakespeare's Othello", the assertion is imperfect. It is vague. But, then, every assertion, every thought, and every perception is inevitably more or less vague. It is implied that if the vagueness were corrected in a suitable way, the proposition could be made precise without any conflict with the truth. The vague parts ought to be made determinate in the way which suits the purposes of the deliverer, that is, so as to make his proposition true.

But when a proposition quotes some other assertion, and there is a vagueness in this second assertion, that vagueness must be corrected in the interest of the quoted proposition which it immediately affects and not in that of the quoting proposition. Thus, that there are some men whose incapacity would be a public calamity, is true; but it is not true that a man who newspaper which says "Some men are incapable" asserts the existence of any public calamity. That depends upon what men that newspaper means to refer to.

If he who refers to an object spoken of by another knows precisely what object that other means, there is no vagueness for him, and though he may refer to it with the same vagueness, the object ranks among other objects to which he vaguely alludes. But if to the quoter the subject of the quoted assertion is vague and if he nevertheless proceeds to make some assertion about it, then in order to make his assertion true, not only must the subject of the quoted assertion be specified according to the intent of that assertion and not to suit the purpose of the quoter, but the quoter must be able to specify what he means without knowing what object

---

something known to itself, that subject at once becomes an object of the universe of G, and in so far, G asserts an ordinary relation to subsist between that individual existent object and the individual existent object, P. Such an object is not treated as being in the universe of P. Thus, of objects which have to be treated as belonging to the universe of P, there is none which can be positively identified with an object of the universe of G. An object of the universe of P may either have characters which absolutely preclude its identification with a given object of G, or it may be indeterminate with respect to such identity.

the quoted assertion intends,—or, at least, he must be able to do so if he knows how his assertion is true. For example, if the assertion is "I know a virtuous man who loves the man to whom John Smith attributes wisdom, although I had no idea what man that is", is as much as to say "I know a virtuous man who loves every man to whom it is possible to attribute wisdom".

Appendix A (Variant)

Illustrations of the Effects of the above Conventions

Taking mankind as the universe of our discourse, let w signify "___ is wise". Then, in Fig. 1, every point of the heavy line is a black dot, denoting, by Convention 4, an indesignate man. By the

| Fig. 1 | Fig. 2 | Fig. 3 | Fig. 4 | Fig. 5 | Fig. 6 | Fig. 7 | Fig. 8 | Fig. 9 |

same convention, juxtaposition must signify identity; for if two ideographs have a common point, that point, as a side of each ideograph denotes a subject of each verb while as a point it denotes existentially identical; for this common point denotes at once a subject of either verb and an individual object existing in the universe of discourse. On this same principle, since every point of the black line is a black dot, its continuity may be regarded as the verb "___ is existentially identical with ___ ". Thus, the whole line is a continuum of verbs "___ is identical with something that is identical with something that is identical, etc. with ___ ". That is, a heavy black line signifies the identity of its extremities. One of these in Fig. 1 is a man that is wise. The other is left wholly vague, except that it is an existing man. Since the graph is written down unenclosed, what is meant is that when this vagueness is removed in a manner favorable to the truth of the proposition, it is true. That is, Fig. 1 asserts that Some existing man is wise.

So if v signifies "___ is virtuous", Fig. 2 will mean, Some wise man is virtuous. In Fig. 3 we have a blank. This is meaningless. Treating it as a verb, we remark that a meaningless verb is true of all subjects, since it cannot conflict with the fact. Moreover, all meaningless verbs are logically equivalent, since none can be false while another is true. To say that individuals existing in the universe of discourse are coexistent is a form of statement void of meaning, since it cannot logically be false. Hence the blank may be interpreted "___ is coexistent with ___ " and Fig. 3 asserts Some wise man is coexistent with some virtuous man. But it may equally be interpreted, Some man is wise and some man is virtuous. Fig. 3 may be delineated with the blank as large as we like, as in Fig. 4. This is a graph in two pieces; and it is evident that, according to Convention 5, writing down two propositions side by side unenclosed asserts them both.

In Fig. 5 a "not" is introduced and the meaning plainly is, Some wise man is other than some virtuous man. So Fig. 6 asserts, Some wise man is other than some wise man, that is there are more wise men than one. So if l signifies "___ loves ___ ", Fig. 7, Some wise man loves some virtuous man.

If *u* is taken to signify "___ is ugly", Fig. 8 will assert, Some wise man is both ugly and virtuous. So if *b* is taken to signify "___ betrays ___ to ___", Fig. 9 will assert, Some ugly man betrays some virtuous man to some wise man.

Fig. 10 asserts, There are, at least, three wise men.

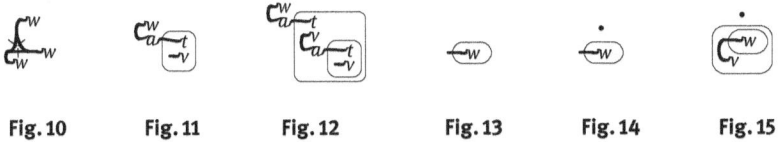

Fig. 10   Fig. 11   Fig. 12   Fig. 13   Fig. 14   Fig. 15

Now passing to a wider universe of discourse, let *a* signify "___ asserts the truth of ___" and let *t* signify "___ is true". Then, Fig. 11 [sic., Fig. 12] asserts that there is something which is a wise man and which asserts something,[6] not true or else there is a virtuous man who asserts that no man is ugly. In short Fig. 11 [sic., Fig. 12] asserts, Some wise man asserts that some virtuous man asserts that no man is ugly.

Fig. 13 asserts, There is something which is different from everything there may be that is wise, that is, Something is not wise. Fig. 14 asserts, There is something which is not coexistent with anything that is wise. That is, nothing is wise. Fig. 15 asserts, There is something which is not coexistent with anything virtuous that is other than something that is wise. That is, Everything virtuous is wise. Here, there existence of something wise is asserted, not absolutely, but in case there is something virtuous.

Fig. 16   Fig. 17

Fig. 16 asserts, Some virtuous man is other than everybody that is other than somebody loved by somebody other than any wise man. That is, there is a virtuous man, and he is other than anybody, M, there may be who while anybody, N, is wise is not somebody who is loved by some-

---

6 [Alt.:] ~~But now the line passes within a circle, and the thing that the proposition is not is to be selected so as to make the whole~~ assertion of the figure false if possible. Moreover in this same circle is the proposition that something is a virtuous man and this something is to be selected so as to make the proposition false if possible. The assertion of the figure is that the thing selected is true and is coexistent with a selected thing that is a virtuous man. The assertion is that these propositions are true though these selections be made in the manner the most unfavourable. That is, the assertion of the figure is that it is true whatever things there may be. It asserts, then, that they are true of everything that is to say, the figure asserts that Some wise man asserts something which is different from anything that is at once true and is coexistent with a virtuous man. That is, what is asserted by the wise man is false or else there is no virtuous man. That is, Some wise man asserts that no man is virtuous.

body who is not that wise man. That is, somebody, L, is virtuous and at the same time is different from anybody M of whom it can be said, that everybody, N, is wise unless M is different from somebody M′ and N from somebody N′ such that N′ loves M′. That is, again, somebody, L, can be found who is virtuous and whoever, M, may be chosen either L differs from M or whoever, N, may be chosen N is not wise or some persons M′ and N′ can be found such that N′ is identical with N and M′ with M and N′ loves M′. That is, again, some virtuous man is loved by every wise man.

Fig. 17 asserts, There is a virtuous man who is different from every man who is loved by every man who is different from some [end]

Appendix B (Alts. 1–5)

[Alt.1:] Each unanalyzed verb is to be represented by a special ideograph, direct (i.e. a picture or other directly suggestive icon) or indirect (as by an initial letter, which is a direct suggestive icon of the word); and to each blank of the verb is appropriated a suitable side of the ideograph. In particular, the circumference of ~~an imaginary~~ a little circle just about the ideograph and supposed to be a part of it may [end]

[Alt.2:]

1. Each unanalyzed verb shall be signified by an ideograph, a suitable point of which is appropriated to denoting each blank, or wholly indeterminate subject, of the verb.
2. A black dot or point shall denote an indesignate individual object existing in the universe of discourse.
3. The writing down of a proposition without any quotation-mark shall be construed as asserting its truth, on the understanding that anything vague in the statement is to be so understood as to be favourable to the assertor's veracity.
4. A lightly drawn endless line encircling a proposition or verb shall be a quotation mark, and whatever is vague in the encircled statement shall be so understood as is most favorable to the veracity of the author of the proposition, after the precise determination of every designation outside the enclosure has been declared. And if the author of a quoted proposition is not given, he shall be understood to be the *advocatus diaboli*, or hypothetical indefinitely clever opponent of the assertion of the whole graph.
5. A blank space shall be understood as void of meaning.

[Alt.3:]

1. Each unanalyzed verb is to be represented by a special character and to each blank of the verb is appropriated a special side of that character, so that any denoting an individual written close to the character on that side of it fills that blank of the verb. The circumference of the character being divided into as many equal parts as there are blanks to the verb, beginning at the left hand side, the blanks in their order may be appropriated to successive divisions between parts of the circumference going round it clockwise.
2. A blank space considered as a verb is meaningless, and therefore necessarily true of any subjects whatsoever.
3. The end of a line is to denote some individual thing existing in the universe of discourse.
4. The unbroken continuity of a heavy line (whether simple or branching) is to be understood as implying the identity of the individual objects denoted by its ends.

5. The writing down of a proposition unenclosed is to be construed as asserting it; and the writing down of two or more propositions is to be understood as asserting them all.
6. The encircling of a proposition by a lightly drawn endless line is to be understood as transmuting that proposition into its denial.

[Alt.4:]

1. Each unanalyzed verb is to be signified by an ideograph which may either be directly suggestive of the idea or (like an initial letter) suggestive of the word expressing it; and to each blank of the verb is to be appropriated a suitable side of the ideograph. In particular, if the four right angles about the centre of the ideograph be divided into as many equal parts as the verb has blanks, beginning at the horizontal left hand side, then the divisions between those parts beginning at the same side and going round the ideograph clockwise may be appropriated in their order to the blanks of the verb in their order.
2. A black dot is to denote an indesignate individual object existing in the universe of discourse.
3. The writing down of a proposition unenclosed is to be construed as asserting it with the understanding that all that is vague in the statement of the proposition is to be so determined as to be favorable to its truth.
4. A lightly drawn endless line enclosing a proposition, or verb, is to have the effect of quotation marks; and if there is no special indication of who its assertor is, it is to be considered as made potentially by the *advocatus diaboli*, or hypothetical indefinitely clever opponent of the truth of the whole graph. Hence, anything vague in its statement is to be determined as will best suit the opponent's purpose, and after the determination of everything vague that is outside the circle has been declared.

[Alt.5:]

1. Each unanalyzed verb is to be represented by an ideograph, which may either be direct (i.e. a picture or other directly suggestive image) or indirect (i.e. directly suggestive of the word expressing the idea, as an initial letter); and to each blank of the verb is to be appropriated a suitably suggestive side of the ideograph. In particular, if a circle (or other oval) about the ideograph be made a part of it, and the circumference of this circle beginning at the left hand horizontal part is divided into as many equal parts as the blanks of the verb, then they may be taken in order going round clockwise, beginning at the left hand horizontal point.
2. A black dot is to denote an indesignate individual object existing in the universe of discourse.
3. The writing down of a proposition unenclosed is to be construed as asserting its truth when all that is left vague is so determined as to be favorable to the truth of the proposition.
4. A lightly drawn endless line enclosing a proposition or verb is to have the effect of a parenthesis in algebra, while at the same time it is a line of demarkation between regions in which contrary rules of determining what is left vague prevails.
5. A blank space considered as a verb is a verb void of all meaning.
6. It will presently appear that in a heavily drawn line every point of it, considered as a verb, signifies "___ is identical with___ ". If a point of ~~not~~ [sic.] the line were left blank its meaning would be lost. If, instead of that, it is traversed by a lightly drawn line at right angles, it is to mean "___ is other than___ ", i.e. "___ is not identical with___ ".

10 [Six Papers on Existential Graphs]

R 497, R 486, R 438, R 485, R 513, R 495; from June 15, 1897 to August 1898. Houghton Library.
This chapter collates the output from the year that followed his ultimately failed battles with the publication of R 482, in six discrete but related texts that have survived at Houghton Library's collection of Peirce's papers. Closely related notes occur on the pages of the *Logic Notebook* written during these months (R 339; LoF 1).

10.1 Existential Graphs (R 497), 1897

R 497, June 15, 1897. Houghton Library. A small notebook, which Peirce had received from Francis Lathorp, contains some refinements to one of the basic rules on the cutting or erasure of a portion of a line of identity on positive areas (later, those rules will be made to pertain to the Beta part of the system). Peirce's letter to Lathrop on July 24, 1898 confirms that he had studied these basic and still somewhat imprecise and incomplete rules since "the last summer".

Existential Graphs. Basic Rules

I. We always have a right to a blank sheet.
II. If we can write two graphs separately we can write them side by side.
III. Every unenclosed part of a graph can be transformed in every way in which and under the circumstances under which it could be transformed if is stood alone.
IV. Two individual indices transformable the one into the other can be joined by a heavy line of connection.
V. Individual indices joined by a connecting line uncrossed by any oval line are mutually transformable.
VI. Every line of connection might be joined to an individual index, did we know what one to choose.
VII. If a graph, A, is transformable into an oval containing only a second graph, B, then this graph B is transformable into an oval containing A.
VIII. If an oval containing only a graph, A, is transformable into a graph, B, then an oval containing only B is transformable into A.
IX. It makes no difference whether an individual index is enclosed in an oval or not. But it does make a difference whether a portion of the connecting line is so enclosed.

Commentary

I. But the only thing we are always entitled to assert is an empty form of proposition, such as, "What I aver is true". Hence the blank sheet means that.

II & III. Hence it appears that writing two assertions together asserts both.

IV. That is, individual identity involves that which the continuity of the line implies.

V. Shows that the continuity of the line implies nothing more than identity.

VI. Shows that when a line of connection is attached to two general verbs unenclosed, the meaning is that there is in the universe of discourse some individual of which they are true.

VII. Shows that the enclosed graph is "distributed". Thus, if every *man* is near *every* dog, then every dog is near *every* man.

VIII. Just so if whatever is cousin of anything but a negro is free whatever is cousin of anything but what is free is a negro. VII and VIII taken together show that the oval precisely denies the assertion it encloses.

IX. A designate individual is known to exist, and is known not to be the *only* existent thing.

10.2 Existential Graphs (R 486), 1897

R 486, summer 1897. Houghton Library. Peirce shares his comments and corrections on the presentation of those rules which Lathrop had written and sent to Peirce in the previous summer, apparently in order to receive Peirce's comments. These rules, written in Lathrop's hand, were derived from one of Peirce's syllabi on logic that he had sent to Lathrop in 1897, perhaps identical to those we find in R 497. After the recovery of Lathrop's 1897 letter that describes those rules Peirce would, in July 1898, check the material, add some explanations and send this amanuensis (R 486) back to Lathrop.

Rules for their (Logical) Illative Transformations
A. Fundamental Rules defining the effects of the different features of the graphs

Rule I. We always have a logical right to a blank sheet. Note: we have a "logical right" to anything not involving any new assertion—i.e. that does not assert anything more than we have assumed to be true.[1]

---

[1] [Peirce's marginal comment:] It is necessary to have a separate rule to enable us to strike erase any unenclosed part of a graph even if connected with other parts.

Rule II. (Originally Rule III.) Graphs which might logically be separately written, can be written side by side—i.e. compounded.

Rule III. (Originally Rule II.) We have a right to transform any unenclosed part of a graph in any way in which we could *logically* transform it if it stood alone in its entirety. Note: This is the converse of Rule XI. ("Converse is not "contradiction"—but is the interchange of subject and object.)

Example. "Supposing A to be true B is true"—the converse would be, "Supposing B to be true A is true".²

Rule IV. If an individual index is illatively (logically) transformable into any graph then it may be written down and connected with that graph by a heavy line.³ *Note:* This rule was first given thus: "Two individual indices logically transformable into each other can be joined by a heavy connecting line".

Example. John—sings (and both names being known   John⊤sings
Jack—sins (to indicate the same person) Jack⊥sins

Rule V. Individual indices joined by connecting lines uncrossed by any line are illatively transformable each into the other.

Rule VI. To any connecting line at least one unenclosed index originating an individual object might be joined, if we know what that index was.

Example. John⌒⟨⊥sins⟩

Rule VII. If a graph is illatively transformable into an oval containing only a second graph, that second graph is illatively transformable into an oval containing only the first.

Example. If "it rains" is illatively (deductively) transformable into ⟨sun shines⟩ then "sun shines" is illatively transformable into ⟨it rains⟩.

Rule VIII. If an oval containing only a given graph is illatively transformable into a second graph, then an oval containing the second graph is illatively transformable into the first graph.

Example. ⟨You pay your fare⟩ ⊰ walk
⟨walk⟩ ⊰ You pay your fare

Rule IX. An index of any individual of the universe may be written down with a connecting line attached to it, the other end of the connecting line being left free.

Note A. Thus connecting lines can be called "bonds".

---

2 [Peirce's comment on Rule III:] This needs amendment. For it may be that a—c ⊰ b—c. Thus, if there is milk there is a cow; but it does not follow that if there is sour milk there is a sour cow. But the word "logically" may save the truth. For strictly illative transformations all take place by insertions and omissions.

3 [Peirce's comment on Rule IV:] This rule is separable into two. Any index is the index of an individual known to exist. This gives Rule IX. Any index may be written. Second, indices mutually transformable may be joined by a heavy line.

Note B. This rule was first given thus: The enclosure of an individual index in an oval has no effect, although the enclosure of a portion of the connecting line has the same effect as upon any graph.

Example. $\left.\begin{array}{l}\text{John}\!-\!\overline{\text{sins}}\\ \overline{\text{John}\!-\!\text{sins}}\end{array}\right\}$ Both mean "John *does not* sin"

$\left.\begin{array}{l}\overline{\text{John}}\!-\!\text{sins}\\ \text{John}\!-\!\ominus\!-\!\text{sins}\end{array}\right\}$ Both mean "John is *other* than somebody who sins"

Note C. "not" means a second person. E.g. "John does not sin" means "Pick out any person as *first* if he sins John is a *second* person.

Rule X is stricken out.

B. Derivative Rules

Rule XI. Any unenclosed part of a graph can be erased.

Proof. Given graph A B, you can infer B, because by Rule I I can erase A standing alone. Hence by Rule II I an erase it if it is an unenclosed part of a graph.

Rule XII. (Corollary from XI.) Any unenclosed connecting line may be broken.

Example. $\mathsf{C}^{\text{sins}}_{\text{sings}}$ can be transformed to $\begin{array}{l}-\text{sins}\\ -\text{sings}\end{array}$

Rule XIII. (An extension of Rule II.) Any unenclosed part of a graph may be separated with all its connections.

Example. sins—sings may be made $\begin{array}{l}\text{sins}\!-\!\!\top\!\!-\!\text{sings}\\ \text{sins}\end{array}$

By Rule III we can write $\left\{\begin{array}{l}\text{sins}\!-\!\!\top\!\!-\!\text{sings}\\ \text{John}\\ \text{sins}\!-\!\!\top\!\!-\!\text{sings}\\ \text{John}\end{array}\right.$

Then by Rule IV $\left\{\begin{array}{l}\text{sins}\!-\!\!\top\!\!-\!\text{sings}\\ \text{John}\\ \text{John}\\ \text{sins}\!-\!\!\bot\!\!-\!\text{sings}\end{array}\right.$

And by Rule XI striking out all we do not want $\left\{\begin{array}{l}\text{sins}\!-\!\!\top\!\!-\!\text{sings}\\ \text{sins}\end{array}\right.$

Rule XIV. A double oval may be inserted or erased.

Proof. Evidently Ⓐ is transformable into Ⓐ. Now call Ⓐ the first graph and A the second graph. By Rule VII, since the first is transformable into the (second), i.e. Ⓐ into Ⓐ so also the second is transformable into the (first), i.e. A into ⓐ. Now call A the first and Ⓐ the second graph. By Rule VIII, since the (first) is transformable into the second, i.e. Ⓐ into Ⓐ, so also the (second) is transformable into the first, i.e. Ⓐ into A.

Rule XV. If our graph can be transformed into a second when the former [is] unenclosed,[4] it can be transformed into the second within any even enclosure; and the second can be transformed into the first within any odd enclosures.

---

4 [Peirce's note:] When both are unenclosed? When the first is unenclosed.

Proof. Suppose A can be transformed into B. By Rule XIV A can be transformed into ⒷⒷ. By Rule VII ⒷⒷ can be transformed into ⒶⒶ. Then also A C can be transformed into B C and A C can be transformed into ⒷⒸ. Therefore B C can be transformed into ⒶⒸ. So that if A can be transformed into B then in our oval B can be transformed into A whether the oval contains anything else or not.[5]

Rule XVI. (Corollary to Rule XV.) Within odd enclosure anything can be inserted. Within even enclosure anything can be erased.

Note. By saying that you have a right to make a transformation, say A into B, you mean that B is as true as A is, i.e. if A is false there is no guaranteeing that B is true. But if A is true B is true, i.e. either A is false or B is true. That is, what you arrive at is fully as true as what you had before, i.e. you have not introduced any falsity that did not exist before.

Rule XVII. (Corollary to [Rule] XVI.) Any two connecting lines under odd enclosures can be joined. And within even enclosures any connecting line can be broken. For instance, if we have this graph:

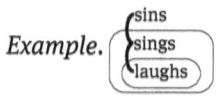 = nobody sins or nobody sings i.e. it is not true that somebody signs and somebody sins at the same time.

We can also write:

(⊂sins⊂sings) meaning "The same person does not sign and sin".

Rule XVIII. Of any transformation can be made irrespective of the oddness or evenness of the enclosures, then the reverse transformation can be made (except possible under no enclosures).

Rule XIX. Any insertion may be made, provided that the partial graph inserted is already present and within no enclosures other than those within which the insertion is proposed to be made. And the connections must be the same of the two occurrences or repetitions.

Example. (sins / sings / laughs)   sins can be inserted in 3 places
sings can be inserted in 2 places
laughs can be inserted in 1 place.

(Proof is postponed.)

Rule XX. The reverse operation can be performed, i.e. any part of a graph may be omitted, which occurs elsewhere with the same connections and not within any enclosures other than those within which lies the part that is to be omitted.

---

5 [Peirce's comment:] But this does not prove that if a—c is transformable in b—c therefore ⓑ—c is transformable in ⓐ—c. Thus from "there is a male dog" we may infer "there is a female dog". But that gives us no right to infer from "there is a dog not female" to "there is a dog not male".

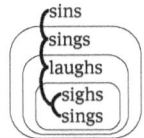

The inner *sings* can be omitted, but the outer *sings* cannot.

Rule XXI. (Corollary from XX.) A part of a graph evenly enclosed may be carried in into two ovals existing in the other.

E.g.

$\overline{\text{man}-\text{loves}-\text{woman}} = \begin{cases} \text{There is a man} \\ \text{who loves all women.} \end{cases}$

"man" can be carried into the two ovals, giving:

$\overline{(\text{man}-\text{loves})-\text{woman}} = \begin{cases} \text{Every woman is} \\ \text{loved by some man or other.} \end{cases}$

Proved by Rules XX and XI.

Rule XXII. Any oddly enclosed part of a graph that is in three or more enclosures can be carried our from two.

Rule XXIII. Any connecting line that is oddly enclosed can be protracted beyond any part or the whole of its enclosures.

10.3 The Logic of Relatives (R 438), 1898

R 438, February 1898. Houghton Library. "The Logic of Relatives". This piece forms the logical part of the first draft of the third Cambridge Conference Lecture which Peirce delivered in February 1898. This earlier draft was probably ready by January or even in late 1897 and was sent to William James for comment. It deals with the question of the nature of assertions. Peirce does not interpret the ovals drawn around graph-instances as denials, but as 'attentional devices' one interpretation of which may be that of negation. Yet there are other interpretations, too, and the oval in the syntactic sense is an operator the interpretation of which varies according to what the semantics is made to be. The final draft of R 438 is what Peirce may have delivered at that Brattle Street gathering, and it has adequately been published in *Reasoning and the Logic of Things* (RLT). A few disorderly snippets were included in the *Collected Papers of Charles S. Peirce* (CP): two paragraphs from this draft version, ending the first (CP 4.4) right where our selection begins, and the second (CP 4.5) starting where our selection below on those graphs ends.

It is now time to explain what the logic of relatives is. Let us ~~agree~~ pretend that any sentence written on the blackboard is asserted. Thus

You are a good girl   You obey mamma

                                                                You are a good girl

Here I assert *both* of two propositions. In other words, I have written a *conjuctive* proposition. When we have occasion to write down a proposition not to assert it, but to say something about it, we will draw an oval round it, to show that it is not asserted, thus,

(You are a good girl)   is important if true.

But the principal thing to be said about a proposition is that it is false. There is no occasion to write that a proposition is true, because it is simpler to assert the substance of the proposition. But we so often have occasions to say

(You are a good girl)   is false

and the like, and, so seldom have occasion to say anything else about a proposition, that we may write

(You are a good girl)

and omit the "is false". Thus

(You are a good girl)
You obey mamma

means you are not a good girl but you obey mamma. The denial of a conjunctive proposition is a *disjunctive* proposition. Thus,

(You are a good girl
 You obey mamma)

means, you are either not a good girl or you do not obey mamma. So

((You are a good girl)
 You obey mamma)

means it is not true that you are [a] good girl but do not obey mama. That is, it is true, that if you obey mamma you are a good girl. That is a *conditional* proposition. All these compound propositions are known to logicians as *hypotheticals*. Be the name suitable or otherwise, it is the established scientific term.

Now let us use a heavy line to assert the identity of the two individual objects represented by its extremities, each extremity denoting an existing individual object. Then

⎧—is a good girl
⎩—obeys mamma

means something is a good girl and is identical with something that obeys mamma. Or some good girl obeys mamma. Or we can better write this

⎧—is a good girl
⎩—obeys the mamma of⎺⎞
                     ⎠

Some good girl obeys her own mamma. This you will observe is a categorical proposition, and the difference between a hypothetical and categorical proposition is simply that the heavy line of identity appears in the categorical. But as long as there is but one such line, whether it branches or not, the logical rules for the illative transformation of such diagrams—Existential Graphs, I call them,—remain just the same as if there were no such line.

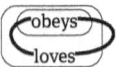

This means, There is somebody whom whoever loves obeys. Here, there are two lines, and wherever there are two there are additional rules of illative transformation, that is modes of necessary inference. The is, there are modes of inference not possible with ordinary propositions. Thus from the diagram just written we can infer

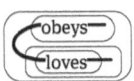

That is, whoever loves everybody obeys somebody. The whole study of such inference and everything connected with it I have named the logic of relatives.

Any part of a graph which only needs to have lines of identity attached to it to become a complete graph, signifying an assertion, I term a *verb*. The places at which lines of identity can be attached to a verb I call its *blank subjects*. I distinguish verbs according to the numbers of their blank subjects as *medads*, *monads*, *dyads*, *triads*, etc. A medad is an impersonal verb, or complete ~~sentence~~ assertion, such as "It rains", "You obey mamma". A *monad* is an intransitive verb such as "___ obeys mamma" or "you obey". A *dyad* is a simple transitive verb, such as "___ obeys ___". A *triad* is such a verb as "___ gives ___ to ___" or "___ obeys both ___ and ___". By a *relation* I mean a fact concerning two or more subjects. By a *dyadic relation* I mean a relation expressed by a *dyad* verb. By a *triadic relation* a relation expressed by a triad verb.[6]

10.4 On Existential Graphs (R 485), c.1898

R 485, c.1898. Houghton Library. "On Existential Graphs". Undated, but likely to be a production from spring–summer 1898. Three points deserve our attention in the fragments transcribed below. In §1, the term "diagrammatic syntax" is introduced, and an alteration (Alt.1) explains most

---

6 [The *Collected Papers* (CP) resumes the selection with "It is a remarkable theorem that no polyads higher than triads are required to express all relations whatever.". See RLT, pp. 154–164 for a continuation of what is likely to be the final version of this third lecture.]

clearly its purpose, which is to capture the specificity of graphical language while emphasising its distance from natural language. In a system of diagrams, the meaning of a diagram is defined by the rules that need to be applied in order to transform it into another diagram. The locution "diagrammatic syntax" will recur only as late as in the writings of 1911. In § 1, the modal notion of "destiny" is introduced; it will reappear in 1906 in the broader context of modal graphs. Here, "destiny" is however pivotal to the understanding of the basic structure of existential graphs, namely the relation of existence. If existence is a relation, the subject of any diagrammatical assertion is a subject of possible experience: "not necessarily all actually experienced, but all *destined* to be experienced". The modal notion of "destiny" adds to the general character of "possibility" the compulsory character of "actuality". § 2, "What assertion is", is one of the first attempts to apply EGs to the analysis of assertions. Peirce's already well-known division of signs into icons, indices, and symbols structures the context of possible experience introduced in § 1. Alteration 2 hints, towards the end, at the "universe of discourse or department of experience", thus underlining the experiential bearing of semiotic activity.

§ 1. What an Existential Graph is

A *graph* is a diagram composed of *spots* of different distinctive qualities, of *bonds*, and of *enclosures*.

A system of *valental graphs* is a system of graph in which all spots of the same distinctive quality have the same number of bonds attached to them.

A system of logical graphs is one in which each graph is susceptible of illative transformations, and must therefore express or partially express an asserted fact. The system will thus be a diagrammatic syntax, if not an entire language.

Two efficient systems of logical graphs are known to me. They are intimately allied. One of these I slightly sketched in *The Monist*, Vol. VII, pp. 168–186 (January 1897). I call it the System of *Entitative Graphs*, because its fundamental symbol expresses an entitative relation. The other is the system herein described. I call it the system of *Existential Graphs*, because its fundamental symbol expresses the relation of existence. I speak of existence as a relation, because it consists in the occurrence of a nature among a collection of individual objects of experience,—not necessarily all actually experienced, but all destined to be experienced, could the experience be rounded out to completion. Any entitative graph may be converted into the equivalent existential graph by, first, enclosing each spot separately and secondly enclosing the whole graph.

§ 2. What assertion is

A *sign*, or representamen, is anything which brings an interpreting mind consciously into relation to an object.[7]

Signs are of three kinds, *icons*, *indices*, and *symbols*. An *icon* is a sign which is related to its object only by a resemblance or analogy with it. It represents object merely as a possibility, or idea. An *index* is a sign which is related to the mind it addresses only by violently forcing it to attend to the object. It conveys no idea but merely excites attention to a familiar experience. There must be resistance wherever there is force; and the presentation of an index involves a reaction. The ~~mind~~ will is overborne by a blind force; and the existence of the object here and now is felt. A proper name of an individual object is the best example of an index. A *symbol* is a sign which expresses a habit, settled and self-satisfied, the antecedent, or occasion of exercise, being the occurrence in thought of the objects of some indices, while the action of the habit is to cause satisfaction with the thought junction to those individual objects of a certain ideal representable by an icon having definite parts to which those indices are ~~connected~~ mentally affixed. For example, a picture of a party of men in medieval costumes landing upon a tropical shore is, in itself, a mere icon. But if the leader of the party is labelled Christopher Columbus, while the beach is labelled "the beach of St. Kitts", the picture expresses a habit of mind of the painter in consequence of which he was content with the [end]

[Alt.1:] Existential graphs is not an entire new language, but is a new grammar, or *syntax*. But it is not a lingual syntax, but a diagrammatic syntax. It is a system of diagrams built out of *proper names*, *verbs*, *heavy connecting lines*, and *enclosing ovals*. The meaning of the diagrams is defined by defining how one can be *illatively transformed* into another. Such transformations are subject to the following Basic Rules:

I. We always have a logical right to a blank sheet.
II. If there are two graphs of which the one and the other might be written separately, they can be written side by side.

---

[7] **[Alt.:]** A *sign*, or representamen, is anything which brings an interpreting idea into relation to an object.

Signs are of three kinds, *icons*, *indices*, and *symbols*. An *icon* is a sign related to its object by resemblance or analogy. An icon does not, in itself, discriminate between itself and its object, or does not represent its object in so far as different from itself to be anything more than an idea. An *index* is a sign related to the interpreting mind by forcing an experience upon it. There can be no force without resistance; there is always a bearing down of the will of the mind to which the index is presented.

III. Every unenclosed part of a graph which is itself a graph can be transformed in any way in which it could be transformed if it stood alone.
IV. Two individual indices, or proper names, illatively transformable the one into the other can be joined by a connecting line.
V. Individual indices joined by a connecting line unenclosed in and uncrossed by an oval line are mutually transformable.
VI. Every line of connection might be joined to an individual index, or proper name, did we know what one to choose.
VII. If a graph, A, is transformable into an oval containing only a second graph, B, then this second graph unenclosed is transformable into an oval containing only A.
VIII. If an oval containing only a graph, A, is transformable into a second graph, B, then an oval containing only this second graph, B, is transformable into A.
IX. Any recognized proper name, or index, of a known individual object of the universe of discourse, can be written unenclosed with a connecting line attached to it. It can also be written enclosed with a connecting line protruding from the oval.

Commentary on the above rules

I. The only assertion we are always entitled to make is an empty form of proposition such as "what I aver is true". Hence, the blank sheet must mean that.

II & III. Taken together, these imply that writing graphs side by side unenclosed has the effect of asserting them all, and has no further effect.

III & IV. These rules imply that a connecting line attached to two individual proper names has the effect of asserting the identity of their objects, and has no further effect. [end]

[Alt.2:] A *graph* is a diagram composed of *spots* of different distinctive qualities, of *bonds*, and of *enclosings*.[8] A system of valental graphs is a system of graphs in which all spots of the same distinctive quality have the same number of bonds attached to them.

---

8 [Alt.:] A *graph* is a diagram composed of *spots* of different colors, or qualities, of *connecting lines*, and of *ovals*, or *enclosures*. A system of *valental* graphs is one in which every spot of any given quality must by its intrinsic nature, have a fixed number of connecting lines.

A system of logical graphs is one in which each graph is susceptible of illative transformations, and as such must represent a proposition, or inchoate proposition.

Signs are of three kinds, *icons*, *indices*, and *symbols*. An *icon* is a sign which is associated with its object by resemblance or analogy. Indeed the icon does not, in itself, discriminate between itself and its object. It does not represent its object to be anything more than an idea. An *index* is a sign which brings its object forcibly to ~~mind~~ experience ~~irrespective of any resemblance~~. There can be no force without a resistance, so that a struggle is expressed in every *index*. A proper name of a known individual object is an index; since when the name is uttered the experience formerly had is recalled as truly, though not as forcibly, as the new experience would be if the object itself were brought into the field of perception. A *symbol* is a sign which so far resembles an index, that it expresses, and tends to convey, a mental compulsion; but it differs from the index in that it expresses not a momentary reaction involving a struggle but a settled, calm, self-satisfied habit, of which the occasion of exercise, or antecedent, arising whenever certain indices are presented, while the consequent of the habit is that those ~~associations with such indices of a certain icon~~ indices become transformed into definite parts of an icon, to which they remain attached ~~by the symbol~~ as labels. Thus, a picture of a party of men in medieval costumes landing upon a tropical shore would be an icon. If their leader is labelled "Christopher Columbus" and the shore "St. Kitts", and if it is understood to be a serious assertion, then we understand that the painter would be satisfied with a picture of a man landing, and a tropical island as representing, at least in part, the pair of objects named Christopher Columbus and the island of St. Kitts, so that the picture, though somewhat indefinite, as far as it goes, would be a satisfactory substitute for that pair of names.

A *valid necessary inference*, or illative transformation, of a symbol, called the *premise*, into another, called the *conclusion*, is such a transformation that either the habit expressed by the premise will ultimately prove unstable and be destroyed or the habit expressed by the conclusion must ultimately prove stable and endure, supposing definite icons ultimately become associated with the different indices belonging to the universe of discourse or department of experience concerned.

Every assertion represents an illative transformation of an index into an icon to be satisfactory.

Two ~~satisfactory~~ effective systems of logical graphs are known to me. They are closely related to one another. One is the system which I slightly sketched in *The Monist* (Vol. VII, pp. 168–186). I term that *Entitative Graphs*. The other is the system of *Existential Graphs* which I here describe. Any entitative graph is converted into an equivalent existential graph by enclosing each spot in an oval and enclosing the whole in an oval.

10.5 [Algebra and Existential Graphs] (R 513), 1898

R 513, "FL", May 1898. Houghton Library. This manuscript is Chapter XI on algebra and existential graphs, from a work written for unknown purposes bearing only the title FL. It was to consist of at least fourteen individual chapters of which only a disappointing amount of 132 manuscript pages have been preserved in the archives. As far as can be told, the main topic of FL is to compare algebraic and graphical logics. (See Introduction to Part II on FL and Peirce's further elaborations on the problem of notation.) What is reproduced below is the first part of a version of Chapter XI. Due to the abundance of lost pages, it is impossible to give a final account of Peirce's views on the comparisons between the algebraic and the graphical systems. An alternative version reports: "My graphs are somewhat disappointing", and the beginning of Chapter XII (*id, ibid.*) reads: "I am a little disappointed with my graphs. My cumbrous General Algebra, with all its faults, seems preferable." R 513 also includes a clear statement of the difference between entitative and existential graphs. Entitative graphs primarily concern *truth*, which can be fully predicated only of individuals (*entia*; see the next selection R 495). In contrast, existential graphs focus on *existence*, as seen above. The rules of illative transformations boil down to (in the fashion of sequent calculus) "*permits to draw* and *permits to erase*." The numerous graphical illustrations include a case of multitude (Figs. 119–122).

XI. Although the "general algebra of logic", as I name the system above described is pretty nearly perfect for its proper purpose, that of analyzing reasoning in the most minute accurate manner, yet it must be acknowledged that it is a very cumbrous machine, utterly wanting in elegance and compactness. In the hope of remedying that defect, I have invented two other methods of representing assertions and performing necessary inferences.

One of these is a graphical method, the other is an algebraic system which seems to have fascinated Prof. Schröder much more than it has me. I will first explain the graphical method. This method has two varieties which I call Entitative Graphs and Existential Graphs. In *The Monist* for January 1897 I have given a very slight and imperfect sketch of the system of entitative graphs. I will here explain the existential graphs which are less philosophical but are much easier to use.

In order to draw such a graph, the first step is to assign some sheet of paper or enclosure upon a sheet, marked out by a bounding line, to represent so much as we know or recollect of the universe.

If on that sheet or in that enclosure we draw a picture, or write a general description, or a letter which is an abbreviation for a general description, the effect is to be understood and agreed upon as being that we *assert* that to something in the universe that picture or description applies. We aver that such a thing *exists*. Hence, I call this the system of *existential* graphs. (On the entitative system the meaning is that being involves necessarily the truth of the description.)

If, however, we draw a "circle" or enclosing line round the picture or description the meaning is that nothing exists that is of that sort.

If we connect two parts by a line, the meaning is that the two descriptions apply to the same thing. Thus, if I draw a man with a beard, it means there exists a man with a beard. If I write the word "blue", it means there is something blue. If I join the word blue by a connecting line to the man's beard, I aver that a man exists in my universe of discourse whose beard is blue.

If however I encircle the whole with a line cutting it off from the universe of discourse, I *deny* that any man has a blue beard.

If I encircle the word blue only, I assert there is a man with a beard which is *not* blue.

The following graph ⟨is mother of–loves⟩ Fig. 1 asserts that something is mother of something loved by it. The following ⟨is mother of–loves⟩ Fig. 2 asserts (in a universe of human beings) that somebody is not a mother of anything that it loves. The following ⟨is mother of–loves⟩ Fig. 3 asserts that nothing is mother of anything without loving that thing.

These rules completely describe the whole system of drawing the graphs. But there are many fine distinctions requiring attention which will present themselves as we go on.

It remains to make out the rules of illative transformation of the graphs.

All such rules are reducible to *permits to draw* and *permits to erase*.

The whole graph is supposed to be in one enclosure marking the limit of the universe. We have to distinguish between parts *oddly enclosed*, that is, within an odd number of encircling lines, including that of the whole graph, and parts *evenly enclosed*, that is, within an even number of enclosing lines, including that of the whole graph. The parts of the graphs are either *spots*, that is, parts having positive descriptive significance, or *lines*, which merely mark the numerical identity of objects to which the descriptions apply. It will simplify matters to assume that only one end of a line is within enclosures that the other end is not within. By simply marking *nodes* on the lines at their outermost or innermost points, these nodes being spots whose descriptive implication is merely existence, we can readily make the lines conform to that condition. Thus, the following ⟨is mother of–loves⟩ Fig. 4 means, "there is something which is not both non-mother of something and non-lover of the same thing", or

$$\Sigma_i \Sigma_j \overline{\overline{m}_{ij} \cdot \overline{l}_{ij}}$$

that is,

$$\Sigma_i \Pi_j\, m_{ij} \,\mathbf{\Psi}\, l_{ij}$$

or "somebody loves everybody except such persons as she may be mother of". And the following, [is mother of / loves] Fig. 5 means "somebody loves everybody of whom she is mother (if she is mother of anybody)". This would, for example, be true of every male, because to say he loves everybody of whom he is mother is to say no more than that he exists, since not being a mother of anybody, the statement does not require him to love anybody at all.

The first illative rule is:

- It is permitted to erase anything oddly enclosed or to insert anything under even enclosure (already existing). But it is not permitted to create an enclosure for the purpose, since that enclosure would be inserted under odd enclosures.

The second illative rule is:

- It is permitted to sever a line (i.e. to erase a portion) under odd enclosures or to connect two loose ends under even connections.

The following [is mother of / loves] Fig. 6 asserts that "there are persons, I and J, whether two or one are the same, such that I is mother of nobody whom J does not love". That is,

$$\Sigma_i \Sigma_j \Pi_k\, \overline{m}_{ik} \,\mathbf{\Psi}\, l_{jk}.$$

Note that this differs from

$$\Sigma_i \Pi_k \Sigma_j\, \overline{m}_{ik} \,\mathbf{\Psi}\, l_{jk}$$

or "somebody is mother only of persons loved", since the latter asserts the existence only of a non-mother, while the former asserts also the existence of a lover. The latter proposition is represented in the graph of Fig. 7, [is mother of / loves] Fig. 7 It might be supposed that the second rule would permit us to connect the two lines under the enclosure; but that is not so. There are no loose ends there. And it makes no difference how a line connecting two lines runs. Fig. 5 and Fig. 8 are precisely equivalent. [is mother of / loves] Fig. 8 The only material question is whether a given line extends out of a given enclosure. As long as the answer to that remains the same, the course of the line is indifferent. But if we have given the graph of Fig. 9 meaning

Fig. 9   Fig. 10

[– – –]⁹ but are also alike in their connections by lines with others. With this terminology the second rule may be expressed as follows:

If submembers of every submember of a term are duplicates, another duplicate is virtually a concomitant of the term, and a concomitant of an enclosure has a duplicate as virtual concomitant of every submember of a submember of the enclosure; and any term or virtual term may be repeated in duplicate, and of two virtual duplicates either may be suppressed. This may be called the *Rule of Tautology*.

Let us illustrate this by examples. Granted the assertion of Fig. 35, that is, "I either play and win or I play and lose", since "I play" is a submember of every

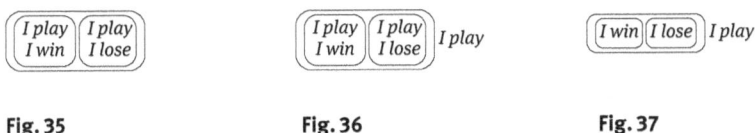

Fig. 35   Fig. 36   Fig. 37

submember of the whole graph, it is a virtual concomitant of the whole, and may be so written as in Fig. 36, whence by the Rule of Superfluity, the I play under two enclosures may be expunged and we get the graph of Fig. 37, "I play and either win or lose".

Again in Fig. 37, "I play" being concomitant of the enclosure is virtually duplicated by concomitants to *I win* and *I lose*, giving Fig. 36. Then by the Rule of Superfluity the unenclosed "I play" may be expunged and we get back to Fig. 35. Thus, Figs. 35 and 37 are equivalent. Granted the assertion of Fig. 38, that is Alexander stands to a king of Belgium in the relation of loving (if anybody) only benefactors of that king. Then by the rule of tautology we can infer Fig. 39. That is, Alexander stands to Belgium in the double relation of first, being to some king of that country a lover of nobody but benefactors of him and second of being to Belgium itself a lover of nothing which is not a benefactor of some king of it. Then by the Rule of Superfluity we can sever the lines connected with the outer "is king of" and remove that dyad, leaving Fig. 40, or Alexander stands to Belgium in the relation of loving

---

9 [Six ms pages and Figs. 11–34 have not been recovered (ms pp. 55–60).]

A—loves—benefits—is king of—B

Fig. 38

Fig. 39

nothing but benefactors of its kings. This assertion is much less than that of Fig. 38, according to which Alexander stands to some particular king of, Belgium in the relation of only loving his benefactors. We thus get the derivative rule following:

Under even enclosures a spot may be introduced under two enclosures and under odd enclosures may be extracted from under two enclosures.

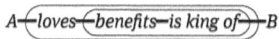

Fig. 40

Granted the assertion of Fig. 12, somebody is loved by all men, we can, by the Rule of Tautology, infer the assertion Fig. 41, "Somebody is at once loved by everybody and is identical with somebody or other". Then, by the Rule of Superfluity, we omit the first somebody and infer Fig. 13, Everybody loves somebody or other.

Granted that assertion of Fig. 42, that Alexander stands to some Belgian in the relation of either loving or benefitting every king of his.

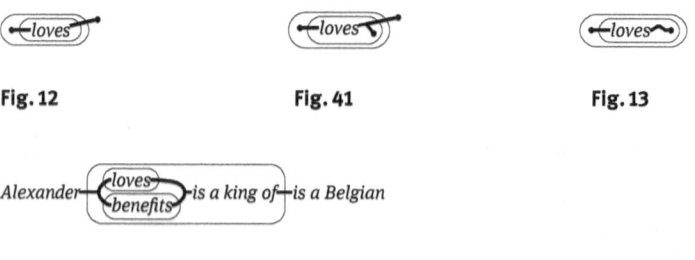

Fig. 12   Fig. 41   Fig. 13

Fig. 42

Then, by the Rule of Tautology we infer Fig. 43.

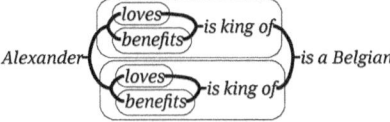

Fig. 42

We can also attach to that the statement that there is in the universe of qualities a certain quality, Q, to which we can attach any conditions not involving contradiction. This is a premise derived from our knowledge of qualities. Then, by the Rule of Superfluity we can insert under the single enclosures such things as to give Fig. 44.

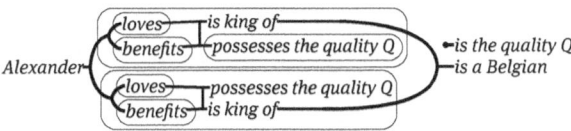

Fig. 44

Now let the quality, Q, be that of being loved by Alexander. Then, without stopping at this moment to analyze the rules of procedure involved, it is evident that wherever we have "___ possesses the quality Q" we can attach to the same blank "Alexander loves ___", and that where both these equivalent verbs are attached either may be omitted. The insertion gives Fig. 45:

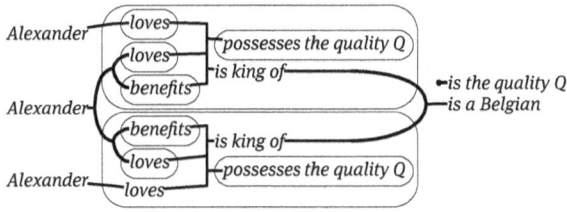

Fig. 45

Next, since Alexander is a single individual, the three lines to Alexander's may all be carried to one Alexander. This gives Fig. 46:

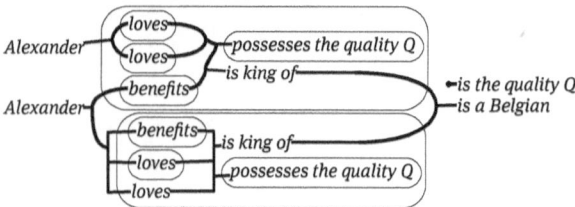

Fig. 46

Now by the Rule of Tautology one of the two "loves" in the upper enclosure can be erased. That done, the other with its "Alexander" can be struck out as equivalent to the "possesses the quality Q". For the lower enclosure we are obliged to call in the aid of a new rule, namely that any verb concomitant with its negative renders all other concomitants (with the same attachments) nugatory. Consequently, the "benefits" can be omitted. Then the lower "loves" can be omitted as equivalent to the "possesses the quality Q". Finally, the quality Q being a single individual, all its occurrences may be joined by a line, and being stated to be existent, it need not be definitely named. We thus get Fig. 47.

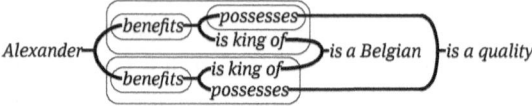

Fig. 47

We have thus succeeded in inferring from Fig. 42, that there is a Belgian of whom Alexander either loves or benefits every king, Fig. 47, that there is a Belgian of whom Alexander at once loves every king who possesses a certain quality and benefits every king who does not possess that quality. The two graphs are in fact

Alexander—loves—is a Frenchman / is a violinist

Fig. 48

equivalent. In much the same way we might show that Fig. 48 that Alexander loves a French violinist is equivalent to Fig. 49 that in every mode of loving Alexander either loves a Frenchman or in some other mode loves a violinist.

10.5 [Algebra and Existential Graphs] (R 513), 1898

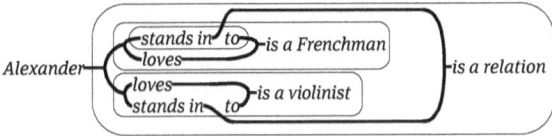

Fig. 49

I have not my papers at hand in which I have with great labor determined the fundamental modes of illative transformation. Consequently, my enumeration here may present some superfluities. But we may take the following as the third rule:

- Whatever can somewhere be inserted under even enclosures, as well as whatever can everywhere be omitted under odd enclosures, can everywhere be omitted or inserted.

For whatever can everywhere be inserted under even enclosures can everywhere be omitted under odd enclosures, and conversely, being true. But anything whatever can be omitted under even enclosures or inserted under odd enclosures. As the fourth rule we may take the following:

- Two enclosures one immediately surrounding the other are equivalent to none. In other words they annul each other.

This is the same as to say that two circles one within the other and vacant and the sole contents of the other can everywhere be inserted and omitted. For this being permitted the first two rules permit anything that is written to be carried into or out of two such enclosures.

As the fifth rule, take the following:

- A vacant odd enclosure is necessarily false.

[– – –]¹⁰ so much as serves to fix the identity of the different references, and also to recover the meaning in the conclusion.

This rule will be sufficiently illustrated in the course of the discussion.

- The sixth rule requires logical relations to be defined.

---

10 [Ten pages and Figs. 50–118 have not been recovered (ms pp. 67–76).]

The above seem to be all the fundamental rules. There are a variety of derivative rules which will abbreviate the process of using the system of graphs.

As a final example of the use of this method, let us employ it for a slight discussion of some elementary points concerning multitude.

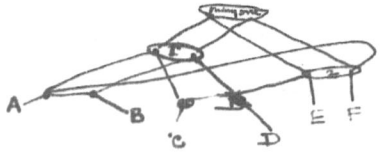

Fig. 119 [P.H.]

To belong as unit to a collection and to *possess* as a quality are substantially the same relation. To abbreviate we will write A—possesses—B meaning A possesses the quality B or A belongs to the ~~class~~ collection designated by B.

Everything about multitude turns upon that class of dyadic relations each of which is such that many things may be in that relation to one and the same thing but the same thing can never be in that relation to two different things. We will call it a *ramal* relation, or better, a *many-to-one* relation. Fig. 119 shows a way of expressing that A stands to B and C stands to D in *one* many-to-one relation, while E stands to F and D stands to A in another many-to-one relation.

In every unit of the collection α stands to a unit of the collection β in the same many-to-one relation, while there is no many-to-one relation in which every unit of the collection β stands to a unit of the collection α, then (as Fig. 120 illustrates) the collection α is said to be *greater than* the collection β. Fig. 121 expresses that there is a many-to-one relation and a quality α and whatever possesses the quality α stands in that many-to-one relation to something which possesses a certain

Fig. 120

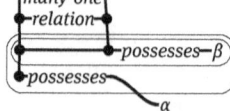

Fig. 121

quality β. Fig. 122 expresses that while there is a many-to-one relation which everything possessing α has to something possessing β, there is no one-to-one relation such that everything that possesses β has that relation to something possessing α.[11]

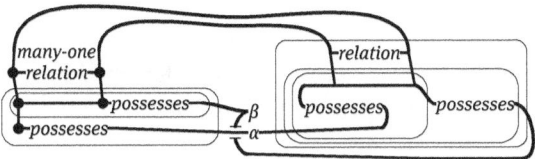

Fig. 122

[– – –][12] Finally we easily express the matter in an existential graph as here shown [P.H.]:

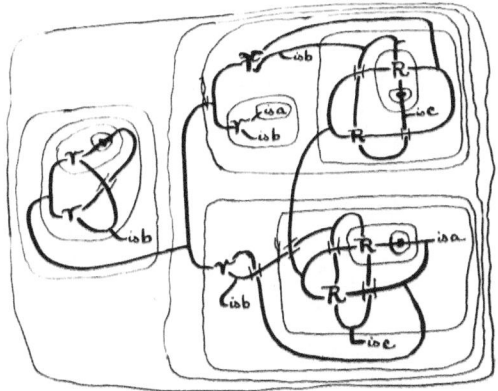

Such are the very simplest of the relations which mathematicians are in the habit of handling! The practical advantage of writing the above in the form $[c] = [a]^{[b]}$ is obvious. Yet for logical purposes the analyzed expression is necessary.

[– – –][13] In the existential graphs

---

12 [Twelve pages missing or omitted. The following is from Chapter XIII (ms p. 91).]
13 [Two pages later, from Chapter IV (ms p. 93).]

 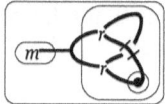

Let us now see what premises are necessary in order to prove that, taking any two characters whatever, whatever object possesses one of them is in a one-to-x relation to some object possessing the other.

That is,

$$\Pi_\beta \Pi_\gamma \Sigma_\alpha \Pi_1 \Sigma_2 \Pi_3 \Sigma_4 \; \bar{q}_{\beta 1} + m_\alpha \cdot r_{\alpha 12} \cdot q_{\gamma 2} + \bar{q}_{\gamma 3} + m_\alpha \cdot r_{\alpha 34} \cdot q_{\beta 4}$$

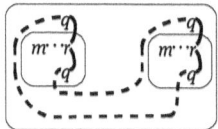

I first assume that whatever characters β and γ may be there is some relation δ such that every object possessing β is δ to every object possessing r.

$$\Pi_\beta \Pi_\gamma \Sigma_\delta \Pi_i \Pi_j \; \bar{q}_{\beta 1} + \bar{q}_{\gamma 2} + r_{\delta 12}$$

---

13 [From the beginning of the next chapter:] **XII.** I am a little disappointed with my graphs. My cumbrous General Algebra, with all its faults, seems preferable. But I have another algebraic system which is not without merit. It expresses things simply. The difficulty with it is that it is so overburdened with identical formulae. This algebra may be combined with the general algebra to any extent. Its peculiarity is that it dispenses with the quantifiers and indices, if not wholly, yet for the most part by introducing two *relative operations* [relative multiplication and relative addition]. There are really *eight* of these operations; but it is not necessary to have special signs for more than two of them in order to accomplish the main purpose of this algebra, which I name my Algebra of Dyadic Relatives.

The algebra of Dyadic Relatives was well explained by me in outline in the book "Studies in Logic" and Schröder has developed it in his third volume at such enormous length that it is not worth while to devote much space to it here.

[Alt.:] My graphs are somewhat disappointing. They do not affect the intuitional swiftness which was expected of them.

There is another algebra, which I name the Algebra of Dual Relatives which does this better. But when it is applied to complicated cases, it too becomes worse than the cumbrous General Algebra.

I next use the principle that if one relation exists, then every relation which differs from it only in excluding certain pairs, exists.

10.6 Logical Graphs (R 495), 1898

R 495, August 1898. Houghton Library. The sixth and final selection in this chapter is a piece from a notebook written in August 1898. The text is closely related to the notes Peirce made in summer 1898 in the *Logic Notebook* (R 339) and to the other selections of the present chapter. R 495 is a recap of the essentials of the system of EGs, now concisely presented in the form and shape that effectively has found its final and definite expression. This study encompasses constitutive conventions, basic formal rules, and reflections on the index-icon relation in the context of graphs: "Every graph is in so far an index in that it asserts something of the actual universe, which *exists* (or rather is the sum of existence) and *is an individual* in as much as of it every proposition is either true or false." In closing, Peirce notes that the process through which a *quality* comes to be regarded as an *individual*, or rather as a quality individuated as a predicate that can be so quantified in our universe of discourse, is a process of *abstraction*. Shortly after having completed the presentation of the system and what now is the complete set of rules, Peirce would fall seriously ill and any further attempt at significant developments of the system had to wait for his *annus mirabilis* of 1903. But for the time being, his job was done.

Existential Graphs: The Constitutive Conventions

1. Each and every conceived fact written (unenclosed) on the sheet of the graph is thereby asserted to be realized somewhere in the universe of actuality.
2. The expression of a conceived fact being enclosed within a lightly drawn oval is thereby not asserted, but is looked upon as a subject of assertion. But if nothing is asserted of it, its being written enclosed on the sheet of the graph *denies* it.
3. Contact of individuals (unenclosed) signifies identity; and every part of a heavy line asserts the identity of its extremities.

Examples

—loves—	Something loves something
(—loves—)	Nothing loves anything
(loves—)	Something does not love anything
(loves)	Something does not love something
((loves))	Everything loves everything
((loves))	Something loves everything
((loves—))	Everything loves something

	Everything has something it does not love
	Some mother loves her child
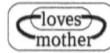	Every mother loves her child
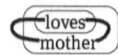	Something loves everything of which it is mother.

The Basic Formal Rules of Existential Graphs, from which all illative transformations are deducible irrespective of the constitutive conventions.

I. The whole graph may be erased.
II. Two graphs that can be written severally can be written side by side.
III. All basic rules for the transformation of graphs apply to unenclosed parts of graphs.
IV. All circumstances authorizing the transformation of any graph, A, into an enclosure containing only B, equally authorize the transformation of B into an enclosure containing only A.
V. All circumstances authorizing the transformation of an enclosure containing only A into B equally authorize the transformation of an enclosure containing B into A.
VI. Every heavy line may be joined to some index; and the writing of a graph virtually joins it (though not its heavy lines) to one constant index.
VII. Unenclosed indices transformable into one another may be joined by a heavy line.
VIII. Every index may be written unenclosed.
IX. Every index has an index, or indices, into which it cannot be transformed.

Existential Graphs. Their Constitutive Conventions

1. Each and every writing upon the sheet of the graph is a representation, or description, more or less indeterminate, of ~~the universe of actuality~~ a universe of discourse, as it is represented in the belief of the writer.
2. A lightly drawn oval removes its contents from the field of the graph. But the whole enclosure is there, and thus the non-application of the contents is asserted as a fact.
3. Contact signifies individual identity; and a heavy line serves to make a continuity of contact between its extremities.

Commentary

The graph ─loves─ describes the universe as involving the fact that *x* loves *y* while leaving it indeterminate what *x* and *y* are, They are individuals of the universe.

The graph ⊂─loves─⊃/⊂is mother of⊃ asserts that some existing individual both loves and is mother of some existing individual.

The graph (loves/injures) asserts that something both loves and injures itself.

The graph ─loves─/─hates─ asserts something loves something and something hates something.

The graph (─loves─/─hates─) asserts that the previous graph is false, that is, it affirms that either nothing loves anything or nothing hates anything.

The graph (⊂loves─/hates─) asserts that taking any individuals A, B, C (different or identical), either A does not love B or does not hate C.

The graph (⊂loves─) or (─loves─) asserts that taking any individuals, A, B, C, whatever (same or different), either A does not love B or is not identical with C; that is, C does not love B. That is, nobody loves anybody.

The graph ⊂hates─/⊂loves─ asserts that somebody, A, hates somebody B, and at the same time is identical with somebody who is not identical with anybody unless that person does not love anybody. That is, somebody is hated by somebody who loves nobody.

The graph (⊂hates─/⊂loves─) asserts that somebody is not hated by anybody unless that hater is a person of whom it is not true that he loves nobody. That is, somebody is hated (if at all) only by a person or persons who love, each of them, somebody.

The graph (⊂hates─/⊂loves─) asserts that somebody is not identical with anybody of whom it is true that he is not loved by a person who hates a person. That is, somebody is loved by whomsoever there may be who hates anybody at all.

The graph (⊂hates─/○) asserts that somebody is identical with whomsoever hates anybody. That is, there is, at most, but a single individual who hates.

The graph (⊖) or (⊖) asserts that there is, at most, but a single individual who is identical with anybody at all. That is, the universe contains but a single object. (This is contrary to the judicial knowledge of logic.)

The graph (⊖) asserts that everything is identical with something.

The graph (⊖) asserts everything is identical with itself. That is, nothing is identical with anything but itself.

It is, in one sense, a defect of the method of graphs here described that an absurdity like ⊖ can be written. But I see no remedy for it except one which would render the method very cumbrous. After all, a method for which a violation of logic is possible must recognize the law of logic it is in danger of violating more explicitly than a method which cannot violate the law very well can do.

An index is a sign which forcibly puts the interpretant into actual relation with the object represented. That object is therefore existent and is an individual. Every graph is in so far an index that it asserts something of the actual universe, which exists (or rather is the sum of existence) and is an individual in as much as of it every proposition is either true or false. (For an individual is a subject of which every predicate is wholly true or wholly false.)

The universe of actuality concerns, or contains, in the first place, individual things, ~~known to us~~ with which we have or may have experiential acquaintance, hypothetically i.e. retroductively through their characters and especially through the continuity of their relations to objects which we do not lose sight of.

These individuals exist, that is, they react in pairs, in the actual state of things which in its singleness reacts upon us.

In the next place, these things have modes of predicates, or qualities and relational qualities (or qualities of ordered pairs etc.).

Each of these qualities becomes familiar to us by inward experience, and forms an individual of inwardly experiential universe, or at least something so far like such an individual that every predicate is either wholly true or wholly false of it.

The mental process by which a predicate becomes added as an individual to the universe of discourse is *abstraction*.

Every assertion can be analyzed into a predicate and subject.

11 On Existential Graphs, F4

R 484, July–August 1898. Houghton Library. F4 is closely related to R 513, FL (see the previous chapter). Its last two pages are dated August 2, 1898; § 1 of R 484 is nearly identical to § 1 of R 482. This manuscript is eye-catching, if only for the reason that Peirce marshals an array of proofs using the graphs, thus creating not only eloquent deductions but also aesthetical experiences of what proofs with graphs look like. His purpose is to establish the set of basic rules of illative transformations and a systematic method of deducing other rules from the set of basic rules. He also aims at proving soundness of many of them. A record number of twenty-eight rules is presented and the correctness of most of them is argued for. Inspection of these rules leaves Peirce ultimately with seven basic rules of transformation, a conclusion consistent with what he had stated in the *Logic Notebook* on August 4, 1898 (R 339; LoF 1). In F4 (it is not known what this acronym means) Peirce reaffirms several points made in the preceding couple of selections. Negation is a derived property of a thin closed line surrounding propositions ("Hence, on the whole the oval denies that which is within") and is primarily to be taken as a description of "what is intended." Peirce even ventures a topological possibility that a double cut is a coarsened form of one continuous line infolded within itself "so as to produce cells and cells within cells." Logical forms of natural-language sentences are given in the graphical system, in the section that entitles those "equivalences." Graphical representations of numerical propositions are also provided, and the illative relation of consequence is interpreted in the deductions of elementary rules from the basic rules as "is transformable into." The analytic virtues of the existential system are demonstrated by applying it to the analysis of the workings of Darii into its smallest details.

§ 1. Of Graphs in General

A *graph*, in the most general sense, would be a diagram composed, first, of *spots*, or parts treated as points having simple visible qualities, or *colors*, and also different *sides*; second, of *nexes*, or parts treated as lines, though they too may have colors and sides; third, of *faces*, or parts treated as surfaces; and so on to higher dimensions.

An *infimal* graph is one which has no faces nor elements of higher dimensionality, nor any distinguishable sides to its nexes.

A *bond-nexed* graph is an infimal graph in which every nex (called a *bond*) has two extremities and no more.

A graph has its Listing numbers. The census-theorem, as applied to infimal graphs, is: The chorisis of the graph less its cyclosis equals the chorisis of the spots plus the singularity of the nexes.

A *valental* graph is a bond-nexed graph in which each color of a spot determines the number of distinguishable sides, called *hands*, that spot possesses; and the end of a bond is attached to each hand. The unattached ends of the bonds are called the *loose ends* of the graph.

Valental graphs receive designations expressive of the numbers of their hands, or *valencies*,

Valency	Name
0	Medad
1	Monad
2	Dyad
3	Triad
> 2	Polyad
2N	Artiad
2N + 1	Perissid

Besides the Listing theorem, the following second sensus proposition holds of valental graphs: The valency of a graph equals the sum of the valencies of its spots less the number of extremities of *connecting* bonds. It follows as a corollary, that no perissid can be composed exclusively of artiads.

Between Listing's theorem and the second census proposition the number of connecting bonds may be eliminated. Let a graph be composed of n_0 medads, n_1 monads, n_2 dyads, n_3 triads, etc. Let K_0 be the sum of the cyclosis of the medads, K_1 that of the monads, etc. and V, N, K denote respectively the valency, chorisis, and cyclosis of the graph. Then,

$$V - 2N + 2N = \sum_{v=0}^{\infty} n_v - 2n_v + 2K_v$$

There are evidently still other topical conditions. We may, as the equation shows, conceive of a tetrad spot as composed of two triads, of a pentad spot as composed of three triads, etc. In a connected whole graph, where $N = 1$, $2 + n_3 - n_1$ may be any number from zero up, while K may be any number whose double does not exceed $2 + n_3 - n_1$. But since $N = 1$, either $n_0 = 0$ or $n_0 = 1$ and all other n's are zero. We may therefore write

$$V + 2K = 2 + n_3 - n_1 = 2 + \sum_{v=0}^{\infty} (v - 2) n_v$$

Thus the medad spot if it enters into such a graph has the paramount effect on $V + 2K$, the dyad has none at all, while the monad and triad act in opposite ways.

A *polar* graph is a valental graph in which there is a distinction between the two ends of each bond.

§ 2. Of Logical Graphs

Of systems of graphs for the representation of logical relations, the simplest in construction, inasmuch as it makes use of but one general sign, is that of Entitative Graphs, sketched by me in *The Monist*. But while simple in one sense, that system is complicated in its mode of representing many logical relations, and it is also quite unnatural in some of its leading conventions. The system of Existential Graphs herein described is very much like that, but this corrects the faults of that, while it misses its chief merit.

§ 3. The Constitutive Conventions of Existential Graphs

1. The first understanding which has to be established between the delineator and the interpreter of the graph is that whatever is written on a certain sheet of paper, or on a certain part of the sheet, individually recognized by them in common, shall be interpreted according to the rules of the system.

In the second place, both parties must recognize a certain state of things, sufficiently known for recognition, as being that of which the graph supplies a partial description. Or, more accurately speaking, there is a pretence at such recognition. The recognition would have to take place were any information really conveyed; but since the object of the system is merely to study reasoning, and not really to reason seriously, a make-believe assertion is sufficient.

2. That the graph is recognized as a partial description of a recognized, or pretendedly recognized, state of things, constitutes it a *proposition*, that is an assertion or feigned assertion.

Signs are of three kinds, *icons*, *indices*, and *symbols*. An icon ~~signifies~~ represents its object by being like it. It appeals to the so-called association by resemblance. This is not an accurate term, by the way, since resemblance *consists* precisely in different ideas being drawn together in our minds by an occult inward force. A *pure icon*, could such a sign exist, would present to us a pure sense-quality, without any parts nor any respects, and consequently without positive generality. But in fact there is no pure icon; and we apply the name icon to any sign in which the force of resemblance is the dominant element of its representativity. An index represents its object by forcibly bringing it before the senses, or before the attention, appealing to "association by contiguity". A pure index would present a pure sense-reaction. But again there is no such thing. Every index is considered as an individual sign; but this individuality will not bear cross-examination, but betrays more or less generality, because there is no pure index. Still we may call a proper name or demonstrative or personal pronoun an index. It appeals to individual recognition. Such words as yard which refer to individual prototypes have much of the index character. "Indefinite" pronouns, *anything*, *something*, etc. which tells us how to proceed in order to experience the object intended,—better called *selective* pronouns,—are almost indices. Now what is a symbol? An icon represents its object as a mere dream, sufficient for itself. An index represents its object as an active, existent, thing, that insists on making me its other. A symbol represents its object as a manifestation, as a representamen having on the one hand a capacity of being *indicated* and on the other hand a capacity of being *iconized*. The object not only exists but has a regularity, a general nature, a reason. It has parts, aspects, continuity, bounds. All signs are more or less symbolic. Take a picture, for example. Here are a lot of colors doubled on a canvas. But I know that they are intended to represent something unlike the canvass in having three dimensions, and the colors represent quite different colors in the object, to which they are proportionate by a scale of values. This is one of the reasons why I must be a connoisseur in order to judge of a painting. The object represented may not exist in the world of sense-experience; but it has an existence in the creation of the artist. It forces itself upon my apprehension much as an object of outward experience would do. Thus, the picture has an indexical nature, and as representing that its indicated object has steady and general characters it is symbolic. It represents its object as something which *manifests*, or represents, an occult *Ding an sich* behind it. Again, I am crossing the street rather abstractedly when I am startled by a sharp shout of "Hi!" It is difficult to imagine a sign more purely indexical, more exclusively calculated to rouse my attention to experience of the moment. Yet, after all, this cry has a meaning. I do not dodge as I might instinctively do if it were the whiz of a bullet. I instinctively jump forward, because the cry means that I should do so. Thus, a particular *quality* of the things about me is asserted in the explanation. Thus, every sign whatever is more or less symbolic. It recognizes its object as manifesting in some grade or manner of existence some general nature which may vary continuously, but not beyond more or less vaguely thought limits. It is a conventional or quasi-conventional sign, which represents its object as conforming to some general rule of representation. Beggars are said to make marks at the entrances of estates which not merely direct attention to those estates, but also classify the families which inhabit them. These marks are *symbols*.

Logicians have always recognized three forms of symbols, to wit, *terms*, *propositions*, and *argumentations*. A *term* is a symbol in which the representative and reactive ~~functions~~ aspects of the object are left entirely vague except so far as they may be determined by the qualitative element, that is, the generalized icon created in the mind. The purest examples are verbs, like "___ shines", "___ loves ___"; although traditionally logicians have usually understood by terms class-names, equivalent to common norms. But these are really mere accidental parts of speech peculiar to certain classes of languages. They have no general logical significance. They are mere fragments of symbols. That is, "___ is a man" is a symbol, but "man" is more nearly an icon. A *proposition* is a symbol in which the representative element, or reason, is left vague and unexpressed, but in which the reactive element is distinctly indicated.

In driving along the road with a compagnon, he points at a house and remarks, "That is a pretty house". It is a proposition. But I make a voyage to a distant island and repeat the remark, "That is a pretty house". "What house", asks my interlocutor. "Oh, a house far way". He will be right in telling me that I do not enunciate anything at all, because I do not indicate what I am talking about. An *argument* is a bad name for a symbol in which the representative element, or reason, is distinctly expressed. It may be used either to produce belief or in various ways.

An existential graph is not only a symbol but it is a proposition. If the subject is not distinctly indicated, it is nevertheless to be understood as an assertion that such a subject might be found in the universe to which the discourse is understood to relate. Thus, -loves- will mean, "Something loves something".

3. If a graph consists of partial graphs, that is of unenclosed points which, written alone, would mean something, each such partial graph has its full effect in rendering the description of the state of things less vague. Thus $\genfrac{}{}{0pt}{}{\text{-sins}}{\text{-sings}}$ will mean, "Somebody sins, and somebody sings".

4. The continuity of a heavy line is to signify the identity of all its parts. Thus $\mathsf{C}\genfrac{}{}{0pt}{}{\text{sins}}{\text{sings}}$ means, "Somebody sins and the same person sings".

The whole graph may be conceived as connected by a heavy line with an index of the individual state of things described. But such line is not drawn.

5. The field within which it was understood that what was to be written should be interpreted as an existential graph may be conceived as marked off by a lightly drawn line surrounding it. That line may be folded in places so as to produce cells and cells within cells, thus:

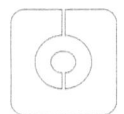 In the practical delineation the canals may be omitted, thus:

Thus whatever is written inside an odd number of lightly drawn ovals is to be conceived as not asserted but merely as describing what is intended and *anything* answering the description is intended. But further every heavy line crossed by the oval, including the imaginary heavy line which unites that which is within with the index of the state of things, is to be taken as signifying the non-identity of that which is denoted by the points on the two sides. Hence, on the whole the oval denies that which is within. Thus ⊂sins⊃⊂sings⊃ signifies, "There is something which sins which is non-identical with *anything* that sings". So ⊂is an angel⊂sins⊃⊂sings⊃⊃ means, "There is an angel which is other than everything which both sins and signs", i.e. some angel either does not sin or does not sing. So ⊂⊂sins⊃⊂sings⊃⊃ means, "there is nothing which sings and does not sin", or whatever there may be that sings, sins.

6. The different spots of the graph can be any verbs which express *relations*, that is to say, which signify that the set of individuals denoted by its hands belongs to a certain class of sets, such as the set composed of buyer, seller, thing sold, and price. Such a verb can only be true if all its subjects (in which name I include the things denoted by the grammatical objects) exist all of them. For instance, the verb may be "___ is at once ___ and ___"; but it cannot be "___ is either ___ or ___"; A may be either B or C, although C does not exist. To write this latter, we must use the form A—⊂⊂B⊃⊂C⊃⊃ that is, A is not anything that is at once not B and not C. To write A—⊂B⊃⊂C⊃ would mean *more*; namely, that there are three things, A, B, C, of which either B or C is A. We shall see later that from this the former graph could be inferred.

§ 4. Remarks on the equivalence between existential graphs and familiar language

It is obvious that the above conventions require us to interpret ___ loves ___ as, "Somebody loves somebody", and -loves- / -benefits- as "Somebody loves somebody and somebody benefits somebody". On the other hand ⌠loves⌡/⌠benefits⌡ means that the same person both loves somebody and benefits somebody. So ⟨loves⟩ means, somebody loves himself.

The last graph but one might be read, "Somebody is loved by a benefactor of something coexistent with him". The last graph might be read, "Something is loved by something identical with it".

The last graph but one might also be read, "there are three things, A, B, and C, whether identical or not, such that A loves B and A benefits C".

The only difficulties of interpretation are connected with ovals. The following graph —⊂loves⊃— may be read, "There are a pair of things, A and B (which may be identical) such that taking any pair of things, X and Y, such that X loves Y, A and B are not identical respectively with X and Y; that is, either A is not X or B is not Y". In other words, there are a pair of things of which the one does not love the other.

The following graph ⊂loves⊃ means, there is something which is not identical with anything which loves something; that is, something loves nothing.

The following graph ⊟loves–/benefits–) means, there are two things, A and B (which may be identical), such that taking any four things X, Y, U, V such that X loves U and Y benefits V, A and B are not respectively identical with X and Y; that is, either A is not X or B is not Y. In other words, either something loves nothing or something benefits nothing.

The following graph ⊂loves–⊃/⊂benefits–⊃ means, something loves nothing and something benefits nothing.

The following graph ⊟loves⊃/benefits⊃ means, there are two things, A and B (which may be identical) such that taking any three things X, Y, Z, such that X loves Z and Y benefits Z, A and B are not respectively identical with X and Y. That is, there are two things, one of which loves nothing benefitted by the other.

The following graph ⊂⊂loves⊃/⊂benefits⊃⊃ means, something loves nothing that is not benefitted by it; or, in other words, something benefits whatever is loved by it.

The following graph (⊂loves⊃/⊂benefits⊃) means, anything whatever is unloved by something that benefits it, or everything is benefitted by something or other that does not love it.

The following graph  means something loves something not itself.

The following graph 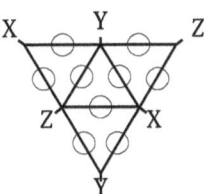 means, there are at least four individuals in the universe.

The following graph [triangle diagram with X, Y, Z, Z', X, Y labels] where, X, Y, Z, are (presumably) unknown individuals, means, there are at least six individuals in the universe.

The following graph –⊂loves⊃– (–benefits–⊂sins⊃) may be read, "Somebody loves somebody not coexistent with anybody who benefits anybody that does not sin"; i.e. somebody loves somebody and nobody benefits anybody but a sinner".

§ 5. Basic Formal Rules of Existential Graphs

The following are the formal properties which justify all legitimate illative transformations of graphs, without reference to the constitutive conventions, that is, without reference to the "meaning" of the graphs.

Rule I. Any graph, once written, may always be written.
Rule II. The entire graph may always be erased.

Rule III. Graphs that might be written separately may be written side by side.

Rule IV. Any detached unenclosed part of a graph may be transformed as if it stood alone.

Rule V. Any unenclosed heavy line may be broken.

Rule VI. No change in the shape of a heavy line is significant so long as it is joined to the same hands and so long as its least enclosed part remains in the same ovals and no others.

Rule VII. Every heavy line can be joined to some individual index, as soon as every less enclosed heavy line has been so joined; but the individual may not be known.

Rule VIII. Every index of an individual of the universe may be written unenclosed, with a heavy line, otherwise detached, attached to it.

Rule IX. Two individual indices joined by a heavy line unenclosed and uncrossed by any line, are everywhere mutually transformable.

Rule X. Mutually transformable indices may always be joined by a heavy line.

Rule XI. If from an unenclosed lightly drawn oval nothing protrudes but heavy lines joined to individual indices, then were the oval removed, in the resulting graph the former contents of the oval could be transformed into any graph whatever.

Rule XII. If a graph (not actually written) consists of two graphs P and Q, P being attached to Q, if at all, only by heavy lines each having attached to it, within Q, an individual index, and if, in this whole graph, P could be transformed into any graph at pleasure, while Q can be written alone, then the whole graph can be written with P enclosed in a lightly drawn oval.

Rule XIII. We can write $\ominus$.

§ 6. Elementary Rules of Illative Transformation deduced from the Basic Rules

I shall here use $\prec$ in the sense of "is transformable into".

Rule XIV. Every unenclosed partial graph, whether attached to the rest or not, can be erased.

For, by V, any attached unenclosed partial graph can be detached by severing the heavy lines attaching it to the rest. It is, therefore, only necessary to show that every unattached unenclosed partial graph can be erased. That is, if the whole graph consists of two partial graphs, P and Q, not attached to one another, it is to be shown that Q can be erased. For, by II, it could be erased if it stood alone. ∴ by IV, it can be erased when it is an unattached unenclosed part of P Q. Q.E.D.

Rule XV. If an unenclosed and detached partial graph, a, could in a certain graph, ac, be transformed into an oval containing only a certain graph, b, then if this graph, b, were substituted for the first named partial graph, a, in the whole graph, ac, it, b, could be transformed into an oval containing only that first named partial graph, a.

That is, if $ac \prec ⓑc$, then $bc \prec ⓐc$.

For suppose $ac \prec ⓑc$. Then since by XIV, $ⓑc \prec ⓑ$, it follows that $ac \prec ⓑ$. Hence, by XI, if ac and b were both scriptible every graph would be scriptible. But, by III, if a and c were both scriptible ac would be scriptible; so that if a, b, and c were all scriptible every graph would be scriptible. That is, if b and c were scriptible, then if in addition a were scriptible every graph would be scriptible. Hence, by XII if b and c are both scriptible ⓐ is scriptible. But, by XIV, if bc is scriptible b is scriptible, and so is c. Hence, $bc \prec ⓐ$. But, by XIV, $bc \prec c$. Now if ⓐ and c are both scriptible, so, by III, is ⓐc. ∴ $bc \prec ⓐc$. Q.E.D.

Rule XVI. If an oval with its contents, a, forming a detached and unenclosed part of a graph ⓐc is in that graph transformable into a graph, b, then were that oval with its contents replaced in the whole graph, ⓐc, by an oval containing only the other graph, b, in the whole graph ⓑc, that oval with its contents would be transformable into the contents a of the first named oval.

That is, if ⓐ$c \prec bc$, then ⓑ$c \prec ac$.

For suppose ⓐ$c \prec bc$. Then it is to be shown that ⓑ$c \prec ac$. Since by XIV, $bc \prec b$, it follows that ⓐ$c \prec b$. And since, by III, if ⓐ and c are both scriptible, ⓐc is scriptible, it follows that if ⓐ and c are both scriptible b is scriptible. That is, by XII, if a could be transformed into any graph at pleasure, and if c were scriptible, b would be so, also. Now if a is not scriptible there is no falsity in saying that if it were written it could be transformed into any graph. Hence, if a is not scriptible, while c is scriptible, b is scriptible; or, in other words, if c is scriptible, either a or b is scriptible, or again, if b is not scriptible while c is scriptible, so also is a. But, by XIV, if ⓑc is scriptible, c is scriptible. ∴ if ⓑc is scriptible and b is not scriptible, a is scriptible. But if ⓑc is scriptible and b is scriptible, since, by XIV, ⓑ is scriptible, and thus, by XI, b is transformable into any graph, including a, it again follows that a is scriptible. Thus, if ⓑc is scriptible, a is always scriptible, or ⓑ$c \prec a$. But by XIV ⓑ$c \prec c$. Hence if ⓑc is scriptible both a and c are scriptible and, be III, ac is scriptible, or ⓑ$c \prec ac$. Q.E.D.

Rule XVII. A heavy line connecting two ~~parts~~ hands of a graph is equivalent to two heavy lines having each one of its extremities attached to one of those hands while the other extremities are attached to iterations of the same vague individual index.

That is, ⓐ ≺ ⓕ and ⓕ ≺ ⓐ.

Let ⓐ be written. Then it is, in the first place, to be shown that ⓕ may be written. By VII, ⓐ ≺ [graph with x] where x is an index of a vague individual. Again by VII, [graph$_x$] ≺ [graph$_{xy}$] where y is an index of a vague individual By IX, x ≺ y and y ≺ x, so that x and y are equivalent and x may be substituted from y, giving [graph$_{xx}$]. By V, [graph$_{xx}$] ≺ [graph$_{xx}$]. By VI, this becomes ⓕ. Q.E.D.

Let ⓕ be written. Then it only remains to show that ⓐ can be written. By X, ⓕ ≺ [graph$_{xx}$]. By XIV, this gives ⓐ. Q.E.D.

Rule XVIII. It makes no difference as to transformations whether a heavy line with an individual index at the end of it protrudes from an oval or remains within it.

If other heavy lines protrude from the same oval, they can, by XVII, be cut off and terminated by individual indices. It is, therefore, only necessary to show that it makes no difference whether a heavy line terminated by an individual index protrudes from an oval or remains wholly within it, when nothing but lines terminated by indices protrude. That is, it is to be shown that B—(ᴬ/a)—x ≺ B—(ᴬ/a—x) and
C etc.   C etc.

B—(ᴬ/a—x) ≺ B—(ᴬ/a)—x.
C etc.   C etc.

First, suppose B—(ᴬ/a)—x is written. Then it is to be shown that B—(ᴬ/a—x) is scriptible.
C etc.   C etc.

For, by XI, in B—a—x, a could be transformed into anything. After such transforma-
C etc.

tion, by XIV, x and its connecting line can be erased. Hence, in B—a—x, a—x can be
C etc.

transformed into anything. ∴ by XII, putting a—x for P and B—| for Q, we can write
C

B—(ᴬ/a—x). Q.E.D.
C etc.

Second, assume B—(ᴬ/a—x). Then B—(ᴬ/a)—x. For by XII in B—a—x, a—x can be trans-
C etc.   C etc.   C etc.
formed into anything. Hence, a in the same graph, can be transformed into any-
thing. For any transformation of a is a transformation of a—x. Hence by XII B—(ᴬ/a)—x.
C etc.
Q.E.D.

Rule XIX. Two ovals, one enclosing nothing but the other and its contents (unless it be parts of heavy lines but not the whole of any), are without effect.

That is, if a written graph consists of two partial graphs a and b joined by any number (or no) heavy lines, ⬭, then we may write ⬭; and second if a written graph has the latter form, the former may be written.

For, first, by I, (x–b) ⊰ (x–b) ∴ by XV x–b ⊰ (x–b) and by IV b–x ⊰ b–x (x–b). But by XVII ⬭ ⊰ b–x x–b etc. And by XVIII b–x (x–b) is equivalent to b–x (x–b) and to b–x x–b. And by XVII, the latter is transformable into ⬭. Hence ⬭ ⊰ ⬭. Q.E.D.

Second, by I, b–x (x–b) ⊰ b–x (x–b) ∴ by XVI b–x (x–b) ⊰ b–x x–b

∴ as above ⬭ ⊰ ⬭. Q.E.D.

Rule XX. If an unenclosed part of a graph would be transformable into another graph, then were the formed replaced by an oval containing the latter this would be transformable into an oval containing the former.

That is, if $ac \prec bc$, then $ⓑc \prec ⓐc$.

For by XIX, $b \prec ⓒ$ so that by IV if $ac \prec bc$, then $ac \prec ⓑc$ whence by XV $ⓑc \prec ⓐc$. Q.E.D.

Rule XXI. If an oval containing one graph and forming an unenclosed part of a graph is transformable into an oval containing another graph, then the last graph being substituted in the second for the oval is transformable into the first.

That is, if $ⓐc \prec ⓑc$, then $bc \prec ac$.

For assume $ⓐc \prec ⓑc$, then by XX $ⓑc \prec ⓐc$. But by XIX $b \prec ⓑ$ and $ⓐ \prec a$, so that $bc \prec ac$. Q.E.D.

Rule XXII. (*Rule of Contraposition.*) If a graph standing alone or a detached and unenclosed part of a graph can be transformed into another, the same transformation can be made wherever (the unchanged part of the graph remaining unenclosed) the former is detached and evenly enclosed (i.e. is within an even number of ovals) while the reverse transformation can be made wherever (the unchanged part of the graph remaining unenclosed) the latter is detached and oddly enclosed.

That is, assuming $ac \prec bc$. Then in every graph where c is unenclosed while a is under $2N$ enclosures, a can be transformed into b, while in every graph where c is unenclosed and b is under $2N+1$ enclosures, b can be transformed into a, whatever finite whole number N may be.

For suppose this were proved so long as N does not exceed a given whole number L. Then, by XX, the same thing would be true so long as N does not exceed $L+1$. But by IV and XX it is true for $N = 0$. Hence it is true whatever whole number N may be.

Rule XXIII. (*Rule of Erasure and Insertion.*) Any part of a graph under even enclosures can be erased; while under odd enclosures any insertion can be made.

Suppose this were proved true for every number of ovals not exceeding a certain number m. Then I say it would be true for $m + 1$ ovals. For in any graph containing $m + 1$ ovals one in another, let a be the part unenclosed and, b the part in one oval only; and let b be any graph from which b would be derivable by this rule. These may be joined by any number of heavy lines. These may all be cut, the ends of section attached to vague indices, and the protruding parts retracted into the oval. Then since $b' \prec b$ by the present rule, it follows that $\text{Y}\!-\!b'^{\text{X}}_{\text{etc.}} \prec \text{Y}\!-\!b^{\text{X}}_{\text{etc.}}$ by this rule. Hence by XX $\widehat{a\!-\!b}_{\text{etc}} \prec \widehat{a\!-\!b'}_{\text{etc}}$. But this is according to the rule, and covers every case of the rule for $m + 1$ ovals. It is thus shown that if the rule is true up to any number of ovals, it is true for a greater number. But by XIV it is true for *zero* ovals. Hence it is true for any number without limit.

Rule XXIV. (*Rule of Iteration and Concision.*) Any partial graph outside any succession of ovals may be iterated within those ovals, provided that the corresponding hands in the iteration are attached to the very same heavy lines as before the iteration; and if any partial graph is so iterated, the inner occurrence may be "concised", or struck out.

1. The rule holds for *iterations*, when iterand and iterate are both unenclosed. That is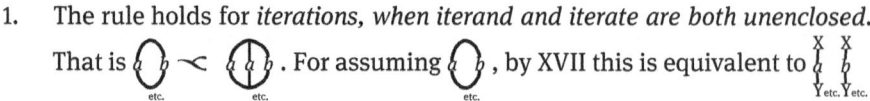

whence, by XIV $\genfrac{}{}{0pt}{}{X}{Y_{etc.}}$ can be written, and by III, $\genfrac{}{}{0pt}{}{X\ X\ X}{Y_{etc.}Y_{etc.}Y_{etc.}}$ can be written. But this, by XVII is equivalent to ⟨graph⟩ which can therefore be written. Q.E.D.

2. The rule holds for *iterations, when the iterand is unenclosed, and the iterate is evenly enclosed*. This follows by XVII and XXII.
3. The rule holds for *iterations when iterand and iterate are evenly enclosed*. This follows from the last and XII.
4. The rule holds for *iterations when the iterate is oddly enclosed*, by XXIII.
5. The rule holds for *concisions when the iterand is in no oval and the iterate is in one*. That is, ⟨graph⟩ ≺ ⟨graph⟩. This follows from the first case, XVII and XX i.e. because ⟨graph⟩ ≺ ⟨graph⟩ it follows that ⟨graph⟩ ≺ ⟨graph⟩.
6. The rule holds for *concisions when the iterand is in no oval and then iterate is in any odd number* (greater than one). By XVII and XXII.
7. The rule holds for *concisions when the iterand is in evenly enclosed and the iterate is oddly enclosed*. Follows from the last and XXII.
8. The rule holds for *concisions when the iterate is evenly enclosed*, by XXIII.
9. The rule holds for *iterations when the iterand is in one oval and the iterate in two*. Namely from the fifth case, by XXII, we have ⟨graph⟩ ≺ ⟨graph⟩.
10. The rule holds for *iterations when the iterand is in one oval and the iterate in any even number*. By the last case, XVII, and XXII.
11. The rule holds for *iterations where the iterand is oddly enclosed and the iterate evenly enclosed*. By the last case, XVII and XXII.
12. The rule holds for *concisions when iterand and iterate are oddly enclosed*. By the third case and XXII.

Hence, in all cases the rule holds.

Rule XXV. (*Rule of Protraction and Retraction.*) An evenly enclosed heavy line (i.e. so enclosed as to its outermost part) may be retracted into an even number of ovals while an oddly enclosed heavy line may be protracted out from any number of ovals.

1. This holds of unenclosed heavy lines. For by VII an individual index may be attached to any such line; and thereupon by XVIII it can be retracted into any even number of enclosures, and finally by XXIII the index can be erased.
2. If the rule, so far as it relates to retractions and protractions through even number of ovals, holds good so long as the retrahend or protrahend is not

enclosed in more than N oval, then it holds good so long as it is not enclosed in more than $N + 1$ ovals.

For any graph of the latter kind consists of a unenclosed partial graph, p joined by heavy lines to a partial graph q inside an oval. And if, according to the rule (so far as it concerns retractions and protractions through even numbers of ovals), q is transformable into r, then according to the same part of the rule r, were it unenclosed would be transformable into q. But by XVII every unenclosed heavy line can be broken and an individual index can be attached to the broken ends, and by XVIII the heavy lines protruding from the outer oval can be retracted within it. Then, because r unenclosed would be transformable into q, it follows by XXII, that in the whole graph as just modified, q may be transformed into r. And that having been done, the former bonds can by X be reestablished, and by XXIV and XXIII the individual indices can be removed. But the effect of this is to perform the transformation which the part of the rule considered.

Hence, it follows that since that part of the rule, by the first case, holds when $N = 0$ it holds in all cases.

3. Any oddly enclosed line may be protracted through any odd number of ovals. For by XXIII any individual index may be attached to such a line. Then, by XVIII, that line with the index may be protracted through any odd number of ovals, and finally, by XXIII, the index may be erased.

Rule XXVI. Under even enclosures any two pairs of ovals, each consisting of one oval in another, but not usually the sole contents of that other, may be *fused*, by breaking all the ovals and uniting the two inner into one and the two outer into one; and under odd enclosures the reverse operation of *segmentation* may be performed.

For, first, the fusion under even enclosures may be performed as follows: The one pair of ovals, with their contents, may, by XXIV, be iterated within the other pair. Then, the otherwise unenclosed contents of the outer oval of the iterated pair may by XXIII be iterated outside of two ovals (i.e. outside the inner oval of the outer pair). Then, the innermost occurrence may, by XXIV, be concised, and the two inner ovals, by XIX, may be removed. The effect is the same as that of the fusion.

Second, the segmentation under odd enclosures may be performed as follows. For, all the unenclosed heavy lines of a graph may be broken and attached to individual indices, and the ends then protruding from the outer oval retracted within it. And then by XXII that transformation can be effected which is the reverse of any which could be made upon the graph it leaves within the oval were the oval removed. And thereupon the heavy line with indices can be protracted and joined to those with corresponding indices and the indices can be erased.

Rule XXVII. A graph consisting of an oval enclosing first any graph, no matter what, and second another oval containing an iteration of the same graph (with corresponding hands joined) can everywhere be written or erased, and with the heavy lines attached to any individual indices.

For if a graph is not scriptible, there is no falsity in saying that it might be transformed into any graph. But in this case, by XII, the graph can be written surrounded by an oval. If a graph is scriptible, by XIX, it can be written within two ovals, and by XXIII, it can be iterated in the outer and outside the inner oval. But if an oval containing the graph is scriptible, by XXIII, it can be iterated in another oval written in that same oval. And by XXIII, any indices can be attached to the different heavy lines, which are all singly enclosed, and by XVIII those heavy lines with the indices can be protracted.

This shows the "dilemmatic conjugation", as I call the whole, for example, can be written unenclosed with any or no indices attached. Whence by XXII it can be written anywhere evenly enclosed or erased when oddly enclosed. But by XXIII it can anywhere be written in odd enclosures or erased in even enclosures. Hence it can anywhere be written or erased.

Rule XXVIII. If an unenclosed oval contains only a graph and another oval containing another graph, whatever heavy lines may join the two, these lines not extending out of the outer oval, then the first graph may be transformed into the second anywhere within even enclosures, those attachments being preserved which join the two graphs in the oval, while all the rest are cut; and within odd enclosures the reverse transformation can be performed.

If the transformand is unenclosed, the transformation can be effected thus:

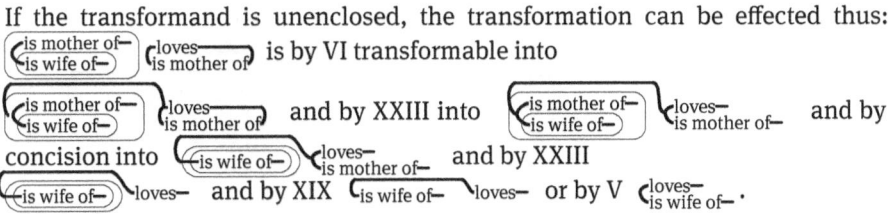

If the transformand is singly enclosed, the transformation can be effected

thus: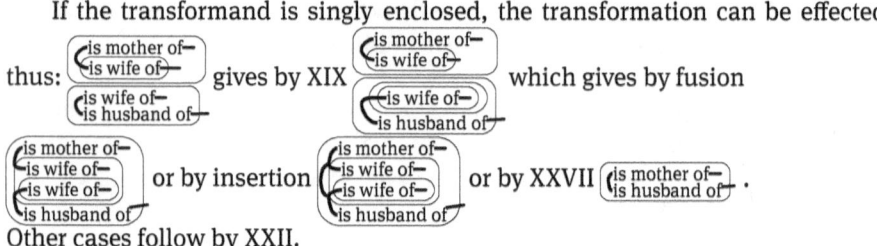
Other cases follow by XXII.

§ 7. Analysis of the Syllogism
August 2, 1898.

Rule XXVIII is the rule of the syllogism. In order to disclose the analysis of the syllogism to which the system of existential graphs necessarily leads, it is desirable to prove that rule directly from the Basic Rules.

Suppose we have given the graph (1) ⟨is mother of—⟨is wife of—⟩⟩ ⟨is mother of⟩loves——

By II and IV	(2) ⟨is mother of⟩loves—— is scriptible.	
By V	(3) ⟨is mother of— loves—— is scriptible.	
By VII	(4) x—⟨is mother of— loves—	
and then	(5) x—⟨is mother of— y—⟨loves— are scriptible.	
By IX	(6) x—⟨is mother of— x—⟨loves— is scriptible.	
By V	(7) x—is mother of— x—loves— is scriptible.	
By II and IV	(8) x—is mother of— is scriptible.	
From (1) by XI	(9) ⟨is mother of—⟨is wife of—⟩ is transformable into any graph.	
By III	(10) if x—is mother of— is scriptible and x—⟨is wife of—⟩ is scriptible, so is x—is mother of— x—⟨is wife of—⟩.	
∴ from (8),	(11) if x—⟨is wife of—⟩ is scriptible, so is x—is mother of— x—⟨is wife of—⟩.	
∴ by X,	(12) if x—⟨is wife of—⟩ is scriptible, so is x—⟨is mother of— x—⟨is wife of—⟩.	
∴ by V,	(13) if x—⟨is wife of—⟩ is scriptible, so is x—⟨is mother of— x—⟨is wife of—⟩.	
∴ by II and IV,	(14) if x—⟨is wife of—⟩ is scriptible, so is x—⟨is mother of— is wife of—⟩.	
∴ by V,	(15) if x—⟨is wife of—⟩ is scriptible, so is x— ⟨is mother of— is wife of—⟩.	
∴ by II and IV,	(16) if x—⟨is wife of—⟩ is scriptible, so is ⟨is mother of— is wife of—⟩.	
∴ by (9),	(17) if x—⟨is wife of—⟩ is scriptible, so is every graph, including x—is wife of—.	
But by XII,	(18) if x—is wife of— could be transformed into any graph at pleasure, x—⟨is wife of—⟩ would be scriptible.	

But if x—is wife of— were not scriptible there would be no falsity in calling it transformable into every graph.

∴   (19) if x—(is wife of—) is not scriptible x—is wife of—
                                        is scriptible.
∴ by (17) and (19),   (20) x—is wife of—   is scriptible.
From (7) by II and IV   (21) x—loves—   is scriptible.
From (20) and (21), by II (22) x—loves—
                                   x—is the wife of—   is scriptible.
∴ by X,   (23) xI loves—
                                   x—is the wife of—   is scriptible.
∴ by V,   (24) x—loves—
                                   x—⊏is the wife of—   is scriptible.
∴ by II and IV,   (25)   ⊏loves—
                                   is the wife of—   is scriptible.

This syllogism in Darii is thus analyzed into a long series of inferential steps. Of these inferences 7 depend on each of II and IV, 6 on V, two on each of III, VII, X, 1 on each of IX, XI, XII. Rules I, VI, VIII, XIII are not explicitly involved. Rule XIII is certainly not involved; but then this is of a different character from the other basic rules, and probably is only one of a number of logical propositions not included among those rules. VIII is a derived rule. For either an oval with some contents is scriptible or not. If not, then if an individual index occurs at all, it occurs attached to an unenclosed heavy line. By V this line may be broken; and by II and IV the individual index can be written unenclosed and attached only to that line. But if an oval can be written, by XI it follows that if the contents of the oval were scriptible anything would be scriptible. Hence, if the contents of the oval were scriptible, as well as an individual index joined to an otherwise free heavy line, then anything would be scriptible. But if a graph consisting of the contents of the oval together with such index so attached were scriptible, so by II and IV, would be each of those parts. Hence, by XII, the contents of the oval may be written in an oval with the individual index attached to an otherwise free heavy line written outside that oval. Now by II and IV the oval and its contents may be erased, leaving the individual index so written.

As to I and VI, they describe the manner or drawing the graphs; but they are not properly basic rules of transformation, any more than saying that if a graph can be written in pencil it can be written in ink, or if a graph can be written when the sheet lies flat it can be written when the sheet is vertical. It is of the nature of a diagram, as an icon, to have innumerable perfectly insignificant characters.

As for rules II and IV, they are only needed together, and should be made one. There are thus only *eight* basic rules; viz.:—II and IV, V, III, VII, X, IX, XI, XII. Moreover, II and IV together with V may be embraced in one generalized rule, making only seven Basic Rules.

12 Peripatetic Talks

R 502–505, R 489; August 1898. Houghton Library. Four pieces of the mysterious "Peripatetic Talks" series have survived: talks number 2, 4, 6 and 7, and a likely addition (R 489) that develops upon the fourth talk and is presented in the appendix. There is no information that Peirce delivered or was even planning to deliver what he here decided to call 'talks'; the Aristotelian term suggests an authorship forced to an isolation and without right to permanent residence or property in which to conduct work with students of logic.

The "Peripatetic Talks" focus on the semantics and on the interpretation of EGs. The question is how EGs can effectively be used to analyse meanings. **Talk 2 (R 502)** outlines Peirce's philosophy of logic and categories in general; the logically fundamental task of recognition is elucidated through the three categories and an analysis of habit. **Talk 4 (R 503)**, together with **R 489** appended to this chapter presents an abundance of natural-language examples and analyses of meanings of propositions according to both the natural and the diagrammatic syntax. **Talk 6 (R 504)** addresses a "grave defect" in the system of quantified (Beta) graphs and in algebraic systems. In modern terms, this relates to the problem of cumulative quantification, or quantification over ternary relations. Peirce's "makeshift" contrivance is to resort to an altogether different type of rhema "___ is a character possessed by the individual___ ", which he would need in order to track the unexpected invariant property involved in such cumulative readings. But using that rhema would at once introduce complications resulting from unrestricted higher-order notions that would take the analysis out of the tidy first-order domain, and Peirce indeed is seen not to be entirely content with his proposed patchwork. Nonetheless, the mere fact that the investigation of language had led him to prefigure not only the necessity of introducing some such generalised types of quantifiers but also that a graphical analysis of complex forms of assertions calls for non-standard types of quantification that refer to the "world of ideas" in addition to the "world of existence", is surely a remarkable achievement on its own. **Talk 7 (R 505)** may be the first instance in which Peirce proposes a language of "graph of graphs", namely a meta-logical representation of fundamental illative transformations. In the 1903 Lowell Lectures he would develop further such language of graphs which can be used to talk about or represent properties of logical graphs. In anticipation of better opportunities to lecture on these topics to students of logic, three properties of illative transformations are represented in such a manner: the transitivity of the relation of illation, its inductive or Euclidean property, and its hypothetical character.

Peripatetic Talks. No. 2[1]

[R 502] Exact logic is restricted to assertions about which there can be no dispute. That condition forces us to proceed slowly, cautiously, and sometimes circuitously. It is one reason why we should put the mathematical part first. You must not complain if what is said seems mere truism. It will be found that by piling truism upon truism we arrive at last at deeply interesting and important results.

Logic supposes that some opinions or thoughts are unsatisfactory and liable to require replacement. They will not stand, while others if not perfectly satisfactory are, at least, relatively so. General experience shows us that. Error is but too well known to us, while some truths, such as that I hold converse with other minds, and that all bodies are perpetually accelerated toward the earth (after allowance is made for other component accelerations), we have never been tempted to suspect. At any rate, in the mathematical part of logic (which passes by the inquiry into the truth of facts and confines itself to the business of tracing their connections) we certainly must assume that this is so; for if it be not so, there can be no such science as logic.

In the next place, it is supposed that there is some general formal rule by which erroneous opinions,—or some class of erroneous opinions,—may be avoided. For that is what logic is. Of course, the truth of this assumption must be carefully examined at the proper time. But in the mathematical part of logic, which does not concern itself with any such examination, it may certainly be

---

1 [Alt.:] Peripatetic Talks. No. 2. We observe in experience three categories of elements,

I. *Feeling-qualities*, which are each *sui generis*, without individual identity (but only more or less likeness to one another), in themselves absolutely simple. I call this the element of Firstness.

II. *Will-reactions*, each of which is between two factors, is a blind exertion of force, is absolutely here and now. I call this the element of *Secondness*.

III. *Habit-representations*, each of which involves three subjects, the representation or sign, its object, its interpreting sign. There is an element of compulsion but it is conditional and permanent. Each instance is essentially one of a class of analogous instances. The sign *brings about* a dyadic relation between the object and the interpreter. It is a *medium* between them. I call this function of mediation, *Thirdness*.

I do not undertake to define these ideas accurately and to show their ramifications here. The statement of it would fill nearly a hundred of these pages, would be dry, difficult, not everywhere entirely satisfactory, and quite unnecessary for our purpose. Suffice it to say, that the Firstness, Secondness, and Thirdness are found in various propositions in a great variety of philosophical conceptions.

[Alt.2:] We observe in experience three categories of elements:

First, *Feeling-qualities*, each of which is *sui generis*, and is all that it is as soon as there is an idea of it or possibility of it. It is what it is in itself without reference to anything else. It is absolutely simple. It has no individual identity but is other than another feeling quality so far as it is different from it. I call its character *Firstness*, or *Monadism*.

Second, *Will-reactions*, each of which subsists between two subjects, and is absolutely here and now. It is a blind exertion of force, without reason, root, or generality. It cannot exist without being opposed: the opposition to it is its life. It is seen equally in will and in sense-impression. We also see similar dyadic relations between pairs both of whose members are outside not only our consciousness but even our sympathy. Thus we see solid bodies in states of stress. I call all this *Secondness*, or *Dyadism*. It is the character of a pair of subjects.

Third, *Habit-representations*, each of which involves three subjects, the sign, the object, and the sign which interprets the former sign. There are some cases in which there is no sign which come under this category. Thus, A causes B to exert a force upon C. But either there is in such a case a representation in a generalized sense; or else [end]

assumed true; since if it is not so there is no such science as logic. For logic supposes, not only that there is error, but also that error is in a measure avoidable, and further that there is some general rule or method by which it can be avoided. If this is the case, it must be some knowledge, or satisfactory state of thought, which enables us to avoid the error. But if that is so, one opinion must produce or tend to produce another opinion. And if there is anything at all that experience overwhelmingly forces us to admit, it is that in fact one opinion does produce another opinion. The former is a *premise*, the latter a *conclusion*. The process, provided it is deliberate, is called *inference*.

It is evident that an error must be capable of being corrected. This does not rest upon experience merely, but upon the nature of error. For if there were nothing to correct an opinion and lead us to change it, it would continue to satisfy us forever and it could not be pronounced to be unsatisfactory. True, one individual's opinion might not satisfy another individual, that is, it would not satisfy him to adopt it as his own. But there is no reason why he should not be perfectly satisfied to have the other adopt it, unless the opinions of one man are to influence those of another. But if they do this, then two individuals could not both be entirely and definitely satisfied each with their own opinion unless those two opinions agreed. Error then *means* an opinion which is liable to be changed, an ill-established opinion.

Now if an opinion is changed, it is either changed in some unaccountable way, for which we cannot be responsible and concerning which there can be not art, or else it is changed by something of which we are conscious, that is by some thought, or reflection, which will be itself satisfactory or unsatisfactory,—that is will be an opinion. Thus, we come again to the result that if there is any such art as logic, one opinion must influence another.

Now, what does it mean to say that one idea produces another? It certainly means something more than that the latter idea follows after the former in time. It means that there is some habit, congenital or acquired, by virtue of which an idea sufficiently like the former would usually be succeeded by an idea analogous to the latter. To say that one idea *deliberately* produces another is to say that that habit is a conscious one and is accepted as a satisfactory habit. In other words, the habit is a belief, which is true or false, satisfactory or unsatisfactory.

A state of mind which he who has it should dignify by the name of a belief and yet would not allow it in any case to influence his conduct is an idle thing without importance. For what can importance mean except an influence upon human conduct, bodily or mental? What I call a belief is a habit has the following essential characters, first, it determines (in conjunction with desires) how its subject will act under some conceivable circumstances, second, it is accompanied with a feeling by which it is recognized by its subject, third, it is accepted by its subject as satisfactory, so that he does not struggle to escape from its influence. Any state of mind which has these characteristics, I term a *belief*, no matter how trivial may be the object of it.

A belief influences human conduct and influences it deliberately. That is, it is recognized that upon a certain description of occasion we should perform a certain description of action (supposing we had a given desire). The description of occasion would have to be recognized as such. Let us see what the elements of this recognition are. First, we find borne in upon us the special *now*, or *this*. Secondly, we have a familiar mode of thought, or idea, making a description of occasion. Thirdly, a habit, or some law influencing our thought, compulsive to attach that idea, or description of occasion, to the special now or this. This recognition of the occasion as being of the given general description is therefore itself a belief. For it in the first place is a state of mind influencing conduct in so far as it leads us to act upon this occasion in whatever way we may have the habit of acting in the general description of occasion. In the second place, it is recognized by its subject, for it is itself a recognition; and a recognition must itself be recognized. Third it must be accepted by its subject as satisfactory. In the next place, the action which the belief leads us to perform it leads us to perform deliberately. It is not an automatic reaction, but must be recognized for what it is. This recognition is again for the reasons just given a belief. Finally the recognition that upon the given description of occasion we should perform such a description of action is a third belief. Thus, every belief is a belief that one belief will produce another.

Peripatetic Talks. No. 4

[R 503] I have invented a system of diagrams called logical graphs. This system has two varieties. One is sketched in *The Monist* 1897.[2] I call that *Entitative Graphs*. The other I have set forth. I call it *Existential Graphs*.

Existential Graphs are based on five fundamental grammatical rules. I say grammatical because the system is a language.

Grammatical Rules

I. The sheet of paper used is understood to relate to a universe or body of experiences, common to the writer and reader; and anything significant written upon this sheet without being enclosed in an oval is asserted of that universe, or, so far as it is indefinite, of some suitably chosen individual of that universe, so as to make the clause of the proposition show as true.

---

2 [The year left blank and afterwards added by pencil.]

II. Two propositions written side by side are both asserted.
III. A continuous heavy line joining two Indices of individuals, or blanks for such indices, asserts the identity of those individuals.

Fig. 1

IV. If a proposition, A, is enclosed in an oval which encloses nothing else except an oval enclosing a second proposition, B, as in Fig. 1, the meaning is that if A be true, B is true. And an individual not definitely specified is to be selected so as to give A the meaning which it would have if it were asserted.
V. An ○ asserts that that which is false is true.

Consequences of the above Rules

1. What does a blank space, considered as a proposition, assert? There is a blank space beside any proposition which may be written, so that by Rule II, it is asserted, as well as the proposition. But by hypothesis nothing but the proposition is asserted. Hence, the blank can mean that which is implied in every proposition, namely, that everything written on the sheet is true of the universe of discourse to which it is understood to relate.

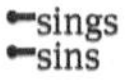

━sings
━sins

Fig. 2

2. Fig. 2 asserts (in a universe of human beings) that somebody sings and somebody sins, or, what is the same thing, "some singer is coexistent with a sinner", in the sense in which a thing coexists with itself.

- A *verb* is a sign which requires only to have a certain blank or blank filled each by an Index of an individual to become a complete assertion. I give verbs certain names according to the number of such blanks requiring to be filled. Namely,
  - A *medad* is a verb having no blank, as "it thunders".
  - A *monad* is a verb having one blank, as "___ dies", "___ is a man".
  - A *dyad* is a verb having two blanks, as "___ loves ___".

- A *triad* is a verb having three blanks, as "___ praises ___ to ___".
- A *polyad* is a verb having more than two blanks.

Fig. 2 does not show what fills the blanks. Only the writing down on the sheet shows that it is asserted that it is something in the universe of discourse. Fig. 3 asserts more, namely, the identity of an individual who sings with one who sins. It means "some singer sins".

Fig. 3   Fig. 4   Fig. 5   Fig. 6

Fig. 4 asserts that if somebody sings then somebody sins (whether singer or listener is not stated). In other words, "Every singer there may be is coexistent with a sinner", where we use the word "coëxistent" in such a sense that everything "coëxists" with itself. Fig. 5 differs from Fig. 4 just as Fig. 3 from Fig. 2.

That is, it means "If somebody signs then *that person* sins", that is "every singer there may be is a sinner". Now compare Fig. 3 with Fig. 6, which is the same as Fig. 2 with one of the assertions erased.

Fig. 6 means then "something sins". That is, while Fig. 3 means "something that sings sins", so Fig. 6 means "something that exists sins". The blank asserts mere existence in the universe, as we saw in the first consequence. Now let us form a graph related to Fig. 6 as Fig. 5 is related to Fig. 3. It is Fig. 7. Then, by Rule IV, and the example of Fig. 5, this must mean "whatever exists (in the universe of human beings) sins".

Fig. 7   Fig. 8   Fig. 9   Fig. 10

If we draw a graph related to Fig. 6 as Fig. 4 is related to Fig. 2, it will be Fig. 8, which will mean "if somebody exists somebody sins", or in other words, "somebody sins". So, Fig. 7 means "everybody sins", while Fig. 8 means "somebody sins", being equivalent to Fig. 6. The two ovals neutralize one another. So then, Fig. 9 will mean, "If anybody sings, everybody sins".[3]

In studying the simple and perfectly regular grammar of graphs, we incidentally are led to reflect upon the grammar of our mother tongue. We do not, in English, express Fig. 4 by saying "If somebody sings, somebody sins", but by "If anybody sings, somebody sins". The rationale of this is that the words *some* and *any* conceive an individual to be selected. *Some* means that a suitable individual is to be chosen by the speaker, or person interested in sustaining the truth of the proposition; while *any* means that the choice of the individual may be left to the listener, or to a person who might be hostile or sceptical to the proposition. Now when we say "if anybody", we carelessly at first (but now by established usage) transpose the words. We mean "Take anybody and if he" for "Take anybody and if he sings, somebody sins", has the same meaning as *ought* in strict regularity to be meant by "If somebody sings, somebody sins", that is, "If I can find a man who sings, I can find a man who sins", For that is the same as "You can select a man; and if that man sings, then I can find a man who sins". But according to the usage of our language, in transposing the *if* and putting it before the *selective* pronoun, though the selection is understood as made at the outset,—according to this usage by "If somebody signs, somebody sins", we mean, "I can find you such a man that if *he* sings, then somebody sins". This proposition is expressed by Fig. 10.

---

3 [Alt.:] Special Consequences of the Basic Rules. [– – –] Fig. 11 according to Rule 4 means "If anybody sings, somebody sins":

Fig. 11

(It is a vicious and illogical usage of our mother-tongue that "anybody" is here used. We ought, were the usage of speech accurately [be] logical to say "If somebody sings, somebody sins", or else "Take anybody and if he sings, somebody sins". These two are equivalent because in order to find an instance that falsifies the proposition, it is necessary it should make the antecedent clause true as the first step to such falsification. ["as the first step to such falsification" added in pencil in P.H.] Now "somebody" implies the suitable selection of an instance by a person favorable to the truth of the clause; while "anybody" implies that an opponent of the truth of the proposition may be allowed to dictate the selection of the instance. Our phrase "if anybody" transposes the two words. "If somebody sings" would be understood as implying that some particular person had this idiosyncrasy that if he sings, it causes somebody to sin (whether by profane objurgations or otherwise). But this would really be equivalent to saying "If all men sing, then some man sins". This illustrates the vices of ordinary language in regard to relations.)

That is the same as to say that "If everybody sings, somebody sins", or "If all men sing, some man sins". This is not obvious; but I can prove that it is so. Two propositions are *logically equivalent* if either being true, the other cannot be false. Now the boast "I can find you a man such that if *he* sings, somebody sins", is very easily fulfilled unless every man sings. Namely, I simply select a man who *does not sing*; and then it makes no difference whether anybody sins or not. If, however, every man sings, then it makes no difference who I select; my promise will be made good if somebody sins, otherwise not. So my boast is true if, and only if, either some man does not sing or some man sins. But that is precisely what is meant by saying "If all men sing, some man sins". The doctrine of graphs will render all such puzzles perfectly clear. I may remark that it is also just the same thing to say, "Somebody, if he sings, sins", as to say "If all men sing, somebody sins". It is certainly a useful thing to have a key to such problems. Yet this is the most insignificant of the utilities of graphs.

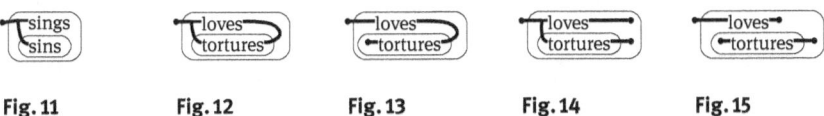

Fig. 11 **Fig. 12** **Fig. 13** **Fig. 14** **Fig. 15**

It may be remarked that while Fig. 11 is equivalent to Fig. 10, yet Figs. 12 and 13 are not equivalent. For Fig. 13 means, there is a man such that if any person is loved by him that person is tortured by somebody, while Fig. 12 means, there is a man such that if any person is loved by him that person is tortured by him. In other words, the one asserts that there is a person who loves (if anybody) only tortured persons, while the other asserts that there is a person who loves (if at all) only persons whom he himself tortures. But Figs. 14 and 15 are equivalent. We thus easily divine that the truth is that *the inmost effective bond between two verbs must be within an odd or even number of ovals to agree with the verbs themselves*. In applying this rule, we must regard the verbs bound together to be, not "loves" and "tortures", but "loves" and tortures . And the bond is enclosed only by such ovals as contain the entire line, in all its branches. In Fig. 14, the verbs are "oddly enclosed", that is, are within the odd number, 1, of ovals, while the only bond is "evenly enclosed", that is, is within the even number, 0, of ovals. Hence, it is not effective, that is, is altogether without effect. But in Fig. 12 this bond is not the *inmost* bond between the verbs. The inmost bond is oddly enclosed, like the verbs themselves. Hence, there is nothing to prevent the bond from being effective and it is so.

3. We have seen that two ovals, one immediately outside the other, annul one another. The question is, then, what can be the meaning *of* an oval enclosing a proposition of known meaning? What, for example, can be the meaning of Fig. 16? The "it thunders" has a blank place beside it. Enclose this in two ovals, which will

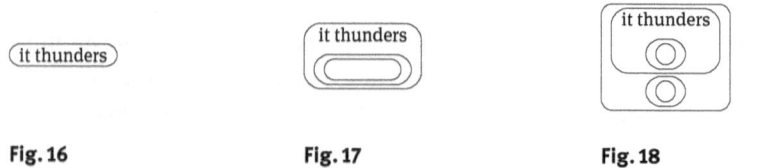

Fig. 16 **Fig. 17** **Fig. 18**

not alter its meaning, and we see that Fig. 16 is equivalent to Fig. 17. But, by Rule IV, this means "if it thunders O is true". The whole question is, then, what can this consequent, O, mean in order that Figs. 18 and 19 may be equivalent?

To say that two propositions P and Q are logically equivalent is the same as to say that if P is true Q is true and if Q is true P is true. Now no matter what consequent X may be, it is always true that if any proposition T is true, it is also true that if it be true that X follows necessarily if T is true then X is true. For example, let T be "you murder", and X "you sin". If it be true that you murder then it follows that it is true that if murder is a sin, then you sin. But the converse is not true for every consequent. That is, it is not generally true, that because if murder is a sin then you sin, that you murder. You may have done something which on the principle that murder is a sin must be accounted a sin. But it need not be murder. For example, if murder is a sin, manslaughter must be a sin, though a lesser sin than murder. The question is then what is the nature of [end]

Peripatetic Talks. No. 6

[R 504] The principle of Existential Graphs may be stated thus:

Whatever verbs A and B may be, ⟨A⟨B⟩⟩ asserts that of every individual object of the universe of discourse of which A is true (if there be any such object) B is true. The heavy line (or the outermost part of it) denotes the individual spoken of, and the continuity of this line signifies its identity; and if there are several separate heavy lines each denotes an individual. The writing of the proposition down asserts it; and if several are written down all are asserted. A lightly drawn oval with its contents is a proposition; and any proposition oddly enclosed is not asserted but only posited as a condition under with some proposition in the same enclosures and one besides is asserted.

This statement [is] useful as showing precisely what the fundamental assumptions of the system are. But in order to comprehend a given graph another form of statement is preferable as follows:

1. Every oval with its contents is a verb.
2. Every place of attachment of a heavy line to a verb is a subject blank of the verb.
3. Every heavy line is the verb "___ is identical with___" or "___ and ___ are identical with ___" etc. according to the number of branches.
4. The outermost point of every heavy line not attached to a designate individual index is to be considered as denoting *some* suitably chosen individual object of the universe of discourse.
5. Every unenclosed proposition is asserted.
6. Every oval with its contents is the precise denial of the proposition it contains interpreted as if it were unenclosed.

For example, read this in a universe of sentient beings [P.H. on the right]:

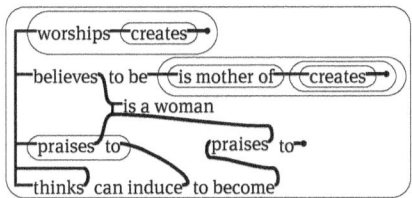 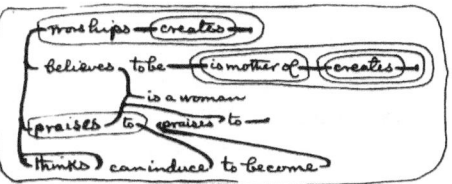

> Every being unless he worships some being who does not create all beings either does not believe any being (unless it be not a woman) to be any mother of a creator of all beings or else he praises that woman to every being unless to a person whom he does not think he can induce to become anything unless it be a non-praiser of that woman to every being.

> That is, every worshipper only of creators of all beings, who believes a woman to be a mother of every creator of all beings praises that woman to every being whom he thinks he can induce to praise that woman to any being.

It will be noticed that the denial of the assertion of two propositions is the assertion either of the denial of one or of the other. On this fact may be based a very practical rule of interpretation of graphs.

1. Make a list of all the lines always naming outer ones before inner ones. Assign an individual index to each, with "*something*" as showing the rule of selection for lines evenly enclosed and "*anything*" for those oddly enclosed.

2. Verbs evenly enclosed are taken *affirmatively*; those oddly enclosed negatively.
3. Verbs under the same enclosure if evenly enclosed are connected by *and*, if oddly enclosed by *or*.
4. The groupings of the enclosures are to be regarded.

To a person trained in logic, it seems inconceivable and inexcusable that a person should commit a fallacy of the kind call "logical". But it is a fact that it is far from unusual to meet with a confusion equivalent to that between Figs. 2 and 3, the one asserting "Every catholic adores some woman"; the other, "Some woman is adored by every catholic". But of course the latter asserts the more; since it says that all catholics adore the *same* woman, while the former allows different catholics to adore different women.

Fig. 2   **Fig. 3**

Interpreted by the last rule Fig. 2 reads:

> Take anybody, A. Then somebody, B, can be found such that, either A is not catholic or A adores B and B is a woman.

Fig. 3 reads:

> Somebody B can be found such that taking anybody, A, B is a woman and either A is not a catholic or A adores B.

There is a grave defect in this system of graphs and in my algebras of logic. It has been known to me from the first; and I have a makeshift contrivance to supply the deficiency. I do not think that even Schröder, who probably understands the subject better than anybody after me, has a clear apprehension of this fault. It is not felt as long as we have only to do with dyads; but when we come to triads, the graphs afford no proper form for expressing such a proposition as this:

> There is some clergyman who praises every lawyer each to doctor, so that for every possible distribution of such praises there is a distinct clergyman who performs the praise.

That is, suppose A and B are the lawyers, X, Y, Z, the doctors, then there are nine clergymen (at least) who praise the lawyers to the doctors as shown in these nine diagrams.

$$\underset{XYZ}{AB} \quad \underset{XYZ}{AB} \quad \underset{XYZ}{AB} \quad \underset{XYZ}{AB} \quad \underset{XYZ}{AB} \quad \underset{XYZ}{AB} \quad \underset{XYZ}{AB} \quad \underset{XYZ}{AB} \quad \underset{XYZ}{AB}$$

But if A, B, C are the lawyers and Y, Z the doctors, there are at least eight clergymen who distribute their praises as shown in these eight diagrams:

$$\underset{XY}{ABC} \quad \underset{XY}{ABC} \quad \underset{XY}{ABC} \quad \underset{XY}{ABC} \quad \underset{XY}{ABC} \quad \underset{XY}{ABC} \quad \underset{XY}{ABC} \quad \underset{XY}{ABC}$$

In short, all the lawyers are praised to doctors by each of the clergymen in question and there is no mode of distribution of all the lawyers each to a doctor for which there is not some clergyman who so performs the praise.

I said above that I had a makeshift contrivance for expressing such things. It is this. I use the dyadic verb "____ is a character possessed by the individual ____" Now I assume that *every collection of individuals whatever possess some common character which no other individual possesses*. I also use the triadic verb: "____ is a dyadic relation in which ____ stands to ____". Now I assume that *every collection of ordered pairs of individuals stand, the first member of the pair to the second member, in some common relation such that no other ordered pair has its first member in the same relation to its second*. By an *ordered pair*, I mean two things so taken that a definite one is *first* and the other *second*, and so that the pair composed of the same individuals in reversed order is a *different* pair. Thus AB and BA are two different ordered pairs. Also AA is an ordered pair, the same individual being both first and second.

By means of these two verbs, I can express all those propositions exemplified by that about the clergymen, lawyers, and doctors. But I consider it a makeshift because I am unable to express in any way those assumptions which I make concerning these verbs.

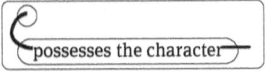

Fig. 6

It is true that the monadic and dyadic logics present each a verb which cannot be defined. In the monadic logic, I cannot define O, otherwise than by saying "If O is true, X is true, no matter what proposition X may be". Fig. 6 may be taken as expressing this. So in the dyadic logic, the verb "___ is identical with ___" can only be expressed by saying, "whatever is true of anything is true of everything with which that thing is identical". But these are only half definitions. For a definition, D, of anything X is a rub composed of simpler parts such that we can say

1   If X is true D is true.
2   If D is true X is true.

Now in the case of ◯ and of identity we only have half a definition, the first form of proposition, not the second.

But, then, the signs ◯ and —, which are these two verbs, are not specially invented or created verbs. They are mere essential parts of graphs. They are parts of the regular morphology of graphs. I should be entirely contented with the verbs "___ is possessed as a character by ___" and "___ is a relation in which ___ stands to ___" if they did not fall back upon the dictionary for their expression. They ought to be mere formal parts of almost any graph; and the system of graphs needs to be remodelled to make them so. But I have never succeeded in fulfilling this desideratum. In that regard I am but the voice of one crying in the wilderness.

I can see in what direction the truth is to come. Namely, although I clearly see that an assertion is the representation that two radically different categories of signs an *index* and an *icon* are applicable the one to the other I have not fully represented the assertion as so formed in my graphs. There is in the assertion a reference to two universes or worlds, the world of existence on the one hand, the world of ideas on the other. It is this second world that I have not sufficiently recognized in my graphs. Instead of representing the selection of the subjects so to be made out of the universe of existence but the idea to be precisely given, perhaps I should have helped matters if I had recognized that it is as impossible precisely to give an idea as it is precisely to designate an individual. Perhaps had I represented "All men are mortal" as meaning, take any individual object whatever and either he has not some attribute of man or he has every attribute of mortality, I should have helped the matter. But investigation, though it may go on indefinitely, yet at any stage of it, no matter for how many years it may be pursued, has a ragged and imperfect border; and here I am at the border of beyond which my reflections have not as yet been carried. I state this matter a little differently from how I should have stated it a month ago, and my statement then would have been a little different from what I should have made a month previously, and so backwards for 300 months. In a few months more, perhaps I shall attain to the *magnum arcarium*. I hope so; as I have hoped all along. Certainly, it seems as if not much labor would be required to better my present conceptions a good deal; and such has been the outlook for many years, and the promise has been fulfilled too. But I always found when one almost obvious improvement had been made, another was still called for. There must probably be some end to that; but I have not reached it yet, nor have I become weary or discouraged in the quest.

For the present, let us make the best of the graphs as they are.

Peripatetic Talks. No. 7
[R 505] *The Fundamental Principles of Existential Graphs restated in a new form.*

Rule I. Any graph, A, that can be illatively transformed into a graph, B, which can be illatively transformed into a third graph, C, can itself be illatively transformed into C. Write t as an abbreviation for "can be illatively transformed into". Then, in a universe of graphs, this rule is represented by Fig. 1.

Fig. 1

(This rule is Aristotle's maxim known as the *Nota notae*, "Nota notae est nota rei ipsius", as applied to graphs. De Morgan's *principle of the transitiveness of the copula* and Aristotle's *Dictum de omni et de nullo* are substantially this.)

Rule II. Every graph, B, such that every graph, A, into which it, B, cannot be illatively transformed, but which, A, can be illatively transformed into it, B, can be illatively transformed in a second graph, C, can itself, B, be be illatively transformed into C. This is represented by Fig. 2.

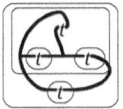

Fig. 2

(This may be called the inductive principle of graphical transformation.)

More clearly stated: Take any two graphs, B and C. Suppose that every graph, A, which can be transformed into B although B cannot be transformed into it, can be transformed into C. Then B can itself be illatively transformed into C.

Rule III. Into any graph, B, such that into every graph, C, that cannot be illatively transformed into it, B, but into which, C, it, B, can be illatively transformed, a given graph, A, can be illatively transformed, this graph, A, can be illatively transformed. Fig. 3 represents this rule.

Fig. 3

(This may be called the hypothetical principle of graphical transformation.)

It may be more clearly stated as follows: Take any two graphs, A and B; and suppose that A can be illatively transformed into every graph, C, which cannot be illatively transformed into B but into which B can be illatively transformed. Then A can be illatively transformed in B also.

Appendix (R 489)

Investigation of the meaning of (It thunders).

We start with the Basic Rule that 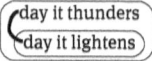 means "if it thunders it lightens" as a consequence *de inesse*. If a range of possibility is taken into account, as for example, supposing that by "if it thunders, it lightens" we mean "On *every* day on which it thunders it lightens" we write

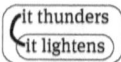

Fig. 1

If we mean that every time it thunders it has lightened within a minute, we can write

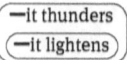

Fig. 2

As an abridged way of expression, we can write

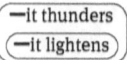

Fig. 3

Whether the line refers to a universe of days, or minutes, or what, is not here stated, but must be supposed to be understood. If we write

Fig. 4

the meaning is, "if it ever thunders, it sometimes lightens", that is "granted that a day (or a minute) can be found when it thunders, then a day (or a minute) can be found when it lightens".[4]

Our first step in the investigation consists in leaving the antecedent of Fig. 4 blank. Now a blank means "what I assert is true",

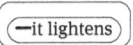

Fig. 5

(which is perfectly empty). Hence, the proposition now is: "If what I assert is true,[5] it sometimes lightens".

But this is the same as to write Fig. 6, "it sometimes lightens".

—it lightens

Fig. 6

Hence, *two enclosures annul one another.*

Our next step is to take Fig. 7, the enclosure of it sometimes thunders

—it thunders

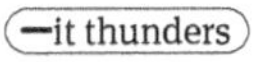

Fig. 7

and remarking that in the enclosure there are blank places, we enclose one of them doubly. This will not affect the meaning in the least, because two enclosures annul one another. Hence, Fig. 8 is equivalent to Fig. 7.

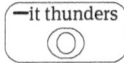

Fig. 8

But, by Basic Rule IV this means "Granted it sometimes thunders, then 0 is true". Hence Fig. 7 means this. It does not assert that it sometimes thunders, but it asserts, as a consequence *de inesse*, that if it sometimes thunders, 0 is true. In other words, *either* it never thunders or 0 is true.

Thus the problem is reduced to that of ascertaining the meaning of the empty oval.

At this point, I introduce a lemma. Namely I assert that $\boxed{\text{T}\boxed{\text{X}}\boxed{\text{X}}}$ means, "Either T is true or X is true". Or, to take a concrete example, I assert that

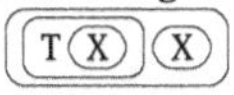

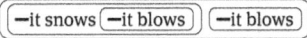

Fig. 9

is equivalent to

---

4 [Marginal note:] "____" stands for "there is a time when".
5 [Marginal note:] i.e. if anything is true or I assert nothing.

Either it sometimes snows or it sometimes blows.[6]

Fig. 10

In order to prove this equivalence, I begin by defining logical equivalence. I say that any two propositions, P and Q, are logically equivalent, if, and only if, first, assuming the truth of P, the truth of Q follows by logical necessity, and second, assuming the truth of Q, the truth of P follows by logical necessity. This definition may be expressed by a graph thus:

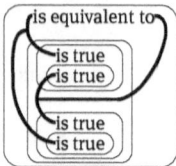 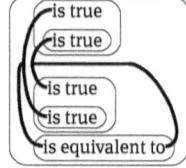

Fig. 11

Two things have therefore to be proved to establish the lemma:

> First, that if Fig. 9 is true, Fig. 10 is true;
> Second, that if Fig. 10 is true, Fig. 9 is true.

I proceed to prove the first proposition involved in the lemma, that if Fig. 9 is true, Fig. 10 is true.
 We assume, then, that Fig. 9 is true, that is, that
 If (—it snows —it blows) is true, then it sometimes blows.
 Suppose, further, that it never blew. Then it would follow that
(—it snows —it blows) was not true. For we assume that, were this true, it would sometimes blow.
 If then it never blew, it would not be true (assuming Fig. 9 true) that if it ~~sometimes~~ ever snows it sometimes blows. For this is the meaning of
(—it snows —it blows). That is to say, if it never blew (assuming Fig. 9 to be true), it would sometimes snow without ever blowing. That is (assuming Fig. 9 to be true), if it never blew it would sometimes snow. That is, it would sometimes snow or else it would sometimes blow.
 But this is precisely what Fig. 10 asserts. Hence we have proved that assuming Fig. 9 to be true, Fig. 10 is true.
 I now proceed to prove the second proposition involved in the lemma, that if Fig. 10 is true, Fig. 9 is true.
 We assume, then, that Fig. 10 is true, that is that

> It is either true that it sometimes snows or it is true that it sometimes blows.

Whether or not in case it were true that it ~~sometimes~~ ever snowed it would be true that it sometimes blew, we do not know; we will call this Hypothesis X. But were this true, it would (assuming Fig. 10 to be true) sometimes blow. For if it sometimes snowed, then it would be true by Fig. 10 be true that it sometimes blows by virtue of Hypothesis X. But if it never snowed, then it would by Fig. 10 be true that it sometimes blows. Thus if Fig. 10 is true, then if Hypothesis X is true, it sometimes blows.

---

6 [Marginal note:] Hyp. X: If it ever knows it sometimes blows.

But that if Hypothesis X is true, it sometimes blows is just what Fig. 9 asserts. For Hypothesis X is "in case it be true that it sometimes snows, it sometimes blows" and Fig. 9 asserts

If it be true that if it sometimes snows it sometimes blows, then it blows.

Hence, we have shown that if Fig. 10 is true, Fig. 9 is true. We have now proved:

First, if Fig. 9 is true, Fig. 10 is true
Second, if Fig. 10 is true, Fig. 9 is true.

That is, we have proved that Figs. 9 and 10 are logically equivalent. That is, we have proved that 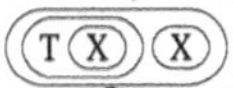 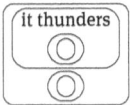 means that either T or X is true.
Our next step is to apply this to Fig. 12

Fig. 12

which by virtue of the lemma means "Either it thunders or ○ is true".

But the two blanks surrounded by two ovals mean nothing, since the two ovals annul one another. Hence Fig. 12 is equivalent to

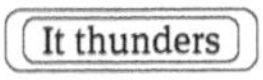

Fig. 13

And because two ovals annul one another, this is equivalent to Fig. 14.

It thunders

Fig. 14

We thus see that "It thunders" is logically equivalent to "Either it thunders or ○ is true".

But by the definition of logical equivalents either follows from the other. Hence, if it is true that it either thunders or that ○ is true, it must be true that it thunders. But this can only be necessary, supposing that if ○ is true, it is true that it thunders. Consequently, we must conclude that *if ○ is true, it is true that it thunders.*

But what has thus been proved in regard to the proposition "it thunders" is, by the same reasoning, proved in regard to any other proposition whatever. Hence we must conclude

If ○ is true, all propositions are true.

Hence, ○ is absurd.

All absurd propositions are equivalent, for if any absurd proposition were true all propositions, including any other absurd proposition would be true. Hence we may interpret ○ by any absurd proposition such as "all propositions are true", or "something false is true" or "what I aver is not true".

Now returning to Fig. 8, we see that it means "if it sometimes thunders what is false is true" or in other words, It never thunders. Thus the enclosure precisely denies its contents.

So likewise

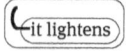

Fig. 15

means "if anything ever happens it *then* lightens", i.e. "it always lightens".

We investigate the meaning of

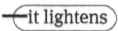

Fig. 16

This is equivalent to

Fig. 17

which means "*Sometimes* if it lightens then at that time ⊸ is true".

Here is a lemma. Fig. 18 is equivalent to Fig. 20

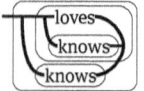   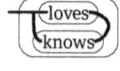   There is somebody who either loves or knows everybody, i.e. Somebody loves everybody except those he knows.

Fig. 18   **Fig. 19**   **Fig. 20**

To prove this, first assume Fig. 18 is true. Let M be the "somebody" of whom Fig. 18 is true. Suppose M does not know a certain person, N. Then it is not true that $M\!-\!\text{loves/knows}\!-\!N$. For if it were, by Basic Rule IV, Fig. 18 (which we assume to be true) would assert that M knows N. But $M\!-\!\text{loves/knows}\!-\!N$ which is thus not true asserts that M if he loves N, knows him. This would not be false unless M loved N. Hence, M does love N. Thus we have shown that assuming Fig. 18 to be true, there be anybody whom M does not know he loves that person. That is, if Fig. 18 is true, Fig. 20 is true.

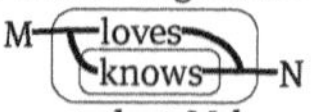

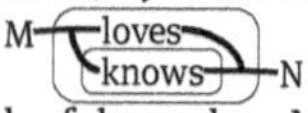

Second, assume Fig. 20 to be true. Suppose the somebody M of whom Fig. 20 is true does not love a certain person N. In that case by Fig. 20 he must know that person. Hence, if it be true that $M\!-\!\text{loves/knows}\!-\!N$ he knows N no matter who N may be. But this is precisely that Fig. 18 asserts.

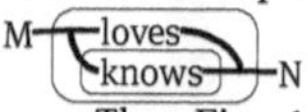

Thus Figs. 18 and 20 are equivalent.

It follows that Fig. 21 means "It either sometimes lightens or else sometimes ⊸ is true".

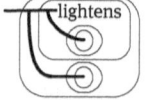   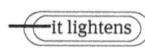

Fig. 21   **Fig. 22**

But Fig. 21 is equivalent to Fig. 22, and means simply "sometimes it lightens".

Hence ⊸ is absurd.

Hence Figs. 16 and 17 mean *sometimes* it does not lighten.

Part III: **Theory and Application of Existential Graphs**

13 The Principles of Logical Graphics

R 493, c.1899. Houghton Library. With its systematic presentation of 126 examples of graphs with only one 0, 1, 2 or 3-ary verb, plus another three dozen more complicated ones, the study that appears on 42 pages of this small red leather notebook is one of the rare pieces on EGs that fall between the first batch that ended with the "Peripatetic Talks" of summer 1898 and Peirce's resolute return to the study of logic with the enormous "Minute Logic" project of early 1902. Peirce recollects his "makeshift contrivance" introduced in the sixth talk of the previous selection, namely a special rhema of "possesses as a character" which is to capture meanings difficult to capture otherwise. The justification comes from the "axiom" that every set of individuals has some unique property. Principle 5 states that a lack of a "head or finish" in the line of identity deprives it from being of the nature of an assertion. A line is usually an assertion, but it needs "an indefinite index" at its end which must be separately denoted by a "swelling or button." Though the notation of a loop at the line's extremity is a *hapax legomenon* in his writings, it is an insightful conceptual innovation, given that the dot is in fact an assertion of self-identity and hence well-definedness (and since a complete classification of manifolds in 0-dimensions is, after all, a loop). Peirce's dissection of the illative rules is also exceptional, as the application of the rules is presented according to which rules are permitted to be applied within even enclosures and which rules are permitted to be applied within odd enclosures. As the principles, definitions and the terminology is not yet fully standard, yet also not exactly those previously encountered (e.g. "the doctrine of forks" is unique nomenclature), we can tentatively date this notebook to the intermittent period of c.1899.

§ 1. The Fundamental Assumptions

Principle 1. It is assumed that writing down a proposition asserts it of the universe to which it is understood the sheet refers.

Principle 2. It is assumed that if two propositions are written down independently, both are asserted.

Corollary 1. A blank asserts nothing. For there is a blank beside every proposition written down. The meaning of this blank is therefore, by Principle 2, independently asserted. But by Principle 1 nothing is asserted but precisely the proposition written. Hence the blank means nothing.

Definition 1. A *verb* is an imperfect assertion having "blanks", or "loose ends", each of which being filled by an *Index*, or sign forcing an object of experience upon thought, makes up an assertion. According to the number of blanks a verb is a *medad* (0), *monad* (1), *dyad* (2), *triad* (3), *polyad* (>3).

Scholium 1. A verb is a conventional sign or ideograph calling up in the mind a familiar idea detached from the occasions of its occurrence. This detachment arises from a "composite photograph" being in the memory of many such experiences. The result of their aggregation is an *icon* [that] comes out strongly while the occasions are slightly impressed, and not clearly in consciousness. Thus, "sings" is a word which brings toward the surface of consciousness from out of its dark places a crowd of auditory images, of which the resultant is strong and clear in respect to the feature they have in common but very dim in regard to the occasions in which they differ.

Principle 3. A continuous heavy line joining two *Indices*, or blanks for indices, asserts their identity.

Thus, Fig. 1 asserts "Nordica is a woman and sings". Fig. 2 asserts (that Nordica exists and) that *something* is a woman and sings. I bracket the first part because Nordica being a proper name is understood to be a common experience of the writer and reader of the graph; so that they both know already Nordica exists. So that this assertion is equivalent to a blank. But this takes for granted as a part of Principle 1, that writer and reader have come to an understanding as to what "universe" they are speaking of.

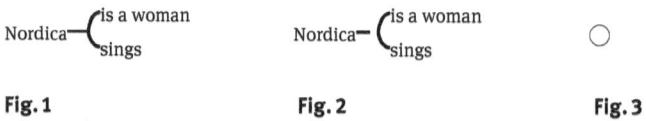

Fig. 1 **Fig. 2** **Fig. 3**

Definition 2. The *Universe of Discourse* is the aggregate of the individual objects which "exist", that is are independently side by side in the collection of experiences to which the deliverer and interpreter of a set of symbols have agreed to refer and to consider.

Principle 4. A lightly drawn oval shall have such a meaning that, if it encloses several independent propositions, that which is asserted is true, provided an oval with any one of these propositions in it alone is true, but otherwise not.

Corollary 2. An oval left blank (Fig. 3) must assert an absurdity; for since there is a blank beside any proposition written in an oval, *every* proposition that could be expressed by an oval with something written in it would be true if the proposition asserted by the empty oval were true. Now a proposition which asserts *every* proposition of a given logical form must be false, or else that logical form is such that it never can convey any information and thus can have no meaning, contrary to Principle 4. Hence, it must be that the empty oval asserts a proposition that must be false.

Scholium 2. In place of Principle 4, we might assume two, of which the first which we may call 4′ ("four prime") is as follows:

Principle 4″. If a proposition, A, is enclosed in an oval which encloses nothing else except an oval enclosing a second proposition, B, as in Fig. 4, the meaning is that there is a *law* of the universe of discourse from which it results that were A true (whether it be true or not being left undetermined) the truth of A would *involve* the truth of B.

Fig. 4   **Fig. 5**   **Fig. 6**   **Fig. 7**

From this principle it follows as a corollary (**Corollary 3**) that a proposition twice encircled is asserted [Fig. 5]. For in this case, A becomes a blank; and a blank, by Corollary 1, asserts nothing. So the meaning is that the truth of a mere empty form of assertion (which cannot be false) *involves* the truth of B. This is as much as to say that the truth of B is involved in the universe of discourse as a consequence of some law. By a law here is only meant something which is true for the universe, so that everything that is unconditionally true is true by some law. Thus, *the two ovals destroy one another*.

At most, when modality is admitted, the double oval asserts the necessity of the included proposition. Thus, Fig. 6 means it *must* thunder some time. But ordinarily this is no more than to say that thunder is a possible event; for every *general* event which can happen does sometimes happen in an infinity of chances. Yet it is not *self-contradictory* to suppose that some throw of the dice never was and never will be thrown, to all *eternity*. Only that would constitute the law of nature.

Thus, that which is *logically* possible may be *naturally* impossible.

As another corollary (**Corollary 4**) we should have that the effect of drawing an oval about a proposition is such that if one proposition B follows from another proposition A, as asserted in Fig. 4, that is the same as to say that (A) follows from (B), as asserted in Fig. 7. For Fig. 7 differs from Fig. 4 only in ((A)) being substituted for its equivalent, A. Hence, we may draw as **Corollary 5**, that the effect of enclosing a proposition in an oval is formally equivalent to asserting that some fixed fact or state of things would be involved in the truth of the enclosed proposition.

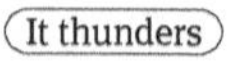

(It thunders)

Fig. 8

(you murder (you sin))

Fig. 9

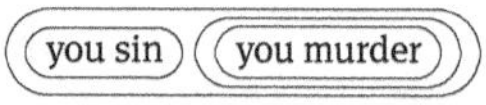

((you sin) (you murder))

Fig. 10

Thus Fig. 8 would mean that if it thunders a certain proposition x is true. For example, x might be "I am delighted", so that Fig. 8 would mean "Thunder delights me".

So as Fig. 9 means, "If you murder then you sin" so its equivalent, Fig. 10 might be read "If your sinning would be sure to delight me, then your murdering would be sure to delight me".

We thus see that if we adopt Principle 4′ we need another principle to show what is the particular consequence x which is asserted to follow from the truth of the proposition enclosed in an oval. We will call it Principle 4″.

Principle 4″. The effect of enclosing a proposition in an oval is to assert that were that proposition true *some thing that is in fact false would be true*.

We must have some way of asserting this consequence; else we could not deny anything, nor could we assert anything manifestly false. In short we should be in a logical paradise before eating of the fruit of the tree of knowledge of good and evil of the cognitive sort.

Principle 5. A heavy line terminating abruptly without any head or finish shows a complete assertion is not intended. But a swelling, or button at the end is an indefinite index.

—sings

Fig. 11

Fig. 12 [P.H.]

•—sings

Fig. 13

Thus, Fig. 11 means "—sings". It asserts nothing. But Figs. 12 and 13 both mean (in a universe of persons) "somebody sings".

§ 2. Illustrations

Fig. 14:   It thunders   It thunders.
Fig. 15:   (It thunders)   It does not thunder.
Fig. 16:   •—sings   Somebody sings.
Fig. 17:   (•—sings)   Somebody does not sing.
Fig. 18:   (•—sings)   Nobody sings.

13 The Principles of Logical Graphics (R 493), c.1899

Fig. 19:	(⊸sings)	Everybody sings.
Fig. 20:	⊸kills⊸	Somebody kills somebody.
Fig. 21:	⊸(kills)⊸	Somebody does not kill somebody.
Fig. 22:	(⊸kills⊸)	Somebody is not killed by anybody.
Fig. 23:	⊸(kills⊸)	Somebody kills nobody.
Fig. 24:	(⊸kills⊸)	Nobody kills anybody.
Fig. 25:	(⊸kills⊸)⊸	Somebody is killed by everybody.
Fig. 26:	(⊸kills⊸)⊸	Everybody kills everybody.
Fig. 27:	(⊸kills⊸)⊸	Everybody is killed by somebody.
Fig. 28:	(⊸kills⊸)	Everybody kills somebody.
Fig. 29:	(⊸(kills)⊸)⊸	Nobody is killed by everybody.
Fig. 30:	(⊸(kills)⊸)	Nobody kills everybody.
Fig. 31:	(kills)	Somebody kills himself.
Fig. 32:	(kills)	Somebody does not kill himself.
Fig. 33:	(kills)	Everybody kills himself.
Fig. 34:	(kills)	Nobody kills himself.
Fig. 35:	⊸praises↓to⊸	Somebody praises somebody to somebody.
Fig. 36:	(⊸praises↓to⊸)	Somebody does not praise everybody to everybody.
Fig. 37:	(⊸praises↓to⊸)	Somebody is not praised to everybody to anybody.
Fig. 38:	⊸praises↘to⊸	Somebody does not praise anybody to somebody.
Fig. 39:	(⊸praises↘to⊸)	Somebody praises somebody to nobody.
Fig. 40:	⊸praises↘to⊸	To somebody nobody praises anybody.
Fig. 41:	(⊸praises↘to⊸)	Somebody is praised by nobody to anybody.
Fig. 42:	(⊸praises↘to⊸)	Somebody praises nobody to anybody.
Fig. 43:	⊸praises↘to⊸	Nobody praises anybody to anybody.
Fig. 44:	(⊸praises↓to⊸)⊸	To somebody somebody is praised by all men.
Fig. 45:	(⊸praises↓to⊸)⊸	To somebody somebody praises all men.
Fig. 46:	(⊸praises↓to⊸)⊸	Somebody praises somebody to all men.
Fig. 47:	(⊸praises↓to⊸)⊸	To somebody all men praise all men.

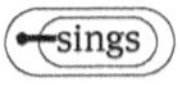

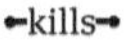

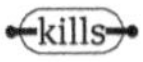

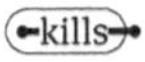

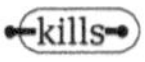

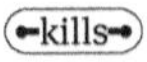

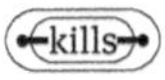

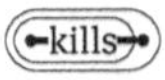

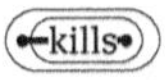

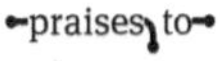

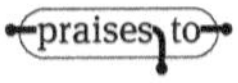

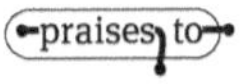

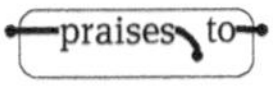

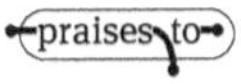

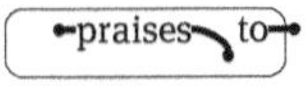

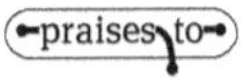

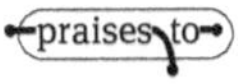

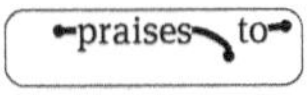

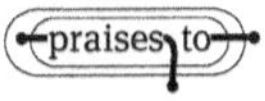

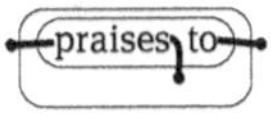

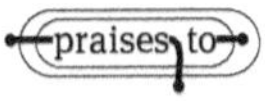

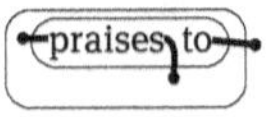

Fig. 48: Somebody is praised to all men by all men.

Fig. 49: Somebody praises all men to all men.

Fig. 50: Everybody praises everybody to everybody.

Fig. 51: To somebody everybody is praised by somebody.

Fig. 52: Somebody is praised to everybody by somebody.

Fig. 53: Everybody is praised to everybody by somebody.

Fig. 54: To somebody everybody praises somebody.

Fig. 55: Somebody praises somebody *or other* to everybody.

Fig. 56: To everybody everybody praises somebody.

Fig. 57: Somebody praises everybody to somebody.

Fig. 58: Somebody is praised by everybody to somebody.

Fig. 59: Everybody praises everybody to somebody.

Fig. 60: To everybody somebody or other praises somebody or other.

Fig. 61: Everybody praises everybody to somebody.

Fig. 62: Everybody praises somebody to somebody.

Fig. 63: There is somebody to whom nobody is praised by everybody.

Fig. 64: There is somebody who is praised to nobody by everybody.

Fig. 65: Nobody is praised to anybody by everybody.

Fig. 66: To somebody nobody praises everybody.

Fig. 67: There is somebody who praises everybody to nobody.

Fig. 68: Nobody praises everybody to anybody.

Fig. 69: There is somebody whom nobody praises to everybody.

13 The Principles of Logical Graphics (R 493), c.1899

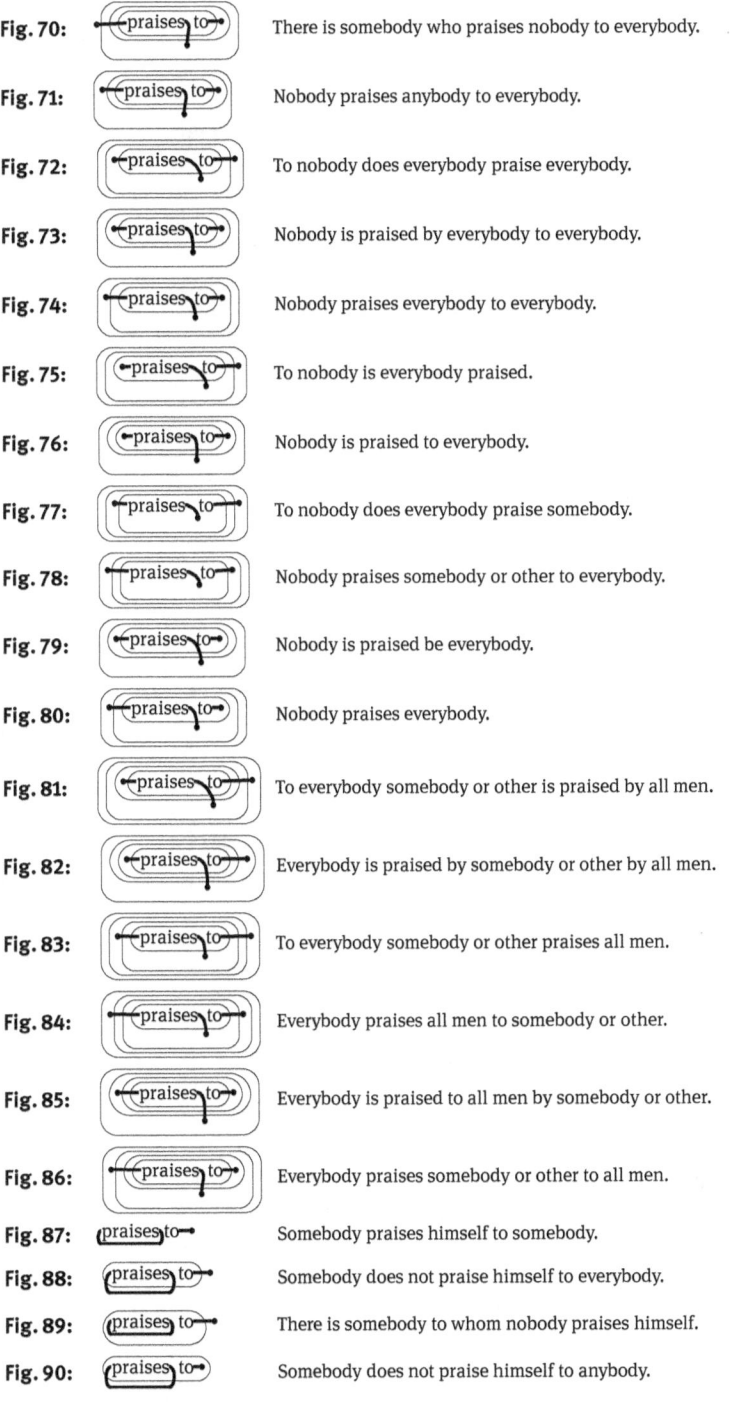

Fig. 70: There is somebody who praises nobody to everybody.
Fig. 71: Nobody praises anybody to everybody.
Fig. 72: To nobody does everybody praise everybody.
Fig. 73: Nobody is praised by everybody to everybody.
Fig. 74: Nobody praises everybody to everybody.
Fig. 75: To nobody is everybody praised.
Fig. 76: Nobody is praised to everybody.
Fig. 77: To nobody does everybody praise somebody.
Fig. 78: Nobody praises somebody or other to everybody.
Fig. 79: Nobody is praised be everybody.
Fig. 80: Nobody praises everybody.
Fig. 81: To everybody somebody or other is praised by all men.
Fig. 82: Everybody is praised by somebody or other by all men.
Fig. 83: To everybody somebody or other praises all men.
Fig. 84: Everybody praises all men to somebody or other.
Fig. 85: Everybody is praised to all men by somebody or other.
Fig. 86: Everybody praises somebody or other to all men.
Fig. 87: Somebody praises himself to somebody.
Fig. 88: Somebody does not praise himself to everybody.
Fig. 89: There is somebody to whom nobody praises himself.
Fig. 90: Somebody does not praise himself to anybody.

13 The Principles of Logical Graphics (R 493), c.1899

Fig. 91: Nobody praises himself to anybody.
Fig. 92: There is somebody to whom everybody praises himself.
Fig. 93: There is somebody who praises himself to everybody.
Fig. 94: Everybody praises himself to everybody.
Fig. 95: To everybody somebody or other praises himself.
Fig. 96: Everybody praises himself to somebody or other.
Fig. 97: There is nobody to whom all men praise themselves.
Fig. 98: Nobody praises himself to all men.
Fig. 99: Somebody praises somebody to his face.
Fig. 100: Somebody does not praise everybody to his face.
Fig. 101: Somebody is not praised to his face by anybody.
Fig. 102: Somebody does not praise anybody to his face.
Fig. 103: Nobody praises anybody to his face.
Fig. 104: Somebody is praised to his face by all men.
Fig. 105: Somebody praises all men to their faces.
Fig. 106: Everybody praises everybody to his face.
Fig. 107: Everybody is praised to his face by somebody or other.
Fig. 108: Everybody praises somebody or other to his face.
Fig. 109: Nobody is praised to his face by all men.
Fig. 110: Nobody praises all men to their faces.
Fig. 111: Somebody praises somebody within himself.
Fig. 112: Somebody does not within himself praise everybody.
Fig. 113: Somebody within himself praises no man.
Fig. 114: There is somebody whom no man within himself praises.
Fig. 115: Nobody within himself praises anybody.

13 The Principles of Logical Graphics (R 493), c.1899

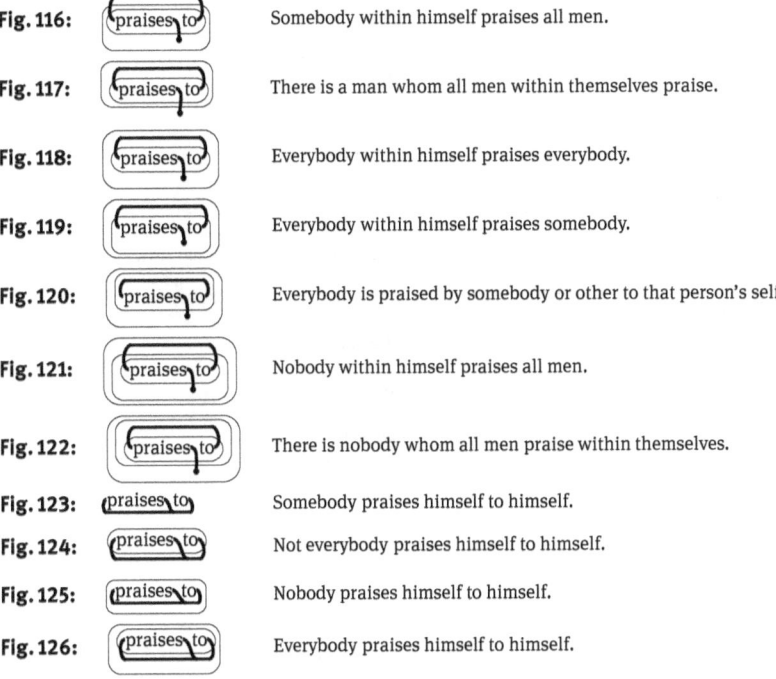

Fig. 116: Somebody within himself praises all men.
Fig. 117: There is a man whom all men within themselves praise.
Fig. 118: Everybody within himself praises everybody.
Fig. 119: Everybody within himself praises somebody.
Fig. 120: Everybody is praised by somebody or other to that person's self.
Fig. 121: Nobody within himself praises all men.
Fig. 122: There is nobody whom all men praise within themselves.
Fig. 123: Somebody praises himself to himself.
Fig. 124: Not everybody praises himself to himself.
Fig. 125: Nobody praises himself to himself.
Fig. 126: Everybody praises himself to himself.

Besides these forms there should be others not easily represented expressing such assertions as the following:

> There is some man to whom all men praise each a single man in every possible distribution and to whom no other man praises anybody. etc.[1]

Let us next consider graphs with two verbs.

Fig. 127: It thunders / It lightens — It thunders and lightens.
Fig. 128: It thunders / It lightens — It lightens but not thunders.
Fig. 129: It thunders / It lightens — It neither thunders nor lightens.
Fig. 130: It thunders / It lightens — It either does not lighten or does not thunder.
Fig. 131: It thunders / It lightens — If it lightens it thunders.

---

1 [Del.:] Every set of men is praised to all men by some man who praises nobody but them.

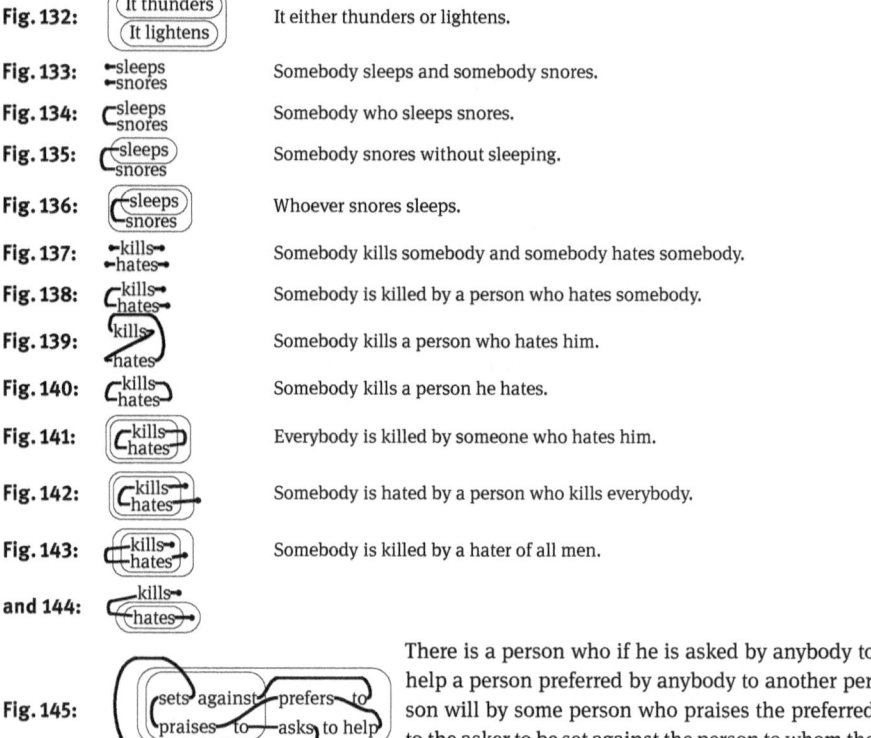

Fig. 132:		It either thunders or lightens.
Fig. 133:		Somebody sleeps and somebody snores.
Fig. 134:		Somebody who sleeps snores.
Fig. 135:		Somebody snores without sleeping.
Fig. 136:		Whoever snores sleeps.
Fig. 137:		Somebody kills somebody and somebody hates somebody.
Fig. 138:		Somebody is killed by a person who hates somebody.
Fig. 139:		Somebody kills a person who hates him.
Fig. 140:		Somebody kills a person he hates.
Fig. 141:		Everybody is killed by someone who hates him.
Fig. 142:		Somebody is hated by a person who kills everybody.
Fig. 143:		Somebody is killed by a hater of all men.
and 144:		
Fig. 145:		There is a person who if he is asked by anybody to help a person preferred by anybody to another person will by some person who praises the preferred to the asker to be set against the person to whom the proposed beneficiary is preferred.

This is given to show how much clearer this machinery is than unaided thought. It is unnecessary to imagine the matter. The graph serves every purpose in reasoning.

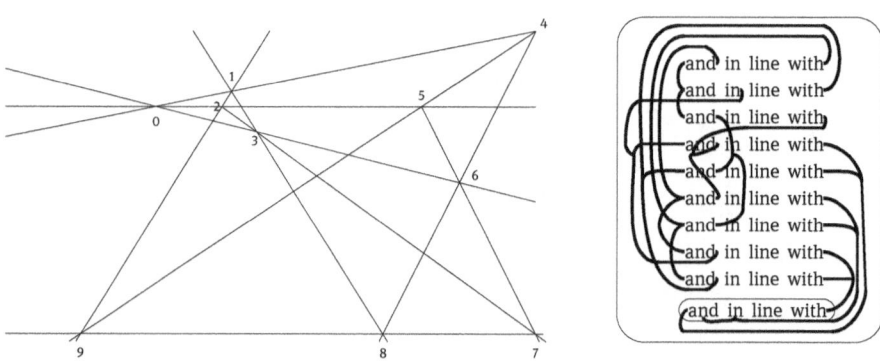

Fig. 146   **Fig. 147**

Given any ten points
0, 1, 2, 3, 4, 5, 6, 7, 8, 9, if

014 are collinear
025 are collinear
036 are collinear
237 are collinear
567 are collinear
138 are collinear
468 are collinear
129 are collinear
459 are collinear
789 are collinear

then

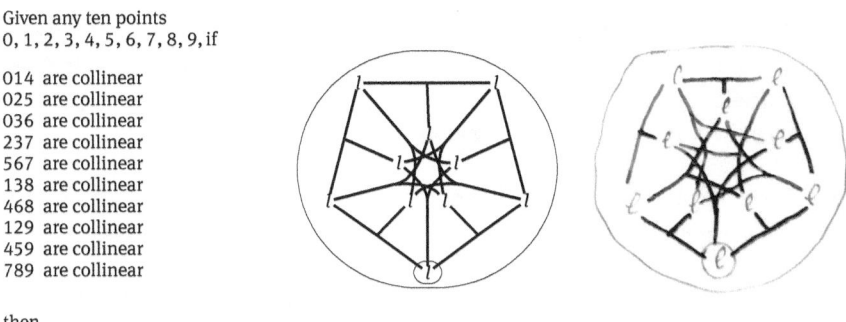

Fig. 147 bis [P.H.]

The expression of many difficult assertions is facilitated by using the verb "possesses as a character". For it is an axiom *that any set of individuals whatever have some character which nothing else has.*

Equally useful is the verb "—is in the relation—to—". For any set of ordered pairs are in a common and peculiar relation, the first member of each pair to the second.

§ 3. Illative Transformations of Graphs

First Rule. If any graph, A, can be illatively transformed into another graph B, when enclosed within any even number (including zero) of ovals, it can be so transformed within every even number of ovals, and within every odd number of ovals, the reverse transformation is illatively valid.

For within an even number of ovals, A, is *affirmed*, conditionally or unconditionally; and if irrespective of the precise nature of such conditions B can be inferred from it, then the affirmation of B must be true whenever the affirmation of A is true.

Consequently if the *denial* of B is true, it must be that the denial of A is true. Now within an odd number of ovals, B is denied (conditionally or unconditionally) so that A may be illatively substituted for it.

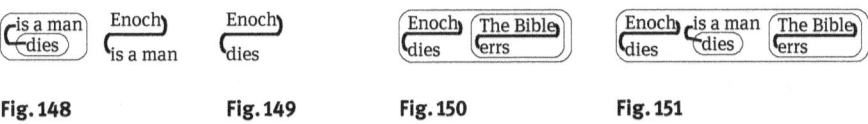

Fig. 148   Fig. 149   Fig. 150   Fig. 151

For example, suppose it to be proved that Fig. 148, meaning "all men die, and Enoch is a man", can be illatively transformed into Fig. 149, meaning "Enoch dies".

Then by this rule Fig. 150 meaning "If Enoch dies, the Bible errs", can be illatively transformed into Fig. 151, meaning "If Enoch is a man, then either some man does not die or the Bible errs".

This is called the *rule of contraposition*.

Second Rule. Within an even number of enclosures any separate part of a graph may be illatively omitted.

Corollary 6. It follows by the rule of contraposition that within an odd number of enclosures any addition of a separate piece of the graph is illatively valid.

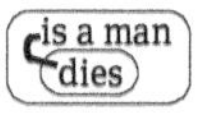

is a man
dies

Fig. 152

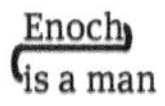

Enoch
is a man

Fig. 153

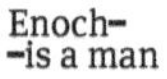

Enoch—
—is a man

Fig. 154

For example, from Fig. 148 may be inferred Fig. 152 and also Fig. 153.

Scholium. The rule extends to any part of the graph which is logically analogous to a separate piece. Thus, within an even number of ovals a line can be broken and within an odd number of ovals two lines can be joined. But it is to be remarked that a *line is virtually within only those ovals which include its outermost part.*

For example, from Fig. 153 we can conclude Fig. 154, or "Enoch exists and somebody is a man", or in other words "Enoch coexists with a man".

Corollary 7. Every evenly enclosed line can be cut and retracted.

Corollary 8. Every oddly enclosed line can be protracted and joined to any other outside of it.

For example, from Fig. 148 we can infer Fig. 155, meaning "Enoch is a man and is either not a man or else dies". From Fig. 76 can be inferred Fig. 98; this may be called the rule of simple omission.

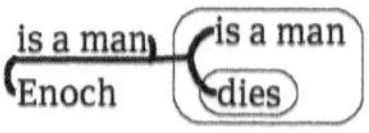

Fig. 155

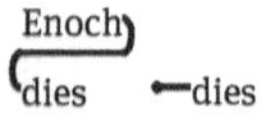

Fig. 156

Third Rule. Within an even number of ovals anything may be illatively inserted which is already in the graph not within any other ovals.

For example, from Fig. 149 can be inferred Fig. 156, or "Enoch dies and somebody dies".

Corollary 9. Within an odd number of enclosures anything can be illatively omitted which is elsewhere in the graph not within any other ovals.

Fig. 157   **Fig. 158**

For example from Fig. 155 can be inferred Fig. 157. And thence by the rule of simple omission can be inferred Fig. 158.

Corollary 10. Within an even number of enclosures, anything may be illatively carried into two ovals one within the other.

Fig. 159   **Fig. 160**

For example, from Fig. 159 "there is a prophet who if he is disobedient is swallowed by a whale", we can infer Fig. 160 "somebody if he is disobedient is a prophet swallowed by a whale". This is a bad example. Take the following.

Fig. 161   **Fig. 162**

Fig. 161 means "There is a person who benefits a brother of a person, yet who loves only servants of that person (if he loves anybody)". Hence, we can infer Fig. 162, "There is a benefactor of a man who loves (if at all) only servants of a person of whom that man is a brother".

Corollary 11. If an oval contains nothing but ovals and each of these contain the same certain verb, then that verb can be taken out of all those ovals.

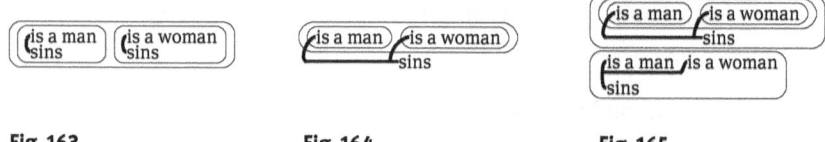

Fig. 163   **Fig. 164**   **Fig. 165**

For example, given Fig. 163, meaning "Either some man sins or some woman sins", we can infer Fig. 164, meaning "Something which sins is either a man or a woman". This is proved by contraposition. For the denial of Fig. 164 is Fig. 165.

Rules of Existential Graphs

Any marked point on a cut is to be regarded as being in the place of the cut.
The doctrine of forks belongs to Rule III.

I. *Rule of Erasure and Insertion.*
   i. In even enclosures,
      1. Any line of identity may be broken at any point. Any part of a line from a loose end may be erased.
      2. Any detached partial graph may be erased.
   ii. In odd enclosures,
      1. Any graph may be inserted detached.
      2. Any line may be extended from a loose end. Any two loose ends of lines may be joined.

II. *Rule of Iteration and Deiteration.*
   i. On any evenly enclosed area,
      1. Any partial graph may be iterated, i.e. copied with identically the same lines of identity joined to corresponding parts.
      2. Any line of identity may be deformed in any way and even made to reach the outside of a cut, in the same area (but not a cut on an outer area), provided its connections are not changed; any line of identity may be extended from a loose end in any way, and a fork may be made at any point of a line of identity.
   ii. On any oddly enclosed area,
      1. Any iterated graph (that is scribed twice with identically the same lines of identity joined to corresponding parts) may be deiterated (by the erasure of one such replica).

2. Any line of identity may be deformed in any way so long as its connections are unchanged, and its extremity even be retracted from the outside of a cut on the same area or so as to annul a fork. And a line returning into itself may be broken.

iii. Where there is an evenly enclosed cut
1. If a graph is scribed on an evenly enclosed area carrying a cut on whose area is a replica of that graph having all its hooks joined to the same ligatures as the corresponding hooks of the outer replica, that graph may be deiterated by erasing the inner replica.
2. A line of identity within the cut and having one extremity loose, and the other on the cut, may be entirely erased.

iv. If an evenly enclosed cut encloses another cut
1. Any graph in the area of the outer cut may be iterated on the area of the inner one.
2. [end][2]

---

2 [R 493 breaks off here. In addition to the completion of the rules Peirce presented here, the rule of adding and erasing double cut rule is needed.

The notebook also contains the following on the last page, omitted from the microfilm edition of the Harvard Peirce Papers:]

Method of investigation: Evolution of time; Evolution of mechanical laws and matter; Evolution of space; Evolution of astronomical systems; Evolution of geological constitution; Evolution of protoplasm; Evolution of species; Evolution of prolonged life.

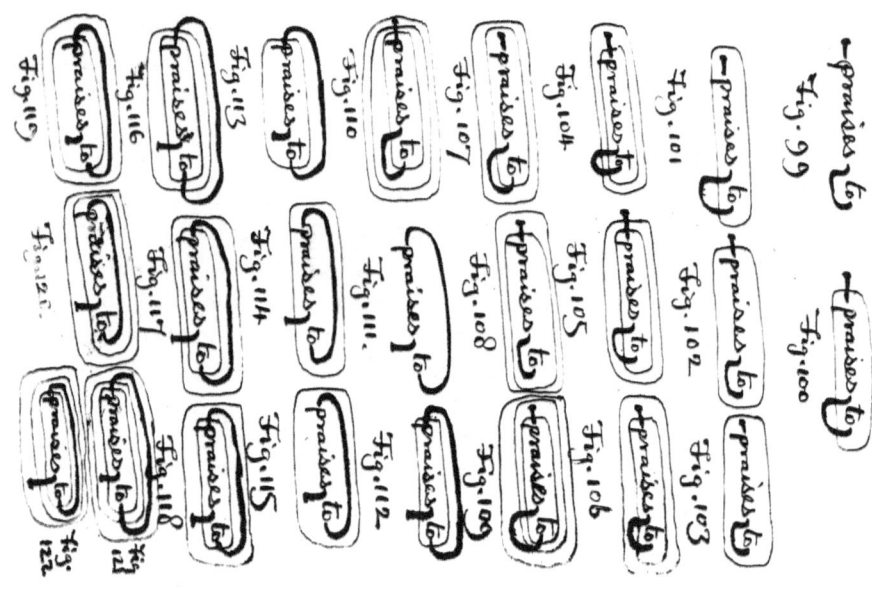

Two holograph pages (Harvard Peirce Papers, R 493).

14 On the First Principles of Logical Algebra

R 515, c.1901. Houghton Library. The next three chapters comprise an interconnected bouquet of writings Peirce produced on general notational aspects of logic. In these papers, all unpublished before, the maxim of the ethics of notation is presented, together with applications to notational issues of logic, thus complementing the ethics of terminology famously articulated in *The Syllabus* of Peirce's 1903 Lowell Lectures. These selections portray novel and often surprisingly modern perspectives to the study of logic. The first, "On the First Principles of Logical Algebra", is a well-preserved run of 34 continuous manuscript pages that may have been written in 1901 or in the early months of 1902 in relation to his *Minute Logic* book project. It could also have been envisioned as the initial third part of what became his *Logical Tracts* project of 1903 (LoF 2), the part which Peirce projected to appear under the title "Logical Algebra".

In the "First Principles", Peirce presents rules of transformations for his general algebra of logic equivalent to those of the rules for EGs. Comparison between the general algebra and existential graphs reveals that there is no significant difference between either using the vinculum or drawing ovals to stand for negation, or indeed that of having the sign of aggregation or encircling ovals around juxtaposed propositions enclosed within ovals to stand for the sign of disjunction. Accordingly, Peirce argues that using either the dot or juxtaposition for the sign of logical conjunction is essentially of the same significance, too. Comparisons between algebraical and graphical notations for quantification follow suit, with an observation that Σ is not strictly speaking the sign for a logical sum but that it merely "simulates" it, since the domains may be uncountable (not "capable of linear arrangement"). He also considers the constraints under which new terms may be introduced in the course of proofs, and investigates whether the treatment of indefinite individuals and singular terms coincides.

§ 1. As the fundamental transformations of any algebra, if strict logical method is desired, choose indecomposable transformations. But an indecomposable transformation is either an omission or an insertion, since any other may be analyzed into an omission followed by an insertion.

§ 2. The algebraic symbols are written on the surface of paper, wherein it is assumed that a surface is capable of representing every logical relation. That the surface must be capable of *iconically* representing every logical relation is not evident; and though it is true, I shall not here have occasion to prove it.

We provide ourselves, therefore, with a surface which we call the *sheet of assertion*; and pretend to hold ourselves responsible for the truth of whatever we may write upon it.[1]

---

1 [Alt.:] We provide ourselves, therefore, with a surface, called the *sheet of assertion*, and pretend to hold ourselves responsible for the truth of what we write upon it. Suppose, then, that we assume that we should be justified in writing a proposition, A, on that sheet, and that we should be justified in writing a proposition, B, on that sheet.

But as long as it remains blank we are irresponsible. Hence, the first rule of transformation will be

Rule I. ~~Everything~~ *The whole of what is written on the sheet of assertion may be erased, without danger of falsehood.*

§ 3. Assume that we should be justified in writing a proposition, A, on the sheet of assertion, and that we should be justified in writing a proposition, B, on the sheet of assertion. It will then be very natural to write A and B in different parts of the same sheet, as if they were written on different sheets. Hence, we adopt as the second rule:

Rule II. *Any proposition may be inserted or erased, as if any other on the sheet,* DISCONNECTED FROM IT, *were not there.*

But two such propositions simultaneously asserted are thereby parts combined into one copulative proposition by logical composition. We have, therefore, in Rule II, adopted a blank space as the sign of logical composition of propositions.[2] As an alternative sign, I use a heavy dot above the line.

Corollary 1. If two propositions are written, detached from one another, on the sheet of assertion, both are asserted, regardless of whether one is to the right, to the left, at the top, or at the bottom of the other. For one might be erased by Rules I and II, and then reinserted in another place by Rule II. Hence follows, the commutative principle of non-relative multiplication, better called composition:

$$x \cdot y = y \cdot x.$$

Corollary 2. If three or more propositions are all written, detached from one another, on the sheet of assertions, the logical relation of any pair of them is the same as that of any other pair. For if x and y were first copulated and then z were copulated with their copulate, thus,

$$xy \cdot z,$$

we should be at liberty to erase $x \cdot y$, thus showing that z could be asserted alone. If, however, we erase z instead, we might erase y, showing that we

---

[2] My habit has been to use the blank as the sign of relative multiplication, as it is used when in trigonometry we write "sin x". It goes against the grain to change this habit; but the above reason forces me to do so.

might assert *x* alone. But let us instead erase *x*, leaving *y*. Then since we might have written *z* alone, we can insert it now, giving *yz*; and then, since we might have written *x* alone, we can insert it now giving $x \cdot yz$. Thus we have,

$$xy \cdot z = x \cdot yz,$$

proving the associative principle.

Corollary 3. Any component of an asserted proposition may be erased without danger of falsehood.

Corollary 4. Any component of an asserted proposition may be iterated to any multitude of times.

§ 4. Suppose we wish to express the conditional proposition, "If *x* is true, *y* is true", and to do so in such a way as to exhibit iconically the relation between *x* and *y*.[3] Such propositions are understood in various senses; but I will suppose the meaning to be, that the assertion that *x* is true and *y* false would be false.

Let us enclose a proposition in an oval, or put a vinculum or obelus over it, to deny it; thus:

$$\textcircled{x} = \overline{x}.$$

Then, the above conditional proposition, being the denial of

$$x \textcircled{y} = x \cdot \overline{y}, \quad \text{will be written} \quad \overline{\left(x \textcircled{y}\right)} = \overline{x \cdot \overline{y}}.$$

If any proposition, *x*, could without danger of rendering it false, be transformed into another *y*, then in case *y* is false, its denial $\overline{y}$ can without danger of rendering it false be transformed into $\overline{x}$, the denial of the first proposition, *x*. For were $\overline{x}$ false, *x* itself would, by the principle of excluded middle, be true; and in that case *y* would be true, so that $\overline{y}$, by the principle of contradiction must be false already, and therefore could not be *rendered* false. The principles of contradiction and excluded middle constitute the definition of denial. Hence we have a third rule:

Rule III. *If any transformation could be made upon an unenclosed and detached component of a proposition, the reverse transformation can be made under one vinculum or oval.* (But the converse is not true.)

---

3 [Alt.:] § 4. Suppose we wish to express, "If *x* is true, *y* is true", and that analytically, so as to exhibit iconically the relation between *x* and *y*. We must, then, in some way, write down *x* and also *y*. But neither being asserted of itself, neither can be written unenclosed and detached from the other.

Corollary 5. By the principle of contradiction, the denial of a true proposition is false; and by the principle of excluded middle, the denial of a false proposition is true. Hence two vincula or ovals, one immediately over the other, with nothing intervening, may be erased or inserted.

Corollary 6. We may insert unenclosed an oval with another within it and with the same proposition within both and repeated within the outer but without the inner; thus

$$\boxed{\boxed{x}\,x} \qquad \text{or} \qquad \overline{\overline{x}\cdot x}.$$

For, by the principle of contradiction, $x \cdot \overline{x}$ is false; and therefore, by the principle of excluded middle, $\overline{\overline{x} \cdot \overline{x}}$ is true.

Corollary 7. Any detached part of a proposition, whether enclosed or not, may be iterated or deiterated under any number (zero included) of additional enclosures already existing. For by Corollary 3 and Rule III, anything may be inserted under odd enclosures; and by Corollary 4 and Rule III, if an unenclosed component is iterated under one enclosure, the enclosed occurrence may be erased; whence by Rule III, it follows that an unenclosed component may be iterated under two enclosures already existing. But since a component unenclosed, if iterated under one enclosure may be erased, it follows that a component of what is once enclosed may be iterated under one additional enclosure already existing. Whence we collect the whole substance of the Corollary.

Corollary 8. If an enclosure contains nothing unenclosed, and if the same proposition is a component of the contents of every enclosure once enclosed, this same proposition may be iterated unenclosed.

That is, from

$$\boxed{\boxed{x\,y}\,\boxed{x\,z}}, \qquad \text{we may infer} \qquad x\,\boxed{\boxed{x\,y}\,\boxed{x\,z}}.$$

For if $\overline{\overline{xy} \cdot \overline{xz}}$ is true, by the definition of a conditional proposition, if $\overline{xy}$ is true xz is true; whence by Cor. 3, x is true. But if $\overline{xy}$ is not true, xy is true, whence again x is true. Hence by Rule II, x may be inserted.

§ 5. In place of $\overline{\overline{xy} \cdot \overline{xz}}$, and $\overline{\overline{x} \cdot \overline{y} \cdot \overline{z}}$, etc. it is very convenient to write $x \curlyvee y$, $x \curlyvee y \curlyvee z$ etc. and to say that x, and y, etc. are combined by logical *aggregation*.

Note. It is improper to call aggregation "addition", since we have

$$x \curlyvee y = x,$$

which violates the fundamental idea of addition. It is, in fact, a "mean function", that is a symmetrical function which when all the variables have one value takes itself that value.

But even if it be called addition, which is not advisable, to signify it by the sign + is not only extremely confusing and inconvenient, especially since aggregation and addition must often appear in the same formula, as in

$$(x \mathbin{\curlyvee} y) + x \cdot y = x + y,$$

but it violates an ethical principle of terminology which is vital to the progress of science.

For unless we can agree upon the technical words and other symbols we employ, the confusion and consequent waste of labor will be intolerable. But every man has his private preferences on such matters, which he will never surrender until they are shown to conflict with a principle which he approves. We ought, therefore, to adopt a general ethical principle of terminology. Now the science which has had the greatest difficulty of this kind, taxonomic biology, has found that the only principle to which men would submit is one which may be generalized as follows:

- The man who introduces a conception into science is entitled to determine the terminology and notation of it, and he should be followed in this, *unless his proposal proves a distinct and serious hindrance to science*, in which case the least modification of his proposal which is satisfactory should be adopted.

This is but justice to those who enrich science with valuable conceptions; and besides that, it is the only rule, that of justice and right, to which candid men will surrender their personal prepossessions.

Applying this principle to the case in hand, Boole created logical algebra, and therefore his notations ought to be followed. Now he used + as the sign of addition, not of aggregation; and since such a sign is indispensable to the most important developments of logic, that sign should be used for that purpose. But it has been found extremely desirable to have a simple sign for aggregation. Jevons was the first to introduce such a sign into logical Boolian algebra; and the sign which he proposed was, ·|· , the old sign of division turned up. This has the merit of suggesting + without being mistaken for it. It is however inconvenient not only as requiring the pen to be put three times to paper, but also more seriously because it may very well be mistaken for three signs.

For that reason I propose to join the two dots to the upright; and I care little how they are joined. ∞ could be written without raising the pen; but I proposed ᛣ before thinking of the other, and I see no sufficient reason to change this until some agreement can be reached or approached.

Corollary 9. That $x \curlyvee y \curlyvee z = x \curlyvee (y \curlyvee z)$ becomes evident on writing the second number in its full form

$$\overline{(x\overline{(\overline{y \cdot z})})} \quad \text{or} \quad \overline{\overline{x} \cdot \overline{\overline{y z}}}.$$

For, by Corollary 5, this is the same as $\overline{(\overline{x}\,\overline{y}\,\overline{z})}$.

Corollary 10. An aggregant can be inserted under even enclosures or vincula, erased under odd enclosures or vincula.

Corollary 11. Aggregation is commutative.

Corollary 12. Aggregation is associative. These corollaries appear from the corresponding properties of composition, as soon as the aggregates are written in their full form.

Corollary 13. We may transform $x \cdot (y \curlyvee z)$ to $x \cdot y \curlyvee z$ without danger of rendering it false. For in $x\overline{(\overline{(y)}\,\overline{(z)})}$ we can, by Corollary 7, iterate x, so as to get $x\overline{(\overline{(xy)}\,\overline{(z)})}$ and we can then erase the outer x by Corollary 3.

Corollary 14. Aggregation and composition are mutually distributive; so that

$$x \cdot (y \curlyvee z) = x \cdot y \curlyvee x \cdot z$$
$$x \curlyvee y \cdot z = (x \curlyvee y) \cdot (x \curlyvee z).$$

The proof [of] the latter formula was given by me in 1867, the former having been substantially given by Boole.

§ 6. Besides the positive, or material, propositions, x, y, etc., we meet, thus far with two propositions of logical provenance. The one is the blank, or ⊚, the purely empty and meaningless proposition, the other, the empty oval, ○, is the proposition necessarily false.

Corollary 15. From ○ anything whatever follows; and from anything whatever ⊚ follows. For by Corollary 4, from ○ follows ○○; and thereby by Corollary 3 and Rule III, follows ○$\overline{(x)}$; whence by Corollary 5 we have ○x, and by Corollary 3, x. Hence, by Rule II follows the other clause of this corollary.

§ 7. A relation r is said to be transitive if the relates of the relate are *included* among the relates of the correlate, so that

> If M is r to P,
> and S is r to M,
> then S is r to P.

Thus, transitiveness depends on a relation of inclusion. Taking any relation, say 'loves',

> If M is loved by every lover of P,
> and S is loved by every lover of M,
> then S is loved by every lover of P.

Such a transitive relation has the special character that

> X is loved by every lover of X,

for which, at present, there is no better designation than an anti-alio-relation. Not all transitive relations have this character. Some are not merely anti-self-relations, but are alio-relations, or such in which nothing stands to itself. But Schröder has shown that all alike depend upon inclusion, every one being compounded from some relation in this fashion:

> M both worships P and worships whatever P worships,
> S both worships M and worships whatever M worships;
> ∴ S both worships P and worships whatever P worships.

- Therefore, M stands both to P and to each person who does not love all that P loves in the relation of loving something that he does not love;
- and if S stands both to M and to each person who does not love all that M loves in the relation of loving something that he does not love;
- then S stands both to P and to each person who does not love all that P loves in the relation of loving something that he does not love.

It is easy to see that every transitive anti-self-relation must be of this form.

We have already virtually encountered a logical transitive anti-alio-relation which is also truly continuous. For when we write,

> It snows
> It blows

we virtually say that these two facts are in the relation of coexistence with one another, and taking coexistence in such a sense that everything that exists is coexistent with itself. By saying that this relation is *truly continuous*, I mean that if A is coexistent with B, I mean that

- A is coexistent with something coexistent with something coexistent with something coexistent with B,
- and that in short intermediaries each coexistent with the next are capable of being inserted up *to any multitude whatsoever*.

If this be admitted as self-evident, then we have at once the extremely important proposition in the logic of collections, that *any collection whatsoever may be taken in linear order*. In another memoir, I shall consider this proposition more narrowly.

The negative of the relation of coexistence I term the relation of *incompossibility*. If we say that it either does not snow or it does not blow (at this moment), I assert that its snowing and its blowing are (at this moment, and under the conditions of this moment) incompossible.

$$\boxed{\begin{array}{l}\text{It snows}\\\text{It blows}\end{array}}$$

Coexistence is the only anti-concurrent anti-alio-dyadic relation, that is, the only relation between all pairs of the form A:A and all pairs of the form A:B. Incompossibility is the only concurrent alio-relation; that is the only relation which subsists between no pairs of the form A:A and between none of the form A:B.

A notation for these two logical relations is thus provided. But there are two others for which notations have to be provided. These are the concurrent anti-alio-relation, which I term *identity*, in which every individual stands to itself alone, and the anti-concurrent alio-relation, which I term *otherness*, in which every existing individual stands to every one except itself.

Identity being the only continuous dyadic logical relation for which a notation has to be provided, may appropriately be represented by a heavy continuous line drawn between its relate and its correlate; which line may be ever so long or may be reduced to a *hyphen*. Thus

Tully   Cicero

will mean 'Tully is identical with Cicero'; that is, an individual *exists* (abstraction being made of tense) who is at once identical with Tully and identical with Cicero. If we enclose this in an oval, we shall precisely deny it, and shall, therefore, cease to assert, what it asserts, that any such individual as Tully exists. Suppose we wish simply to assert that Tully exists. Since this is less than is asserted in saying that Tully is Cicero, according to the fundamental principle of our notation that the erasure of what is unenclosed result in asserting less, we shall naturally change

Tully——Cicero   into   Tully——

thus changing 'Tully is Cicero' into 'Tully is something', or 'Tully exists'.[4] On the same principle, going one step further, we may write

———

or 'Something exists'.

---

4 A proposition is either *universal*, *particular*, or *singular*. A *universal* proposition is one which leaves to its interpreter the liberty of choosing the singular subject (from out of its universe) of an instance by which he may seek to refute the proposition. A *particular* proposition is one which transfers this liberty of choice to the other party, the utterer, and consequently the defender of the proposition. A *singular* proposition is one which leaves no liberty of choice, as to the singular instance, to either party. These statements follow as consequences of more essential definitions. Every proposition, and every sign, must be, in every aspect either *definite* or *individual*. That sign is *definite* to which the principle of contradiction applies. 'Some man' is not definite, since it may be true that 'Some man dies and some man is translated'. The definite sign leaves no ambiguity of interpretation: that states the same thing in another form. That sign is *individual* to which the principle of excluded middle applies. 'Whatever man there may be' is not individual, since it may be false that 'Either whatever man there may be dies or whatever man there may be is translated'. A universal proposition is non-individual (and consequently, necessarily definite) in respect to its subject. A particular proposition is indefinite (and so necessarily individual) in respect to its subject. A singular proposition is both definite and individual in respect to its subject.

A proposition is commonly said to have one subject and one predicate; and in a certain sense this is true. In another sense, it is not true. Thus, if we say 'Every man is the son of some woman', we are just as much speaking of women as of men. What we mean is that the interpreter is at liberty to instance any man he pleases, and then we (under favorable circumstances) shall be at liberty to instance a woman and under favorable circumstances can instance a woman of whom that man is the son. If, then, we insist that this proposition has but one subject, and still wish to view it analytically, so as to bring out its reference to women, we must say that that single subject is the single pair of which the interpreter must name the first member before the utterer and defender can be called upon to name the second. By "naming", here, we mean assigning a proper name, which applies only to a definite individual. Regarding a proposition as having, in general, a multitude of subjects, which must, in general, be "named" in a certain order, there is one first subject to which all propositions whatsoever may be regarded as referring; namely, the Truth, or the absolute reality, or the total universe. This Truth, or total universe, is singular; that is, is a definite individual. For the principles of contradiction and excluded middle apply to all propositions, in that respect.

Here we have two new rules. For each of these transformations may be resolved into two steps, of which the first simply ruptures the line of identity, while the second is an erasure justified by Corollary 3. We find then

Rule IV. *A line of identity may be ruptured where it is unenclosed.*

Moreover, the fact that we at all inquire about a universe shows that we already have sufficient familiarity with it to say that 'There is something'. For a "universe" is a collection or continuum of objects which the two interlocutors which every proposition or judgment supposes (in the latter case both included in the same person) understand each other to mean. Hence we have the rule,

Rule V. *Any undetached line of identity may be written unenclosed.*[5]

Let us now see how it is the same thing to say that 'Tully is something' and that 'Tully exists'. When we say, for example, 'A sinless man exists', we do not, therein, predicate anything of a sinless man. This has been shown by several logicians; particularly by Scotus, and very clearly by Kant in his discussion of the ontological proof. On the contrary, the utterer of the proposition 'A sinless man exists' and its interpreter must well understand one another, or else there is no proposition *in actu*, and both must be familiar, to some extent, with the universe referred to, and what is meant is that in that universe a sinless man "occurs", that is, reacts with the other objects in that universe, and under favorable circumstances, *might* be "named", or instanced. Every proposition whatever supposes that its subject can be instanced, and therefore in saying that some sinless man exists you assert no more than in saying "some sinless man is a sinless man". If I say that the color vermillion exists, I mean that unless one is color-blind, one can meet with it in the universe of colors. This capability of an object of being met with consists in its reacting with everything else in its universe, so that if we place ourselves in such a position to be sufficiently in reaction with the objects of the universe we shall be in reaction with it. The sign which forms the subject of any proposition always acts upon its interpreter through association by contiguity, which sort of action calls up a reaction between *ego* and *non-ego*. The only objects of whose existence we have underived and uncriticizable knowledge are objects of perceptual reaction in perceptual judgments. These are the only objects to which the principle of excluded middle applies in all its strictness. We say that 'Phillip of Macedon' is an individual term; yet we can neither say that Phillip is drunk or that Phillip is sober. It is only with reference to certain characters that the principle of excluded middle applies to Phillip. The instantaneous reaction at the common limit of two times is alone absolutely individual. To say that the principle of excluded third applies to A is to say that taking any predicate, P, either A occurs as P or A occurs as not P; for if it does not occur at all, neither assertion is true. Hence individuality implies existence, and existence individuality.

5 [Alt.:] It thus appears that each unenclosed point marked on the sheet of assertion denotes some individual object. Every individual "exists", that is, exerts reactions in its own universe; and every designate individual must be well known to do so. But it does not follow that our symbolization should be restricted to objects of a single universe, or even that the individual existences should all be ultimate reactions independent of all reason. There is no reason why some of the

We see that every unenclosed point of a line of identity denotes an indefinite individual, "Something". Consequently, two non-individual terms being joined by a line of identity, the meaning will be that there is some individual which both represent. Thus

$$\begin{matrix} \text{—is a patriarch} \\ \text{—is translated} \end{matrix}$$

means 'Some patriarch is translated'; and

$$\begin{matrix} \text{—is mother of———} \\ \text{—is wife of—is father of} \end{matrix}$$

means 'Somebody is mother of somebody and a wife of a father of the same'.

A logical principle which is the very sole leather of mathematics, so continually is it used, is that upon any indefinite individual of which anything can be

---

individuals should not be individual collections, for example, or even individual collections of pairs or other sorts. The logic of collections will be touched upon below.

An *individual* term is a term to which the principle of excluded middle applies. A *definite* term is one to which the principle of contradiction applies. A *singular* term is one both individual and definite. Points merely marked on the sheet of assertion are individual but not necessarily definite. A proper name is singular; and therefore we have a fifth rule:

Rule V. *Two occurrences of the same singular term may be joined by a line of identity.*

Thus if we have $\begin{matrix}\text{Tully—is an orator}\\ \text{Tully—is a Roman}\end{matrix}$ we may write $\begin{matrix}\text{Tully—is an orator}\\ \text{Tully—is a Roman}\end{matrix}$, whence, by Rule IV, $\begin{matrix}\text{Tully—is an orator}\\ \text{Tully—is a Roman}\end{matrix}$ and by Corollary 3, $\begin{matrix}\text{Tully—is an orator}\\ \text{is a Roman}\end{matrix}$. But if we had started from $\begin{matrix}\text{—is an orator}\\ \text{—is a Roman}\end{matrix}$, 'Something is an orator and something is a Roman', we should have no right to unite the two lines of identity, since 'something', though individual, is indefinite.

How shall we express analytically 'Some Roman is not an orator'? One excellent way, quite in the spirit of mathematics, is to suppose the indefinite Roman who is not an orator to be definitely known, and write $\overline{\begin{matrix}\text{X—is a Roman}\\ \overline{\text{X—is an orator}}\end{matrix}}$. This give us a new rule:

Rule VI. *Every indefinite individual may receive a singular designation.*

But we may also extend our notation so as to permit a line of identity to intersect an oval, and allow Rule V to apply to this case. We shall then have, successively, $\overline{\begin{matrix}\text{X—is a Roman}\\ \overline{\text{X—is an orator}}\end{matrix}}$, $\begin{matrix}\text{X—is a Roman}\\ \overline{\text{X—is an orator}}\end{matrix}$, $\begin{matrix}\text{X—is a Roman}\\ \overline{\text{—is an orator}}\end{matrix}$, $\begin{matrix}\text{X—is a Roman}\\ \overline{\text{—is an orator}}\end{matrix}$, $\begin{matrix}\text{—is a Roman}\\ \overline{\text{—is an orator}}\end{matrix}$. From the last of these we can also obviously deduce the first, under certain restrictions. Namely knowing that Tully exists is a Roman, I cannot write $\begin{matrix}\text{Tully—is a Roman}\\ \overline{\text{—is an orator}}\end{matrix}$. Having broken the line of identity unenclosed, I cannot simply reunite it. Still less can I change $\overline{\text{—is an orator}}$ into $\overline{\text{—is an orator}}$. I must invent a new Proper name and write $\begin{matrix}\text{Y—is a Roman}\\ \overline{\text{—is an orator}}\end{matrix}$. I can then iterate Y within, thus $\begin{matrix}\text{Y—is a Roman}\\ \overline{\text{Y—is an orator}}\end{matrix}$, and now the connection between the two Y's may be broken; thus, $\begin{matrix}\text{Y—is a Roman}\\ \overline{\text{Y—is an orator}}\end{matrix}$.

predicated we may confer a proper name, or peculiar designation.[6] It is true that a proper name is definite; and as long as an individual is utterly indefinite, a mere 'Something' unidentifiable, no designation can really function as a proper name. But as soon as we know that 'Somebody was translated', the principle of contradiction begins to apply. We know that *this* somebody is not both translated and untranslated; and commonly we shall know much else. So then if we know that somebody is a patriarch and is translated, we may invent the designation E for that translated patriarch, and may write

$$\begin{array}{l} \text{E—is a patriarch} \\ \text{E—is translated} \end{array}.$$

We are thus enabled to express, what we have hitherto had no means of expressing, that some patriarch is not translated. For we may write

$$\begin{array}{l} \text{F—is a patriarch} \\ \overline{(\text{F—is not translated})} \end{array}.$$

The notation which I employ in my general algebra of logic for such a proper name applied to an indefinite individual is this. If p means 'is a patriarch' and [t means] 'is translated', instead of writing

$$p \cdot e \cdot t \cdot e \qquad \text{I write} \qquad \Sigma_e \, p_e \cdot t_e$$

The sign Σ *simulates*, and merely simulates, a sign of logical aggregation. If there are only five individuals in the universe, 1, 2, 3, 4, 5, we should have

$$p-1 \cdot t-1 \,\text{✢}\, p-2 \cdot t-2 \,\text{✢}\, p-3 \cdot t-3 \,\text{✢}\, p-4 \cdot t-4 \,\text{✢}\, p-5 \cdot t-5 = \Sigma_e \, p_e \cdot t_e$$

and so it would be for any multitude whatsoever, assuming that a collection of any multitude is capable of linear arrangement. But if I were talking of the points of a line, there could be no logical aggregate of these, since they do not constitute a collection; yet I should still use the notation employing Σ.

The notation with Σ has the advantage of showing at once that the arbitrary proper designation written subscript to it is a peculiar kind of term. We did not

---

6 [**Alt.:**] [...] upon any indefinite individual we may confer a proper name, or special designation, as soon as this individual can be identified in two presentations. It is true that a proper name is definite; and as long as an individual is utterly indefinite, merely 'Something', though you may say you give it a proper name, yet this name will not function as such until two presentations can be identified. As soon as this is the case, it ceases to be utterly indefinite. The principle of contradiction begins to apply to it.

14 On the First Principles of Logical Algebra (R 515), c.1901 — 397

contemplate such a term as this when we adopted Rule III; and were we, on the strength of that rule, because from

$$\text{—is translated} \quad \text{we can pass to} \quad \text{X—is translated}$$

to think ourselves authorized to pass from

$$\overline{\underline{\text{F—is translated}}\atop\text{F—is a patriarch}} \quad \text{to} \quad \overline{\overline{\text{—is translated}}\atop\text{F—is a patriarch}}$$

we should commit a blunder. For, in point of fact, we are *not* authorized to pass from

$$\text{—is translated}\atop\text{F—is a patriarch} \quad \text{to} \quad \text{F—is translated}\atop\text{F—is a patriarch}\;.$$

If we wished to treat designations for indefinite individuals as ordinary terms, instead of writing 'Some patriarch is not translated' in the form

$$\text{F—is a patriarch}\atop\overline{\text{F—is translated}}$$

we should have to write something like this:

$$\overline{\overline{\text{F—is a patriarch}\atop\overline{\text{F—is translated}}}\atop\overline{\text{F—is wrongly chosen}}}\;.$$

But in order to avoid, at once, too much complication in writing any comparatively simple proposition, and any too complicated rule,[7] I simply allow the line of identity to cut an oval, and write —$\overline{\text{is translated}}$ to mean 'Something exists which is not translated'. In the general algebra, this is written

$$\Sigma_i \overline{t_i}$$

the *i* being under the obelus, and at the same time, outside the obelus. Then, 'Everything is good' will be written

$$\overline{\text{—is good}} \quad \text{or} \quad \overline{\Sigma_i \overline{g_i}}\;.$$

---

[7] **[Alt.:]** [...] complicated rule, I simply allow the line of identity to cut the oval. (Two other systems of notation in perfect harmony with that here described will be given below. The present system I term that of Existential Graph, as contradistinguished from a nearly similar system of Entitative Graphs which I described in *The Monist*, Vol. VII pp. 161–217.)

But since the negative of an aggregate is a composite, the very definition of aggregation being

$$a \curlyvee b \curlyvee c \curlyvee \text{ etc.} = \overline{\bar{a} \cdot \bar{b} \cdot \bar{c}} \cdot \text{ etc.}$$

I also, and most usually in the algebra, write this

$$\Pi_i g_i$$

The proposition 'Something loves all things' will then appear as $\overline{\boxed{\text{loves}}}$ while the proposition 'Everything is loved by something or other' will appear as $\boxed{\overline{\text{loves}}}$. In the algebra I distinguish between these by the order of "quantifiers", Σ and Π, writing the former proposition

$$\Sigma_i \Pi_j l_{ji} \quad \text{and the latter} \quad \Pi_j \Sigma_i l_{ji}.$$

Thus in the algebra, the expression of a proposition consists in a series of "quantifiers",—which collectively I propose to call the Hopkinsian, not ~~knowing~~ remembering now whether Mr. O. H. Mitchell or I first introduced this, at the Johns Hopkins University,—followed by an expression which I call the Boolian, since it comes under the rules of Boole's algebra of logic as modified by Jevons.

15 On the Basic Rules of Logical Transformation

R 516, c.1901. Houghton Library. This second paper on the philosophy and ethics of notation is another and slightly more matured development of the previous one, in a continuous run of 51 manuscript pages, with variants. It demonstrates how both the logic of relatives and the graphical method of logic are built up from Peirce's earlier work on Boolean algebra, and how those earlier principles are to be conserved to the fullest degree. The focus is on two notions, scriptibility and transformability, and the soundness and validity of the latter, which at once show the generality of basic principles in philosophy of notation: such basic rules are not meant to advance the philosophy of logic in particular but are the very principles for setting up such philosophy in the first place. Again, it is conceivable that this piece or its still later versions were planned to be one of the first sections of the second chapter of Part 3 of the 1903 *Logical Tracts*, given that the plan of the *Tracts* contains the section "Basic Principles" which was to explain the principles of illative transformations in its first part on existential graphs (LoF 2). As can be learned from coeval writings, Peirce is led to these notions by making three important generalisations to fundamental theoretical notions of logic: that of (i) propositions to all signs, (ii) truth to scriptibility, namely "capable of being written conformably to the purpose" (R 501, late 1901), and (iii) derivation to transformability, namely "capable of being transformed without changing anything scriptible into anything non-scriptible" (R 430, early 1902; LoF 1).

§ 1. The purpose of this paper is to show what appear to be the first principles of the Boolian algebra of logic, as extended by me to the logic of relatives and at the same time to develop certain other notations.

Shall we aim to make as few rules as possible? A single rule would suffice, if it were made complicated enough. Shall we endeavor to carry the analysis of distinct principles as far as possible and so make as many rules as possible? They may be made innumerable by making them special enough. It seems to be desirable, in the first place, to analyze every operation into as many radically unlike steps not destructive of one another as possible. If every permissible transformation, that is, every transformation proceeding upon a general rule, which can never result in a transformation of truth into falsity, can be analyzed into two steps one a permissible insertion and the other a permissible erasure this should be done. All the radically different categories of signs required should be recognized. The rules should be as general as possible. They should not afford two different cases for any transformation. Under those conditions, the greater their number the more completely full and the more completely analytic would they appear to be. I shall not undertake to prove that the analysis I offer is the best possible; but I think it will be manifestly better than any heretofore presented.

§ 2. A logical notation is a system of symbolization by which (if it is perfect) any proposition can be expressed; and there are certain "rules", that is, statements of conditions under which certain transformations of the expressions are permissible; and this body of rules is so complete that any proposition that can be necessarily deduced from the propositions originally expressed can be obtained by a skillful employment of these rules of transformation.

§ 3. Since we have to frame a system for symbolizing propositions, a philosophical mind would judge that the first thing to be done would be to analyze the nature of a proposition. But I purpose confining myself as far as I am able to the mathematical or purely formal method, and avoiding logical analysis as much as I can. A proposition is defined as that which is either true or false. But I will avoid these words, and content myself with saying, at first, that a proposition is intended to conform to a certain purpose. I will use adjectives in *-able* and *-ible*, implying possibility, to mean possibility agreeable to this purpose. Thus, *scriptible* shall mean capable of being written conformably to the purpose; *transformable*, capable of being transformed without changing anything scribtible into anything non-scriptible.

We are going to use visible marks upon a surface as our symbols. We will provide ourselves, therefore, with a surface which we will call the *sheet of assertion*, and will pretend to hold ourselves responsible for, that is to *assert*, the perfect conformity to our purpose of whatever proposition we write upon it. But let us not talk of propositions; but let us call what is written, or might be written, and might under circumstances not necessarily the actual circumstances conform to our purpose, a *graph*. As long as the sheet of assertion remains blank let us conceive that we are irresponsible. Having once written something upon it, we have judged that to be conformed to our purpose. All that we have to do is to avoid all danger of transforming the scriptible into the non-scriptible. By a "rule" of transformation, we mean a general *permission* to make certain transformations under certain circumstances on the ground that such transformation can never transform anything scriptible into anything non-scriptible. Perhaps, then, we ought to call it a rule of transformation that,

Rule 0. Whatever graph is written on the sheet of assertion may be allowed to remain.

For we shall make abstraction of tense; and therefore if any graph ever was scriptible, it remains so. But since there is some doubt of the relevancy or utility of such a rule, I shall number it Rule 0.

Since a blank sheet involves us in no responsibility, we have the more positive rule,

Rule I. A graph written on the sheet of assertion may be erased.

§ 4. Suppose that each of two graphs is scriptible; so that we might, conformably to our purpose, write either of them on the sheet of assertion. Then it will be extremely natural to write both on different parts of the same sheet of assertion, treating these parts as different sheets of assertion, and that without regard to their greater or less distance from one another or their relative direction from one another. Let us adopt this so natural convention, in the following rule:

Rule II. Detached graphs may be inserted or erased, as if no others were on the sheet, and that regardless of distance and of direction.

We shall naturally be prepared to find reason, later, to extend or even to restrict the meaning of the word "detached", here.

In consequence of the convention embodied in this rule, I term the particular system of symbolization that is here in process of development that of *Existential Graphs*, as opposed to a system of *Entitative Graphs* which I sketched in "The Logic of Relatives" (*The Monist*, Vol. VII, pp. 161–217). The pertinency of the name will appear below.[1]

Suppose that L, written alone on the sheet of assertion, would express that 'Art is long'; and suppose that W, in place of L, would express that 'Time is weary'. Then

$$L \ W$$

would, by Rule II, express that 'Art is long and time is weary'. The mode of combination of the two clauses of this proposition is traditionally called *copulation*; but a more familiar term, due to De Morgan, is *composition*. The clauses combined will be termed *copulants*; the resulting whole, the *copulate*. Rule II, then, has the effect of making the blank space a sign of copulation. It will be convenient to be provided with a second sign for the same purpose; and I shall use a heavy dot above the line between the copulants, with the same signification; thus,[2]

$$A \cdot T.$$

As a third sign, an inverted caret may be employed; thus:

$$A \smallsmile T.$$

---
1 [Alt.:] There is no restriction upon the distance at which the two simultaneously written graphs shall be placed. One may follow the other with a short blank.
2 [Hereon A means 'Art is long' and T 'Time is weary'.]

Boole called copulation "logical multiplication"; and in this he has been followed by his entire school. But this is a mere confusion of ideas, and no genuine extension of the conception of multiplication. The idea was undoubtedly suggested to him by the circumstance that if p and q are the probabilities of two independent events, pq is the probability of the *copulate*, or *composite*, of those events. But this is merely because the problems in probability that happen to be the most usual are of such a nature that it is convenient to measure probabilities upon a certain scale. It is a property, not of probabilities themselves, but of a particular system of measuring them. This was judged by Boole to be a good reason for using 0 and 1 in logical algebra for falsity and truth, or for nothing and being; which being done, the product of two algebraical expressions for propositions becomes *one* out of an infinite multitude of ways of *expressing* the compound of them. But Boole's followers have, by giving up the use of addition, quite relinquished all connection with probability; and they speak of logical composition *itself* as multiplication, not of multiplication as merely one way of expressing copulation. Copulation, mathematically considered, is of the nature of a "mean function"; that is, a symmetrical function which, when all the variables have the same value, itself takes that value.

Of two of my signs, the dot suggests the sign of multiplication, but is not exactly that. As for the blank, it is forced upon me by the general idea of my system. Early in 1880 (*Am. J. Math.* II p. 33) I quite correctly[3] defined logical copulation by means [of] the copula of inclusion. The definition (substituting for the copula its definition) is as follows:

Clause 1. Whatever graph, x, would, if written, be transformable (consistently with our purpose) into a, and would be transformable (instead) into b, would be transformable into $a \cdot b$.

Clause 2. Whatever graph, x, would, if written, be transformable into $a \cdot b$ would be transformable (instead) into a, and would be transformable (instead) into b.

I proceed to show that both clauses are corollaries from Rules I and II. I shall refer to them as **Corollaries 1 and 2**. To prove the first, suppose x to be written, and that, in consequence of its being written, a and b are separately scriptible. But by Rule II whatever graphs are separately scriptible are scriptible together, detached. Hence, $a\,b$ or $a \cdot b$ is scriptible. Q.E.D.

To prove Corollary 2, I remark that if a were written, it could, by Rule I, be erased; whence, by Rule II, if $a \cdot b$, that is, $a\,b$, were written a could be erased.

---

3 Prof. Schröder's criticism will be answered below.

Whence, if, in consequence of x being written, $a\,b$ should become scriptible, this could be transformed into b, so that x could be transformed into b; and the same reasoning applies to the transformation into a.

Previously to 1880, the associative and commutative principles were regarded as the fundamental characters of copulation, along with a distributive principle. I proved the two first from the above definition; but Rule II shows them in their true light, as mere negations which in no way touch upon the real essence of composition. It is no more necessary to refer to them than it is to state that the graphs can be written in blue ink, if desired.

Corollary 3. Any detached partial graph may be erased.

Corollary 4. The whole graph written or any detached part of it may, consistently with our purpose, be iterated, and may be regarded as iterated up to any multitude of replicas whatsoever.

This last clause assumes that there is room upon a surface for a collection of any multitude whatsoever.

§ 5. We must enable ourselves to express that a given graph, if it were written as an entire graph, would be transformable into another given graph, without danger of passing from the scriptible to the unscriptible. To accomplish this, two steps of enlargements of our notation are requisite which, although they are of the same general nature, are distinct from one another. For to say that A is transformable into B, is to say that under any circumstances whatever, although we are not prepared to say whether A will be scriptible or whether B will be so, we are prepared to say that *if* A is scriptible, B will be so. At present, we can combine two graphs only by saying that both are scriptible. But this is not all. It may be that A does not happen to be scriptible; and yet it may not be transformable into B without *danger* of passing from the scriptible to the unscriptible. For it may be that A, though not scriptible under present circumstances, may become so. I shall separate these difficulties; in the present section assuming that the law of excluded middle applies, so that A is either scriptible or unscriptible, and that we have only to avoid passing from the now scriptible to the not scriptible; while in the next section I shall reconsider our conclusions to see how they are to be modified in case A should become scriptible.

As a first step toward the attainment of an analytical method of expressing that a given graph, A, if it were written as an entire graph, could be transformed into another given graph, B, let us begin by writing to express this; that is, this graph is scriptible, if, and only if, A, if written as an entire graph, would be transformable into B.

We may now simplify this notation, and render it more analytical, by means of the following theorem; where the Hebrew letters, א, *Aleph*, and ב, *Beth*, are for the nonce used as signs either of which is replaceable (in conformity with the general purpose) by any graph whatever; so that, for example, B א shall be such a graph that if it be scriptible as an entire graph, B, if scriptible as an entire graph would be transformable into any graph whatever. Then the theorem is that the graphs

are alike in respect to scriptibility; that is, are either both or neither scriptible. In setting forth the proof, I propose to attach to different propositions such letters as (A_1), (B_1), (C_1), (A_2), (B_2), (C_2); etc. to show that the proposition to which C is attached with a subjacent number, follows by one inferential step, or syllogism from the propositions to which A and B are attached with the same subjacent number.

Proof. In this proof, I shall refer to the graph A B as P, and to the graph A B א ב as Q.

The three following cases include (one or more of them) every possibility:

- Case 1. A is not scriptible;
- Case 2. B is scriptible;
- Case 3. A is scriptible, but B is not so.

In Case 1, By the definition of this case,

$(A_1) \cdot (B_4)$ A is not scriptible.

By the definition of *transformable* given in § 3,

$(B_1) \cdot (B_5) \cdot (B_7)$ Any graph is transformable into any given graph, unless such transformation would transform anything scriptible into anything not scriptible.

$(C_1) \cdot (A_2)$ ∴ A is transformable into B.

By the definition of the scroll ◯ given above,

$(B_2) \cdot (B_9)$ P is scriptible if A is transformable into B.

$(C_2) \cdot (A_3)$ ∴ P is scriptible.

By Corollary 3,

(A_4) If A B א were scriptible A would be scriptible.

(C_4) · (A_5) ∴ A ⦅B⦅ℵ⦆⦆ is not scriptible.
(C_5) · (A_6) ∴ A ⦅B⦅ℵ⦆⦆ is transformable into ⊐.
    By the definition of the scroll,
(B_4) If A ⦅B⦅ℵ⦆⦆ is transformable into ⊐, Q is scriptible.
(C_6) · (B_3) ∴ Q is scriptible.
(C_3) · (A_7) ∴ In Case 1, P and Q agree in respect to scriptibility.
    In Case 2, by the definition of the case,
(A_8) · (B_{14}) B is scriptible.
(C_8) · (A_9) ∴ A is transformable into B.
(C_9) · (A_{10}) ∴ B is scriptible.

By the definitions of P and Q, they are graphs. Hence, if there were no graph not scriptible, P and Q must agree in respect to scriptibility (both being scriptible), and the Theorem would be true. Hence, we may assume, for the purposes of argument, that

(A_{11}) Some graph is scriptible.
    But, by the definition of ℵ,
(B_{11}) ℵ, written as an entire graph, would be transformable into any graph that might be instanced.
(C_11) · (A_12) ∴ ℵ, written as an entire graph, is transformable into a non-scriptible graph.
    But it is of the essence of transformation that,
(B_{12})   If anything is transformed into a second, thing, any third thing that is transformed into the second would be transformed into the second would be transformed into the third.
(C_{12}) · (A_{13}) ∴ If B were transformable into ℵ, it would be transformable into a non-scriptible graph.
    But, by the definition of what is *transformable*, in §3,
(B_{13}) · (B_{16}) No scriptible graph is transformable into an unscriptible graph.
(C_{13}) · (A_{14}) If B were transformable into ℵ, B would be unscriptible.
(C_{14}) · (A_{15}) B is not transformable into ℵ.
    But, by the definition of the scroll,
(C_{15}) If ⦅B⦅ℵ⦆⦆ were scriptible, B would be transformable into ℵ.
(C_{15}) ∴ ⦅B⦅ℵ⦆⦆ is unscriptible.
    Hence, by reasoning similar to that under Case 1,
(B_{10}) In Case 2, Q is scriptible.
(C_{10}) · (B_7) ∴ In Case 2, P and Q agree in respect to scriptibility.
(C_7) ∴ In Cases 1 and 2, P and Q agree in respect to scriptibility.
    By the definition of Case 3, in this case,
(A_{16}) A is scriptible, but B not so.

(C_{16}) · (B_{17}) ∴ P is not transformable into B.

But, by the definition of the scroll,

(A_{17}) If P is scriptible, A is transformable into B.

(C_{17}) ∴ In Case 3, P is not scriptible.

By (A_{16}), no transformation of B into another graph would be a transformation of a scriptible into an unscriptible graph. Hence, by (B_1), B is transformable into any graph. Hence,

(A_{18}) B⦅ℵ⦆ is scriptible.

But by (A_{16})

(B_{18}) A is scriptible.

Hence by Rule II,

(C_{18}) A B⦅ℵ⦆ is scriptible.

Consequently, just as under Case 2, B⦅ℵ⦆ was proved unscriptible, in this case Q is unscriptible, and again P and Q agree in respect to scriptibility. Thus,

(B_{19}) In Cases 1, 2, 3, P and Q agree in scriptibility.

(C_{19}) ∴ P and Q invariably agree in scriptibility. Q.E.D.

This proof has been set forth with some approach to fullness, in order to make manifest the practical necessity and good sense of large abridgment of proofs.

It follows from the above theorem that a graph expressing that a given graph if it were written as a complete graph would be transformable into a given graph can be analytically expressed as soon as we adopt a sign enabling us to write a graph which shall be scriptible, if, and only if, a given graph X is transformable into any graph that is capable of being instanced. Let us for that purpose draw a simple oval round the graph X. We shall then have the following rule:

Rule III. An enclosure is scriptible, if, and only if, all that it encloses, being written as a complete graph, would be transformable into any graph.

Corollary 5. Any graph, A, is scriptible, if and only if, a graph ⦅Ⓐ⦆ consisting of the same graph enclosed in two ovals containing nothing else is scriptible.

For if A is not scriptible it is transformable into any graph whatever, since the transformation will not change a scriptible into an unscriptible graph. Consequently, Ⓐ will be scriptible. Now Ⓐ being scriptible is not transformable into A, which is not scriptible. Consequently, Ⓐ is not transformable into any graph that may be proposed. Hence ⦅Ⓐ⦆ will be unscriptible like A.

But if A is scriptible, and there is no unscriptible graph, ⦅Ⓐ⦆ is scriptible, like A. But if there is any unscriptible graph, A, being scriptible is not transformable into any graph whatever, and therefore Ⓐ will be unscriptible. Since Ⓐ is unscriptible, it will be transformable into any graph whatever without transforming a scriptible into an unscriptible graph; and therefore again ⒶⒶ will be scriptible like A. In any case, therefore, A is scriptible if and only if ⒶⒶ is scriptible. Q.E.D.

Corollary 6. Any graph A is transformable into a graph consisting of the same graph enclosed in two ovals enclosing nothing else. And two ovals unenclosed and with nothing between them are removable without transforming a scriptible into an unscriptible graph.

Corollary 7. Any graph A which, if it were written as an entire graph would be transformable into another graph B, will be transformable into the same graph whenever it is detached and "evenly enclosed", that is, is within a finite even number of enclosures; and the graph B, will be transformable into A whenever it is detached and "oddly enclosed", that is, is enclosed in an odd number of ovals.[4]

Suppose the graph A to be transformable into the graph B. Either of these may be a blank; for a blank is a graph, subject to all the rules of graphs. Its only peculiarity is that it accompanies every graph; so that if it is erased, it still remains. Now suppose B to be written within a single oval. Some other graph is written, besides, in that oval, if it be only a blank. For this other may be substituted, by Corollary 5, a graph consisting of an enclosure containing another graph. Let all beside B that is enclosed in the outer oval be represented by Ⓒ. Then what is written is ⒷⒸ. But by the above theorem, this asserts that were B written as an entire graph, C could be substituted for it. By the essential nature of transformation, this means that whatever is transformed into B is transformable into C. But A is transformable into B. Therefore A is transformable into C. Hence we may write ⒶⒸ. But in doing this we have transformed B into A. Consequently, if any graph, A, is written as an entire graph, would be transformable into another graph, B, then B written detached within one oval is transformable into A.

Now suppose there is a finite number, N, such that if any graph, B, is enclosed in any less number of ovals, and if the number of these ovals is odd, then B is transformable into any graph, A, that would, were it written as an entire graph, be

---

4 [Alt.:] Since the proof of this proposition is not very simple, it would, by most mathematical writers, be reckoned as a theorem rather than a corollary. But I undertake to make the distinction between a *theorem* and a *corollary*, a precise distinction. Namely, if a proposition be such that the meanings of terms and the truths already demonstrated are held distinctly in mind, we have only to apply them to the new proposition in order to make its truth evident, I call it a corollary, however long the process of proof may be; while a proposition which cannot be proved without the introduction of some construction which definitions and previous propositions do not call for I call a *theorem*.

transformable into B; while if the number of ovals enclosing B is even, then any graph, A, that, written as an entire graph, would be transformable into B, is still transformable into B within this even number of ovals less than N.

Since N is finite, $N-1 < N$. Suppose, then, that as a necessary consequence of the state of things supposed, any graph P within $N-1$ enclosures is transformable into a graph, Q. Then, let there be another oval within the $N-1$ ovals, this inner oval enclosing Q and let the rest of what it encloses be written in the form ⓡ. We have, then, within the $N-1$ enclosures ⓠⓡ. Consequently, as above, within $N-1$ enclosures Q is transformable in R and therefore P is transformable into R. That is, we may write within the $N-1$ enclosures ⓟⓡ. In other words, Q is transformable into P within N enclosures. Thus if the rule holds for $N-1$ enclosures it holds also for N enclosures. It therefore holds for any finite number of enclosures.

The same thing may be proved in another way. Supposing that the rule holds for any number of enclosures less that N. Then, let V be a graph containing $N-1$ enclosures; and let us suppose that a transformation authorized by the rule being made within these enclosures U would be transformed into a graph v. Suppose, then, that v is written within one additional enclosure; and call the remainder of the contents of this enclosure ⓦ; so that ⓥⓦ is written unenclosed. Then, as before, we have ⓤⓦ and v is transformable into u under one enclosure. But this is the authorization of the performance within N enclosures of the inverse of the transformation which the rule authorized within $N-1$ enclosures.

These proofs, being evident, are perfectly satisfactory as proofs. But when we come to the analysis of the reasoning of the theory of numbers; it will be necessary to bear in mind that a proposition concerning numbers has been used in establishing these propositions; so that they cannot be safely used in the analysis of that reasoning. But as long as we confine ourselves to a definite number of exhibited enclosures, the principles may be applied to them without danger.

Corollary 8. Under odd enclosures, anything may be inserted, detached.

Corollary 9. Any detached part of a graph, however enclosed, is iterable under any additional enclosures; and if already so iterated the inner replica is erasible.

For the graph A B C is, by Corollary 4, transformable into A A B C. Consequently, by Corollary 7 A ⒶⒷ C is transformable into A Ⓑ C. Consequently A ⒷⒸ is transformable into A ⒶⒷⒸ and so forth. The other transformations are obviously permissible.

Corollary 10. If an unenclosed oval contains nothing but ovals all of which contain, otherwise unenclosed and detached the same graph, this graph may be iterated unenclosed. That is (AB)(AC)(AD) may be transformed into A (AB)(AC)(AD) and consequently into A (B)(C)(D). For by Rule II, Corollary 4, (AB)(AC)(AD) is transformable into 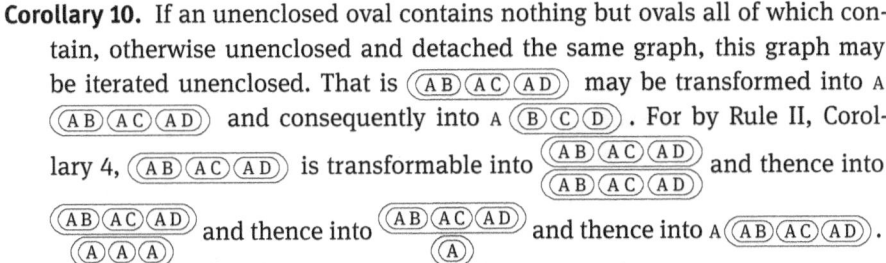 and thence into (AB)(AC)(AD)⁄(A)(A)(A) and thence into (AB)(AC)(AD)⁄(A) and thence into A (AB)(AC)(AD).

Corollary 11. If a graph is scriptible, consisting of an oval enclosing two graphs, then either of these, if written as an entire graph, would be transformable into an enclosure containing only the other.

For if (AB) is scriptible, then A B is transformable into any graph, C. That is, under any circumstances under which A and B are both scriptible, C is scriptible. If, then, either of these is scriptible, the other when scriptible as an entire graph would be transformable into C. Now since C may be any graph whatever, if A is scriptible (B) must be scriptible. That is, the transformation of A into (B) cannot be a transformation of the scriptible into the non-scriptible.

Scholium. There is a common expression, "That is as false as anything can be". This is just the effect of the oval. The graph (A) does not quite express that A is unscriptible, but only that if anything is unscriptible, A is so. This Hegelian sort of denial is the only one our system expresses. It will practically answer the purpose of flat denial. As such, it is a sign of denial if there can be any such sign, and is identical with the *obelus*, or black horizontal spit written over a word or sentence to deny it; a sign which Isodorus Hispalensis about A.D. 600 refers to as an old sign. It has been used ever since, giving rise to the use of the same mark to indicate an omitted *n* (*non*) or *m*. It is used by writers on probability and by Boole in the same sense. We may use it as an alternative sign equivalent to the oval.

§ 6. We have now to consider the second of the difficulties mentioned at the beginning of the last section. When we write a graph, we may agree that it shall mean that the graph is scriptible under present circumstances, or that it is sometimes scriptible, or that it is always scriptible. But by Rule II, whenever we should mean by writing A and B severally we equally mean by writing them together. If by writing A, we merely mean that A is sometimes scriptible, then by writing A B we meanly mean that A is sometimes scriptible and that B is sometimes scriptible, without implying that they are ever scriptible together. Then by saying that A is transformable into B, we merely mean that by the transformation we shall not change what is sometimes scriptible into what is never scriptible. If on the other hand, by writing A we mean that A is scriptible under some definite circumstances, such as the present circumstances, or all circumstances, then by saying that A is transformable into B we shall merely mean that if A is now scriptible, so is B, or that if A is always scriptible so is B. In any case, we are without means of expressing that under *some* circumstances not definitely known A and B are scriptible together. This is the defect of Boole's algebra of logic which I first pointed out in March, 1867. We are also unable to express that B is scriptible *whenever* A is scriptible, without saying that it is always scriptible so long as definite conditions are fulfilled or that A is never scriptible under those conditions. The logic of relatives, by a single device, enables us to do these things and far more.[5]

---

5 [Alt.:] For this reason, Jevons, and all subsequent students of Boole, following De Morgan (whose pupil Jevons was) have adopted the operation of logical *aggregation* as fundamental. That is ought not to be considered as a primitive operation, if copulation and negation, are to be taken as primitive, appears from my paper of March, 1867.

There is, however, no doubt that it is extremely convenient in logical algebra to have a special sign for aggregation. This is sufficiently proved by the fact that De Morgan, in 1858, having given appropriate signs to the two operation of composition (or copulation) and aggregation, without employing the Boolian algebra was followed in this by the Boolians, Jevons, in 1864, Peirce in 1867, Robert Grassmann in 1872, Schröder in 1877, and M[a]cColl in 1877, each being unaware of the works of his predecessor (and the last three, doubtless, unaware also of the work of De Morgan). In short, all the followers of Boole, with the distinguished exception of Mr. Venn, have given up the use of the operation of addition and have substituted for it that of aggregation. If we represent addition by + and aggregation by ψ, the relation of the two is

$$a + b = (a \psi b) + a \cdot b.$$

That the temptation to call aggregation by the name of *logical addition* is strong, I must admit, since I, in common with most of the others was led independently to do so. But a further study of what has been said by Boole and Venn, together with reflexions of my own, have convinced me that aggregation is *not* addition in any properly extended sense, but is only another operation considerably resembling addition.

Even if aggregation be a sort of addition, I hold that to represent it by the sign + (a sin into which I myself was led at one time) is not only highly inconvenient, since addition and aggregation much often appear in the same formula, but is also an offence against ethical principles of terminology which are vital to the health of this branch of science. I am sure that nobody will understand that in saying this I am accusing my esteemed friends who have so used the sign + for aggregation of disregard of morals. I simply hold that they have overlooked certain considerations which, duly weighed, must forbid such notation.

Almost any science is liable to fall into confusion in respect to the use of technical terms and notations. The useless multiplication of synonyms is to be deprecated; although when synonyms mark distinctly different and valuable points of view they are not useless. But the use of one word or other symbol in two different senses, both exact and scientific, is an intolerable evil.

Individuals, however, will have their preferences which they will only yield to some principle the justice of which they must acknowledge. Taxonomic biology is the science which has found this difficulty the most serious; and the other sciences will do well to imitate the method in which the difficulty has been conquered in taxonomic biology. If we generalize the rule which has there approved itself, we get something like the following:

- The person who introduces a conception into science has the right and duty of supplying a terminology and notation for it; and these should be followed, unless there is a positive scientific advantage in departing from them; and no such departure should be greater than necessary, and if possible should involve some recognition of the original inventor or discoverer.

Let us apply this principle to the case in hand. Boole, immortal, if for nothing else, for the invention of logical algebra, used the signs of algebra in their strict algebraic senses; and it was merely a consequence of a certain convention adopted by him that they became, not logical signs, but algebraic equivalents of logical signs. In particular, + as used by him was *not* an equivalent for a sign of aggregation; and there is a positive scientific disadvantage in so using it. It was Jevons who first introduced into logical algebra a sign for aggregation; and the sign which he decided upon as appropriate was ·|·, which sufficiently resembles + to mark the resemblance of the operations. This sign is objectionable because it requires the pen to be put down three times, and also (what is more important) because it is liable to be mistaken for three signs, and would inevitably be so mistaken. But both objections may be obviated by trifling modifications. The best of these I believe to be Υ which only requires the pen to be placed on paper once. But before this occurred to me, I had joined the two dots thus ψ, and until there is some prospect of a general recognition of the ethics of notation, I may as well continue to do so, although the other sign Υ appears to me distinctly preferable. But I hope others may be led to consider the matter from the ethical standpoint,—the only one upon which any uniformity can be attained; and when that is done any sign I might now adopt would be liable to modification.

In 1880, along with the definition of composition given above, I proposed the following definition of aggregation.

Clause 1. If a is transformable into x, and b is transformable into x, then $a \psi b$ is transformable into x.

Clause 2. If $a \psi b$ is transformable into x, then a is transformable into x, and b is transformable into x.

By means of these definitions I proved the commutative and associative principles. But as to the double distributive Principle

$$(a \psi b) \cdot c = a \cdot c \psi b \cdot c$$
$$a \cdot b \psi c = (a \psi c) \cdot (b \psi c)$$

I remarked that it was "easily proved; but the proof is too tedious to give". It turned out, however, that the proof was so far from obvious that I was unable to reproduce it, myself, upon challenge;

The blank space has hitherto been regarded as a sign of copulation. It may equally be regarded as a sign of the relation of co-scriptibility. In the sense in which I use the word *relation*, there can hardly be said to be any relation which is the negative of co-scriptibility. At any rate, there is no pair between which it subsists. It is altogether similar to *nothing* considered as a class. You may, in a sense, say there is such a class; but no individual belongs to it.

There is another logical relation the expression of which at once constitutes the logic of relatives. This relation is that of *identity*. It resembles the relation of co-scriptibility in being *affirmatively transitive* and *truly continuous*. I call a relation *affirmatively transitive* if, and only if, the *dictum de omni* applies to it; by which I mean that to say that A is in the given relation to B signifies that whatever is in the given relation to A is in the given relation to B, just as to say that A is, all of it, B, is to say that whatever is, all of it, A is, all of it, B. I call a relation *truly continuous*, if, and only if, a collection of intermediaries of any multitude whatsoever can be interposed in series between any relate and correlate, all previous ones being in the same relation to all subsequent ones; just as between any two separate instantaneous events in time any multitude whatsoever of distinct events are capable of being interposed. Or between any two marked points on a line any multitude whatsoever of points are capable of being marked. But identity differs from co-scriptibility in that each individual is in this relation to but one single individual instead of being in relation to all individuals. For this reason, it will be appropriately symbolized by a heavy line drawn from one partial graph to another, its ends abutting upon them. The line may have any shape and length. It may, in particular, be reduced to a *hyphen*.

With this convention, we shall write

$$\text{A}\!\!-\!\!\text{B}$$

---

and my friend, Prof. Schröder, went so far as to undertake to demonstrate that no such proof is possible. He admitted that it is easy to show that $a \cdot c \,⅋\, b \cdot c$ is transformable into $(a \,⅋\, b) \cdot c$. Further, if one could prove that $(a \,⅋\, b) \cdot c$ were transformable into $a \,⅋\, b \cdot c$, it would be easy to show that, by the same principle, it must be transformable into $a \cdot c \,⅋\, b \cdot c$. But this Professor Schröder thought he demonstrated to be impossible. I will first submit to the reader my "tedious proof", and then Prof. Schröder's "demonstration" that there can be no such proof.

My "tedious proof", from the definitions of aggregations and composition that $(a \,⅋\, b) \cdot c$ is transformable into $a \,⅋\, b \cdot c$ is as follows:

If $(a \,⅋\, b) \cdot c$ is not transformable into $a \,⅋\, b \cdot c$, let m be a graph transformable into $(a \,⅋\, b) \cdot c$ but not into $a \,⅋\, b \cdot c$.

Since m is transformable into $(a \,⅋\, b) \cdot c$, it follows from the definition of composition that m is transformable into $a \,⅋\, b$ [and] m is transformable into c. But because [end] to signify that A and B are scriptible *under the same circumstances*, or *at once*, without definitely saying under what circumstances, or when. It will be remarked that the use of this sign in this indefinite sense compels us, when we write any graph, G, to mean that G is *sometimes* scriptible, unless G involves some definite individual circumstance. I may note, by the way, that circumstance, the *hic et nunc*, is the only sort of object that is, strictly speaking, individual. A person, for example, like Phillip of Macedon, is not individual, since an individual is, by definition, only a term to which the principle of excluded third applies. Now Phillip is neither always drunk nor always sober. But Phillip under any individual circumstance is the one or the other.

Postponing, however, the consideration of definite individuals a little, let us first consider the rules for parts of graphs that are attached by means of lines of identity, these lines never cutting ovals.

It may be remarked that even without any line of identity there is a graph which is always admissible to the sheet of assertion. This graph is the blank. With the line of identity there is such a graph which distinctly involves matter of observation. Namely, we have the following rule:

Rule IV. A detached and unenclosed line of identity is scriptible.

Identity is what I call a relation. Any proposition refers to one or more singulars, each of which is either named, indefinitely described, or indicated by showing where it may be met with. The parts of the proposition containing these indications (including what are grammatically called the subject and objects) are called by me the *subjects* of the proposition. There is, in general, a determinate order among them; for it is not the same to say that for every catholic there is a woman whom he adores. Now if we remove from the proposition and leave blank certain of the subjects beginning with the first, as for example " ___ is adored by every catholic", " ___ is adored by ___ ", " ___ is a woman either adored by or not coëxistent with a catholic that is ___ ", " ___ is not a catholic or else adores some woman", " ___ is not a catholic or else adores a woman that is ___ ", " ___ is not a catholic or else adores ___ ", " ___ adores ___ "; I term any such blank form which is convertible into a proposition by filling each blank with a proper name, a *rhema* or *term*. The practice of logicians is to use the word *term* for a name, especially a *common noun*, or something equivalent to a possible common noun. But a common noun is a part of speech which, as well as I can make out, is restricted, or almost restricted, to the small and extremely peculiar groups of language—which we call Aryan or Indo-European.[6]

My 'rhema', for example, in the proposition 'Man breathes' is 'breathes'.[7] The other logicians say that 'object which breathes' is the predicate 'term'. To attach it to the subject, they say a special sign, which is not a 'term', but a 'copula', is requisite. That, I grant, is equally true of the rhema; only I add that a special sign is needed to connect this copula with the predicate, and another to connect it with the subject; and if these signs are specially expressed, still other signs will be requisite to connect them; and so on *ad infinitum*. It appears to me that the continuity of the line of identity sufficiently represents the infinite series of connections. Meantime, the difference between 'breathes' and 'object which breathes' is chiefly apparent, not real; and that real difference is not sufficient to forbid my designating the *rhema* by the more familiar designation of *term*. Of terms, or *rhemata*, those which contain more than one blank each, like '___ loves ___', '___ gives ___ to ___', are called *relative terms* by me. The other logicians say that the relative terms are 'object which loves something', 'object which gives something to something'. I do not think this a convenient analysis. I should not call '___ loves something' a relative term, but a monadic, or non-relative term. A rhema is an indispensable part of speech in every language. Every verb is a rhema. But a common noun is a singular and superfluous formation. Its function is the same as that of the Proper Name. That is, it merely draws attention to an object and so puts its

---

6 The word Aryan is objected to as seeming to imply that these languages are spoken by people descended from a people that once inhabited Arya. But since nobody any longer too closely connects language with race, or pretends to know much about an *uralt* Aryan race, but we are all inclined to think that these languages began to take their peculiar development in the cradle of the human race, in Malaysia, or wherever it may have been, I do not see any dreadful consequences to be feared any longer from reverting to the simple and pretty appellation 'Aryan' for these languages. There is no longer an eminent opinion that the races of men were distinct creations, that Europeans are a very pure breed, or language depends almost exclusively upon blood.

7 [Alt.:] My 'rhema' is, for example, '___ is a man'. The logician's 'term' is 'man'. The only difference is that my rhema has suggested identity in it so that it needs only to be connected *in a certain way* with a proper name to ~~become~~ produce a proposition. The logicians' 'term' also involves identity implicitly. For certainly 'what is a man' is the same term as 'man'. Only it is supposed to have the stopper 'what' added to it, which is a distinct word, the 'copula', has to remove, before a proper name can be connected with it. The case is closely analogous to the relation of a proposition to an argument. Certainly, no proposition fulfills its function unless it argues something, or determines some idea or other representation. I knew a person who added the word 'So!' to almost every speech. "There is a visitor; so!" This was strictly logical. Everything said is supposed to be said to some purpose. But it appears to me that the distinction between by 'rhema' and the ordinary 'term', or rhema with 'that which' attached to it, is so slight that it will be permissible for me to call the schema by the familiar name of 'term'.

interpreter into condition to learn whatever there may be to be learned from such attention. Now attention can only be drawn to what is already in experience. A proper name can only function as such if utterer and interpreter are already more or less familiar with the object it names. But the peculiarity of a common noun is that it undertakes to draw attention to an object with which the interpreter may have no acquaintance. For this purpose it calls up to his mind such an image as a verb calls up, appeals to his memory that he has seen different objects the subjects of they [sic.] image,—and it is the peculiarity of the common noun that it has a regular plural formation,—and then of those which might be so recollected or imagined, the noun indefinitely names one. A language which, like the Greek, does not need to insert the verb "is" in such a sentence as "The man is wise", plainly has not yet fully developed the conception of the common noun. Its noun retains something of the *rhema*. This is the case with the Semitic languages, which moreover have few common nouns which are not regular formations of verbs. In these languages, also, plurals are for the most part irregular and are modified like singulars. When we come to a language which in place of the verb "is" puts a demonstrative pronoun, as the ancient Egyptian does, it is pretty clear that its nouns are more *rhemata* than names. In my very moderate acquaintance with languages, there is but one which is constructed in accordance with the logicians' analysis of the proposition; and that is the Bask, which has no verbs except two three serving as connectives like "is", "has", etc. Geographically at the extreme limit of Aryan extension, it seems to have carried the Aryan conception of language to its extreme.

The proper names, or indices, then call attention to individuals existing within the "universe", or general field of experience common to the interlocutors which every sign supposes. The *rhemata* simply call up images, which in the proposition are represented to be applicable to the objects of the names. A rhema for which there is no set of existing objects may be said not to exist, although the image it calls up be ever so positive and distinct. If we form an abstract noun from the rhema, which is a sort of proper name for a factitious singular, that is, for a singular whose being consists in the possibility of its being conceived; say for example, sinlessness; we cannot say that that does not exist,—has no place, in its own proper universe of objects conceivable,—simply because nothing in quite another universe is found to be in relation to it. The pertinence of these remarks to mathematics will appear below.

If a person says, "Somebody was a harlequin Plato", he conveys pretty nearly the same idea to a person who does not know Galiani as if he had said "The ablé Galiani was a harlequin Plato". "Something" is an individual whose proper name is withheld, thus giving the utterer liberty to justify his assertion by a choice of instances. On the other hand, it may be said that the very sole-leather of the mathematician, —the implement he uses at every step, —is the invention of a proper designation for a something.

At first, this designation is perfectly arbitrary; but when it has once been used it ceases to be so. We may write $C{}^{\text{is a patriarch}}_{\text{is translated}}$ to signify that some one individual is at once a patriarch and translated. This we may equally signify by writing $\substack{\text{E—is a patriarch}\\\text{E—is translated}}$ where E is an arbitrary individual designation; perfectly arbitrary when it is applied in the first line, ceasing to be altogether so in the second line. The transformation of the first form of expression into the second may be analyzed into the following steps. First,

Rule V. A new proper name may be attached to any line of identity, after every less enclosed line has received a name.[8]

We thus write $\text{E-}C{}^{\text{is a patriarch}}_{\text{is translated}}$. I will consider presently whether this can always be done. In the next place, as we have already seen that any detached graph may be iterated under the same or additional enclosures, so it will easily be shown that

Rule VI. Any partial graph may be iterated under the same or additional enclosures, with the same attachments, as in its original occurrence.

It follows that we can write $\substack{\text{E}\top\text{is a patriarch}\\\text{E}\bot\text{is translated}}$. We may then avail ourselves of the following rule:

Rule VII. Any line of identity may be severed where unenclosed.

We shall thus have $\substack{\text{E—is a patriarch}\\\text{E—is translated}}$. We can make the inverse transformation by means of the rule

Rule VIII. Different replicas of the same proper name may always be joined by a line of identity.

Hence the last graph is transformable into $\substack{\text{E}\top\text{is a patriarch}\\\text{E}\bot\text{is translated}}$. Then by Rule VII we have $\substack{\text{E-}\ulcorner\text{is a patriarch}\\\text{E-}\llcorner\text{is translated}}$ and by Corollary 3 $C{}^{\text{is a patriarch}}_{\text{is translated}}$.

It remains to examine into the validity of these four rules. Rule VII is very easily justified. Let there be an unenclosed line of identity, and call all the rest of the graph G. Then the whole will be Ⓖ. Now if the line of identity be severed at any point so as to give ⁽ᴳ⁾, the only difference is that the latter asserts the coexistence of a something and a something, the terminals produced by the rupture, while the

---

8 [This corresponds to a common restriction in the semantic tree method, for example.]

former asserts their identity. Coexistence does not exclude identity. It only asserts existence. But identity being a "relation" asserts the existence of its correlates. Therefore, nothing is asserted in the latter graph that is not asserted in the former.

Rule V is evident as long as the line of identity is unenclosed. When we invent a name for something we create a fact, and are justified in asserting the fact so created. Only we must take care that the "something" to which the name is given is individual, that is, is of such a nature that the principle of excluded middle is applicable to it. A mere ideal thing is not of that nature; but if it is to be realized, it will become of that nature. I may, for example, wish for an automobile; and then by a dilemma prove that no particular kind of automobile would please me. This will prove that there is no automobile that I wish for but not that I do not wish for an automobile. For wishing does not consist in a relation to any existing thing.[9]

If the same arbitrary individual designation occurs unenclosed and again in one enclosure, it is the outer occurrence which is the original creation of the designation. Thus, $\frac{\text{F—is a patriarch}}{(\text{F—is translated})}$. This must be understood to mean that "Some patriarch is not translated". For since K—is translated means "Something is translated", (K—is translated) must mean "Nothing is translated",—that is "Anything is untranslated unless it cannot be designated as K", as anything can be. If, therefore, in the last graph but two, the inner occurrence created the name, F, the only meaning possible would be that "Nothing is translated but everything is a patriarch". But here the two subjects would be independent and there would be no sense in writing them with the same letter. This principle then being established $\left(\frac{\text{F—is a patriarch}}{(\text{F—is translated})}\right)$ will mean "Take anything, F, you please, and either F is not a patriarch or F is translated", i.e. whatever patriarch there may be is translated.[10]

---

9 [Alt.:] If, then, I prove that neither a live horse nor a dead horse would suit me, I may continue to wish I had a flying horse, but only on condition that the facts on which the dilemma is based were otherwise. Thus, the merely possible [end]

10 [Alt.:] [R 516(s)] $\frac{\text{Thingumbob—is a patriarch}}{(\text{Thingumbob—is translated})}$

is to be ~~translated~~ interpreted thus: "I will call a certain patriarch Thingumbob and nobody is translated unless he is other than Thingumbob"; that is "Some patriarch is not translated". So the graph

$\frac{\text{Who do you call him—is a man}}{(\text{Who do you call him—is a ~~mortal~~ sinner})}$

is to be interpreted thus: "Take any object in the universe you like, and it is either not identical with any man or you do not designate it as 'Who do you call him', or (if there be a man whom you designate as Who do you call him) Who do you call him is a sinner"; that is, "Whatever man there may be in existence is a sinner".

The reason of the restrictive clause of the rule does not yet appear, but it will appear shortly.

Rule VIII introduces an entirely new element of notation; that of a line of identity intersecting an oval. For the rule is that replicas of the same proper name may *always* be joined by a line of identity. Therefore, $\overset{\text{F—is a patriarch}}{\text{(F—is translated)}}$ may be transformed into $\overset{\text{F⊤is a patriarch}}{\text{(F⊥is translated)}}$. By deiteration we can now write $\overset{\text{F⊤is a patriarch}}{\text{(is translated)}}$ and thence by Corollary 2 $\overset{\text{(is a patriarch}}{\text{(is translated)}}$ or "Some patriarch is not translated". This must be the meaning, since the inverse transformation is permissible. Namely, by Rule V $\overset{\text{F⊤is a patriarch}}{\text{(is translated)}}$. And then because a line of identity may be ruptured unenclosed and any graph detached can be erased, it follows that under one enclosure F— can be inserted, and the two lines of identity can then be joined giving $\overset{\text{F⊤is a patriarch}}{\text{(F⊥is translated)}}$ whence by deiteration $\overset{\text{F—is a patriarch}}{\text{(F—is translated)}}$.

Since the whole line of identity denotes the same individual, a line of identity cannot be considered as enclosed in any oval in which it is not entirely enclosed.

We now see the reason for the restriction upon Rule V. For consider the graph 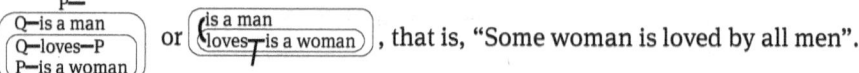. This reads "Every man loves some woman". But if we were to attach a proper name, say P, to the inner line of identity, without attaching one to the outer, the meaning would be "Every man loves some individual woman, P", which since it would name that line before the other would be equivalent to

$\begin{pmatrix} \text{P—} \\ \text{Q—is a man} \\ \text{Q—loves—P} \\ \text{P—is a woman} \end{pmatrix}$ or $\begin{pmatrix} \text{(is a man} \\ \text{(loves⊤is a woman)} \end{pmatrix}$, that is, "Some woman is loved by all men".

Now we may as well extend the convention embodied in Rule VII to these cases, and join the two lines of identity, [end]

16 A Proposed Logical Notation

R 530, late 1901. Houghton Library. Peirce continues redrafting his contributions to the philosophy and ethics of notation with the present piece, which proceeds from where he had left off with the previous attempts. A total of 62 running manuscript pages from R 530 are published plus the most significant variants; some 75 additional pages of text mostly on history of logic remain dormant in the folder. Peirce's enterprise is now well underway, and we find in these transcribed pages his lists of the sixteen binary connectives (the "Box-X" notation), among numerous other notations. Peirce accentuates "the order in which the selections of instances are to be made" as an indispensable property that needs to be reflected in one's logical notation, while the maxim of the ethics of notation dictates that notational considerations must nowhere be overlooked. R 530 stands out as a benchmark for the maxim at work also as regards to editorial practices. In reproducing this remarkable piece, the typography and the design features of its notation have to be taken into account by closely observing Peirce's ethics of notation.

I set out from the following ethical principle which must appeal to the conscience of every right-minded person:

– The person who introduces a conception into science has both the right and the duty of prescribing a terminology and a notation for it; and his terminology and notation should be followed except so far as it may prove positively and seriously disadvantageous to the progress of science. If a slight modification is sufficient to remove the objection, a ~~very great~~ much greater one should be avoided.

Although, in my opinion, the deliverance of conscience upon this matter is clear and is much more trustworthy than any other criterion, yet because there are many logicians who prefer to be guided by utilitarian reasoning, I will argue the matter on that basis. In the first place, then, uniformity in terminology and notation avoids a frightful waste of energy of thought. Yet every man has his individual preferences in terminology and notation which he will only surrender to some general principle the advantage of which he cannot but admit; and in particular a large part, even of logicians, among scientific men, will hold a plain principle of right and wrong to be sacred, and will not compromise on any other basis. Even if the votes of this party could be disregarded as insignificant in numbers and influence, which is not the case, still scientific experience goes to show that the above rule that the terminology and notation of the introducer of a conception should be followed, in the absence of a decided scientific reason to the contrary, is the only basis upon which it is possible to ~~produce~~ effect uniformity of usage. The scientific experience to which I allude is that of the sciences of taxonomic biology, which have been confronted with confusion in terminology far worse than that which has plagued any other science. They have been driven to substantially the above rule; and it has had the happiest effects.

There are many cases in logic, however, for which this rule does not provide. Those in which the introducer of a conception has not provided a terminology are too few to require a general rule; and I do not think that there are more cases in which there is any difficulty owing to his failure to prescribe a notation. But there is many a conception of logic which is so old that it is impossible to make sure who did introduce it, or what terminology he used for it. There are also conceptions which are distinctly due to Aristotle (not as conceptions, but as conceptions of logic), and for which certain Latin names are in universal use. The above rule is certainly not to be understood to mean that we are bound to introduce into the English language Greek or Roman words contrary to the spirit and taste of the language. The words of Latin origin which we use to translate Aristotle mostly translate his words, syllable by syllable, almost; such as *induction* for ἐπαγωγή, *contradiction* for ἀντίφασις, *infinitated* for ἀόριστον, less exactly, *proposition* for πρότασις. In cases in which English usage has been perfectly settled since some time in the seventeenth century,—say from 1700 down to Victoria's reign, during which the uniformity of terminology suffered considerably in some respects, I think we ought to follow that usage, especially when it is supported by ~~the great~~ general medieval ~~logicians Shireswood, Scotus, and Ockham~~ use as represented by Boethius, Albertus Magnus, Petrus Hispanus, Aquinas, Scotus, Ockham, etc.

Although the chief purpose of this paper is to endeavor to do something toward bringing about uniformity of logical notation, yet I desire to preface what I have to say upon that subject by some remarks on a few logical ~~words~~ terms of a quasi-mathematical character, in the use of which there is some lack of uniformity.

Postulate. The Latin *postulatum* was probably used in classical times in the mathematico-logical sense, to translate αἴτημα. The Greek word is defined by Aristotle (I Anal.Post.x), who had some acquaintance with mathematics. We have, besides, Euclid's use of the word, and the explanation of Proclus. By the postulates of geometry were meant those fundamental hypotheses which, though not evident, the geometer did not concern himself to prove. Later, though evidently very early, considerable confusion arose between the postulates and the axioms; ~~and ultimately~~ but still in English and in French, the original meaning prevailed. To that we ought to adhere. In German, the influence of [Christian] Wolff caused the *Postulat* to be generally understood as an indemonstrable practical proposition, a signification of considerable antiquity, but a confusing corruption of the original meaning.

Axiom. The Latin *axioma* occurs in Apuleius, but its meaning was never very well settled. The Greek ἀξίωμα is defined by Aristotle and by Proclus. Euclid happens to use the synonym κοινή ἔννοια, ~~generally~~ "universally accepted notion, maxim of common sense." It meant a proposition which needed no proof for the reason that nobody doubted it. It is correct logic that that which is not doubted neither needs nor is capable of proof. Among the axioms of Euclid, one only is geometrical; and this is of doubtful genuineness. It is that two lines cannot enclose a space, (contrary to the doctrine of modern geometry). But it is plain that Euclid was unable to get any clear idea of anything infinite. There seems to be no occasion for the word "axiom" in modern logic.

Theorem and *Corollary.* The word *corollarium* in the logical sense is used by Boethius. Heiberg admits 27 corollaries as genuine in the *Elements* [Heiberg & Menge 1883]. Broadly speaking, the corollaries were consequences drawn by commentators, mostly very obvious. At present, the word merely means an obvious consequence, and is not a term of science. I intend, however, in another paper, to borrow these words to mark a scientific distinction between two kinds of mathematical consequences. I can now only say, vaguely, that I shall apply the word corollary to a consequence which is seen to be true by anybody who has a perfectly clear apprehension of what is already accepted; while a theorem can only be seen to be true by means of a new construction or other act of invention.

Hypothetical proposition. This term having been applied in Greek in several senses, but never in that of a conditional proposition, ultimately, ~~as in Boethius~~ with the Stoics, received a settled signification as a proposition formed by any mode of conjunction of independent propositions. Hypotheticals were divided into copulatives, conditionals, and disjunctives. But this division is bad. The proper division is into *copulatives*, or propositions which can be most simply analyzed into independent propositions the truth or falsity of which follows from the truth of the copulative proposition, into *disjunctives*, or propositions most simply analyzable into independent propositions the truth or falsity of which follows from the falsity of the disjunctive, and into propositions which can with equal simplicity be analyzed in either way. Thus, the proposition 'The Propositions A and B are equivalent', may be equally well considered as a copulative proposition whose two ~~parts~~ members are the disjunctive propositions, 'Either A is true or B is false', and 'Either A is false or B is true', and as a disjunctive proposition of which either member is the copulative proposition 'A and B are both true' or 'A and B are both false'. The *conditional proposition* is ~~simple complication~~ a necessary mode of the disjunctive proposition. 'Either A is false or B is true' is a simple disjunctive proposition. The conditional proposition 'If A is true, B is true', merely means 'In any possible state of things either A is false or B is true'. The proof of the correctness of this view is very simple. Whatever is true or false is a proposition; and anything asserted may be denied. Then there must be some kind of proposition which denies a disjunctive proposition. That is evidently a copulative proposition. But if the conditional proposition is essentially different from the disjunctive proposition, then its denial must be essentially different from the denial of the disjunctive. But the denial of 'If A is true, B is true', is 'There is a possible state of things in which A is true, while B is false'. This, however, is nothing but the copulative proposition in the possible mode.

Those who were ignorant of usage or ignored it, determining the meaning of the term *hypothetical proposition* by what they thought it ought, from its formation, to mean, confused *hypotheticals* with *conditionals*. Finally Kant, wishing to make a triadic division, instead of dividing propositions into hypotheticals, non-relative categoricals, and relative categoricals, which would have been sound, and instead of dividing hypotheticals as above, divided propositions into Categoricals, Disjunctives, and Hypotheticals, meaning by the latter Conditionals; and most erroneously regarded Disjunctives *de inesse* as of a more complex order than Conditional propositions, and both as more complex than Categoricals, wherein he completely reverses the true order of complexity. He separated Disjunctives and Conditionals, which differ only in mode, and left no place for Relative propositions or for Copulatives. Yet this mass of error, which contains but one item position on which any rational stand can be made (that Categoricals are simpler than Hypotheticals)[1] has been accepted entire by the general body of nineteenth-century German logicians. The traditional meaning of the term *hypothetical proposition* ought, at least, to be insisted upon.

Copulation, Composition, Multiplication, and *Disjunction, Aggregation, Addition.* *Copulation* is traditionally applied to that mode of conjunction by which two signs, whether terms, propositions, or arguments, are united conjoined into a sign which is applicable to, and only to, what all the conjoined signs are applicable to. *Disjunction* is traditionally applied to that mode of conjunction by which two signs are conjoined into a sign which is inapplicable to, and only to, that to which all the conjoined signs are inapplicable. But *copulation* and *disjunction*, although so used, were not so analytically defined; their perfect balance was seldom noticed; and their connection with the doctrine relation of logical depth and breadth could not be emphasized, seeing that that doctrine relation was much obscured by the doctrine of predicables. To De Morgan we owe the important service of directing attention to these things. But he did not perceive that names were already provided for these two modes of conjunction. Apparently even the word *conjunction*, as a term of logic, was not familiar to him. The medieval logicians looked at logic

---

[1] But that it is erroneous will be shown in another paper.

from a grammatical point of view; De Morgan from the point of view of a mathematician. Thus, he failed to perceive that Conjunction was the relation for which he invented a needless name Combination, whose only merit is that it looks away from words to mathematical forms. He called *Copulation* by the name of *Composition*; *Disjunction* by the name of *Aggregation*; and certainly his service to logic in making the relations of these modes as clear as, by degrees, he did, was such as to justify him in conferring the new names; and we ought not to reject them. Yet there is no reason why we should not recognize the old names, too.

About the time at which De Morgan was making his first studies in Logic, Boole reached his illuminative *aperçu*.[2] This really was (though he perhaps did not distinctly so regard it) that a problem in deductive logic could be considered as a problem in common algebra in which, in consequence of the Principle of Excluded Third, each quantity was restricted to one or other of two values, by a quadratic equation. There was no ~~reason why~~ necessity for the two roots of this equation being identified by any two definite numbers; but Boole, no doubt under the influence of the doctrine of chances, did identify them with 1 and 0. Why are these two numbers made to represent certainty *pro* and certainty *con* in the doctrine of chances? It is merely because the simplest problems in probabilities happen to be of such a nature that this convention puts their solutions into simple and familiar forms. There is no inherent necessity for it. Boole, however, so influenced, as I presume, took 1 and 0 to signify existence and non-existence. That done, the product of two quantities became the simplest, out of an infinite variety of forms by which the logical *copulate* or *composite* of the terms or propositions represented by those quantities could be represented. But addition did not have the same relation to logical *disjunction*, or *aggregation*; and Boole does not seem to have been struck by the balance between composition and aggregation, even if he remarked it. But to any student of Boole who has imbibed the ideas of De Morgan, whether at first or second hand, it was so obvious that one could imagine an algebraical operation somewhat analogous to addition which should correspond to aggregation, that first Jevons (a direct pupil of De Morgan), then C. S. Peirce (a reader of De Morgan), then Robert Grassmann, Schröder, and M[a]cColl (who got De Morgan's ideas from Bain) successively and independently introduced such an operation into the Boolian algebra. The new operation was $x + y - xy$ or what is the same thing (because of the quadratic $x^2 = x$, $y^2 = y$ etc.) $\frac{1}{4}(x+y)^2 + \frac{3}{4}(x-y)^2$. It ought to have been obvious that the new operation was not addition, if the quadratic equation was to stand. For that reason, I proposed the transformation of x, y, etc.

---

[2] De Morgan's first paper is dated October 3, 1846; Boole's *Mathematical Analysis of Logic* appeared in 1847.

Boole's quantities, into ξ, η, etc., new quantities having the same logical signification, by means of the equations, $x = 1 - e^{-\xi}$, $y = 1 - e^{-\eta}$, etc. But that proceeding only made it still clearer that the connection of multiplication and addition with the logical modes of conjunction was an accidental one. It would always remain that there was an infinite variety of other functions equally corresponding to the logical conjunctions. Calling Fx, y any such function representing composition, and calling $\Phi x, y$ any such function representing aggregation, it would always be true that

$$Fx, x = x \qquad \Phi x, x = x$$
$$Fx, y = Fy, x \qquad \Phi x, y = \Phi y, x$$

$$Fx, \Phi y, z = \Phi(Fx, y), (Fx, z)$$
$$\Phi x, Fy, z = F(\Phi x, y), (\Phi x, z)$$
etc. etc.

These and other formulæ continue to hold in all the infinite variations of the arithmetical operations. The logical operation and the arithmetical operation are distinct and independent operations.

The effect of these facts, not of their being perceived, was that the logicians were led to disregard the numerical meaning of the algebra, and to consider the signs as directly signs of composition and aggregation. Mr. Venn alone, who was particularly interested in probabilities, retained addition in its strict sense; and there is an unquestionable advantage in doing this. Mrs. [Ladd-]Franklin adopted my suggestion of ~~considering~~ using logarithmic infinity as the sign of existence, thus making addition represent aggregation. For it is to be observed that while ordinary infinity has no *plus* or *minus* sign, so that $-\infty = +\infty$ ~~and consequently~~ but $\infty + \infty$ and $\infty 0$ are indeterminate, while $\infty\infty > \infty$, it is not so with ∞^0; but on the contrary

$$(+\infty^0) + (+\infty^0) = +\infty^0$$
$$(+\infty^0)0 = 0$$
$$(+\infty^0)(+\infty^0) = (+\infty^0).$$

Since, however, for brevity, ∞ was written in practice, instead of $(+\infty^0)$, and since the properties of logarithmic infinity are not very familiar, especially to persons who interpret infinity by the doctrine of limits, Schröder and others put exclamation marks after such formulæ. All, even Venn, seem to be infected with the notion, so marked in Boole and in his widow, that the way to investigate logic is to listen to the mumblings of a mysterious instinct which ~~pronounce~~ affirms a secret affinity between certain arithmetical operations and certain logical relations. For my part, I will welcome an idea from whencesoever it comes; but it would seem that if there be any field where distinct thought is in order, it is logic. All except Venn and Jevons apply the terms multiplication and addition to the logical conjunctions with which they have a merely accidental connection. I can see no advantage in this practice.

The conception of multiplication has been generalized by mathematicians, so that they speak of functional or operational multiplication. This operational multiplication is very nearly, if not precisely, what I have called *relative* multiplication; as appears in multiple algebra, where the two are quite indistinguishable. This is a true generalization. For $5a$ signifies that for the object which a represents are to be substituted a set of 5 replicas of it. The etymology of the word *multiplication* involves that idea. Then $2 \times 5a$ signifies that for that set of 5 replicas is to be substituted a pair of replicas of each. The idea is that the product is the result of substituting for the multiplicand something related to it in the manner which the multiplier represents. Hence, it is a mere generalization of multiplication to say that, in the expression 'sin x', x is multiplied by 'sin', or that in the expression 'lover of a woman', 'a woman' is multiplied by 'lover of'. Since, then, 'operational multiplication' is a well-established term of mathematics, and is open to no objection, there can be no positive objection to the term "relative multiplication". At the same time, there are other aspects of this mode of application of a relative term to ~~its object~~ a correlate which seem to call for recognition in the designation of it rather than this analogy to multiplication. The name 'relative addition' by which I formerly called another mode of application of a relative term is utterly vicious, as suggesting analogies which do not exist. I now propose the following terminology. There are many modes (of which eight are simple) in which *complication* may be made of any two relatives, say 'lover of', as *preplicant*, or *plicant*, and say 'benefactor of', as *applicant*, or *plicand*, to form a *complicate* relative. Among these modes especially prominent are two. Namely, *composition*, or relative composition, may be made by *preponing* 'lover of' to 'benefactor of', the latter being *apponed* to the former, or the former being *ponent* or *preponent*, the latter *ponend* or *apponent*, to form the *composite* relative 'lover of a benefactor of'. Another mode of complication is *conjunction*, or relative conjunction, where 'lover of' being *prejoined* to 'benefactor of', and the latter *adjoined* to the former, the *conjunct* 'lover of everything but a benefactor of' is formed, in which 'lover of' is the *jungent*, or *prejungent*, and 'benefactor of', is *jungend, adjungent*. Another mode of complication is *convolution*, forming the *convolute* 'lover of every benefactor of', where we *prevolve* 'lover of' as *volvent*, or *prevolvent*, to 'benefactor of' as *volvend*, or *advolvent*, the latter being *advolved* to the former. Another mode is *contorsion*, where we *pretort* 'lover of' to 'benefactor of' to form the *contort* 'lover of nothing but a benefactor of', 'lover of' being the *torquent* or *pretorquent*, and 'benefactor of' the *torquend*, or *'attorquent'*. We may term the complicate 'Non-lover of something not a benefactor of', *colligate* in which 'lover of' is *preligated* to 'benefactor of' and the latter is *alligated* to the former; the former being the *ligant* or *preligant*, and the latter the *ligand* or *alligant*. The operation will be *relative colligation*.

Notation

I now pass to the principal subject of this paper, the consideration of the best algebraical signs for logic.[3]

I will take my start from an idea of Mrs. [Ladd-]Franklin's the merits of which are such that it is worth while to endeavor to reconcile it to our ethical principle.

To explain this idea, I must mention that De Morgan introduced, in 1846, the conception of a system of eight simple propositions, in 1850 supplied a notation for them, systematic and having some peculiar merits (but not that of blending well with Boole's algebra, which as he himself remarked at that early date, "is sure to occupy a prominent place in [its] ultimate system"), and in 1858 furnished an ample a considerable, though not in every particular an unobjectionable nor on every side a complete terminology for his propositional system.

---

3 [Alt.:] It is, however, chiefly the algebraic notation of logic which I wish to consider here. I will take my start from an idea of Mrs. [Ladd-]Franklin's that seems to me so good that it seems worth while to endeavor to reconcile it to our ethical principle. But first I must go back to De Morgan, who, in 1846, introduced below, condenses a far greater amount of meaning and truth than appears at first blush; but in carrying it out into detail she has either quite overlooked the above ethical principle or shown a complete contempt for it. This was quite unnecessary; for if she had had any desire to do justice to others while bringing out her own idea, the way of doing so would have been obvious enough. I entertain a sanguine hope that as soon as I point this out, I shall gain in her a most fortunate accession of strength for my present proposal.

If I should be disappointed in this, it will probably be because she unfortunately clings to De Morgan's narrow conception of "copulas" as essentially different from signs of conjunction, such as those of disjunction (or aggregation) and copulation. In the Johns Hopkins *Studies in Logic*, there appears, beside an article of Mrs. [Ladd-]Franklin, whose high merit nobody can fail to perceive, another by Prof. O. H. Mitchell of which the extraordinary and truly great originality places it among the two or three landmarks in the history of modern logic;—an originality so very great that it can only be appreciated by long study. No three months of my life more advanced my understanding of logic than those which I devoted to the consideration of this work. My paper of two years later in Vol. VII of the *Am. Jour. of Math.* was written before I had sufficiently digested all its ideas. One of the lessons of this memoir is that copulas are nothing but conjunctions. Mr. Mitchell in this paper regards a proposition as a sign of the universe. Certainly, a proposition is a sign; and of what else can a proposition be a sign except of the universe? Any other sign is but an incom-

16 A Proposed Logical Notation (R 530), c.1901

The fact that De Morgan's notation cannot be applied to Boole's algebra, or to any modification thereof, at least renders an alternative notation desirable.

De Morgan's eight propositions consist of two sets of four, those of each precisely denying those of the other. Mrs. [Ladd-]Franklin has had the elegant idea of turning one sign over into four positions to represent the four "copulas" of each set [Ladd-Franklin 1883]. This idea, as will sufficiently appear in the sequel, condenses more meaning and truth than the bare statement suggests. But in carrying it out she seems to have had no concern to do justice to her predecessors.

Prof. O. H. Mitchell, in his epochal paper in the Johns Hopkins *Studies in Logic* [Mitchell 1883], shows that every proposition may be regarded as a description of the universe. It follows from this that every 'copula' is of the nature of a logical sign of combination. Thus, De Morgan's eight copulas are as follows:

X)) Y   Every X is a Y; i.e. Anything is either not X or is Y.
X)·(Y   No X is a Y; i.e. Anything is either not X or not Y.
X (·) Y   Everything is either X or Y.
X ((Y   Every Y is an X; i.e. Anything is either X or not Y.

---

plete sign. To say that 'Every man is a sinner' is to say that 'Anything in the universe is either a non-man or a sinner'. To say that some man is not a sinner, is to say that 'Anything in the universe is coexistent with something at once a man and a non-sinner'. Thus every copula is a conjunction.

Now there is no simpler way of representing the relations of two classes than by the Eulerian diagrams, which go back at least to Laurentius Valla, which Venn improved by blackening excluded combinations, and which I have further improved by dots where existence is asserted. I begin then with this Eulerian diagram:

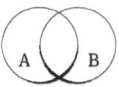

I mark the lower intersection by thickened lines. This part gives sufficiently the whole diagram. There are four cases: S P, S not P, not S not P, not S P.

Now Jevons was the first to introduce the idea of adopting, in Boolian algebra, a simple sign to signify *abstraction*, regardless of any correspondence between the logical universe and the realm of number. It follows, according to our ethical principle, that the sign which he prescribed should be used, except so far as it may be seriously objectionable. That it requires the pen to be placed three times upon paper is no infinitesimal objection, considering how frequently the sign is to be used; but that it is liable to be mistaken for three signs is still more serious. I think, therefore, that the two dots must be joined in some way. The character will not thus cease to commemorate the work of Jevons. I have in some writings joined the two dots, thus: ᛘ. But the sign would be made by one stroke of the pen by allowing the upright to double itself, thus ⚭.

[discont.] For any one individual there are 16 possible states of knowledge respecting his being S and being P. I number these on the secundal system nearly after Mrs. [Ladd-]Franklin &

X (·(Y   Some X is not Y; i.e. Anything is coexistent with an X that is not Y.
X () Y   Some X is Y; i.e. Anything is coexistent with an X that is Y.
X)(Y   There is something besides X's and Y's; i.e. Anything is c, with a non-X non-Y.
X)·) Y   Some Y is not X; i.e. Anything coexistent with a non-X that is Y.

It will therefore not be necessary or advisable to have independent signs for copulas and conjunctions; for every copula is so closely connected with a conjunction that the notation should show the connection. I will, therefore, at once consider signs of conjunction.

Any conjunction of classes or of relatives can be reduced to a conjunction of propositions, after we have introduced a series of proper names which are to be assigned, in a certain order, each to whatever individual in the universe an enlightened defender or an enlightened opponent of the proposition may choose. Thus, to say that every mother loves something of which she is a mother, is the same as to say, "Take any individual, *i*, then there is an individual, *j*, such that either *i* is not mother of *j* or *i* loves *j*". We have, therefore, first to consider signs for the conjunction of propositions.

De Morgan Universe of 1.

Code	Symbol	Description	Notation
0000	⊠	It is nothing (absurd).	
0001	⋈	It is S and P.	S () P
0010	⊠	It is S but not P.	S (·(P
0011	⋈	It is S.	
0100	⊠	It is neither S nor P.	S)(P
0101	⋈	It is both S and P or neither.	S ‖ P
0110	⊠	It is not P.	
0111	⋈	It is S or not P.	S ((P
1000	⊠	It is not S but is P.	S)·) P
1001	⋈	It is P.	
1010	⊠	It is not both S and P, but is one or other.	S ⊬ P
1011	⋈	It is either S or P.	S (·) P
1100	⊠	It is not S.	
1101	⋈	It is either not S or is P.	S)) P
1110	⊠	It is either not S or is P.	S)(P
1111	×	It is.	

There is no simpler way of representing the relation of two propositions than by a Eulerian Diagram; thus:

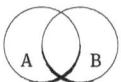

I have thickened the lines at the lower intersection, and all the rest of the diagram may be dispensed with. If now we close by a transverse bar any possible combination which a given conjunction bars and leave open every compartment corresponding to a possibility which the conjunction leaves open, we shall have the following sixteen representations of conjunct propositions.

A ⊠ B. Every thing impossible (absurd).
A ⋈ B. A and B are both true.
A ⊠ B. A is not true, but B is true.
A ⋈ B. Neither A nor B is true.
A ⊠ B. A is true, but B is not so.
A ⋈ B. A and B are equivalent, as to truth.
A ⊠ B. A and B are contradictory, in effect, one only being true.
A ⋈ B. A is false.
A ⊠ B. B is false.
A ⋈ B. A is true.
A ⋈ B. B is true.
A ⊠ B. Either A or B is true.
A ⋈ B. If A is true, so is B.
A ⊠ B. Either A or B is false.
A ⋈ B. A is true or B false.
A × B. Meaningless.

Let us now inquire whether these signs cannot be modified so as to fulfill the rule set forth at the beginning of this paper.

⊠. This is wanted so extremely seldom, that there is at present no such sign. It best stand unmodified, so that it may be understood.

⋈. The sign of copulation. I would propose to reduce this sign to one of the forms $\vee$ (which was proposed by Mrs. [Ladd-]Franklin, in this sense, in 1883), ˘, ·, and the blank. Common signs may advantageously be used in different states of cursivity, especially when they are not associative, the rule being that the more cursive signs are to signify the closer conjunctions. Then the associative principle could be written

$$x \bigvee y\breve{\,}z = x\breve{\,}y \bigvee z$$
$$\text{or } x\breve{\,}y \cdot z = x \cdot y\breve{\,}z$$
$$\text{or } x \cdot yz = xy \cdot z.$$

⌦. This sign may be reduced to <; for it is an innocent concession to the tendency to employ numerical signs with logical significations to admit that the true has a greater value than the false. Then $(a < b) < c$ may mean c is true, but some b is not a. While if we consider < to be a more cursive form, $x < y < z = y < x < z$.

⌧. I would reduce this to $\wedge$, being Mrs. [Ladd-]Franklin's $\vee$ inverted. $A \wedge B$ will mean "To something (or some state of things) neither the description A nor that of B is applicable". Written small $\wedge$ it will be more cursive.

⌧. I would reduce this to >, as with the last sign but one. In these four signs, I adhere closely to Mrs. [Ladd-]Franklin's idea. Written small it will be treated as more cursive.

⌦. The sign of equivalence. Of course, [Robert] Recorde's[4] = can never be given up. But it is not infrequently desirable to write together propositions of equality and propositions of equivalent truth, or logical coextension; and it is most confusing to have but one sign for the two. Therefore, without abandoning the use of the more cursive sign of Recorde, I would reduce the present one to the form

$$A \mathrel{\infty\!\!-} B$$

to signify 'A and B are applicable to the same thing, quantity, or state of things'. This sign would be found convenient by mathematicians, who now often write $y + x \equiv x + y$.

The sign with three lines could then be restricted to numerical congruence.

⌧. The sign of ~~precise~~ contradiction. I would reduce this to $\{$. Used as a copula, we should write

$$\bar{x} \{ x$$

---

4 [Robert Recorde (ca. 1512–1558), a Welsh mathematician and physician. See *The Whetstone of Witte* (1557). Recorde's original notation for the sign of equivalence is a long form of such notation, composed of a "pair of parallels" in which the lines of "one length" are used, "because no two things can be more equal". Recorde's own notation, meant to be a continuous one, was in *The Whetstone of Witte* printed as '=====', presumably because of typographical limitation.]

to mean that the *obelus* is a sign of negation. It would also be very useful as a sign of conjunction. Thus

$$x \backsim (y \mathbin{\S} z)$$

would mean that x is applicable to and only to such a thing, etc., as is either y or z, but is not both.

⋈⋈⋈ ⋈. These signs being of the extremest rarity, should remain unmodified.

⋈. The sign of disjunction or aggregation. In order to bring this sign as nearly as possible to Jevons's ·|· I would shape it thus:

$$x \infty y.$$

At the same time ⼛ could stand as an alternative sign, ~~especially when used as a conjunction. If it should be desirable to distinguish between~~ and a more cursive one, because more unlike the Eulerian diagram. If then one wished to distinguish a copula and a conjunction, ∞ could be used for the former purpose, ⼛ for the latter. We should have

$$(x \infty y \mathbin{\curlyvee} z) \backsim (x \mathbin{\curlyvee} y \infty z).$$

⋉. The sign of inclusion. Since I was the first to introduce a sign of inclusion into the Boolian algebra, in 1870, I claim that my sign should be used if not seriously objectionable. I first wrote this sign in the form —<, and remarked upon introducing it that I had adopted this form as not implying that a disjunction of two relations was implied, which I was anxious to do since the idea signified by this sign is simpler than either of those signified by = and <. Since this view is now generally accepted, I ask logicians to do me the justice of using my sign. Its stiff form may, however, very well be modified, as I have done, to ⃔< or still better to ⚲. The latter is intended as a representation of the Eulerian diagram at the same time that it is a cursive form of my —< of 1870. It has the advantage of being easily ~~struck of~~ written with one stroke of the pen.

I would treat the form ⚲ as the least cursive, because its loop makes it most like the Eulerian diagram, which, indeed, it was designed to imitate. Next will come —< which reduces this loop to a line, and most cursive is ⃔< which arose as cursive modification of —<.

⋊. I would reduce this to ∇, the wedge used by Mrs. [Ladd-]Franklin in this sense in 1883, of which she developed the properties. In a less cursive form, it could be written ⋏.

⋈. This could be written ∞. In the *Geometry* of Descartes and other writings following that, this sign was used apparently often as substitute for Recorde's =. But I am inclined to think that what was meant when for example

$$\sqrt{4} \infty 2$$

was written was "*a* value of the square root of 4 is 2". In that sense the sign might advantageously be retained; for it offends a logician to be told that $\sqrt{4} = -2$.

✕. If this sign is ever wanted, it should be written so large as not to be mistaken for X or for a sign of multiplication.

The sign of negation. The *obelus* (spit), or heavy horizontal line over the term or proposition to be negated, is mentioned about A.D. 600 by Isidorus Hispalensis (*Etymologiarum* lib.I.cap.xxi.3) as being an old sign, as placed above words or sentences "in iis locis ubi lectio aliqua falsitate notata est". I presume it to be the origin of the line often still written above a letter to show that an *n* (*non*), or even an *m*, has been omitted. It was early placed above a probability to mark the probability of the negative; and has been used by Boole, and by all logical algebraists of fine notational sense to negative the term or proposition over which it is written. It should unquestionably be retained. I would employ a circle round a symbol as an alternate mark of the negation of it. I must postpone my reason for this.

Signs of Nothing and of Being. For Nothing, or that term which is defined as being included under every term, all the logical algebraists, so far as I remember, have used 0. There can be little objection to this. Perhaps it might be better to make it circular, ○; but there seems, in any case, to be no danger of confusion.

The case is very different with that term which is defined as including every term. Any number is objectionable; but especially, 1, which is the natural symbol of identity. There is no symbol which is specially appropriate. We might, of course, write $\overline{0}$; and I have thought of the sign of Taurus, ♉, as suggesting this. It has also occurred to me that, since 1 and ∞ have been used to represent this term, the sign of Aries, ♈, might suggest either or both of them. If an oval is used as the sign of negation, ⓞ would express this. A blank must also express it; and to show that a blank is meant, we might write a blank square ⌐ ⌐. Of these suggestions, it appears to me that the sign of Taurus, ♉, especially if it were properly cut, as it never is now-a-days, would be the most convenient.

Parentheses, *Brackets*, *Braces*, etc. The ordinary algebra-books treat these as matters of secondary importance, hardly worth mention. It is true that they need little explanation, so perfectly suggestive. But it would be nearer to the truth to say that all other algebraic signs are adjuncts to these. For mathematics might almost be defined as the art of grouping things so as to render them intelligible; and the distinctive signs of grouping are these. In logical algebra the number of these enclosures that are requisite is most embarrassing; and that is the reason that I propose alternative signs for the commoner modes of conjunction, so as to economize these rather cumbrous signs. At present, mathematicians are too profuse in the employment of them. How is $f(x)$ more intelligible than fx? If the parentheses do not render the expression more perspicuous, the use of them is unquestionably in bad taste. I do not believe they do have that effect. Usage is to make parentheses the interior enclosures, next square brackets, then braces, then heavy parentheses. The new form $\langle x + y \rangle$ ought, I should think to intervene between the parentheses and the square brackets. A form $[x + y]$ might intervene between the braces and the heavy parentheses. All these forms will be often needed in logical algebra, unless special ~~means are employed~~ letters are introduced to simplify expressions by separating them into parts.

I would write

$$a \vee b \propto c \infty\ d\breve{\ }e \prec f \curlyvee g \cdot h \prec i \curlyvee jk$$

for $a \vee \left\{ b \propto \left[c \infty \left\langle d\breve{\ }\left(e \prec [f \curlyvee \{g \cdot [h \prec \langle i \curlyvee (jk) \rangle]\}]\right)\right\rangle \right] \right\}$.

Notation for the General Algebra of Logic

A proposition in the general algebra of logic consists of two parts. The first is the series of quantifiers, or directions for the order and manner of choosing the individuals of the set to which the second part of the proposition, called the Boolian (since it is an expression of the Boolian algebra) is written. The first part collectively may be called the *Hopkinsian*, since it was developed in the Johns Hopkins University. According the practice now in vogue (introduced by me in 1870) the letters Σ and Π are employed for this purpose. Of course, Σ stands for Σύμ and Π for Πρόδυκτ, which I do not now approve. But even if we overlook the objection that a composite is not exactly a product nor an aggregate a sum, the interpretation is restricted to cases in which the universe is a collection of individuals, even if not to cases in which it is a finite collection. But there is no necessity even for the lesser restriction. The liberty of choosing and naming of each individual instance is a fact which ought to be expressed like any other fact by the ordinary resources of logical algebra; and the order in which the selections of instances are to be made is another fact which ought to be expressed in the same way.

So, at least, it is from my point of view. The question depends upon whether it is logic or mathematics that we are interested in. The mathematician is interested in finding methods of solving problems. The logician, on the other hand, is interested in analyzing methods, in determining the essential nature of their different steps, in ascertaining why they are appropriate to special problems, and in discovering a general method for creating methods appropriate to given problems. The majority of my co-workers in logical algebra are more logical algebraists than algebraic logicians. They have a skill in solving problems (mostly simple ones) in a specially easy way, which I admire but do not try to emulate. It does not seem to me that logical algebra, considered as a calculus having now fifty years of life, has proved to be anything very wonderfully successful. Compare its achievements, for example, with those of the differential calculus, during its first half century, with those of the calculus of probabilities, with those of the calculus of finite differences. I do not think that its real utility lies in that direction, but in the analysis and study of the constituents of thought. It is this, at any rate, that has occupied me.

If the question be simply what is the easiest way to take account of the order of succession of the selection of the different indices, then undoubtedly the best way is simply to set them down in that order. Let p mean 'praises', p_j 'praises j', p_{jk} 'praises j to k', p_{jki} 'i praises j to k'. Then in order to express, that 'Each person praises some one person to all persons', in a universe of persons, the usual way $\Pi_i \Sigma_j \Pi_k p_{jki}$ is very good; while $\Sigma_j \Pi_i \Pi_k p_{jki}$ would mean 'There is some one person whom everybody praises to everybody'; and $\Pi_i \Pi_k \Sigma_j p_{jki}$ will mean that 'Everybody to each person praises somebody or other'. From the second proposition the first follows; and thence the third. For a Σ can always be carried further toward the right and a Π toward the left. The precise denials of the three propositions are: $\Sigma_i \Pi_j \Sigma_k \bar{p}_{jki}$ or 'There is somebody who fails to praise each person to somebody or other'; $\Pi_j \Sigma_i \Sigma_k \bar{p}_{jki}$ or 'Everybody is unpraised by somebody to somebody'; $\Sigma_i \Sigma_k \Pi_j \bar{p}_{jki}$ or 'There exist two persons (or they may be identical) of whom one praises nobody to the other'.

We come nearer to an analytical expression, if we write the first proposition thus: $0_i \text{ ⚭ } \text{ʊ}_j \check{\ } 0_k \text{ Ψ } p_{jki}$. That is, "For whatever individual there may be designable as i, there is an individual designable as j such that whatever individual be designable as k, i praises j to k". The other five propositions will then be

$$\text{ʊ}_j \bigvee 0_i \text{ ⚭ } 0_k \text{ ⚭ } p_{jki}$$
$$0_i \text{ ⚭ } 0_k \text{ ⚭ } \text{ʊ}_j \check{\ } p_{jki}$$
$$\text{ʊ}_i \bigvee 0_j \text{ ⚭ } \text{ʊ}_k \check{\ } \bar{p}_{jki}$$
$$0_j \text{ ⚭ } \text{ʊ}_i \check{\ } \text{ʊ}_k \check{\ } \bar{p}_{jki}$$
$$\text{ʊ}_i \bigvee \text{ʊ}_k \bigvee 0_j \text{ ⚭ } \bar{p}_{jki}$$

Whether my translation into words of the first of these six forms is a perfectly accurate analysis or not, the notation itself is entirely correct. Of that I feel sure, since it is the same in principle with a mode of writing propositions in my Algebra of Dyadic Relatives that has been subjected to the most careful scrutiny. But

16 A Proposed Logical Notation (R 530), c.1901

this notation is open to two objections. In the first place, there is too much mere formalism about it: the characters ȣ and 0 have no real meaning. Even the i, j, k, are mere means of identification, like the letters on a geometrical figure. But then it is not particularly desirable to eliminate such signs; for they materially aid the mathematician. But another objection which strikes very deep indeed is that p is treated as if it were a sign having nothing in common with i, j, k. This is not true; for there are definite and individual characters, just as much as there are definite and individual things or persons. For these maladies of the notation, I propose the following remedy:

Let us use heavy lines each of which may be reduced to a hyphen, -, lengthened dash, − or ⎯, and curved into any convenient shape, as a sign every point of which shall denote an indefinite individual, "something", which its continuity shall express the identity of this "something" with the object of any sign upon which it abuts in the proper way, that way being defined in the definition of that sign. Such heavy lines shall be called *lines of identity*. [Alt.]

But different individuals may in the same proposition belong to different "universes"; say for example, one to a universe of persons, another to a universe of things. In such a case, it may sometimes be convenient to distinguish between these universes by giving different textures to the line of identity. In particular, an individual may be an ultimate individual, or an individual "set" or ordered collection, and that either a set of ultimate individuals or a set of sets or a set of characters, or it may be an individual general character, and that either a character of ultimate individuals, of sets, or of characters. An *individual* sign is a sign which allows its interpreter no latitude of choice as to what he will consider it applicable to, so that the principle of excluded third applies to it; namely, every predicate is either altogether true of it or altogether false of it: no distinction is possible. But this has to be understood in a modified sense in logic. We cannot strictly mean that this is so of every predicate. Otherwise we should be reduced to confining individuals to instants of time and points of space; and even then there would be difficulties. For if we were to take a point where there was a discontinuity, as for example, a point on a surface at the boundary between two colors, how could we say that it had either one color or the other exclusively? While to take a point where there was no sort of discontinuity whatever would be impossible. The mere marking or noting of it as a definite individual would be to establish a discontinuity. But there is no need of examining these subtleties. It suffices that our ultimate individuals should be individual, or subject to the principle of excluded third as far as the characters which we propose to take into account go.

By a *set* we understand an individual whose existence is determined by the existence of certain individuals between which there is such a relation of earlier and later in the set that taking any two of them, not identical, one is earlier than the other, and other not earlier than the first, and to say that A is earlier than B, is to say that A [is] earlier than anything than which B is earlier.

Appendix (Variant)

~~Let us use the lower case italics to denote ultimate~~[5] **[Alt.:]** [...] individuals; meaning individuals of the universe which we treat as ultimate; generally things or persons. Metaphysically, it is not true that a thing or person is an ultimate individual, absolutely *hic et nunc*; but there is no falsity in so treating it. Let us use the Greek minuscules, $\alpha\,\beta\,\gamma\,\delta\,\epsilon\,\zeta$ etc., to denote a 'set', or individual ordered collection (so that $\alpha\beta$ and $\beta\alpha$ are different sets), whether this set be a set of ultimate individuals or whether it be a set of sets, or whether it be a set of unordered collections. Strictly, perhaps, an unordered collection is a special variety of ordered collection. That is to say, if i and j are ultimate individuals, α is the set ij, β is the set ji, ω is the set $\alpha\beta$, and א is the unordered collection of i an j, then to say that i is a member of א is to say that it is first member of a set that is first or second member of ω. But because this requires us, in some form, to say that an object is *some* member of a set, it virtually treats that set as an unordered collection. This circumstance would render it convenient to treat unordered collections differently from sets. But besides that, the possible logical breadth or scope of a general term, that is, the totality of the possible objects to which it is applicable, is not a collection at all. For every collection (*Menge*) has multitude (*Mächtigkeit*), as can be proved; and it is further demonstrable that there is no maximum multitude. That is, given any collection there is a greater collection. But no collection whatever is greater than a possible collection to each member of which any given general term would be applicable. Let us, then, take the letters of the square Hebrew alphabet to denote each the scope of a general term (whether relative or not), or as an unordered collection. Then to say that i loves j is to say that there is a dyadic set, or *couple*, α, of which i is the first member and j the second member, which α is an individual of the scope of the general, 'couple of a lover and beloved'.

Let us adopt the general convention that the top of a Greek minuscule or Hebrew square letter is the part of it upon which a line of identity must abut in order to signify that something is identical with it in the *collective* sense, or that in which it is an individual. Let the left-hand side be the part of a Greek minuscule upon which the line must abut to signify that something is the first member of the set it denotes and let the right-hand side have the same identification with the second member. If the set denoted has more than two members, let the requisite number of dots be placed under the minuscule and be identified, in their order from right to left, with the third, and succeeding members. Let the under side of a Hebrew square letter be the part of it upon which a line of identity must abut in order to signify that something is an individual of the general or of the unordered collection which it denotes. But if several such lines abut upon the under side of the same Hebrew square letter, they must be entirely separated from one another in order to avoid signifying that they are the same. Being separated, they will neither signify that they are the same or are different. In order to signify non-identity, or *otherness* (aliety),[6] let a line of identity be crossed by a fine line. We are thus provided with an apparatus almost as superior to

---

5 [This crossed-out sentence and the long variant that follows begins after "Such heavy lines shall be called *lines of identity*."]
6 [See Peirce's definition in the *Century Dictionary*, "The state of being different; otherness", CD 1889, Vol. 1, p. 140.]

my General Algebra of Logic as that is to my Algebra of Dyadic Relatives of which Prof. Schröder has so high an opinion. In order to provide a name for it, I will call it the *Algebra of Sets*.

I will postpone the consideration of how much and what can be expected from this algebra as an aid in reasoning until I have illustrated the manner in which it expresses propositions. Let Lameth [sic., in Hebrew lamed or lamedh, ל.] ל, denote this general: 'triad of which the first member praises the second to the third'. Then the expression

will signify that there are three individuals (some or all of which may be identical) which compose an existing triad, a, which is one of the triads to which the description Lameth applies. Since a has not been identified with any definite triad, it serves (at present) no purpose to write it. We might as well have written

What is expressed amounts simply to this: "Somebody praises somebody to somebody". Using the oval to deny what it encloses, the following expression,

would precisely deny the previous one, and mean, "Nobody praises anybody to anybody"; i.e. take any three individuals (different or some or all the same) and take any triad whatever, then either individual number one is not the first of that triad, or individual No. 2 is not the second, or individual No. 3 is not the third, or this triad is not one of which the first member praises the second to the third". If the Lameth had remained outside the oval, the effect would have been precisely the same. Let us examine this case.

Here the assertion is that there is such a general. But a general is merely of the nature of a possible representation: its being is not existence but merely being represented. The assertion is that "Any three individuals being take in their order, they are either not the 1st, 2nd, and 3rd members respectively of any triad or if they are (the line of identity being intersected by a line and thus negatived) anything whatever (represented by a point of the upper line within the oval) is either not identical with that triad or is not identical with something (represented by a point of the same line outside the oval) that is a triad of which the first member praises the second to the third". Such a triad has a mode of being belonging to anything represented; but no real individuals compose it.

Suppose, however, that we allow one of the three lower lines to protrude from the oval; thus

Then (in a universe of persons), the meaning will be that 'There is somebody who does not praise anybody to anybody". If all three protrude, we have this

That is, "There are three individuals (not necessarily different) of whom the first does not praise the second to the third".

If this is entirely enclosed in another oval, we have this:

That is, "Everybody praises everybody to everybody". If two lines protrude, we may get this:

That is, "There are two persons such that taking any third, the first praises the second to that third", i.e. "Somebody praises somebody to all persons". Denying this, we have the following:

That is, "Everybody fails to praise each person to somebody or other". Let the first lower line protrude, and we have this:

That is "Somebody fails to praise each person to somebody". Finally denying this, we get the first of the above six propositions

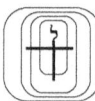

By introducing italic letters we shall be enabled to use the signs of ~~operation~~ conjunction, and so avoid the bewildering number of ovals or other signs of negation. Thus,

$$-i \propto -j\breve{\ } -k \prec i\text{-}q\text{-}j \cdot \breve{\ }.$$
$$\phantom{-i \propto -j\breve{\ } -k \prec i\text{-}}k a$$

If it is desired to treat 'identical with' and 'other than' as relative terms, no sign for the former can be more appropriate than |, which strongly resembles 1, the sign inevitably used for this purpose in functional multiplication. For other than, the simplest sign is T, which is | with an obelus joined to it.

The *Algebra of Dyadic Relatives* is characterized by the employment of certain modes of combination of relative terms by means of which the quantifiers and the signs of indefinite individuals are eliminated. There [are] eight simple modes of combination, in two sets of four. But one of each set is sufficient. Of one set, the most appropriate signs are ∨ < ∧ > crossed by a line of identity. Instead of ∨ the blank or dot may be used. Thus,

$$(l \not\lor b)_{ik} = (l - b)_{ik}$$
$$= (l \cdot b)_{ik}$$
$$= \Sigma_j l_{ij} b_{jk} = i - l - b - k$$
$$(l \not\land b)_{ik} = \Sigma_j l_{ij} \wedge b_{jk}$$
$$(l \not< b)_{ik} = \Sigma_j l_{ij} < b_{jk}$$
$$(l \not> b)_{ik} = \Sigma_j l_{ij} > b_{jk}$$

For the other set no such natural signs present themselves; but I think the best way will be to add tails to the signs ⩑ ⩓ ⊂ ∞ or their equivalents; thus

$$(l \, \natural \, b)_{ik} = \Pi_j l_{ij} \, \natural \, b_{jk}$$
$$(l \, \flat \, b)_{ik} = \Pi_j l_{ij} \, \flat \, b_{jk}$$
$$(l \, \sharp \, b)_{ik} = \Pi_j l_{ij} \, \sharp \, b_{jk}$$
$$(l \, \natural \, b)_{ik} = \Pi_j l_{ij} \, \natural \, b_{jk}$$

I add translations taking l for 'lover of', b for 'benefactor of':

$l - b$ = is lover of a benefactor of.

$l \not\land b$ = does not fail of being a lover of merely of benefactors of.

$l \not< b$ = is not a lover of every benefactor of.

$l \not> b$ = is a lover of something besides benefactors of.

$l \, \natural \, b$ = is a lover of everything but benefactors of.

$l \, \flat \, b$ = is a lover of no benefactor of.

$l \, \sharp \, b$ = is a lover of nothing but benefactors of.

$l \, \natural \, b$ = is a lover of every benefactor of.

I have now completed the review of logical notation which was the purpose of this paper. But since the answer to the question what is the best notation depends upon what work is to be done with the algebra of logic, and since I seem to be in disaccord, upon this point, with many of my coworkers with logical algebra, I will briefly consider the question what utility may be expected in such an algebra.

It appears to me that many logical algebraists expect a logical algebra to be a calculus which being employed according to certain fixed rules will draw conclusions from given premisses which could not otherwise have been drawn so readily.

I do not think that this is true. But even supposing it were true, I cannot admit that this would answer the purposes of those who aim at this effect. For if the procedure is to follow fixed rules, it will be, in so far, blind, and might as well be performed by a machine. I do not doubt that there are logical algebraists who think that if logical problems of the kind mentioned could be solved by machinery, that would be a most glorious achievement, answering every purpose of a logical algebra. But we are already in possession of logical machines which will solve problems that have baffled the whole race of mathematicians; and yet no use is made of these machines, but the problems continue to be studied in the old way without machinery. There is no more difficult problem than that of determining what the motion of a viscous fluid,—to add to the difficulty, let us suppose it elastic,—will be in a confined space in which a solid maintains a simple harmonic motion, but is neither a sphere nor an infinite cylinder. It need not be said that we are in possession of a logical machine that will furnish the solution of that problem. Yet, strange to say, the solution has not been sought in that way. Why not? Obviously, because it is not so much the *solution* of that problem that is desired as its *logical analysis*.

The notion that *any* calculus, worked in a straightforward manner, ever solves any great problem is a delusion. One might as well say that the truths of elementary geometry were discovered by means of writing materials. The demonstration of every great theorem (as I would restrict the word, of every theorem) requires a new construction (or equivalent invention) not directly ~~suggested~~ pointed out by the terms of that theorem and the truths already at hand; in particular, therefore, not to be found by any mere analysis of the meaning of the proposition. But a logical ~~calculus~~ algebra can do absolutely nothing but state propositions so as to exhibit the anatomy of their meanings. Undoubtedly, this may be very useful to the ~~inventor~~ seeker for a demonstration: it may show him what kind of a construction he is to search for. But a logical algebra will not automatically turn out any consequence which a clear-headed man cannot quite as easily (usually more easily) perceive to be a consequence without that apparatus of rules. In this respect, logical algebra must always remain very inferior, we will say for example, to Schubert's [1879] *Calculus of Geometry*, which, worked in a strictly routine way, will furnish myriads of results not otherwise easily made out. It is true that every calculus and every algebra is, in a broad sense, a logical calculus or algebra. Dedekind holds mathematics to be a branch of logic. But what I mean by a logical algebra is an algebra which deals with no other system of values than a dichotomic one. Such algebra would more accurately be called *Dichotomic Algebra*. When every quantity is restricted to one or other of two values,—say, to that of being true and that of being false,—necessarily consequences are so readily perceived by the unaided mind that the help to be derived from a calculus for this purpose is outweighed by the trouble of bearing its rules and symbols in mind. The real utility of logical algebra lies in a different direction.

In order to show that such real utility there is, and what it is, an illustration or two is needed. Unfortunately, the illustration needs to be, not a fancy ~~picture~~ of what might be, but a veracious narrative, and thus, from the nature of the case, I am restricted to drawing my illustrations from the processes of mind of a man who has no pretensions to strictly mathematical ability above ~~the average~~ mediocrity. ~~In short, I have to~~ In plain words, I am compelled to take as my illustrations theorems discovered and demonstrated by C. S. Peirce. I will mention two and will describe truthfully the simple line of thought actually followed in each case.

The first relates to linear associative algebra. I had already been led by the study of the logic [of] relatives to remark a class [of] multiple algebras of which my *novenions* (the which I prefer to *nonions*, the designation given by Clifford) is an example. This algebra, when brought to my father's standard form, presents this multiplication table:[7]

	i	j	k	l	m	n	o	p	q
i	i	j	k	0	0	0	0	0	0
j	0	0	0	i	j	k	0	0	0
k	0	0	0	0	0	0	i	j	k
l	l	m	n	0	0	0	0	0	0
m	0	0	0	l	m	n	0	0	0
n	0	0	0	0	0	0	l	m	n
o	o	p	q	0	0	0	0	0	0
p	0	0	0	o	p	q	0	0	0
q	0	0	0	0	0	0	o	p	q

Evidently, for every square number there is such an algebra, called by my father a *quadrate*. My theorem was that every linear associative algebra may be expressed in terms of a quadrate, a proposition which, at its first enunciation, appeared far from evident, even upon close consideration. I was led to it from the algebra of logic in this way. In the first place, pure algebra is a purely formal affair, a matter of mathematical possibilities. Now anything is mathematically possible that involves no contradiction. But linear associative algebra has but two fundamental operations each of which has its perfect analogue in the algebra of dyadic relatives. But a dyadic relative is a quasi-aggregate of individual pairs. Consequently, nothing prevents our assuming perfect analogues of these in linear associative algebra. But if we identify relative composition with multiplication, the multiplication table of a complete set of individual pairs, considered as relatives, is of the form of the multiplication table of a quadrate algebra. Consequently, every linear associative algebra ought to be capable of statement in terms of a quadrate. In this way I was led to *discover* the theorem; but it remained to *demonstrate* it. [end]

---

[7] [See e.g. "A Communication from Mr. Peirce". *Johns Hopkins University Circulars* 2(22), April 1883, pp. 86–88 (P 245). Reprinted in W4, p. 470, and Introduction to W4 by Nathan Houser.]

17 The Simplest Possible Mathematical System

R 430, R 431a, January–March 1902. Houghton Library. Peirce's gargantuan undertaking to write a detailed account of his theory of logic and analysis of reasoning resulted in four long unpublished chapters and the brutally rejected Carnegie Institute application (R L 75). The selection below consists of two alternative and unpublished sections from Chapter III ("Mathematics. Section 1"): "The Essence of Mathematics" and "Section 2: Specimens of Mathematical Reasoning". The first and the only subsection Peirce wrote of the latter, "A. The Simplest Possible Mathematical Systems", is also the only place in which he explored the logic of EGs in the context of his "Minute Logic" project. In these two sections Peirce applies EGs to the analysis of mathematical reasoning, logical problem-solving, and representation of linguistic meaning. He gives detailed analyses of the basic signs of the system, namely the cuts (ovals) and the lines of identity, indeed more detailed than anything we have witnessed so far during their five-year history. Peirce distinguishes five "offices" of the ovals, only one of which is negation. He then argues that "even when there are no lines of identity", the ovals "fulfill three distinct offices, and that in introducing these lines we have imposed upon them two more." The graphs "fulfill all five with success", yet they hamper progress in mathematical pursuits, as "all mathematical inquiry advances by means of experimenting upon schemata." As "there are a few cases in which [ovals] do not give us the freedom of manipulation which is desirable in mathematics", Peirce is seen to propose several innovative ways in which one could minimally change the notation of the language of Beta graphs to overcome such limitations.

Section 1. The Essence of Mathematics

It was Benjamin Peirce, whose son I boast myself, that in 1870 first defined Mathematics as "the science which draws necessary conclusions". This was a hard saying at the time; but today, students of the philosophy of mathematics generally acknowledge its substantial correctness.

The common definition among such people as ordinary schoolmasters still is that mathematics is the science of quantity. As this is inevitably understood in English, it seems to be a misunderstanding of a definition which may be very old,[1] the original meaning being that mathematics is the science of *quantities*, that is, of forms possessing quantity. We perceive that Euclid was aware that a large branch of geometry had nothing to do with measurement (unless as an aid in demonstration); and, therefore, a Greek geometer of his age (about 300 B.C.) or later, would not have defined mathematics as the science of quantity. But a line was regarded as **a** *quantity*, or *quantum*, so that even perspective could be said to be a science of

---

[1] From what is said by Proclus Diadochus, d. A.D. 485, it would seem that the Pythagoreans understood mathematics to be the answer to the two questions 'how many' and 'how much'.

quantities.² That this is what was originally meant by saying that mathematics is the science of quantity is shown by the fact that those writers who first enunciate it (Ammonius and Boethius) make astronomy and music branches of mathematics, as well as by the reasons they give for doing so.

Aristotle regards mathematics as characterized by a peculiar kind and degree of abstraction (consult the same passage of the *Metaph.* cited in the footnote), greater than that of physics but less than that of metaphysics. This is only a modification of the view of Plato in the Sixth Book of the *Republic* (510C to the end).³ Plato, with Aristotle after him, recognizes that mathematics deals wholly with hypotheses, and asserts no matter of fact; and that this is the reason of the necessity of its conclusions.⁴ Such is the view of all modern mathematicians. Kant regards mathematical propositions as synthetical judgments *a priori*, which is perhaps not in such irreconcileable conflict with the mathematicians' view as it has been assumed to be. Whether a mathematical theorem is "synthetical" or "analytical", in Kant's sense, can hardly be answered: it is neither. Meantime, if the propositions of arithmetic are forms of true cognition, this circumstance is quite aside from their mathematical character. That would be a virtue which the pure mathematician, as such, has not aimed at and does not value. Kant, however, correctly says that mathematical reasoning proceeds from constructions of concepts. He adds that philosophical reasoning proceeds from the concepts themselves. Nevertheless, the efforts of the philosophers to make it appear that philosophy is scientifically higher than mathematics are simply a fit subject of amusement. Perhaps its problems—of God, Freedom, and Immortality,—are more exalted than, for example, the question of how many hours, minutes, and seconds, it will be before two courriers come together. They sound so: they have not been proved to be so. But in method of thought, from whatever side viewed, metaphysics is far inferior to mathematics.

Beyond the two features of being based on pure hypothesis, and being schematic in its mode of reasoning, there is no general character of mathematics which need be noted just now, except the very obvious ones, of, first, the skeleton-

---

2 Aristotle often speaks of Optics as if it were often, if not usually, regarded as a branch of mathematics; though he himself thinks it is a part of physics. This Optics no doubt included perspective and perhaps all that was known of projective geometry. If there had been in Aristotle's day any current opinion that mathematics treated only of quantity, Aristotle could scarcely have failed to alluded to it as supporting his refusal to consider optics as mathematics. But on the contrary he says that mathematics treats the how much and the continuous (*Metaph.* K.iii.1061a33).
3 In the *Laws* his conception is different and more nearly correct.
4 J.S. Mill in his *Logic* (II.v.§§ 1, 2) rather comically alludes to this as "the important doctrine of Dugald Stewart."

like and fleshless build of its propositions, second, the peculiar difficulty of its reasonings, third, the perfect exactitude of its results, and fourth, their practical infallibility. It is easy to be exact if one abandons all ambition to be certain; and easy to be certain if one desists from seeking exactitude. To be, like mathematics, exact and certain at the same time, is not easy.

Of these six characteristics of mathematics, the last five are necessary consequences of the first, which, to restate it, is that, alone of all the sciences, mathematics utterly disregards all matter of fact, and confines itself to ascertaining what would be true in given imaginary states of things. The creation of these hypotheses is a part of the business of the mathematician in which admirable genius is often displayed; but it is difficult to assure oneself that there can be in the work of unfettered imagination anything that can fitly be called science. For there is no truth or falsehood in it. But whether or not of a state of things of a given description, a certain proposition would under all circumstances be true, is, on the other hand, a question to which either Yes or No, but not both, must be the true answer. The given description of the state of things contains every relevant fact. Since, therefore, either Yes or No,—one or the other—must be true, and we are in possession of every fact upon which this necessity depends, it follows that nothing is needed but the work of the mind to render the true answer apodictically, and with absolute exactitude. When a course of reasoning by which this answer is deducible has been discovered, it will be easy to omit from the general description every special feature which is not needed in the demonstration; and hence it is that the propositions of mathematics are so hideously skeletal. For since the reasoning relates, not to what does happen in the living world, but to what would happen in every possible universe, nothing is relevant but formal relations, as will appear more clearly, I hope, when the end of this chapter is reached than it perhaps does at the beginning.

It will also be seen that the reasoning must in all cases be at bottom schematic, or diagrammatic, or else it will not be reasoning at all, but the mere practice of the rule of thumb; and furthermore, the diagram must be made very prominent by alterations being made in it, in the course of the demonstration, or else no vigorous advance in knowledge will be made. As a general rule the diagram will be so complicated that ordinary language is put to a severe strain to express it at all, even though facile perspicuity be not attempted; and naturally the clear mental representation of the problem, and then the invention of the proper alteration of the diagram, call for the closest of thought.

Thus all the marked general characteristics of mathematics are consequences of its being a scientific study of imaginary states of things. That it is so is implied in my father's definition that mathematics is the science which draws necessary conclusions. For imaginary states of things are the only ones of which we can have complete and absolutely exact knowledge. Now without such knowledge no absolutely necessary conclusion can be drawn, since a necessary conclusion is one which not only holds good in the existing universe, but would hold good in any universe whatsoever. For example, nothing can be more certain, as to this world, than that I shall die. Yet it may not be so. Even if all men die, I can have no positive assurance that I am a man; and that all human beings die is a mere generalization, by no means apodictic. True, there is far more solid knowledge in the predication that I shall die than there is in all the pure mathematics in the worlds, which is no knowledge at all, except of fancied states of things. But real solid knowledge is not apodictic; for necessity consists in the application of a proposition to imaginary universes.

The philosophical mathematician, Dr. Richard Dedekind, holds mathematics to be a branch of logic. This would not result from my father's definition, which runs, not that mathematics is the science *of drawing* necessary conclusions,— which would be deductive logic,—but that it is the science *which draws* necessary conclusions.[5] It is evident, and I know as a fact, that he had this distinction in view. At the time when he thought out this definition, he, a mathematician, and I, a logician, held daily discussions about a large subject which interested us both; and he was struck, as I was, with the contrary nature of his interest and mine in the same propositions. The logician does not care particularly about this or that hypothesis or its consequences, except so far as these things may throw a light upon the nature of reasoning. The mathematician is intensely interested in efficient methods of reasoning, with a view to their possible extension to new problems; but he does not, *quâ* mathematician, trouble himself minutely to dissect those parts of this method whose correctness is a matter of course.

The different ways in which the two men will regard an algebra of logic shows the contrariety of their aims. The mathematician asks what value such an algebra has as a calculus. Can it be applied to unravelling a complicated question? Will it at one stroke produce a remote consequence? The logician does not wish the algebra to have that character. On the contrary, the greater number of distinct logical steps into which as algebra breaks up an easy inference will for him constitute a superiority over one which moves more swiftly to its conclusions. He demands that the algebra shall analyze the reasoning into its ultimate parts. Thus, that which is a merit in a logical algebra for one of these students is a demerit in the eyes of the other. Moreover, logic is a study of positive truth; it seeks to know what is,

---

5 [*Collected Papers* (CP 4.239) has misled later interpreters in wrongly italizing the two phrases in a related passage that concerns this Benjamin–Charles definition of what makes logic and mathematics different.]

as a fact, the nature of reasoning; while mathematics is a study of the matter of hypotheses.

In one respect, however, I am in doubt whether my father's definition is adequate or not. It seems to make the deduction of the consequences of hypotheses the sole business of the mathematician. Now it cannot be denied that immense mathematical genius goes into the framing of those hypotheses. Consider, for example, the idea of the field of imaginary quantity, and the connected idea of a Riemann's surface. Consider such ideas as that of a non-Euclidean system of measurement, that of ideal numbers, that of a perfect liquid. Even the framing of the particular hypotheses of special problems has often required great intellectual power. Yet, regarded from the point of view of pure mathematics, which utterly disregards actual fact, the mere creation of imaginary states of things is less science than poetry. It is only when a hypothesis is considered as an approximate rationalization of those phenomena of nature that suggested it, that it can be reckoned as a contribution to science. But even poetry in the narrow sense may be said to be a sort of science when it is considered as a partial interpretation of the facts of life. Perhaps we might escape this doubtful objection if we were to define mathematics as the study of exactly imagined systems.

There is one characteristic mode of good mathematics which, if not quite essential, seems to be worth mention. The mathematician seeks to make his imaginary state of things as homogeneous and free from arbitrary exceptional features as the general regularity of it allows. If he imagines the surface of a sphere to be divided up into stripes, there must inevitably be at least one exceptional point; but he will not imagine an arbitrarily bounded part of the sphere. He prefers to consider a regularity extending over the complete surface, from which he can afterward cut his bounded portion. Chess is mathematics: only it is a crabbed and unbeautiful kind of mathematics, with its bounded board, its sixteen pieces of six kinds in each of two colors, its unsymmetrical king and queen, its exceptional castling, queening of pawns, and captures by pawns. It is unmathematical mathematics.

Section 2. Specimens of Mathematical Reasoning

Subsection A. The Simplest Possible Mathematical System

It is of the essence of mathematics that it should draw conclusions. There can be no reasoning where there was not previously room for doubt. Hence, the simplest mathematical hypothesis must allow the possibility of two answers to a question, and thus must involve at least two elements. Let us begin with the case in which it involves nothing more. We are to suppose, then, two independent units, or objects, which we may call $\mathbb{V}$ and $\mathbb{F}$. What the nature of these units may be is of no consequence. It is so indeterminate that they might be two atoms, or two worlds, or two virtues, or two values, or an orange and a dimension, or an assertion and pure nothingness. The hypotheses of pure mathematics are determinate only in respect to certain formal relations. These two units are determinate only in being distinct from one another. The general problem in this branch of mathematics will ask whether an object concerning which there are certain data is $\mathbb{F}$ or is $\mathbb{V}$. A more general problem will be to find a regular form of procedure for solving all such special problems. We set out with two postulates, as follows:

Postulate I. Nothing is both $\mathbb{V}$ and $\mathbb{F}$.

Postulate II. Everything (in the supposed system) is either $\mathbb{V}$ or $\mathbb{F}$.

The only assertions relevant in this system about a single object, x, regardless of every other, are two:

$$x \text{ is } \mathbb{V}; \qquad (1)$$

$$x \text{ is } \mathbb{F}. \qquad (2)$$

The only assertions possible concerning two objects, x and y, which neither imply any assertion of form (1) or (2) about x or y, or are implied in any single assertion, are two:

$$x \text{ and } y \text{ are the same}; \qquad (3)$$

$$x \text{ and } y \text{ are different}. \qquad (4)$$

For the sake of brevity we may write the single statements, thus: $x = \mathbb{V}$, $x = \mathbb{F}$; and the dyadic statements, thus: $x = y$, $x = \bar{y}$. Then we have four forms of inference as follows:

$x = y$	$x = y$	$x = \bar{y}$	$x = \bar{y}$
$x = \mathbb{V}$	$x = \mathbb{F}$	$x = \mathbb{V}$	$x = \mathbb{F}$
$\therefore y = \mathbb{V}$	$\therefore y = \mathbb{F}$	$\therefore y = \mathbb{F}$	$\therefore y = \mathbb{V}$

Really the same as the last two, though they appear different owing to the imperfection of the notation use, are the following:

$x = \bar{y}$	$x = \bar{y}$
$y = \mathbb{F}$	$y = \mathbb{V}$
$\therefore x = \mathbb{V}$	$\therefore x = \mathbb{F}$

17 The Simplest Possible Mathematical System (R 430), 1902

The mathematician always extends and generalizes his notation. Why not write $x = \overline{\mathbb{V}}$ and $x = \overline{\mathbb{F}}$, forms which yield the following inferential forms?

$$x = \overline{\mathbb{F}} \qquad\qquad x = \overline{\mathbb{V}}$$
$$\mathbb{F} = \mathbb{F} \qquad\qquad \mathbb{V} = \mathbb{V}$$
$$\therefore x = \mathbb{V} \qquad\qquad \therefore x = \mathbb{F}$$

The premisses $\mathbb{F} = \mathbb{F}$ and $\mathbb{V} = \mathbb{V}$ are no new postulates. For a postulate expresses in part the hypothesis of the system. But these are mere empty formulae arising from the superfluities of the notation. For $x = \overline{\mathbb{F}}$ is but a superfluous form for expressing $x = \mathbb{V}$; and $x = \overline{\mathbb{V}}$ of expressing $x = \mathbb{F}$.

We may strip off these superfluities of notation. But, unless we do so by arbitrarily forbidding certain combinations of symbols, which would be in conflict with the spirit of mathematics, we can only do so at the expense of the symmetry of the notation. We may, for example, continue to write $x = \mathbb{V}$, but instead of $x = \mathbb{F}$, we may write $\mathbb{V} = x$. Then our four forms of inference will be

$$x = y \qquad x = y \qquad x = \overline{y} \qquad x = \overline{y}$$
$$x = \mathbb{V} \qquad \mathbb{V} = x \qquad x = \mathbb{V} \qquad \mathbb{V} = x$$
$$\therefore y = \mathbb{V} \qquad \therefore \mathbb{V} = y \qquad \therefore \mathbb{V} = \overline{y} \qquad \therefore y = \mathbb{V}$$

But since $x = y$ and $y = x$ are two forms of writing the same thing, we shall have, as apparently different forms,

$$x = y \qquad x = y \qquad x = \overline{y} \qquad x = \overline{y}$$
$$y = \mathbb{V} \qquad \mathbb{V} = \overline{y} \qquad \mathbb{V} = \overline{y} \qquad y = \mathbb{V}$$
$$\therefore x = \mathbb{V} \qquad \therefore \mathbb{V} = \overline{x} \qquad \therefore \mathbb{V} = x \qquad \therefore \mathbb{V} = \overline{x}$$

The symmetry of the equational form necessarily entails superfluity. In order to get rid of this, let us abandon equations and use a non-reciprocal relation instead of the reciprocal relation of equality. For that purpose let us write $x \prec y$ to mean that one of the following three pairs of assertion is true:

$$x \text{ is } \mathbb{V} \qquad\qquad x \text{ is } \mathbb{F} \qquad\qquad x \text{ is } \mathbb{F}$$
$$y \text{ is } \mathbb{V} \qquad\qquad y \text{ is } \mathbb{V} \qquad\qquad y \text{ is } \mathbb{F}.$$

Thus, the only possibility which the statement $x \prec y$ excludes is $x = \mathbb{V}, y = \mathbb{F}$. Then if we write:

$$x \prec y \qquad\qquad\qquad y \prec x$$

we shall exclude the truth of $x = \mathbb{V}, y = \mathbb{F}$ and also the truth of $y = \mathbb{V}, x = \mathbb{F}$, while we shall allow either $x = \mathbb{V}, y = \mathbb{V}$ or $x = \mathbb{F}, y = \mathbb{F}$. These two expressions then will together amount to writing $x = y$. Then $x \prec \mathbb{V}$ will permit $x = \mathbb{V}$ or $x = \mathbb{F}$, as will $\mathbb{F} \prec x$. But $\mathbb{V} \prec x$ will be equivalent to $x = \mathbb{V}$, and $x \prec \mathbb{F}$ to $x = \mathbb{F}$. We shall now have the following inferential forms:

$$x \prec y \qquad\qquad x \prec y$$
$$\mathbb{V} \prec x \qquad\qquad y \prec \mathbb{F}$$
$$\therefore \mathbb{V} \prec y \qquad\qquad \therefore x \prec \mathbb{F}.$$

Both of these come under the general formula, which invariably holds good,

$$x \prec y$$
$$y \prec z$$
$$\therefore x \prec z.$$

Still, as soon as we undertake to express that x is different from y we again encounter superfluity, because difference is a reciprocal relation, or equiparance. For $x \prec \bar{y}$ will be the same as $y \prec \bar{x}$. The best way to accomplish our purpose of finding one way to express one thing will be to abandon the signs $\mathbb{V}$ and $\mathbb{F}$ and simply write x for $x = \mathbb{V}$ and $\bar{x}$ for $x = \mathbb{F}$. We may then write xy, or yx, or $\overset{x}{y}$, or $\overset{y}{x}$, etc. to express $x = \mathbb{V}, y = \mathbb{V}$. That is, we simply write both to express both. Not that we are debarred from writing a proposition without asserting it; but when we write it on a certain sheet of paper it is to be understood that we assert it (or pretend to do so). If we sever a portion of the sheet by drawing an oval line round it, it shall be equally understood that what is written therein, taken in its entirety, is precisely denied, so that ⒡ is $\mathbb{V}$ and ⒱ is $\mathbb{F}$. Thus the oval has the effect [of] interchanging $\mathbb{F}$ and $\mathbb{V}$.

The resulting diagram, which is called an *existential graph*, may be transformed according to the following *rules*, or permissions.

Rule I. *Any unenclosed part of the graph may be erased, together with whatever it may enclose.*

Proof. For the original graph asserts that each unenclosed part of it represents $\mathbb{V}$. It, therefore, asserts that the part remaining after the erasure represents $\mathbb{V}$. But this graph consisting of this part by itself asserts no more than that that part represents $\mathbb{V}$. Hence, the effect of the erasure is merely to cause the graph to desist from asserting a part of what it had previously asserted.

Rule II. *Two ovals, the one enclosing nothing but the other with its contents, may be brawn round the graph, or being drawn, may be erased.*

Proof. For let G be the entire graph, then the holds provided that of the following two graphs G and ⓖ neither asserts anything not asserted by the other. The first, G, asserts only that G is $\mathbb{V}$. Then the graph ⓖ precisely denies this, and thus asserts simply that G is $\mathbb{F}$. Then ⓖ precisely denies this; and thus asserts simply that G is $\mathbb{V}$. Thus the two graphs assert precisely the same thing, Q.E.D.

Rule III. *Whatever transformation would [be] permissible upon a graph if it were written alone, is permissible upon any detached portion of a graph within an even number of enclosures; and the reverse transformation is permissible within an odd number of enclosures.*

Proof. I will first show that this holds good for a single enclosure. That is, if G is a graph which written by itself would be transformable into Γ then ⟨ΓH⟩ K, whatever graphs H and K may be (or if they are blanks, which are a kind of graphs), is transformable into ⟨GH⟩ K. That is to say, if Γ asserts nothing not asserted by G, then ⟨GH⟩ K asserts nothing not asserted by ⟨ΓH⟩ K. For ⟨ΓH⟩ K asserts that K is $\mathbb{V}$ and ⟨ΓH⟩ is $\mathbb{V}$. Asserting that ⟨ΓH⟩ is $\mathbb{V}$, is to deny that ΓH is $\mathbb{V}$. To assert that ΓH is $\mathbb{V}$ is to assert that Γ is $\mathbb{V}$ and H is $\mathbb{V}$. Hence, to deny that ΓH is $\mathbb{V}$ is to assert that either Γ is not $\mathbb{V}$ or that H is not $\mathbb{V}$. But the hypothesis is that to say that Γ is $\mathbb{V}$ is to assert nothing not asserted in saying that G is $\mathbb{V}$. If then the former contains a falsity this is contained in the latter. Hence, to say that Γ is not $\mathbb{V}$ is to deny that G is $\mathbb{V}$. But if either G is not $\mathbb{V}$ or H is not $\mathbb{V}$ then GH is not $\mathbb{V}$; for if GH is $\mathbb{V}$, G is $\mathbb{V}$ and H is $\mathbb{V}$. And if GH is not $\mathbb{V}$, ⟨GH⟩ is $\mathbb{V}$. And if ⟨GH⟩ is $\mathbb{V}$ and K is $\mathbb{V}$, then ⟨GH⟩ K is $\mathbb{V}$ and the graph ⟨GH⟩ K may be written. Thus, if G could be transformed as an entire graph to Γ, then ⟨ΓH⟩ K can be transformed to ⟨GH⟩ K, whatever graphs H and K may be; and the rule holds for a single enclosure.

If the rule breaks down for any number of enclosures, there must be some smallest number of enclosures for which it can break down, being valid for every smaller number. Then, let G' be a graph involving one fewer enclosures than the smallest number for which the rule can break down, and suppose that by virtue of the rule and the fact that G is transformable into Γ, G' is transformable into another graph Γ'. Then any graph of the smallest number for which the rule can break down may be put into the form ⟨Γ'H⟩ K, by putting H for all the rest of the graph within the outermost enclosure containing G or Γ, and K for all outside that enclosure. But as just shown, if G' is transformable in Γ', as it is by virtue of the rule, then ⟨Γ'H⟩ K is transformable into ⟨G'H⟩ K, which accords with the rule. Hence, there can be no smallest number of enclosures for which the rule breaks down; and therefore, it does not break down at all.

17 The Simplest Possible Mathematical System (R 430), 1902 — 451

Rule IV. *Any part of a graph may be iterated, within the same or additional enclosures, provided these already exist; and if any part of a graph is iterated so that one occurrence of it is within whatever enclosure the other is within, the former may be erased.*

Proof. It being evident that the unenclosed iteration of an unenclosed part has not effect, I will begin by proving that if a graph contains two ovals one inside the other, any unenclosed part of it can be iterated within the two ovals. For let the unenclosed parts to be iterated be A, and the rest that is unenclosed be B. Let the simply enclosed part be C, and the doubly enclosed part be D. Then the graph before iteration will be A B (C(D)) while after the iteration it will have become A B (C(DA)). I have to prove that if what the former asserts is true, so is what the latter asserts. (D) asserts that D is not V; C(D), that C is V and D is not V. (C(D)) asserts that if C is V, then D is V. A B (C(D)) asserts that A is V, that B is V, and that if C is V, then D is V. A B (C(DA)) asserts the same thing, except that if C is V then both D is V and A is V. But since A is asserted to be V in any case, the addition is without effect. Hence, the rule holds in this case.

I will next prove that an unenclosed part of a graph can be iterated within any even number of enclosures. For if not there must be some smallest even number for which the rule may break down. Let it then be iterated within the greatest even number of enclosures for which the rule holds. That done, since we have just seen that an unenclosed part of a graph can be iterated within two enclosures, it follows from Rule III, that this part may be inserted a third time within two more enclosures. That done, the middle occurrence of it can be erased by Rules I and III. The rule will hold for the number of enclosures for which it was supposed to break down, if it breaks down at all. Hence, it cannot break down, as far as the iteration within even enclosures of an unenclosed part is concerned. If follows, then, by Rule III that any evenly enclosed part of a graph can be iterated within any even number of additional enclosures.

I will next prove that if an unenclosed part of a graph is iterated within one enclosure, the inner occurrence of it can be erased. That is, if the graph A B (CA) can be written, so can A B (C). For the former asserts that A is V, B is V, but that not both C and A are V. It follows that C is not V. Now all that the second graph asserts is that A is V, B is V, and C is not V. Q.E.D.

I will next prove that if an unenclosed part of a graph is iterated under any odd number of enclosures, the inner occurrence of it can be erased. For we have just seen that an unenclosed part of a graph can be iterated within any even number of enclosures. It can therefore be iterated just outside the inmost enclosure of the iteration within odd enclosures; and then by Rule III applied to what has just been proved, the inmost iteration can be erased, after which by Rules I and III, the evenly enclosed occurrences can be erased.

Rule III now extends what has just been proved, so that if any evenly enclosed part of a graph is iterated under any odd number of additional enclosures the inner occurrence can be erased.

But by Rules I and III anything can be erased within even enclosures or inserted within odd enclosures.

Hence it will be seen that the entire rule holds good.

But it is proper to remark that A B (C(A)) or A B (C(D(A))) will thus give A B (C(○)) and A B (C(D(○))).

The interpretation of these graphs is not obvious. Considering the first, by Rule I it can be transformed into A B; and on the other hand, starting from A B we get by Rule II A B (○) and then, by Rules I and III, A B (C(○)). Thus this graph and A B are mutually transformable, and denote the same state of things. The graph A B (C(D(○))) gives, by Rules I and III, A B (C(○)), and thence, by Rules II and III, A B (C); while A B (C) gives at once, by Rules I and III, A B (C(D(○))). Hence, these two are equivalent.

In order to show that even this simplest possible mathematics is not quite foolishness,[6] I will apply it to an example or two. The following by Mr. Venn is taken by me from Mrs. [Ladd-]Franklin's paper in Johns Hopkins *Studies in Logic*. The wording is mine.

Every member of a certain board of directors is either a bondholder or a shareholder; but no director is both bondholder and shareholder; and every bondholder is on the board. What is the relation between bondholders and shareholders? Every student of logic will see instantly what the answer is; but we will work it out by our mathematics.

Let us speak of the *value* of a proposition meaning one of the two attributes, *truth* and *falsity*. Truth shall be $\mathbb{V}$; falsity, $\mathbb{F}$.

---

[6] **[Alt.:]** [...] In order to show that this simplest kind of mathematics is not useless, I will apply it to the solution of a problem already solved by M[a]cColl in substantially the same way. The problem is easily explained to the least mathematical head. It is to reverse the order of integration of the following

$$\int_a^{2a} dt \int_{-t}^{2t} dx \int_{-x}^{2x} dy \int_{-2x}^{\frac{y^2}{2x}} dz\, \phi(t,x,y,z)$$

We will suppose that a peculiarly shaped solid body composed of heavy materials is guided along a certain path and is attached to a mechanism so that it does work as it moves [end]

17 The Simplest Possible Mathematical System (R 430), 1902

Now we will consider any man, no matter who. Let D be the 'value' of the proposition that this man is one of the directors in our problem; let s be the 'value' of the proposition that the same man is a shareholder; and let B be the value of the proposition that this man is a bondholder. Then the graph ⟨D S B⟩ expresses that the proposition that this man is at once director, stockholder, and bondholder is not true, no matter who the man is; that is, as premised, no director is both stockholder and bondholder. The graph ⟨D S B⟩⟨B ⟨D⟩⟩ expresses, in addition, that our man (whoever he may be) is not a bondholder without being a director. That is, as stated, every bondholder is on the board. By Rule IV, we iterate the left hand graph in the inner enclosure of the right hand graph, thus: ⟨D S B⟩⟨B ⟨D ⟨D S B⟩⟩⟩. By the same rule, we strike out the inner second occurrence of D and B, thus: ⟨D S B⟩⟨B ⟨D ⟨S⟩⟩⟩ By Rules I and III, we strike out the left hand unenclosed part, and the evenly enclosed D, thus: ⟨B ⟨S⟩⟩. By Rule II, we erase the double oval about s, thus: ⟨B S⟩. This means that our man (whoever he may be) is not both bondholder and stockholder. That is, the two collections of bondholders and stockholders have no common member.

Another by Mr. Venn: It is stated, in reference to a certain examination that there was no candidate but juniors who took Latin and seniors who took composition; that there was no junior but [those who] took Latin or composition; and that there was none who took composition but juniors who took Latin. What sorts of candidates could there have been?

Considering any candidate, whoever he may be, let J be the value of the proposition that he was a junior; s that he was a senior; L that he took Latin; c that he took composition. Then the premises form the following graphs

$$\langle J \langle L \rangle \langle S C \rangle\rangle \tag{5}$$

$$\langle J \langle L \rangle C \rangle \tag{6}$$

$$\langle C \langle L J \rangle\rangle \tag{7}$$

To these, since no junior is senior, we add

$$\langle J S \rangle. \tag{8}$$

Iterating (8) in (5), we get

$$\langle J \langle L \rangle \langle J S \rangle S C\rangle\rangle \text{ whence } \langle J \langle L \rangle \langle J \rangle S C\rangle\rangle \text{ whence } \langle J \langle L \rangle \langle J \rangle C\rangle\rangle. \tag{9}$$

The last (9) gives

$$\langle\langle L \rangle \langle J \rangle\rangle \text{ whence } \langle L J \rangle; \tag{10}$$

and (7) gives

$$\boxed{c\ \boxed{J}}.\tag{11}$$

Iterating (10) in (11), we get,

$$\boxed{c\ \boxed{J\ \boxed{J\ L}}}\ \text{whence}\ \boxed{c\ \boxed{J\ \boxed{L}}}\ \text{and}\ \boxed{c\ \boxed{\boxed{L}}}\ \text{and}\ \boxed{c\ L}.\tag{12}$$

But (7) gives

$$\boxed{c\ \boxed{L}}.\tag{13}$$

Iterating (12) in (13) we get

$$\boxed{c\ \boxed{L\ \boxed{L\ C}}}\ \text{whence}\ \boxed{c\ \boxed{L\ \boxed{C}}}\ \text{whence}\ \boxed{c\ \boxed{\boxed{C}}}\ \text{and}\ \boxed{c\ C}\ \text{and}\ \boxed{c}.\tag{14}$$

Now (5) gives

$$\boxed{\boxed{L}\ \boxed{C}}\ \text{whence}\ \boxed{L\ \boxed{C}}.\tag{15}$$

Iterating (14) in (15) we get

$$\boxed{L\ \boxed{c\ \boxed{C}}\ \boxed{C}}\ \text{whence}\ \boxed{L\ \boxed{c\ C}\ \boxed{C}},\ \text{whence}\ \boxed{L\ \boxed{\ }\ \boxed{C}}\ \text{and}\ \boxed{L\ \boxed{C}}.\tag{16}$$

Iterating (6) in (5) we get

$$\boxed{J\ \boxed{J\ L\ \boxed{C}}\ \boxed{L}\ \boxed{S\ C}}\ \text{whence}\ \boxed{J\ \boxed{\boxed{C\ L}}\ \boxed{S\ C}}\ \text{and}\ \boxed{\boxed{L}\ \boxed{C}}.\tag{17}$$

Finally (16) and (17) give

$$\boxed{L}\ \boxed{C}\ \boxed{\boxed{L}\ \boxed{C}},\ \text{whence}\ \boxed{L}\ \boxed{C}\ \boxed{\ };\ \text{whence}\ \boxed{\ }.\tag{18}$$

But this last is the sign of absurdity, since if x is the value of the proposition A is A, it gives $\boxed{x}$ or A is not A. Hence, the hypotheses of the problem are absurd; that is, there were no candidates.

Presuming that the subject is new to the reader, I suppose he is impressed with the idea that great ingenuity is required to work this calculus. But I shall now proceed to show that none is needed; that he has only to follow a straightforward method. The method I shall develop is not the most expeditious possible; but in my opinion it is the best on account of its extreme simplicity.

Problem 1. *To reduce any existential graph to a simple combination of graphs each of the form* P $\boxed{Q_1\ Q_2\ Q_3\ \text{etc.}\ \boxed{R_1}\ \boxed{R_2}\ \boxed{R_3}\ \text{etc.}}$.

17 The Simplest Possible Mathematical System (R 430), 1902

Solution. I begin by showing that a graph of the form P(Q(RS)) is equivalent to P(Q(R))(Q(S)). This will be the case if each of these forms is transformable into the other. Beginning with P(Q(RS)), we iterate the last part, giving P(Q(RS))(Q(RS)). Then, by Rules I and III, this gives P(Q(R))(Q(S)). This shows that the first form is transformable into the second. Next starting with the last result, we get by iteration P(Q(R(Q(S))))(Q(S)). By the rule of iteration, this gives P(Q(R(S)))(Q(S)) which gives P(Q(RS)). This shows that the second form can be transformed into the first.

It follows that if there is more than a single letter or single enclosure within two ovals the number can be reduced until there is but one letter or one enclosure within any enclosed oval. But if this is an enclosure instead of a letter, it can be further simplified by erasing the ovals by Rule II. Thus P(Q((R))) is equivalent to P(QR). It is therefore a perfectly simple matter to free the graph from all ovals within enclosed ovals. But if this is an enclosure instead of a letter, it can be further simplified by erasing the ovals by Rule II. Thus P(Q((R))) is equivalent to P(QR). It is therefore a perfectly simple matter to free the graph from all ovals within enclosed ovals.

Thus the first premiss of our last problem is (JL)(SC). This is equivalent to (JS)(JC)(LS)(LC).

It is only necessary to take every possible combination, preserving the numbers of enclosures, modified only by Rule II. So (A B(C(DE))) is equivalent to (AB)(ACD)(ACE).

Problem 2. *To eliminate a letter from a graph in the canonical form above given.*

Solution. We will consider seven cases, as follows:

- *First Case.* The letter only occurs doubly enclosed. It can only be erased by Rules I and III.
- *Second Case.* The letter only occurs singly enclosed. The only way is to erase each oval containing it, by Rule I.
- *Third Case.* The letter only occurs unenclosed. It can only be erased.
- *Fourth Case.* The letter occurs only singly and doubly enclosed. The base way is to iterate each entire double enclosure as many times as there are occurrences of the letter under one enclosure, and then to iterate each of the latter inside the double enclosure, erasing them elsewhere. The letter may then everywhere be erased. Thus A(BX(C))(D(X)) will give A(DB(C)) and (AX(B)(CX(D))(E(X))(F(X))(G(X)) will give (EA(B))(FA(B))(GA(B))(EC(D))(FC(D))(GC(D)).

- *Fifth Case.* The letter occurs only unenclosed and singly enclosed. Here A X (B X Ⓒ)(D X Ⓔ)(F X Ⓖ) gives A(B Ⓒ)(D Ⓔ)(F Ⓖ).
- *Sixth Case.* The letter occurs only unenclosed and doubly enclosed. It is to be simply erased.
- *Seventh Case.* The letter occurs unenclosed and both singly and doubly enclosed. A X(B X Ⓒ)(D X Ⓔ)(F X Ⓖ)(I Ⓧ)(J Ⓧ) gives A(B Ⓒ)(D Ⓔ)(F Ⓖ).

Most problems are problems of elimination, like the last. Let us treat that according to our method.

The premiss-graph is (J Ⓢ)(J Ⓒ)(L Ⓢ)(L Ⓒ)(J Ⓛ Ⓒ)(C Ⓛ)(C Ⓙ)(J Ⓢ). We eliminate s, thus: (J Ⓙ)(J Ⓒ)(L Ⓙ)(L Ⓒ)(J Ⓛ Ⓒ)(C Ⓛ)(C Ⓙ) We eliminate L; after dropping (J Ⓙ) which is meaningless: (J Ⓒ)(C Ⓙ)(C Ⓒ)(J Ⓒ)(C Ⓙ). We eliminate J, after dropping (C Ⓒ): (C Ⓒ)(C Ⓒ) whence Ⓒ c; whence ○ c; whence ○.

Some problems, instead of seeking the conclusion from given premisses, seek a premiss needful to establish a given conclusion. The method is to take the denial of the derived conclusion as a premiss; and then the denial of the conclusion so reached will be the requisite premiss. Such is the following by Mr. W. B. Grove. Every member of a certain society who is a member of section A but not of section B, or of B but not of C, or of C but not of A, and who has paid his subscription may lecture. If he has not paid, he cannot lecture. Every member of A but not of C, of C but not of A, or of B but not of A and who has paid may experiment. If he has not paid he cannot experiment. Every member lectures or experiments. What addition to the rules is required to compel every member to pay?

Considering any member, whoever he may be, let A be the value of the proposition that he belongs to section A; B, that he belongs to section B; C, that he belongs to section C; E, that he experiments; L, that he lectures; P, that he pays.

The existing rules are expressed as follows:
(P A(B)(L))(P B(C)(L))(P C(A)(L))(L A(B)(P))(L B(C)(P))(L C(A)(P))
(P A(C)(E))(P C(A)(E))(P B(A)(E))(E A(C)(P))(E C(A)(P))(E B(A)(P))
(E(L)).

To this we join the expression of the state of things to be presented namely Ⓟ.

Observe that a graph of the form (M Ⓝ N) has no meaning, and may as well be erased (which we have anyway a *right* to do) since it follows from anything say x, thus x x; A (Ⓧ); x (M N Ⓧ); x (M N (N X)); (M N Ⓝ). Unless we eliminate P we shall take no account of the result we wish to bring about. The result is as follows:
(L A Ⓑ)(L B Ⓒ)(L C Ⓐ)(E A Ⓒ)(E C Ⓐ)(E B Ⓐ)(E Ⓛ).

The negative of this expresses the least requisite addition to the rules. But to simplify the matter we may eliminate first E and then L. The elimination of E gives

17 The Simplest Possible Mathematical System (R 430), 1902

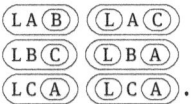

The elimination of L gives (A B C)(A B C)(A B C)(A B C)(A C). This is equivalent to (A C)(A C)(B C)(A B) or c(A B).

Hence the convenient rule will be (c(B(A))) or (c(B)(C A). That is every member of section c must be treated as a member of section B; but nobody can belong to sections A and c, both.

The logical value of this schematic of existential graphs is very considerable. Not that there would twice in a life-time be occasion to use it for the solution of problems; but the practice of it aids us to form a habit of getting distinct logical ideas of what we read and write. However, from a logical point of view, this schematic would, as it stands, so far, be inferior to another system, called (incorrectly) by the name of "Euler's Diagrams", which I shall describe in an appendix to this chapter. But I shall now go on to describe three modifications, or supplements, of it, which immensely enhance its utility. The first consists in introducing, besides the letters (of course, words may be written instead of letters; but it is convenient to speak of them as letters) *heavy lines* connecting some of the letters. It will be a material circumstance on what side of a letter the heavy line joins it; but the form of the line will be indifferent. Thus A—B and A⏤B will be the same; but A⏤B will be different. So (A—B) will be different from (A/B) ; because different sides of the letters are joined, but (A⊤B) and (A/B) will be the same; because continuous lines join the same parts. These heavy lines will be called *lines of identity*.

If it be asked what is the signification of these lines of identity, I reply that I shall presently give formal rules showing under what circumstances they can be drawn and erased. To ask for more is to misunderstand pure mathematics, where form subject to rules is all that is pertinent. Suffice it to say that the graphs may be used to represent any relations to which their rules render them analogous. Nevertheless, since I began by supposing a system of two objects V and F with one or other of which each letter was supposed to be identical, I may explain that now, it is each detached piece, as A—B, considered as one whole, which is identical with V or with F. But it is important to remark that since we adopted the system of writing anything to show that it is identical with V and of writing two things to show that each of them is identical with V, while their combination, being written, is also identical with V, the leading idea has become transformation. For whatever may be written, say A, we can always juxtapose V; for A V only means that the A is V (which A alone means) and that V is V, which is an empty formula. Then since we can always refrain from asserting anything without thereby falsifying, we can erase A, leaving only V. Thus, anything written unenclosed may be transformed into V. In like manner, since whatever is not V is F, F can be transformed into anything, although it is absurd to write F, because this would signify that F was identical with V. However, supposing that in consequence of our having unwarily started from false premises we are led by legitimate transformations to F. Now F is the same as (V) and since anything, x, when unenclosed, can be transformed into V, so can (x), for this whole is unenclosed. Then by Rule III, within an oval V can be transformed into (x); so that (V) becomes (x) or by Rule II, x. Thus, F can be transformed into x, whatever x may be. This being the case, V and F, are no longer, in the schematic which we have developed, mere undefined objects. But V is that into which everything can be transformed; while F is that which can be transformed into everything.

Notwithstanding what has been said of the absolute formality of mathematics, it will be convenient to attach some interpretation to lines of identity to serve as an aid in establishing rules for their transformation; remembering that this interpretation is only accidental and that the resulting schematic will be applicable to any subject presenting analogous relationships. We have hitherto supposed that every detached part of the graph represents a proposition, that writing it unenclosed asserts the proposition and that writing it within an otherwise empty oval precisely denies it. Let us continue that convention. Let us only assume that the heavy lines signify identity. Let us further suppose that as Rule I permits us to erase any detached part of a graph, se we can pass from the assertion man—wounded implying some sort of identity between men and wounded things, to —wounded.

We shall, then, naturally make the former mean that something is identical with a man and a wounded thing, that is, that 'some man is wounded', while the latter means that something is wounded. So man— —wounded will express that something is a man and something is wounded. Then (man—wounded) will deny that any man is wounded. man— (—wounded) will assert that something is a man, but will deny that anything is wounded. Then, we shall naturally write man—(—wounded) for 'some man is not wounded'. Thus we shall understand that the continuity of the identity is quite unbroken by the oval.

Consider this graph man—C$_{\text{disgraced}}^{\text{wounded}}$. This asserts that something is at once, a man, wounded and disgraced. Then the following man—C$_{\text{(disgraced)}}^{\text{wounded}}$ will mean that something is identical with a man wounded but not disgraced. The following man—(C$_{\text{disgraced}}^{\text{wounded}}$) will mean that something is identical with a man who is not at once identical with [a] wounded thing and with a disgraced thing; that is, some man is either not wounded or not disgraced, while man—C$_{\text{(disgraced)}}^{\text{(wounded)}}$ will signify that something is a man who is not wounded *and* not disgraced. The continuity of the identity is unaffected by the oval. Then, —(wounded) will mean 'something is not wounded'; while (—wounded) will mean 'it is not true that something is wounded';

i.e., 'everything is unwounded'. It thus makes a difference whether a line of identity is or is not completely enclosed; for in the one case it is not and in the other is attached to something unenclosed, though it be but a point.[7] But the enclosure does not make the line signify non-identity unless the latter is wholly enclosed. Of course no elongation or branching of a line has any effect: its continuity and connectivity is alone significant.

Lines of identity may be transformed according to the following rules:

Amendment of Rule I. *An unenclosed part of a line of identity may be broken; but not at an oval.*

Thus from man⎯⎯(wounded) or 'some man is unwounded' we may pass to man⎯ ⎯(wounded) or 'some man is coexistent with something unwounded'. But we cannot pass to man⎯ (⎯wounded) since this might be understood to mean man⎯ (⎯wounded) or 'some man coexists with nothing wounded'.

In like manner, any two lines of identity can be joined when under the same single enclosure. Thus, given (man⎯(respects)⎯American) or 'any man (that may exist) respects any American that may exist', we may write (man⎯(respects)⎯American) or 'any American man there may be respects himself'.

Amendment to Rule IV. *The whole rule of iteration applies to attached parts of graphs with the understanding that a part of a graph is not iterated unless it has identically the same lines of attachment in all occurrences.*

---

7 **[Alt.:]** With regard to the line of identity, it is to be remarked that their continuity is not broken by crossing ovals; but a line of identity cannot stop just at the oval; it must [sic.] Changing the shape of such a line, producing it, giving it a new branch etc. have no effect. But if it enters an oval, that is a different thing. It is subject to the following rules:

Amendment of Rule I. *An unenclosed part of a line of identity may be broken.*

Amendment of Rule IV. *A part of a graph attached to others by lines of identity can be iterated as if undetached, provided its attachments remain identically the same; and a part of a graph may be erased by virtue of an iteration, as if there were no attachments, provided the attachments are the same in both occurrences.*

Rule V. *An unattached and unenclosed line of identity can always be drawn.*

There may be cases in which it would be convenient to abrogate this rule. But it is practically all but if not quite universal. [end]

Thus, given the graph

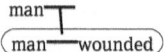

or, 'there is a man but there is no man wounded'. We iterate the outer line of identity thus:

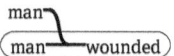

We join the two lines by Rules I (amended) and III, thus:

man⌐
(man══wounded)

We erase the inner occurrence of "man" by Rule IV amended, thus:

man─(wounded) or 'some man is not wounded'.

It might appear, at first glance, as if the reverse transformation could be effected. But it is not so. Starting from the last, we could get by iteration

or 'some man is cöexistent with something besides wounded men'. But we could never get (man══wounded).

As another example, take this

(catholic─(adores)─woman   or 'some woman is adored by every catholic'.

By iteration

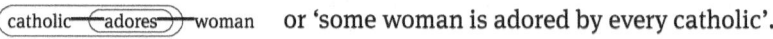

and by Rule I

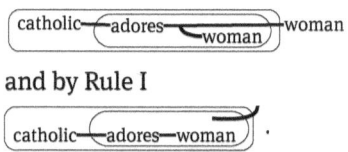

By the rule of iteration, we now get

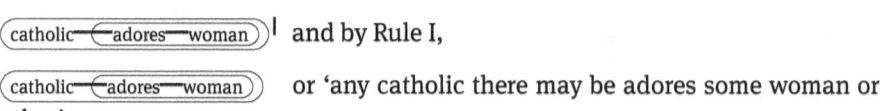

or 'any catholic there may be adores some woman or other'.

The beginner should be on his guard against creating an enclosure in order to place something within it. That cannot be done by any rule. It may be that the whole enclosure with contents can be inserted; but otherwise insertions can only be made in places already existing or previously created according to some rule.

17 The Simplest Possible Mathematical System (R 430), 1902

Rule V. *A detached line of identity may be drawn unenclosed.*[8]

Thus given the graph  or 'nobody is wounded', we get by this rule 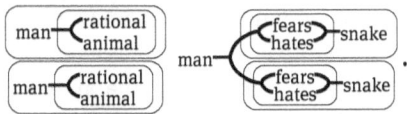. Then by iteration and by Rules I and III 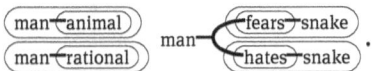 or 'somebody is not wounded'.

The lines of identity do not prevent our reducing such forms as the following so that there shall not be two parts in an enclosed oval:

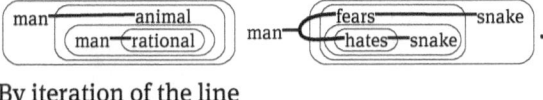

For by iteration we have

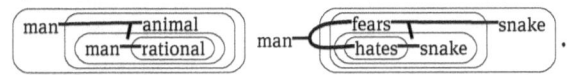

Thence by Rule I, we get

From these forms we can pass back to the originals, thus showing that these are equivalent to the originals. Namely, by iteration we get

By iteration of the line

By Rules I and III, the lines are joined under odd enclosures. Then by de-iteration, we get

Omitting the double ovals, we finally get

This method fails when we attempt to apply it to such a case as this:[9]

---

8 [Alt.:] This holds good as long as there is anything in the universe considered; and even if not, we are simply driven to absurdity, as we must be in such case.

9 [Alt.:] This method fails when we attempt to apply it to such a case as . The reason it fails is that in the line, in order

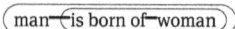

Let us inquire why the method fails in such a case: the investigation will repay the exertion both in understanding of this schematic and as an exercise in this kind of thought. If we attempt to apply the method, we get the following graph:

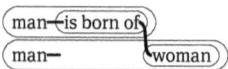

This means, 'There is a woman who is coëxistent with (a blank interpreted as a relative can be proved to mean "is coëxistent with") whatever man there may be, and from whom is born any man there may be'; while the original graph expressed that 'whatever man there may be is born of some woman'. Thus, the new graph misrepresents the original one, first, in asserting positively that there is a woman, which the original only asserted in case there is a man; and second, that it makes one woman a mother of all mankind, while the original only gave each man some mother or other. It is not that no such separation as we attempt is possible; we can effect it [in] words, as follows:

---

to connect 'is born of' to 'woman' has to pass outside the ovals; so that what is asserted is that there is some individual of whom any man there may be is born, and this individual, in case there exists any man, is a woman. Thus, the difficulty is the purely geometrical one that our graphs are written in such a kind of space, that it is impossible to pass from one oval to another without traversing a region outside them both. The ovals were chosen for negation because they would at the same time show the order of connection. They answer ~~this~~ the two purposes well in ~~most~~ all cases, where there is no identification. But when there is identification, a third office is imposed upon the ovals, that of determining the order of the lines of identity. Even this they will always do fairly well; but there are a few cases in which they do not give us the freedom of manipulation which is desirable in mathematics. Three dyadic relatives may be combined in four general ways in a proposition. Two of these ways, which are very common, are illustrated by these examples:

- There is a benefactress of everybody whom anybody she has not rejected must love.
- Everybody has some benefactress who rejects everybody that does not love her.

The other two modes of combination are uncommon. They are, for example,

- Anybody has either been rejected by somebody or loves some benefactress of himself.
- Somebody rejects everybody that does not love some benefactress of him.

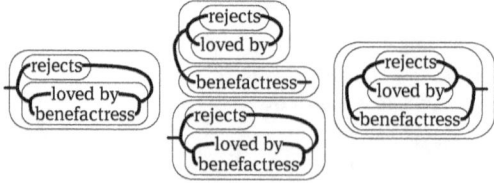

Any man there may be is born of something, X; and any man there may be is coexistent with a woman who is that X.

It is simply that our schematic affords no means of expressing these. We can write

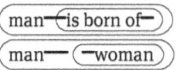

But we cannot identify that woman with the progenetress, without drawing a line of identity which shall pass outside the enclosures, and in doing so, is asserted absolutely to exist and to be one mother of all men.

Why have we made use of these ovals in our schematism? What do they effect? Careful attention will show that, even when there are no lines of identity, they fulfill three distinct offices, and that in introducing these lines we have imposed upon them two more. They fulfill all five with success. Only, in performing the last they slightly hamper that freedom of manipulation which mathematics requires;—for, in the course of this chapter, the reader will perceive more and more clearly that all mathematical inquiry advances by means of experimenting upon schemata.

The first office which the ovals fulfil is that of negation. A term is taken affirmatively when in case 'existent' or 'coexistent with' be substituted for it, the resulting assertion must be true if the original assertion is true; while it is taken negatively when the original assertion must be true if the result of this substitution is true. Thus, in the assertion, 'Whatever man there may be is born of a mom', if we substitute 'existent' for 'man', we get 'Whatever exists is born of a woman'. If this were true, the original assertion would be true. Hence, man is taken negatively, and is oddly enclosed. But if we substitute 'coëxistent with' for 'is born of', we get 'Whatever man there may be coëxists with a woman'. This is necessarily true, if the original is true; and hence, 'is born of' is taken affirmatively, and must be evenly enclosed.

The second office of the ovals is that of associating the conjunctions of terms. By this I mean, for example, distinguishing between such assertions as

'This man is either at once civilized and a redskin or is a negro'; and 'This man is at once civilized and either a redskin or a negro'.

This is the office of parentheses in algebra. In Boole's logical algebra, for instance, if we put T for 'this man', c for 'civilized', r for 'redskin', and n for 'negro', the above propositions may be written

$$T \leq (c \times r) + n \qquad T \leq c \times (r + n).$$

The ovals are able to combine these offices because the last does not refer to single terms; so that we have only to use the ovals so as rightly to associate the elementary parts of the assertion we wish to express; and then, if any such parts have the wrong *quality* (which is the technical term for the distinction between affirmative and negative), it only needs to have an oval drawn around it so as to enclose nothing else. To illustrate this, let us express the last two assertions; first, understanding by 'this man', some man where I point, and second, understanding whatever man there may be where I point. In the first sense, they are

$T\overline{(cr)(n)}$, which is resolvable to $T\overline{(c)(n)}\,\overline{(r)(n)}$

$Tc\overline{(r)(n)}$ from which the other is deducible by first enclosing c in two ovals and then inserting $\overline{(n)}$ into the outer of these. In the second sense, the propositions are

$T\overline{(cr)}\,n$ which is reducible to $T\overline{(c)}\,n\,T\overline{(r)}\,n$

$T\overline{(c\overline{(r)}\,n)}$ which is reducible to $T\overline{(c)}\,T\overline{(r)}\,n$

from which the other is at once deducible by inserting $\overline{(n)}$ in the first oval.

The third office of the ovals is to distinguish the modes of conjunction of the parts of propositions. The modes of conjunction of two unattached parts of propositions are six, as follows:

It both hails and rains. It either does not hail or does not rain.
It hails without raining. If it hails, it rains.
It neither rains nor hails. It either hails or rains.

These are expressed as follows:

grandinat pluit $\overline{\text{grandinat pluit}}$
grandinat $\overline{\text{pluit}}$ grandinat $\overline{\text{pluit}}$
$\overline{\text{grandinat}}\ \overline{\text{pluit}}$ $\overline{\text{grandinat}}\ \overline{\text{pluit}}$

The circumstance which enables the ovals to add this office to the first two is that by means of negations all six modes of conjunction are expressible by means of any single one; and without using the negation of the whole are expressible by two, *copulative conjunction*, which is that of *grandinat pluitque* and *disjunctive conjunction*, which is that of *grandinat aut pluit*, both of which modes are *associative*. That is to say grandinat pluitque et ningit is the same as grandinat et pluit ningitque; and grandinat pluitve aut ningit is the same as grandinat vel pluit ningitve. The consequence is that it is only necessary (or even desirable) to distinguish which of two conjunctions is first used unless they are, the one copulative, the other disjunctive. Thus, every time an associative sign is wanted, the mode of conjunction changes from copulation to disjunction or the reverse. All that is needed, then, is to see that the outer mode of conjunction is right, and all the others follow a rule. If the outermost conjunction is not that one of the two which is expressed by simple juxtaposition (which is copulation in the schematic of existential graphs) we simply enclose the whole in an outer oval, and then correct the quality of each smallest part.

The fourth office of the ovals is to indicate the order of succession of the identifications. In order to understand what this means let us compare these two graphs:

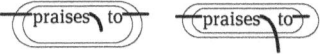

Examining the first we find a tail protruding from an oval. That means that something, X, exists which is not of the description found in the oval. What is found in the oval? Again a tail protruding from an oval, which were it unenclosed would signify that there is something, Y, of which what is within the inner oval is not true. What is in this oval, the assertion that something is praised to Y by X. Thus, the whole graph means 'there is something X of which it is not true that there is something Y of which it is not true that to Y X praises something'. That is, there is somebody, X, of whom it would be false to say that there is somebody to whom he, X, does not praise a thing. That, again, is to say that there is somebody who to each person praises somebody or other. Or, we may express it thus: A person, X, there is such that, taking any person Y you please, there is something Z which X praises to Y.

Now consider the second graph. Here there are two tails protruding from an oval, asserting that there is a pair of individuals, say X and Z, of which what is within the oval is not true. But what is within the oval is a tail protruding from an oval, which unenclosed would assert that there is something Y of which what is within the inner oval is not true. But what is within the inner oval is as before that assertion that X praises Z to Y. Hence, the whole means that there are two individuals, X and Z of whom it is not true that there is a person Y to whom X does not praise Z. That is, there is somebody who praises something to everybody. Or we may say: A person, X there is such that there is something Z such that, taking whatever person Y you please, X praises Z to Y.

Compare this with the final statement of the meaning of the first graph, and you will see that the only difference is in the relative order of settling upon the persons taken as Y and Z. The effect is, that the former asserts that somebody praises to each person some one thing or another, while the latter asserts that he praises the same thing to all persons. A graph with heavy lines is an assertion about a set of individual objects as many in number as the separate heavy lines (each of which may branch to any extent). Each individual of the set which forms the subject of the assertion is either *to be suitably chosen* by the speaker or by an omniscient being desirous of supporting his assertion or else is *to be taken at pleasure* by the auditor or by the most knowing antagonist of the assertion. It is of the set so made up that the predication is made. When the proponent or opponent has to designate an individual object as a member of the set, he is entitled to know what are the objects so far selected, so that he may shape his choice accordingly. Now every heavy line is regarded as enclosed only in those ovals which entirely enclose it. All these heavy lines which are evenly enclosed (that is, are wholly within an even number of envelopes) represent members of the set of subjects to be selected by the proponent in a suitable manner. All the heavy lines oddly enclosed represent individuals which the opponent is free to select as he likes. Individuals represented by less enclosed lines are to be selected before individuals represented by more enclosed lines. In all cases in which this rule leaves the order of choice indeterminate it makes no difference which order is pursued. The reason this convention is sufficient is that if either proponent or opponent has, at any stage, several individuals to select successively, it is obvious that the order in which he names them will be indifferent, since he will decide upon them in his own mind simultaneously.

The only defect of this system is that it may require us to multiply the ovals merely for the sake of enclosing lines of identity. Thus we may write as a sort of solution of our difficulty,

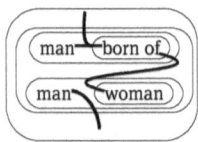

Another way would be to bring the ovals into contact thus:

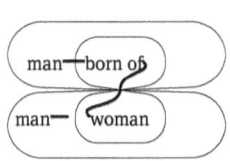 [P.H.]: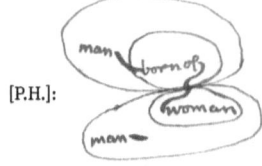

A third way would be to mark a nodule on a line of identity when it is to be considered as enclosed in any oval in which its outermost part is not enclosed; thus:

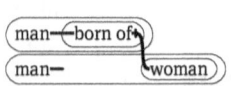 [P.H.]: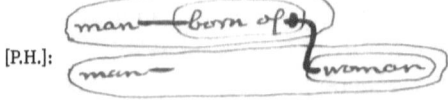

A fourth way would be to use certain signs, as for example signs of the zodiac as signs of individuals, writing, for example:

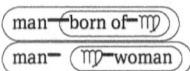

The difference between variations in the association of conjunctions and in the order of identifications may be illustrated by the following four propositions:

N. Some benefactress of all people rejects every flatterer of her.
W. Everybody has a benefactress who rejects him if he flatters her.
E. Some woman rejects everybody who flatters her as well as all but those of whom she is benefactress.
S. Whoever flatters every benefactress of him is rejected by somebody.

The reader's *logica utens* will show him that the truth of N entails that of W and of E, and that if either W or E is true, so is S; but it will probably not be keen enough to make him feel that W follows from N and S from E in one way while E follows from N and S from W in another way. But this will appear if we express the propositions as graphs; thus:

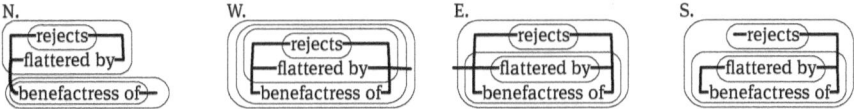

Graphs W and E have what might be called *expanded forms* as follows:

In order to pass from the first form of W to the expanded form, we first surround "flattered by" by two ovals, by Rule II. We then iterate "benefactress of" both inside the outer of these ovals and inside the oval of "rejects". We then erase the original occurrence of "benefactress" by Rules I and III. We get rid of the projecting tails by deiteration. We then have two ovals, one immediately enclosing the other and nothing else. Erasing these, we get the expanded form. Let us now pass from the expanded form to the original. For that purpose I wish first to make a transformation during which it will be convenient to call the contents of the two enclosed ovals of the expanded form a and b, for the sake of brevity that form then is 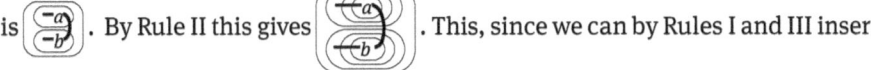. By Rule II this gives . This, since we can by Rules I and III insert what we please within odd enclosures, gives 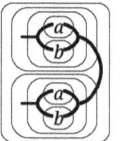. Thence by deiteration

we get .

This, on substituting what *a* and *b* represent, becomes 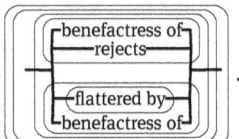.

By Rule II we can now put two ovals round 'rejects', and using only the initial letters, and also not writing the heavy lines, the regularity of which makes it needless but merely indicating their outermost points, we have 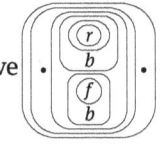 . 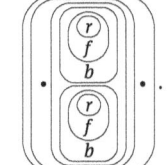 .

Now Rules I and II allow us to insert what we please under odd enclosures. Accordingly in the fifth oval from the outside above we will insert *f* with the regular connections, and in the fifth oval below *r* with the same connections. We thus get the graph shown which contains duplicates within its third oval [above right]. By the rule of iteration, we erase one of these duplicates. This brings two ovals together, one within another, just outside of *b*. Erasing these by Rule II, we have the original form of w.

17 The Simplest Possible Mathematical System (R 430), 1902

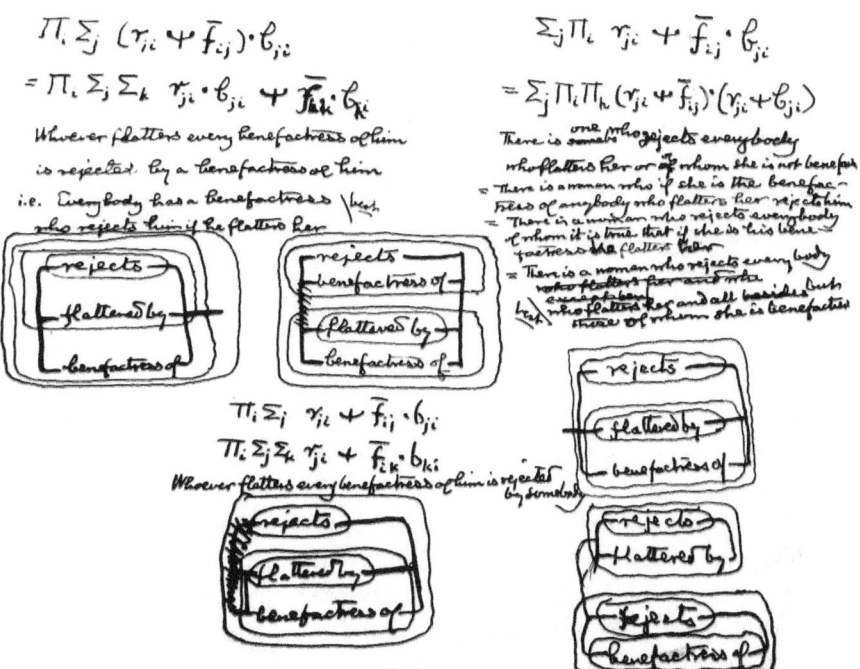

One holograph ms page (Harvard Peirce Papers, R 507), with the graphs N, W, S and E as in R 430.

18 Multitude and Continuity

R 316a(s), May 1903; plus R S-36, R 1584. Houghton Library. With the subtitle "A Lecture to students of Philosophy to be delivered in Harvard University 1903 May 15 (by Charles S(antiago?) Peirce)", the draft in R 316a(s) on "Multitude and Continuity" represents Peirce's sketchy plan for the additional eighth lecture he gave to the Division of Mathematics at Harvard University, calculated to supplement the seven lectures on "Pragmatism as a Principle and Method of Right Thinking" that were arranged for him by Harvard's Department of Philosophy. What survives from that eight lecture is a fragmentary set of notes, with an autobiographical tone, on Cantor, Dedekind, and Peirce's own system of existential graphs. Not much may have been delivered on the announced topics of multitude and continuity, a proper treatment of which would in any case have had to presuppose knowledge of the logical system of graphs. Additional pages from the related writings and notes in R S-36 and R 1584 suggest that Peirce rather attempted in this lecture, or at least in its first part, to draw a connection between EGs and pragmatism. Conventions of EGs were much elaborated later during the year, and arguments to establish their philosophical and pragmatistic kernels would grow into colossal proportions during the next couple of years (LoF 3). Since this supplementary lecture was presented to an audience that consisted of students of mathematics, Peirce might have wanted to speak further on the basic illative rules of insertions and omissions. (This eighth lecture was not included in the 1997 publication of Peirce's 1903 Harvard Lectures (PPM), but it was published in NEM III(1), pp. 128–131, with minor omissions.)

Gentlemen (and Ladies?): I address you as students of philosophy. You are no doubt aware that the last generation has seen the most wonderful development of pure mathematics. It was in 1862 that I took my degree in chemistry; and chemistry was at that time in such a state that one could carry in his mind pretty much the whole of it, and as we students used to say, could keep up with the progress of it provided one only devoted twenty-five hours a day to reading, and has a good chemical memory. The Jahrbuch which covered the whole subject consisted of one thick volume. Today the Berichte of the German society of chemists consists of several unwieldy volumes a year, and is almost confined to one branch of the subject. But the world of ideas is no less rich and teeming than the world of outward perception and I do not think that the progress of chemistry has been a bit greater than that of mathematics, or that its rate of advance is today undergoing greater acceleration. Nobody can think of keeping up with the pure mathematical discoveries in anything more than some very special department. And the quality of the work, its profundity, generality, originality, improves almost as rapidly as its quantity. In particular in precision of reasoning mathematics has undergone a radical revolution during the time that I have known something of it. But do not understand me as meaning that this revolution has been accomplished once for all, so that tranquil state of logical security has been attained. Not at all: it is easy to see that very great changes cannot be long delayed, although we cannot say precisely what they will consist in. There are great lessons in logic here. Mathematicians always have been the very best reasoners in the world; while metaphysicians always have been the very worst. Therein is reason enough why students of philosophy should not neglect mathematics. But during the last thirty years, there has been an extraordinary mathematical development of the general doctrine of multitude (including, of course, infinity) and of continuity. Philosophers would fall short of their well-earned reputation as dunces if they paid much attention to this until it begins to ring in their ears from all quarters. But you would not have come here tonight unless you were philosophers rather in the etymological sense of the word that according to the wont of those profess logic and metaphysics—unless you were philosophers of the school of Royce rather than of the school of Hamilton.

The leader in this investigation, with whom no other ought to be put into comparison, is Dr. Georg Cantor.

My own first contribution to this branch was made in the autumn of 1867.[1] It contained an idea to which I intend to return, and I received some warm letters about it. But I myself became doubtful of its value.

I may remark that this has invariably been my experience. I have no itch at all to go into print and never will do so until I have gone over the subject so many times and have elaborated so clear an idea of it that it seems a great pity that it should not be recorded. It is always anywhere from five to twenty years from my first having written the matter out. Of course I don't speak of newspaper contributions, though I sometimes have these standing in type for months before I will consent to their going to press. This is because I know of the castigation that is coming to me from myself. For no sooner is the paper out that I set to work to raise all the objections I possibly can both of the trifling kind and of the dynamite kind. And the result has always been that I have found that there were other men who were far better satisfied with them than I myself have been.

The truth is that I am far too well acquainted with the depths of my own stupidity to know what it is to be satisfied with any product of my mind.

---

1 [Alt.:] My own first contribution to this branch was made in the autumn of 1867. It seemed to interest students. I received some warm letters about it, but I myself became quite sceptical about its value.

I may remark that this has happened to me in other cases. I am never in a hurry to go to print and will be never done so until the special matter I have to communicate to us was gone over many times and elaborated thoroughly. No sooner as a paper of mine is worked up to a finish and printed than I immediately begin to take a critical attitude toward it and go to work to raise all the objections to it big and little that I can.

My second contribution was 1881.

My third [end]

That is all I have printed. My work has been, I believe, completely independent of Cantor. I never knew anything definite about him until ~~after my about~~ 1884.

I have seen it stated in some book that I modified the statements of Dedekind. But the truth is that Dedekind's *Was sind und was sollen die Zahlen* first appeared in [1887].

It contains not a single idea which was not in my paper of ___, of which an extra copy was send to him and I do not doubt influenced his work. It is true that certain of Dedekind's appendices to Le Jeune Dirichlet's Theory of Numbers developed the application of the concept of the *Abbild* to numbers. But I had never read those appendices and of course the *Abbild* idea has been perfectly familiar to everybody for decades before either of us wrote.

Understand me. I am simply defending my own ~~positive profession of not having~~ position which is that of Göethe's "*Quidam*", except that my results coincide in the main with those which any competent analyst must reach in the nature of things on these subjects.

As for Dedekind's book, it is worked out with great ability, although it might have been done better.[2]

I will first show you my way of analyzing these ideas. Namely I require they should be expressed in a certain form of diagram.

The system I call that of *existential graphs*. I do not believe it the best possible; but it is the best I have been able to invent for the purpose.

Should be *analytic*.

Not to be a good *calculus*.

I proceed to explain my system of existential graphs.

According to the ~~principle~~ doctrine of pragmatism, this must connect them with familiar everyday ideas.[3]

---

2 A—is a man   A—possessed—humanity   A —> h

$\Pi_i \Sigma_j w_j . a_{ji} \curlyvee \bar{c}_i$

$\Sigma_j \Pi_i w_i . (a_{ji} \curlyvee \bar{c}_i)$

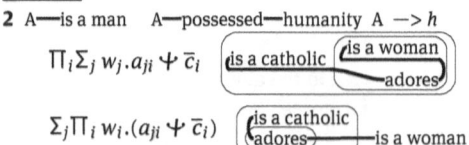

3 [Alt.:] [From R S-36] The principles connecting existential graphs with everyday ideas are three: My first Principle is this.

The blackboard or paper, whether something be already written on it or not is supposed to be a representation of any state of things you like of a certain general description and if I now write any proposition quite outside of anything else that may be written, I determine the board

The *first principle* explains what I shall mean by writing a proposition on the board. Namely, I suppose that the board on which I write, whether anything is already written on it or not, represents *a universe* perfectly familiar and well-recognized by the *writer* and the *writee*, the person who writes and the person who interprets the graph.

And if I write any proposition on the board *quite outside of anything else that is written there*, I simply say that this proposition is true as well as that [it] may be written.

Second Principle. That a line of a certain color (or texture) called a line of identity will mean that there is an individual existing i.e. *occurring* in this universe whom every part of this line denotes, and anything is true of it which is written abutting on this line. ―lives   ―loves―   ―loves―loves―   ―loves―hates―

Third Principle. That a slightly drawn oval denies whatever is written within it and denies the identity of parts of a line crossing it. (―loves―)   ―(loves―).

But all this will be made a hundred times clearer by investigating the Rules of Transformation of Existential Graphs. When I speak of *Rules* of Transformation, I use the word Rule in the same sense as it is used in Algebra. It really means a Permission. There are two Basic Rules according to which certain changes may be made in a graph after it is written without any danger of rendering the assertion false. Here they are:

No transformations except insertions and omissions.

Five rules of *insertions* and *omissions*.

Rule I. What is written can be erased.
Rule II. Whatever transformation of all that is written is permissible is permissible of any part under even enclosures (i.e., ovals) and the reverse under odd enclosures.
Rule III. Double ovals with nothing between are of no effect and can be erased or inserted.
Rule IV. Any part can be *iterated* preserving its connections, under the same enclosures or any additional enclosures *already written*.
Rule V. A line of identity may be broken where unenclosed.

---

to be a representation not of any state of things you please of the same description as before but of any state of things of that description in which this new proposition is true.

My second principle is that any part of a line of a certain color is taken as asserting that the two ends of that part of the line represent the same *existing individual*, that is, occurring in the universe. This implies that a *point* marked in the [end]

[R 1584] Nothing can be done with a conception until it enters into prop[osition].[4]

- Every conception a predicate.
- The three kinds of Reasoning that the question of Pragmatism is the question of Abduction.
- The question of Pragmatism affected by the logic of Relatives.
- The Maxim of ~~Pragmatism~~ Abduction.
- Relation [to] Comte's Maxim.
    - Nothing is admissible in theory which is no[t] experimentally verifiable.
    - But this does not say that nothing else can be perceived. It would seem [that] he has much to say that nothing inadmissible can be conceived.
    - There are now two functions that the maxim has to fulfil.
        * First it ought to free us from ideas essentially unclear. To say less dangerous than when written.
        * Secondly, it has got to take some attitude towards elements of Thirdness. Pertinence of this to the question.

I shall ~~assume~~ take it for granted that Thirdness is a distinct element of thought not reducible to Secondness. Then granting this three attitudes may be taken:

- First, that Thirdness, though an element of the phenomenon never ought to be admitted into a theory because it is not experimentally verifiable.
- Second, that Thirdness is experimentally verifiable, although it cannot be directly perceived.
- Third, that it is directly perceived.

I set forth the nature of these positions:

First, the man will admit no general law. He will, so far as possible, abstain from prediction, or limit his predictions to experiments he ~~intends~~ expects to make. But Thirdness is too much interwoven with our thoughts to make that practicable.

Second, the man will hold that Thirdness is an addition made to abductions not involved [in] their premisses and that experiment while not perceiving any such thing justifies it. Then he will have a conception of ~~reality~~ the real that completely sunders it from perception and the question arises why should perception be allowed so much say about it?

---

[4] [From a Houghton folder R 1584, a small notebook in which apparently Peirce revisits the Harvard Lectures on Pragmatism in a synoptic manner, perhaps in preparation of this supplementary eight lecture (R 316a(s)).]

Then the question arises how far is Thirdness verifiable?

Take an event between two events. Shall we say that this is true to an indefinite extent but that we have no right to say that between every part of events an event might be interpolated. In that case, we get down to a series of motionless states. And when we say there are a series

[P.H.]

we can only mean that to a certain extent one order renders them more intelligible than another. We have no right to say more.

No law can then ~~mean more~~ be justified further than that for a good while things will be so. Whether there be any meaning at all in saying more or not, any such further meaning will be completely banished from the mind of the logical man.

Then the real will be to him what men would be convinced of by sufficient inquiry. But this is in turn a real fact. It means that men would be convinced [that] all there would be [are] laws and could only mean that for a considerable time men will probably so think.

Third, this man who accepts the causes will evidently have no difficulty with Thirdness. The only question will be whether he will deal satisfactorily with unclear ideas.

He will find given in the very judgment of perception every element contained in the purpose of action.

He will hold with the firmest of grasps to the conception that all that ~~self-controlled part~~ of the mind over which you or I exercise some self-control which gives us some right to call it yours or mine reposes upon two things, on the one hand upon a part of the mind connected with our individual organisms, and with our racial germ plasm or whatever it may be which makes our solidarity with other men and women and with the lower animals and again upon a constituent of mind which belongs no more specially to biological organisms than it belongs to planetary systems, to crystals, and to radiations [*illeg.*]. These two parts of the mind being equally beyond our control are no more subject to logical criticism than are the solar sun spots or the growth of hair and nails. To say that the man has a *faith* in human instincts misrepresents his position, for the reason that to have a faith in anything implies that conceivability of distrusting it, while this man will look on those two parts of the mind as constituting the very bedrock of fact to which he desires to make his voluntary thoughts conform.

1. To add anything is to make the board a representation of a state of things of the same description that it already represented but further determined in that what is written is true.
2. To unite two indefinite signs of individuals with a ~~heavy~~ line means that they are identical.
3. To enclose anything in an oval is to deny it.

Rule I. Anything unenclosed can be erased.
Rule II. Any permissible transformation of all that is written is permissible under even enclosures and the reverse under odd enclosures.
Rule III. Double enclosures with nothing between annihilate one another.
Rule IV. Any ~~detached part~~ can be iterated under the same enclosures or additional ones (already existing) its connection being joining.
Rule V. A line of identity may be broken where unenclosed. [end]

19 [A System of Existential Graphs]

R 514, 1904. Houghton Library. Among a confusing set of assorted pages and segments in R 514 there remain 28 fragmentary leaves of a sequence, of which the first four pages are lost and which might have existed as a continuous run of a considerably longer and finalised text. This sequence appears to be the only text on EGs in which Peirce prefers to use the term "the Sheet of Truth" in place of the standard "Sheet of Assertion". Indeed truth-values take the central stage of this treatise on the fundamentals of the Alpha and Beta graphs. An important observation is made on what is commonly thought to be among the basic rules of the Alpha system, namely the insertion of a double cut around any graph, which is not a primitive rule of proofs but a consequence of three more fundamental permissions: (i) the rule of 'soundness', namely that any rule that "can never change a true graph into a false one" is permissible, (ii) that any graph "that we know to be true" is permitted to be scribed on the sheet of truth, and (iii) the rule of "truism" (tautology), namely the blank on any area is a graph "regarded as meaning anything that is too obvious to take the trouble to say." To draw a light circle around a blank graph twice is not primarily a double negation of a blank, either, but an implication from an obvious truth, truism or tautology, to an equally obvious truth. The importance of having a notation for an absurdity, or a denial of a truism (elsewhere termed the "empty cut" or the "pseudograph") in the system is to signal "absurd alternatives" or those of "unmeaning supplements." The maturing three-fold classification of sentences into 'inquiry-making' interrogations, those involving perlocutionary acts such as commands and imperatives, and those of propositions that have a force in influencing the 'conduct of thought', suggests that this piece was written in tandem with his revisions of the classification of signs that began in 1904, as it is those revisions that came to accommodate various forms of such speech acts.

Well, What is this thing, anyway, that I propose to teach you?[1] Why it is nothing but a particular way of making a diagram to express any fact that one says or imagines is true. This particular way of expressing what might be said in ordinary language is called the *System of Existential Graphs*. A *graph* is a diagram composed of lines and dots, with or without other parts. These *graphs*,—this particular kind that I am going to explain, are called *existential*. But as I am not going to talk of any others, I shall call them *graphs* without the long word *existential*. A graph then will be the expression in a particular way, or the particular way of expressing anything that must be either true or false. A graph is generally partly *written* and partly *drawn*. I shall say that it is *scribed*. "Scribed" will mean either written, or drawn, or partly written and partly drawn.

We must have a sheet of paper upon which everything that is scribed is to be understood to be true. For you might write on at most any old scrap of paper,

---

[1] [The segments begin at manuscript page 5, with the preceding sentence "can only come gradually to understand the chief advantage of it." The first four pages have not been found.]

"The father goes out", simply to practice handwriting without meaning it. But if it is scribed on the sheet that has been set aside for our graphs, we make believe that it is true. For that reason we will call that sheet by the name of "the sheet of truth". Whatever is scribed on the Sheet of Truth is true (according to our make-believe). Therefore *if two graphs are scribed on the sheet of truth*; such as

The father g.o.   (g.o for "goes out")

The mother g.o.

both are to be understood as true. And now we have this rule, or rather this permission: *We may erase,* or strike out, *any graph that is scribed on the sheet of truth.* For if

The father g.o.

The mother g.o.

then it is true that

The father g.o.

For we cannot undertake to set down on the Sheet of Truth *everything* that is true. We might imagine that our paper sheet of truth is merely a part of a possible Sheet of *All* Truth.

Namely that our Sheet of Truth is so much of the Sheet of All Truth as we have in mind at the time. We have a right if we please, to pay no attention to a part of it that we had before attended to. That will be the same as scratching out a graph. I may here make one remark about the meaning of the word "Graph". The following

The father g.o.

The mother g.o.

is a graph which is composed of two graphs, "The father g.o." and the mother g.o." If there is nothing else on our Sheet of Truth, each of the two graphs is a "partial" graph while the two together make up the "entire" graph. Oh there is another explanation I have to make about the word graph. "The father g.o." is a *graph*, even if it is not scribed on the sheet. For a graph is what is true or false, and its being scribed does not make it so. Also suppose we have on the Sheet of Truth

The mother g.o.   The mother g.o.

The mother g.o.   The mother g.o.

Then there is only *one* graph on the sheet, but there are *four graph-instances*. This is a very useful distinction to prevent misunderstandings. A *graph-instance* is a single scribing according to this System of that which must either be true or false. A *graph* is the one *form* of all possible graph-instances which express the same meaning in precisely the same way. Thus

The MOTHER g.o.   and   The mother goes out

are two instances of the same graph because their differences are entirely *insignificant*, that is do not amount to different ways of expressing the fact, but only to different ways of writing. But

The mother g.o.   and   The mother g.o.   The mother g.o.

are two different graphs, though their meaning is the same.

I have now to explain another contrivance of the System of Existential Graphs. Suppose we have on the Sheet of Truth the following entire graph:

The father g.o.
(The mother g.o.)

That fine oval line round "the mother g.o." is called a *cut*, and is supposed to cut off the part of the paper inside of it, which is called "the *area* of the cut" from the part of the paper outside of it, which is called "the *place* of the cut"; so that the area of the cut is no part of the place of the cut. The cut, together with its area, and together with the entire graph on that area is called an *enclosure*. This enclosure is a graph which means that the entire graph on the area of the cut is cut off from the place. In the present example the place of the cut is the sheet of truth, and therefore the meaning is that

The mother g.o.

is *not* true; and the whole represents that the father goes out but the mother does not go out. Here is another example:

Boaz and Dan are together
(The father has gone out
The mother has gone out)

This being on the Sheet of Truth means that Boaz and Dan are together but it is not true that both father and mother have gone out. That is, *either* the father *or* the mother is at home. That is quite different from scribing on the sheet of Truth

Boaz and Dan are together
(The father has gone out)
(The mother has gone out)

For this means that it is true that Boaz and Dan are together but it is false that the father has gone out, and it is false that the mother has gone out, i.e. *Both* father *and* mother are at home.

All this is excellent exercise in accurate thinking. Take another example. Let the following be scribed on the sheet of truth, using h.g.o. for "has gone out".

```
┌─────────────────────┐
│ The Father h.g.o.   │
│┌───────────────────┐│
││ The Mother h.g.o. ││
│└───────────────────┘│
└─────────────────────┘
```

This means: It is false that the father has gone out while the mother has not; or in other words, if the father has gone out so has the mother; or still in other words, if the mother is at home so is the father; or once again in other words, Either the father has not gone out or else the mother has.

The word "if", however, has different meanings in different cases. I should first define a few words. Any expression or sign, that must be true or false, whether addressed to another person or to oneself, is called a "*proposition*". Every graph is a proposition expressed according to the System of Graphs. A proposition which says that two things (or things that might otherwise be true) are or are not the same single thing is called a "categorical" proposition, or a "categorical". Thus "the father has gone out" means "Something is a father and that very same object has gone out". "No father is a mother" means that no matter what father you may select and no matter what mother you may select, those two will not be the very same thing. A proposition which asserts or denies *two* or more identities is a "relative" proposition. Thus, to say "There is a Being who has created all the worlds" is as much as to say, that there is a being such that no matter what world you may select this Being is identical with the Creator of an object identical with that world.

A proposition that does not positively assert or deny any identity, or does not so nearly assert it as it does something else, is called a "hypothetical proposition" or a "hypothetical". Thus "A father of something has gone out, and it is raining hard", does assert that some father is identically the same as something that has gone out; but the *principal* thing it asserts is that the father is going out and the hard rain, are true together. A proposition that consists of saying that two or more propositions are all true is called a "*copulative*" proposition or a "copulative". Scribed as a graph, it will consist of two or more graphs on the sheet of truth. The denial of a copulative,—for example, to say it is not true that it is both snowing and hailing,—denies of two or more propositions that they are all true,—says they are not all true, which amounts to saying that their precise denials are not all false, such as in the form of a graph consists of two separate graphs on the area of an enclosure on the sheet of truth,—is called a "disjunctive proposition", or a "disjunctive", simply. Thus, "It either snows or it rains" is disjunctive. There are some propositions which can with equal reason be regarded as copulative or as disjunctive. They must be called "ancipital" propositions. Here is an example: "If it lightened it thundered, and if it thundered it lightened", which is the same as to say "Either it lightened and thundered or else it neither lightened nor thundered". Expressed as graphs, and putting l for it lightened, t for it thundered, this ancipital proposition is either

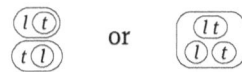

So if a coin is turned up, let *h* mean it will turn up heads, *t* it will turn up tails, then

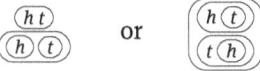

will equally express that it did not turn up heads and tails both but did turn up one or the other, which is the same as to say that it either turned up heads and not tails or else tails and not heads.

A *conditional* proposition, or proposition expressible by the aid of an "if", has the form (g ⓖ) where *g* and ɢ are any graphs. The graph *g* is called the *antecedent* proposition, the graph ɢ is called the *consequent* while those that are together and oddly enclosed are to be connected by "or". For example ℛ (ꜱ ℋ) will be translated It rains *and* it does *not* snow *or else* does not hail.

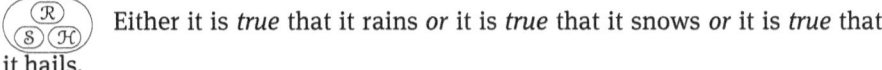 Either it is *true* that it rains *or* it is *true* that it snows *or* it is *true* that it hails.

ℛ ꜱ (ℋ/𝒥 ℒ) It is *true* that it rains *and false* that it snows *and* it is (either) *false* that it lightens or it is *true* that it hails *and false* that it thunders.

I will now show what changes we are permitted to make in graphs after they are scribed.

1. *We are permitted to follow any rule of changing a graph provided it can never change a true graph into a false one.*
2. We are permitted, therefore, to scribe on the sheet of truth any graph that we know to be true.
3. A blank place on any area regarded as a graph may be regarded as meaning anything that is too obvious to take the trouble to say; such as "Something is not true", "Any graph is either true or false".

Consequently, we have a right to scribe on the sheet of truth this graph Ⓞ. For this only means that if a truism (or obvious truth) is true, a truism is true. This is quite an important permission.

On the other hand ○ which denies a truism cannot possibly be true.

Something called "common sense" makes most people think that an absurd graph, like this, can be of no sort of use. My boy, you are yet too young to discuss such questions; but I will say to you, and you can remember it later, that there is something called "common sense", which might rightly be called the voice of our Creator, and it is the refuge of minds pressed with deceptive reasonings. But the greatest achievements of the greatest minds are entirely opposed to that kind of common sense that supposes an absurd conception to be without value. This absurd graph ○ furnishes us with the key to many problems. Not, of course, that we are to accept an absurdity; but it is the best aid to keeping us clear from nonsense.

Let us now see what the effect of the absurd graph ○ is. Let us first suppose the absurd graph to be oddly enclosed and let A be the graph that is in the same area with it and let B be the graph that is in the place of the cut in whose area it is; thus: B(A○). Then the meaning will be that under certain circumstances (expressed by whatever is less enclosed than B, if there be anything less enclosed) B is true and if A is true then what is true is true, where "what is true is true" may be replaced by any other truism. But this means no more than simply to say that under the expressed circumstances B is true; and the entire enclosure containing the absurd graph may as well (and better) be erased. Next suppose that the absurd graph is evenly enclosed, but is not directly on the sheet of truth. Let A be the graph within the same cut, let B be the graph in the *place* of that cut, and let C be the graph in the place of the cut in whose area B is; thus C(B(A○)). Then the meaning will be that under circumstances expressed by parts of the entire graph exterior to C, C is true and if B is true then A is true and something true is not true, the last words representing the absurd graph. This reduces B to absurdity and we might as well (and better) simply write C(B) i.e. under the circumstances expressed C is true and B is not true. Here again the effect of the absurd graph is to recommend the entire erasure of the whole area in which it is contained. But what if the absurd graph should not be in any enclosure at all? In that case it would be flatly asserted that that which is manifestly absurd was true. That could only come about by a great error in what was originally assumed to be true or by some blunder subsequently. In either case, the only thing to be done is to rub out all that is on the sheet and begin all over again. So the rule is that the absurd graph in all cases permits and recommends us to abolish the entire area on which it occurs, together with all that is scribed there. At the same time it will be well to notice that the reasons for abolishing evenly and unevenly enclosed areas that contain the absurd graph are quite opposite. Evenly enclosed areas that contain the absurd graph are to be abolished because they are absurd alternatives while unevenly enclosed areas that contain the absurd graph are to be abolished because they are perfectly unmeaning supplements to what is said. For instance, (*L*(*T*○)) means "It either does not lighten or else it thunders and thunders quite terrifically and as quietly as a mouse" (for as long as the absurd is to be said, it makes no difference in what shape it is made absurd). This is the case of the *absurd alternative.* But *D*(*R*(*S*)(*H*)○) means "It is day, and it either rains or snows or hails or else at any rate twice two is four". This is the case of the *unmeaning supplement.* It is better to say simply, *D*, "It is day".

4. I have already shown that we have a right to erase any graph on the sheet of truth. I now add that we have a right to erase any evenly enclosed graph. For let the graph in question be A, and suppose there is another graph, B, on the same evenly enclosed area. Then, the effect of erasing A will be that whereas we had a right to say that, under certain conditions both A and B will be true, we abstain from saying whether A will be true or not, and merely say that under those conditions B will be true. There is no falsehood in silence. It is true that if there be nothing else on the evenly enclosed area, our erasure will leave an absurd graph. But it will be a case of unmeaning supplement merely, not of falsity. For example, if we have accepted this graph: 𝒟(ℒ(𝒯)) meaning "It is day, and if it lightens it will thunder", the 𝒯, being evenly enclosed, may be erased and the result will be 𝒟(ℒ ○) which means substantially "It is day and moreover if it should lighten, once one will be one". All that amounts no more than to simply saying "It is day"; but still we have introduced no falsity, and have a right to keep silence about the thunder. We only undertake to tell *nothing but the truth* and do not attempt the absurd requirement of the law that we should tell "*the whole truth*", which no man can do about any event or fact.[2]

[...] we can erase the right hand  that occurs along with the  because the same thing precisely has already been premised:[3] "If Roosevelt favors tariff-reform and Root does the same, then Cannon will come down to the floor and Taft will hold his tongue and Root will not favour tariff reform or Lodge will not make the effort of his life". [– – –][4]

[...] that ◎, the "double cut", or "empty scroll" can always be scribed on the sheet of truth. For let  be a graph meaning "Truth is truth".[5] This is true and can always be scribed on the sheet of Truth. It is also true that if Truth is truth then truth is truth. Therefore we can always scribe on the sheet of truth

2 [The following is very fragmentary and eleven manuscript pages are altogether missing among the pages numbered 27–40 until the next section begins.]

3 [These original images drawn by Peirce look like the trunk and the roots of a tree (the first) and a house (the second). The preceding and following pages of what may be an altogether a discrete variant sequence of this writing are lost.]

4 [Four pages are missing here and the next paragraph (ms p. 33) is marked as crossed out.]

5 [The following four graphs and images are in Peirce's hand. The image of an open book, which stands for a tautology, or the top unit element (the *verum*), is apparently that of a bible. Peirce uses it to emphasise the important fact that the blank sheet of assertion (the blank sheet of truth) is not empty.]

That done, the Rule of Deiteration permits us to change what we have scribed to

and then the Rule of Erasure permits us to change this to ⬭ .

In that way, then, it is always permissible to scribe the "empty scroll" or double cut, on the sheet of truth.

We now come, at length, to the fourth and last permission, which is rather a difficult one, so I will begin a fresh page for it.

4. Fourth Permission: called the rule of the pseudograph (*pseudon* is the Greek for 'false', 'pretended', and the like; and a pseudograph is something which has the form of a graph and can be treated like a graph, but lacks the essence of the graph, which is that it might be true or might be false, since this pseudograph does not represent anything that ever could be true.)

When a cut with nothing at all in its area, ○, is contained in the area of another cut, B (A ○), it is permissible to abolish the whole of the outer enclosure, with all it contains, reducing B (A ○) to B or to B (○) (that all that is contained in the outer enclosure except the vacant cut can be erased). Or instead if the vacant enclosure, ○, occurs on the sheet of truth, it proves that there has been some mistake, and that which was supposed to be true (either at the outset or at some transformation) is not true; and everything on the sheet should be denied by making a cut round the whole of it, or if we prefer, the whole can be erased by Permission No. 1.[6]

The Second Part of Existential Graphs. Spots and Ligatures

This system of Graphs, as distinguished from other systems of graphs, is called *Existential* Graphs. Before long, I shall be able to explain why it is so named.

What is called a sentence in Grammar is a sign sufficient for one person to influence another; although if he merely says "mermaid" or "heroic self-sacrifice", he does inevitably excite an idea in the person who heard him. Sentences either

---

6 [The following pages that might be six in number are not found. This manuscript resumes with the next section "The Second Part" on ms p. 41.]

make inquiry and are called Interrogations or Interrogatories, or they are intended to make the person addressed perform a single definite voluntary act, and are called Commands or Imperatives, or they are intended to influence the conduct of those they address by bringing their thought to bear upon something; as when I say "The planet Mars is easily seen from the Earth, but the Earth is very badly placed to be seen from Mars", or if I say "Nitroglycerine is not so good as lard to fry a doughnut in". Those sentences are called *propositions*; and every proposition must be either true or false. Our system of graphs deals with propositions, and with no other kind of sentences.

If we take a proposition and strike out certain parts of it, leaving spaces called *blanks* which can be variously be filled up, so as to make a proposition again, that is called a *blank form* of proposition. The law-stationers sell a hundred different kinds of printed blank forms. A blank form whose blanks are so placed that if each is filled with a proper name, or name of any one person, thing, or attribute, the result is a complete proposition, no matter how wildly absurd, a blank form of proposition is called a *rheme*. Here are a few examples

___ gives ___ to ___
Roosevelt gives a horse to ___
LaFollette gives ___ to Tillman
Carnegies gives ___ to ___

Now in the System of Existential Graphs, we may erase part of a graph and leave a *rheme*. That rheme may appear, as it is scribed, as built up out of several rhemes, as I shall soon show. But if the graph does not indicate or show how it is compounded, then that *rheme*, as scribed according to this system is called a *spot*. For example, we might agree to use BEATS as a spot, and with its aid might build up graphs meaning "Roosevelt beats Bryan" or "Either Roosevelt beats Cicero or Webster beats Gladstone", or "If Craft beats honesty, then beauty beats wealth"; all non-sensical enough but still *propositions*. But if we are to use BEATS as a spot we must have some way of distinguishing between "Roosevelt beats Bryan" and "Bryan beats Roosevelt"; and if we use "praises" as a spot we must have some way of distinguishing between "The Tsar praises Roosevelt to the Kaisar" and "The Tsar praises the Kaisar to Roosevelt" and "Roosevelt praises Kaisar to the Tsar" and "Roosevelt praises the Tsar to the Kaisar" and "the Kaisar praises Roosevelt to the Tsar" and "the Kaisar praises the Tsar to Roosevelt". For this purpose, we must not only write 'praises' to make a spot. That is not enough. We must also agree upon three places around the outside of the written word where what is attached shall be in one place the 'praiser' in another place the thing or person 'praised' and in a third the thing or person to whom or to which the praise is addressed. So it is not sufficient, in order to create a spot, merely to write a verb; it is necessary also to distinguish places upon its "periphery" or outside, at which the several different things that it connects may be each placed. These places on the periphery (a Greek word meaning the 'goingaround') of a spot are called the 'hooks' of the spot. So then, be it well understood that the mere word 'beats', or this word as written, cannot be a spot in the System of Logical Graphs. But if we connect with the written word the agreement that the beater shall be joined to the top of the writing and the beaten with the bottom of the writing, then the written word with that agreement tacked on to it, will make a *habit of mind*, the expression of which according to this system is what we call a 'spot'. So 'gives' cannot become a spot until it is agreed that the giver shall be attached at one point of the periphery, say the left hand, and the gift at another point, say the right hand and the person to whom the gift is made at another point say the bottom. Those agreements being well understood between the two parties, the 'graphist', who makes the graph-instances, and the 'interpreter' who takes in their meaning, 'gives' becomes a *spot*. As to the 'graphist' and the 'interpreter', I may mention that whenever a person thinks over any question in his own mind, he carries on a sort of conversation. His mind of one minute appeals to his mind of the next minute to agree with it and say whether so-and-so is not reasonable; and then the mind of the next minute may say either 'Certainly by all means, and I wish all future minutes of my mind to take note that this is my decided opinion, after close examination' or else he may [say], 'Well, that seems so, at first glance, but I don't feel quite so sure of it as that mind of the last minute wished me to be' or he may even think 'Well, look you, my mind of the future, before whom my last minute mind and I, *this* minute's mind are arguing (for we both submit to you as knowing more than either of us do),—it appears to me that that last minute's mind was a goose and entirely failed to perceive the real state of the case', etc. etc.

That mysterious thing called Reason which, without the exercise of any force, renders Truth and Justice the mightiest of all powers in a world of fierce and greedy men, only acts through signs, spoken and written or "scribed or imagined". That which has made all our wonderful engines, wireless telegraphs, telephones, phonographs and a thousand other wonders possible has been the differential calculus, by which scientific men are instructed how to make the experiments that will be important. What is this "differential calculus"? It is a system of *signs* invented by the great philosopher Leibniz though Sir Isaac Newton independently invented something like it, and other mathematicians such as the great reasoner Fermat, approached doing it. What reason is in itself,—whether it is anything all by itself,—we cannot say. It is mysterious. It is what makes man's life noble. It is what gives a man self-control. It acts through words or other signs. Napoleon Bonaparte sits on his horse watching great battle and thinking "to himself" about it. Up rides an officer, and whispers something in his ear. What is that? It is little vibrations, little jars he gives to the air from his throat, without power to disturb a fly. They enter Napoleon's ear. He pulls out a pad and makes some marks on a sheet and hands it to an orderly. What result can these little things produce? The effect is that presently thousands of men lie dying on the field, and in another day a mighty government and the people that it rules are brought to their knees in abject despair. How could those forceless waves of air do that? They were animated by that mysterious thing called Reason, which only appears, apparently only has its being in *communications*. The Book of Genesis says, "God *said*, Let there be light!" and there was light. To whom or to what did God say it? The whole thing is mysterious. Of course, it does not mean that God spoke either in English or in Hebrew or with any air vibrations at all. But it does seem to mean that in communication of some kind there may lurk, without any brute force, a persuasive power that can even create such a world-boon as light.

Ah, well; let us leave these high mysteries and get down to things that the high mysteries have brought about but of which there are certain aspects or sides that we can comprehend. A 'spot' is not a graph: it is not true or false. It is not even scribed: no blank form can be scribed. The scribed part of it can be scribed, but not the blanks. Their significance lies in the *mutual understanding*, the *habitual* mutual understanding, between the scribe who draws up the blank form and the user of it, that the different blanks shall refer to the different several ways in which it is meant that the signs that are to fill them up shall be considered as related to the signification of the blank form.

You cannot put a habit upon a paper. But now if a heavy dot be placed at each of the *hooks* of the spot it becomes a *graph*. Thus, this, •gives• means "*somebody* gives *something* to somebody". For it is one of the principles of this system that every heavy dot denotes some single existing thing or single existing person, or single actual time, or single actual place, or some single actual occurrence, or some single abstraction, and that a single dot never denotes but one single subject no matter what universe. *But nothing prevents two separate dots from denoting the same single subject*. (By a "subject" I mean a single thing whether definitely thought or not that a truth or falsehood *relates* to.) Thus if I say "John gives Eliza the dome of the statehouse", the subjects are John, Eliza, and the dome of the statehouse. If I say "all men are liars", the subject is any single man you please. If I say, "There must have been some brave men before Agamemnon", the subjects are, first, some unnamed man, we know not who, second, Agamemnon. If I say "A man's body will soon rot, after its life is gone", the subjects are, first, that single aggregation of a million cells that makes up the body of any man you may choose to pitch upon, and second, that mysterious condition of this single body that brings it under the control of sense, of will, and of reason.

Next, imagine a heavy dot, with its power of denoting a single subject, to move; and imagine that as it moves it both carries along its singleness and also leaves it behind in its "wake". What will that result in? It will come to this, that whereas the single dot was but a *name*, a proper name of a single individual thing *not described* or distinctively designated,—"something"—and nothing more, the *line* is no longer a mere name. It is a *graph*. It is true or false, since it asserts that the "something" denoted by one end of it is the very same individual "something" that is denoted by the other end of it. In consequence of this, the following (where the spot HAS PRAISED has the hook for the praiser to the left, the hook for the object praised to the right, and the hook for the person to whom the praised was addressed at the bottom).

⟨gives/praises⟩ means "somebody gives something praised to him by somebody to that person". Let us see how this combines with a cut. If we scribe ⟮—is a phoenix⟯ it reads "there either is nothing at all or it is not identical with anything unless that thing be other than a phoenix", or in other words, "there is no phoenix". The following ⟮—phoenix⟯ means "there is something but it is identical with nothing that is a phoenix"; in other words, "*something* is not a phoenix". The following ⟨is a man / loves—is a woman⟩ means that there is a man and there is a woman whom that man does not love. The following ⟨is a pole of the earth / —is a pole of the earth⟩ means "there is a pole of the earth and there is a pole of the earth that is not the same as that pole", or in other words "there are at least two different poles of the earth".

20 Reason's Conscience
A Practical Treatise on the Theory of Discovery; considered as Semeiotic

R 693b, R S-26; summer 1904. Houghton Library. Inspired by Kant's *Critique of Practical Reason*, Peirce's next big project *Practical Treatise on the Theory of Reasoning*, written to fill up six Harvard notebook volumes, was meant become a new book on reasoning. The general title for the text that altogether comprises some 280 autograph pages was "Reason's Conscience: A Practical Treatise on the Theory of Discovery; considered as Semeiotic". In this aptly named "practical treatise", Peirce argues that logic ought to depend on the three sciences of mathematics, phenomenology and ethics. The plan was to devote a chapter on each before moving on to the topic of logic. He manages to address mathematics, and to some extent phenomenology and ethics, after which the part on logic, largely unwritten, was supposed to follow.

The first and the main variant below is from Volume 4 of the treatise, of which Peirce completed four sections (§ 23–§ 26). They provide a convenient introduction to the topic of existential graphs. Peirce indicates that the variant he had written is to be replaced by what is included Appendix A of the present selection as the second variant, which is on the analysis of the nature of mathematical reasoning. The first variant differs from the version in the appendix in introducing the logic of existential graphs; it is previously unpublished. Appendix B is an alternative version of § 24 from R S-26, "The Alpha Part of Existential Graphs", here numbered § 24–§ 25. In it, Peirce presents a practically complete glossary of key terms of the Alpha part of the theory. Another such list was prepared for the *Logical Tracts* dating from the previous year; together the two may now be taken to accomplish what Peirce wanted to write already for his 1896 seminal paper on logical graphs (R 482), namely a glossary of "some hundred terms". The abundance of such terms can be explained by the need to precisely define the notation and the working of the ovals. (The version given in Appendix A is Volume 5 of the *Practical Treatise*. It was published, with minor omissions, in NEM IV, pp. 185–216.)

Volume 4

§ 23. The *pons asinorum* has not the reputation of being abstruse; but I am sure you will find the kind of mathematics called Dyadics, to which I now propose to introduce you, reader, because of its great utility in logic, to be much easier. All reasoning in mathematics is performed by the aid of diagrams, using this word in a broad sense. In pure mathematics, we do not trouble ourselves much about the *meanings* of the diagrams. We can, upon occasion, assign to them any appropriate meanings we like. The principal thing is to learn how to work with the diagrams, and to go through the motions of reasoning. For it is performed in the same way whatever the special meanings may be. You want to look upon the diagrams as things that are governed by certain rules. It will make a sort of solitaire game; and later we will look into the possible interpretations.

Let us begin with a system of Diagrams called the *System of Existential Graphs*.

§ 24. I regret that I shall here have to set down an entire glossary of technical terms. The system could not be clearly described without them; and clearness is of the first importance in mathematics. When you come to find how useful the system is, and what valuable ideas are embodied in the technical terms, you will begin to forgive the trouble they put you to at first.

The system of Existential Graphs has three grades, called *the Alpha Part*, *the Beta Part*, and *the Gamma Part*. The Alpha part, or foliage and verdure of the whole system, is so much of the system as is requisite for any use of it. The entire signs are here all separated from one another. *The Beta Part* introduces ~~heavy~~ thick lines ~~joining~~ running from ~~graph to graph~~ entire sign to entire sign, and coalescing with these signs. It could not exist without the Alpha part of which it is a further development, or flowering. *The Gamma Part* supposes the reasoner to invent for himself such additional kinds of signs as he may find desirable. It grows out of the beta part and is the fruit and uberty of the whole. I begin with

The Alpha Part of Existential Graphs

The signs are drawn upon a sheet of paper or other surface appropriated to the purpose. This surface must ~~have a single boundary and~~ be in one piece, and must not be capable of containing a filament that could not shrink in the surface to nothing or that could shrink to nothing, in two ways such that no part of the surface would be passed over in both ways. Certain parts of the whole sheet are severed from the rest by having fine lines drawn round them, called *cuts*. What is inside a cut is not regarded as a part of the sheet. The whole sheet less what is thus severed from it is called the *sheet of assertion*. Any place where entire signs may significantly be placed, whether blank or not, is called an *area*. But when *opplete* (a term defined below) an area ceases to be such.

Now for the signs that are to be put upon this sheet. The operation of placing an entire sign on the sheet is called *scribing* it. A sign which is not composed of signs, corresponding to single letter in an ordinary book, is called a *symbolical atom*.

A sign which does not contain as parts any other signs which have the same signification in their situation as parts of it that they have in. The complete sign is said to be instantaneously created.

The entire signs are called *Graphs* or *Replicas*. A graph and a replica are nearly, but not quite, the same thing, as I shall explain presently. ~~The cut is linear; it has length without breadth or thickness. Any sign whatever, however composed, which is actually "scribed", that is drawn or written, and which occupies~~ They are distinguished from all other signs by occupying *superficial* spaces. The only difference between a graph and a replica is that a *graph* is any quite definite type of sign (not that it need have a perfectly determinate signification but that the sort of sign it is the type of is incapable of further significant determination) while a replica is a single scribed embodiment of the graph. The distinction is the same as that which distinguishes two senses of the word "word". For instance, the word *the* is likely to occur about twenty times on a printed page; and it is always one and the same "word", in a sense, in which each "word", like each graph, is a certain perfectly definite *type* of sign; while the twenty 'thes' are twenty "words" in a sense in which each 'word', like each replica, is a single embodiment of its type of sign. A replica must be scribed, or it has, no being at all; a graph can, in absolute literalness of speech, never be scribed; only replicas are scribed. Yet for that very reason, there can be no inconvenience in talking of "scribing a graph", meaning "scribing a replica of that graph". We shall see presently that in one point of view the expression "scribe a graph" is rather more correct that "scribe a replica".

A *graph* (as well as its *replicas*) is by no means necessarily a symbolical atom. Not only may a graph be composed of graphs, but all that is on the sheet of assertion is the replica of a graph. Nay so is the sheet itself with all that is on it. Moreover, one graph is the *blank*, so that if we extend the term *replica* to occurrences of this, though they are not actively "scribed", it would follow that every area contains an infinite multitude of replicas of this graph. For the same reason, neither is the scribing of a graph the creation of a replica, nor the erasure of a graph the destruction of a replica, but each of these operations is a transformation by which a replica is modified so as to become the replica of a different graph from that which it had previously represented. Moreover, following this rather fine distinction is of importance. Namely, a cut is not a replica, still less a graph. But a cut makes up with its enclosed area and with whatever replicas may be scribed thereon, a whole which is called the *enclosure* of the cut, and which is the replica of a graph, which is regarded as scribed on the sheet of assertion or on whatever other area it occurs upon. The enclosure is a replica upon the area outside of it, which is called the *place* of the cut and of the enclosure, and what is scribed upon its area is the replica of a *different* graph upon a different area. A graph within an even number of cuts is said to be *evenly enclosed*; within an odd number, to be *oddly enclosed*.

All that is actively scribed upon any area (exclusive of blanks) is called the *entire scribed replica* of that area; and the graph of which it is an embodiment is called the *entire scribed graph* of the area. Graphs that are parts of entire scribed graph are called *partial scribed graphs*; and their scribed replicas are *partial scribed replicas*.

An *instantaneously created replica* is a replica which is feigned to have been scribed in an instant, because a part of it scribed while the whole was incomplete violated some rule of graphs. To avoid that inconvenience we make believe it was all made at once. In particular an enclosure is regarded as having been, in the first instance an instantaneously created replica, because it would not be generally permissible to scribe the vacant cut nor yet to scribe upon the place of the cut the entire graph of its area. But this inconvenience may sometimes be avoided by making a *scroll*, or *double cut*, that is, one cut inside another, in this form and by these successive steps.

A *nest* is any series of cuts each enclosing the next one. An area is said to be *oppleted*, or *opplete*, when it is virtually quite filled up, all graphs having replicas upon it. This is represented by completed blackening it. An enclosure whose area is opplete is equivalent to a blank.

A *vacant enclosure* is an enclosure whose area is entirely blank.

§ 25. The rules, or rather the permissions, of graphs relate almost exclusively to what it is permitted to *insert*, or inscribe, and what is permitted to *erase*. The rules for the Alpha part are as follows:

Permission No. 1. It is permitted to scribe whatever one pleases on the sheet of assertion whatever is needed to represent the conditions of the special problem in hand.

Permission No. 2. It is permitted to erase all that may be on the sheet of assertion.

Permission No. 3. If it would be permitted to transform one graph into another upon a given area were there no other replica upon any area, then the same transformation is always permitted on the same area, regardless of what else may be on the same or other areas.

Permission No. 4. It is permitted to scribe anywhere on the sheet of assertion any graph which might permissively be scribed, on the inner area of an otherwise vacant scroll.

Permission No. 5. The reverse of any transformation that would be permissible on the sheet of assertion is permissible on the area of any cut that is upon the sheet of assertion.

Permission No. 6. An area upon which it is permitted to scribe a replica of any graph is opplete; and an enclosure whose area is opplete may be created on any area or, where existing, may be abolished.

§ 26. The above six fundamental permissions involve an endless series of others, of which I proceed to state and prove the most important, continuing the numbering of the permissions already given.

No. 7. Whatever transformation is permissible in any area is permissible within any nest of an even number of cuts that may exist in that area, while the reverse transformation is permissible within any nest of an odd number of cuts.

A permission does not relate to individual replicas but is general and extends to all cases of the description given. A permission for a transformation within an area is to be understood as regardless of what there may be in exterior areas, because otherwise, it would not be a general permission to transform in the interior area, but would only be a *general* permission if understood as a permission to transform in the exterior area. Consequently, a permission to transform a replica of a graph, R, into a replica of a graph S, within a given number, n, of cuts would be a permission to transform upon the sheet of assertion any replica of any graph containing a nest of n cuts in the area of which nest there should be a replica of R, into a replica of a graph exactly similar to that excepting only in the respect that S should be substituted for R. But that being permitted, according to Permission No. 6, it becomes permissible to transform a replica of any graph whatever that contains a nest of $n + 1$ cuts with a replica of S in its area into a replica of a graph differing from that only in having R in place of S. But this, again, amounts to a general permission that, provided it be permissible within any number n of cuts to transform a replica of a graph, R, into a replica of a graph, S, one may then, within $N + 1$ cuts, transform a replica of S into a replica of R. Since this holds whatever whole number may be substituted for n, it holds when for n we substitute $n + 1$. And since it holds for any graphs, R and S, that may satisfy the proviso, it holds for S and R, if these satisfy that proviso.

That is to say, provided it be permissible, in the area of every nest of $n + 1$ cuts, to transform S in R (should S occur there), then, in the area of every nest of $n + 2$ cuts, it will be permissible to transform R to S, should R occur there. Thence, joining these two results, if in the area of a nest of n cuts it be permissible to transform any given graph, R, into a given graph, S, then in a nest of $n + 2$ cuts the same transformation is permissible. But n, here may be any whole number we please. Assume it, then, to be $n + 2m - 2$, where m is any number we please. Then, what has just been said, applied to this case, is that if any transformation is generally permissible in the area of a nest of $n + 2m - 2$ cuts, the same transformation is generally permissible in a nest of $(n + 2m - 2) + 2$, or $n + 2m$, cuts, whatever whole number m may be. But this is the same as to say that if a transformation permissible in the area of a nest of n cuts is *not* generally permissible in the area of a nest consisting of some even number, $2m$, more than n cuts, then there will be a number of cuts smaller by some even number (namely, $n + 2m - 2$) in which the transformation will not be generally permissible. Hence, there can be no smallest number of the class of numbers within which it is not permissible. But every class of whole numbers has some smallest number. Hence, it is absurd to suppose that a transformation is universally permissible in a given number, n, of cuts and yet is not permissible in all numbers of cuts that exceed n by even numbers.

This being, thus, proved, Permission No. 5 at once shows that the reverse transformation will be permissible in all numbers of cuts that exceed n by odd numbers. For what has just been shown may be stated thus: If the sheet of assertion any replica of a graph containing a nest of any number, n of cuts, having on its area a replica of a graph, R, is transformable into a replica of a graph differing from that only in the respect that in place of R is scribed S, then the same permission will hold good for a case differing from that only that in place of n cuts there are $n + 2m$ cuts, where m is any whole number. But applying Permission No. 5 to this case, we find that under the same proviso being satisfied, within one cut more, that is $n + 2m + 1$ cuts, S maybe transformed to R. Now, $2m + 1$ may be any odd number. Hence if any transformation is universally permissible within any given number of cuts, the reverse transformation is universally permissible in any number of cuts, greater by an odd number.

No. 8. It is permitted to erase any evenly enclosed graph and to insert any graph so as to be oddly enclosed. This is called the rule of insertion and omission.

For Permission No. 2 allows a graph on the sheet of assertion to be erased when there is no other on the sheet; and Permission No. 3 extends this to the case where others are present. Then No. 7 extends this to all evenly enclosed graphs and justifies the reverse transformation within any odd number of cuts.

No. 9. It is permitted upon any area to create a vacant scroll, or cut upon whose area is a second cut and anything else, this area of the second cut being vacant; and any such vacant scroll that may exist upon any area may be permissively abolished.

No. 10. It is permitted, upon any area, around any replica upon that area, to create two ends, one within the other, with nothing between them, or wherever two cuts exist one within the other with nothing between, to abolish them.

For, by Permission No. 5, it is permitted to create such a pair of cuts on the sheet of assertion around a blank place. If then the replica of any graph is scribed upon the sheet, by Permissions No. 2 and 3 it might permissively have been alone upon the sheet. For Permission No. 2 would allow the transformation of any other replica there may be upon the sheet into a blank if it were alone upon the sheet, and Permission No. 3 extends this permission to the case in which there is another graph on the sheet. Hence, if the replica of any graph is on the sheet, a blank sheet of assertion might have been transformed into a replica of that graph. Hence, by No. 8, after the blank has been enclosed in the two cuts, this blank might be transformed into a replica of any graph of which a replica is on the sheet of assertion; and then by Permission No. 2 that replica of this graph which remains outside the two cuts could be erased; and the whole of this permissible operation would amount to creating the two cuts around the graph on the sheets.

Secondly, if there is on the sheet of assertion such a pair of cuts with nothing between then, Permission No. 4 permits us to scribe on the sheet of assertion a replica of whatever graph has a replica within them; and then Permissions 2 and 3 permit us to erase the two scrolls with their contents; and the effect of this is that we are permitted to abolish the two cuts with nothing between them and leave their contents standing upon the sheet of assertion.

Thirdly, these two reverse transformations being thus both permissible upon the sheet of assertion, by No. 8, they are permissible upon every other area.

No. 11. Any graph of which a replica is scribed upon any area may be *iterated*, that is to say, have a second replica of it scribed upon that area or on the area of any nest of cuts that is upon that area; or if it be so iterated, may be *deiterated*, that is to say, may have the innermost of its two replicas erased. This is called the rule of iteration and deiteration.

For, by No. 9, the rule of erasure and insertion, if a replica is scribed upon the sheet of assertion, all else might permissively be erased, so that it would be permitted to scribe a replica of the same graph upon the blank sheet. Whence, by Permission No. 3, a replica of it may be scribed upon the sheet of assertion no matter what else is scribed there, including another replica of itself. Thus a graph having a replica on the sheet of assertion may be iterated on that sheet.

If a graph having a replica on the sheet of assertion is also iterated there, it may, by the rule of erasure and insertion, No. 9, be deiterated.

Then, by No. 8, it follows from the former of these two results that a graph having a replica on the sheet of assertion may be iterated upon the area of any even nest of cuts, and if it be already iterated upon the area of any odd nest of cuts, it may be deiterated there. While from the latter of the two results, it follows that if a graph having a replica on the sheet of assertion is iterated on that sheet or on the area of any odd nest of cuts, it may be deiterated, while upon the area of any even nest of cuts it may be iterated.

Thus, a graph having a replica upon the sheet of assertion may permissively undergo either of these two reverse transformations, either upon the same area or within any additional cuts. Whence, by No. 9, the same two transformations are permissible for any graph having a replica either evenly or oddly enclosed.[1]

Appendix A (Volume 5)

§ 23. The *Pons Asinorum* has not the reputation of being abstruse; and no person who has any intellectual self-control can find it unsurmountable. The tradition is that this once conquered one will find nothing very redoubtable in the rest of mathematics. At any rate, it is certainly true that the further one penetrates into mathematics the more intrinsically easy it becomes, as a general rule, apart from the facility that one gains by the habit the facility that one gains by the habit of intellectual exertion. The part of mathematics which it is necessary for the student of reasoning to be thoroughly skillful in, I mean Dyadics, is far easier than the Pons Asinorum.

In addition to that branch, however, it is quite indispensable for a good reasoner to understand the doctrine of chances. This is a subject of difficulty in two ways. In the first place, the mathematics of it is a little difficult in places. But these can be smoothed down considerably. In the second place, the greatest difficulties of the theory of probabilities are not strictly speaking mathematical, or at least not what is usually recognized as mathematical, but are logical; and

---

[1] [Cut pages:] [...] feelings being connected with the percept. And further that, always connected with one another of these perceptual memories, there seem to be certain volitional memories, and that it frequently happens that there seems to be subsequent to one of these yet not subsequent to it, still another kind of phenomenon connected with a perceptual memory, which may be called a satisfactional memory; and further more, that connected with some pairs of memories occupied by a replica, and a replica may be situated wholly within a cut.

[...] occupied by a replica; and a replica may be situated wholly within a cut. The whole surface outside all the cuts extending up to and including the cuts themselves, but excluding everything within them is called the *sheet of assertion*. The whole surface within any cut, extending up to and including every cut that, is although within it, yet not within any intermediate cut that is in its turn within it, and excluding every point within such immediately interior cuts, is called the *area of the* exterior *cut*. In general, by an *area* is meant either the sheet of assertion or the area of some one cut, that is to say, a superficial space everywhere within which there either are or may be scribed replicas, and which is not traversed by any cut. An area is not regarded as containing [discont. "A hundred real dollars contain] not a bit more than a hundred possible ones. [...] Let me think of a thing by what predicates I will, if I then think that the thing exists, I do not thereby in the least modify my notion of the thing". [From Kant's *Sämmtliche Werke*, Vol. I, p. 510, Philosophische Bibliothek, 1867, concerning the ontological argument. Peirce's own translation.] The clever psychologist Hans Cornelius endeavors to meet this by saying that there are various ways in which an existing thing differs from a non-existing one. He enumerates quite a list of these points of difference; but it is sufficient to speak of the fact that an existing thing reacts with other things while a non-existing thing does not.

[...] in an instant. Only one more definition need be added. It sometimes happens (and one may anticipate that it is not an unimportant circumstance) that an area is so circumstanced that it becomes permissible to scribe upon it replicas of any or all graphs while at the same time it becomes permissible to erase from this same area the replicas of any and all graphs that may be scribed there.

the discussion of these can be postponed until the reader has gained from previous parts of this book, a proper equipment for grappling with them.

§ 24. Before taking up dyadics, it will be necessary, in order that the reader may have the sort of understanding of mathematics that the study of logic requires,—a somewhat different kind of understanding of it from that which he would need if he desired only to understand mathematics,—that we should make some preliminary reflections upon the nature of mathematics.

Now the feature of mathematics which separated it widely both from Philosophy and from every special science is that the mathematician never undertakes (*quâ* mathematician) to make a categorical assertion from the beginning of his scientific life to the end. He simply says what *would be* the case under hypothetical circumstances.

The higher branches of Physics and of Psychics,—the nomological sciences,—likewise discover and enunciate general laws which are very properly expressible in the same grammatical forms. But they only mean *at most*,—if they do generalize so far, which may be questioned,—that experience forces them to believer that such are the laws of this universe in which we find ourselves. The mathematician, however, snaps his fingers at experience and at this little universe: what he means to pronounce upon relates to any and every universe in which the antecedent of his proposition might be true. Even the normative sciences,—logic, for example,—go far beyond objective experience. The logician reasons about objects that are not even real. Still, all the normative sciences necessarily make themselves responsible for certain characters of objects of thought. The mathematician alone does not unconditionally assume or assert anything at all.

What does he rely upon, then? Ah, that is a question-begging question. He no doubt works with his imagination and his generalizing intellect; and if they were to work wrong, he would fall into error. But there are two circumstances to be taken into account, and to be taken into account, *together*. They have no relevancy to mathematics; but they are relevant to the irrelevant question that has been asked. One of these circumstances is, that in point of fact, the mathematician's imagination and intellect do *not* work wrong,—although once in a while, from inattention, he adds up a column wrongly, and says that 2 and 2 make 5. But such blunders are so promptly rectified, when attention is directed to them, and are so extremely rare, that they are not regarded as belonging to the general course of the mathematician's work. You might as well say that his success in answering how much seven times eight is, is due to his not being struck by lightening before the has given his answer. A bold sailor contrives to sail round the world alone in a small boat. As he lands at the end of his achievement, a person at the landing says to him, "Do you know that your success was due to whales?" "How so?" "Why if every whale in the ocean had not abstained from butting your boat you never would have brought it to port". The sailor, I think, might properly reply, "Oh, do have a little good sense!" A sound logician would certainly say that the sailor was right, as we shall see, in due time.

The second circumstance that has to be borne in mind at the same time with the first, is that the mathematician, as such, never knew that he had any such faculties as imagination and intellect. Consequently, he cannot be said to have relied upon them. The fact that they did not go wrong was simply one of the million matters of course the absence of which if they had been replaced by something almost miraculous, might have resulted in his making a mistake in some few sporadic cases. If you do not agree with me you ought to find fault with a physician who reports yellow fever as the cause of a death instead of attributing it in part to the deceased not having lived in Judaea at the time of Jesus Christ and his apostles and subsequently not having been healed by one of them. If you reply that the mathematician's imagination and intellect are the "direct cause" of his success, I shall rejoin that that is metaphysics too stale for me to deal with at this date.

The mathematician does not "rely" upon anything. He simply states what is *evident*, and notes the circumstances which make it evident. When a fact is evident, and nobody does or can doubt it, what could "reliance" upon anything effect?

§ 25. If Euclid's geometry is regarded, as he no doubt regarded it, as the science of real, physical space, it is humanly speaking certain to a closer degree of approximation than any other special science. It is, in that case a branch of idioscopy; for the most refined methods of observation have to be employed in order to determine, for example, how great the area of a triangle must be in order that the sum of its angles should depart from 180° by as much as one thousandth or one ten-thousandth of the angular diameter of the moon as seen from the earth. But it does not, in that case, approach,—literally, *does not approach*,—the degree of precision of pure mathematics. For that purpose, the postulates, after having been thoroughly revised, must be considered as purely hypothetical; and the question that the geometer is answering must be understood to be, 'What *would be* the properties of spatial figures, in a space having the properties embodied in the postulates?'

To answer the question, he needs no external observation. Strictly speaking, he does not need even to look at his own diagrams. Indeed, a mathematician of good habits ordinarily only puts pen to paper to record his results, except in intricate work of a low order. The objects [of] the studies are the creation of his own conscious volition, so that no part of their nature can be hidden from him.

There is thus nothing to surprise one in the (theoretical) infallibility of mathematics. The puzzle is how it can present any difficulties. Anybody who should take up that question, and give a thorough-going answer to it, would write an exceedingly helpful book. It would require a book, since the causes of difficulty are various. I can only indicate in the briefest terms a few of them. One is that much intellectual strength is required at each step of one's progress to put the really pertinent, pressing, and readily answered question. Then, although we say that the mathematician is dealing only with the creatures of his own conscious volition, yet, after all, who is this self? His whole discourse of reason is a dialogue between a past self with a future self; and much that was the creation of one in his skin is now strange to him and expressed in foreign language. He has gone on complicating his ideas to an extent of which nobody but logicians, and few of them, have any adequate idea. To grasp his entire hypothesis clearly at one time has passed beyond his power. Moreover, his two selves are unavoidably talking to each other in two different languages, the one a language of images, necessary for tracing out results, the other a language of abstractions, necessary for the generalization.

Those items will serve well enough such ends as a bald list, even were it more nearly complete, could alone serve. What I am aiming at is to deduce from the mathematician's purposes and circumstances those features of his general method of procedure which it concerns the student of logic to understand before taking up the study of those parts of mathematics that are indispensable for any true comprehension of the nature of the different kinds of reasoning.

It is obvious, to begin with that precision is everything in the kind of inquiry in which he is engaged, whether he is dealing with metrical branches of his science or not.[2] Rough statements are sometimes useful; such as Simpson's Rule, and Poncelet's Theorem, and some methods of trisection of angles, but their utility lies mostly outside of pure mathematics, and they generally must be mere abridgements of exact knowledge. Precise statement being thus the very staff of life to the mathematician, he is forced to use abstract statements of all his results. For in no other terms could anybody dream of precisely enunciating very general propositions, as those of the mathematician always are of their very essence.

But one can never trace out consequences by the help of general terms. That is a proposition which very few logicians have seen. John Stuart Mill partly saw it: I cannot say more. Friedrich Albert Lange fully saw it; but he restricted the means of tracing consequences too narrowly, by far. As for such writers as Boole, De Morgan, Schröder, together with another class of whom the Abbé Gratry is a typical example, I am astonished that they should have failed to grasp a truth so near to their own constant practice. They must have been deceived by the old syllogistic, where it is true that deductive conclusions,—very puerile ones, though they be,—are obtained by no other apparent machinery than that general language. But in those cases, the conclusion comes so instantaneously that direct observation of how we come by it is impossible. It is not the question what is the process by which I am led to conclude that Socrates was mortal or Andree who was lost in the Arctic regions, or that I myself shall die; because those are not pure deductions. But to say how, from the pure *hypothesis* that every three-legged animal has two heads and that every inhabitant of Mars is a three-legged animal, I trace out the consequence that every inhabitant of Mars has two heads, that is a question to which direct observation can furnish no even tolerably certain reply. The conclusion comes too quickly. It is so even with the least obvious of the old syllogisms, *Frisesomorum*, of which I will give an example. Now watch your process of thought, reader, and see if you can catch a glimpse of it, as it flashes by Now! On the hypothesis that

Some minstrels know the Basque Language and that
Among the fireworshippers there is no minstrel

How are you led to be certain that

Somebody who knows Basque is not a fireworshipper.

I will venture to guess that, as well as you can make out, you found out the conclusion by imagining a minstrel who know Basque, and considering that the absence of minstrels among fireworshipper would preclude this Basque-speaker from being a minstrel. If so, you resorted to an image and did not perform your reasoning in general terms, as syllogistic prescribes. But in order to make sure of how necessary conclusions are drawn, you must take one which is more difficult. Watch again, if you please! Suppose we admit as true the testimony of two witnesses one of whom testifies that in the course of a single calendar year there was not a single monk in a certain monastery against whom at least one formal criminal accusation had not been laid by some monk of the same monastery; while against some there had been several such accusations. The other witness testifies, however, that no one monk had ever made accusation against more than one monk.

---

2 I do not think that this precision is by any means so evident. The mathematician is tracing out necessary consequences. Now that which is necessary must be definite. But the only way will be to rewrite a part here on sheets that I shall insert.

Then I ask, does it follow or not, that Every monk during that year made an accusation of crime against a monk?

You may say, off hand, that it does not follow. But think again and see how else it could be. There were only just so many monks. Every mother's son of them was accused. You might think, from the first witness's testimony, that perhaps someone malicious and half-cracked fellow had accused all his fellows and finally, publicly confessing, had accused himself. But no; the other witness avers that no monk accused more than one. Then each one accused had his own distinct accuser; and the accusers must have been as many as the accused. Since then the accused were all, the accusers were as many as all. Could that be if any were not accusers? How now, reader who said it did not follow. You see, you depended on the general terms.

However, it is true that the conclusion does not necessarily follow from the premises, as you have doubtless remarked; because all that follows is, that every monk must have had among the monks a distinct and separate accuser. But since we are considering a pure hypothesis, and the evidence of experience is wholly discarded, there might have been, for ought we know, an infinite number of monks that year. They might have been numbered from 1 up indefinitely, as far as whole numbers go, which is beyond all limit. Then each monk may have been accused by the monk whose number was double his own. Thus all monks would have been accused, while only these who bore even numbers would have been accusers. This shows how circumspect one must be in necessary reasoning.

The abstract expressions and the images are all that the mathematician deals with. There is no third object that they both represent. The images, being the creations of an intelligent man, conform to some purpose; and a purpose, being general, can only be thought in abstract or general terms. Thus, in one way, the images represent, or translate, the abstract language; while in another way, it is the latter which represents the former. The mathematicians certainly always have considered the images an external world, not supposed to be experienced, and sometimes (of late years always) acknowledged to be imaginary, as of course a universe not experienced must be. Nearly every image is regarded as standing, not for a definite individual object in that universe but for an individual object, yet as truly any one of a class as any other. Thus, when the geometer draws a straight line upon his diagram, he understands that, within what restrictions there may be, it represents any straight line. The imaginary universe to the parts of which all the images and propositions refer is always thought of as a single individual whole of individual parts. No particular purpose is subserved by this individualization of the mathematician's imaginary universe; and the explanation of it must be awaited in another part of this book. Yet it may be remarked here that nothing would be gained by making the universe general.

The mathematician always describes his universe, usually in some individual features of it and always, at any rate, as to certain regularities which he supposes to be without exception in it in a list of postulates or otherwise. This description always leaves it indeterminate what color the imagined objects are. To specify anything of that sort would be considered grotesque. Why? Because so long as those which might have been imagined blue, or any other color, are represented to be in some way distinguished from others, the distinguishing color chosen could make no difference as to the forms of necessary conclusions that might be drawn. Now the mathematician's whole interest in these forms of necessary conclusions; and whatever does not concern them is regarded by him as foreign to ~~logic~~ mathematics. It is the same in regard to relations. Only a few relations between the individuals of his imaginary universe are noticed at all by the mathematician, and as to these few, what he cares for is the presence (or absence) of an unbroken rule as to the identity of objects in different sets of objects between which the relation subsists. If there is no such rule, which might serve as the means of drawing some necessary conclusion, he will regard the relation as having no mathematical interest. The obvious reason is that dealing with creatures of the imagination, exclusively, nothing that he can say will be of any consequence except that if certain propositions are true certain others are infallibly true; and this would be a necessary consequence.

Of course, the unfailing universality of the mathematician's conclusions are due to every conclusive step being evidently nothing but the application of a plain rule to a manifest instance under that rule. In that sense, those logicians are quite right who say that the mathematicians whole inferential proceeding is of the type called *Barbara*, or the form of

Any M is P;
S is an M;
∴ S is P.

On the other hand, the very same general fact justifies those who say that all the mathematician's reasoning consists in observation; for whatever is "evident" or "plain", or "manifest" is so only to observation of it. Logicians of each of these classes are, however, apt to deny what the other class says, wherein they fall into opposite errors; while both kinds commit the same rash assumption that having found out one universal characteristic of a large variety of reasonings, they have thereby mastered the whole secret of the subject. That is just as if the first chemist who discovered that matter never alters its weight,—Sir Walter Raleigh assumed this according to a tradition,—should have supposed that chemistry had no further secret for him.

These hypotheses which form the matter of the postulates are of permanent and immutable states of things,—mostly imagined laws as to how changes would take place; but so far, the mathematician has not created any moveables to obey those laws. As long as nothing else is imagined, very few and trifling consequences, if any, can be drawn. For what he imagines simply remains as he imagined it. To bring to light any result that was not obvious at the outset, it is necessary that changes should take place. Now imaginary and unreal things have no forces to move of themselves; it must be the mathematician's own will that changes them. To do this, he must have a purpose: he must be aiming to bring about some result. If, however, he could foresee what the result would be, he would be able to draw those consequences which he cannot draw. I will not undertake to say how he grows to asking what would happen if some changes in the mutable objects which he has now imagined were to take place according to the immutable laws expressed in his postulates. He has to do something similar to Euclid's moving one triangle over into coincidence with another. But when he has supposed this change to take place he cannot be satisfied to trust to his imagination of what the result has been. He must appeal to the general rule contained in one of his postulates, and to the manifest fact that this comes under that rule, and to the evident result of the rule in that case.

Thus, hypotheses of objects imagined to be mutable furnish the mathematician with the data of his problems. It often happens that there are some questions about the relations between the parts of such an image which he can answer with certainty without making any changes in it. They are all obvious enough. Such make the chief substance of those *corollaries* which editors of Euclid have added to his text.[3] Hence, I propose to call this class of inferences *corollarial deductions*.

---

3 In Weiberg's text of the 13 books of the *Elements*, there are 132 definitions, 5 postulates, 9 axioms, 401 theorems, 64 problems, 17 lemmas, 2 scholia, or remarks, and 27 corollaries or πορίσματα. They are parenthetical inferences of an obvious kind. As to the genuineness of these 27 there are special reasons for doubt in many cases. The other corollaries, of which for example,

But all the consequences not readily seen, are only to be discovered or proved after making changes in the image, requiring more or less ingenuity. How the mathematician can guess in advance what changes to make is a mystery that deserves a life-time of study. Books have been written about it; but they are mere collections of empirical recipes for accomplishing what has substantially been done before, and are no help to any really great step, because they do not go into the rationale of the matter. The truth is that mathematicians have not at present any knowledge of how to plan an attack upon a problem altogether novel. This is shown by the fact that such a problem as that of proving how many colors will suffice to distinguish the regions upon any map on a given kind of surface has remained prominent for half a century without being solved.

Appendix B

[R S-26] **The Alpha Part of Existential Graphs. § 25.** In all mathematics it is essential that there should be a multitude of objects which the student can perceive (usually see, but it would be sufficient if he could imagine them), and is able to modify at will (he usually creates and destroys them), but in doing this obeys certain general rules (usually conventional in part and physically compulsory in part). Then, his work consists in imagining problems which suppose the changeable objects to be at the beginning in a state defined in general terms and which require the discovery of an infallible general method by which they may be brought (without violation of the rules) to another state defined in general terms.

It would be, I suppose, psychologically impossible for a man to devote much energy to any branch of mathematics unless he supposed it likely that the rules of it were so analogous to the general laws of some relations of real objects, that the former might be considered as representing the latter; and thus we find that mathematicians usually speak of the mutable objects they study as signs, symbols, images, and the like. But their being such has no relation to any part of the mathematician's business except that of the formation and adoption of hypotheses.

The purpose and uses of the system of existential graphs cannot be explained until the system itself has been set forth. Certain features of the system have been adopted for trivial reasons; and it will be well that this should be understood at the outset.

The *replicas* (1), or things which the student sees and subjects to transformations, are represented as superficial objects, or films. This is convenient, because it is necessary that they should exhibit a great variety of easily recognized differences even in their *atoms* (2), that is, in those parts of them which are never cut in the transformations or even usually thought of as composite. The advantage, for this purpose, of making them visible surfaces is obvious; or at least a part of it is so. The different recognizable *types* of the atoms are called *elements* (3). Thus, the distinction between an *atom* and an *element* is no greater than that which we observe between two senses of the word "word". The word "the" usually occurs about a score of times upon a printed page. In one sense, it is always the same "word"; in another sense it is twenty different "words". The former sense is analogous to that of the term *element*, the latter to that of the term *atom*. The atom is the individual object that is seen and transmuted; the *element* is the perfectly definite *type* which is associated with atoms that are alike in their essential characters, though not in their existential

---

there are a score in the first book of Playfair's Euclid, they are all the work of editors, and are almost all trivial things that Euclid did not deem worth mention. It is supposed they were called corollaries because marked by a marginal wreath of triumph.

relations of place, etc., this type being, in itself, such as it is, incapable of mutation, and only recognized by thought, not in itself a direct object of experience. The atoms and the objects that are composed of atoms are called *replicas* (4). The complex types, any one of which belongs only to replicas that are exactly alike in all essential respects and are different only in existential respects, are called *graphs* (5).

The replicas are imagined to be written or drawn,—*scribed* (6) is the term employed,—upon a sheet of paper or a blackboard. This is obviously convenient, since they are in great variety and must be recognized, made, unmade, and modified by the student. But there is hardly anything about the graphs which is analogous to any essential properties of a surface. In the Alpha Part all the atoms stand separate from one another; so that there is nothing like continuity. In the Beta Part, there is a relation sufficiently analogous to continuity to make its representation by means of continuity decidedly apt. But the restriction to a surface is severely felt as inconvenient and essentially unsuitable; but a third dimension, which is needed, would be still more inconvenient. No replica is scribed wholly or partly over another. But as to this certain explanations will be given presently.

Besides the replicas, we place upon the sheet certain fine self-returning lines which we do not regard as "scribed" and which we call *cuts* (7). No two cuts ever intersect; but there are frequently cuts within cuts. A series of cuts one within another is called a *nest* (8) of cuts. A nest of two cuts (generally drawn as one nodal line) is called a *scroll* (9). Two nests of cuts may have cuts in common; and one nest of cuts may be within another so as to constitute with it another nest. But of every pair of cuts of the same nest one is immediately or mediately within the other. One cut is said to be *immediately within* (10) another if it is within that other but is not within any third cut that is within that other.

The entire extent of that part of the sheet which is not within any cut, including the linear space occupied by the cut itself, is called the *area of assertion* (11), and relatively to any cut that does not lie within any other, it is called the *place* (12) of that cut. I intend very slightly to modify this statement and some others presently; but I think the easiest way to make the matter clear will be to state it as I am doing, in the first instance. The entire surface that is contained within any cut but is not contained within any cut within that cut is called the *area of the exterior cut* (13) and is called the *place* (14) of any cut immediately within that cut. The *area of a nest* (15) of cuts is the space within all the cuts of the nest; but in speaking of a scroll we often speak of the *outer* and *inner close* (16). By an *area* (17), simply, is meant either the area of assertion or the area of some cut. It is a superficial place which does not include its outer limit but does include any inner limit that it may have. An area either is, or may be, in part or in whole occupied by replicas; and the part occupied does not cease to be a part of the area.

Every replica is situated upon some one area which is its *place* (18), and is never traversed by a cut. Every area may have a replica scribed upon it. But now a fine distinction has to be noticed. Although a cut is not a replica, and surely is far from being a graph, yet every cut taken together with whatever replica is upon its area is regarded as constituting a replica (called an *enclosure* (19)) whose *place* (20) is the place of the cut. The area of the cut is called also the *area of the enclosure* (21). Since this is not an easy conception to grasp surely and steadily, I will suggest a way of gaining a sort of image of it. It is with reference to this that I said just now that some of my statements would be slightly modified. Instead of conceiving a *cut* (22) as separating the surface into two parts, it may be imagined to be a line of splitting of the surface such that inside the cut there are two sheets. Upon one of these sheets (say the under one, in order to "fix the ideas") are scribed whatever replicas are in the area of the cut; and this sheet is regarded as being no part of the main sheet outside. The other sheet that overlies that one is simply a part of the outer area, and is occupied with a replica the character of which depends upon the graphs that have replicas on the under sheet, but not in the same way as if they were scribed on this very same sheet. According to this, there would be two ways in which a graph may govern the character of a replica; namely, firstly, by a direct action of the graph upon a part of the sheet determining a replica of itself; and secondly, by the graph's acting directly in this way to produce a replica upon another sheet, which, being then brought under the main sheet, acts as a sort of photographic negative, to produce a second replica on the main sheet. Then, in case there is another cut within the first, this is to be conceived as a line of splitting of the lower sheet; so that there is first a direct replica of the graph upon the lower sheet of the split lower sheet, which is the area of the inner close; that influences a secondary replica upon the main sheet of the lower sheet, which is the outer close, and that again produces a tertiary replica upon the upper sheet, which is the place of the scroll. I do not know as every reader will find this fancy a help; but at any rate, he must in some way contrive to understand that while the area of a cut, together with what replicas there may be scribed upon it, are severed from the outer area which is the *place* (23) of the cut, yet the *enclosure* (23) is a replica which is upon that outer area as its place, and the peculiar graph of this enclosure is not the graph of the replica in the area of the cut but is determined to be the graph of the enclosure by the fact that the replica of the area of the cut is severed from the place of the cut. Moreover, when we come to the rules of these graphs, it will be found that the different areas, one within the other, of the cuts of a nest alternate in their natures in a way that harmonizes very well with the idea of the photographic negative. For this reason, it will be useful to distinguish replicas as *evenly enclosed* (24) and *oddly enclosed* (24) according as they are within even or odd numbers of cuts.

It will be necessary to correct what I have been saying in still another particular. For I have talked as if there might or might not be a replica upon the area of a cut. But it is far better to regard the parts of the sheet where nothing has been scribed and which remain in their original condition, nothing being there but *blank spaces* (25), as the phrase is, as being occupied with replicas of one graph, the *blank* (25). The view ought, at first blush, to recommend itself to mathematicians, to whom nothing is always a quantity when they are speaking of quantities. So when we are speaking of replicas filling a space, these spaces are filled with the absence of scribed replicas. In applying the system to logic, as I shall do later, this conception will become still more imperative. In this view, scribing and erasing are simply special cases of transformations of replicas; and this simplifies the rules. It will then be necessary to distinguish the *entire replica* (26) of an area from its *entire created* (27) (or *factitious* (28)) *replica*, the latter excluding the blank; while the *entire scribed replica* (29) will exclude enclosures. Graphs may be distinguished in the same way. *Partial replicas* and *partial graphs* (30), meaning replicas there are parts of the entire replica and their graphs, will also be distinguished, if necessary, by the adjectives *created* (31) (or *factitious*) and *scribed*.

I may mention here that it sometimes becomes necessary to speak of replicas as being *instantaneously created* (32). This means that although the graphist may be obliged to construct a replica part by part, and although in doing so he may perforce make something that seems to be a replica, yet it must be understood that all power of functioning as such is suspended until the construction is complete; as if it had been created in an instant.

There now remains, I believe, but a single group of definitions that need be added. It sometimes happens (and I leave the reader to guess whether the circumstance is unimportant or not) that there is upon an area a replica which renders it permissible to erase any and all other replicas upon that area and equally renders it permissible to scribe any and all other replicas upon that area. It is thus left to the option of the graphist to produce any effect that a replica in that area can bring about. How great, then, is likely to be the force of a replica in that area? An area so affected is said to be *opplete* (33) or to be *oppleted* (34) (from *opplēre*, to stuff up). Or we may prefer to say that it is the *annulus* (35), or annular space, comprising all that area except that occupied by the replica that effects the *oppletion* (36) that is *oppleted* (37). Or again, we may say that the enclosure in the area of which the *opplent* (38) replica occurs is *opplete* (39). Connected with this conception is that of a vacant *enclosure* (40), which is an enclosure whose area is entirely blank.

I have numbered in the margin the definitions of this section, and I now add an alphabetical index to them.

Annulus 35	Graph 5
Area 17	Immediately within 10
Area of assertion 11	Inner close 16
Area of a cut 13	Instantaneously created 32
Area of an enclosure 21	Nest 8
Area of a nest 15	Oddly enclosed 24
Atom 2	Opplent 38
Blank 25	Opplete 33, 39
Close 16	Oppleted 34, 37
Created 27, 31	Oppletion 36
Cut 7, 22	[Partial 30]
Element 3	[Place 12, 14, 18, 20, 23]
Enclosure 19, 23	Replica 1, 4
Entire 26, 27, 29	To Scribe 6, 9, 29
Evenly enclosed 24	Scroll 9
Factitious 28, 31	Vacant 40

§ 26. Those of the rules, or rather the permissions, of the system of existential graphs, may, which are first principles, the essential definitions of the working of the system, be properly termed *postulates*. They relate, almost, if not quite, exclusively to what it is permitted to *scribe* or *insert*, and to what it is permitted to *erase* or *omit*.

Postulates of the Alpha Part. It is permitted

A. To scribe on the area of assertion whatever is needed to represent the data of the problem in hand;
B. To erase all there is on the area of assertion;
C. To make any transformation on the area of assertion, regardless of what else there may be there, that would be permissible if the subject of transformation were alone on that area;
D. To insert upon the area of assertion a replica of any graph of which it would be permissible to scribe a replica upon the inner close of a vacant scroll;
E. Instantaneously to create on the area of assertion, when entirely blank, a vacant scroll:
F. To perform on the area of any cut placed upon the area of assertion the reverse or any transformation that would be permissible on the area of assertion.

21 Topical Geometry

R 145, 145(s) (R 96 in the microfilm edition), plus R 507, R 839, R 1575, R S-31; April–May 1905. Houghton Library. On November 16, 1904, Peirce read a paper entitled "On Topical Geometry" at the National Academy of Sciences meeting in New York City. Manuscripts R 145 and R 145(s), together with a number of loose and alternative pages collated from several other folders (R 507, R 839, R 1575, R S-31), portray his slightly later attempt to write up a fuller account. This fuller account, written in April–May 1905, reveals Peirce finally having a chance to integrate his work on topology, hypostatic (or "subjectal") abstraction and map coloring, now also encompassing existential graphs. These attempts at a longer version—though written with a potential publication in mind and advancing yet another unfulfilled prospectus to evolve into a book-length treatise—represent a relatively hurried hand, resulting in an uncompleted and sketchy version of the presentation from the previous autumn. Yet it is not without new ideas, and in one of the variants found in a supplementary folder (R 145(s)) Peirce for instance proposes representing hypostatical abstraction in graphs by a purple line that blends the colours of the spots (red and blue) connected by the abstracted line of identity, together with a reference to the map-coloring problem.

An Attempt to state systematically the Doctrine of the Census in Geometrical Topics or Topical Geometry, more commonly known as 'Topology'; Being, A Mathematico-Logical Recreation of C. S. Peirce following the lead of J. B. Listing's paper in the "Göttingen Abhandlungen"[1]

Preface

The definition of mathematics as the science of quantity seems now at last to be happily exploded. In its later years is was a capital example of the disposition of the "vulgar" among the educated to hold on to phrases without minding much whether their meanings be retained or no. For the three principal terms in this definition, *mathematics*, *science*, and *quantity* had long been completely revolutionized in meaning before the phrase itself lost any of its favour. The definition is given by Boethius, with whom "mathematics" meant the whole quadrivium, including astronomy, music, and an "arithmetic" which was little but a system of nomenclature, while it excluded "logistic", or what we call arithmetic nowadays. By "science" was meant scientis, ἐπιστήμη, which comes nearer to what we call

---

[1] [The title given in R 145(s):] "An Attempt to state systematically the Doctrine of the Census in Geometrical Topics, or Topical Geometry, more commonly called 'Topologie' in German books; Being, A Mathematico-Logical Recreation of C. S. Peirce following the lead of J. B. Listing's paper in the 'Göttingen Abhandlungen'. Preface."

comprehension than to what we call science; and finally by "quantity" was evidently meant *quanta*, things which are subject to being measured or counted.

What I purpose writing in this book is a rough draught, even more hurried than hasty (suggested by Professor Cook Wilson's book on *Traverses*), of an exposition I never expected to find time to finish of ideas that, for years and years have been dismissed from my mind. That it should be crammed with mistakes and other vermin of stupidity is inevitable under the circumstances.

Geometrical *Topics* is that branch of Pure (or Ideal) Geometry which is related to Geometrical *Graphics* (as Clifford conveniently called strictly Projective Geometry) as this is to Geometrical *Metrics*. Metrics is well defined by Cayley, in the 1st Chapter and 1st Article of Salmon's *Higher Plane Curves*, which chapter was contributed by Cayley to the 2nd edition, as that geometry of the[2] consequences of the relations of places in Space (the place of all places) to that *definite individual* (if I have the patience to do so, I will write logical terms that are to be understood in their strict acceptions in blue ink) place which, being the limit, or superficies of Space, is not in Space, and consequently is supposed to be (for Pure Geometry rests on Pure hypothesis) a non-existent place. Cayley does not thus elicit the paradox of the idea.[3] All other geometry is called Descriptive. This negative department consists of two departments which may be positively defined.

The one, Graphics, deals with Projections and Sections, by the projectionally and sectionally simplest kinds of places. In all places of dimensionality, N, whatever integer N may be, it distinguishes the places therein of dimensionality $N-1$, into those that are of such a kind that any N of them each of which N places of dimensionality $N-1$, may have any element (point) common to them all and besides any $N-1$ other elements, and the entire collection of N such places will have no other element common to them all than that one, unless they have a continuum of common elements. Such places are particularly distinguished in Graphics from other places which, through N of them necessarily have in common a collection of elements, yet do not necessarily have one sole element in common, even though they be not so related as to have a continuum of common elements. Thus, in a Space of three dimensions, this kind of Geometry, Graphics, distinguishes among

---

2 [On a verso page:] A is a lover of every pope

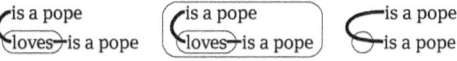

3 Cayley's is the scientific definition, because it gives the term "metric" a *depth* over and above what is necessary for determining its *breadth*, or as I called it, in a paper of November 13, 1867 (*Proceedings* (Boston) *American Acad. of Arts and Sci.* VII, 412), it has *information* [Peirce 1867b]. Thus, this makes the curved-ratio *descriptive*, not *metrical*.

surfaces, particularly those of which any three necessarily have one point in common, unless they have a common line. This supposes that the place of dimensionality, N, is of such a character there is any such class of places, or as topics teaches us to say is perissid. If not, Graphics would no doubt consider this place as within a Space that was perissid.

Graphics having thus distinguished the simplest kind of surfaces, lines, etc., classifies all the rest by means of their relations to these. Thus in Space of three dimensions, it classifies surfaces as those which have *one*, *two*, *three*, etc. or an endless number of possible points in common with a *ray* or unlimited simplest line; as well as according to the number of tangent planes containing a given ray, etc.

The other kind of Descriptive Geometry is *Topics*. It utterly ignores the essential distinction of Graphics. It does not know the difference between a straight line and a curve or a crooked line, nor that between a plane and a curved surface or a bent surface. It does not distinguish a cusp or an inflexion from an ordinary point.

It considers two kinds of objects; immovable *places*, and *Movables*, which are things occupying, that is, being in every part of, places, and at different places at different instants, but only by continuous movements and deformations which do not alter the connectivity of their parts. That is, the mode of possible *generation* of their instantaneous places remains the same.

A *point* is an indivisible place, of which any one is, in itself, indistinguished as different, from any other, though it is recognized as *other*. In other words pairs of points are either the same or different.

A *particle* is a Movable which at every instant occupies a *point*.

A *particle-collection* is an object composed of separate particles.

A *line-figure* is a place of which even part can be occupied at *some* instant during a course of time by a *particle-collection*, but not the whole at one instant.

But at no instant during the course of time can any particle be at once at two points, as would be the case if it made an instantaneous leap. [- - -][4]

Pure Topics is not limited to Space of three dimensions but is the full account of all forms of Continuity. In so far as it is limited to Space, it is the complete account of all the properties of Space itself. For graphics is only the doctrine of a particular general reticulation in Space and discourses only of the Topical characters of that Reticulation, and Metrics was shown by Cayley in his immortal "Fifth Memoir on Quantics" [Caley 1858] to be nothing but a special problem of Graphics.

Cayley's definition of Metrics in the first Article of Chapter the First of Salmon's *Higher Plane Curves* [Caley 1879], which chapter was contributed to the second

---

4 [Six ms pages are omitted.]

edition by Cayley, is the only scientific definition of Metrics,—the only definition which goes down to the substance of the theorems and does not stop at their dress. To say that a Metrical theorem is one which relates to measure is to consider merely the form of expression. The true definition is that a Metrical theorem is one whose truth depends upon the special characters of the Absolute. Space is that Place which includes all Places. The Absolute Place is the limit, or superficies, of Space, and as the limit of Space is not in Space. It is, therefore, the Place which is not among the collection of all Places. It is the impossible Place which it is necessary to consider in order to comprehend the metrical properties of Space. I use the word *metron* to denote a rigid body filling all Space and capable of motion like a rigid body interpenetrating all other bodies without resistance. There is a ~~surface~~ superficial film of this Metron which moves in its surface but no part of which ever leaves that surface and no other part of the metron ever can reach that surface. ~~In Euclidean~~ This surface is a real or imaginary surface of the second order. You may call it a sphere without loss of generality, or you may equally call it a *plumus* or *pyrgus*, meaning a one sheeted hyperboloid. In Euclidean geometry it degenerates to two coincident places connected with each other only along an imaginary circle. This is a different idea from the *metron*, but like that it is a *definite individual object*.

As for Graphics, Sylvester picks out a single proposition and declares, with his characteristic emphasis, that it is altogether non-quantitative. Yes, particular propositions may be so regarded; but as a whole, this branch of geometry is exclusively quantitative. Only instead of using fractional and surd quantities like Metrics, it confines its quantity to integers. It is in fact identical with the enumerative geometry of Hermann Schubert [1879], whose *Kalkül der abzählen den Geometrie* is specially interesting to the logician on account of its resemblance to Boole's algebra of logic. This deserves more study than it has received. The barycentric calculus also which may be based on a network derived from 5 arbitrarily taken points in space (no 4 being complanar) is also pure Graphics and covers the whole of Graphics in its cumbrous fashion.

Topics is equally quantitative throughout. We may say so with confidence although only one department of the subject has ever yet been brought to light. More may be hoped for as the ultimate fruit of Kempe's studies in the logic of relations [Kempe 1887]. The part that is known is the doctrine of the Census, which is developed from a proposition discovered by Descartes. See M. Cantor's *Geschichte*, Vol. II, pp. 683, 684 [1900]. But this was not brought to light until 1860, having been discovered among the papers of Leibniz. There is no reason to suppose that Euler knew anything about it and a particular aspect of the proposition is known as Euler's theorem of 1758. It is proposition 25 of Livre VII of Legendre's *Eléments de géométrie* [1794]. There have been a great many different extensions of this theorem; but the only one that has any great importance is by J. B. Listing, who was a colleague of Gauss in Göttingen. He published two papers on *Topologische Studien*. One of these in an octavo publication called as well as I remember *Göttingen Studien* [1847], or something like that, the other later on in the quarto *Göttingen Abhandlungen* [1848]. This latter contains the curious and excessively important Theorem of the Census. I have improved it in detail and brought it into harmony with modern ideas (for Listing preceded Riemann with his doctrine of connectivity, and far outdid Riemann, though the latter worked out all he had need of). I have also added a study of the singularities of places.

This subject is of special interest to the logician on account of the great difficulty mathematicians have found in making it demonstrative. The map-coloring proposition has never yet been satisfactorily proved.

Topics. Part I. Preliminary Considerations. Chapter I. Logic

I do not think that there is any one ultimate analysis of logical relations which, from a purely logical standpoint, excluding all psychological considerations, can be said to be *the* true analysis to the exclusion of all others. I think, on the contrary, as in mathematics an imaginary quantity may equally be defined by its modulus and argument, as $R\partial^{\theta i}$, or by its real and pure imaginary part, as $X + Yi$, where the *number* of the coördinates is alone invariable, so in my opinion when the minimum number relations has been assumed as fundamental, there is absolutely no purely logical criterion to determine which set is simpler than all others. This appears to me evident.

My system of existential graphs is, I hold, as good an analysis as any, and is the *only* satisfactory analysis that I have seen, except one substantially the same given by myself. In existential graphs, we have the following signs: First, a sheet upon which every proposition *scribed* (so I say, since the symbols used may not be written rather than drawn), is understood to be *asserted*; second, two states of things expressed by propositions scribed simultaneously on the sheet are understood to be *coexistent*; third, a heavy dot scribed upon the sheet, whether alone, or as a part of a heavy line, or attached to a relative term, is understood to assert 'something exists'; fourth, a heavy line, however long or short, is understood to assert the identity of the individuals represented by its points, and that of the corresponding subjects of the propositions upon which it abuts. Thus, Fig. 1

•is a man   •is a king   ⸨is a man
                                is a king

Fig. 1   **Fig. 2**   **Fig. 3**

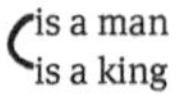

supposed to be on the sheet of assertion, asserts 'Something is a man', Fig. 2 'there is something that is a king', Fig. 3 'there is a man that is a king'. Fifthly, a finely drawn oval on the sheet of assertion denies the truth of what is scribed upon its enclosed area, as a whole; and if a heavy line crosses from the outside to the inside of the oval, or even touches the oval from the inside the effect is that the denial is limited in its application to the individual denoted by the point or points of that

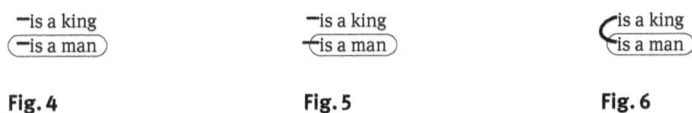

Fig. 4 **Fig. 5** **Fig. 6**

line that reach the oval. Thus Fig. 4 asserts that there is a king and denies that there is any man. Fig. 5 asserts that there is a king and that there is something that is not a man. Fig. 6 there is something that is a king and is identical with

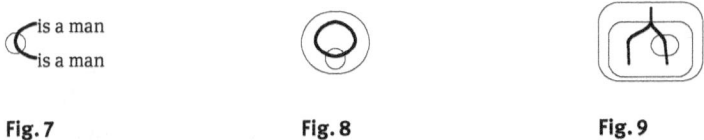

Fig. 7 **Fig. 8** **Fig. 9**

something that is not a man. Fig. 7 asserts that there are more than one man.[5] Fig. 8 asserts that everything is identical with itself. Fig. 9 asserts that everything is identical with something and is other than something.

The system as thus far developed is called the Beta development, the Alpha development being the system without the lines of identity. A Gamma development is required. For example, Fig. 8 does not express the *principle of identity* since it merely asserts, as a fact, that everything is identical with itself. The Beta development is limited to the expression of propositions *de inesse*.

---

5 [Alt.:] [R 507, pages cut out from R 145 notebook] Fig. 7 asserts that there are more than one man. Fig. 8 expresses the principle of identity, as nearly as it can be expressed in the system as thus developed which I call the *Beta* part of the system (the *Alpha* part has no line of identity). The *Gamma* part has been a good deal considered, but has not been settled. The Beta part only expresses propositions *de inesse*. Thus Fig. 8 does not express the principle of identity, but only that nothing exists that is not identical with itself, as a matter of fact. The principle of identity is that nothing could by logical possibility be other than itself. What the Beta part of existential graphs fails to express is Possibility and Necessity. Subjective possibility is simply the character of that which we do not know to be false. But [end]

In order to represent the reasoning of mathematics in all its fullness, two improvements must be made. In the first place the operation of *hypostatic abstraction* must be rendered practicable. This has been the object of jeers since Moliére died in enacting the *recipiendaire* in the 3me Interméde of the *Malade Imaginaire*:

BACHELIERUS. Mihi a docto doctore
    Domandatur causam et rationem quare
        Opium facit dormire.
        A quoi respondeo
        Quia est in eo
        Vertus dormitiva
        Cujus est natura
        Sensus assoupire

CHORUS
Bene, bene, bene, bene respondere.
Dignus, dignus est intrare
In nostro docto corpore.
Bene, bene, respondere.

Nevertheless, this operation of clipping the wings of words, as it may be called, if definite terms are called ἔπεα ἀπτερόεντα and indefinite ἔπεα πτερόεντα 'Solomon is wise'. Here, 'Solomon' is definite in its denotation; 'wise' is indefinite, for it is *a* wise man, *some* wise man, not in itself specifying which among wise men. But change it to 'Solomon is a possessor of something that is wisdom', and though *possessor* is in itself vague, both as to its subject nominative and its genitive, yet *wisdom* is the name of a single quality, a proper name of an *ens rationis*, whatever that may be,—apparently it is something which does not affect the senses but is discovered by thought. I suppose, then, a man is an *ens rationis*,—I mean the man himself, not his carcase. The operation of hypostatic abstraction consists in substituting for any predication that of possessing a quality, or that of standing in a relation. It is so that in mathematics an operation is itself made the subject of operations. The hypostatically abstract quality or relation is necessarily *general*, that is, is not subject to the *principle of excluded middle*. The universe of characters is thereby quite outside the universe of existents.[6]

---

6 [From R 145(s)/96] [...] the inadequacy of this definition appears in its leading to no stronger necessity than that which we know to be true. We certainly have the notion of objective possibility, whether there be such a thing or not. It may be defined as that mode of being which is not subject to the principle of contradiction since if it be *merely* possible that A is B, it is possible that A is not B. Necessity, on the other hand, is that mode of being which is not subject to the *principle of excluded middle*, since it may neither be that A is necessarily B, nor that A is necessarily not B. How can the principle of contradiction fail to apply to anything? By something being held in reserve and not expressed. A man is rich; and yet a man is poor. That may be because you do not say what man. Possibility is that mode of being in which something is held in reserve, so that actuality is not attained. How can the principle of excluded middle fail to apply? By the function

The second needed improvement is that there should be some way of expressing *collective* wholes. From a collective assertion one can pass to a distributive general, provided the collective assertion were universal. The reverse transformations can be effected under certain conditions. The collection of Spaniards is an adorer of the whole collection of women, provided every Spaniard adores a woman and every woman is adored by a Spaniard. That every Spaniard adores a woman shows that all Spaniards are adorers of *women*, but not that all Spaniards are adorers of *a woman*. It is sometimes desirable to speak of a collection of Spaniards, and at

---

of determination being given over to the person addressed. It is not true that *any* man you please is rich nor is it true that any man you please is poor. That is because you have surrendered to another person your right to say what you are talking about. Necessity is that mode of being the determination of which does not lie with the subject of being.

Another thing which the Gamma part of existential graphs, or some subsequent part, must enable us to express is *hypostatic abstraction*. *Abstraction* names two wholly different operations. One of them consists in supposing some feature of the fact to be absent, or at least leaving it out of account. I call that *prescissive abstraction*. The other changes 'This man is shy' to 'This man is affected with shyness'. It may be called clipping the wings of words provided we call these words in a sentence which show us upon what our attention is to rest because something is about to be said of that, the ἔπεα ἀπτερόεντα and those words which say something of these subjects the ἔπεα ἀπτερόεντα. In non-prosaic language it changes a predicate into a subject (extending the term subject beyond the subject nominative to the subject accusative and subject dative,—in short, to what are called the direct and indirect *objects* of the verb). "The rose smells very sweetly" is by hypostatic abstraction converted into "The rose possesses a delightful perfume". So "Cain killed Abel" is changed to "Cain caused the death of Abel". Perfume and death are *hypostatical abstractions*. They denote *entia rationis*, whatever that may mean. They are predicates; namely, qualities, dyadic relations, triadic relations, etc. Logically simple predicates are easily shown to be necessarily of one of these three kinds. For a tetradic relation between A, B, C, and D may be regarded as a triadic relation between A, B, and a combination of these, which combination is in a triadic relation to C and D. It is impossible to analyze a triadic relation in this way, because *combination* is essentially a triadic relation or combination of such relations.

The difficulty of representing a hypostatic abstraction in existential graphs (which I trust may be conquered eventually) is that what suggests itself is to distinguish individuals regarded as determinate in every respect, so that the principle of excluded middle applies to them, by (for example) using a different colored ink say red from that say blue used in scribing predicates such as 'is wise'. But then the dot which denotes 'something', should be red while the continuous line which has a dot at even part of it should be blue. Perhaps the remedy would be to make this line *purple*.

Solomon———is wise   [P.H.:]

But when the operation of hypostatic abstraction is performed, the proposition takes the form 'Solomon *possesses wisdom*' or 'Solomon is possessor of wisdom'. I must interpose a special dyadic relative between two parts of the line, as well as changing the color of 'is wise'.

other times, though rarely except in the theory of numbers, to speak of the collection of whatever Spaniards there may be. Usually, a collective is indefinite. It always refers to existents, for possibilities are not units of collections. In the rare cases in which we wish to say, for example, that the number of all Spaniards is divisible by seven, we can say that there is a collection of Spaniards such that there is no exclusive collection of Spaniards which is a collection of seven collections of Spaniards. The collective certainly refers exclusively to what is, not to what might be, and it is best taken as indefinite, like any ordinary class-name, as a Spaniard.

Corresponding to every abstraction, to every predicate is a possible collection but whether or not there actually *is* a collection of say 1001 phoenixes is another question. Such an object may or may not have existential being, like a phoenix.

In short, a collection of indefinite like any ordinary predicate. A collection of 7 phoenixes is of course a different object from a collection of 1001 phoenixes. But the peculiarity is that a collection of 1001 phoenixes not coexistent with a collection of 7 phoenixes is impossible.

Any collection whatever such as the 10th satellite of Saturn, the pillow that smothered Desdemona, and Julius Caesar's crossings of the Rubicon has some character common and peculiar to its members, as De Morgan very simply showed. Kant had stated it as a *regulative* proposition, but it is a constitutive principle.

A collection is an object whose mode of existence is that of an indefinite object, that is not in all respects subject to the *principle of contradiction* whose existence consists in the existence of certain objects, its members, which are such that the existence of none of them consists in the existence of the collection.

A hypostatical abstract is an object whose being consists in the possibility of a predicate and which stands in a peculiar relation, that of being possessed by, to whatever there may be of what that predicate is true.

I have not yet discovered a suitable mode of representing such objects in existential graphs.

Representation, by which I mean the function of a sign in general, is a *combinant*, or *trifile*, relation; since it subsists between the *sign*, the *object* represented, and the *interpretant* or sign of the same object determined by the sign in the mind of the person addressed, or in other field of signification. The object is something external to and independent of the sign which determines in the sign an element corresponding to itself; so that we have to distinguish the quasi-real object from the presented object; or some may say, the external from the internal object. And the external object as it is in itself is to be distinguished from the feature of the external object that is represented. The interpretant is created by the sign; and since the sign *as such* determines the interpretant, it is in some sense represented in the sign, that is, it is called up by the sign while in itself it is acted on by the sign. It is so acted upon as to represent the sign to be a sign of the object. Thus, while the object is bifiss, the interpretant is trifiss or trifissile. It is very easy to distinguish the interpretant as actually acted upon from the interpretant as announced in the sign or as representing the sign to be a sign; but it is not so easy sharply to distinguish these two from each other. In the actual interpretant has to be divided into the actual interpretant in these features in which it is a determination of the field of representation and the actual interpretant in those features in which it is acted on by the sign. The representative interpretant is either the interpretant as the sign designs it to represent the sign to be related to its object, the interpretant as it actually does represent the sign to be related to its object, and the interpretant as it ought to represent the sign to be related to its object. For example, a proposition or other asserting sign, such as a portrait with a legend telling of whom it is a portrait, which I call a dicisign, in itself as asserting, intends its interpretant to represent its immediate or internal object as being really related to its external object[7] so that its representation is determined as a brute compulsory effect of the real state of things;—"brute", I mean, in so far as no reason for it is presented. An argument, on the other hand, intends its representative interpretant to represent its immediate object, not now as a brute effect, but as a *sign* of its external object. The dicisign is accordingly obliged to represent its external object twice over, once (in the subject) to distinguish it in itself from other objects, and

---

7 [Alt.1:] [From R 839] [...] so that its representation is determined as a brute compulsory effect of the real state of things. An argument on the other hand intends its representative interpretant to represent its immediate object not as a brute effect but as a rational sign of its external object. The dicisign is thus obliged to represent its external object twice over, once to distinguish the external object as it is *in itself* from other objects, and again to represent the external object in its represented characters. The argument, on the other hand, is obliged to address the representative interpretant in three ways, first in the premisses, especially in the minor premiss as informing it as a dicisign does, second, in the suggested principle of inference or in the major premiss recalling to present representation the interpretant's own representation of the represented character of the external object, and third as it ought to represent the relation of the previous part of the sign as a sign of the external object.

[Alt.2:] [From R 1575] [...] so that its representation is determined as a brute compulsory effect of the real state of things. An argument on the other hand intends its representative interpretant to represent its immediate object not as a brute effect but as a rational sign of its external object. The dicisign is thus obliged to represent its external object twice over, once to distinguish the external object as it is *in itself* from other objects, and again to represent the external object in its represented characters. The argument, on the other hand, is obliged to address the representative interpretant in three ways, first in the premisses, especially in the minor premiss as informing it, as a dicisign does, second in the suggest principle of its presence as in the major premiss, recalling to present representation the interpretant's own representation of the represented character of the external objects, and third as it ought to represent the relation of the previous part of the sign as a sign of the external object.

again (in the predicate) in its represented characters. The argument is in a similar way obliged to address its representative interpretant in three ways; namely, in the premisses, especially in the minor premiss, as informing it, as a dicisign does, again in the suggested principle of the reasoning, often expressed as the major premiss, to recall to present representation the interpretant's own representation of the represented characters of the external object, and finally, in the conclusion, in an appeal to it to represent how the premisses ought to be interpreted as a sign. Of course, such distinctions might be traced out much further, but I limit myself to the distinctions which are needed in present study.

22 Logical Analysis of some Demonstrations in high Arithmetic

R 253, June 11, 1905. Houghton Library. Though a slightly later production, this item could also be considered as forming the fourth piece in the sub-theme on the philosophy and ethics of notation, of which R 515, R 516 and R 530 are the previous three. This summer he mentions to William James his work on arithmetic (CSP to WJ, July 23; LoF 3), and in the same month proposes to Victoria Welby a new logical schema of abduction (CSP to VW, July 16; LoF 3). Both of these letters were unsent drafts. The present draft is mostly concerned with notational prerequisites of general algebra of logic and EGs, perhaps to fill in the slot left in the book-length draft of *Logical Tracts* written two years previously, which he still might have hoped to find some use for, as it is in its prospective third chapter of the first part concerning existential graphs that we find an unwritten section on "Logical Analysis". Peirce planned to apply the results to the discovery of logical forms of mathematical proofs, including Fermat's and Wilson's famous theorems; a bold statement that he soft-pedals by noting this 20-page piece to have been "written for my eyes solely". This does not make it any less interesting, however, as it is not just a strict continuation of his philosophy of notation project which had started some two decades ago. What we find him doing is a comparison of algebraic and graphical notations which he would wish to help tackle the "most vexed of questions of logic", namely the analysis of the meaning of propositions equipped with the "Peircians", that is, with complex strings of first-order quantifiers.

Preface

It is not my purpose in this paper to study the nature of number in its distinction from other kinds of quantity as I did in the *Am. J. Math.* Vol. IV pp. 85–95 [1881] where I anticipated all the leading results which Dedekind, six years later, made far clearer in his admirably ingenious little book, in which his spirit is that of a mathematician, not a logician, as is conclusively shown by his dissent from Schröder's just criticisms. My purpose here [is] to show in ~~pretty~~ sufficiently strict logical form, just what the demonstrations of Fermat's and Wilson's theorems are, with all that is required to lead up to them; my motive in undertaking the task being to provide myself with examples for use in treating of logic. It is written for my eyes solely, like all my logical papers of the last twenty years.

Logical Introduction

(June 11, 1905.) Since I may, some time, wish to refresh my memory concerning the logical algebra I propose here to use, and may even possibly some time wish to show the paper, I will say what is necessary to understanding the notation which is only imperfectly described in my paper in the *Am. J. Math.* Vol. VII. I wrote out in 1885 a full systematic exposition of the notation and its use; but I did not print it.

Indeed, it was, in effect, refused by the editor of the *Am. J. Math.*, Simon Newcomb, who said he would print it, if I would declare that it was a mathematical paper. That I could not do.

I shall expect the reader to have an understanding of, and indeed some familiarity with, the system of Existential Graphs, and its terminology as given in my *Syllabus* of 1903.

The system of algebraic notation which I shall here use is called Peirce's Universal Algebra of Logic, and is not my Algebra of Dyadic Relations which Schröder chiefly employed in Vol. III of his *Algebra der Logik*. The expression of a proposition in this system consists of two parts, the Boolian and the Peircian. The Boolian expresses a proposition concerning individuals each denoted by a distinct letter called an *index*. These individuals are called the *subjects* both of the proposition expressed by the Boolian and of the other proposition expressed by Boolian and Peircian taken together. In grammar, the designations of them would usually be called either subjects or objects, direct, indirect, or prepositional. But in this system no one of the individuals to which the proposition relates is given that prominence and principal attention which distinguishes the grammatical subject from the objects and other designations of individuals.

The indices are written small and below the line and are attached to letters on the line which express their predicates. Thus, that the individual i is mortal, might be written, m_i; that the individual i loves the individual j, might be written l_{ji}. Though there is no rule about it, I usually place the more prominent index last. That is to say the letters on the line are always taken with the some understanding as to the relations of the individuals expressed by indices; and that understanding is usually such that the more active and prominent of the subjects shall be denoted by the last index. The reason is that for example, if g_{jki} means that the individual i *gives* the individual object k to the individual (though possibly, in a legal sense, the artificial) person j, then g alone will express a triadic relation, g_j a dyadic relation, g_{jk} a non-relative predicate or character. Now, if the giver is the most prominent and active individual in an act of giving, it is the giving of k to j, rather than the being a recipient of k as a gift from i, or than the being given by i to j, that is most prominent of these non-relative characters. This is a matter entirely without importance. Yet it is well enough to make a record of the reason for an arrangement of indices which might seem rather eccentric.

The letters of the Boolian that [are] written on the line are equivalent to the Spot-graphs (*Syllabus*, p. 17, Convention IV, ¶1), of Existential Graphs. The indices are equivalent to the Selectives (*Syllabus*, Convention VI), and the several *places* subjacent to the letters on the line which are suited to indices of the subjects are equivalent to the Hooks of the Spot (*Syllabus*, Convention IV, ¶1). The attachment of an index to a letter on the line fulfills a function of a line of identity.

22 Logical Analysis of some Demonstrations in high Arithmetic (R 253), 1905

The scribing of Graph-replicas together on the same evenly enclosed area is represented in this system by writing the corresponding partial propositions, one after the other, with a heavy dot above the line between them; as $m_i \cdot l_{ij}$, which might mean, "i is a mortal and is loved by j". But if the area is oddly enclosed, the dot is replaced by the sign ⴕ, otherwise drawn thus, ⚭. This sign is a cursive form of Jevons's ·|·. It might be called Aries. It is intended as such as simplification of Euler's diagram a ⚭ b being (a◯b) as shall sufficiently conform to Jevons's precedent to satisfy the ethics of notation. At the same time, it recalls the algebraical *plus* sign, as Jevons intended that form of the sign should do. At the same time it is distinctly a different sign; because the analogy of the logical operation of aggregation to mathematical addition is by no means close. It was different with Boole's use of + in logic; for his operation was not aggregation simply. As for the dot, it is governed by the fact that Boole, the creator of logical algebra, used any sign of multiplication in precisely this sense. This consideration would permit ✕ regarded as a simplification of an Euler diagram, thus (a◯b). But owing to the usage in regard to Klammern (parentheses, brackets, and braces, for which, as far as I am aware, there is no general name in English), it is necessary that the sign for logical composition should be small. Moreover, the dot sufficiently accords with the present prevailing usage to be readily understood by logicians.

The Cut of Existential Graphs serves three distinct purposes. In the first place, it is a sign of negation. In the second place, it serves, more completely and perspicuously, though but a single sign, ~~to replace all~~ the purposes of all parentheses, brackets, braces, etc, which, notwithstanding their diversity, are often found insufficient. In the third place, [it] dispenses with the necessity of having two signs, the dot and the aries, to represent logical combination. The Klammern, which are commonly spoken of in the elementary algebra-books as mere subsidiary signs, are in reality the very heart of algebraic notation. (They were used by Cardan; but according to Moritz Cantor, in their present shape first by Albert Girard in 1629.) They show that the whole of what is written within them is to be subjected to the combination signified by the dot or other sign of combination placed outside. Thus, $(A ⴕ B) \cdot C$ is what would be represented in Existential graphs by (Ⓐ Ⓑ) c, where the inner cuts are required to show that A and B are taken affirmatively. A *vinculum*, however, or *obelus*, a heavy bar over an expression to be negated, is in the Universal Algebra, exactly equivalent to a cut. Thus, $\overline{A} \cdot \overline{B} \cdot C = (A ⴕ B) \cdot C$. So $\overline{A}$ ⚭ B is the same as (Ⓐ Ⓑ) or $\overline{A \cdot B}$.

The Klammern are usually omitted when they would enclose no other sign of combination than a dot.

Thus, $\overline{a} ⴕ b \cdot (c \cdot d ⴕ \overline{e}) ⴕ \overline{f} \cdot g$ means 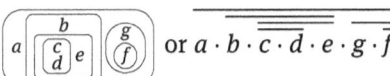 or $a \cdot b \cdot \overline{c \cdot d \cdot e} \cdot g \cdot \overline{f}$.

An obelus below another must never extend beyond the upper one at either end.

The Boolian taken by itself is always ~~an assertion~~ in form, a proposition concerning the individuals designated by the indices. I say, "in form", because, usually, there is no convention as to what individual objects those indices denote; so that the proposition is indefinite in respect to every subject, unless some of the indices happen to be proper names.

It may be remarked that the indices being placed to the right of the letters on the line which refer to the individuals denoted by those indices, since most, if not all, the languages with which most of us are familiar usually put the grammatical subject before its predicate, it is natural to regard the Boolian as proceeding from right to left.

I will now go on to treat of the *Permissions of Transformation of the Boolian*. Any letter on the line, with or without an obelus extending over nothing else, taken in its connexion with its indices, makes up what is called a Simple Term, and expresses a Proposition. (By a Proposition, I do not mean a linguistic expression, nor act of judgment or ~~mental sign~~ an actual psychical sign of any kind, but what I mean is the *intellectual purport* of a symbol which is fitted to *express* evidence and to compel belief; and by the intellectual purport, I mean that possible conditional resolution which most directly, but completely, covers all the possible effects of the sign upon the conduct of the interpreter, so far as they are intended by the utterer of the symbol.) In the Boolian, these propositions are conjoined and otherwise modified by the two ~~signs~~ Conjunctions, as I call them, the dot and the aries, by the Klammern and by the obelus. I will first treat of the Conjunctions taken by themselves. Either of the two Conjunctions establishes, in any Instance (called in the *Syllabus* a *replica*; but the term is not suitable), a relation between the conjungends, or terms conjoined, the same general relation as the Conjunction would, but under a different modification, as is plainly seen in the equivalents in Existential Graphs. This relation is essentially one of equiparance between the members of a collection, which may have any multitude. If I were to write you a letter on the first day of every month for a year, all that I assert in a single letter might (we may suppose so, at any rate) be expressed as a simple term. The total of my assertions would be the compound of all twelve propositions. The composition is the same general relation whether I wrote in each of the twelve solar months or in each of the thirteen lunar months. Owing to the Boolian being written along a line instead of over a surface, as Graphs are scribed, it is necessary to put a separate Instance of the dot between every two consecutive components. But this is an effect of a physical necessity. It is different with continued numerical conjunctions since these represent, at bottom, operations performed by the arithmetician each upon the result of the preceding operation, while logical composition consists in the combined truth, in fact, regardless of what we may opine about it. This relation

22 Logical Analysis of some Demonstrations in high Arithmetic (R 253), 1905

being of the nature of an equiparance, there is no serial order in the facts represented by the conju[n]gends. Hence, $a \cdot b \cdot c \cdot d = a \cdot c \cdot b \cdot d = d \cdot c \cdot b \cdot a$ = etc. and $a \curlyvee b \curlyvee c \curlyvee d \curlyvee e = b \curlyvee d \curlyvee a \curlyvee c \curlyvee e = c \curlyvee a \curlyvee d \curlyvee b \curlyvee e = d \curlyvee c \curlyvee b \curlyvee a \curlyvee e$.

This equiparance involves the *Commutative Principle* as an immediate consequence.

It does not involve the Associative Principle; but the *Associative Principle* follows from the fact that the Conjunction merely unites the Conjungends, without modifying them.

A person not familiar with existential graphs might see clearly enough the force of this reasoning as to Composition but not clearly as to Aggregation, which he would naturally suppose to be another relation altogether, if properly speaking, a relation at all. But such a person will see that since $x \curlyvee y = \overline{\overline{x} \cdot \overline{y}}$ and since $\overline{x} \cdot \overline{y} = \overline{y} \cdot \overline{x}$, $x \infty y = y \infty x$; and that since $(x \infty y) \curlyvee z = \overline{(\overline{x} \cdot \overline{y}) \cdot \overline{z}}$, and since $(\overline{x} \cdot \overline{y}) \cdot \overline{z} = \overline{x} \cdot (\overline{y} \cdot \overline{z})$, it follows that $(x \infty y) \curlyvee z = x \infty (y \curlyvee z)$. And not only are the associative and commutative principles rendered evident by the purely junctional character of the conjunctions, but, what is not the same thing, the absolute independence of the conjuncts of the order and association of the conjungends, *whatever their multitude*, which is not true for arithmetical addition or multiplication.

There is another kind of mixed associativeness which gives a permission of transformation to be noticed below.

By a *term* of the Boolian is meant, *not* an aggregant of it by any part of it which neither separates indices from their letters on the line, nor, if it contains a part of what is outside of a Klammer, contains a part of what is within unless it contains the Klammer with all that is within it. The *Rule of Omission*, in the form which it takes in the Universal Algebra of Logic, is that *Any component of any term of the Boolian can be struck out, provided some component remain,*—a rule first given by O. C. [sic., H.] Mitchell. The correlative *Rule of Insertion* is that *Any term may have any term ~~conjoined~~ inserted as an integrant part of it.* Perhaps this had likewise never been stated before O. C. [sic., H.] Mitchell. The validity of the Rule of Omission is evident from the nature of composition. There can be no falsity in non-assertion; for falsity is the assertion of something not wholly true. Now in order that there should be room for omission, you must already have made two assertions. The omission consists in not insisting upon one of them in repeating the rest of what you said. But the Rule of Insertion, though I enunciate it by the side of its mate, is by no means so obvious, but depends upon the principle of ~~negation~~ contraposition.

The principle of contraposition is that if ~~an assertion~~ a possible affirmation, A, could, were it made, be transformed into another affirmation, B, without danger of introducing any falsity, then, were B to be denied, this denial could equally be transformed into the denial of A, without danger of introducing any falsity. This is obviously true; but in my profound paper of April, 1867, "On the Classification of Arguments", of which no logician of my time has been adept enough [to] comprehend the importance, I analyzed this principle, or rather recognized in two different analyses of it two constituents which, though simpler, are not so obvious. This was, in my own judgment, a remarkably subtle piece of work, considering that, at that time, I was unacquainted with the Logic of Relations (as is shown in my §7 on "mathematical syllogisms") with the aid of which the doctrine becomes more easily intelligible.

In order to state it in this way, I must somewhat anticipate the treatment of the Peircian. Namely, if R_x, though written as a simple term, be understood as any proposition concerning an individual designated as x (in the full expression of which x may occur more than once), then the two expressions $\Sigma_x R_x$ and $\Pi_x R_x$ will alike result from conjunctions of a series of propositions $R_1, R_2, R_3, R_4, \ldots R_{100\,000\,000\,000}$, etc. $\ldots R_\infty$ necessarily concerning all the individuals of the universe, such that

$\Pi_x R_x \;=\; R_1 \cdot R_2 \cdot R_3 \cdot R_4 \cdot R_5 \cdot R_6 \cdot R_7 \cdot$ etc. asserting R of *every* individual

$\Sigma_x R_x \;=\; R_1 \mathbin{\text{\textpsi}} R_2 \mathbin{\text{\textpsi}} R_3 \mathbin{\text{\textpsi}} R_4 \mathbin{\text{\textpsi}} R_5 \mathbin{\text{\textpsi}}$ etc. asserting R of *some* individual object

It must also be explained that the symbol $\prec$ is taken in such a sense that $A \prec B$ means that if A is true, B is true; so that, in case A and B have no generality, but relate exclusively to individual subjects and facts, $A \prec B$ is the same as to say that either A is false or B is true. Now the four direct moods of the first figure of syllogism, as applied to relative terms, are as shown on the next page.

The moods of the Second Figure may be derived from those of the First by contraposition; that is, by interchanging the minor premiss and conclusion and precisely denying both each, as on p. 21. But they may equally be derived by merely changing the consequents, as on p. 22.[1]

---

1 [R 253 ends at the following page (ms p. 20). Manuscript pages 21 and 22 are not extant.]

First Figure *Barbara*

$$\Pi_a M_a \prec \Sigma_b k_{ab} \cdot b$$
$$\Pi_c l_{cd} \psi S_c \prec \Sigma_d M_d$$
$$\therefore \Pi_c l_{cd} \psi S_c \prec \Sigma_b k_{db} \cdot P_b$$

Celarent

$$\Pi_a M_a \prec \Pi_b k_{ab} \infty P_b$$
$$\Pi_c l_{cd} \infty S_c \prec \Sigma_d M_d$$
$$\therefore \Pi_c l_{cd} \infty S_c \prec \Pi_b k_{db} \infty P_b$$

Darii

$$\Pi_a M_a \prec \Sigma_b k_{ab} \cdot P_b$$
$$\Sigma_c l_{cd} \cdot S_c \prec \Sigma_d M_d$$
$$\therefore \Sigma_c l_{cd} \cdot S_c \prec \Sigma_b k_{ab} \cdot P_b$$

Ferio

$$\Pi_a M_a \prec \Pi_b k_{ab} \infty P_b$$
$$\Sigma_c l_{cd} \cdot S_d \prec \Sigma_d M_d$$
$$\therefore \Sigma_c l_{cd} \cdot S_d \prec \Pi_b k_{db} \infty P_b$$

[end]

23 A New Deduction of the Properties of Positive Integers

R 70(s), August 9, 1906. Houghton Library. In this Harvard Cooperative notebook 'night study' Peirce presents a definition of properties of positive integers by the Peano axioms of natural numbers, defining (i) the two-place successor function (namely that each positive integer N has a successor S(N)), (ii) that successor to be unique, and that zero is not a successor of any positive integer, and (iii) the principle of finite induction. He then derives further axioms such as that being a successor of two positive integers implies the identity of those integers, and the property that 0 is the only integer (natural number) not a successor of any integer, among other things. What is distinctive about the present piece is of course the definition of these axioms and the derived properties in the language of Beta graphs.

Defining Propositions of Integers

August 9, 1906. 0:30am.

A definition is a composite term which can be truly affirmed *per se primo modo* of its definitum and its definitum of it.

The Definitum predicated of the Definitum.

There is a certain dyadic relation 'being S to' (*secundum*, next after).

1. Given any integer X, there is an integer I, such that I is S to X (I write N for integer):
2. Whatever appellative U may be, if Every U is an integer, then Some U is not S to any U:

   There is a certain integer, 0 (zero), which is not S to any integer: 0⊸S—N⟩
   This is only a definition since it follows from 2. that
3. Whatever predicate V may be
   - either 0 (a certain integer which is not S to any integer) is not V, or
   - Every integer is V, or

– Some integer, I, such that no integer that is S to it is V is itself V. (And if every N that is V has an S that is V then Every N is V.)[1]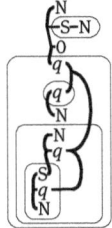

I do not know whether these premisses are sufficient or not.

It is easily shown that no integer comes next after itself. For we have only to make the U of Premiss 2, any simple integer.

That is, in the graph, —*q*— is to be replaced by ⟩-N. Then (N over N) disappears and the whole becomes (S^N).

In the same way it can be shown that no two integers can be reciprocally S to each other. In the graph —*q*⟨ is to be replaced by (N/A over N/B) . The (-N) (-N over -N) disappears as before. The two outer ovals collapse and we get (N/A over N/B over N/A over N/B) i.e. Something which is either integer A or integer B is not next after anything that is either integer A or integer B.

It is obvious that the same premiss renders impossible any cycle of integers each S to the next one of the cycle. There is some difficulty in expressing this, not owing to any imperfection of the system but simply because in order to express my meaning in this system it is necessary to know just what that meaning is, and

---

1 [From R 1575] 1. Every number has a different number next after it that is next after no other number. 2. There is a number, 0, that is next after no number. 3. Whatever is true of 0 and if true of any number is true of some number that comes next after it, is true of every number. It is not true that there is a property possessed by 0 and by any number either unpossessed or possessed by some P to it and yet unpossessed by a number

it is some trouble to analyze the idea of a number of objects forming a single cycle. I shall not here attempt it.

There is no difficulty in proving from Premiss 3 that there is no other integer but 0 which is not S (next after) any integer. For we have only to make V mean 'either 0 or S to some N' when the three alternatives of that premiss become as follows:

- Either 0 (an N not S to any N) is neither 0 nor is S to any N; which is absurd, or
- Every N is either 0 or is S to some N, or
- Some N, such that no N that is S to it is either 0 or S to every N is itself either 0 or is S to some N. Also absurd.

The second alternative being alone not absurd must be the truth.

It can also be proved from Premiss 3 that every integer except 0 is the sole S to some integer. I will prove it by a reduction *ad absurdum*.

We will start then from the hypothesis that there is a certain integer B such that every integer to which it is S has some other integer, not B, likewise S to it.

Now in the three alternatives of Premiss 3 we will opt for V, which may be any predicate we choose, 'not B' which will make all three alternatives contrary to the hypothesis, thus:

- Either 0 is B (which cannot be since B is supposed to be S to several integers and 0 is S to none), or
- No integer is B (directly contrary to hypothesis), or
- Some integer such that every integer that is S to it is B, is not itself B. (But of such integer B would be the sole S contrary to hypothesis.)

Hence it cannot be that any integer is only one among two or more that are S to each integer of which it is S.

It cannot be that any integer is either non-S or is one of several S's to each integer.

I do not feel confident that no more can be done with these premisses. Still, it is pretty clear that they are insufficient. Perhaps I might provisionally take these:

4. No integer is S to two different integers: $\left(\begin{smallmatrix}S & N\\ N & \bigcirc\\ S & N\end{smallmatrix}\right)$.
5. Given any two integers, P and R, there is a class of integers, the W, to which those integers belong and there is one of them, say P, to which no W is S, while the other, R, is S to no W; and every other W is S to a W and has a W that is S to it.

6. Given any one integer, K, all the integers of which none is of such a nature that K is S to none of them and that if any integer belongs to this class so does any S to it, are capable of being separately specified.

What this ill-expressed 6 seems to mean is that taking that class of integers which includes a given integer K and every integer which is S to one of this class but which embraces none which this rule and the S-relations of integers does not necessitate its belonging to the class, then the integers that do not belong to the class are such that if there is a relation R such that every integer not belonging to the class is R to some other not belonging to the class and is uniquely so then to every integer not of this class some one is R.[2]

Let that integer which is the unique S of any integer be termed a P of that integer.

And let any integer which is a unique S of any integer that is termed a P of a third integer be likewise termed a P of that integer.

And let no integer be termed a P of another unless relations of S among integers together with the above rules necessitate its being a P to that integer.

According to the idea which governs the present attempt to improve upon the method of deducing the properties of integers (of which whole idea I have some doubts), (Alas! I cannot twice in a month get a chance to write an entire page without interruption; and the interruption is always of an agitating nature. What wonder I grow old!) I must endeavour particularly to provide a foundation for the proposition that no integer is S to two integers—or is sole S to two. Now this, as it seems to me, depends essentially on the fact that there would not be enough to go round if a number were allowed to have two numbers from which it was derived by being S to them. In other words it depends upon *finiteness* in some way. Now finiteness of multitude is that peculiarity of the class of Hottentots required to render this as valid deduction:

Every Hottentot kills a Hottentot
No Hottentot is killed by more than one Hottentot
∴ Every Hottentot is killed by a Hottentot.

This is a case of the general syllogism

Every A is R to at least m different A's
No A is R'd by more than n different A's
∴ [end]

---

[2] [This paragraph is inscribed on the verso leaf.]

August 12, 1906. I think I have found the (Bad interruption) secret of the matter. In the first place *if necessary* but I don't believe it will be, the first premiss may receive the addition that the S is S of no other integer.

I doubt if I have made sufficient use of Premiss 2, which perhaps might be enlarged.

Finally Premiss 3 should be treated in this way. That taking any integer K, let the "extensions" of K comprise K and every integer S to K of S to any extension of K (call any such extension EK) and in the original premiss instead of S put S_K meaning 'S provided it be not the integer K' and let all such integers be called the pre-K's, and then the assertion should be that every integer is either a pre-K or an extension of K (call any such extension FK);—either EK or FK.

To get the simple premiss put K = 0, then the FK obviously doesn't exist (Bad interruption), and consequently all integers are EK.

I begin afresh, then. In order to define integers, I first define (or partially define) two or three relatives S, F.

S is either a dyadic or a triadic relative. When it is dyadic some integer may perhaps be S to an integer. I say no more. When it is triadic an integer is S_K of an integer L if the former be not any integer called K and if it be S of the integer L. But if it be either K or not S of L it is not S_K of L.

(Long interruption.)

F is a triadic relative. Whatever predicates X and Y may be (Bad interruption.) No Y is $F_Y X$. Every X not Y is $F_Y X$ and every integer is either not S_Y to any integer that is $F_Y X$ or it is $F_X X$ and whatever predicate Z may be, if X is Z, and if for whatever integer that is both Z and $F_Y X$ whatever integer that is S_Y to it is Z, then whatever integer is $F_Y X$ is Z.

For if rational animal is the definition of man, I say

Every man is rational

Every man is animal

and then

Every rational animal is a man.

But instead of this I can say, let U be what predicate it may.

If every rational animal be U then Every man is U.

(Put U = rational animal and you will see what this comes to.)

(Interruption.) The last is a strange piece of nonsense for me to set down even with a sick headache (Interruption.) According to the *dictum de omni*, to say that every rational animal is a man is to say that if anything is a rational animal it is a man or if anything is not a man it is not a rational animal or if every man is U every rational animal is U. I have the cart before the horse.

The integers that are $F_Y X$ are all those integers and only those of each of which is true every ~~character~~ predicate which is at once true of X and is true if of any integer that is $F_Y X$ then also of some integer which is S to that integer unless Y is S to it. [end]

24 A Contribution to the Amazes of Mathematics

R 201, summer 1907. Houghton Library. The three-part publication of "Amazing Mazes", which appeared in 1908–1909 in *The Monist*, was Peirce's testimony to his career as a publishing academic, as well as an unfulfilled and somewhat derailed finale to his ambitious series during the unforgiving years of 1904–1908. The "Amazing Mazes" papers arose from some 750 draft sheets he worked on during summer 1907, probably soon after his return to Arisbe in July from Cambridge. The present selection of 40 manuscript pages from R 201 begins with the definition of the cyclic systems at the ms page 75; overall the segment below complements the material found in NEM III(1) (pp. 555–622) and those in the original publications of the series. Peirce's major quest during 1907 was the puzzle of continuity; his argument aimed at showing that the Cantor–Dedekind approach captures only the imperfect or pseudo-continuum, not the true continuum. The draft of the published articles carries the working title of "A Contribution to the Amazes of Mathematics" and it is intended to bring forth a few additional glimpses into that quest. Those include the role of non-mechanical, or as Peirce's choice of the word goes, *theoric inferences* (misspelled in NEM p. 622 as "*theoretic* inference"; in his published papers the term is the "theoric *step*") that take place amidst mathematical reasoning and mathematical proofs. He assures the reader that what is meant by the "theoric" is a real mode of inference and not a singular creative step, element or moment encountered in the course of proofs, and that an account of those inferences is best exposed in the language of EGs.

I enunciate the governing principle of succession of numbers in a finite cycle as follows:

– *A cyclical system of numbers is such a system that every number belonging to it stands to some number of it or other in a certain relative capacity,* A, such that, taking any ~~absolute~~ definite predicate whatever, if this predicate is not true of any number of the system without likewise being true of ar least one number of the system that is A'd by that number, then this predicate is true either of all or of none of the numbers of the system.

From this definition of a cyclical system (for so I shall regard it), all the properties of the system necessarily follow, without exception. It is particularly remarkable that it follows from this that the multitude of numbers composing the system is enumerable, or finite; for this, one would say, could only be by a logical mode of inference hitherto unrecognized. The proofs will be indicated below.

The governing principle of succession of the system of *all positive integers* is as follows: *In this system there is a certain relative capacity,* A, in which every number stands to some number, and there is a certain number, 1, to which no number is A; and whatever definite predicate is not true of any number of the system without

24 A Contribution to the Amazes of Mathematics (R 201), 1907

likewise being true of at least one number to which that number is A, is either true of all numbers of the system or is false of 1.

The governing principle of succession of the system of *all real integers* is as follows: *In this system there is a certain relative capacity,* A, in which every number of the system stands to at least one number of the system, while in the converse respect all numbers of the system are alike; and if any definite predicate is not true of any number of the system without at once being true of some number to which it is A, and being true besides of some number that is A to it, then from both these conditions conjointly, but not from either of them alone, it follows that that predicate is true either of all or of none of the numbers of the system. It is remarkable that from this principle, which differs so little from that of a cyclical system, far from following that the multitude of numbers of the system is enumerable, it follows that it is denumeral.

The governing principle of succession of the *Cantorian system of ordinals*, if I rightly understand that system (which I am not quite sure has been logically described by Cantor), is as follows: In this system there is an ordinal, 1, to which none of the ordinals of the system is A_1, where I use A_1 as a relative term, that is, followed by the construction with *to*, to signify a relative character to which that which is denoted by the word or symbol following *to* is correlative; and the character of A_1 is such that every ordinal of the system is A_1 to another. The character subjacent to the A is an ordinal of the [sic., system] here used to distinguish the relative character signified by A_1 from other more or less analogous relative characters which will be signified by A with other ordinals subjacent to it. Moreover, there is a relative term, B_1 (the ordinal subjacent to which is used like that subjacent to A_1) such that if any ordinal, l, is A_1 to an ordinal, m, then l is also B_1 to m; and if m is B_1 to a third ordinal, n, then l is B_1 to n; but no ordinal is B_1 to any other unless this rule determines it to be so. But no ordinal is A_1 to any ordinal that is B_1 to it. The rule of A_1-ness, as I shall call it, is that every ordinal is A_1 to some ordinal that is not B_1 to it. There is, moreover, a relative term, A_2, such that if, by the C_1's, we denote the entire collection of all the ordinals of the system whose existence in it is necessited by the existence of 1, according to the rule of A_1-ness, then the collection of the C_1's is A_2 to an ordinal that is not a C_1. There is, moreover, a relative term, B_2, such that if one ordinal is B_1 or A_2 to another it is always B_2 to that other, which, however, is not B_2 to it; and further any ordinal that is B_2 to another that is B_2 to a third is always B_2 to that third, while that third is not B_2 to it. And calling the C_n's the entire collection of the ordinals whose existence is necessitated by that of 1, according to any part of the principle of succession this collection is always A_2 to an ordinal that is not one of the C_n's; and every C_n is B_2 to this new ordinal, which is not B_2 to any of the C_n's.

It is by no means clear that Cantor's ordinals fulfill the purpose for which they were designed. Schönfeld [sic, Schönflies] positively denies their doing so; and I much doubt it. I have, however, devised a system of ordinals which seems to leave no doubt of the truth of the propositions that Cantor thought he had proved by his own.

Returning, then, to the cyclical systems, I will first give demonstrations of the chief properties that are common to them all; endeavouring to render them logically instructive, by explaining how I am led to take each step.[1] The process of drawing a necessary conclusion is not quite so purely mechanical as the old doctrine of syllogisms would make it to be, where people could talk of *the* conclusion from two premisses, as if but a single conclusion were possible. Were this true, how many propositions would there be in all in cyclical arithmetic, which has at most but two premisses? At the same time, if one gives not only the premisses, but *how many times*, each is to be introduced, what "middle terms" are to be eliminated, and a few other particulars, it is certainly true that a machine would seem to be capable of performing the work; and most treatises on the logic of necessary

---

1 [Alt.:] I now return to the subject of cyclical systems. My definition of such a system may very well be thought queer. I venture, on the contrary, to think that it is the simplest and most straightforward of all possible definitions,—that really are definitions,—of this system. I can imagine somebody asking why I do not say simply that it is a system that returns into itself. My answer would be that that conception is a confused, unanalyzed, and indefinite one. I might be asked why I do not say that the numbers succeeds one another regularly until they reach or exceed the value of the modulus, when the remainder after subtracting from each the highest possible multiple of the modulus is substituted for the number. I answer that that is a highly artificial, not to say false, way of conceiving the system, which has no break in its law of succession, and has, in its pith and marrow, no connection with any system of endless numeration. My definition introduces the relation of A-hood without any complete definition of it. I only say how it enters into every cyclical system; and since these properties are introduced into the *definition* of a cyclical system, it follows that A-hood, or A-age, is only defined as a certain relation that enters, in a described way into some possible collections. But the truth is that, further than that, A-age may be any relations. The "numbers" of a cyclical system are not necessarily those vocables which we are accustomed to call numbers. The days of the week, Sunday, Monday, Tuesday, Wednesday, Thursday, Friday, Saturday, are cyclical numbers; and if we choose to take them in their Ptolemaic planetary, or horary order, Monday, Wednesday, Friday, Sunday, Tuesday, Thursday, Saturday, then Monday becomes A to Wednesday instead of to Tuesday, and so on. In short A-age, or immediate antecedence in a cyclical course, belongs essentially to a given cyclical system.

But, partly that the Reader may be brought to comprehend the real simplicity of my definition of a cyclical system, and partly on account of the logical interest and instruction there is, in the entire universe of conceivable attributes (I begin at the extreme right-hand, and proceed to the left), any one, such that there is a number of the system that does not possess it, while there is a number of the system that does possess it, and while it is possessed by two numbers (though it is not said that they are different) of which it is not true that one is A to the other.

reasoning overlook the chief fact about such reasoning, which is that this process is not the whole of it. The most important part of a demonstration is a step in reasoning of a kind which I call the *theoric inference*. Although I have for a quarter of a century had in mind the importance of systematizing theoric inference, it is only of late that I have begun to do some real work upon it, and what I have done so far is but little. Nevertheless, I am sure that such comments as I can make will be useful to all who have not a natural genius for mathematics, of which I have myself but a small share.

Everybody knows that mathematics, which covers all necessary reasoning, is as far as possible from being purely mechanical work; that it calls for powers of generalization in comparison with which all others are puny, that it requires an imagination which would be poetical were it not so vividly detailed, and above all that it demands invention of the profoundest. There is, therefore, no room to doubt that there is *some* theoric reasoning, something unmechanical, in the business of mathematics. I hope that, before I cease to be useful in this world, I may be able to define better than I now can what the distinctive essence of theoric thought it. I can at present say this much with some confidence. It is the directing of the attention to a sort of object not explicitly referred to in the enunciation of the problem in hand, yet whose properties have a decisive bearing upon that problem. The great work upon which I am ambitious to have my share in breaking ground,—since at my age I can hope for nothing more,—is that of profitably discussing the different categories of possible relationship to different problems of necessary reasoning of that object upon which theoric thought focusses the attention. Not that I am quite so foolish as to anticipate that any cut-and-dry rules can in the least supersede that ἀγξίνοια,—that penetrating glance at a problem that directs the mathematician to the point from which it may be most advantageously viewed,—but that I am fully persuaded that a comprehensive study of all the data that are at our hand will help that faculty to fulfill its office with less random casting about and to develop itself in ways better calculated to that end.

One condition, for example, that has since antiquity been clearly seen to be requisite, is that the theoric thinker should substitute in place of thought through *general terms*, indispensable as these are in carrying rules of procedure in our minds, thought through proper names and other *singular signs*;—that substitution which the algebraist makes when he says, "Let x denote" the unknown quantity. This may be called the *first direction* of theoric thought: it carries us but a very little way, but it carries us, by that little stretch, straight toward our goal. A *second direction*, a pretty vague one, it is true, in its present formulations, is that the idea that theoric thought should endeavour to summon up should be the most concrete and concentrated possible quintessence of the pertinent relation to be thought. I will try to contrive an early example of the application of this rule which may bring its meaning into a light somewhat less dim and reduce the blur upon it. But the present subject is too simple to bring out any but the most prominent features of theoric thought.

I must now hasten to fulfil my promise and establish, as consequences of the above definition of a cyclic system, all the fundamental properties of such systems. For the definition taken by itself may well seem rather queer. But when one finds how simply these properties flow from it, it will be perceived that whatever is strange in the definition arises from the substitution in it for familiar expressions which are used without any exact apprehension of their meaning, of the really simplest relations that those expressions conceal. First of all, however, I will express that definition in the Existential Graphs explained in *The Monist* Vol. XVI, pp. 524–544 (but note the *Errata* in Vol. XVII, p. 160), since to think relations in that system is to think them in a remarkably iconic and theoric form.

I will begin by establishing some simple facts, that we all recognize about cyclical systems; for it is important to show how they follow from the original definition of such a system that I have given above. I will write $-\mathrm{I}$ or $\mathrm{I}-$ or $-\mathrm{I}$ or $\mathrm{I}-$ to express the relation of any thing or object of any kind to any kind of attribute of it. The tail at the right or left shall connect with a sign denoting the thing, while the tail at the top or bottom connects with an abstract sign expressing the attribute. Thus, Fig. 7 asserts "Some man possesses or is a subject of deafness"; that is, "Some man is deaf".

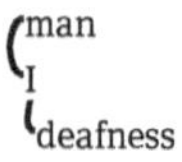

⌠man
⌡I
⌡deafness

Fig. 7

In like manner, I will use the sign $-\mathrm{II}-$ or $-\mathrm{II}-$ to express a dyadic relation, the left-hand tail being joined to the relate, the right-hand tail being joined to the correlate, and the tail at the top or bottom being joined to an abstract expression of the relation. Thus,

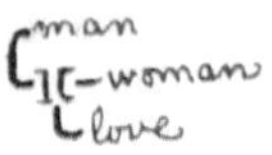

⌠man
⌡I⌡—woman
⌡love

Fig. 8 [P.H.]

will assert that "Some man stands to some woman in the relation of loving her". In like manner, I might employ $-\text{\scriptsize III}\!\!=$ or $-\text{\scriptsize III}\!\!=$ and so on. Then, using $-\text{A}-$ to assert that the number of the system joined to the tail at the left of the A is A to the number joined to the right-hand tail, and adopting for the universe of things considered all the numbers of any one cyclical system, and for the universe of attributes all attributes by whose assertion or denial of such a number anything could ~~conceivably~~ be meant.

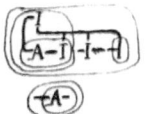

Fig. 9 [P.H.]

I shall scribe Fig. 9 to express the above definition of a cyclic system. Namely, the lower enclosure *denies* that there is a number of the system of which it is *false* that it is A to a number of the system; that is, it asserts that whatever number of the system there may be is A to a number of the system. The upper enclosure (if I make the interpretation begin at the right and proceed left-wards), *denies* that there is, in the whole universe of ~~conceivable~~ attributes to which any meaning can be attached, any which some number of the system does not possess while some number of the system does possess it, and of which, at the same time it is not true that it is possessed by some number of the system that is not A to any number of the system that possesses it. In other words, any predicate whatever that is true of some number of the system and is false of another is true of some number of the system that is A only to numbers of which that predicate is false; or again in other words, if any predicate is of such a nature as to be true of some number among those to which any one number of the system of which it is true is A, then this predicate is either true of all or false of all the numbers of the system. A very obvious transformation of the definition is effected by introducing as a premiss, the logical principle expressed by Fig. [10a], that given any predicate, p, there is a predicate, q, such that whatever individual object i may be, either p is true of i while q is false of it, or else p is false of it and q is true. For anybody who cares to become a master of necessary inference, it will be a rather pretty and very useful exercise to trace out exactly how from the rules of existential graphs and from these premisses the truth of Fig. [10b] follows, that if any predicate is true of one number of a cyclic system but is false of another, then there are two numbers such that of one of them the predicate is true while it is false of every number to which that number is A, while of the other the assertion is false while true of even number to which that number is A.

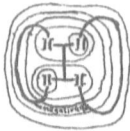

Fig. [10a] [P.H.]

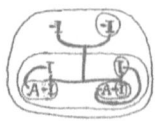

Fig. [10b] [P.H.]

I will now prove that no number of a cyclic system is A to itself except in the case where, the modulus being *one*, there is no other number to which it could be A. (One may, of course, question the propriety of considering a single number as forming a cycle; but whether one does so or not being a matter devoid of all importance, it is certainly not worth while to complicate our definition of a cyclical system in order to exclude that case. Indeed, to do so would be a violation of the principles of sound logical terminology.) The demonstration of this theorem is all but purely *corollarial*, a term which I apply to necessary reasoning such as alone the writers of logic-books seem to be competent to perform, which involves no theoric step whatever.

The only theoric step that will be needed in this consists in the general enunciation, or πρότασις (the *proposition*), of the theorem to be proved, is translated into that form of statement which is called the ἔκθεσις, or *exposition*, where the *general* subjects of the proposition are replaced by *singular* terms, or proper names, each of which, it is explained may be taken as designating any single object the reader may please to which the corresponding general term applies. Euclid, in his *Elements*, hardly ever omits the ecthesis, which, in substance, is indispensable to all theoric reasoning. But I am wrong in saying that absolutely no theoric step [is needed] beyond drawing up the exposition. The theoric step proper, which in Euclid is represented by the κατασκευή, the construction, the part that calls for invention, is here so slight and obvious that I momentarily overlooked it. It here consists in the selection of the particular predicate to which the rule of the definition is to be applied. An assertion in existential graphs is always in ecthetic form. Very well, then; let *l* stand for the proper name of a single number in a single cyclical system, but of any number the reader may choose, in any cyclical system he may choose; and suppose that *l* is A to *l*. Then consider the predicate "is *l*". Since this predicate is true only of this one number, and since this is A to a number of which this same predicate is true, it follows by the definition of a cyclical system, that this predicate, "is this very number, *l*", is true either of none or of all the numbers of the same cyclical system. But by the supposition it is true of one, and so cannot be true of none. Consequently of every number of the system it follows that it is true that it is this very number, *l*. Now if the reader had chosen any other number in the same or any other cyclical system, the same thing would follow, namely, that if it be called *l* (which cannot affect its real characters), then if it be A to itself, every number of the system must be this very number, *l*; or in other words, if any number you or anybody may select from among the numbers of any cyclical system is A to itself, it is the sole number of that system. Q.E.D. Now observe the importance of selecting, for the predicate to which the rule of the definition was to be applied, the *narrowest predicate that would apply*. If I had selected, in place of "is *l*", the predicate "is A to itself", all that would have been proved would have been that every number of a system is A to itself if any one is so. I should not even have proved that the numbers could not, at the same time, be A to other numbers. In all demonstrations care must be taken to make the theoric imagination as characteristic of the case in hand as possible.

I will now introduce a mere *corollary*,—a term, hitherto vague, to which I assign the definite signification of being demonstrable without any *theoric* step, at all. It is that no cyclical system contains another cyclical system as a part of it; for if it did, by the definition of a cyclical system the members of the partial system would either be none or all of the members of the larger system.

I have given the above two propositions in order to illustrate the distinction between *theorems* and *corollaries*, in the definite senses to which I propose to restrict these terms. But now that they have fulfilled that office, both had better be superseded by the following extremely simple theorem.

No cyclical system can contain, as a part (without being the whole), of it, a class of numbers of which every one is A to a number of that same class. For considering the predicate "belongs, or would belong, to that class", it follows from the definition that either all or none of the numbers of the system belong to that class.

This theorem, which I will call the "Simplissimum", obviously covers the two previous propositions as corollaries of it. It likewise so covers most of the other properties of cyclical systems; or, at any rate, will do so with the aid of the theorem which I now proceed to prove. Indeed, after that, but one important property of cyclic systems will remain to be proved.

But that I may even so much as enunciate this new theorem it will be necessary to introduce a term to express a conception that has not been employed in what I have hitherto said of cyclic systems. Namely, if r be any dyadic relative term; so that it has a definite meaning to speak of one thing being r to another; then I shall employ the prefix *trans-* in such a sense that anything, X, is "trans-r" to anything Y, if, and only if, it follows necessarily that X is trans-r to Y, from the two principles that whatever is either r to anything is trans-r to it; and that whatever is *r* to anything that is trans-*r* to anything, is itself trans-*r* to the last. Thus, to say that a woman is trans-child to William the Conqueror means that she is a descendant of that great man. Adopting this conception and his locution, the new theorem is that, in every cyclical system, some number is trans-A to itself, or, as we should usually express it, by passing successively from a number of the system to a number of which it is A (or to a number that is A to it), one may "come round" to some initial number. But this last form of expression being of an only half-defined kind, whose sense is not exactly analyzed, would have been of no use in strict demonstration, until the analysis had been performed, as it now has been in the other phrase. This is a genuine theorem, requiring a quite unmistakable theoric step for its demonstration. Wherever a theoric step, or invention in reasoning, is called for, there are usually several that might be employed; and as commonly happens in the business of invention, the first one upon which one lights almost always turns out, afterwards, to have been most curiously and needlessly complicated, the cause of which circumstance is that the first inventor has not a clear logical view of the whole problem. My plan for demonstrating the proposition to be proved (and mark that the *plan* of a demonstration involves, in some form, the theoric imagination that it is to employ) may, very likely, be subject to this imperfection; but it will answer the purpose. It consists in showing that if the successive A-taking could not come round into itself, then if the process had begun one step later, it would have failed to be probative concerning every number of the system, as the definition of a cyclical system requires that it should be. I carry out this plan in the following way. I will suppose that from among the numbers of any cyclical system, you compose a class of numbers in the following manner. You choose any number of the system arbitrarily as the first member of the class; and after that you add to the class number after number singly, always taking a number to which a number already adopted is A, this number that is A to the new number not being A to any number already taken into the class, and you continue this procedure, either *ad infinitum* or until it is impossible to take a new number according to the rule. Now all I have promised to prove will be proved when I shall have shown that the procedure will *not* continue *ad infinitum* but will stop because you "come round" to a number which is A to the number first arbitrarily chosen. In point of fact, much more than this will have been proved, as we shall see. My plan for proving that there will not be an endless succession of adoptions will be to suppose that having thus formed your class, you begin again and retrace exactly the same steps, except that instead of beginning with the number which you originally took first, you begin with the number that you took second. I shall then show that you must obtain the same class as before, the number you originally took first being, in the repetition, taken last; and yet that if there had been an endless succession this number would, in the repetition, not be taken at all. That both proceedings will give you precisely the same class of numbers follows by applying the definition of cyclical system to the predicate "belongs to the class so formed". For every number of which this is true will, owing to the rule of forming the class be A to a number that will be taken into the class, whence it follows from that definition that every number of the system will be taken into the class, both in the first proceeding and in the second. So as each class consists of all the numbers of the system, the two classes must be identical; and every number that is in one must be in the other. Nevertheless, were there an endless series of adoptions of numbers in the first proceedings, the number originally arbitrarily chosen would not get adopted into the class in the second proceeding. For in your first process of forming your class, at any stage of it subsequent to the first arbitrary choice, let us (as a nonce-expression), term any number there may be such that you are able, according to the rule to adopt as your next accretion to your class a number to which that number is A, an "open" number. Then your next adoption, when you make it, will "close" that number, that is will render it no longer an "open" one, since the rule of formation forbids your adopting into your class a number to which a number is A, that is A to a number already taken into your class. It is true that the adoption will at the same time give you a new "open" number, provided the number you then take in be not A to any number already taken in; but the adoption can give you no more than this one new open number, which is set off by the same adoption having "closed" a number that is A to the new number. Consequently the multitude of "open" numbers can never be increased; and since immediately after your first arbitrary choice, the number then chosen is the only "open" number, it follows that there never can be but one "open" number at any one stage of the proceeding. Hence, at any stage of the proceeding, if the number that was last taken is an "open" number, it is the sole open number; but if it is A to a number that has already been taken into the class, the adoption of it into the class "closes" the last previously taken number without replacing it by a new "open" number, and the proceeding is brought to a close. Consequently, if the proceeding never were brought to a close but went on endlessly, a number A to a number already taken into the class would never be taken into the class. Hence, in your first formation of your class you never take in any number that is A to your first arbitrarily chosen number; and since your second proceeding follows exactly the footsteps of the first (as far as they go), from which it never differs except in beginning with the number that in the first proceeding was taken second, unless it differs from the first in taking numbers after it has taken all the numbers (after the first) that had been taken in the first proceeding, it follows that in the second proceeding no number that is A to the one arbitrarily taken in the first proceeding will ever get taken unless subsequently to all the numbers taken the first time after that first arbitrarily chosen number. But after an endless series of adoptions the rule allows of no number being taken; for it never allows any number to be taken in after the first except after taking the *last* of those previously taken. Now there is no *last* member of an endless succession; and therefore the rule will allow no number to be taken in your second proceeding that was not taken in the first; and thus the number at first arbitrarily chosen will not get taken at all in your second proceeding. But this contradicts the necessary consequence that this second formation of your class includes all the numbers of the system; and hence it cannot be that there is an endless series of adoptions. Q.E.D. The contradiction, however, disappears now that we find that there is no endless series. For, as we shall presently see, in the second proceeding, the first having been brought to an end by the number last adopted into the class being A to the number first arbitrarily chosen, this first arbitrarily chosen number will be adopted before further adoption ceases in accordance with the rule. Along with what I promised to demonstrate, I have now virtually proved two other propositions which now become corollaries to the theorem proved.

- The first of these is that no number of a cyclical system is A to more than one number of the system. For, by the mode of formation of your class, no member of it can be A to two members; and your class comprises all the numbers of the system.
- The second is that for an altogether similar reason to every number of a cyclical system some number of that system is A.

I will now demonstrate that no two numbers of any cyclical system are A to the same number of the system. This is a very simple theorem. Let l be the proper name of any member of the cyclical system to which you choose to apply it. Then since the class you formed embraced all numbers of the system, l must at some time have been adopted into the class; and either in this first or second formation l must have been other than the first member assigned to your class, since there was, each time, but one such member, and that one was changed. Then in one formation of your class (and we need not consider the other), some member of the class, which we may call m, was A to l; and immediately after adopting m into the class, l was adopted into the class.

For take any member, l, and suppose several numbers are each of them A to l. Then form your class starting from l as your first choice and suppose that k is the first of the numbers you take in that is A to l. Then as soon as you have taken in k the formation of the class must stop. For it has been proved that every new number

24 A Contribution to the Amazes of Mathematics (R 201), 1907

taken must be one to which the last previously taken is A. So only one number A to *l* can be taken into your class. Yet all the system belongs to that class. [– – –]²

[pp. 448–451:] I shall now employ the first corollary [that "no member of a cyclical system is A to itself unless it is the only member of the system", pp. 448] to prove that every member of a cyclical system is A'd by some member [the second corollary of R 201 above]. For take any member you please of any such system you please; and I will assign to it the proper name N. If then N is the only member of the system, by the definition N is A to itself. But if there be another member, it is one of which the predicate "is N" is not true, though there is some member, namely N, of which that predicate is true. Consequently, by that first corollary, there must be a member of which it is not true that it is N which is A to nothing of which this is not true. But, by the definition, every member of a cyclic system is A to some member; and therefore that member which is not A to any member of which "is N" is not true, must be true of a member of which "is N" is true, which, by hypothesis, is only N itself; consequently any member of any cyclic system which one may choose to select is A'd by some member, and by another than itself, if there be another. Q.E.D.

Further investigation of the properties of cyclic systems will need a somewhat more recondite theoric step. Certainly, however, I must not convey the idea that I claim to be quite sure of this. As yet, I have not sufficiently studied the methodeutic of theorematic reasoning. I only have an indistinct apprehension of a principle which seems to me to prove what I say; and I must confess that of all logical habits that of confiding in deductions from vague conceptions is quite the most vicious, since it is just such reasonings that to the intellectual rabble are the most convincing; so that the conclusions get woven into the general common-sense so closely, that it at length seems paradoxical and absurd to deny them, and men of "good sense" cling to them long after they have been clearly disproved. However, whether it be absolutely necessary or not, the only way I see, at present, of demonstrating the remaining properties of a cyclic system is to suppose a predicate to be formed by a process which will seem somewhat complicated. I shall not state what this predicate is, but only suppose it to be formed according to a rule; and even this rule will not be exactly stated but only a description of its provisions will be given. I shall suppose that one member of the system is selected by the rule as one of the class of subjects of which the predicate is true, and that the remaining members of this class shall be taken into it from among the members of the system *one by one*, according to the rule that when the member last taken in is not A

---

2 [Next six manuscript pages are missing (ms pp. 102–107); that part is supplied from the published paper (Peirce 1908b, pp. 442–443), following the next insert of pp. 448–451.]

to any member already taken in, one and one only of the members of the system not yet taken in to which that last adopted member is A is to be added to the class; and this new addition may, in the same way. require another. If the system were infinite (as we shall soon see that it cannot be), this might go on endlessly; and so far, we have not seen that this cannot happen. But as soon as it happens that the member last admitted to the class is A to a member already admitted (and consequently that every member admitted to the class is A to an admitted member) the admissions to the class are to be brought to a stop. There are now two supposable cases to be provided for which we shall later find will never occur; but if we did not determine what was to be done if they should (this not being proved impossible) our first proof would involve a *petitio principii*. One is the case in which the finally adopted member is A to a member already having an A that had previously been admitted to the class. The other is the case in which the last (but not necessarily the final) adopted member is not only A'd by the *last previously* adopted member (for the sake of providing which with a member A'd by it, the very last was taken in) but is also A'd by an earlier adopted member. In the latter case, in which the member last adopted, which we may name V, is not only A'd by the last previous one, which we may name U, but is also A'd by a previously adopted member of the class which we may name K, we are to reject from the class all that were admitted after K to U inclusive; so that we revert to what would have been the case, as it might have been, if next after K we had admitted V, to which K is A. We should thus make the class smaller, which we shall soon see could not happen. In the other case, where the last adopted member, which we will name Z, is A to a previously adopted one, which we will name J, which was not the first member adopted into the class, but is A'd by another, which we will name I, we reject from the class both I and all that were adopted previously to I.

After these supposititious rejections, there is no object of which the predicate, "is a member of the class so formed", is true that is not A of any object of which the same predicate is true, and therefore, by the definition so often appealed to, this predicate cannot be both true of a member of the cyclic system and false of another such member. Now it plainly is true of some member, since the first object taken into it as well as every one subsequently taken into it were members of the cyclic system. Therefore, this predicate cannot be false of any member of the cyclic system. In other words, the class so formed includes all the members of the cyclic system. Consequently, there cannot have been any rejections.

Since there were no rejections, the first member adopted must remain a member of the class; and since we have seen in a former corollary that every member of a cyclic system is A'd by a member of the same system, this first adopted member must be A'd by some member of the system, that is, by some member of the class. But by the rule of formation of the class no member of it except the finally adopted one can be A to a previously adopted member. It follows that there must be a finally adopted one; and by the same rule no member of the class except the first was adopted without there being a *last previously adopted member*. It follows that the succession of adoptions cannot, at any part of it, have been endless. This is one of the most difficult theorems that I had to prove.

Moreover, every member of the class is by the mode of formation A to one, and only to one, member of the class; and consequently the same is true of all the members of every cyclic system.

Moreover, every member of the class except the first was only taken in so as to be A'd by the last, or, at any rate, by one member only; and the first adopted member as we have seen is A'd by the finally adopted member. It cannot be A'd by any other, since by the rule of formation, such another would thereby have become the finally adopted member. Hence, no member of a cyclic system is A'd (in the same sense) by any two members of the system; or no two members are A to the same member.[3]

[pp. 442–443:] Owing to my Existential Graphs having been invented in January of 1897 and not published until October, 1906, it slipped my mind to remark when I finally did print a description of it, what any reader of the volume entitled *Studies in Logic by Members of the Johns Hopkins University* (Boston, 1882) might perceive, that in constructing it, I profited by entirely original ideas both of Mrs. [Ladd-Franklin] and Mr. Fabian Franklin, as well as by a careful study of the remarkable work of O. E. [sic., H.] Mitchell, whose early demise the world of exact logic has reason deeply to deplore.

My reason for expressing the definition of a cyclic system in Existential Graphs is that if one learns to think of relations in the forms of those graphs, one gets the most distinct and ecthetically as well as otherwise intellectually, iconic conception of them likely to suggest circumstances of theoric utility, that one can obtain in any way. The aid that the system of graphs thus affords to the process of logical analysis, by virtue of its own analytical purity, is surprisingly great, and reaches further than one would dream. Taught to boys and girls before grammar, to the point of thorough familiarization, it would aid them through all their lives. For there are few important questions that the analysis of ideas does not help to answer. The theoretical value of the graphs, too, depends on this.

Strictly speaking, the term 'definition' has two senses,—Firstly, this term is sometimes quite accurately applied to the composite of characters which are requisite and sufficient to express the signification of the 'definitum,' or predicate defined; [R 201 resumed:] but I will distinguish the definition in that sense by call-

---

3 [This is the first corollary of R 201 above.]

ing it the definition-term. Secondly, it is the double assertion that that composite of characters by any object would be both requisite and sufficient to justify predicating the definition-assertion part. This I will distinguish as the definition. But in the majority of cases, and in our case now, in place of the strict definition, in the latter sense, it suffices simply to predicate the definition, in the former sense, of the definitum, or rather of whatever the definitum may be true of.

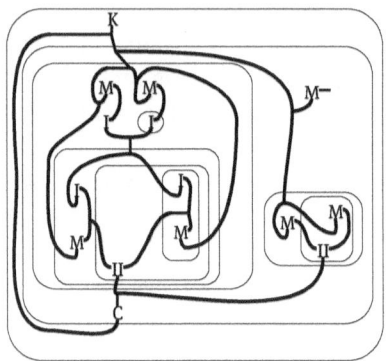

Fig. 11

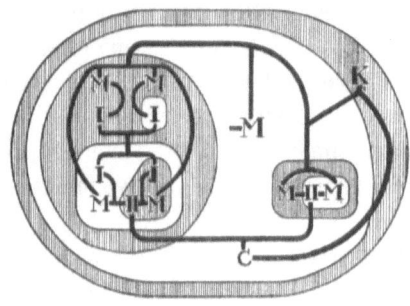

[Fig. 11, from Peirce 1908b, p. 445]

Fig. 11 expresses this.[4]

- ᴋ means that the object denoted by the peg is a cyclic system;
- ᴍ— that the object denoted by the side-peg is a member of the object denoted by the bottom peg.
- ċ means that the object denoted by the top-peg is a state of things involved in the existence of that denoted by the bottom-peg.
- ɪ— means that the object denoted by the bottom peg is true, as a definite predicate, of the object denoted by the side-peg; where by a "definite" predicate, I mean one which, unlike "rather pleasing" is necessarily either quite true or down-right false of each object in the universe.
- —ɪɪ— means that the object denoted by the bottom peg is a recognized relation in which that denoted by the left-hand peg stands to that denoted by the right-hand peg.

---

4 [The innermost cut around the spots I and M in the graph on the left may be Peirce's slip of the pen.]

Then the graph may be read as follows: It is not true that there is any cyclical system, unless (see the upper right-hand part) there be some existing object that is a member of it, and unless it involved a state of things of such a kind that, at the same time is (lower right-hand part) such that there is no member of the system that does not stand to a member of the system in a relation (call it A), which is that state of things, while moreover (left-hand part, beginning at the top), taking any predicate, P, whatsoever, either this is not true of any member of the system, or it is not untrue of any member of the system, or else, if it be both, it is true of a member of the system which stands in the relation A to a member of the system to which the same predicate, P, is untrue.

I will at once call attention to an excellent example of a corollary, in my strict sense of the term, which can be drawn from this definition. For it is a logical principle that every predicate is contradictory of another predicate, which is true of every singular subject of which the former is untrue, and *vice versa*. Consequently, what the definition makes to be true of every predicate must be true of the contradictory predicate and *vice versa*; so that since if any predicate P is neither true of all nor false of all the members of a cyclical system, it follows that it is true of some one member that is A to another of which that predicate is false, then this holding good for every predicate, it holds good for the predicate that is contradictory of P, which can neither be true of all the members, if P is not false of all, not can be false of all if P is not true of all, and hence there must be some member of which this predicate contradictory of P is true, and therefore of which P is false, while this member is A to another of which the predicate contradictory of P is false and P itself is true. Thus, unless a predicate is either true of all the members or false of all there must not only be a member of which it is true but which is A to another of which it is false, but there must further be a member of which this predicate is false but which is A to another of which it is true. Here is an inference drawn by means of a general logical principle without necessary resort to any theoric step. For not even designating the first predicate by the letter P was indispensable. It was only done to avoid confusion of language.

Another remark of a logical nature is this. That member that I have scribed of the pair of propositions making up the definition of a cyclical system declares a certain kind of relation to be *essential* to a cyclical system. That is to say, in order that there should be a cyclical system, there must be such a relation. The other proposition of the pair, the one I have not scribed, which predicates the definition of the definition-term, makes the existence of a relation of that kind among the members of a collection to be *constitutive* of a cyclical system; so that the definition defines at once a cyclical system and the kind of relation which makes a collection to be a cyclical system. Now we have already called one such relation THE relation of "immediate antecedence". But since every such relation is equally constitutive of a cyclical system, it would seem to be equally proper to call every such relation "A relation of immediate antecedence". It is pretty nearly evident, since no essential difference exists between the members of a cyclical system, that is to say, no difference that need be noticed in the definition of the system, that the interchange of any two members, X and Y, in the sense that whatever stands in either of two relations to X stands in the other to Y, and whatever X stands in one of the relations to, Y stands in the other relation to,—it is nearly evident, I say, that such an interchange will result in a new "relation of immediate-antecedence", provided there be two members that can be so interchanged without giving the same relation over again; and therefore it is nearly evident that in a system whose members are somewhat numerous, there must be a great multitude of such relations. In their relation to the essence, or definition, of a cyclical system, they all stand quite on a par. It is therefore a very narrow and unphilosophical view to bind down the "immediate antecedence" of a cyclical system to that particular kind of immediate antecedence which is found in the system of all positive integers and in the system of all real integers. The members of a cyclical system are not essentially numbers at all; for a certain single order of succession is essential to numbers but is not essential to the members of a cyclical system. That is to say, they are not *unchangeable* numbers; but we shall comprehend this better when we come to consider cyclical addition, multiplication, etc.

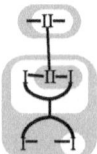   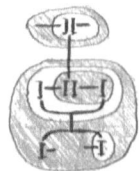

Fig. 12   [P.H.]

[discont., from Peirce 1908b, p. 446: All that we require of the definition may be put into a simpler] shape by omitting the M's, which we can do by regarding our universe of *things* (not of predicates or relations) for the time being as consisting of all the members of one cyclic system. We thus get the graph of Fig. 12, which asserts that there is a relation in which everything (that is to say, every member of any one cyclic system) stands to some one, and that if any definite predicate whatever is true of one and is untrue of one, then it is true of one that is not in that relation to any. The graph obviously quite as well serves as a definition of the relation of A-ness, or immediate antecedence in a cyclic system [end, one page is missing in R 201 (ms p. 117)]

[From Peirce 1908b, p. 452:] A corollary from what has already been proved is that if we regard the definition of Fig. 12 as the definition of A-hood, or cyclical immediate antecedence, then A-hood is not a single relation but is any one of a class of relations which, if the collection of all the members of the system is not very small, is a large class. For taking any two members of the system, and naming them Y and Y, we may form such a relation, that of A′-hood, that whatever is neither Y nor Y, nor is A to Y nor to Y is A′ to whatever is A′d by it, while whatever is A to Y is A′ to Y, whatever is A to Y is A′ to Y, whatever is A′d by Y is A′′d by Y, and whatever is A′d by Y is A′′d by Y; and then A′ will have the same general properties as A. Thus, if the number of members of a cyclic system is m, the number of relations of A-hood is $(m-1)!$ If m be seven, the number of A-relations is 720; etc.

[R 201 resumed (ms p. 118):] [...] true of any to which that member is A; or, in other words the original predicate will be false of some member without being A to any to which that member is false, as well as being (as the definition directly says), true of some member without being A to any member of which it is true.

The second corollary is that if there are many members in any cyclical system there will be not one sole relation only of immediate antecedence but very many such relations. This follows from the purely logical principle given by De Morgan, that any collection of objects whatsoever constitute a general class of which some predicate is universally true that is true of no other object. (A proof of the principle is that "belongs to that collection" is such a predicate.)

25 Logical Critique of the Creed of Religion

R 855–856, plus R 514, R 846; April 1911. Houghton Library. Peirce's another late attempt to bring his ideas on logic and its applications to a book-length fruition is spread over a number of folders (R 846–856) written between January and May. His plan was to write the "Critique" in two parts: one on the theory of logical critic, which concerns the justification and validity of different types of reasoning, and the second part on the application of critic to metaphysical questions concerning religion and faith. In this previously unpublished selection (R 855–856, plus additions from R 514, R 846), Peirce explains at length the abductive mode of reasoning (retroduction). An important part of the task of logical critic was to exhibit a theory of the degree and quality of assurance provided by the three different but interconnected modes, or stages, of reasoning: abduction, deduction and induction. We find pertinent remarks on how retroduction guides us to the grasping of different states of things which facts of the matter alone do not reveal, rendering those surprising facts that we are confronted with "comprehensible", "likely", or "comparatively simple and natural." One of Peirce's accounts of deductive reasoning takes him to the domain of EGs, as it is that mode that gives the highest level of security reasoning can possibly provide, while at the same time being the "language of self-communion" when ordinary language fails to do so. In R 846 Peirce further explains that the logical consequence relation that defines deduction concerns reasoning under general states of affairs, not relations between singular events. Consequently, experimental science does not claim demonstration from single experiments, as it is the general form of relations that scientists are on the lookout for in designing, conducting and interpreting results of their experiments. Multiple variants are collected in the appendix on Peirce's repeated attempts to show the non-existence of modes of reasoning beyond these three.

Contents of Rough Draughts of Logical Critique of Religious Faith

§ 1. The appearance (though doubtful) of contempt of Religious Faith in scientific circles.

§ 2. Intention of this work. Three and only three essentially different kinds of reasoning. *The three kinds defined.* The best proof that there is no fourth kind is inductive.

§ 3. My subject of Logical Critic coupled with facts of human life. This purpose is vague and needs rewriting—that is what the intention is. Earliest conscious knowledge consists in percepts. First impressions of sense. The process of formation of percepts perfectly analogous to reasoning. Yet not reasoning because not *controlled*. It may be objected that reasoning is equally forced upon us. And this will naturally be joined to denial of Free Will. Thus we are brought to the question of whether or not all phenomena are governed by immutable laws. But this had better be postponed until the principles of Critic are settled.

A Logical Criticism of the Articles of Religious Belief

§ 1. I doubt very much whether men who devote their lives to scientific research are in general, or on the average marked with any decided color of opinion upon matters of religion, distinguishable from that of other thoughtful men. For the true scientific man is averse to expressing, and even to entertaining an opinion upon a subject until he knows, of his own experience if possible, something about it worth communicating that others do not know. But we naturally oftener hear in scientific circles disparaging remarks about current religious beliefs than earnest words in support of them; and the result is that there is a pretty widely spread impression that the tendency of scientific work is to produce skepticism, if not disbelief, regarding religion, as distinguished from a deistic philosophy. Now, under these circumstances, having for many years made the precise justification of all the different modes of reasoning, and the different kinds and amounts of confidence to which their conclusions are entitled under different circumstances a chief subject of study I have determined to free myself, as much as possible from all irrational prejudices and to reconsider the grounds of the most important articles of religious belief, and the kinds and degrees of confidence to which those articles are logically entitled.

§ 2. I begin, then, with showing the nature of the justification of the different kinds of reasoning.

There are three, and only three, essentially different kinds of reasoning, which I shall distinguish by the names Deduction, Induction, Retroduction.

By Deduction, or mathematical reasoning, I mean any reasoning which will render its conclusion as certain as its Premisses, however certain these may be. (By the way, although I admit the advantage and truth-of-form of regarding the premisses of a simple reasoning as being two, yet I often find it more to the purpose to regard them as united by an "and" into a single Copulative Proposition, or proposition consisting of two or more propositions all of which it asserts; so to speak of its "premiss", instead of its "premisses".)

By Induction, I mean a reasoning which provisionally concludes something to be true of every member of a collection, or, more frequently, of whatever there *may be* of a definite general kind, for no other reason than that firstly the same thing has been found to be true of a part of that collection, or of a finite collection of things of that kind, and secondly, that the manner in which this partial collection had come to be known to have the character which is concluded to belong to the whole, compels, or at least authorizes, us to regard it, provisionally, approximately, and probably, as an image of that whole.

By Retroduction I mean that kind of reasoning by which, upon finding ourselves confronted by a state of things that, taken by itself, seems almost or quite incomprehensible, or extremely complicated if not very irregular, or at least surprising, we are led to suppose that perhaps there is, in fact, another definite state of things, because, though we do not perceive any unequivocal evidence of it, nor even of a part of it (or independently of such evidence if it does exist), we yet perceive that this supposed state of things would shed a light of reason upon the state of facts with which we are confronted, rendering it comprehensible, likely (if not certain), or comparatively simple and natural.

That these three are the only kinds of reasoning that there are, excepting mixtures of these, I am satisfied by the circumstance that since I first ventured to assert, in 1865, or earlier, I have constantly been on the alert for the fourth kind of reasoning, and yet have never found the least vestige of any; nor has my attention been called to any claim by any other student of his having met with any fourth. In addition, there are some appearances of ways of regarding the matter of reasoning which would render it *evident* that there cannot be any fourth kind. [Alts. 1–4][1] Surely, if there *can* be any fourth, sooner or later there will be; and after that some student of reasoning will have his attention drawn to it. Indeed, every possible form of valid reasoning that is of so general a kind as to be fundamentally unlike every coordinate form, must be capable of being applied [to] all sorts of subjects, or so nearly so that every reasoner of broad mind will be apt to use it, and that being the case, every student of reasoning who pursues his study in a thorough way ought, one would suppose, to have his attention drawn to it within a few hours. When therefore, I review my unwearied and energetic search during half a century for a fourth form of reasoning without the least success, I think myself entitled to presume for the present, that there is no such fourth form. When we consider that logic has been actively studied during two thousand years, this argument appears very strong, even though we make all proper allowance for this science never having been illuminated by the earnest blaze of modern research in all coöperative energy. I, for my part, believe that we shall not have to wait much longer for a satisfactory demonstration that there can be no fourth kind.

§ 3. I proceed, then, to consider the precise kind and degree of justification for each of the three great Types of Reasoning, as well as of those different Classes of Reasoning under each type in each of which the justification of that type is applied in a general way essentially different from the application of it in every other Class of the same type.

The department of logic whose business it is to make this investigation is properly denominated Critic.

---

[1] [Alts. 1–4 branch off here and are given in the appendix.]

I shall find it convenient to begin by considering the justification of Deduction, although this seems to be, in two fundamental respects intermediate between Induction and Retroduction. For true as this seems to me to be yet certainly if we have the justification of Deduction already clearly before our mind's eye, before we approach the questions of the Critic of Induction, which is of a more complicated kind, or that of Retroduction, which is elusive from its very simplicity, its tenuity, or, what I shall say,—its lubricity, not presenting any hold for discussion,—we shall find those problems greatly simplified, and the road of Critic made straight and relatively smooth.

I have defined Deduction as that kind of Reasoning which renders its conclusion as certain as its Premisses, however certain these may be.[2]

---

2 [Alt.:] [...] certain these may be. This means that when assent to the copulate premiss has once been granted one can no longer in consistency admit the possibility of the conclusion being false. Now this is as much as to say that this conclusion has already been in substance asserted in asserting the copulate premiss. To assert a fact is, in substance, to represent it as Real. The fact which the conclusion of a sound Deduction represents to be Real has been so represented, however cryptically, is the copulate premiss.

Various systems for expressing propositions have [been] invented by different logicians in order to detect "fallacies", or faults in Deduction. These are quite distinct from those which have been used by mathematicians in order to facilitate reasoning about quantity,—such as the so-called "Arabic" notation for numbers, algebra, the differential calculus, quaternions, etc.—these all confining their applicability to certain perfectly regular systems of values, and being incapable of much essential improvement. The chief aim of the logicians' systems is to prevent "any" or an equivalent from being used where "some one or other" is called for and *vice versa*. Of these logicians systems, the one that most clearly and fully exhibits the real nature of Deduction is unquestionably the system of *Existential Graphs*, which I shall therefore at once very briefly describe. Fuller descriptions of all the systems with which I am acquainted will be found in an appendix to this volume.

In Existential Graphs, when there is no object in dissecting an assertion, it is expressed by writing or drawing (it is called "scribing" in the lingo of the system) in almost any fashion. Thus, Fig. 1 might be understood to assert (or more commonly, to pretend or make-believe to assert) that it rains.

rains   (rains)

Fig. 1   Fig. 2

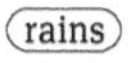

If two or more ~~assertions~~ propositions are separately scribed on the sheet, they are to be understood as, *all* of them, asserted.

If, however, a "Graph", as any expression of a proposition in the system is called, be surrounded by a fine oval line (called a "cut", and not being a "graph", since it does not, in itself

The copulate premiss and the conclusion are *assertions*, using the word "fact" to signify any possible state of things, whether instantaneous or permanent, and whether of the nature of actuality (including an existence) of a possibility, or of a necessity (i.e. an impossibility) and using the word "real" to signify something which is as it is independently of its being so represented in any individual mind or minds, even though it be not independent of *all* that may be in some individual mind or minds,—we may say that the copulate premiss and conclusions in their character of assertions, are signs each of which represents some fact to be Real.

---

express any proposition) so enclosed proposition is to be understood as thereby denied. Thus, Fig. 2 asserts that it does not rain. It will be convenient to say that while a cut is not itself a "graph", yet the cut together with whatever is scribed within it is a "graph"; and in particular is called an "enclosure". Further, the space within the cut is called its "Area", while the surface surrounding it is called the "Place" of the Cut, as well as of the Enclosure.

In conformity with what has been said, Fig. 3 must be understood to assert that it both rains and blows, Fig. 4 that

rains blows	rains (thaws)	(thaw freeze)	(rains (thaws))	(rains) (thaws)	(thunders (has lightened))
Fig. 3	Fig. 4	Fig. 5	Fig. 6	Fig. 7	Fig. 8

it rains but does not thaw; Fig. 5 that it does not both thaw and freeze, i.e. that it either does not thaw or it does not freeze; Fig. 6 that it does not rain without thawing, i.e. that if it rains, it thaws; Fig. 7 that it does not both non-rain and non-thaw, i.e. that it either rains or thaws. So Fig. 8 asserts that it does not thunder without having lightened; i.e. If it thunders, it has lightened.

A heavy dot will denote some individual thing or person or state of things; so that Fig. 9 will assert "somebody is asleep". If the dot is prolonged into a line, it will assert the identity of the individuals denoted by its two extremities. Thus Fig. 10 asserts Somebody talks in his sleep. The heavy line is evidently a Graph: it is evidently a Graph. That is to say, it is so when we say that this same line appears in Fig. 11. But if we regard the lines of Figs. 11 and 10 as different, they are two "Graph-instances". The line of Fig. 12 is not a "Graph-instance", because it is not scribed upon a single area: it is made up of three graph-instances. But the whole is called a single "ligature". Fig. 13 asserts that it is not true that an individual both sleeps and walks and is not a somnambulist: i.e. If anybody both sleeps and walks, he is a somnambulist.

·sleeps	(sleeps talks	(wakes is silent	(sleeps) talks)	(sleeps walks somnabulist)
Fig. 9	Fig. 10	Fig. 11	Fig. 12	Fig. 13

If every fact and part of a fact that the conclusion asserts, i.e. represents to be Real, is equally represented to be Real in the copulate premiss, there the conclusion is as certain as the copulate premiss after they are accepted as true. But if it be not so, and something is represented as Real in the conclusion which is not represented as Real in the premiss, then the acceptance of the truth of the premiss does not oblige a person to admit the truth of the conclusion, and there is no sound Deduction.

There is a method of expressing any assertion—or at least almost any that has a definite meaning and is likely to occur in deductive reasoning, ~~which renders it very easy~~ any so expresses it as to render that, by an almost mechanical process to determine whether a Deduction, however intricate it may be, is justified or not. It is called the *Method of Existential Graphs*; and since it is extremely simple, I will describe it. Let it be fully understood at the outset, however, that I do not say that this method is insusceptible of improvement. I only say that it has more to recommend it than any of the numerous rival methods.

1. If one has occasion to assert anything, without having any occasion to analyze the assertion, one will appropriate a sheet of paper to such assertions, and call it the Phemic Sheet. One side of this is to be called the *recto*, and on that any proposition which is "scribed", that is represented according to this system, is to be regarded as thus having its truth *affirmed*. One way of scribing is simply to write that sentence. Thus, "rains" being written on the recto of the Phemic Sheet will be supposed to declare that it rains.

Notes for my Logical Criticism of Articles of the Christian Creed

[R 846] First of all I must establish, as well as I can, the proposition that all Reasoning is either Deduction, Induction, or Retroduction.

Unfortunately, I am unable to make this as *evident* as would be desirable, although I think there is very little room for doubting it, since in the course of a long life of active study of reasoning, during which I have never met with any argument not of a familiar type without carefully analyzing and studying it, I have constantly since 1860, or 50 years, had this question prominently in mind, and if I had ever met with an argument not of one of these three kinds, I must certainly have perceived it. But I never have found any such kind of argument except Analogy, which, as I have shown, is of a ~~mixed~~ nature,—a mixture of the three recognized kinds. Therefore, it may be taken as substantially certain that I have never in 50 years met with a reasoning of any fourth type. Now I have not been the only man whose attention would have been roused by the appearance of any such reasoning; and if anybody in the civilized world had found such an argument, I should have heard of it.

Now it is of the nature of a genus of reasoning that it applies to any kind of matter in inexhaustible variety. It is therefore very difficult to believe that there is any kind of reasoning that has not been familiarly employed and known by all the world from time immemorial. On the whole, then, I think my negative experience ought to be pretty convincing, inductively.

Though I do not profess to render it, strictly speaking, *evident* that there are but the three types of reasoning, yet it will be interesting to see how nearly I can approach that desideratum.

A sound reasoning justifies us in some kind of belief in the truth of a proposition that in the absence of the reasoning we should not have been so much justified in believing. In reasoning, one is obliged to *think to oneself*. In order to recognize what is needful for doing this it is necessary to recognize, first of all, what "oneself" is. One is not twice in precisely the same mental state. One is *virtually* (i.e. for pertinent purposes, the same as if one were) a somewhat different person, to whom one's present thought has to be communicated. Consequently, one has to express one's thought so that that virtually other person may understand it. One may, with great advantage, however, employ a language, in thinking to oneself, that is free from much explanation that would be needed in explaining oneself to quote a different person. One can establish conventions with oneself, which enable one to express the essence of what [one] has to communicate free from signs that are not essential. For that reason, for example, a mathematician has, in thinking of mathematical subjects an immense advantage. Thus if he has to express to himself a force he will think of $D_t^2 s$, which, he will remember, or can readily see if he should not remember it is the same as $Ds[\frac{1}{2}(D_t s)^2]$. Or he may express the same thing by means of a geometrical diagram, and that in anyone of various forms. In like mathematical fashion Existential Graphs enable me here and there greatly to abridge the labor and increase the exactitude of my thought by putting intricate logical relations into forms that display to me precisely what they involve.

In particular, Existential Graphs shows clearly that all logical relations are compounds of the relation of *consequence, provided we look upon identity as so composed.* But Existential Graphs does *not* so regard identity. That is, it does not assert that to say that the Battle of Waterloo was the final downfall of Napoleon is precisely the same as to say that if the Battle of Waterloo was the final downfall of Napoleon then for Napoleon to lose that battle as completely as he did, necessarily involved his final overthrow, while if he had not so lost that battle, he would not then and these have been finally overthrown.

My reason in constructing the System of Existential Graphs for not allowing such an identity was that no single *actual event* can follow as logically consequent upon any other, since if it be otherwise in the smallest particular, it would be a different event. If in the Battle of Waterloo one man's wound were shifted a hundredth of an inch, or if it had occurred a tenth of a second earlier or later, the Battle would not have been that actual event that did take place; and we never can be in a situation to affirm that underspecified circumstances which did take place must have taken place with such absolute precision; and it is the merest moonshine to claim to know only that if as any describable circumstances had taken place the Battle of Waterloo or any other actual historical event *must* have taken place *precisely* as it did. It is a pretty theory although there are grave objections to its precise truth, but to claim to know it is a pretension that I do not think any soberminded man who sufficiently considers the subject will allow himself to make. It has all the earmarks of the *doctrinaire*, the man who is willing to accept theories as absolutely true. All the difficulties into which metaphysicians contrive to snarl themselves up are traceable to just that doctrinaire disposition. Certainly, I will take care that my system of logic is not inoculated with that easily avoidable but fatal infection.

Therefore, the System of Existential Graphs is so constructed that nothing can be recognized as an apodictic proof that in any circumstances defined in general terms, an event *must* have happened precisely as it did.

But as long as we have to do with general states of things, Existential Graphs analyzes all logical relations into cases of the one relation of *consequence*, that is the relation between one general description of event, A, an antecedent, and another general description of event, C, a consequent, the relation consisting in the fact that whenever A is realized, C will be realized. All known laws of dynamics as well as all other truths consist of such relations.

I will not, therefore, admit that we know anything whatever with *absolute certainty*. It is possible that twice two is not four. For a computer might commit an error in the multiplication of 2 by 2; and whatever might happen once might happen again. Now 2 has never been multiplied by 2 but a finite number of times; and consequently all such multiplications may have been wrong in the same way. It is true that it would be difficult to imagine a greater folly than to attach any serious importance to such a doubt. Still foolish as that would be, its folly would not be so great as to assert that there is some number of repetitions or a multiplication that renders their result, if all agree, absolutely certain. For if this be the case there is some number which is the *least* that is sufficient to produce certainty. Let this number be denoted by N. Then $N - 1$ repetitions of the multiplication do not yield an absolutely certain result, but one more, if it agreed with all the others, will have that result. Consequently a single multiplication will be sufficient to give it *absolute certainty*, that the result is the same, unless some other one of $N - 1$ repetitions should give a different result. Thus disregarding the particular proposition in question one is driven to maintaining that a single experiment (no matter how carelessly performed) is capable of giving us certain knowledge as to the result of any number of experiments. This is sufficient to show that such an assumption is dangerous in the extreme. It is also absurd from various points of view. The only safety is to say that man is incapable of absolute certainty.

But someone will ask me, "Do you, then, really entertain any doubt that twice two is four?" To this I must answer, "No, as well as I can perceive, there is not the slightest real doubt of it in my mind". "But", he will say, "how can that be? You say it is not certain. Ought you not then to entertain a doubt of it"; and if you feel that it ought to be doubted, do you not, *ipso facto*, actually doubt it?" I reply: "Doubt is a certain kind of feeling. It has not only grades of intensity, but also varieties of quality. Now if I were able to modify my state of mind by sufficiently slight tincture of the right kind of doubt, I ought to do so. But if I were to attempt really to feel any doubt at all, I should certainly either feel none at all or else millions upon millions of times too much. For I could not in the least recognize a tincture so small nor even one that should be millions of times too great. If I were to devote my whole life to the useless task of trying to make such slight distinctions in my feelings, I could not come near to the requisite delicacy. My feeling of doubt is one of the coarser of my sensations; and there would be no practical use in making it more delicate than it is; for it is already so far more delicate than that of almost all the persons with whom I converse, that I often find an insufferable difficulty in making them comprehend the slighter grades of my feeling, and there is no practical difference in my conduct whether, say $\frac{3}{8}$ or $\frac{5}{13}$ be the proper degree of doubt about a matter not measurable. It would be a waste of time to adjust my feeling of doubt more accurately, since it neither would have, nor ought to have any effect upon my scientific conduct. Instead of wasting effort on my feeling, I devote my energies to learning more about the subjects concerning which I have any considerable doubts, while very small doubts I neglect until I can reduce the amount of my doubt concerning subjects of greater importance." [End of R 846]

Appendix (Alts. 1–5)

[Alt.1:] [...] *evident* that there *cannot* be any fourth kind. None of these considerations suffices to remove all reasonable doubt; and for that reason I will not attempt to state any of them, since it is precisely because it is difficult to produce in another mind a just estimate of the value of doubtful reasons for holding a given state of things to be *necessary* or *impossible*. But perhaps I may, without impertinence, assert my personal belief, founded upon those imperfect reasons joined to the failure of my fifty-years' ardent search for such argument, that before very long a perfect proof of the impossibility of any fourth kind of reasoning will be discovered. This belief of mine is analogous to, though better founded than the belief that has, in our days, been held by many students of the mathematico-logical doctrine of multitudes, or of "cardinal numbers", that a perfect proof would before very long be discovered of the proposition that if of two collections, that of the A's and that of the B's, it be impossible that every A should be in a given relation to a B to which no other A should be in the same relation, then it must be that there is a relation in which every B stands to an A to which no other B is in the same relation.

For the present, my subject must be Logical Critic, or the doctrine of the nature of the justification for reasonings of each of the three types. Yet since I am to apply this doctrine to determining how far Religious Faith is justified, I shall take care, in my treatment of Critic, not to lose sight of its relations to the main facts of human life, and to that end must bestow a glance upon psychology.

Before a child begins to reason, the only kind of conscious knowledge, or to speak of the language of psychology, the only kind of cognition, that he has is perception. Now although percepts seem to us to be produced immediately by outward objects, there is a mass of facts that show conclusively that this cannot be the case, but that our percepts must be constructed in our minds out of mental materials more directly due to our senses. Psychologists have often called these materials "the first impressions of sense." I will omit the word "first", which involves, as I hold, an unwarranted assumption. Some psychologists have insisted that the process by which the mind constructs Percepts out of Impressions is, strictly speaking, a Reasoning, "Schluss"; while others have denied this. I will not say how the process ought to be classed *psychologically*; for psychology is not my *Fach*, but, from a logical point of view. I am certain that in all its minutest details, so far as they have as yet been brought to light,—saving only one, with its consequences, the process is exactly analogous to the type of reasoning here called Retroduction. But the one exceptional feature of it which forbide my calling it "Reasoning" at all, is that its result is forced upon us, without any appeal for our approbation, and is thus an automatic act, or rather *performance*, of our organism, and not our own free act. Now it is the very essence of Logic to distinguish *good* from *bad* in reasoning, just as ethics distinguishes good from bad conduct, and not merely to distinguish them but to recommend the good to us and to urge us to avoid the bad. This *normative* character of Logic implies that reasoning is our own free act and no mere performance of our organism; and I do not recall that anybody throughout the twenty-two centuries during which Logic has been studied has ever disputed this. There is therefore a great gulf between the formation of a percept and any kind of Reasoning, notwithstanding the minute analogy between the two.

Some readers may be inclined to question this. He may say, "When I read a mathematical demonstration of Lejéune Dirichlet or of Weierstrass, I find it quite impossible not to assent to the conclusion in my own mind; and even in the case of a merely probable reasoning, if it be sound, I cannot help being inclined to the belief that that reasoning supports. Suppose that at a church fair a young lady show me a great sack and assures me that it contained, at the opening of the fair, a thousand little boxes of each of which contains an order for a prize. Among the prizes there are a house and lot, gold watches, and so on down to penny dolls and testaments. I ask the price of a 'grab'; that is, of permission to draw out a box. 'Only a dollar', says she; and I immediately plank a fifty-dollar bill, and proceed to draw fifty boxes, after stirring them all well up, and drawing from all parts of the bag indiscriminately. Having drawn my fifty orders for prizes, I find, on examining them, that I am the happy owner of 39 penny dolls and eleven testaments. Hence I cannot help concluding that the gold watches are few, that about four fifths of the prices are penny dolls and about one fifth of them are testaments, although it may be otherwise and I may have been merely unlucky. But while I admit this, I *cannot help* inclining strongly to a belief that my fifty drawings represent pretty fairly the whole body of prizes." So you ought to see, this reader will continue, that as long as a man thinks logically, there is but one conclusion that he can come to in reasoning; and talk of free-will in reasoning can express nothing but a desire to stick obstinately to preconceived opinions, in spite of Reason.

However, if this Reader is not talking at random, but is expressing a definite and well-considered opinion, he will not stop here, but will go on to attack the doctrine of free-will in morals as well as in reasoning. He will say, "Your actions must precisely represent the necessary effects of your motives upon your character. It is contrary to experience to say that a drunkard when his glass is half way to his mouth is able to put it down and never touch a drop of alcohol. He cannot, because he has not the horror of alcohol that the total abstainer who sits in a corner, watching him, has. Without that horror he can no more act so contrary to his motives, than the abstainer could possibly get up and deliberately intoxicate himself and then go home to beat his wife; or than the young man who wakes up in the middle of the night to find a beautiful woman by his side can refrain from doing just what he will do. Our conduct is governed by our physiology; that is to say, by our impulses and our habits, as certainly and as immutably as the physical universe is governed by the immutable laws of nature; and Free-Will is a mere illusion resulting from our knowledge that we can do as we like. If *can* implies freedom to do what we prefer on the whole *not* to do, we have no such power."

Such a reader strikes me as a candid man, and I am interested in his opinions accordingly. He does not understand what I mean by Free-Will, however, and as for his notion of Nature being exclusively governed by immutable laws, I can only say that it flies in the face of the phenomena, meaning by that it conflicts with what the phenomena appear to show, and with what, if I am not mistaken they are now unanimously understood to show. For consider what a law must be. I distinguish—though perhaps needlessly, *in the present* context,—between a law and an expression of that law; the former being a habit of nature and the latter a form of human statement, and this I may properly, although we cannot conceive of the law except as somehow expressed or expressible. The law itself consists in the invariability with which one kind of fact is realized whenever another kind of fact to which the former has a perfectly definite relation is realized. But there will be various ways of stating this. For example, if a body is attracted to or repelled from another, this law consists in the generality of the character of its motion relative to that other; but this may be expressed in three ways; first, by saying that it always has its motion accelerated along the straight like joining it to that other, second, by saying that its *vis viva* depends on its distance from that other, and third, by saying that it describes areas round that other at a uniform rate.

A law must unite two logical characters that are ordinarily usually opposed: namely, it must be entirely *general*, and yet, at the same time, perfectly *explicit*; and to this end whatever *singular* is referred to in its *consequent* must be indicated and distinguished from every other in its *antecedent*. In order that this may be rendered perfectly clear, I will show its application in two examples. In the first place, then, there may be a law that one body shall have its motion accelerated in a direction either directly towards and directly away from another by an amount depending on its distance from that other and on the mass of the latter. But there can be no law that it shall move in any other direction relatively to that other, unless something be mentioned in the antecedent towards or away from which it shall move. This is obvious.

It follows from this that the operation of a law of nature can never increase the number of independent entities; and accordingly we find that by the laws of dynamics the number of independent constants necessary to describe two systems before they encounter each other can never be increased as a result of their encounter.

It follows that it can never be a result of law that the variety or complexity of the totality of reacting objects should receive any increase or augmentation. But now the telescope shows us apparently nebulae becoming solar systems, the earth inhabited as it now is with a marvelously varied flora and fauna must surely be less simple than it was when it was all a mass of molten metal and slag, the individual animal appears during its growth to become more complex than the original egg from which it has grown, and in the mental world was not the Greek mind far simpler than the modern mind, and is not the way in which good grows out of evil an example of increasing complexity that cannot be attributed to law? To what, then, are such increases of complexity to be attributed?

Remember what revolution happened about A.D. 1800 in scientific opinion. Committee after committee of the most distinguished members of the French Academy of Sciences had reported positively that no stones ever fell from the sky. Scientific prejudice was even more opposed to a belief in that than it ever was to the possibility of human flight. Why, the prejudice was so rooted and so diffused that even an English bishop, though I dare say he was given in the pulpit to thundering against "science falsely so called", chancing to be in Sienna one day when a whole shower of stones fell,—white hot, I suppose,—in a public square in that city, wrote Rome that he had received the testimony of so many and so competent witnesses of the occurrence, that—what? that he was convinced, think you? Oh no, prejudice, especially scientific prejudice, is too strong for that; but that—he "did not know what to think". You know that, nowadays, it is calculated that ten million of these stones fall on the earth's surface every twenty-four hours!

Now nothing has happened during the subsequent century to weaken the force of *scientific prejudice*. Students of logic,—genuine students of reasoning,—have hardly ever been fewer. Here and there, there has been one, Augustus De Morgan and myself,—and no doubt there has been a general increase of self-control, slight yet perceptible, among respectable people during the last two generations, which has made men on the average less obstinate in their prejudices, more ready to listen to reasons for new opinions. On the other hand, however, the average scientist has become far more specialized, and instead of being the man of general and broad culture that he used to be, he is turned into an ignorant fellow, very little, if at all, intellectually higher than an average photographer, outside of his specialty. His peculiar and narrow but deep training has made him a queer mixture of enlightenment and of what is equivalent to superstition. If he happens to be a physiologist, he will very likely be well aware of the dubious nature of that belief which used to be the stock instance of the highest certainty, namely, the belief in his own personal existence; but in spite of the overwhelming reasons for doubting it, the absolute uniformity of the action of the physical universe, will be for him the first article of his faith. It becomes so in his mind because his whole attention is confined to those sequences of phenomena which seem to occur most uniformly. It is these that he is continually on the watch for, while those of a contrary appearance he passes by as insignificant.

(I here break the current of my thought in order to explain a verbal expression that I find convenient. Neither St. Augustine nor Bishop Butler is willing to regard the miracles in which he believes to be really violations of what we, in our days, call the "laws of nature", but which in former days was called "the course of nature". But the conception of a miracle has come so generally to be made synonymous with such a violation of law, that those departures from law, mostly far too minute ever to be detected by us, but in whose occurrence I find reason to believe, I propose to denominate "ultra-miracles".)

There is a logical principle, as I shall show the reader in the proper context, that forbids us to believe any definite occurrence,—this occurrence or that occurrence definitely designated,—to be an "ultra-miracle". But it does not forbid our opinion that there are such occurrences. On the contrary, there may be, and I shall show reason for believing that there is a general law of nature according to which no uniformity in nature ever can be absolutely perfect.

It seems to me that the idea that is stamped upon Nature in all its departments, the moral, the intellectual, that of physical life as revealed [end]

[Alt.2:] [...] evident that there can be no fourth kind. But as nothing that has occurred to me is satisfactory, I pass it over and proceed to consider at once how the three kinds of reasoning are justified and what their chief varieties are.

As for Deduction, the only way in which the truth of one proposition can render that of another *certain* is by the latter not asserting any fact that is not asserted in the former, and this is always the case in legitimate Deduction.

The chief division of Deduction is into the *Necessary* and the *Probable*. Probable Deduction is a Deduction which concludes that a definite state of things has a given Probability because this is substantially asserted in the Copulate Premiss.

In order that this statement may be distinctly understood, it will be requisite that Probability, by which I invariably mean Mathematical Probability, be accurately defined, which, so far as I am aware, has never, hitherto, been correctly done. It will be convenient to begin with defining it in a particular case. What, then, is meant by saying that the Probability that a certain die will, when it is thrown, turn that face of it uppermost that is marked 6? If the die were perfect, the probability would be exactly $\frac{1}{6}$, and we will suppose that some pains have been taken to [sic.] But since it cannot be perfect (or rather, since, although it might quite as well be perfect as have any exact kind and degree of imperfection, yet there is no probability that it *will* be so), what the probability of its turning up six actually is can only be ascertained by Induction. We will suppose, however, that the die has been made as near perfect as it conveniently could be made, so that the probability does not greatly differ from $\frac{1}{6}$. Many books on the doctrine of chances follow Laplace in making Probability consist in a mixture of knowledge and ignorance. But Laplace is only great as a mathematician; while this is a question of logical analysis. I shall completely refute his analysis before I have done. In this place, I will content myself with pointing out that Probability, in the sense in which I employ the term, is the basis of a gigantic business than which no other is more secure, if indeed any other is as secure. Is it credible that such a business is based in any degree upon the ignorance of those who carry it on? It is based upon tables of statistics laboriously compiled. Can one reason from what one does not know? Can one turn one's own ignorance to any account whatever? But when one does not know what will happen in the single case, one can almost always make a good use of *a knowledge of how often, under apparently similar circumstances, a given kind of result* WOULD *occur* IN THE LONG RUN. Now it is, as we shall see, the function of Induction to infer what *would* be from what *has* been; but in order to understand precisely what it is that it teaches us in such a case, we must get a distinct and exact idea of what is meant by "in the long run". Now how often our die will turn up its "six"-side, in a finite number of throws we cannot know *for certain*. We can only know the *probability* of that; and it is no definition of probability to say that it means that something is probable. That would be what is called "a vicious circle" or *circulus in definiendo*. By "the long run" must, then, be understood an *endless* series of objects, or rather of occurrences of objects, everyone taken into the series because it belongs to a given genus, and quite regardless of any other circumstance, and in particular, regardless of what may be the character of any others in the series. In short, the causes that operate to include those that are included in the series, must only be such as always operate. These conditions can only be *inductively*, that is, approximately and provisionally, satisfied.

Now supposing that the particular die in question, instead of turning up its six-side once in six throws, turns it up once in $6 + e$ throws, where e is the small discrepancy, positive or negative, in question. This is in the long run, which, as has been seen must be *infinitely* long, or else we can only say what the character would *probably* be, which will not do when we are defining probability. Now among an infinity of throws there will be an infinity of throws of 6, unless it be a miracle to throw 6, when there *may* be but a finite number.

(Leibniz's doctrine of infinity, which is taught in some of the old text-books on the calculus is illogical and false. The true doctrine is as follows: The smallest *multitude*, or magnitude of a *collection* that is greater than any finite collection may be called "the denumeral multitude", and may be denoted by ∞. Then, if F is a finite multitude, we have $F + \infty = \infty$, and $F \times \infty = \infty$ and $\infty \div F = \infty$ and $\infty^F = \infty$. But $2^\infty = \infty^\infty > \infty$ and $2^{(2^\infty)} > 2^\infty$ and so on, *ad infinitum*. 2^∞ is the multitude of all irrational values possible, while the multitude of "algebraic numbers" or possible roots of algebraic equations is only ∞. I believe it was I who first proved that $2^\infty > \infty$ and in fact that $2^x > x$ if x is any infinity (such as $x = 2^\infty$). I will below give that proof as an illustration of Deduction.) [end]

[Alt.3:] [...] evident that there cannot be any fourth kind. Certainly, if there can be, sooner or later we shall come upon an example of such reasoning. But if that were possible, it would seem that I must have come upon an instance of it in my fifty years of incessant search for such a thing. I am therefore led to believe that there must be some faultless proof that there cannot be any fourth type, although I have not yet found any such.

I proceed, then to consider how the three great types of reasoning are justifiable, and what those of the classes under each Type are, each of which that justification is applied in a way peculiar to itself. This study is properly denominated Logical Critic.

Deduction is the only kind of reasoning which is *apodictic*, that is, which renders its conclusion absolutely certain, provided its premisses are precisely true. It must do this regardless of any other consideration or reason whatsoever. For if any such reason were needed, the reasoning would not be apodictic until that consideration had been taken into account as one of its premisses. On the other hand, it is needless to insert, as a separate premiss, any explanation of the meaning of another premiss, since we do not reason from forms of expression but from the *facts* which the language of the premisses asserts to be real.

It renders the apodictic character of Deduction more obvious to express the same meaning in the same terms throughout the premisses and the conclusion. A single system of expression is particularly useful in case one of the premisses has, unawares, been left unexpressed, since that system will greatly facilitate the discovery of the precise premiss needed. For the purpose of investigating all the forms of deduction such a system is practically indispensable. It is specially valuable, in such research, in pointing the way from the forms that one has already taken into account to others that have been omitted.

The best system yet invented *for these purposes*, which must on no account be confounded with those of a "pasigraphy", is that called "Existential Graphs", which I will at once describe in a simple way. A much more elaborate description of the system will be found in *The Monist*, Vol. XVI pp. 492–546. (Some bad misprints are corrected in the following number of the same journal.)

I will here give the briefest possible account of the system of Existential Graphs. But if the reader is willing to take it upon trust that in all necessary reasoning the fact asserted in the conclusion must have been asserted in [Alt.5] the copulate premiss, then it will not be indispensable that he should acquaint himself with Existential Graphs, although, if he has turn for Logic, he will find the system interesting and instructive. However, since many may prefer to skip the description of this system, I will facilitate their doing so by placing the mark ¶ before each paragraph of this description and at the end of the whole of it.

¶ The word *graph*, now familiar to mathematicians, was introduced into their nomenclature by Clifford, to denote a diagram in which lines running from one spot to another had significations analogous to the lines in chemists' formulations of the structures of organic compounds, where each line running from a symbol of an atom of one element to a symbol of an atom of another (or even of the same) element indicates the neutralization of one unit of valency of each of the two atoms represented.

¶ Now in Logic two entirely unlike methods of diagrammatizing the structure of an assertion are in vogue, one of which is strikingly analogous to a chemical graph, while the other seems to have no resemblance at all to such a diagram.

The latter kind is extremely pretty and represents universal syllogisms charmingly; and when I say "charmingly", I do not refer to the impression it might make on an artist,—a being of wonderfully true perceptions, but no reasoner, or at any rate, no logician, or an anatomist of reasoning, at all; but I mean that it delights the logician. Such diagrams are commonly called "Euler's diagrams"; but Friedrich Albert Lange, in his posthumous *Logische Studien* (in which he attained such an approach to a correct view of the subject, as makes his little book one of those that a serious student must read, though he was unable to push his discoveries far), pointed out Ludovico Vives was the real originator of the system. In this system Fig. 1 asserts that every man

Fig. 1   **Fig. 2**

is mortal; Fig. 2 that no man is mortal. This is beautiful. For here the *existence* of no kind of object is affirmed, Fig. 1 merely denying that there exists any non-mortal man, and Fig. 2 denying that any mortal man exists. But instead of these *denials*, merely, Fig. 1 might be understood as *affirming* the existence of mortals not men, of mortals that are men, and of beings not mortal; and three analogous affirmations might mistakenly be read into Fig. 2. It was therefore a considerable improvement of the system that was made in this system in 1881 by Mr. John Venn in always drawing the circles so as to intersect one another, and *shading* the compartment representing the possible class that he meant to deny. In this way Fig. 3 can only mean "No man is mortal"; Fig. 4, only "No man is immortal"; Fig. 5, only "None but men

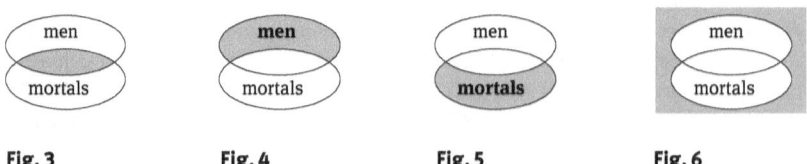

Fig. 3   **Fig. 4**   **Fig. 5**   **Fig. 6**

are mortals"; and Fig. 6, only "Immortals, if there be any, are all men". But it is a curious instance of the failure of logicians to make the most obvious generalizations, that it did not occur to Mr. Venn that he ought to use a second kind of shading or tinting to mark any kind of thing whose existence (or possibility) he meant to affirm. Thus, he might have made Fig. 7 assert that "Some man is mortal"; Fig. 8, that "Some man is immortal"; Fig. 9, that "Something besides men is mortal"; and Fig. 10, that "Something is neither a man nor mortal". But there is another defect of this system that I must confess I see no simple way of remedying

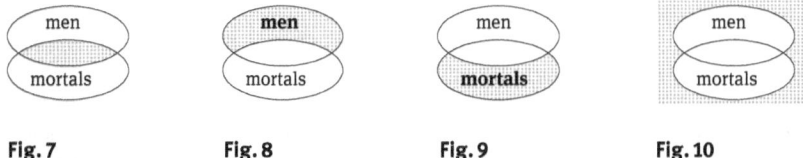

Fig. 7   **Fig. 8**   **Fig. 9**   **Fig. 10**

except by a resort to graphs. Namely, how is one to express either of the following assertions?

There is a man who loves whatever woman there may be.

There is no woman who has not some man who loves her.

The first affirms the existence of a one kind of object such that the existence of another kind of object having a given kind of relation (that of being unloved) to him can be truthfully denied. The second denies the existence of a kind of object of which the existence of a certain relation to another kind of object can be denied.

Now there are kinds of reasoning which depend essentially upon such forms of reasoning as this.

[Alt.4:] [From R 514] [...] evident that there cannot be any fourth kind. Surely, if there can be a fourth, sooner or later some student of reasoning will light upon an example of it. But it would seem that were there any such fourth kind, I must have come upon an instance of it, in the course of my half-century search for such a thing. I might argue, too, that I have not been the only hunter after it; though I must confess that there I have come upon more evidence of the carelessness than of the thoroughness of logicians. However, on the whole, I think myself warranted in believing for the present that we shall one of these days, not distantly future, discover some faultless proof that there can be no fourth type of reasoning.

§ 3. Although my subject is that branch of logic called *Critic*, which studies the precise kind and degree of justification for each possible manner of reasoning, yet in order to couple this justification, conditional as it is upon the hypothesis of our reasoning in the particular way under consideration—to couple it, I say, to real life, it will be requisite to give a glance at some patent facts of human existence. Without this the connexion between logical critic and religious faith would be lost to sight.

Before a child begins to reason, the only kind of conscious knowledge he has is perception. Now percepts are certainly built up out of something; and these somethings are called by the psychologists to whom I am contemporary the *first impressions of sense*. These "first impressions of sense" appear to me to be, in a sense, fictions. In order to explain myself, I resort to a hypothetical simile. Imagine a solid body that is not composed of molecules, atoms, and electrons, or [sic.], but that, on the contrary, is absolutely homogeneous. This body must have some shape; and, for the sake of simplicity, I will suppose this shape to be that of a tetrahedron; that is, of a triangular pyramid. Suppose the lowest point of this tetrahedron to be one of its four vertices. Suppose further, that the tetrahedron continuously moves vertically downward without rotation until it dips into a liquid equally homogeneous having an upper level surface that is plance, and that the motion continues after the solid dips into the liquid. Now after the solid has dipped into the liquid the part of it that is at the level [end]

[Alt.5:] [From R 514] [...] the premises, he may skip the account of the system of Existential Graphs, if he prefers to do so; and to enable him to do this without losing anything else, I will put the sign ¶ at the beginning of every paragraph of the account of it, as well as at the end of the last paragraph of that account. At the same time I will say that even if one is willing to take the writer's word for it that whatever state of things is asserted in a Sound Deductive conclusion to be Real must equally have been asserted to be Real in the premises, still to do so without examination is merely to yield an implicit faith to the writer, without at all ~~understanding~~ or comprehending the truth to which one so asserts.

A proposition expressed in the System of Existential Graphs is usually in part written and in part represented by a diagram that [is] *drawn* rather than *written*. It thus becomes convenient, in describing this system to have a word to mean, "either written, or drawn, or partly written and partly drawn". It will further be convenient, in describing the system, to illustrate what is said [end]

If two or more assertions are scribed on the *recto*, they must be understood as all of them affirmed. Second, on the other hand, if a piece be cut out of the Phemic Sheet and turned the other side up, any assertion scribed on that "verso" side is to be understood as *denied*. Practically we do not go to that trouble but write the assertion to be denied within a fine oval line, which we call a *cut*. Thus ⌒rains⌒ will mean that it does not rain; ⌒rains blows⌒ will mean that it does not both rain and blow; or in other words, it either does not rain or does not blow. One "cut" may be included within another, and the piece of the sheet within the inner cut having been twice reverted, will show its *recto* side, on which affirmations are written. Thus, Fig. 3 will mean that it is not true that it thunders but has not lightened, or, in other words, "If it thunders, it has lightened". An area within an even number of cuts or none at all is said to be "evenly enclosed" and carries affirmations, since it shows the recto side of the Phemic Sheet while an "oddly enclosed" area, or one within any odd number of cuts, shows the "verso side" and carries only *denials*, that is, anything scribed upon it is denied. [end]

26 Assurance through Reasoning

R 670, R 669, May 25–June 17, 1911. Houghton Library. The following text reproduces two manuscripts of the same title, R 670 written on June 7–17, 1911, and its earlier but independently significant discrete version R 669 written from May 25 to June 2, 1911. These two manuscripts may have been drafts of the paper Peirce planned to deliver in the upcoming autumn meeting of the National Academy of Sciences, where he was invited to give two presentations. Manuscripts 669 and 670 are his last (namely the ninth and the tenth) attempt to complete the series of papers on the grounds and rationale of reasoning he had worked on since summer 1910, in view of publishing a collection of his essays on reasoning. They might also be the ones that were to become his contribution to the *Festschrift* in honour of Victoria Welby.

The two versions of "Assurance through Reasoning" present one of Peirce's most successful attempts to explain both the logic of existential graphs and the philosophy of its diagrammatic syntax. The notions of identity, teridentity, composition of graphs, plurality, conditional, scroll, and the derivation of the idea of negation as a consequence of the scroll, all get their fair shares of exposition. Peirce observes that in diagrammatic syntax, logical constants ought to serve both the roles of collectional signs expressing their scope, and the truth function that those constants have in the context of making assertions. He then notes that "there is no reason why a single sign", "as it is seen by the mind's eye", "should not perfectly fulfill both these purposes." Moreover, tinctures are reintroduced to enable logic to assert, among other things, modalities such as necessities and metaphysical possibilities, that call for changes in the nature of the universes of discourse. In the final paragraph of R 669 Peirce observes that his transformation rules "will suffice to enable any valid deduction to be performed", and that even in the presence of such a relatively simple set of rules of transformation, any attempt at an automated or mechanised theorem-proving unaided by a "living intelligence" would fall short of completing the performance of deductive inferential tasks.

Deductive Reasoning

[R 670, June 7–17, 1911] The word "Deduction" will here be used, in a generalized sense, to include any necessary, or mathematical, reasoning,—any reasoning of which the premisses,—or, as they will here often be called, the "Copulate Premiss",—having been asserted, the conclusion cannot consistently be denied by the same assertor. But though all deduction is thus necessary reasoning it will, nevertheless, be convenient to divide deduction into "Necessary Deduction" and "Probable Deduction", the latter expression denoting any deduction concluding that, under stated conditions, a given kind of "Event" would have a stated probability, whether the statement of it be numerically precise or be as vague as it may; while by a Necessary Deduction is to be understood a Deduction which simply reaches the conclusion that a certain state of things would necessarily result from the facts asserted in its copulate premiss without resorting to any calculation of probabilities. Thus, the kind of reasoning herein termed Necessary Deduction is no more necessary reasoning than is Probable Deduction, the reasoning of which, being mathematical, is of course necessary. The designation here applied to the former ought, strictly speaking to be, "deduction which concludes a necessary, or apodictic, conclusion, without the introduction of the concept of probability in the process of deriving that conclusion"; but it is presumed that the indulgent reader will be willing to put up with the name "Necessary Deduction", in view of its brevity and of the fact that nothing whatever would be gained in discussing this kind of deduction, by reminding the reader in almost every sentence that there is a complication of Deduction with which, for the time being, he has nothing whatever to do.

The reader's study of the reason of the validity of deduction will be greatly facilitated by practicing the expression of the copulate premiss and conclusion of every a variety of deductions that comes under his consideration in such study, not in the ordinary syntax of any spoken tongue, but in a certain *diagrammatic syntax* which has been specially devised for such purpose, and which shall forthwith be here described.[1] This system supposes that every single word expresses it uses is an assertion. Thus, if the word "man" is put upon a sheet appropriated to expressions in this syntax, it will be understood to mean "There is a man", i.e. "Something is a man". So if "loves" appears on the sheet, it will be interpreted as asserting that "Somebody at some time did love or will love somebody or something". Of course, one cannot *speak* in this syntax, since it is diagrammatic; for nobody can talk a diagram. It is essentially superficial: a surface on which assertions are to be made must be devoted to the purpose of receiving the diagrammatic expressions, and this surface is called the Phemic Sheet. Are those expressions written, drawn, or incised? All three of these methods are employed; though the last is only used in pretence a make-believe incision represented by a fine line. Because we generally both write, and draw, and else pretendedly incise, in almost every expression assertion made in this syntax, we cannot say we write it, or that we draw it, or that we incise it. We say that we *Scribe* it; and that assertoric form to which, when we say we "scribe" it, we mean that we "give it a local habitation and a name", that we *embody* it, i.e. give it existence in a single "instance", though in itself it is only a *kind*, and so a "May-be", not a definite individual person or thing.

---

[1] I must acknowledge that my assertion that the reader's study of the reason of critic of necessary deduction will be greatly facilitated by the study practice of this diagrammatic syntax is merely an analogical inference from my own experience. I had studied and practiced the whole theory of reasoning for many years and perhaps was unconsciously puffed up with my acquisitions as a true the ideal student never will be. All I can say for certain is that after some years' acquaintance with this syntax I found it had taught me a good deal more than I had at all suspected that it could. Beyond that I cannot know how much a reader will gain from similar practice.

Just so, the word "the", though it be printed twenty times on an ordinary page, is only one single word, those twenty occurrences of it being so many *instances* of the single word. In this diagrammatic syntax in which every word is an assertion, the form which *would*, were it scribed be embodied in an instance, is called a "Graph". It is a graph whether it be composed of many graphs, or whether it ~~is an atomic~~ be a "Graph-atom". ~~The sheet upon which it is pretended the student of logic exercises himself by scribing the premisses that making believe to scribe he makes believe he asserts is called the "Phemic Sheet."~~

The fact that according to this syntax any single word is an assertion classes the syntax, but does not characterize it. With that understanding, "man" by itself would most naturally mean what this syntax makes it mean, and the same may be said of "loves", "gives", "sells", etc. Yet "man" might mean "Everything is a man"; and "love", "everything loves everything" etc. This latter was, indeed, the first proposal which led up to the syntax here to be described. That first proposed may be named "the Syntax of Entitative Graphs" and that which is here to be described is "the Syntax of Existential Graphs".

There are but three peculiar signs that the Syntax of Existential Graphs absolutely requires. ~~The first of these is a Sign which shall deny Graph or a scribed assertion. Such a sign is required, since "Not man" would only mean, "There is something besides some man", or else, "There is something that is not a man".~~ The first of these is a sign of identity. An ordinary word or abbreviation would not answer this purpose because it would not show what two objects were said to be identical, which is the sole end of a sign of identity. To write one before and the other after the graph of identity could only be suggested by a person who had no experience of the cases in which such a sign is needed. How, for example, should we express "Somebody loves himself"? A practicable suggestion and one which may occasionally be used is to attach duplicate marks of reference, such as asterisks, obelisks, double daggers, sections, parallels, and paragraphs. But a much more diagrammatic method is commonly used. ~~Namely, when every graph except a "Medad", i.e. one expressing an entire assertion ought to carry a heavy dot, at a point of its periphery to be agreed upon to be settled by a convention to denote each of its "Subjects", a word used in this syntax to denote indifferently a Subject nominative or any variety of object. If a graph is a "Monad", that is, has but~~[2] Namely, every "Simple Graph", or "Spot", that is to say, every graph that is not composed of other graphs, unless, indeed, it be a "Medad" (i.e. unless it be, in

---

[2] [Continues undeleted on an alternative page:] [...] a single subject, such as "man", "dies", etc., it makes no difference at what point of its periphery the dot is placed. If it be a "dyad", or Graph of two subjects, the Subject Nominative, or more actual or active of the two should usually be put to the left, and the more ~~potential~~ passive to the right, or the more concrete may be placed

itself, a complete assertion, such as "rains", meaning "it rains", and as such has no subject), ought to carry at a point of its periphery to be decided upon by convention, a heavy dot to denote quite indefinitely, each of its subjects. Thus, "•dies" will naturally mean "Something dies", this something being denoted by the dot; and •kills• will naturally mean "Something kills something", the left-hand dot denoting the killer, and the right-hand one the killed. So •gives• may very well be used to mean "Somebody gives something to somebody", the left-hand dot denoting the giver, the right-hand dot the gift, and the dot below the recipient of the gift. For to give is not a simple physical act, like to illumine, to hear, to push, to pull. If it were it would be "dyadic", that is, the assertion of it would be sufficiently completed by two subjects. But it is a transfer of something created by the mind, to wit, a legal right; and such actions are mostly "triadic", at their simplest. These heavy dots attached to spots and indefinitely denoting their different subjects are called the "pegs" of the spots. They have their analogues in chemical graphs. Now we have only to stretch such a heavy dot into a heavy line, and it automatically becomes an assertion of the identity of the two graph-subjects denoted by its two extremities. Thus, Fig. 1 asserts "Mary is a woman". Fig. 2 asserts "Cain kills Abel". Fig. 3 asserts "Somebody kills himself". This way of asserting identity, along with

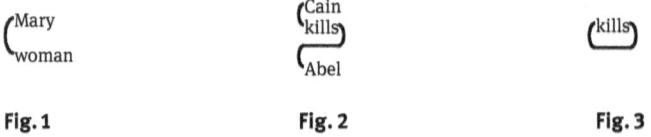

Fig. 1 **Fig. 2** **Fig. 3**

other important advantages, has that of automatically furnishing *the second general sign required by the syntax of existential graphs*. This is the "Spot of Teridentity". At first blush it is likely to seem to the reader that the identity of three subjects is nothing but the simple identities of the first with the second, and of this with the third; whence follows the identity of the first and the third. But in the Critic of Deduction it is needful to think more accurately than that. It is true that if the three can be definitely and distinctly identified, their teridentity is given in two simple identities. But from the premisses "Some wise man is identical with some virtuous man" and "Some virtuous man is identical with some able man", it by no means follows that "Some wise man is identical with some able man",

---

indifferently to the right or left, and the more abstract, indifferently above or below; as, •kills• and •İ = •I = İ• = I• . If there be a Subject nominative, direct object, and indirect object, the dots denoting these may be placed respectively to the left, to the right, and below (or above); and so on.

much less does it follow that because "Some wise is identical with some virtuous, some virtuous is identical with some able, and some able is identical with some wise", that some wise, some virtuous, and some able are coidentical; and consequently the existence of coidentity is far from consisting in the existence of two or in three simple identities. It thus becomes evident that we must have a Spot of Teridentity, and that no Existential Graph of Teridentity can be built up of instances of the graph of simple identity. However, a simple point of branching on a line of identity automatically signifies teridentity, as in Fig. 4, and teridentity once ~~scribed~~ conquered we have the means, by it alone, of expressing any grade of multi-identity, as in Fig. 5.

Fig. 4   **Fig. 5**

We thus perceive that the essence of Plurality is not perfectly realized in the number two, while it [is] in three; which, by the way, indicates the truth of those numerous languages of every type that distinguish the grammatical dual number from plural. Moreover, it furnishes a hint toward explaining why perfectly comprehended and essential logical divisions are often trichotomies, but never result in a number of parts having any prime factor greater than three. There is more to be said about the Line of Identity, after the third ~~essential~~ indispensable peculiar sign of the Syntax of Existential Graphs has been considered.

This third is one that shall deny a Graph-instance, or scribed assertion. For without that we could not, in Existential Graphs, express any proposition [in] that form which is, *par excellence*, Critical; namely, the conditional form, "If Antecedent then Consequent". No more could we in Entitative Graphs (whose development starts from the conditional form) express a proposition of the particular form with which the development of Existential Graphs begins. But that Conditional Proposition just written may be expressed by the aid of a sign of Negation in the form, "That the Antecedent is true and the Consequent not true, is not true". This example shows us that along with the sign of negation we require one of those *Collectional Signs*,—"Klämmern", Schröder calls them,—such as in algebra are the parentheses, brackets, braces, the vinculum, ~~and, in the principal effect~~ period. The functional signs when more than single letters are attached to them belong to this class of Collectional Signs, which class is the most important,—it would, indeed, be strictly true to say they are the only indispensable,—signs of algebra. But the whole of the strict truth is, in this case, not important. What *is* important is to understand that the essential power of algebra is due exclusively to collectional signs. It will not be surprising, then, to find that logical critic cannot be firm upon its legs and able to progress until it is provided with convenient collectional signs. However, they are only first needed in Existential Graphs after this syntax has been provided with a sign of negation; for whether one says "To assert that the assertion of A would be *true*, and that the assertion of B would be true, and that the assertion of C would be true is to assert nothing but the truth", or whether one says "To assert that the assertion of C would be true is to assert nothing but the truth", or whether one says "To assert that the assertion of A would be true and that the assertion of B and C together would be true", or whether one says, "To assert that the assertion of A and B together would be true and that the assertion of C would be true" is perfectly indifferent: they all come to the same thing. On the other hand to say that "To assert that the assertion of A would be *false*, and that the assertion of B would be false, and that the assertion of C would be false" would be to assert nothing but the truth", would amount to much more than either to say "To assert that the assertion of A would be false, and that the assertion of B and C together would be false, would be to assert nothing but the truth" or to say "To assert that the assertion of A and B together would be false and that the assertion of C would be false would be to assert nothing but the truth" would be very different. But while the syntax of existential graphs thus needs both a sign of negation and an endless series of collectional signs, there is no reason why a single sign should not perfectly fulfill both these purposes. Here immediately follows an explanation of this sign as it is seen by the mind's eye; and this shall be supplemented by an account of how this ideal sign can be conveniently represented on paper.

Let the descriptions of things or of events of each of which one wishes to say that something of the sort exists or sometimes occurs be scribed in black upon the white surface of the phemic sheet. Then if of some description of object one wishes to deny that it ever exists, let a part of the sheet be blackened but with white spot left in it, so shaped as to compose in their entirety an instance of a description in question, and let the interpretation be that no such thing or event is ever actualized as that description in its entirety. Thus, Fig. 6 will affirm A and affirm B while denying C and denying D. But Fig. 7, while affirming A and B will only deny that *both* C and D are true; that is it will assert that no C ever occurs at the same time, or occasion, as D. On precisely the same principle Fig. 8 must be interpreted as asserting that if A is ever true either C or D will sometimes be true; for this is precisely the same as to assert that to say that A is sometimes true and that C and D are each sometimes false would be to assert something not altogether true.

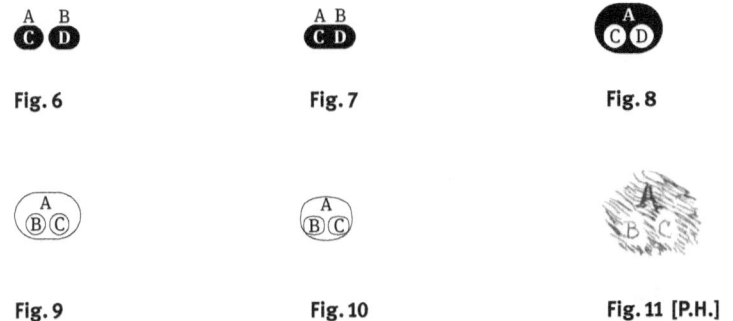

Fig. 6   Fig. 7   Fig. 8

Fig. 9   Fig. 10   Fig. 11 [P.H.]

It is needless to say that the process of making a black surface with a diagram in white upon it is insufferably inconvenient. For that reason in practice one substitutes Fig. 9 or Fig. 10 in place of Fig. 8. This sufficiently overcomes the inconvenience of making the diagrams; but it is accompanied by a serious danger. For though the bounding ovals be drawn in as fine lines as they may,—and they must be so drawn,—one is but too apt to think of these ink-lines as signs, like the graphs, and to forget that they have no meaning at all, but are mere boundaries between black and white. They are called "cuts",—that is, girdling-edges; for the black areas usually carry white areas within them, and may be thought of as taking away the presence of that which the graphs they carry denote. It is only the color of the area itself which has the force of affirming, if it be white or *evenly-enclosed* (i.e. is enclosed by an even number of cuts, or by none) or of denying if it be shaded or *oddly-enclosed*. It is a help to shade the oddly-enclosed areas and omit the lines that represent the cuts, as in Fig. 11, which is equivalent to Fig. 10.

Though the cuts in themselves have no meaning whatever, but are, at most, mere punctuation-marks separating "particular" affirmations from general negations, yet an *enclosure*, that is, an area together with all that it carries, including whatever other ~~area or areas~~ enclosure or enclosures it may carry is a graph-instance. The area upon which a given area lies is called *the place* of the latter area, or *the place* of the cut which is its outer boundary; while an area within a cut is sometimes called *the area* of the cut. The "place" of any graph-instance is the outermost of the areas which any part of it enters. But an instance of a simple graph, i.e. one not having parts that are themselves graphs, must be wholly in one area: and this is not an unimportant fact.

Let us now exercise ourselves in interpreting a few graph-instances. Fig. 12 reads "If it thunders it must have lightened"; for it denies an occurrence of thunder without its having lightened. Fig. 13 reads "If there is anything there is a mind". Fig. 14: "If anything is possible there must be a mind". Fig. 15 is an absurdity; for it denies that which does not assert anything. Fig. 16: "Either there is a mind or there

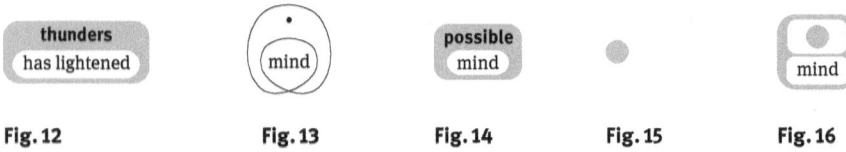

Fig. 12 **Fig. 13** **Fig. 14** **Fig. 15** **Fig. 16**

is an absurdity". This may be considered as asserting that the existence of a mind is an absolute necessity. It does not quite say this because it does not say there *would* be a mind under all circumstances. To express that explicitly, it would be necessary to indicate, upon the very outermost, or border, area, [that] the logical universe is that of metaphysical possibility, so that oddly-enclosed graphs express necessities. The nature of the universe or universes of discourse (for several may be referred to in a single assertion) in the rather unusual cases in which such precision is required, is denoted either by using modifications of the heraldic tinctures, marked in something like the usual manner in pale ink upon the surface, or by scribing the graphs in colored inks. In the former method it is usual to employ the different metals (or, argent, fur, and plomb) to ~~signify~~ mark the different kinds of existence or actuality, the different colours (azure, gules, vert, purpur) for the different kinds of possibility,—possibility consisting of ignorance, of variety, of power, of futurity; and the furs (sable, ermine, vair, potent), for the different kinds of intention. But when what is scribed has not to go to press, nothing else is so simple as the use of colored inks, of which excellent mauve, crimson, scarlet, maroon or reddish brown, buff or yellowish brown (the so-called bismarck brown) olive or greenish brown (in *appearance*; for it is really nothing but darkened gamboge), blue, violet, and royal purple, are easy to be had. The pale colors may be used for possibility, the dark for actuality, and the high for intentions. To express the metaphysical necessity of mind, one may on a pale reddish ground make a deep red area bearing a white spot in its turn on which is written "mind". This will express, "It is metaphysically impossible that there should not actually exist a mind". But it is to be remembered that an assertion,—although in itself, either a command, usually obeyed (like other ~~customary~~ commands that the interpreter is ~~habituated~~ accustomed to obey), by force of habit; or else, taken as the tota~~lity~~ composed of the appearance of the assertor, and all the interpreter's experience of him, of that assertor's tone and manner, together with the proposition considered as asserted and by whom it is to be regarded as a retroductive argumentation tending to persuade its interpreter of the ~~breadth~~ reality of its substance,³—yet, when it is to be made the premiss of a yet undeveloped necessary deduction, it ought to be regarded merely in its syntactical *form*, carrying significant matter, it is true,—but that matter packed up as concisely as it may, and not to be undone and scrutinized until the deductive conclusion shall have been drawn, so that the energy of attention may not be wasted upon it. Every part of the ~~composite~~ copulate premiss that does not need to be dissected for the purpose of drawing the conclusion is best represented by a single letter with the requisite pegs about its periphery; while at the nodal point of the argumentation no subtilty can be useful in drawing any part of the conclusion ought to be spared. But before we consider deductions, we need to exercise ourselves in correctly so scribing graphs that involve both enclosures and lines of identity as to express various familiar forms of thought.

In the first place, if the reader can put up with another technical term, it must be remarked that the line of identity, that heavy kind of line that when evenly enclosed affirms that that individual object that is denoted by one of its extremities *is identically the same as* the individual denoted by its other extremity. Since no concept stands less in need of analysis in the process of deduction than does that of identity, it ought to be regarded as a *simple graph* expressing that "Something (denoted by one of its extremities) *is* the *same individually as*" (that which its other extremity denotes); and consequently it must be scribed, if at all, upon some single area within the border of the phemic sheet. Any instance of it is, however, scribed as a continuous line, which is divisible into and consists of as many parts as one may like.⁴ Now it is not the question how it may be with a real line; for let us assume that our conception of a line is correct, or, at any rate, is all we are talking about. Then there can be no question that there is room upon it for a multitude of points at least as great as the multitude of all numbers, rational or

---

3 By the "Substance" of an assertion is to be understood that state of things or event whose Reality it asserts.

4 **[Alt.:]** [...] consists of as many parts as one may like; so that it might be urged that what it actually expresses [is] something more like this: "Something (its one end) is something that is something that is something that is something that is something that is something that is something that is something that is something that is (its other end)". Only instead of a finite series of "somethings", there is, not an infinite number, (for that would not suffice) but a continuum of somethings! This might be urged, but it would not be correct; and in this case, as in many others, the difference which amounts, quite absolutely, to nothing at all in substance, is of high importance in logic and will sometimes make the difference practically of falsehood in place of truth, ~~of going to hell by mistaking its door, in the~~ especially in that long and dark corridor of metaphysical ~~for that of heaven~~ speculation it might be so easy to mistake the cellar door of hell for that of heaven.

irrational, between any two values,—say between 2 and 4. The mathematicians assume that any simple line *is composed* of just so many points, and no more. The present writer ventures to disagree with them;—and let it be well understood that, as just said, it is a disagreement in regard to our notion of a line. His reason is that if we cut a line in two thus making two new ends, our notion is that there will be a point at each of those ends while if we cut the series of all real numbers in two so as to leave a number on one side next to the cut, then on the other side however close to the cut any number may be there will be an *endless* series of numbers yet nearer. For example if we cut the series of numbers so that 3 shall be the highest of all the numbers below the cut, then there will be above it 3.5 3.05 3.005 3.0005 and so on *endlessly*. For 3.00000 *et cetera ad infinitum* 1, is the same as 3, or, if it be not, then the number expressed by substituting 0001 for the last 1 is higher that 3 and lower than 3.00000 *et cetera ad inf.* 1. No competent mathematician will hesitate to endorse the statement that if the series of real numbers be cut so that there shall be a number nearest to the cut on one side of it, then the series as one approaches the cut on the other side is *endless*, whether the series embraces all real numbers or only all real rational numbers. It is one of the recognized truths of arithmetic, demonstrated by Euclid. The cause of the misrepresentation by mathematicians of the concept of a line is ~~simply~~ that their representation is faithful to every measure of line; or at least is so nearly as faithful to the concept of a measured line as to result in no measurable error, and they would not correct their concept without going into logic deeper than it is pertinent to measurement to go. But Kant sometimes defines the continuity of time in a manner which solves the difficulty and is perfectly applicable to a line, although Kant himself fails distinctly to appreciate the merits of his definition. He says that the continuity of time consists in the fact that every part of a time is a time; that is time is not wholly nor partially composed of instants.[5] The continuous parts of a line, i.e. where there is neither a node, or point of branching, nor an extremity, nor any marked point, contains no point. But as soon as a point is marked upon a line the continuity is broken at that point and nowhere else; and a point on a line occupies no part of the line. To be sure, if you choose to *call* a point a part of a line, by an arbitrary misuse of the word "part", then you must define the continuity of a line differently. You may say that every *constituent part* of a continuous line is a line. Or you may say that every part of the *room* on a line affords *room* for a line. This is merely a variation of nomenclature. The multitude of rational numbers is demonstrably no greater than the multitude of whole numbers; but the multitude of real irrational numbers is greater. There are still greater and greater multitudes endlessly. The

---

5 C.d.r.V. 1ˢᵗ Aufl. S. 169ff.

reason the mathematician can conceive of no more points on a line is not at all that there is no room for more on the line; for no multitude whatever of points can fill any linear space; but the reason is that he has exhausted his vocabulary for distinguishing the units of a multitude. He can only approximate to distinguishing the irrational numbers, and for distinguishing the different individuals in higher multitudes than that of the irrational reals, the human mind is not capable even of approximating to doing so.

The line of identity does no more than assert the individual identity of the objects denoted by its extremities. Identity is a dyadic relation; and among dyadic relations it belongs to the type to which belongs the relative term "is loved by whatever loves". For to say that "some woman is identical with something that is beautiful" is precisely the same as to say that "some woman is identical with whatever there may be that a certain something that is beautiful is identical with".

The term "line of identity" is taken in such a sense as to limit it to *graphs*. Now a graph-instance must be scribed in some one area and be limited to that. But a line of identity may be continuous with another line of identity in another area, as

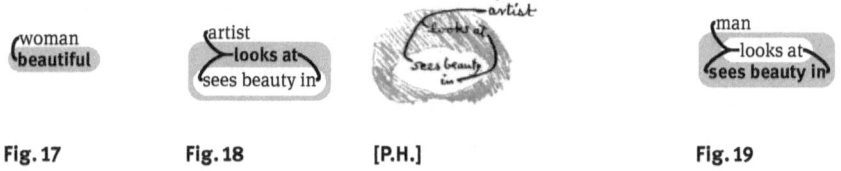

Fig. 17   Fig. 18   [P.H.]   Fig. 19

in Fig. 17; and such a series of lines of identity thus continuous each with the next is called a *ligature*. Fig. 17 may be read, "Some woman is identical with something which is not identical with anything unless it be with something that is other than everything except what is other than anything beautiful", which comes to saying, "Some woman is other than everything beautiful", or "Some woman is not beautiful". Thus a ligature which has its outer end evenly enclosed and its inner end oddly enclosed has no other effect on the whole than asserting the identity of something denoted by a graph in the outer area with some thing that is *not* of the description signified by a graph in the oddly enclosed area. Fig. 18: "Some artist sees beauty in whatever he looks at". Fig. 19: "Some man sees beauty only in things he looks at".

All the strictly synthetical elementary signs essential to this syntax have now been explained. But the writer has been led by fourteen or fifteen years experience of it to rate its utility so very high that he will here insert examples of all the propositional forms up to a certain limit of complexity, so as to familiarize the reader with the use of it, and following these will make the briefest possible restatement of the definitions of the signs.

It will be understood that the system is not a complete syntax, but is only a *syntax of assertions*. It is a question whether an assertion should be regarded as a command to believe, that is, as an action on the part of its Utterer,—a word which will throughout this writing be applied as much to one who puts forth a sign by writing or by any other kind of action as to one who does so by means of his voice,—as an action, then, on the part of its Utterer with the deliberate purpose of causing belief in the mind of its Interpreter, through a habit in that mind, much in the same way as an officer's command causes a soldier to obey with very little reflexion, if any at all; or whether, on the other hand, the assertion ought not rather to be regarded as the voluntary manifestation of the utterer's belief usually, but not necessarily, with more or less hope that the fact of belief so manifested will appeal to the interpreter's reason as a sufficient premiss to make him conclude that it is true; or whether finally it should be considered, neither as a command nor the manifestation of a premiss of reasoning, but rather as a third ~~genus~~ species of sign more or less resembling each of those others. In order to solve this far from easy problem, let us turn our attention back to the essential nature of a *Sign*, in general, and consider whether that does not point out to us the nature of that fundamental division of signs which will furnish us with the concept of the Assertion as one of its members. A Sign, then, is anything whatsoever,—whether an Actual or a May-be or a Would-be,—which affects a mind, its Interpreter,—and draws that interpreter's attention to some Object (whether Actual, May-be, or Would-be) which *has already* come within the sphere of his experience, and beside this purely selective action of a sign, it has a power of exciting the mind (whether directly, by the image or the sound or indirectly) to some kind of feeling, or to effort of some kind or to thought; and so far as it has any such effect *quâ* sign—for besides being a sign, it may also be a music,—but so far as it excites feeling, will, or thought *as a* sign, it connects the feeling, will, or thought in the mind of the Interpreter with its Object as due to it, as the interpretation of it. The writer is not altogether satisfied with this attempt to analyze the nature of a sign; but he believes that the sign calls up its Object or Objects, for there may be several, and besides that excites the mind as if it were the Object that had this effect. If a person reads an item of news in a newspaper, its first effect on his mind will probably ~~depend on his habits; upon someone—upon anyone, perhaps, of little experiences—its first effect will~~ be to cause ~~him to believe the truth of what is asserted, that is, to believe the reality of the substance of it; upon another the first effect~~ something that may conveniently be called an "image" of the event, without any judgment as to its reality.

Appendix: Assurance through Reasoning

[R 669, May 25 to June 2, 1911][6] **Deductive Reasoning.** The word Deduction will here be used in a generalized sense to include all necessary, or mathematical Reasoning,—every reasoning of which the premisses,—or, as they will here be termed, the *Copulate Premiss*, having been asserted, the Conclusion cannot consistently be denied ~~without self-contradiction~~; so that all that the latter asserts has really been already asserted in the former.[7] Although all Deduction, ~~as I use the word,~~ is thus Necessary Reasoning, it will, nevertheless, be convenient to speak of "Probable Deduction" as distinct from "Necessary Deduction"; the term "Probable Deduction" being used to denote any Necessary Reasoning that concludes that under stated conditions a given kind of event would have a stated Probability. *Example*: That any homogeneous cubical die will, at any given throw, turn up six is ~~a chance against which the odds are 5 to 1.~~ decidedly improbable. Therefore, it is very improbable that a pair of quite disconnected good dice should turn up ~~sixes at any given throw~~ without referring to any calculation of Probabilities.

The study of Necessary Deduction is much facilitated by expressing the Copulate Premiss, not in ordinary grammatical form, but in a sort of "diagrammatic syntax" of which an explanation shall forthwith be described, along with the terminology required in this description. A piece of paper having been taken for this use, and noun or verb written upon it is to be understood as *asserting* that the object, action, or state signified by what is written is actualized somewhere at some time, past, present or future. If two such words are written, both assertions are made. But if one or more of the words is surrounded by a fine line, that which would have been asserted if it had not been so enclosed is to be understood as being thereby, precisely and *as a whole*, denied. For example, Fig. 1 would assert that it does not both rain and thunder. Strictly it ought to mean that it either never rains or never thunders, but unless the reasoning turns on such an interpretation, it will not be worth while to be particular on such points, and when nothing to the contrary is asserted it is to be understood that all that is on any one of the sheet refers to some one place and some one time. Common sense on the part of the interpreter is supposed in this special respect, although in others a free rein must not be accorded to that useful servant to him who holds it with a firm hand.

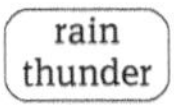

⎯ rain ⎯
⎯ thunder ⎯

Fig. 1

---

6 [R 669 is an important alternative and slightly earlier version of R 670 which Peirce designates as a "Chapter" with a "full glossary" of "technical expressions" provided in the appendix.]

7 Any dispute on this point must, I think, be a dispute about words. For all I mean is that if a diagram, or model, or true representation of any kind that any being could make, should represent the Copulate Premiss to be true, it would *ipso facto* represent every Deductive Conclusion to be true, although, these being endlessly manifold, it could not *expressly* represent this of every such conclusion. That is it could not concentrate attention on them all; although it would *mean* all that consistency would make it mean; and being an assertion, it would *assert* all that.

It is not *words* that are "asserted", but *facts*: any dictionary ought to say that. Consequently, "Cain killed Abel", "Abel was killed by Cain", and "The death of Abel was directly due to the intentional agency of Cain" are not three assertions, but only three forms in which of one and the same assertion may be clothed.

A heavy dot before a verb will denote the perfectly indefinite subject of the verb. A similar dot after the verb will denote with the same indefiniteness its direct object; and such a dot close under the verb will usually denote the dative indirect object. But such conventions must yield to convenience. Similarly, places about other words may be appropriated, each to denote "something" in a particular relation to that which the word signifies. Any such heavy dot may be prolonged into a heavy line; and when this is done the whole line continues to denote the same identical individual. If such line joins another, the junction asserts the identity of two "somethings". But if it be desired to draw one such "line of identity" across another without joining them, there are two ways of doing so. The first is to make a little bridge, as in Fig. 2 which may be read "Somebody is husband of somebody that loves him". The other way is to do away with the line and use one of the usual marks of reference, such as, *, , ‡, ‖, §, ¶, as in Fig. 3. In either case, it is to be

Fig. 2   Fig. 3

carefully observed that this syntax is *endoporeutic*. This means that a "line of identity" is to be understood as lying in the outermost of the "areas" within which any part of it lies, meaning by an "area" (here and everywhere), all of the surface that lies inside and outside of

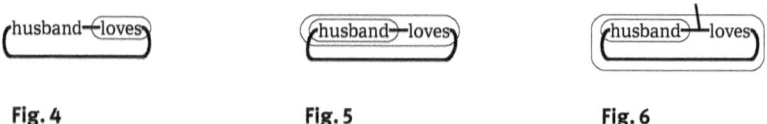

Fig. 4   Fig. 5   Fig. 6

precisely the same "cuts", or fine oval lines. Thus, Fig. 4 means "Somebody does not love some husband of hers"; Fig. 5, "Somebody is husband of whoever loves him" = "Somebody is loved, if at all, only by those (or some of them), of whom he is husband"; Fig. 6, "Somebody does not love anything that is not husband to her" = "Somebody has for her husband whatever there may be that she loves" = "Somebody if she love anybody, it is some husband of hers that she loves".

These two features, the finely drawn oval *cut* that denies as a whole, whatever it includes and the heavily drawn *ligature* that expresses the identity of whatever it abuts upon or is continuous with make the sum total of the essence of this Syntax. There is, therefore, no other difficulty in using it except that of knowing precisely what it is that one desires to express, without which one cannot think or do anything at all, to good purpose. There are, to be sure, a few signs besides those two, that are occasionally convenient; but they are never indispensable, and are not often wanted. The merit of this syntax is that when, by means of it, one has expressed one's premisses, with sufficient distinctness (i.e. analytically enough), it only remains to make, according to three general permissions, suitable insertions, followed by suitable deletions, the effect of such insertions and deletions amounting only to the omission of a part of what has been asserted, and one will be able to read in what will then be on the sheet, whatever sound deductive conclusion from those premisses that one may have aimed at in the insertions and deletions. A false logic has caused the habit of speaking of *the* conclusion from given premisses, as if there were but one.

The truth is that the number of conclusions deducible from any proposition is strictly infinite.[8] It is, therefore, necessary to determine what sort of conclusion one desires to draw or by what sort of operation one proposes to proceed before one can deduce a definite conclusion.

Before going further it will be well to define a few technical expressions that have been found almost indispensable in describing the properties of this Syntax. A full glossary shall be appended to this chapter.[9]

The *Phemic Sheet*, or the *Sheet* simply, is the surface on which the premisses are to be expressed, and from which, after insertions and deletions have been made, the deductive conclusion can be read off.

To *scribe* is to embody an *infima species* of *pheme*, or assertional sign, by writing or drawing.

A *Cut* is a fine oval line. It is called a Cut because, being the only kind of sign used in this system of syntax that does not, of itself express an assertion, and is in other ways *sui generis*, it is not convenient to speak of it as "scribed"; and besides imagining it to be cut through the sheet, we further imagine and speak of the part of the sheet within the "Cut" as if it were turned over so that what were exposed to view were the *Verso* side, unless the Cut in question be itself enclosed within another, or within any other odd number of others, in which case, of course, the even number of reversals will be imagined and spoken of as exposing the *Recto* again within it.

By an *Area* is meant so much of the exposed surface as lies wholly within and without the same identical Cuts. The Area within a Cut is called *the Area of* that Cut; while the Area in which the Cut has been made is called *the Place of* that Cut.

An Area that is enclosed in an even number of Cuts, or in none at all, is said to be "evenly enclosed". Any other is "oddly enclosed", since no Cut is allowed to intersect another.

The word "Graph" was introduced by the still lamented William K. Clifford to mean a diagram expressive of relations by means of lines abutting upon spots, after the fashion of those employed in organic chemistry. The syntax I am describing employs Graphs modified by Cuts. They are called *Existential* Graphs to distinguish them from another system of logical graphs[10] called Entitative Graphs. But ordinarily it will be convenient in the present essay, for the sake of abbreviating the long name Existential Graphs, the adjective is dropped. A *Graph*, then, as the word is used ~~by the present~~ when it is plain that an *Existential* Graph is meant, is *not* a sign or mark or any other existent or actual individual, but is a *kind* of sign ~~not any instance of~~ which if scribed on the Phemic Sheet (i.e. if an *Instance* of it stood on the Sheet) would make an assertion. The individual sign that results from the scribing of a Graph has been called an "*Instance*" of the Graph. This word "Instance" might conveniently be introduced into ordinary parlance. For example, only two words in our language are called articles; but one of these, the definite article, *the*, will commonly occur, on an average page of novel or essay, over twenty times. They are reckoned by the editor who asks for an article of so many thousand "words" as distinct words; but in fact they are only twenty or more *instances* of the same word; and if the editor takes any pleasure in speaking accurately he should call for an article of so many thousand "word-instances". At any rate, it would be highly inconvenient to call "Graph-instances" Graphs.

---

8 The number of *interesting* propositions deducible from the definition of ~~such a single proposition as the def~~ the series of positive integers is very great, while that deducible from the definition of projective space is enormous.

9 [Peirce either did not write such glossary or else it has been lost. R S-26 (1904) is an earlier glossary of nearly 200 terms on EGs included in R 693b, LoF 1.]

10 See *Monist*, Vol. VII, pp. 168 *et seq.*

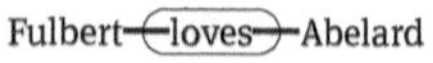

Fulbert—(loves)—Abelard   Fulbert—⊂⊃—Héloise

Fig. 7    **Fig. 8**

The "line of identity" is a graph. For just as Fig. 7 asserts that "Fulbert does not love Abelard", so Fig. 8 asserts that "Fulbert is not identical with Héloise". But each Instance of a Graph must be either affirmative or negative, and consequently must lie wholly in one area. For that reason we must call the "*ligature*" of Fig. 8 not a Graph-instance, and consequently, not an Instance of the "Line of Identity", but as a composite of three graph-instances. This gives rise to a subtile and difficult doctrine about ligatures, with which common-sense finds it hard to have patience, because in its eyes a ligature is the simplest thing in the world. Namely, only the outermost, or least enclosed, part of it signifies anything, and the rest only serves to point out the two individuals objects, each of which the identity it signifies is affirmed or denied, according as that outermost part is *evenly* or oddly enclosed (i.e. enclosed in an even or an odd number of cuts, zero being, of course, divisible by two and so even). We may pat common sense on the back for this facile method of interpretation; yet there is no difficulty at all in the more formally logical view that a ligature consists of as many separate graph-instances as are the areas into which parts of it enter, these different graph-instances being connected by the *dot* or *dots* where they cross a cut or cuts. At such a dot—theoretically, a mathematical point—there can be no predication, since there can be neither affirmation nor denial of that which is neither within nor without the cut. It must be borne in mind that Fig. 9 and Fig. 10 are both absurd. For Fig. 9 asserts that something is not identical with anything at all—not even with itself.[11] Now Fig. 11 denies, not A, B, *and* C, but

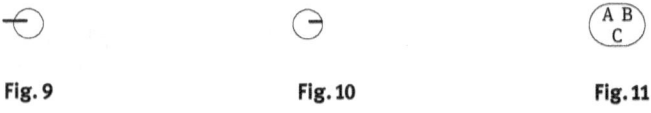

Fig. 9   **Fig. 10**   **Fig. 11**

either A or B or C. For it only denies the truth of A, B and C as one copulate. Fig. 7 may therefore be read, "Fulbert is something that is something, that is something etc. that is either nothing (not even when it is), unless it be nothing except something that is nothing etc. but something that does not love anything that is something that is Abelard"; which comes to this that "Fulbert does not love Abelard". The number of times the ligature crosses the cut is immaterial, since at a crossing it merely transmits the identity from an outer line of identity to an inner one.

It will be well to give examples of the most frequently occurring forms; and the reader is counselled to reason out for himself the interpretation of each. Fig. 12 reads "something is a dog"; Fig. 13: "Nothing is a phoenix". Fig. 14: "If it lightens, it thunders". Strictly this should mean "If it ever lightens, it sometime thunders". The truth is that it is very seldom requisite, in the critic of Deductive reasoning to observe distinctions of time. In order to do so, however, it would only be

---

11 [Likewise, the graph in Fig. 10, for which Peirce did not provide a reading, asserts that it is not the case that something exists that is identical to itself, in other words a denial of well-definedness, namely that the universe of discourse is empty.]

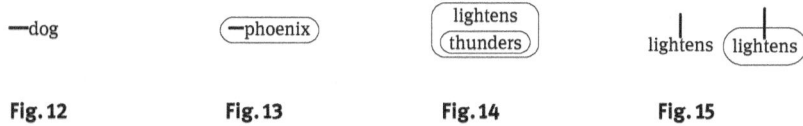

Fig. 12   Fig. 13   Fig. 14   Fig. 15

requisite to agree that a point on the upper part of the periphery of any graph of action or other change should denote an instant during such action or other change. Then Fig. 15 will read "It sometimes lightens and sometimes does not". Fig. 16: "If it ever lightens it will shortly after thunder". For were the outer cut of the figure not there, the interpretation would be "It sometime lightens without thundering at any shortly subsequent time". Fig. 17: "Every multicellular animal dies". Fig. 18: "There is a man who loves nothing but women". Fig. 19: "There is a man who loves every woman". Fig. 20: "Nothing but a man loves any woman". Fig. 21: "The only positive integer that is not higher than One is One itself". Fig. 22: "Philip is identical with whatever is Philip"; i.e. the name Philip denotes a definite Individual.[12] ("Some man" is an indefinite individual. "Any man there may be" is an indeterminate individual according to the terminology herein adopted.)[13]

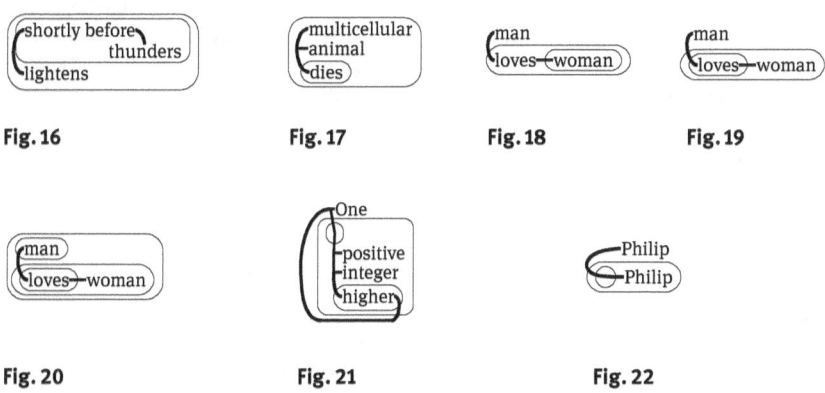

Fig. 16   Fig. 17   Fig. 18   Fig. 19

Fig. 20   Fig. 21   Fig. 22

The Syntax of Existential Graphs has thus been described. The elementary signs this syntax may require are, in the first place, such as,

thunders,   •man,   •lover•,   •giver•,   •seller•,   •beauty,   •water,

---

12 [Figures 21 and 22, which Peirce did not draw in the main sequence of this manuscript, are found among the loose pages (ms p. 15) and have been added and renumbered.]
13 [Alt.:] In order still further to make the reader acquainted with the *Syntax of Existential Graphs*, a series of problems shall at once be proposed, each requiring something to be expressed in this Syntax, with their solutions, as follows:
    1. Required to express all those independent properties of Positive Integers, which are independent of any application of them. *Solution.* Let $-w$ mean something is a positive integer; and let $x-l-y$ mean x is lower than y. Let $x-t-y$ mean x is true of y. [end]

•possessor• (as of a character or quality), •stands• (in the dyadic relation),

•stands• (in triadic relation), •a collection that includes and excludes, •is a collection,

•is something that includes•, •is something that excludes•,

•its members are in one to one correspondence to• .

In addition to signs of this sort, which may be multiplied indefinitely and can cannot[14] be considered as constituent parts of the syntax, the only signs it so constantly requires that they may be individually regarded as almost inseparable parts of the syntax, are the following: First, the *cut*, or perhaps more properly, the *"Scroll"*, which is a pair of cuts, the one enclosing the other, so that a scroll has two areas, its *"outer close"* and its *"inner close"*. In the order of the actual mental evolution of the syntax of existential graphs, the Scroll was first adopted as a sign required before all others because it represented a necessary Reasoning, as in Fig. 23,[15] which reads: "If the Copulate Premiss is true, the Conclusion is true".

The Cut came to be thought of because of the immense frequency of occasions on which it was necessary to express the assertion "If X be true, then every assertion is true". It was forced upon the logician's attention that a certain development of reasoning was possible before, or as if before, the concept of *falsity* had ever been framed, or any recognition of such a thing as a false assertion had ever taken place. Probably every human being passes through such a grade of intellectual life, which may be called the state of paradisaical[16] logic, when reasoning takes place

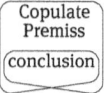

Fig. 23

but when the idea of falsity, whether in assertion or in inference, has never been recognized. But it will soon be recognized that not every assertion is true; and that once recognized, as soon as one notices that if a certain thing were true, every assertion would be true, one at once rejects the antecedent that leads to that absurd consequence. Now that conditional proposition "If A is true, every proposition is true", is represented, in the model of Fig. 24, "If A is true, C is true" by blackening the entire inner close, as if there were no room, in reason, for any additional consequence. This gives Fig. 25: "If A be true whatever can be asserted is true", which is as much as to say that "A is not true and the inner close being cut very small", we get, first Fig. 26 and finally Fig. 27, in which the idea of flat falsity is first matured.

---

14 [Peirce wrote both "can" and "cannot" inline and did not notice to strike out "cannot".]
15 [Numbering has been corrected from Fig. 22 to Fig. 23.]
16 [Peirce wrote "paradisaical" instead of "paradisiacal"; cf. "The Logic of Relatives", Peirce (1897, p. 184).]

26 Assurance through Reasoning (R 670, R 669), 1911 — **583**

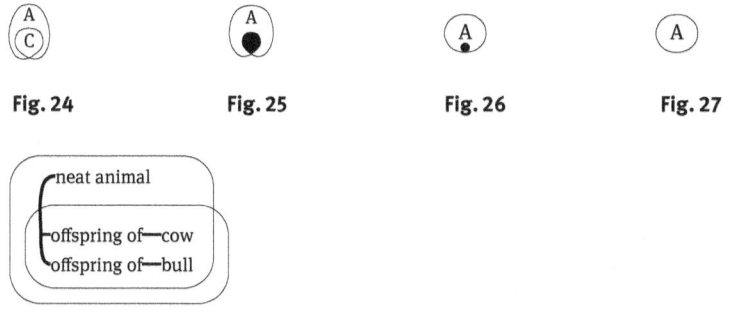

Fig. 24 **Fig. 25** **Fig. 26** **Fig. 27**

Fig. 28

Beside the Syntax of Existential Graphs involves no other sign as essential to it except the Line of Identity, and the signs that grow out of that, such as the *Point of Teridentity*, where, as in Fig. 28,[17] a line of identity furcates, the *Peg*, or heavy dot which indicates that place on the periphery of a graph that denotes an individual kind of *Subject* of that graph (since, in this syntax, we have to recognize various other kinds of "Subjects" than the "subject nominative", as for example, the Object Accusative, which this Syntax shows to be as much a Subject as the other, if "subject" is to have any real meaning; the Object Dative; the Instrumental Object; the Locative; and others usually in the Aryan languages expressed by adverbial phrases). There is also the place on the cut where a Ligature crosses it. All these are so many Graphs, whose general significations are forced upon them by that of the line of identity. The only other is the bridge, which is required simply to save the trouble of pasting the two ends of a paper ribbon on the sheet to make a real bridge.

It will be acknowledged that a simpler Syntax, capable of expressing any proposition, however intricate, would be difficult to imagine. ~~A proposition too intricate for any living human mind to grasp could be set down without ambiguity, by means of this Syntax with a very moderate amount of trouble.~~ A proposition too intricate to be clearly expressed in a single sentence in any living tongue can be expressed without ambiguity in this syntax as soon as it is distinctly apprehended.

It now only remains to ~~state~~ formulate those general permissions to modify what has already been scribed which express the ~~elementary~~ logicality of those several forms of elementary deductive inference, out of which all other deductions can be built up. There are but two of these general illative permissions; but before stating them there is one other thing that has to be said. Namely, it is to be imagined that every graph-instance anywhere on the sheet can be freely moved about upon the sheet; and since a scroll both of whose closes are empty asserts nothing, it is to be imagined that there is an abundant store of empty scrolls on a part of the sheet that is out of sight, whence one of them can be brought into view whenever desired.[18] What is here said ought to be reckoned as a permission, but it is not an illative permission, i.e. a permission authorizing a species of inference.

---

17 [The graph in Fig. 28 may be read, "If there is a neat animal then it is offspring of something that is a cow and offspring of something that is a bull".]

18 [This amounts to the double-cut rule, and together with the first and the second illative permission will "suffice to enable any valid deduction to be performed."]

- *First Illative Permission: the Rule of Deletion and Insertion.* From any evenly enclosed area any enclosure or other graph-instance may be deleted, even if it involves the rupture of lines of identity on that area; and upon any oddly-enclosed area any enclosure or other graph-~~instance may~~ may be scribed and any connections made by lines of identity.
- *Second Illative Permission: the Rule of Iteration and Deiteration.* Any graph may be iterated on the same area or within any number of cuts in that area, the graph-instance so inserted having identically the same connections as that which it imitates; and if a Graph occurs twice in the same area or in two areas one within a series of cuts within the area where the other occurs, and two having identically the same connections, then a deiteration may be executed by deleting the innermost of the two or if they are on the same area by deleting either of the two.

These two permissions will suffice to enable any valid deduction to be performed. The few examples that shall forthwith be given might tempt a lively mind to exclaim: Why, this syntax draws conclusions of itself, automatically. This would be extravagant; but one may say that the Syntax together with the application of the two illative permissions does so, provided it be ~~borne in mind~~ not overlooked that such application can only be made by a living intelligence.

26 Assurance through Reasoning (R 670, R 669), 1911

A thr R
17
1911
June 12
P.M.
6:15

at most, mere punctuation-marks separating ⟨general⟩ affirmations ⟨"particular"⟩ from ⟨an⟩ negations, yet ~~the~~ enclosures, that is, ~~the~~ an area together with all that it carries, including whatever other ~~area or areas~~ ⟨enclosure or enclosures⟩ it may carry is a graph-instance. The area upon which a given area lies is called "the place" ~~of the latter area~~, or "the place" of the cut which is its outer boundary; ~~&~~ while an area within a cut ~~may be~~ ⟨is sometimes⟩ called "the area of the cut. The "place" of any graph-instance is the outermost of the areas which any part of it enters. But ~~a simp~~ an instance of a simple graph, i.e. one not having parts that are themselves graphs, must be wholly in one area: and this is not an unimportant fact.

Let us now ~~practi~~ exercise ourselves in interpreting a few graph-instances. Fig. 12 reads "If it thunders it must have lightened; for it denies an occurrence of thunder without

A thr R
18
1911
June 12
P.M.
7:10

its having lightened. Fig. 13. reads "If there is anything there is a mind." Fig. 14. "If anything is possible there must be a mind." Fig. 15 is an absurdity; for it denies that which does not assert anything. Fig. 16: "Either there is a mind or there is an absurdity. This may be considered as asserting that the existence of a mind is an ~~absolute~~ necessity. It does not quite say this because it does not say there would be a mind under all circumstances. ~~For that purpo~~ To express that explicitly, it would be necessary to indicate, upon the very outermost, or border, area, the logical universe is that of metaphysical possibility, so that oddly-enclosed graphs express necessities. The nature of the universe or universes of discourse (for ~~there~~ ⟨several⟩ ~~may be severed~~ may be referred to in a single assertion) in the ~~more~~ ⟨rather unusual⟩ cases in which such precision is required, is denoted by using modifications of

Two holograph pages, ms pages 17 & 18 (Harvard Peirce Papers, R 670).

27 [Logical Graphs, from the *Prescott Book*]

R 277, May 1907–September 1910. Houghton Library. This paginated notebook of 171 pages consists of elaborate notes mostly on mathematics, topical geometry, logic of graphs, theory of signs and pragmatism. Peirce named it the "Prescott Book" as he began writing it while lodging in Prescott Hall next to the Harvard campus from December 1906 until his return to Arisbe, Milford, the following July. The selection below provides nine excerpts that concern the logic of graphs and related topics. A few additional entries from the *Prescott Book* on the theory of signs are interpolated to the end of the *Logic Notebook* (R 339, the next chapter).

[Collections]

[May–June, 1907] Is every possible collection of A's r to an A to which no other collection of A's is r?

A possible collection of A's is that one which contains no A that is contained in the collection that is r to it but contains every A that is not contained in the collection that is r to it.

Let any B be distinguished from any other by the fact that one is q to an A to which the other is not q. And given any B that is not q to every A, and let A_1 be any A to which B_1 is not q, let there be a B which is q to A_1 as well as to every A to which B_1 is q but to no other A to which B_1 is not q.

Now I ask whether or not every B is r to an A to which no other B is r.

- Let any A be an A′ if and only if one and only one B is r to it and if this B is also q to it. No B is r to an A′ without being q to it.
- Let any A be an A″ if and only if one and only one B is r to it and if this B is not q to it. No B is both r and q to any A″.
- There is a B that is q to whatever A″ there may be and is not q to any A′.
  ∴ This B is not r either to any A′ nor to any A″.

Given two classes the A's and B's and two relations p and q:

- Let these be such that taking any two objects that are not both p to the same A and calling either of these objects you please the first and the other the second there will be a B to which no A will be q to which either the first object is p or to which the second is not p.
- The two "objects" may be taken as two qualities p is "belonging to".
- B may be a collection of A's.

- q may be "is excluded from" or with the oval crossed out in pencil "is included in".[1]

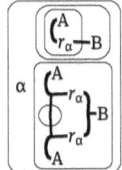

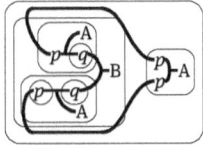

Fig. 1   **Fig. 2**

What I want to know how to prove is that,

- Whatever the A's may be and whatever relation ρ may be there is either some collection of A's that is not ρ to any A or some collection of A's that is ρ to two different A's: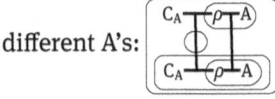

What I want is to know what proposition true of collections of A's it is that renders that true.

The naturally suggested method is to assume the proposition not to be true and see what follows about collections of A's:

- If C_1 includes whatever A that C_2 includes and if C_2 includes whatever A that C_1 includes, then C_1 and C_2 are identical considered as *collections of* A's and conversely if C_1 and C_2 are identical considered as collections of A's then C_1 includes whatever A is included in C_2; C_2 includes whatever A is included in C_1.

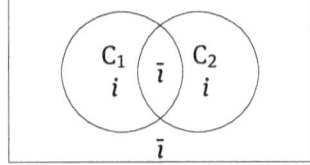   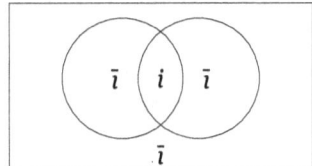

---

[1] ["Crossed out in pencil" are the two innermost cuts surrounding q's in Fig. 2.]

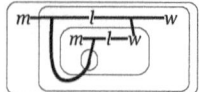 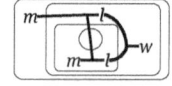

Assume then that there is a relation ρ such that Every C_A is ρ to an A to which no other C_A is ρ.

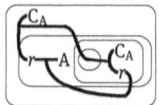 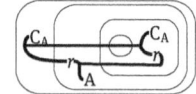

[Holding]

[October 16, 1907] I shall use the term *holding* to denote any collection or class of objects, which class is connected with a triadic relation "___ is r_m to ___ for ___", where r_m is any particular relation of a certain class of relations called the *r*'s, the object whose designation might in a true proposition fill the first blank is to be called the *subject nominative* of the relation, that whose designation might so fill the second is to be called the *direct object* of the relation, and that whose designation might so fill the third blank is to be called the *indirect object* of the relation; and if a and b are any two members of the class and c is such an object that c is r_m to a for b, or is such that c is r_m to b for a, then c is always a member of the *holding*. Farther, such a collection shall be more specifically termed a "*r*-holding", and the class of relations of *r*-hood shall be termed the *title* or *titular-relation-class* of the holding and every member of the title shall be called a *titular relation* of the holding.

If any part of a holding, consisting, we will say, of the g's, be such that from the fact that the g's are members of the holding, together with the fact that the class of r's is the title of the holding, and with all the facts expressible in the form x is r_t to y for z; it either necessarily follows that of any object that it is a member of the holding or else it is not a member of the holding, then the class of g's shall be said to be a *grant* of the holding, and a grant of a holding from which no object could not be excluded without the class ceasing to be a grant of the same holding shall be called *an original grant* of that holding.

If every *titular relation* of a holding is the relation of the *result* of a mathematical operation to an *operator* of it, for an *operand* of it, then the holding shall be termed an *operational holding*.

Number

Meanings of the word. Every plural has a *multitude*, or maniness. All the different multitudes form a linear series. If the count of the collection comes to an end, the multitude of it differs from that of a collection which should consist of the same members with [end]

Every collection, or *plural* of distinct members, has a *multitude* or degree of maniness; and all possible multitudes form a conceivable linear series; that is to say any two only differ in that one is greater than all than which the other is greater, and than more besides. If any correct count of a plural, by marking each member of it with one of a limitless series of marks, this mark being officed to no other member, and every mark earlier in the series being officed in like manner to some member of the plural [end]

Modality

[January 1908]

Potentiality is the absence of Determination (in the usual broad sense) not of a mere negative kind but a positive capacity to be Yea and to be Nay, not ignorance but a state of being. It is therefore *Inchoateness of Being. Nothing* is the Egg of Being. It is self-contained ability to be this and that. Latent Being.

Actuality is the *Act* which determines the merely possible. It is the act of direct determination itself arbitrary. The act of arbitrary determination.

Necessitation is the support of Actuality by reason. The generalization or continuity of Actuality.

The primitive variety of the idea of Low Modality, which I here, for conformity to usage, express by "possibility" through potency, δύναμις, comes nearer to it, is extremely difficult rightly to conceive on account of its vagueness; which is so essential to it that vague being or the being of the vague, is still nearer to the idea. This vagueness renders it most difficult to conceive, and it will be best to begin by explaining the idea of "actuality" or "existence". The Latin words *actus* and *actualitas* are marvels of expressiveness.

On Continuity

April 15, 1908.
§ 1. *Definition of a Unidimensional Pseudo-Continuum.*

Let r be any dyadic relative term, but best such a one that of two great class of things, the A's and the B's, it is true that if one A, say A_1, is r to a B to which another A, say A_2 is not r, then the former A_1 is r to every B to which A_2 is r.

Then let P (prae) be the relative term ___ is both r to whatever is r'd by and is also r to something not r'd by ___

Then a Unidimensional Pseudo-Continuum is any collection, say the X's, of which these four things are true:

1. that of any two X's X_1 and X_2 is either X_1 is P to X_2 or X_2 is P to X_1
2. that if one X, say X_2 is P to another, say X_4 then there is a third X, say X_3 which is P to X_4 and is P'd by X_2
3. No matter what objects the Ξ's may be, if Every Ξ is an X and if Every Ξ, say Ξ_n, is P to a Ξ, say Ξ_{n+1}, but Ξ_n is not P to any Ξ that is P to Ξ_{n+1} and if there be an X to which every Ξ is P, then there is an X, say X_Ξ, to which every Ξ is P such that X_Ξ is P to every X that is not X_Ξ to which every Ξ is P.
4. No matter what objects the ξ's may be, if Every ξ is an X and if whatever ξ_n may be there is a ξ that is P to ξ_n but is not P to any ξ that is P to ξ_n and if there be an X that is P to every ξ, then there is an X, say X_ξ, such that X_ξ is P to every ξ but is not P to any X that is P to every ξ.

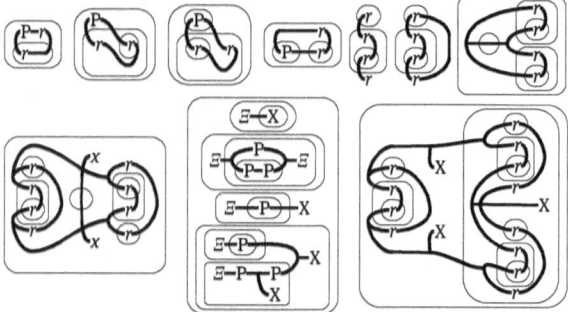

A perfect continuum is an object having material parts, and any two parts of it that have the same Listing numbers are themselves separable in precisely the same ways, into parts, that when put together at the original whole will be connected in precisely like manners.

A peneperfect continuum is an object that violates the definition of a perfect continuum only in having an ~~finite~~ enumerable multitude of topical singularities.

A quasi-perfect continuum is an object which violates the definition of a perfect continuum only in having ultimate parts.

A quasi-pene-continuum is an object which differs from a penecontinuum only in having ultimate parts.

[Distance]

    x is equally distant from y, z, and &.

    a is the distance of *b* from *c*.

    w is the ray through *u* and *v*.

R—○<k/○   *k* is a circle whose centre is ○ and the length of radius R.

p—P—*l*   *p* is a point on line *l*.

ᵃ/ᵦ>S—*c*   Of the two points *b* and *c*, *b* is nearer point *a*.

a—L<l/b   *l* is distance of *a* to *b*.

Σ/ab—*r*   *r* is the sum of *a* and *b*.

Analysis of the Relation of Whole and Part

[April 1908–October 1909][2] First, suppose whole to be a *collection*.
    Let *p* be a predicate true of every individual of the collection and true of nothing else.

A—*u*—C   A is a member of C.

    If anything is *p* it is a member of some C.

    If anything is a member of any C it is *p*.

    asserts that *u* is either nothing or else is a single individual.

    expresses that there is a predicate and two subjects of *both* which that predicate is neither true nor false.

---

[2] [The most likely date is February 1909; cf. LN [343r], R 339, dated February 17, 1909.]

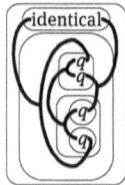

Unless any two things, *x* and *y*, are "identical", there is a predicate that is neither true of both nor false of both.

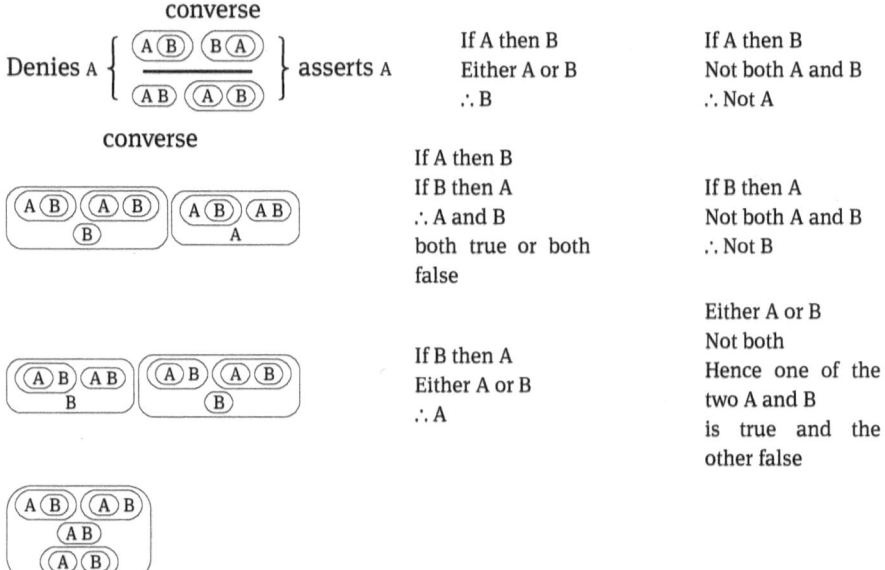

I intend to analyze the relation of Whole and Parts with care; but as this was only introductory to another subject, and I have simply wasted time, not being in time, I shall content myself with saying that the *parts* are a collection of independent objects, whose characters and relations would determine by themselves without any further principles all the essential characters of another object, their whole, and will determine nothing more. This is unsatisfactory and does not go deep; but it will "do" perhaps for my present purpose.

[Attachments]

October 31, 1909 Noon.

1. There may be one simple i.e. homogeneous being complete in itself.
2. There may be a being that needs *one* attachment only to complete it.

[P.H.:]

The two are necessarily of different kinds. Otherwise the two would make one simple and complete being. *Different* means of two kinds. Every complete being whose parts are merely single-needing consists of two. $\mathcal{M}$ being the number of kinds of parts which must be two or more, $\frac{\mathcal{M}(\mathcal{M}-1)}{2}$ is the number of different kinds of complete being.
3. There may be a being that needs *two* attachments. And there may be but two such parts

[P.H.:]

If there are only two kinds, the number of parts in the complete being must be even and half of one kind and half of the other. The two attachments of any one part must be of the same kind, the ABABAB number of parts must be even and the number of kinds two. If the attachments of each part must be unlike (BAC) (BACBAC) there must be at least three kinds and if only three the numbers of the several kinds must all be equal.

If there are four kinds and each is joined to two unlike parts there must be somewhere on the chain a succession of all four.

Then there may be four  or six or seven

[Modality]

September 13, 1910 [171][3]

It is my duty to investigate Modality more closely.

    A certain existing man *might* be attacked without defending himself.

    A person may dream that Theodore Roosevelt attacks him.

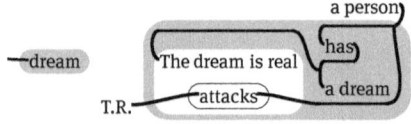

Field of may-be.

---

[3] [The pagination [171] that appears on the top right corner of the ms page is a post-microfilm addition on the physical leaves of the notebook.]

28 [Existential Graphs, from the *Logic Notebook*]

R 339, June 9, 1898–November 1, 1909. Houghton Library. This final chapter collects Peirce's entries on EGs as they appear in the *Logic Notebook* (LN). Between the Novembers of 1865 and 1909, he kept detailed notes on his ideas and the progress of the study of logic and semeiotic. This notebook, of which 340 non-blank pages survive, is a treasury of logical insights (see W1, p. 555 for its compositional history). Over the years, however, the notebook became unbound and its sheets loose and displaced, and many of its pages appear to have been lost.

Peirce's entries in LN on EGs are numerous and are from [102r]–[345r] of the notebook's pagination that was inscribed by later editors of Peirce's writings. The copy-text of the present selection comprises over sixty manuscript pages, and they represent some of the most intensive periods during which he drafted his notes. LN reveals that there are four peaks in Peirce's devotion to the development of EGs and which altogether are not much more than 12 months in duration: the summers of 1898 [102r]–[140r] and 1903 [236r]–[239r], from late 1905 until early March 1906 [264r]–[273r], and from late 1908 until early 1909 [319r]–[345r]. The first period concerns the setting up of the constitutive conventions and his revisions to the earlier permissive rules of transformation. (Peirce did not carry the notebook with him during his stays in New York City and there are no entries from the first, 1896–1897 phase of the development of the theory.) The second period, which falls between the Harvard and the Lowell Lectures and which is preceded by a five-year hiatus of making no records of EGs in LN at all, portrays Peirce's preliminary studies in view of bringing the theory into full fruition. These notes seem to have assisted him in composing a pedagogically thought-out presentation of the logical architectonic in the style of what can be found first in the *Logical Tracts* and then in the Lowell Lectures (LoF 2). The surprising "Studies of the Eight Systems of Existential Graphs", which is interpolated from a separate note (R 1483), derives from this period of initial planning of the Lowell Lectures. The third period consists of the study notes as he prepared for *The Monist* series on pragmaticism. It is here that Peirce is struck by his realisation of how to express necessity in graphs; his coveted "special sign" is no more and no less than the verso of the sheet of assertion.

Peirce's last logical notes from September 1908 to February 1909 are written in the somber mood of finally realising that plans for bringing his later logic before the public in any book-length form had to be forfeited. These notes portray an assortment of modifications, deviations and proposals for new kinds of graphs and types of graphs, and their potential applications. Among them one can mention explanations of "Peirce's Puzzle" ([319r, 320r]); plans for a new book entitled *Logic* and its planned preface on assertions, followed by a proposal for a graphical analysis of assertions ([329v–332r]); a non-trivial definition of the property of 'next after' ([335r]); proposals to extend the interpretation of the line to that of quantification over time ("is true under some circumstances"; "is true some times", etc., [340r]); and, in particular, three further stand-alone excerpts interpolated from non-LN sources but which coincide with the LN entries both topically and chronologically. The first is from the *Family Record* (R 1601), the second, "The Calculus of Existential Graphs", is interleaved from R 124 (February 7, 1909), and the third, "The System of Existential Graphs applied to the Examination of Itself" is taken from the Harvard sketchbook that derives from 1903 but was written in mid-February 1909 (R S-3).

With the editorial title of "[Collections]", the first of these non-LN additions is found on the pages of another notebook named "Family Record", which Peirce began writing as early as in June 1864. "[Collections]" is an unusual late study of the logic of collections, higher-order logic, and some modalities (alethic, epistemic, presumptive, temporal), with the shading of areas instead

https://doi.org/10.1515/9783110651409-032

of encircling by cuts. The dating of the relevant pages of the notebook is uncertain, but topically it fits well within the closely related topics in LN and in R 124 that are from early 1909. The *Family Record* may indeed have been Peirce's preferred place to continue recording logic entries after they ended in LN in early 1909. The second (R 124) deals with matters that are both preceded by the LN sketches on modal and temporal logic of events as well as followed by [343r] on "Geometrical Topics" and the part-whole considerations. The third is a belated follow-up on the 'graph of graphs' theory he had fleshed out in the Lowell Lectures but which he fell short of actually presenting to the audience. Instead, in that occasion he had announced that he would send material on that idea to anyone interested (LoF 2). His late attempt in R S-3 is too sketchy to make a communicable presentation, but at least two new things stand out: graph types that represent the assertion that "something *justifies* some other thing", and the beginnings of the "Logic of Time" that "involves more than one state of things." The next day, on February 16, 1909, Peirce would embark on the development of three-valued (triadic) logics, under the heading "Studies of Modal, Temporal, and Other Logical Forms which relate to Special Universes" [341r]. Since those studies on three-valued logics are presented in non-graphical notation, they are not included here (see Fisch & Turquette 1966 for the original study of Peirce's triadic logic). An orphan manuscript page of an unknown and lost paper from R S-36, dated February 12, 1909, is also interleaved here.

The closing sentence of the entire LN concludes the semiotic entries from the late 1909: "Let it be admitted then that no act of thinking can involve thinking about that very act of thinking." This can be read as an epitome of Peirce's lifetime of accomplishments: in one way or another his graphical method of logic was intended to tackle those "vexed questions of logic", which by now are fully conceived as semeiotic, and include the maxim of pragmaticism, abstraction and scientific reasoning, relationship of signs to minds, meta-logical theory of graphs of graphs, and the analysis of assertions and propositions, all emerging from the plurality of systems developed within the framework of the method of EGs.

June 9, 1898 [102r]

Existential Graphs: A system of logical expression
The Constitutive Conventions of this language

1. We pretend that the "graph", that is, what is written in a certain place agreed upon and called the "sheet of the graph" is a general description of a certain recognized state of things. With this state of things it is essential that the writer and reader of the graph should have sufficient common experience to identify it. For this purpose, the writer must act upon the reader to such effect that, first, the latter shall be forced into a dynamic, or experimential, reaction with the state of things referred to, and second, that he shall be further forced to regard the graph as standing for that state of things. A general description is a sign of such a nature that, on the one hand, it calls to mind [an] image, "like", that is to say, by virtue of the occult inward nature of the mind associated with, images of the object described, and like them in a constant respect, that is to say, mentally attracted to each other in being attracted to the images they are like, and with a special liveli-

ness of consciousness of this circumstance, while on the other hand, the images it calls up are not attracted to one another when the attention is so directed that they are not attracted to the images to which the object described calls up.

We "pretend" that it is so; for our purpose is merely to study formal logic. The graph is a mere specimen of an assertion for whose matter we care nothing.

The graph is a sign. A sign is the third member of the triad, Quale, Relate, Sign. A quale is something considered only as in itself as embodying an idea. A relate is something considered as paired with something. Every brutally physical relation is dyadic. Every triadic relation has some intellectual character. A triadic fact is degenerate, if it is a mere sum of dyadic reactions. It is [end]

June 9, 1898 [105r]
Existential Graphs
The Constitutive Conventions of this system of ~~assertion~~ expression

1. We pretend that the "graph", that is, what is written in a recognized place called the "sheet of the graph", is a general description or qualitative representation more or less vague, of a certain state of things. With this state it is essential that the writer and the reader of the graph should have a sufficient common experience to identify it. For that purpose, the writer must ~~communicate~~ so act upon to the reader that the latter shall be forced into a dynamic, or experiential, relation to the state of things in question and further be forced to connect the graph with it as its object. At the same time, the reader is supposed not so completely to know the writer's belief, or settled representation, of that state of things that he cannot receive further information. And it is hoped that further experience would establish the truth or falsity of the graph.
2. This descriptiveness is understood not merely of the whole graph collectively but of each part distributively.
3. Every ordinary graph is equivalent to a representation that a vaguer description applies to an individual.

June 10, 1898 [106r]
Existential Graphs: a system of logical expression
Chapter I. The Constitutive Conventions of the language of graphs

1. A certain place is called the sheet of the graph, and what is there written is called the graph.

We pretend that the graph is a general description of a certain recognized state of things.

We "pretend" it is so, for our purpose in experimenting with graphs is merely to study formal logic, the matter is a mere specimen ~~not to aver any real convictions of positive science. We therefore do not care whether we really believe~~ [of] what we pretend to assert or not.

The graph is a sign. That is, we do not care for its ~~character~~ nature or quality in itself, not for its dynamic reactions which pair it with other things, but we care for it as a medium whereby one thing, the idea in our mind, is brought into correspondence with an object. Every triadic relation is somewhat intellectual. Thus, if I accidentally upset my inkstand and make a spot on the tablecloth, the purely physical act is upsetting the inkstand. The effect on the tablecloth is a separate transaction between the ink and the cloth in which I have no hand. I am only responsible in that I might have known what would result; that is, it is an affair of knowledge. Even if the wind had upset the inkstand, it would have produced the effect only so far as the effect was necessary. But this supposes a law, and a law is an affair of intellect. Let us call a triadic fact genuine if it is not a mere ~~aggregate~~ sum of dyadic facts. Signification or representation is the principal kind of genuine triadic [end]

June 11, 1898 [107r]
Existential Graphs: a system of logical expression
I. The Constitutive Conventions of the language

1. We pretend that the "graph", that is, what is written in a certain place called the "sheet of the graph", is a general description of a certain recognized state of things.

With this state of things it is essential that both the writer and the reader of the graph should have sufficient common experience to identify it. For this identification, the writer must act upon the reader so that the latter shall be forced into an experiential reaction with that state of things, either then first becoming acquainted with it or having his attention directed to it. Not only that, but furthermore the reader must be forced to regard the graph as standing for that state of things.

A general description is a sign having several essential characters. In the first place, it calls up in the mind the idea of a quality like that of the object described. To say that an idea is *like* another is to say that by virtue of an inward occult disposition of mind it is associated with that other idea. But, in the second place, not only is the idea called up by the general description more or less like the true idea of the object, but a certain *respect* is isolated, or emphasized, in the mind in which it specially is like the object, and whether it is so in other respects or not is of no consequence. The general sign has not only the power of directing the mind of the reader to particular sensitiveness to a special [*illeg.*, a word torn out (quality?)] of likeness, but also has the power to make the reader see that [end]

June 11, 1898 [108r]
Existential Graphs: a system of logical expression
The constitutive conventions of existential graphs

1. A certain place may be called the "sheet of the graph" and what is there written may be called the graph.

We pretend that the graph is a general description of a certain recognized state of things.

We only "pretend" that it is so; for our purpose is merely to study formal logic, and the graph is a mere specimen of an assertion for whose matter we care nothing.

In the contents of consciousness we recognize three sorts of elements, Firstness, Secondness, Thirdness. A First is whatever it is in itself regardless of all else whether exterior to it or parts of it. It is feeling-quality. What a Second is depends partly on another, but is regardless of any third, and thus of any reason. It is brute reagent. What a Third is depends on two other things between which it mediates. Firstness is feeling-quality; secondness is brute reaction; thirdness is mediation. Secondness is *generous* or *degenerate*. A degenerate secondness is such a pairing as gives to each member of the pair only such a character as it would retain were the other non-existent. Generous secondness imparts a character to which the existence of the other member is essential. Generous secondness is an accident of individuals. Existence is that mode of being which is constituted by generous secondness. It only belongs to individuals. An individual is an object determined in respect to every character. Thirdness is either generous, degenerescent or perdegenerate. Perdegenerate thirdness imparts to its members as might belong to them though they were not existent. Degenerescent thirdness is a thirdness which imparts to its member such characters as involves their brute existence but not their *significance*, or conformity to general law. Generous thirdness is such as involves the significance of the members of the triad. By significance, I mean that mode of being which is constituted by generous thirdness. It is the mode of being of a continuum or law.

A sign has an object and an interpretant. In the interpretant, which is a partially indeterminate thing, the sign determines a Firstness, not absolute but relative to the object. The pairedness it brings about is not absolute or brute, but recognizes the sign as its creator.

Signs are of three kinds: Icons, Indices, Symbols. An icon is a sign in so far as it is *like* its object and produces an idea which being like itself is like its object. "Like" ideas are ideas attracted to one another by an occult inward law. Indices are signs acting by brute reactions. Symbols are signs which bring about ideas like their objects in certain definitely designated respects.

Symbols are either Terms, Propositions, or ~~Syllogisms~~ Arguments. A term is a symbol which only represents its object in so far as it embodies an idea which is formally a first. A proposition is a symbol which separately indicates with more or less definiteness to what object it refers; it presents in form a first and second. An arguments is a symbol which separately shows by what sign it is led to accept its proposition.

June 14, 1898

2. If a graph consists of graphs, that is, of parts that would have a meaning if written alone, then every such partial graph has its full effect in rendering the description less vague.
3. Continuity of a heavy line signifies the individual identity of all its parts. The whole graph may be conceived as connected by a heavy line with an index of the individual state of things described, but this line is not written.
4. A general description within a lightly drawn oval applies to whatever there may be of that description and is not asserted of the state of things considered.
5. A lightly drawn line crossing any graph denies they are all true. Thus ⦅is a man / is good⦆ means "something is a man and is not identical with anything that is good". But ⦅is a man / is good⦆ means "something A is a man and something B is good and A is not identical with anything X or else B is not identical with anything, Y, if X is identical with Y".

Questions. What is the connection between these two characteristics of symbols: first, that unlike an *icon* it has reference to a particular respect; second, that it represents itself as representing something otherwise known?

Answer: the latter is not a characteristic of all symbols, but only of propositions.

But as an *icon* represents the simple idea which it excites by inward association and the *index* represents the individual object which it excites by *outward* association, so the *symbol* represents that some individual of a collection indicated resembles certain ideas in so far as they resemble one another.

June 15, 1898 [114r]

Basic Formal Rules, from which regardless of the constitutive conventions all illative transformations are deducible

  I.   A graph, once being written, may remain.
  II.   The graph may be erased.
  III. Graphs which can be separately written may be written side by side.
  IV.   Every rule of illative transformation of a whole graph applies to every unenclosed part of a graph.
  V.   If any graph A is illatively transformable into any other B, then an enclosure consisting of an oval containing only B is transformable into an enclosure consisting of an oval containing A.
  VI.   Any graph may have two ovals drawn round it.
  VII. Every graph is equivalent to an enclosure consisting of an oval containing some graph.
  VIII. Every heavy line is a graph and can have attached to it a capital letter (index of some individual).
  IX.   Any two capital letters, transformable into one another, can be joined by a heavy line.
  X.   Any capital letter may be written unenclosed.
  XI.   Some possible graph cannot be written [end][1]

June 19, 1898 [125r]

The Dozen Basic Formal Rules

  I.   Some possible graph cannot be written unenclosed.
  II.   A graph once written, may remain, written.
  III. Any unenclosed part of the graph may be erased.

---

1 [Omitted here are Peirce's numerous derivations of theorems from these basic formal rules that occupy the next fourteen LN pages (Theorems XII–XXVIII, LN [115r]–[124r]). At this point Peirce notices, among other things, that "The basic rules given above are incorrect in regard to their effect on attached parts of graphs which are not in all respects like other parts. They are also ~~defective~~ redundant in regard to this that contraposition can be proved two ways. [...] All illative transformations can be effected by insertions and erasures; and every insertion or erasure illative for the whole graph is illative for every unenclosed partial graph" [122r].]

IV. Graphs that might be written separately may be written together.
V. Any graph which, standing alone, might be transformed into another may be so transformed wherever it is unenclosed, and detached.
VI. Every graph is equivalent to an enclosure containing some graph.
VII. Every graph may have two ovals drawn round it.
VIII. If any graph is transformable into another, then an enclosure containing only the transformed graph is transformable into an enclosure containing only the untransformed graph.
IX. Any graph of the kind called an index may be written unenclosed.
X. Any two indices transformable into one another may be joined by a heavy line, such line being a graph.
XI. Every heavy line can have some index attached to it.
XII. The shape of a heavy line (especially whether a furcation occurs at an enclosed or unenclosed part) is indifferent.

June 20, 1898 [126r]

The list of basic rules seems to be very bad.
I. Any unenclosed partial graph may be erased. [end]

August 4, 1898 [127r]

The Basic Rules of Existential Graphs are only ~~eight~~ seven

I. Any unenclosed part of a graph (except a part of an oval) can be erased (with all it encloses if it encloses anything) whether attached or detached.
II. Graphs scriptible separately can be written side by side.
III. Every heavy line can be joined to some individual index, after all less enclosed lines are so joined; but the individual may not be known.
IV. Mutually transformable indices can *always* be joined by a heavy line.
V. Two individual indices joined by a heavy line unenclosed and uncrossed by any lightly drawn line are mutually transformable.
VI. If from an unenclosed oval nothing protrudes but lines joined to indices, then were the oval removed, in the resulting graph its formal contents could be transformed into any graph at pleasure.
VII. If in a graph (not actually written) consisting of two graphs P and Q, joined, if at all, only by heavy lines each attached to an index in Q, P could be transformed into any graph at pleasure, while Q is scriptible, then a graph differing from this only in that P is in an oval can be written.

August 4, 1898 [128r]

We now come to **An Extension of Existential Graphs, permitting Abstraction**

It is the abstractive power of ordinary speech which renders it more logically powerful than any algebra of logic hitherto developed.

Abstraction consists essentially in regarding a set of things, ordered or unordered, as an individual object, and denoting it by an index.

But it is hard to define a "set" of things. Since, then, the idea of a *sign* is presupposed in logic, it is but to endeavor to define abstraction in terms of signs instead of sets. Abstraction consists in asserting that a given sign is applicable instead of merely applying it. Thus, I say Napoleon was a man to whom the term Great could be applied, instead of merely saying Napoleon was a great man.

Instead of saying A loves B, we may first say to A as first B as second may be applied the terms lover and loved. Or, what amounts to the same thing "A represents B in so far as the lover represents the loved", where "represents" is used in a very wide sense. "A is a sign of B to those for whom the lover is the sign of the loved".

Now we can carry abstraction one step further and say, to A as first and B as second may be applied a sign of which lover and loved is a sign. Or A is a sign of B to a representing sign represented by the sign of lover and loved.

What I mean is that A and B form an ordered pair which belongs to the *set* of pairs designated by lover and loved.

Try to define a pair, an ordered pair. You are driven to the idea of a sign. An ordered pair, or couple, is an object of which whatever is true is *ipso facto* true of a first object in one sense and of a second object in another sense. Or an ordered pair is an object in respect to which one object corresponds to another.

An ordered pair is an object whose essence consists in one existing object being taken as first and another as second.

We want a symbol to say that one thing is the first in a certain ordered pair of which the other is second.

 A is the first, B the second of the ordered pair C.

 It will be convenient to allow the line from C to emerge on either side.

No. 1. This is merely what is true of any relative.

No. 2. Nothing is everything.  No. 2. bis.

No. 3. Some character belongs to nothing. ──●

No. 4. Given any two things there is some character they both possess such that taking anything it is either identical with one or the other or does not possess that character.

We also need a ~~sign~~ symbol to express that A belongs to the general unordered collection B: ●━

Thus A loves B may be written [is a pair of which the first loves the second] or [the relation of lover to loved]

These two signs may be joined in one [symbol] meaning A stands to B in the relation C.

Take any two characters there is some character such that taking anything whatever either it has neither of the first characters and does not have the third or it has one of the first characters and has the third.

$$\Pi_\alpha \Pi_\beta \Sigma_\gamma \,\bar{p}_{\alpha i} \cdot \bar{p}_{\beta i} \cdot \bar{p}_{\gamma i} \curlyvee (p_{\alpha i} \curlyvee p_{\beta i}) \cdot p_{\gamma i}$$

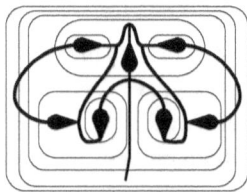

No. 5. Given any character there is another such that taking anything whatever it either possesses the second and not the first or the first and not the second.

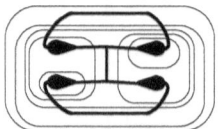

No. 6. Anything (or the same thing) forms a pair

No. 7. No two things form more than one pair

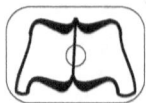

No. 8. The same pair is formed by one only two things [sic.] in a given order.

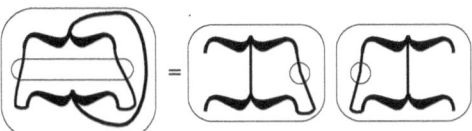

The facile abstraction of ordinary language brings these two into one proposition.

No. 9. Given any relation there is a relation such that taking any two things either the first is not in the first relation to the second or the second is in the second relation to the first and either the first is in the first relation to the second or the second is not in the second relation to the first.

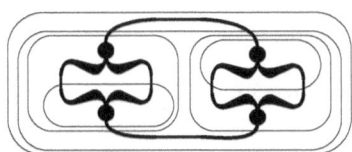

No. 10. The universe here requires attention. But for simplicity in these graphs different universes are not distinguished.

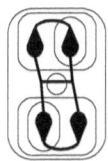

No. 11.

August 5, 1898 [132r]

Let a sequence be defined as follows:

First, take any object. Then,
  it is either not a sequence
  or there is a relation such that
    First, there is another relation
      and taking any two objects whatever
        either the one is not in the former relation to the other
        or taking any object whatever
          either the former of the first two is in the latter relation to the third
          or the latter of the first two is not in the latter relation to the third
          and further there is something such that
            the former of the first two is in the latter relation to the fourth
            while the latter of the first two is not in the latter relation to the fourth
      and further taking any two objects whatever
        either the former of the two is in the former relation to the second
        or there is an object such that
          the former of the first two is not in the latter relation to this fifth
          while the latter of the first two is in the latter relation to this fifth
          or taking any object whatever
            either the former of the first two is not in the latter relation to this sixth
            or the latter of the first two is in the latter relation to this sixth
    and second, taking any two objects whatever
      either one or the other does not belong to that sequence
      or they are identical
      or the one is in that first relation to the other
      or the latter is that relation to the former.
Second, take any object.
  It either is a sequence
  or taking any object
    it is not a relation of the above description.

But it is not necessary to introduce the first relation.

First, take any object.
  A. It is either not a sequence
  B. Or else—There is a relation such that two things are true
    C. First, taking any two objects
      E. Either the one or the other does belong to the sequence
      F. Or two things are true
        G. First, taking any third object the first is in that relation to this object
        J. Or the second is *not* in that relation to the third object
        H. And second
          There is an object such that
            K. The first is in that relation to this fourth object
              L. and the second is not in that relation to this fourth object
    D. Second, taking any two objects, one or other of 3 things is true

M.1. Either both belong to the sequence
  N.2. Or there is an object of which two things are true
    P. First, the first object is not in that relation to this
    Q. Second, the second object is in that relation to this
  O.3. Or taking any object whatever
    R. Either the first is not in that relation to it
    S. Or the second is in that relation to it.
Second, take any object
  It either is a sequence
  Or there is no relation of that description.

[136r]

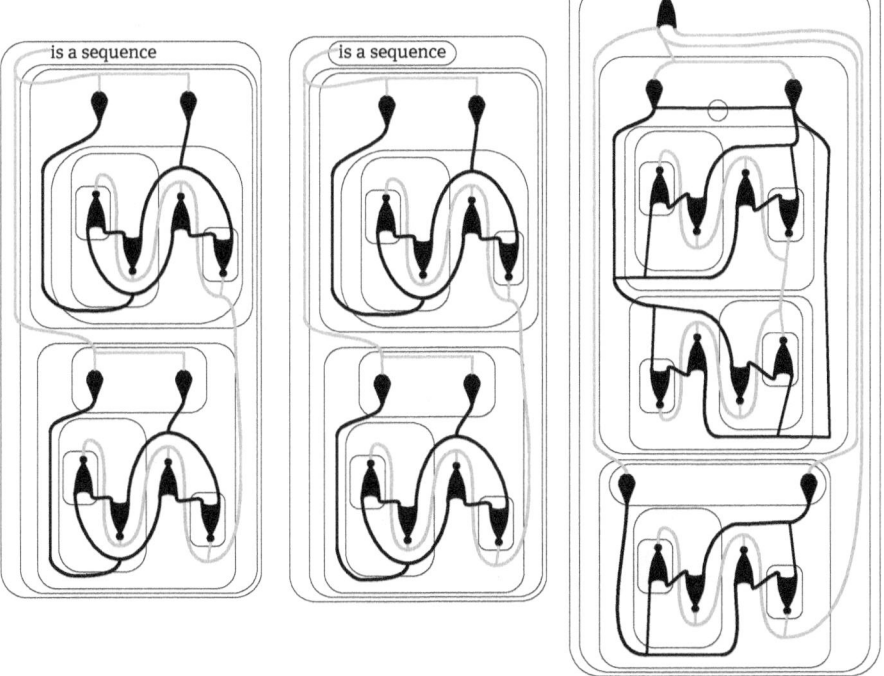

[138r]

But the above leaves out an alternative, namely that it may be the *second* that is in the relation to the *first*.

August 6, 1898 [139r]

The whole numbers form a sequence which has this property, where —g— means —exceeds—. The universe is that of the numbers.

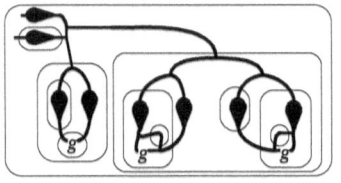 Hence follows the important Fermatian theorem: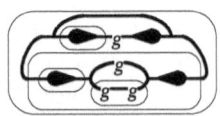

Addition of whole numbers defined by
$$0 + 0 = 0$$

Multiplication is defined by
$$0 \times 0 = 0$$
$$x \times Ey = (x \times y) + x$$
$$Ex \times y = y + (x \times y)$$

Let Ex be no. next greater than x
$$x + Ex = E(x + y)$$
$$Ex + y = E(x + y)$$

Involution
$$x^1 = x$$
$$X^{Ex} = x \cdot x^y$$

August 8, 1898 [140r]

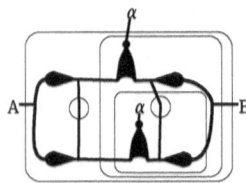 A's are at least as small in multitude than the B's.

December 11, 1900 [178r, 179r]

A New Logical Algebra.[2]

---

[2] [Included are two holograph pages of autograph manuscript sheets [178r] and [179r], substantially suffered from wear and tear, entitled "A New Logical Algebra". Not included is a third page, [181A], which is a draft from the same date entitled "A New System of Graphs", which hardly gets beyond the title in describing new system of graphs or of algebra, only stating two principles: "Writing propositions together means that each is scriptible alone" and "$\begin{pmatrix} x \\ y \end{pmatrix}$ means that x is transformable into y." A familiar transformation is then described, namely that "Any unenclosed part of a graph may be erased, or $\begin{pmatrix} x\,y \\ y \end{pmatrix}$", followed by a page-long list for several other transformation rules given in algebraic form. The ideas on this page may nevertheless have sparked off

28 [Existential Graphs, from the *Logic Notebook*] (R 339), 1898–1909

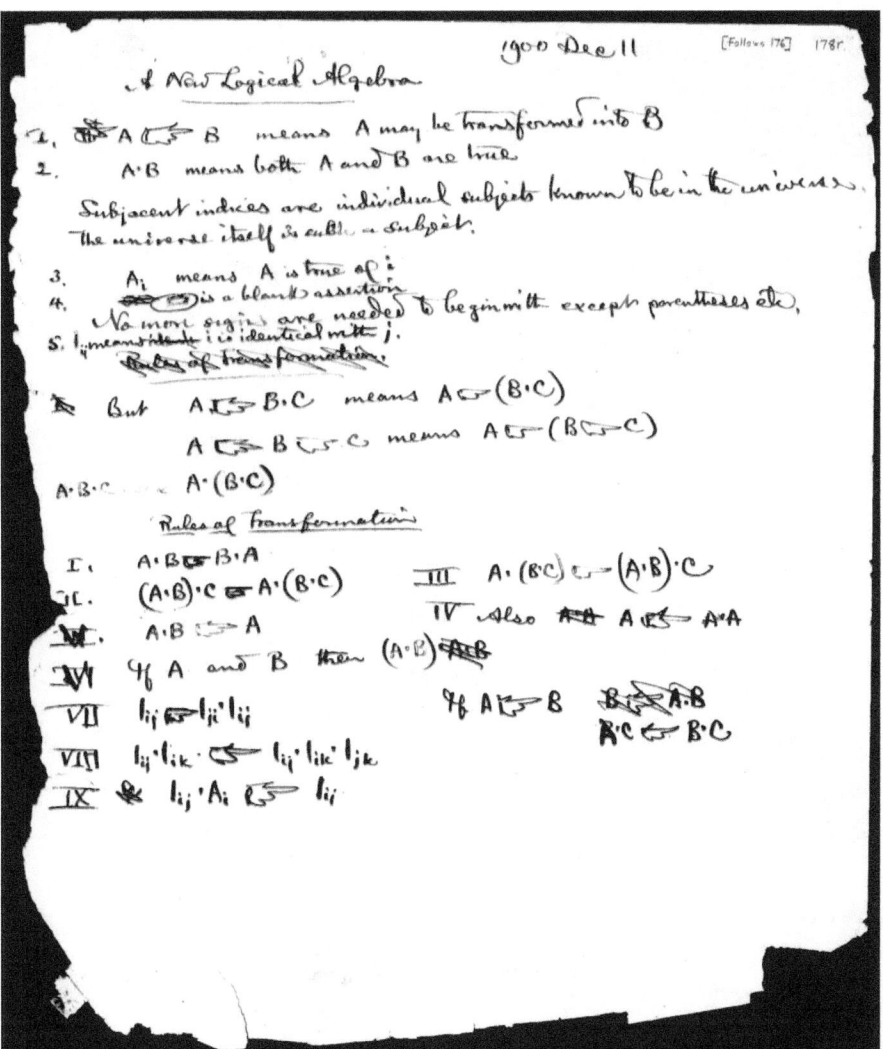

A holograph page [178r] (Harvard Peirce Papers, R 339)

Peirce's drafting of the worksheets on the Dragon-Head and the Dragon-Tail notation (R 501 and the adjacent pages; see Ma & Pietarinen 2019).]

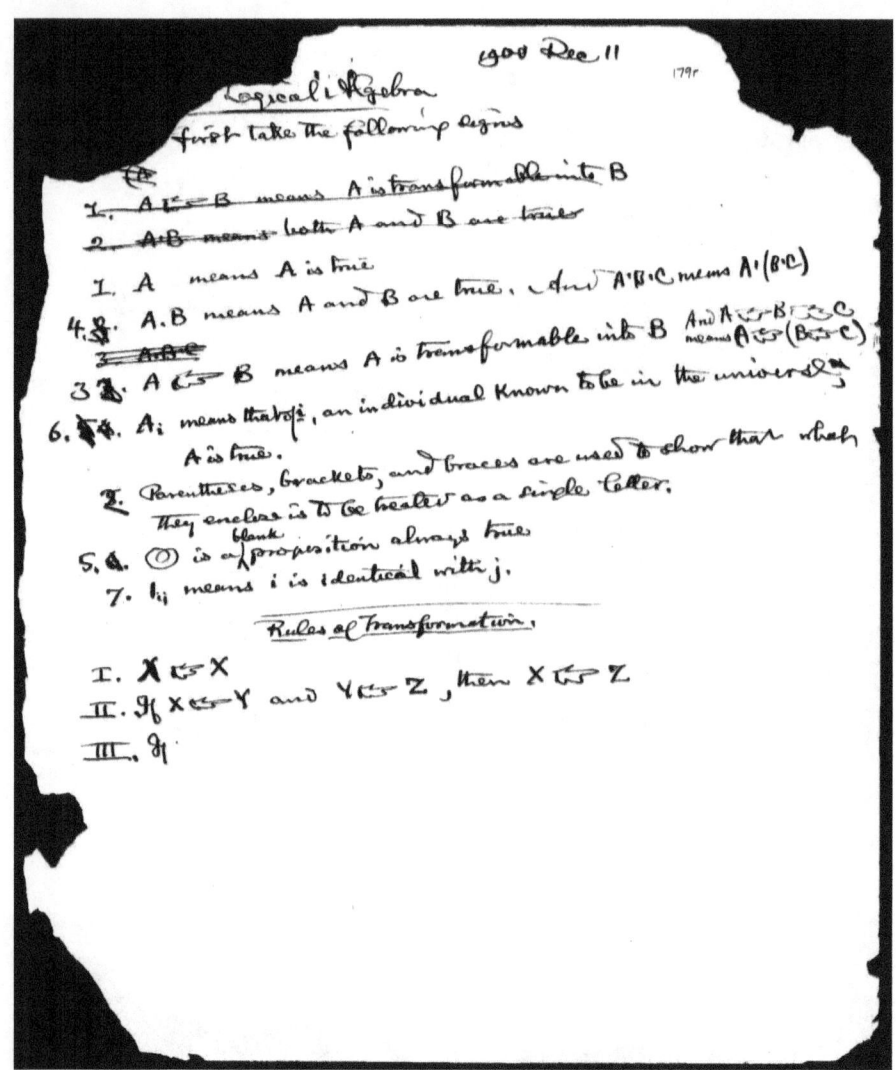

A holograph page [179r] (Harvard Peirce Papers, R 339)

June 11, 1903 [236r]

- Principle of contradiction (not) Nothing is other than itself.
- Principle of excluded middle (not) Everything is other than everything explicitly.
- Given (is a man / not — a fool), by simple insertion (is a man / not — a fool). By principle of contrad[iction] (not)(not — is a fool). By iteration (not)(not / not — is a fool). By deiteration (not)(not / is a fool). By simple erasure (is a man / is a fool). By two ovals (is a man / is a fool).
- A being an index A—x is the same as A—x.
- Any onoma may be changed to an outer onoma evenly enclosed.
- Any oddly enclosed onoma may be changed to any outer onoma.
- Any two connecting lines may be connected, unless the outer is oddly the inner evenly enclosed.

June 27, 1903 [237r]

There are eight possible systems of Existential Graphs, as follows:[3] [R 1483]

Studies of the Eight Systems of Existential Graphs

First I will draw up Rules for my ~~standard~~ usual system.

- A heavy line enclosed or not enclosed is a graph.
- But a line where it crosses a sep is not a graph.
- $\ominus m$ means Something is not m.
- That is *on* the sep virtually crosses the sep.

Hence $\ominus g$ can be transformed to $\ominus g$ but *not* to $(-g)$. For to do so would be to erase in the close.

---

[3] [Peirce does not present these "eight possible systems" in LN [237r] beyond a couple of doodles; R 1483 contains a related proposal up to the fourth system, and is presumed to have been written around the same time.]

On the contrary ⊂-g⊃ can be transformed to ⊂-g⊃ because we can insert in the close; and ⊂-g⊃ is equivalent to ⊂-g⊃. Hence ⊂-g⊃ by mere shortening becomes ⊂-g⊃ and then because evenly enclosed graphs can be erased (⊂-g⊃).

Now let us see how it is when there are other lines.

⊂—loves—⊃ $\Sigma_i P_{ij}\, l_{ij} = \varphi_{11}.\varphi_{12}.\varphi_{13}.$ etc $\curlyvee \varphi_{21}.\varphi_{22}.\varphi_{23}.$ etc $\curlyvee$
           $P_{ij}\Sigma_i\, l_{ij} = (\varphi_{11}\curlyvee \varphi_{21}\curlyvee \varphi_{31}\curlyvee$ etc$).(\varphi_{12}\curlyvee \varphi_{22}\curlyvee \varphi_{32}\curlyvee$ etc$)$

⊂—loves—⊃ by elongation becomes ⊂—loves—⊃ $l_{12} \cdot l_{13} \curlyvee l_{23}$
                                              $l_{12} \curlyvee l_{23}\, l_{13} \curlyvee l_{23}$

The proof is this:

- If ⟨man—loves—woman⟩ either —woman or ⟨—woman⟩.
- In the latter case ⟨man—loves—woman⟩ is not true because it gives —woman.
- In the former case ⟨man⟨loves⟩woman⟩ / ⟨man—loves—woman⟩ whence $m\!\!-\!\!b\!\!-\!\!w / m\!\!-\!\!b\!\!-\!\!w$ whence $m\!\!-\!\!b / m\!\!-\!\!b\!\!-\!\!w$ whence $m\!\!-\!\!b / m\!\!-\!\!b$ whence $m\!\!-\!\!b / m\!\!-\!\!b$ which is a contradiction.
- This may be arranged thus: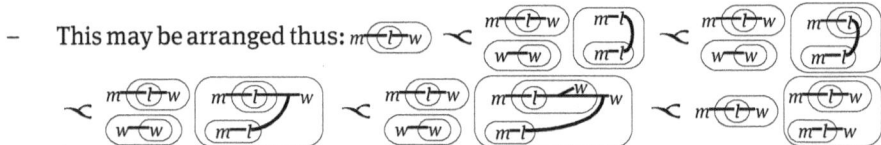

This is on the principle that $a\!\!-\!\!\text{⟨}b\text{⟩} = a\!\!-\!\text{⟨}b\text{⟩}$ and $a\, \text{⟨}\!\!-\!\!b\text{⟩} = a\, \text{⟨}\!\!-\!\!b\text{⟩}$.

Why can we pass from $\Sigma_i \Pi_j\, l_{ij}$ to $\Pi_i \Sigma_i\, l_{ij}$?

The only proof known is based on the supposition that the i's and j's

Try reduction *ad absurdum*. If ⟨-b⟩ then ⟨⟨-b⟩⟩ and also ⟨⟨-b⟩⟩ and also ⟨⟨-b⟩⟩.
$\Sigma_i \Pi_j\, l_{ij} \prec \Sigma_i\, l_{ij}$
$\Pi_i\, l_{ii} = \Pi_i \Sigma_i\, l_{ij}$

Rules.

(1)   An unenclosed graph can be erased.

(2) Every transformation permitted on sheet is permitted in every even close and the reverse in every odd close.
(3) Any graph can be iterated within same or additional *seps* and either of two iterations can be erased.
(4) ⟨a⟩=⟨a⟩   b─○ = b─○   A sep is outside its close.
(5) Point in close of sep may be identical with point on sep. Every oddly enclosed line of identity can be joined to every one not additionally enclosed. Not basic. Every oddly enclosed line can be cut so as to leave inner part evenly enclosed. Sheet is pseudo-continuous.
(6) Rule of two ovals.

There are besides rules for proper names and for abstractions.

Second System. This differs from my usual system only in regarding a partially enclosed line of identity to be enclosed; so that man─⟨good⟩ usually means $\Sigma_i \Sigma_j \Pi_k m_i \cdot l_{ij} \cdot (t_{jk} \curlyvee \bar{g}_k)$ but now is to mean $\Sigma_i \Pi_j \Pi_k m_i \cdot l_{ij} \cdot (t_{jk} \curlyvee \bar{g}_k)$.[4]

This *condemns* the system.

Third System. This system differs from my usual one only in this that instead of expressing "If *a* then *c*" *de inesse* by ⟨⟨a⟩c⟩ it is expressed by ⸨a⸩c.

Of course as to erasures and insertion it is only the heavy line that counts.
The rule of identification will be considerably more complicated.

Fourth System. This system differs from my usual one only in this that a line of identity unenclosed refers to *everything* in the universe.
Hence

a—b	a line outside entirely has no effect
a─⟨b⟩	no effect
⟨a—b⟩	no effect
⟨a⊥b⟩	Everything is either $\bar{a}$ or $\bar{b}$
⟨a⊥b⟩	Something is both *a* and *b* (You have to give up the interpretation as conditional)
⟨b⊥a⟩	Anything if *a* is *b*
⟨─loves─⟩	Anything you please is such that not anything you please is unloved by it
⟨─m⟩	Everything loves something
⟨─loves─⟩	Something loves everything [end R 1483]

---

4 [...] ~~means taking anything whatever there is a man that it is or else it is not good.~~

June 29, 1903 [238r]

The great *défaut* of my graphs (and of course any logical algebras) is this:

I can say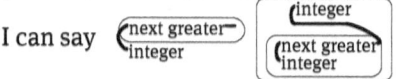

But now I want to say that there is no integer except what these two conditions

necessitate: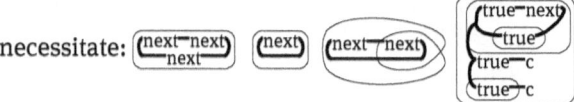

July 10, 1903 [239r]

Endless Nests of Seps:

[P.H.]

The graph asserts nothing since $\bar{x} \prec x$ so that it must be true while a must be absurd.

December 14, 1905 [264r]

In existential graphs on the sheet we erase what we like that is to say we erase depth, and therefore what is scribed on the sheet is scribed in depth. What is scribed oddly enclosed is on the other hand scribed in breadth. It may be that the *negation* element is essential to all that is scribed in breadth but one would suppose not and that many relations not to existents but pseudo-relations, as for example to qualities etc. would be of the same nature, so that we should have some more elementary kind of cut.

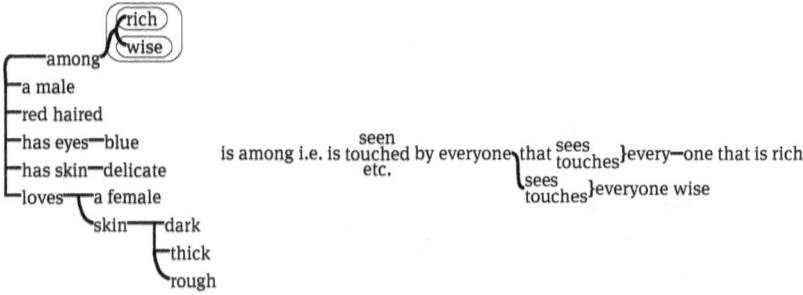

Any part can be erased.

28 [Existential Graphs, from the *Logic Notebook*] (R 339), 1898–1909

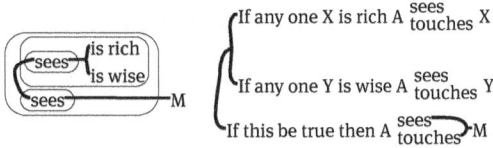

If M is unseen by somebody that person does not see somebody who is both rich and wise. But we want to make this *necessary*. At present it states a mere accidental fact.

December 14, 1905 [265r] continued

What I am after is to remove the anomaly by which in existential graphs "other than" is expressed differently from any other relation,—or appears to be so. Will not this anomaly be removed if ⌜wise/virtuous⌝ be understood not merely to express the fact *de inesse* that there exists nothing that is wise and is not virtuous, but to express that the essential idea of the wise requires its object to be virtuous as part of its logical depth? But if so how shall we express the fact that a wise object not virtuous does not happen to exist? In answer to that I would suggest that we might make individual existence a predicate. ⌜wise/existent now/virtuous⌝ I do not know that I am pronounce definitely that this won't do. But I hardly believe it would do. I should be more inclined to have some special sign to show that the world spoken of in the general proposition is an ideal world.

December 15, 1905 [266r]

(At 5:30 this morning, as I was standing back to the heater ruminating upon the problem of the last page, it suddenly struck me that all my observations led logically to the idea that completely answer the riddle. I haven't any very definite idea of it as yet. But that I am going to proceed to evolve.)[5]

I set out from the remark that if I scribe on the sheet of assertion ⌜is a woman/is an angel⌝ I do not therein assert that there is any such thing as an angel. I do assert that there is such an **idea** as the idea of an angel. It means that the woman in question has some character that no angel has. Or differs from angels in some respect in which all angels would necessarily agree. She lacks some essential character of an angel.

– Some woman either does not possess *x* or else *x* is a character of *x* or else *x* is not an angel: ⌜is a woman/possesses—is a character of—is an angel⌝

---

5 [Paragraph written in blue ink.]

– This woman possess no characters except such as are common to all angels:

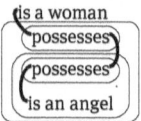

(December 20, 1905.) Whatever is to have its existence affirmed unconditionally must be scribed on the sheet.

Whatever has not its existence affirmed, but only has it hypothesized is to be singly enclosed; as ⊂man/fool⊃.

Whatever is to have its existence affirmed conditionally upon the existence of something B unconditionally supposed must be scribed in a cut upon the same area as B. ⊂man lover of ⊂virgin⊃⊃ "Some man is a lover, if at all, only of a virgin".

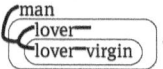. This follows from the other and so on.

January 30, 1906 [271r]

A sign is a species of medium of ~~inter~~communication.

The object, O, determines the sign, S, and S determines the Interpreting sign, I, to being determined by O through S.

There are now five questions to be considered.

(1) What would be the effect of adding to the condition that S must *correspond* to O according to some system?
(2) What would be that of adding that I is to be determined by the very determination of S by O?
(3) How would it be to require that I should be determined in such a manner as to contract a habit?
(4) How would it do to say that a sign is a consciousness of a habit; that is, that an instance of a sign is a present determination of a quasi-mind brought about by the direct action of a habit of that quasi-mind. That is, that the mere truth of the proposition that under certain circumstances it *would* be determined in a certain way, directly determines an actual determination of that quasi-mind?
(5) Is every sign a proposition as in Existential Graphs? And does every proposition relate to the future as its object? Is every knowledge or even conjecture a sign? Is every sign determined by its object? Is all real determination a determination of the relatively past by the relatively future? How are these propositions to be escaped or reconciled?

28 [Existential Graphs, from the *Logic Notebook*] (R 339), 1898–1909

To begin with it is necessary to distinguish between the *immediate* and the *dynamic* object of a sign.

March 7, 1906 [273r]

⌐γ   is a graph

D⌐$\genfrac{}{}{0pt}{}{B}{C}$ D is an instance of graph B on area C

A always stands for the area of the sheet

E⌐ϵ⌐H   E is an enclosure or cut on the area F of which enclosure or cut [of]
  F   the area is H

ε⌐K   K may be erased, K being a single *graph-instance*

ⲓ⌐L   L may be scribed, L being a single *graph*

P⌐W$\genfrac{}{}{0pt}{}{M}{N}$ P is a graph consisting of two graphs M and N. Or put

R⌐W⌐S   R contains as a part S.

March 9, 1906 [274r]

In all discourse there is but one symbol. Its parts are joined by lines of identity *solely*. Every object to which it refers must be immediately or mediately joined through the graph of coexistence with a known object of the same universe.

Every object (by which I mean that which determined the interpreter's intention through determining the sign, the "object" of a proposition being for example the *fact*, real or not, which the proposition expresses) is of one or other of two kinds which I know not how to characterize without suggesting some idea that I do not mean. Otherwise I would say "represented as external" and "represented as imaginary". But to avoid the wrong ideas these suggest, I will take the colorless designations "active" and "passive".

The interpreter has no logical right to admit any active object without the specific assurance of a sign. He has a logical right to admit all the passive objects he can conjure up. When a sign has given him the right to admit an active object he can still refrain from thinking it if he likes. But he cannot logically refuse to admit a passive object without a specific sign authorizing him to do so. Therefore active objects may be termed *actualities* and passive objects *possibilities*.

He cannot think of an object as an actuality without a sufficient sign. But he may refrain from thinking of any object as actuality whenever he pleases. He can think of an object as a possibility from his thought without a sufficient warrant of a sign.

Consequently, to avoid setting down an infinity of objects we represent the actualities whose admission to thought is warranted on one side, recto of the sheet, and on the *verso* the possibilities whose exclusion is warranted.

September 5, 1906 [286r]

The purpose of a Diagram is to represent certain relations in such a form that it can be transformed into another form representing other relations involved in those first represented and this transformed icon can be interpreted in a symbolic statement.

It is necessary that the Diagram should be an Icon in which the inferred relation should be perceived. And it is necessary that it should be in so far General that one sees that accompaniments are no part of the Object.

The Diagram is an Interpretant of a Symbol in which the signification of the Symbol becomes a part of the object of the Icon.

No other kind of sign can make a truth *evident*. For the *evident* is that which is presented in an image, leaving for the work of the understanding merely the Interpretation of the Image in a Symbol.

The Dynamic Interpretant is the *Action* of transforming the Diagram.

The Eventual Interpretant is the Symbol interpreting the transformation or is it the transformed Diagram? The latter is the first Eventual Interpretant.

September 6, 1908 [319r]

I consider the graph (wife of—fails / —suicides) $\Sigma_i \Sigma_j w_{ji} \cdot (\bar{f}_i \,\Psi\, s_i)$.

A = There is a married pair and if the husband fails the wife suicides.
B = If every married man fails some married woman suicides.

$$\Sigma_m \Sigma_n \Sigma_p \Sigma_q w_{nm} \cdot \bar{f}_n \,\Psi\, w_{qp} \cdot s_p.$$

Let w be a state of things and f_{wu} means u fails in state of things w.

$$A' = \Sigma_i \Sigma_j \Pi_w \bar{f}_{wj} \,\Psi\, \bar{w}_{wji} \,\Psi\, s_{wi}$$

There is a man and a woman and under all circumstances if the man is married to the woman and he fails she will suicide.

$$A = \Sigma_i \Sigma_j \Pi_w w_{ji} \cdot (\bar{f}_{wj} \,\Psi\, s_{wi})$$

There is a married couple and under all circumstances if the husband fails the wife will suicide.

$$B = \Pi_w \Sigma_i \Sigma_j \, w_{ji} \cdot (\bar{f}_{wj} \, \Psi \, s_{wi})$$

Under all circumstances, there is a married couple and if all husbands fail some married woman will suicide.

$$C = \Sigma_j \Pi_w \Sigma_i \, w_{ji} \cdot (\bar{f}_{wj} \, \Psi \, s_{wi})$$

There is a married man and under all circumstances if he fails some wife of his will suicide.

Let h_{uv} mean u and v live in the same house. c_{tu} means that u comes home on say t. e_{tu} means v eats dinner on say t.

$\Sigma_u \Sigma_v \Pi_t \, h_{uv} \cdot (\bar{c}_{tu} \, \Psi \, e_{tv})$. There is somebody living in a house who has one or other of two things, either he eats dinner every day he comes home or is on such terms with another person in the house that every day on which he comes home that other eats dinner. [That is,] Some person is on such terms with some person (himself or another) living in the same house that if the former comes home the latter eats dinner.

$\Pi_t \Sigma_u \Sigma_v \, h_{uv} \cdot (\bar{c}_{tu} \, \Psi \, e_{tv})$. On every day somebody or other eats dinner unless there be somebody living in the same house who does not come home, or what is the same thing, on every day on which if everybody that lives in a house at all comes home somebody in the same house eats dinner.

$\Sigma_u \Pi_t \Sigma_v \, h_{uv} \cdot (\bar{c}_{tu} \, \Psi \, e_{tv})$. Every day there is somebody that does not come home unless there be somebody living in the same house who eats dinner. [That is,] There is some person of whom it is true that on every day on which he comes home somebody living in the house with him eats dinner.

See January 7, 1909.[6]

September 7, 1908 [320r]

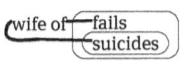

There is a married woman and should her husband fail she will commit suicide (under the actual circumstances). But it is not said that his failure will have any connexion with her suicide.

---

6 [See also the facsimile holograph page [319r] at the end of the present selection, and the related [319v] (facsimile page) and [340r] (transcription below) both of which Peirce inscribed on January 7, 1909.]

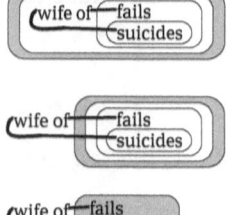

Under all circumstances there would be a married woman who, should her husband fail, would commit suicide.

There is a married woman and under all circumstances, *the fact would be*,[4] that if her husband fails she will commit suicide.

There is a married woman; and if her husband *might* fail she will suicide.

There is a married woman and should her husband fail she might commit suicide.

October 15, 1908 [329v–330r, 331r–332r]

I will begin my *Logic* like this:[7]

If nobody ever reads what I have set down, it goes virtually unuttered. In other words, if it be uttered it is interpreted by a Reader; and to this Hypothetical Reader I say, You necessarily know the English language, which implies a certain likeness between your mind and mine. Not only that, but you and I inhabit the same world and are acquainted with many of the same things in it (whether directly or indirectly does not much matter). Each of us well knows that the other has this common ground of experience with himself. Each knows the other knows it; each knows the knows that *he* knows it; each knows the other knows he knows the other knows it; and so on *ad infinitum*. I will term this ~~infinite~~ endless series of knowings a *mutual understanding*. Do not lose sight of the fact that our mutual understanding implies much common experience, mostly indirect. Thus, we have a common experience of the city of H'Lassa, though I was never there, and should be surprised if you were. By one's "experience" I mean the substance of the knowledge and seeming knowledge that the course of his life has forced him to acknowledge to himself, to recognize.

These two facts, then—(1) our mutual understanding and (2) your understanding of the dialect I employ—render it certain that when I assert something, that is, endeavour by my utterances to induce you to recognize it as true, you will (if not invariably, at least sometimes) know what it is to which I intend to bring you to assent; for otherwise you would not be my Reader; and were you to deny it you

---

4 Qu[estion]: What precisely does this mean?

7 [The analysis of assertion in graphs into subjects and predicate in the next paragraph [332r] is motivated by this "Preface" to a book on logic that Peirce began to sketch here. That book, which he planned to be "a smallish and popularish book on logic" [327v] did not appear to have progressed beyond a couple of pages of prefatory remarks.]

would *ipso facto* demonstrate its truth. In the first place, by virtue of our former common experience and our mutual understanding of it, you will recognize one or more of things I mention or allude to. These I term the *dynamical subjects* of my assertion. In the second place, by virtue of your knowledge of the language I employ, you will understand what it is that I mean to predicate about the subject or subjects.

I need not tell you that any assertion is composed of *subject* and *predicate*; for grammar has taught you that. Grammar, however, looks upon these matters in a superficial way; and the traditional logic is scarcely better. Permit me to suggest you are regarding the matter from a different point of view, from which I am confident that, as soon as you become familiar with it, you will agree with me that the true composition of an assertion is revealed much more distinctly than from that of grammar. In the first place, then, when I speak of the *subject* I do not mean the grammatical subject nominative, nor do I necessarily mean that real thing which the subject nominative denotes. I cannot in a single brief sentence give you a perfectly definite distinct plea of what I mean. I shall have to be a little vague at first. By the subject I mean that about which the assertion is made, whether the name of it be in the nominative or not. You must consider the *meaning*, not the linguistic expression merely. For instance, in the assertion "Rienzi was on the borderline between a great man and a fool", the dynamical subject is Rienzi. In the assertion, "The greatest mind of the tenth century was Gerbert", there are two subjects, the man Gerbert, and the European men of the tenth century. In the assertion "Julius Caesar died at the foot of a statue of Gnaeus Pompeius", the subjects are the two men Caesar and Pompey. For though some statue is mentioned, it only serves to describe the event, which concerned Caesar chiefly but Pompey, too. Two remarks will serve to give you a clearer notion of what I mean by a dynamical subject of an assertion. The first is this. I have said that the subjects and predicate are the two parts of an assertion. (Abelard reckoned the copula as a third part; and in a certain sense, it is a part of an assertion, but not in the sense in which the subject and predicate are parts. It is nothing but a mark that the predicate is to be understood predicatively, that is, as increasing the interpreter's inform conveying information, and not as limiting the denotation of the grammatical subject.) Now while the predicate may call up in the mind an entirely express a novel combination of characters, such as the interpreter never dreamed before of any subject possessing, no assertion can make us acquainted with its dynamical subject, but can only point it out among the things with which some collateral experience must make the interpreter acquainted before the assertion can convey its meaning to him.[8] Thus if anybody were to tell me Bartolomé y Herrera was ~~living in 1639~~ not alive in 1650, and if I never heard of any person of that name, it would convey no information whatever. But if I were subsequently to come into possession of a portrait so signed, it might at once convey an important fact to me.

(October 18, 1908.) The second remark about the subject of an assertion is that more or fewer may be regarded as subjects while the remainder of the assertion is the predicate. Moreover instead of regarding the subjects as plural one may regard the whole set as forming the *Collective Dynamical Subject*. The *Complete* Collective Dynamical Subject includes *all* that it is necessary to be acquainted with in order to understand the assertion, excepting the forms of connection between the different *Single Subjects*. Thus in the assertion "Every catholic adores some woman", the Complete Subject embraces, first, the character of being catholic, second, the character of the relation of adoring, third, the character of being a woman; and the proposition is that, the character of being catholic determines anything to be in the relation of adoring to something having the character of a woman.

October 20, 1908 [332r]

To analyze an assertion into Subjects and Predicate, comes to making the Subjects to be all the simple monads that can be imagined that with Predicates will make up the Assertion.

> The Great Pyramid is white

Its subjects are "The Great Pyramid" and "whiteness"

> The Great Pyramid *possesses* the character of whiteness or
> The Great Pyramid *stands in the relation of to* a character possessed that is at once a possession of something—and—is whiteness
>
> Pyramid—Possesses—whiteness
> Pyr.—is in relation to—whiteness / of—possessing
> Brutus—kills—Caesar
> Brutus—is in the relation { of—killing / to—Caesar
> Brutus—has—the relation { of—killing / to—Caesar

---

[8] [Del.:] Thus, if while you or I are upon a pedestrian tour through a country where we had never been before, an aeroplane flying with prodigious speed were to descend from an immense height to a level where the aeronaut could make himself heard; and he were to shout out there is a house on fire, ~~and the flames are bright green~~ and a man has been burned to death, and on our asking "where do you come from?" he were to call out "From China", and hie away, ~~we should~~ [end]

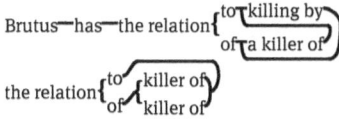

December 4, 1908 [335r]. Definition of Next After

If F is *next after* E in the Series, S, in respect to Π,

(1) There is a genus, Γ, of qualities such that there is a member, L of the collection, S, such that whatever quality, g, of the genus, Γ, be considered, L possesses g

(2) and there is a member, A, of the collection, S, such that whatever quality, q of the genus, Γ, be considered, A does not possess q

(3) and there is a quality, ⊙, of the genus, Γ, such that whatever member, t, of the collection S be considered, ⊙ is possessed by t

(4) and there is a Ω of the genus, Γ, such that whatever member, r of the collection S be considered, Ω is not possessed by r.

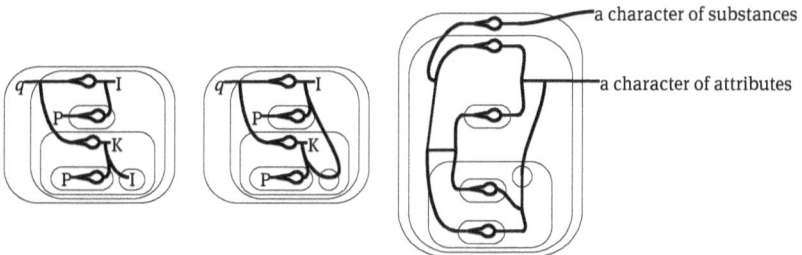

[336r]

(1) There is a genus, Γ, of qualities such that taking any member, g, of the collection, S there is a member, P, of the collection, S and there is a quality, I, of the genus Γ such that I is possessed by q but not by P and taking any quality, κ, of the genus Γ either κ is not possessed by q, or it is I, or it is possessed by P.

(2) Taking any quality, κ', of the genus Γ there is a quality I', of the genus Γ and a member P', of the collection S such that P' possesses κ' but not I' and taking any member q' of the collection S either q' does not possess κ', or is P', or possesses I.

January 7, 1909 [340r]

♭	*p* is true under some circumstances
ⓑ	*p* is true under all circumstances
♭ ♭	*p* is true some times and *q* true some times
♭͡♭	*p* and *q* are some times true
♭͡♭	*p* is true under some circumstances and *q* under others
$\Pi_k \Sigma_i \Sigma_j w_{li} \mathbin{\text{Ψ}} l_{kj}$	Under all circumstances somebody wins and somebody loses
$\Sigma_i \Pi_k \Sigma_j w_{li} \cdot l_{kj}$	There is somebody who wins under all circumstances and under all circumstances somebody fails

Write $\Sigma_u \Sigma_{(\bar{u}) \cdot v} h_{uv}$ to mean there are two *different people* living in the same house or better $\Sigma_u \Sigma_{\bar{u} \cdot v} h_{uv}$.[9]

[Collections, from the *Family Record* R 1601, c.1909]

—A includes (as a collection) —B every B (A—B)   [P.H.:][10]

- If of two things (they may be identical) of which one does not include the other
    - either the one is not an A
    - or the other is a B
  i.e. Every A includes every B: B↘A
- If anything includes a B it includes an A.
- If there is a predicate that applies to a B it applies to an A.

x—⍺⟨ᵧₓ	applies to Y
x—x—y	x is a character of y
x—ρ—y, z	x stands in the relation z to y

---

9 [See the facsimile holograph page [319v] at the end of this selection for a related sketch Peirce inscribed on the same day, and [319r] from September 6, 1908.]
10 [In the original figure there is a character that looks like an ϵ on the innermost area connected to A and to B.]

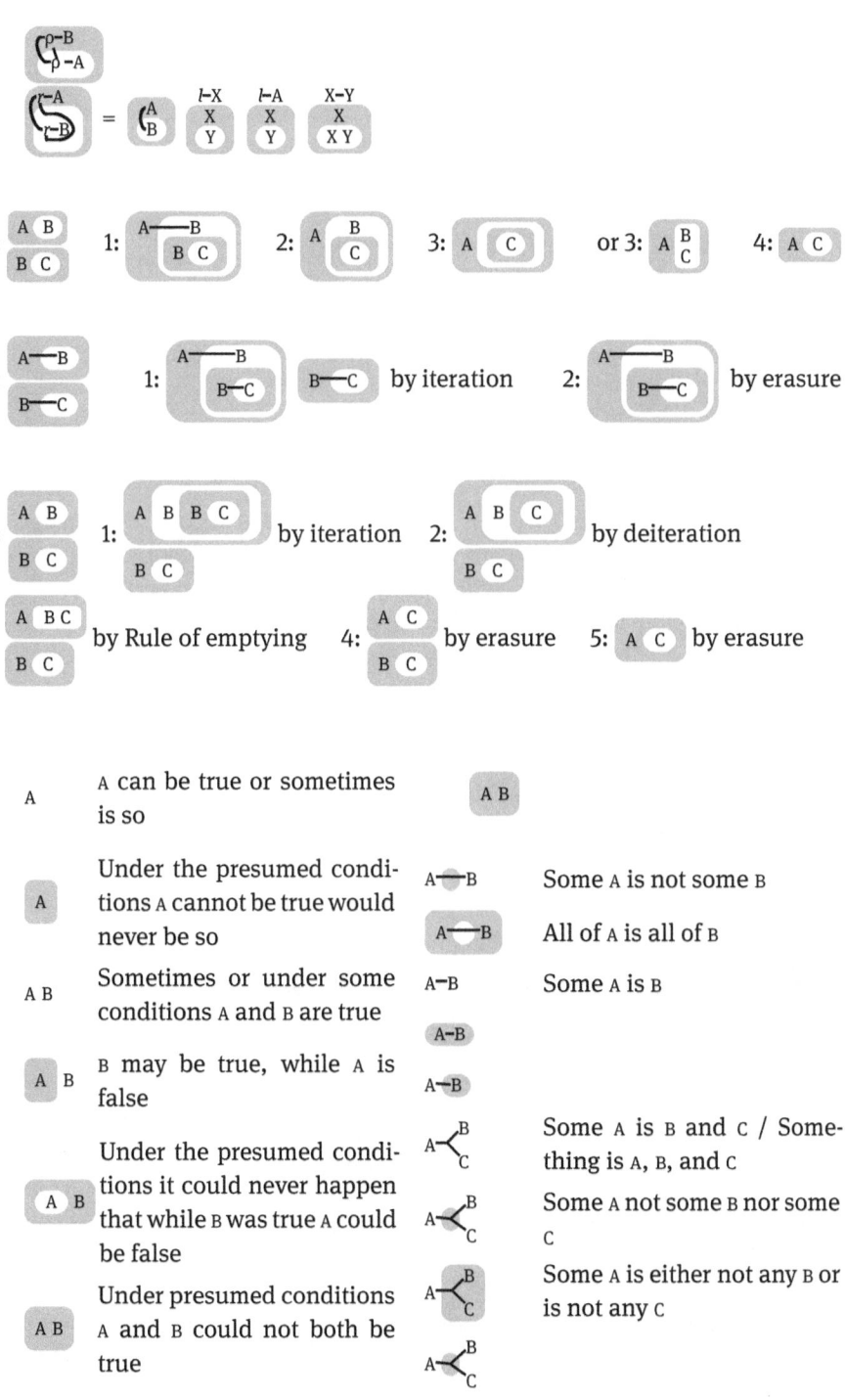

The Calculus of Existential Graphs (R 124)

February 7, 1909.

1. The Universe of Medads ~~assumed Individual~~.

   Let V be a graph ~~necessari~~ certainly true.

   Let F be a graph certainly false.

   Let $\boxed{x}$ be a certain graph regarded as involving x. Let $\boxed{\overline{x}}$ be another graph involving x.

   Let $\boxed{x\;y}$ be a certain graph regarded as involving x and as involving y.

   Let $\boxed{\tfrac{y}{x}}$ be the graph $\boxed{x}$ after y has everywhere been substituted for x.

Then $\boxed{x} = \left(\boxed{\tfrac{V}{x}}x\; \boxed{\tfrac{F}{x}}\overline{x}\right) = \left(\boxed{\tfrac{V}{x}}x\;\boxed{\tfrac{F}{\overline{x}}}\overline{x}\right) = \left(\boxed{\tfrac{V}{x}}\;\boxed{\tfrac{F}{\overline{x}}}\right)$.

These formulæ suppose x to be a medad, and that the universe of medads, or "events", is individual. In that case the proof of them is as follows. $\boxed{x}$ can only assert that if the universe has a given character, x is ~~true~~ veracious (i.e. not false, though may be meaningless), while if it has a certain other character x is false. Then A and B being, for the present, indeterminate, $\boxed{x} = (A\,x)(B\,\overline{x})$. Now if x is veracious (i.e. if $\boxed{x} = \boxed{\tfrac{V}{x}}$), we have $\boxed{x} = (AF)(BV) = B$; so that $B = \boxed{\tfrac{V}{x}}$. But if $\boxed{x} = \boxed{\tfrac{F}{x}}$, $\boxed{x} = (AV)(BF) = (A)$; so that $A = \boxed{\tfrac{F}{\overline{x}}}$. Thus, in general $\boxed{x} = \left(\boxed{\tfrac{F}{\overline{x}}}x\;\boxed{\tfrac{V}{x}}\overline{x}\right)$.

On the other hand, we may assume $\boxed{x} = (M\,x)(N\,\overline{x})$. On this assumption, if x is veracious; i.e. if $\boxed{x} = \boxed{\tfrac{V}{x}}$, we have $\boxed{\tfrac{V}{x}} = (M) = M$. But if x is false, i.e. if $\boxed{x} = \boxed{\tfrac{F}{x}}$, $\boxed{\tfrac{F}{\overline{x}}} = N$ and in general $\boxed{x} = \left(\boxed{\tfrac{V}{x}}x\;\boxed{\tfrac{F}{\overline{x}}}\overline{x}\right)$.

2. But now suppose the universe of Medads, or possible "events", to be a collection of discrete Medads, without any definite maximum possible multitude. In this case a Medad Graph may be true (i.e. as before, not false) in *all*, in *some only*, or in *no* Medad objects, i.e. "events" of possible states of the Universe; and there is no further alternative. A Graph should be interpreted as having the least Signification (i.e. Logical Depth = *Inhalt* = "Comprehension" = "Connotation") which the Rules of Interpretation permit, or render seriously supposable as having been intended. Its Application is simple, that is if it bears the same signification in all its Application (i.e. Logical Breadth, Denotation, *Umfang*, Extension, Subjection) may be to a single Event, or State of the Universe, or to a Part only, or to all events, or to a Part at Most, or to a Part at Least, or to all or none, or certain possible numbers of Events excluding others, or to this number at Most, or at Least, etc. A Part

may be Designate or Indesignate or an Indesignate part of a Designate Part.⁵ But it is not necessary to have more than two elementary forms of application, unless one wishes to take account of absolute numbers and ratios, the consideration of which must be postponed to quite another part of this writing, being an extensive subject. One form ~~makes application to all events~~ expresses what will happen at all events; and this form, by means of negation, ~~takes application to no event~~ will make express what will happen in no event; it will take account of ant Designate part. The other form makes application to some indesignate part at least, of the whole universe of ~~Events~~ Occasions (such as days). It easily makes an application as well to an indesignate part at most; by a slight complication such as "None except some part at least".

As to the Truth of a Graph, only the presence and the absence of Error are taken account of. The amount of Error is naturally not considered until number is considered.

[Definitions of Monad and Dyad Graphs, R S-36]
February 12, 1909

[...]¹¹ problem. Its premisses shall be *seven*, constituting the definitions of a monad graph $-c$ (= $c-$) and of a dyad graph $-w-$. But in order to define the latter, I find it needful to define a subsidiary dyad $-x-$.

Two propositions are requisite to define $-x-$, namely,

1ˢᵗ ⊖$-x-$⊖ ; and

2ⁿᵈ (ˣₓ) .

Two more propositions are requisite to define $-w-$, namely,

3ʳᵈ ⊖w⊖ ;

4ᵗʰ A—(ˣₓ)—B .

Finally three more are needed to define $-c$:

---

5 An example of the last (an indesignate part of a designate part) is when we say In every day of some week in the June of some years it is pleasant weather. Here the designate Part is the June, of all the years during the period some millions of years, for which Newcomb's *Tables of the Sun* are sufficiently correct, while the Indesignate part is some week in some year of the Designate part.
11 [This is the only surviving page (ms p. 8) of an unknown but dated piece located in the supplementary folder R S-36 of assorted fragments, cut pages and rejects. It may be the last page of a segment that coincides with other February 1909 sketches on EGs. In this piece, too, Peirce appears to have come up with ideas not found in other surviving writings.]

5th (–w–c);

6th 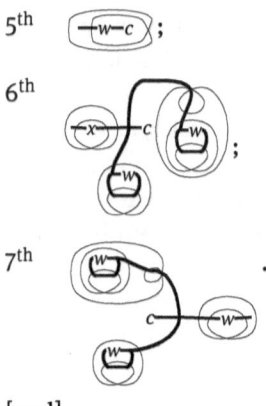 ;

7th

[end]

The System of Existential Graphs applied to the Examination of Itself [R S-3, February 1909]

Let x—a or a—x or $\int_X^q$ or $\int_a^X$ mean that X is an *area*.

Let x—$e^{[0]}$ = x—e mean that X is not enclosed and x—$e^{[n]}$ mean that X is just n times enclosed.

Let $\overset{X}{\underset{Y}{\}}}$ mean that X is scribed on Y.

Let $\underset{X-\vert-Z}{\overset{Y}{\vert}}$ mean that X–*may permissively* undergo the transformation Y so as to give Z (?)

Let x—u—A mean X may be *deleted* from the area A.

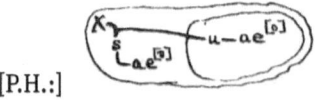

[P.H.:]

The first principle is —$ae^{[0]}$ i.e. *There always is an unenclosed Area.*

The second is ⊂$\overset{ae^{[0]}}{\underset{ae^{[0]}}{}}$⊃ i.e. *There is but one unenclosed Area.*

February 15, 1909

I will begin again. But let the notation for an area stand? *No.* But x—a X is an area. Let ⓔ a̸x mean X is the sheet, the *phemic sheet*.

x—e—y   X is a cut enclosing Y.
x—p—y   X is the first peg of Y.
x—p'—y   X is the second peg of Y.
x—p"—y   X is the third peg of [Y].

$\overset{\vert-p'-z}{\underset{p-y}{C}}$ The first peg of Y is joined by a ligature to the second peg of Z.

x—j—y   X justifies Y.
x—g   X is a graph.
x—s—y   X is scribed on Y.

[P.H.:]

Logic of Time. Involves more than one state of things.

A makes B

Universe of Possibility. $\displaystyle\int_x^a$ *a* is true at an ~~time~~ instant *x*.

l later than $\displaystyle\int_x^a$.[12]

February 17, 1909 [343r] Geometrical Topics

Let   x—l   mean *x* is a place

Let   x—i—y   mean some part of *x* is in *y*

If $\left(_{il'}^{il}\right)$ *l* is a part at least of *l'*

If $\left(_{il'}^{il}\right.$ some part at least of *l* is a part at least of *l'*

If $\left(_{il'}^{il}\right.$ some part at least of *l* is out of *l'*

Let   x—s   mean *x* is a part at least of space $\left(_{s}^{il}\right.$

To be in a place is to be $\begin{smallmatrix}x—p\\y—p\end{smallmatrix}$.

February 26, 1909 [345r] Note on the Tinctures

To illustrate the need of the Tinctures, take the fact that no matter what particles there may be on a Line, there will be a point place on that Line (if nothing but Particles are on it) where there is no Particle but where a particle can be placed.

---

12 [On February 16, 1909 [341r], Peirce begins the development of three-valued (triadic) logics, first under the heading "Studies of Modal, Temporal, and Other Logical Forms which relate to Special Universes", continuing it on the 17th and the 23rd [342v, 342r, 344r]. See Fisch & Turquette 1966 for the first study of Peirce's triadic logic.]

Let x—s mean x is a *particle* (or existent without spatial parts) στιγμή (Lat. a tattoo-prick) Euclid (and Aristotle too, for that matter) uses σημεῖον; but that is too indeterminate. The definition is [end]

July 6, 1909 [347r]

The distinctive features of my System of Logic are as follows:

First, using "cognimen" (*not* cognomen) to mean that which is before the mind when one actively makes an approximation toward *knowing*, and using the word *infer* to signify the act making a cognimen because of other cognimen, I say that to draw an inference is virtually to assume that there is a real cause that tends to make the universe conform to something similar to human reason; so that, just as the fish ~~and~~ or the bird know by nature how to coordinate the efforts for swimming ~~and~~ or for flying, and just as many insects know where and how to dispose of their eggs so as best to insure their producing new individuals, although they can have had no experience pertinent to such a talk, so man by nature has a power of guessing at the truths which he has not experienced. And, therefore, although we know that we cannot always guess right, yet it would be the height of folly to hesitate to accept, provisionally, any cognimen which we feel an inward impulse to accept; while ~~always bear~~ never losing sight of the possibility of its being false.

Secondly, because we see that the instincts of animals have no other value than that of guiding their actions, as well as for several other reasons, I maintain that the whole *intellectual* signification proper to any sign is summed up in the effects which it could rationally have upon our conduct. William James seems inclined to say that the word "pleasure" signifies that sort of immediate consciousness that we call "pleasure"; and no doubt this is true in a certain sense. But what is the *intellectual* sign's [end]

July 11, 1909 [348r]

The meaning of any sign is its rightful *effect*. And its rational meaning is its rightful effect upon that which ought to be governed by my reason; that is to say, upon my conduct.

This follows from the definition of a sign.

August 9, 1909 [349r]

The clear superiority of the genuine, undegenerate Greeks, the Micenean, classical, and the ancient Greeks generally, to all other breeds of the species *homo albidus* is exhibited in various ways; in their sculpture, and the accuracy of their taste generally; in their exploits; in their language which none of the modern scholars who have discovered in it a thousand excellences unnoticed by the Greeks themselves has ever been able to cope with and to domesticate; in their science; their assimilation of christianity. But in order justly to gauge the intellectual capacity of any people, since the works of intellect consists in making and in establishing theories, we must inquire what it has accomplished or endeavoured toward ascertaining the relation between data and conclusions; in other words toward an understanding of logic. Now we find that, excluding from consideration the present scientific era of which we cannot well judge because we breathe its atmosphere, there has been no other people than the Greeks that ever really originated or broke the ground for the construction of any system of logic whatsoever; while we may say that they did that not once alone nor twice, but something like five times over. For without attempting to disinter works that may have been forgotten, and without reckoning such apparently unsystematic observations as those of the sophists and of Parmenides, we may reckon in the first place the inductive system of inquiry of Socrates, and secondly the Analytics of Aristotle. Thirdly, we find in the Elements of Euclid, and in what we know of his other works, a fully self-conscious method for reaching necessary conclusions, a method sharply distinguished from that of Aristotle in several respects, especially by its recognition of the necessity of having before the mind's eye a diagrammatic image of the relations between the parts of the subject of the ratiocination. It was further recognized that individuals exactly alike must in reasoning be distinguished by arbitrary lettering or other designations; and the system had other peculiarities. In the fourth place Chrysippus and the early stoics had a logical system of their own well filled to their uncompromising ethics. It was distinguished particularly by its nominalism, its necessitarianism, and its endeavour to make the *reductio ad absurdum* (really a mere device of exposition), supply the place of induction, which was utterly rejected as illogical. Last comes the Epicurean logic which, as set forth by Philodemus in papyrus recovered in a fragmentary condition from Herculaneum, prefigures in astonishing detail, all the merits and all the errors of the system of J. S. Mill. Like that it breathes an individualistic nominalism; yet represents Induction as the sole form of reasoning, and bases it upon uniformity, without observing that a uniformity that can lend any support to induction, a uniformity which is more than a chance coincidence, is a real law the actual occurrence of which its nominalism denies.

Taking these five systems together, they more than tolerably well represent the methods of scientific thought among the Greeks.

Throughout the Middle ages, all their science nor [sic.] philosophy either intentionally carried the only part of it into practice that skeleton of Aristotle's system that was those ages understood and appreciated or else resulted from the application of their own logical doctrine of realism.

But throughout our scientific era, which I reckon from the epoch of 1543, as I do the preceding Humanistic era from 1453, logic, despite the attention we pay to methods of doing everything except to think, has been most strangely neglected. We have methods of reasoning, but we fail to recognize them as such, and consequently confine them to the fields in which they first happened to appear. For example, to illustrate my meaning, I may mention that the whole method of algebra apart from special details and apart from the general plan of representing quantitative relations by arrays of letters, such as that of a determinant, or set of equations lucidly arranged, depends upon the use of parentheses, square brackets, braces, and the vinculum to show that all that is described within such an enclosure is to be conceived as describing a single object. Thus, $a \cdot (b + c)$ means the product of a and the quantity resulting from increasing c by b (or "linearizing b by c"; but where a rule has to be followed, the rule of writing must be followed, I prefer the active factor before the passive one, since such is our usual and the natural way; as when we say 'Isabella horse' not '*cheval alezan*', and 'the laughing man', not '*l'homme qui rôt*', 'four-and-twenty', not twenty-four).

Yet disease has so weakened our power of logical analysis that I have never seen brackets and other 'Klämmern' referred to as the most indispensable of all algebraic signs; they are usually treated as unimportant because insignificant. Even Schröder relegates his rules for their use to an "Excurs".

Linear perspective, rectangular coordinates, the differential calculus, and so called "symbolical" algebra are powerful instruments of reasoning but the by far chief contribution to logic that the scientific era has witnessed has been the opening up of the *doctrine of chances*; otherwise called the "calculus of probabilities".

This high rating of it would not be justified by the improvements this method has introduced into physical and biological science and into business, but is justified by its placing at a point of view whence we are enabled to solve the riddle of the validity [of] reasoning about realities in general.

Although mathematicians and physicists always,—I do not say have done full justice to its importance but have always recognized its importance as great, it is lamentable, it is humiliating to note the puerile weakness of all their treatments of it that crosses the threshold of pure mathematics.

November 1, 1909 [360r]

During the last three years I have been resting from my work on the Division of Signs and have only lately—in the last week or two been turning back to it; and I find my work of 1905 better than any since that time, though the latter doubtless has value and must not be passed by without consideration.

Looking over the book labelled in red "The Prescott Book", and also this one, I find the entries in this book of "Provisional Classification of 1906 March 31" [275r][6]

---

6 March 31, 1906 [275r] **Provisional Classification of Signs.**

A Sign is
in its own nature

A Tone	A Token	or A Type
which has all its being whether it exists or not	whose being consists in dyadic relations	whose being consists of the order of whatever may come hereafter to be or in the order that will be shown whenever certain kinds of action shall take place

in reference to its Immediate Object
is either

| Indefinite | Singular | or General Sign * |

in reference to its nature of its Real Object
is either

| Abstract | Concrete | or Collective * |

in reference to its relation to its Real Object
is either

| Icon | Index | or Symbol * |

in reference to its Intended Interpretant
(August 30, 1906 Transpose first and third)
is either

| Ponitive | Imperative | or Interrogatory |

in reference to the nature of its Dynamic Interpretant
is either

Poetic	Stimulant	or Impressive
or excitant of feeling	or excitant of Action	or determinant of a Habit
Eidoseme	Ergoseme	Logoseme

in reference to its relation to its Dynamic Interpretant
is either

| Sympathetic | Compulsive | or Rational |

in reference to the Nature of its Normal Interpretant
is either

| Strange | Common | or Novel |

in reference to the Passion of its Normal Interpretant
is either

| ~~Substitute~~ Suggestive | ~~Suggestive~~ Assertive | or Argument |

in reference to the Significance of its Normal Interpretant
is either

| Monadic | Dyadic | or Triadic ? ? |

April 2, 1906. **Notes on my Provisional Classification of Signs.** I have thought of the Object of a Sign as that which determines the sign; and this is well thought. I have thought of the Interpretant as that which the Sign determines or might determine or should determine, but this is not so well. For my idea of determination is dyadic while the idea of the relation of the interpretant to the sign is triadic.

Say the Interpretant is that which the Sign brings into the correspondence with the Object.

The Object is plainly twofold. The Dynamic Object is the Real Object according to the above definition. The Immediate Object is the Object as presented in the Sign.

The Interpretant is Threefold. The Normal Interpretant is the Genuine Interpretant, embracing all that the Sign could reveal concerning the Object to a sufficiently penetrating mind, being more than any ~~possible~~ mind, however penetrable, could conclude from it, since there is no end to the distinct conclusions that could be drawn concerning the Object from any Sign. The Dynamic Interpretant is just what is drawn from the Sign by a given Individual Interpreter. The Immediate Interpretant is the interpretant represented, explicitly or implicitly, in the sign itself. I have thus omitted the *intended* interpretant. So far as the intention is betrayed in the Sign, it belongs to the immediate Interpretant. So far as it is not so betrayed, it may be the Interpretant of *another* sign, but it is in no sense the interpretant of *that* sign.

As to the Matter of the Sign itself, it is either a Tuone or a Token or a Type. The word T[u]one is a blend of Tone and Tune. It means a quality of feeling which is significant, whether it be simple, like a Tone or complex, like a Tune. But the latter is not *pure* feeling. By a Token, I mean an existing thing or an actual historical event which serves as a Sign.

By a Type, I mean a general form which can be repeated indefinitely and is in all its repetitions one and the same sign. Thus the word *the* is a Type. It is likely to occur over a score of times on a page of an English book; but it is only one word twenty times repeated. The distinction between a Type and a Token is obvious. There may be some confusion between the Tuone and the Type. They may, however, be distinguished in various ways. In the first place, a [Type] is absolutely identical in all its *instances* or embodiments, while a Tone cannot have any identity, it has only similarity. Thus the sound of any vowel will be slightly different every two times it is pronounced and then so far as it is so, it is two Tuones. But any two vowels in so far as they are alike are the same Tuone, in the only case in which there can be any sameness to a tuone. Anything then that could conceivably be made absolutely definite, bearing in mind that no two things can be exactly alike in any quality whatever, cannot be a Tuone. Another test is that a Tuome [Peirce occasionally misspells Tuone as Tuome.] though it may be composed of many ingredients is, like a chemical compound of many elements, perfectly homogenous and structureless in effect, while a Type, though it may be indecomposable, must be more or less complex in its relations. Tests might be multiplied; yet after all, it will often require subtlety to decide whether a given sign is a Tuone or a Type. Take for example a given melody, say the Last Rose of Summer. Considered as to its structure it is a Type; but considered as a whole in its esthetic effect which is not composed of one part due to one note and another to another, it is a Tuome. As ordinarily conceived it is a Tuone, slightly different however every time, it is sure, but from the point of view of contrapoint, it is absolutely the same every time it is rendered so with substantial correctness (though it be a trifle out of tune and time) it is a Type. But any one singing of it is neither Tuone nor Type but a Token. Notwithstanding these difficulties in many cases there is no room for an instant's hesitation, and the distinction is not only useful but practically indispensable.

The immediate object of a sign may be of quite a different nature from the real dynamical object. Let the object really be ever so complex, yet if it is presented without analysis, and in such

and of October 13, 1905 [262r]⁷ particularly important from my present (accidentally limited, no doubt) point of view; particularly in regard to the point made in

---

a way as to have no definite identity, the *Immediate* Object is a simple quality. This substantive with the indefinite article has a simple quality for its object. A proper name on the contrary has a well-known existent thing for its object, even if like Othello, it be a fictitious object. But this cannot be the case for an interpreter who has never heard of the thing or to whom the name is new.

A sign may have for its immediate object a determining course of nature, or habit of things. Thus if I say every President of the United States has been a high-minded man, I conceive that the operation of some natural law has made them so. This is a way in which the precise meaning *may be* expressed; and it is the first rule of logic that in pure thought in whatever way a thing can be accurately conceived in that way it is; because pure thought has no other being than that of representing its object. This is not only the way the matter may be regarded but the way it *must* be regarded subject to an exception I shall mention presently. The reason it must be so regarded is that a sign cannot have two objects. You may represent a pair of things, or a triplet, etc. other collection number, but it will be a single pair, a single triplet, or a single other collection. So the exception I alluded to is that the sentence (which is in so far ambiguous) may be taken to mean that the succession of Presidents of the U.S. (which succession is a unique object) is a succession uninterrupted of honorable men of certain sentiments. Usually as when we say "All men have two legs" we plainly refer to the nature of men, since some monstrosities reckoned as men have different numbers of legs.

7 October 13, 1905 [262r]
A   Nature of Sign in Itself
       Abstraction = Qualisign
       Existent = Sinsign
       Combinant Type = Legisign
B   Of Object
     a.   Immediate
          In what form object is represented in sign
          {Indef[finite]/Sing[ular]/General As far as effects form of signs
     b.   Dynamical.
        α.   Nature of Object in Itself
             {Abstraction/Concrete/Collection As far as it affects nature of sign
        β.   Causation of signs representing Obj[ect]
C   Of Interpretant
     a.   Immediate
          In what form interpretant is repr. in sign
          {Interrog[ative]/Imper[ative]/Significant
          As far as it affects form of sign
     b.   Dynamical
        α.   Nature of Interpretant in Itself
             {Feeling/Fact/Sign As far as that affects Nature of sign
        β.   Causation of sign affecting Interp[retant]
             {Sympathy/Compulsion/Representat
     c.   Representative

the Prescott Book 1909 Oct 28 and what immediately preceded that in that book but is not dated.[8]

α. In what form sign is represented in Interpretant
As far as this affects form of sign.
β. Causation of representation of Sign by Interpretant.
As far as this affects the nature of the Sign.
γ. *Rationale* of Connection between Sign and Object effected by Interpretant.

[8] October 28, 1909. 6:30pm. **Another endeavour to analyze a Sign.** A Sign is anything which represents something else (so far as it is completed), and if it represents itself it is as a part of another sign which represents something other than itself, and it represents itself in other *circum*stances, in other connections. A man may talk and he is a sign of what he relates. He may tell about himself as he was at another time. He cannot tell exactly what he is doing at that very moment. Yes, he may confess he is lying, but he must be a false sign, then. A Sign, then, would seem to *profess* to represent something else.

Either a Sign is to be defined as something which *truly* represents something or else as something which *professes* to represent something.

[These are the "immediately preceding passages":] Of the distinction between the Objects, or better the "Originals" and the Interpretant of a Sign.

By A "*Sign*" is meant any Ens which is determined by a single Object or set of Objects, called its Originals, all other than the Sign itself, and in its turn is, capable of determining a Mind, something called its Interpretant, and that in such a way that the Mind is thereby mediately determined to some mode of conformity to the Original or Set of Originals. This is particularly intended to define (very imperfectly as yet) a Complete Sign. But a Complete Sign has or may have Parts which partake of the nature of their whole; but often in a truncated fashion.

The *Interpretant* ~~brings a state of things to appear, either in Imagination or in Facts, or in Tendency~~ is the Effect upon the mind or venues ~~exerts upon the mind,~~ brings to pass, either causing a state of feeling, or an Imagination, ~~or concentrating attention, or it may~~

or may stimulate to action whether external, or an exertion of attention

or it may cause a state of mind of the nature of a disposition or habit.

A sign is in regard to its Interpretant in one or another of three grades of Completeness, which may be called the *Barely Overt*, the *Overter*, and the *Overtest*. The Barely Overt sign, of which a name is an example does not expressly distinguish its Original from its Interpretant, nor its reference to either from the Sign itself. The *Overter* sign of which an Assertion is an example.

Thus the Sign has a double function.

First, to affect a mind which understands its "*Grammar*", or Method of Signification, which signification is its Substance Significate or Interpretant.

Second, to indicate how to identify the conditions under which ~~sign~~ its significate has the mode of being it is represented as having.

October 29, 1909, 10:45am. It will probably be profitable to trace out the varieties of signs of themselves. Take, first, icons. A ring bearing a repeated pattern, considered as starting at any point may be an indefinitely exact icon of itself considered as starting at any corresponding point. [P.H.:]

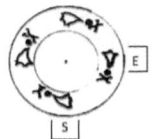

Yet it is necessary that these points should be individually identified; and that requires that there should be something which is not copied, each as the E and S of the figure. This is true of every icon. If it were in all respects a perfect *icon* it would be indistinguishable from and for all intents and purposes the very same thing as its Object. It thus seems to be of the very essence of an icon that it should not be perfect; and if this be so, then unquestionably an icon may represent nothing but itself, by every part of it representing a different part and there being a cycle of representation. Instead of a cycle there may be an endless sequence of representations. Thus imagine the series of all real positive rational quantities to be expressed in the order of their values as a doubly endless series of fractions in their lowest terms. Then the whole series of their numerators may be regarded as an icon of the numerators of their doubles and those of their triples and so on and may be regarded as represented by the series of numerators of their halves their thirds etc. and so on ad infinitum both ways and in all these their limits (which may be regarded at will as included areas excluded) remain the same.

October 29, 1909, 2:00pm. When the cause as appearance is so connected with a state of things as to indicate the presence of the latter it is an *index* of that state of things.

Thus the woman's coming out of the weather-houses is an *index* of moisture in the atmosphere. A purple precipitate an addition of a salt of tin is an index of the presence of gold. The communication of blue to starch paste is an index of the presence of free iodine etc.

So the appearance of a faint light in a particular point of the heavens as viewed through a great telescope is an *index* of such a light there whenever one looks there even without a telescope. Is this not an index of itself? Intensification of any sensation comes under the same head.

But one of the functions of an Index is to call attention to something, as when one points a finger. Now is there any reason why a thing should not call attention to itself? It is true that if a sign calls attention to anything, it is in order to bring something else to attention. But it may be that that is at bottom itself, in some cases.

May not a testimony be emphatically a witness of its own truth, so that it is impossible not to believe it?

October 30, 1909. 1:00pm. As for Indices, it is plain that a man may point to himself and the purpose of many an exclamation is chiefly to call attention to itself and its neighbours in space and time of whatever description they may be.

Or say "*whatever* they be". (And by the way, why should not a scientific dialect have a special grammar, selective pronouns, prepositions, conjunctions, and perhaps even interjections.)

Such to be retained *of what description* (G[er]. *was für ein–*) *whux*, pron, *whŭggs*, *whugs* or *whiks of what guess whuxever*, of what description you please
- *anybut* or *ambut* lover of ambut servant
- si—ud means ( ) thus *A* is a si lover of ambut servant ud of some man
- *A* stands to some man *B* in the relation of loving every thing that servants of his

Namely, a good deal of my early attempts to define the difference between Icon, Index, and Symbol, were adulterated with confusion with the distinction as to the Reference of the Dynamic Interpretant to the Sign.

The amount of labour still required upon the ten trichotomies of signs (and more than these ten I don't inquire into, not because I don't think they are in truth there, but simply because it will be all I possibly can do to *define* and to *prove* these ten) is enough of itself to occupy the 10± years of efficient thinking that may remain to me if no accident cuts them short.

The light which the two trichotomies referred to in the last paragraph but one above throws upon each other suggests a ~~mode~~ method of study that I have hitherto employed only in getting as clear ideas as I have (and they ought to be more definite) of the first and second trichotomies or (using the excellent notation of October 12, 1905) A and Ba.[9] I am now ~~employing~~ applying the same method to Bbβ and Cbβ. It ought to be applied not merely to A and Ba but further to A, Ba, and Ca taken together. Also to A Ba Bbα to A Ba Cbα to Bbα Cbα. Then to A Bβ Ccγ etc. to Ba Bbα Ccα to A Bbα Ccα etc.

A "Sign" is an Ens (i.e. something, and it may be of any category of being) which, ~~in addition to~~ not only has a capacity of being either imagined, perceived, or conceived, as anything of the same category of Being of which one ~~has sufficient~~ happens to have enough of the right kind of dealings may be but also has the prop-

---

- while *A* is a si lover of ambut servant of some man ud.
- $(l \, \S \, s)B_i$ *A* is a lover of anything but servants of *B*
- $\Sigma_j \Pi_i (l_{Ai} \, \Psi \, S_{ij}) \cdot B_i$ ~~(l)(s)~~m tan tin lov nitin serve nit nat a man
- $\Sigma_j \Pi_i (l_{Ai} \, \Psi \, S_{ij}) \cdot B_i$ ~~(l)(s m)~~ tan tin lov nittin servman nit nat
- $l \, \S \, sm$ ·l~~(s)(m)~~ lov tantin serv nittin man nit nat.

One incidental remark may be made here. The question may be asked whether a photograph is an *Icon* or an *Iconic Index*, since similarity with its object is produced by physical necessity. Now if the distinction between Icon, Index, and Symbol be, as I have defined it, a distinction in the relation of the Sign to its Real or Dynamical Object, then the Photograph is certainly not an Icon but is an Index, and the phrase "Iconic Index" seems to be self-contradictory. But using my terminology of $\frac{13}{3}$ years ago, its relation to its Actual Interpretant and still better the *word* (though not exactly the definition) that I proposed October 12, 1905, it is an *idoseme* (then spelled *Eidoseme*). That is to say that it directly *exhibits* its signification, or Dynamic Interpretant (But Qu[estion]: Is it the *dynamic* interpretant? It is rather the "signification" or interpretant as embodied in the Real Object.)

That is to say, it brings up the ideas which are referred to the object by Association by Resemblance and neither by Association by Contiguity, or yet by the third mode of Association as that which is capable of accounting for the facts exhibited.

9 [Pietarinen (2015c) contains a transcription of this notation and Peirce's ordering of sign classes in a tree-structure, in the article "Division of Signs".]

erty of producing ~~in a mind which perceives it and which has skill, or practical un~~ through upon a person ~~who fulfills~~ in whom certain conditions are fulfilled effects that another thing or a collection of other things would ~~fulfill~~ produce, those conditions being the possession by that person of a practical understanding of the system of correspondence.

But this definition ought to be prefaced with the remark that no ~~know event of cognition~~ event of learning anything brings *per se* any other knowledge than ~~its content~~ that which it has in learning; and in particular does not include any knowledge about that event of learning itself. Thus seeing does [not] include a sight of the eye or any knowledge about the learning itself. True, Hamilton and others insist that to know includes the knower's knowing that he knows; and in the limited sense in which he here used the word know, one must admit that something is true which those words seem to express. Nevertheless, merely knowing a fact does not include the knowledge that that very act *per se* includes any knowledge about itself, any more than seeing includes any vision of the event of sight itself. When one first comes to assent to this truth in any solid that has no hole through it nor any hole enclosed in it, the number of edges is less by two than the sum of the numbers of its distinct surfaces and of summits (supposing everyone of the former is bounded ~~has an edge all round it~~ by three or more edges and that every one of the latter simply extends from one summit to another), ~~he is thinking~~ his thought is exclusively occupied with the solid and its parts, and he is not thinking at all of himself or his knowledge. And if Hamilton does not call an assent, however unqualified and confident, by the name of "knowledge" unless it be accompanied by a recognition of its acceptance by the knower, then it is undoubtedly true that to know is to know that one knows that which one knows, but it still remains false that to know is to know that one knows *that one knows* one's knowledge of the ~~former~~ knowing that one knows it, in the sense of actively thinking it, though one undoubtedly has what the scholastics call an habitual knowledge of it, that is to say a disposition to accept it as soon as the question occurs to the person supposed.

Let it be admitted then that no act of thinking can involve thinking about that very act of thinking. [End of the *Logic Notebook*]

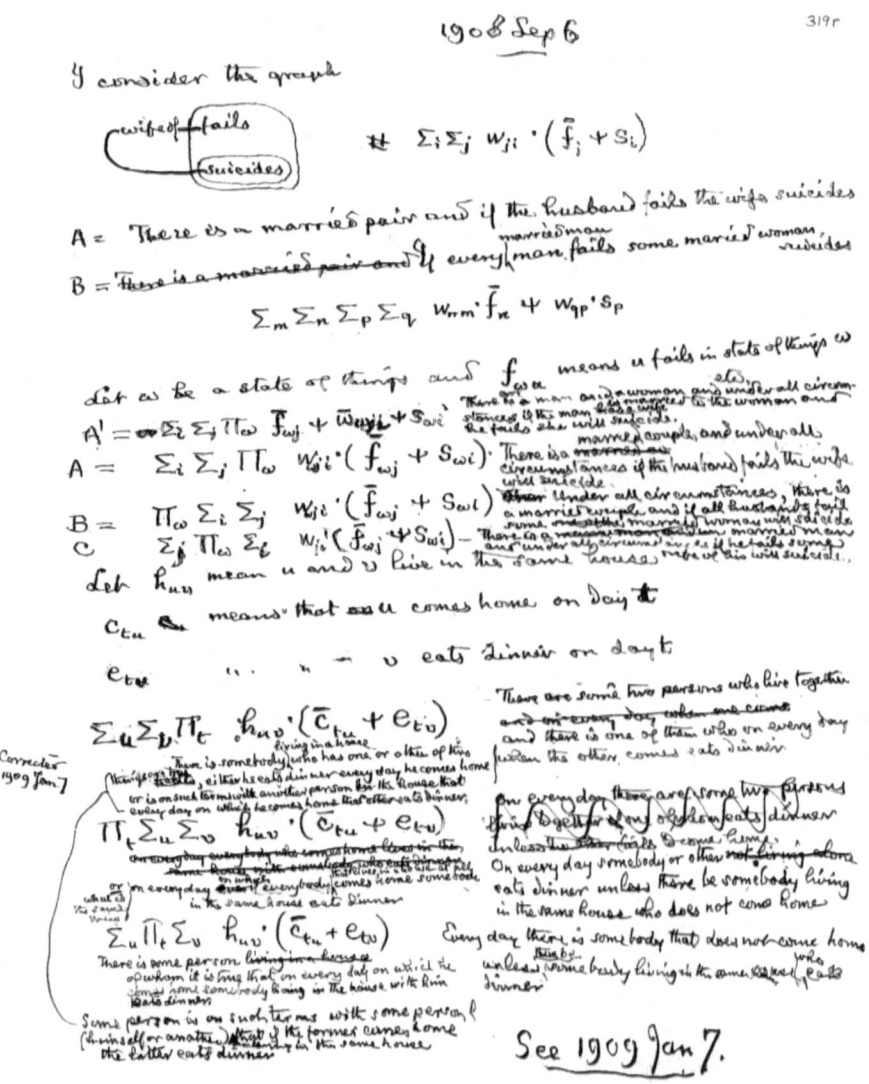

A holograph page [319r], September 6, 1908 (Harvard Peirce Papers, R 339).

28 [Existential Graphs, from the *Logic Notebook*] (R 339), 1898–1909

$h_{0\underline{2}} \cdot h_{23} \cdot \bar{c}_{a0} \cdot \bar{c}_{a3} \cdot \bar{c}_{b0} \cdot T_{b3}$

$+ \bar{h}_{01} \cdot \bar{h}_{23} \cdot \bar{c}_{a0} \cdot e$

$h_{01} \cdot \bar{c}_{a0} \cdot \bar{c}_{b0} \qquad + h_{0.3} \, \bar{c}_{a0} \cdot \bar{c}_{b0} \qquad = \Sigma_u \Sigma_v \Pi_t$

$+ h_{01} \cdot \bar{c}_{a0} \cdot e_{b1} \qquad \text{etc} \qquad h_{uv}(\bar{c}_{tu} \psi e_{tv})$

$+ h_{01} \cdot e_{a1} \cdot \bar{c}_{b0}$

$+ h_{01} \cdot e_{a1} \cdot e_{b1}$

$h_{01} \cdot \bar{c}$

1909 Jan. 7.

Write $\Sigma_u \Sigma_{(a)v} h_{uv}$ to mean there are two different people living in the same house or better

$\Sigma_u \Sigma_{\bar{a}v} h_{uv}$

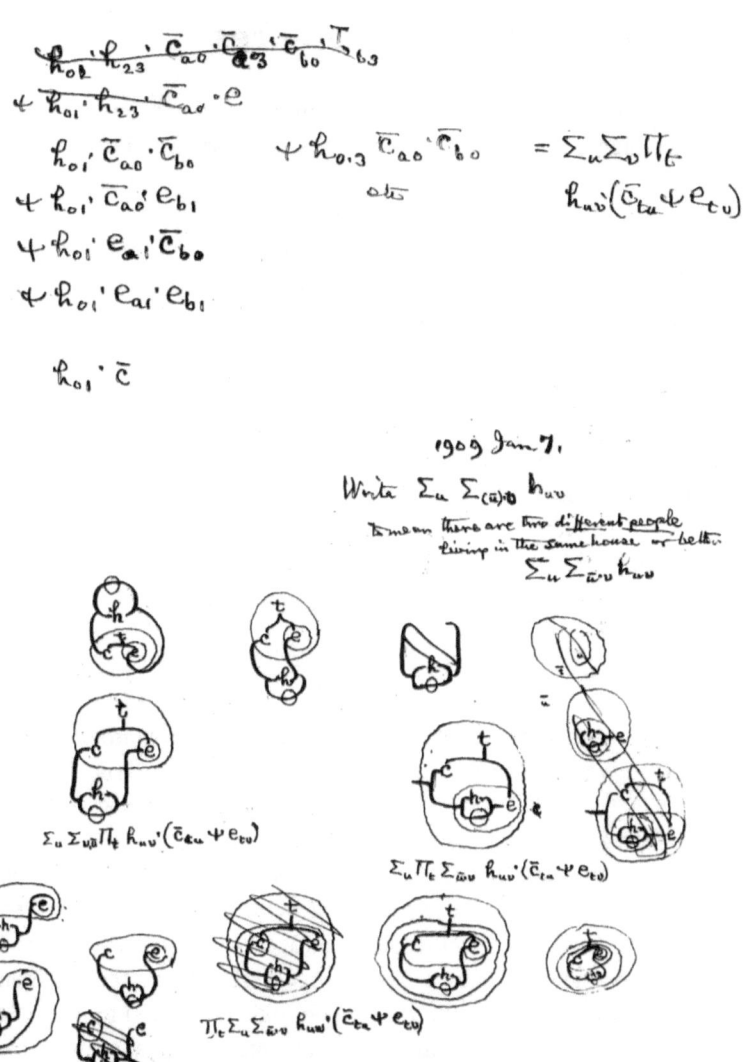

$\Sigma_u \Sigma_{u\bar{v}} \Pi_t \, h_{uv}{}'(\bar{c}_{tu} \psi e_{tv})$

$\Sigma_u \Pi_t \Sigma_{\bar{a}v} \, h_{uv}{}'(\bar{c}_{ta} \psi e_{tv})$

$\Pi_t \Sigma_u \Sigma_{\bar{a}v} \, h_{uv}{}'(\bar{c}_{tu} \psi e_{tv})$

A holograph page [319v], January 7, 1909 (Harvard Peirce Papers, R 339).

Bibliography of Peirce's References

This bibliography encompasses those books, volumes and editions that Peirce referred or is most likely to have referred to in the relevant parts of the texts included in the three volumes of the *Logic of the Future*. His self-references are included in the bibliography at the end of the introductory chapters of each volume.

At various times in his life, Peirce owned extensive and valuable collections of books, journals and reference works that was likely to consist of several thousand items. Details of the editions that Peirce owned or had in his possession when producing the relevant studies are included after the item information, and if known, with their present provenance (JHU = Johns Hopkins University, Special Collections).

The list below comprises approximatively some 1/30 of the books that Peirce might have acquired during his lifetime. Sadly the bulk of his collection, including countless books rife with marginalia, is no longer recoverable as most of the items that once belonged to his library have been lost, damaged, discarded, destroyed, stolen, given away or sold to collectors over the years.

Abelardus Petrus. *Ouvrages Inédits d'Abelard Pour Servir À l'Histoire De La Philosophie Scolastique En France*. Edited by Victor Cousin. Paris: Imprimierie Royale, 1836. (Peirce's Library) [Only mentioned by name, no specific book detailed. This edition was owned by Peirce.]

Aquinas, Thomas. *Opuscula sancti Thome: quibus alias impressis nuper hec addidimus videlicet Summam totius logice. Tractatum celeberrimum De usuris nusquam alias impressum*. Venice: cura & ingenio Giacomo Penzio mandato & expensis Peter Liechtenstein, 1508. (Peirce's Library) [Peirce's reference is: "Aquinas ... or the writer of the treatise on logic attributed to him" (LoF 3), probably referring to the *Summa logicae*. It is this particular edition that was in Peirce's possession.]

Aristotle. *Aristoteles Graece*. Two volumes. Edited by Theodor Waitz. Leipzig: Georg Reimer, 1831. (Peirce's Library, JHU) [Peirce mentions a few books in Aristotle's œuvre by name: *Metaphysics*, *Prior Analytics*, *Posterior Analytics*, *Perihermeneias* and *Sophistical Elenchi*.]

Aristotle. *Aristotelis Organon graece*. Edited by Theodor Waitz. Lipsiae: Sumtibus Hahnil, 1844–1846. (Peirce's Library, JHU)

Arnauld, Antoine & Pierre, Nicole. *The Port Royal logic*. [*l'Art de Penser*] Translated by T. S. Baynes. 5th edition. Edinburgh: James Gordon, 1861. (Peirce's

Library) [Peirce refers to the 5th edition of 1861 (R 454; LoF 2). This translation contains Leibniz's *Mediationes de Cognitione, Veritate et Ideis* (1684).]

Bachmann, Carl Friedrich. *System der Logik: Ein Handbuch zum Selbststudium*. Leipzig: F. U. Brockhaus, 1828. (Peirce's Library, JHU)

Bayes, Thomas. "An essay towards solving a problem in the doctrine of chances". *Philosophical Transactions of the Royal Society* 53(1763): 370–418.

Berkeley, George. *A Treatise Concerning the Principles of Human Knowledge*. Dublin: Jeremy Pepyat, 1710.

Berkeley, George. *The Works of George Berkeley, D.D. Late Bishop of Cloyne in Ireland—To which is added An Account of His Life, and several of his Letters to Thomas Prior, Esq., Dean Gervais, and Mr Pope*. In Two Volumes. Dublin: John Exshaw, 1784. (Peirce's Library, JHU)

Bertrand, Joseph Louis François. *Calcul des probabilités*. Paris: Gauthier-Villars et fils, 1889.

Boethius. *Anitii Manlii Severini Boethi: opera omnia*. Two Volumes. Basileæ: ex officina Henricpetrina [1570], 1546. (Peirce's Library, JHU)

Boltzmann, Ludwig. "Über die Grundprincipien und Grundgleiehuugen der Mechanik". In *Clark University 1889–1899: Decennial Celebration*, Edited by W. E. Story et alii, (261–309). Worcester, Mass.: 1899.

Bolzano, Bernard. *Wissenschaftslehre: Versuch einer ausführlichen und größtentheils neuen Darstellung der Logik mit steter Rücksicht auf deren bisherige Bearbeiter*. Sultzbach: J. E. v. Seidel, 1837.

Bolzano, Bernard. *Paradoxien des Unendlichen*. Leipzig: C. H. Reclam sen., 1851.

Boole, George. *The Mathematical Analysis of Logic: Being an Essay Towards a Calculus of Deductive Reasoning*. Cambridge: MacMillan, Barclay, and MacMillan, 1847.

Boole, George. *An Investigation of the Laws of Thought On which are founded the mathematical theories of logic and probabilities*. London: Walton & Maberly, 1854.

Bosanquet, Bernard. *Knowledge and Reality. A Criticism of F. H. Bradley's "Principles of Logic"*. London: Swan Sonnenschein & Co., 1892.

Bossuet, Jacques-Bénigne. "Logique". Oeuvres inédites de Bossuet, évêque de Meaux dédiées à S. A. R. Monseigneur le Duc de Bordeaux. Paris, 1828.

Boutell, Charles. *The Handbook to English Heraldry*. London: Cassell, Petter, & Galpin, 1867.

Bradley, Francis Herbert. *The Principles of Logic*. London: Kegan Paul, Trench & co., 1883.

Bradley, F. H. *Appearance and Reality: A Metaphysical Essay*. London: Swan Sonnenschein & Co, 1899. (Peirce's Library, Robbins Library)

Byrne, James. *General Principles of the Structure of Language*. Two volumes. London: Trübner & Co, 1885.

Cantor, Georg. "Beiträge zur Begründung der transfiniten Mengenlehre". *Mathematische Annalen* 49(1897): 207–246.

Cantor, Georg. *Zur Lehre vom Transfiniten: gesammelte Abhandlungen aus der Zeitschrift für Philosophie und Philosophische Kritik*. Halle: Pfeffer, 1890.

Cantor, Georg. "Une contribution à la théorie des ensembles". *Acta Mathematica* 2(1883): 311–328. [Peirce's reference is: "Acta Mathematica Vol. II, p. 321" (LoF 3).]

Cantor, Georg. "De la puissance des ensembles parfaits de points". *Acta Mathematica* 4(1884): 381–392.

Cantor, Moritz. *Vorlesungen über Geschichte der Mathematik*. Volume 2. Leipzig: B. G. Teubner, 1900.

Carus, Paul. *Ursache, Grund und Zweck: Eine philosophische Untersuchung zur Klärung der Begriffe*. Dresden: R. von Grumbkow, 1883.

Castrén, Matthias. *Grammatik der samojedischen Sprachen*. St. Petersburg: Buchdruckerei der Kaiserlichen Akademie der Wissenschaften, 1854. [Mentioned by name ("...Castrén, a grammarian of those [Samoyeed] languages...", LoF 1).]

Cayley, Arthur. "Fifth Memoir on Quantics". *Philosophical Transactions of the Royal Society of London* 148(1858): 429–460.

Cayley, Arthur. "Metrics". In: Salmon, George. *A Treatise on the Higher Plane Curves: Intended as a Sequel to A treatise on Conic Sections*, (108–128). Dublin: Hodges, Foster & Figgis, 1879.

Clarke, Frank Wigglesworth. *Data of Geochemistry*. Bulletin No: 330. Series E, Chemistry and Physics, 54. Washington: Government Printing Office, 1908.

Davidson, Thomas. *Aristotle and Ancient Educational Ideals*. New York: C. Scribner, 1892.

Dedekind, Richard. *Stetigkeit und irrationale Zahlen*. Braunschweig: F. Vieweg und sohn, 1872.

Dedekind, Richard. *Was sind und was sollen die Zahlen?* Braunschweig: Vieweg, 1887.

Dedekind, Richard. *Essays on the Theory of Numbers, 1. Continuity and irrational numbers. 2. The Nature and Meaning of Numbers*. Translated by Wooster Woodruff Beman. Chicago: Open Court, 1901.

De Morgan, Augustus. "On the Structure of the Syllogism". *Transactions of the Cambridge Philosophical Society* 8(1846): 379–408.

De Morgan, Augustus. *Formal Logic, or The Calculus of Inference, Necessary and Probable*. London: Taylor & Walton, 1847. (Peirce's Library) [This book's has Peirce's abundant marginalia and its provenance had been at the Harvard

University's Library System in the past. The item is no longer to be located in its collections.]

De Morgan, Augustus. "On the syllogism no: II. On the symbols of logic, the theory of the syllogism, and in particular the copula". *Transactions of the Cambridge Philosophical Society* 9(1850): 79–127.

De Morgan, Augustus. "On the syllogism no: III and on logic in general". *Transactions of the Cambridge Philosophical Society* 10(1858): 173–230.

De Morgan, Augustus. "On the syllogism no: III and on the logic of relations". *Transactions of the Cambridge Philosophical Society* 10(1860): 331–358.

De Morgan, Augustus. *Syllabus of a Proposed System of Logic.* London: Walton & Maberly, 1860.

Descartes, Rene. *Geometria.* Second Edition. Amstelædami: apud Ludovicum & Danielem Elzevirios, 1659. (Peirce's Library, Harvard Robbins Library)

Diogenes Laertius. *Diogenis Laertii de vitis, dogmatibus et apophthegmatibus clarorum philosophorum libri X, Graece et Latine.* Volumes 1 and 2. Amstelædami: Apud Henricum Wetstenium, 1692. (Peirce's Library, JHU)

Drummond, William. *Academical Questions.* London: W. Bulmer and Co., 1805. [Peirce refers to Diodorus Cronus, "as related by Cicero toward the end of the Lucullus' book of his Academical Questions" (LoF 3).]

Erdmann, Benno. *Logik. I. Band: Logische Elementarlehre. Zweite, völlig umgearbeitete Auflage.* Halle a. S.: Max Niemeyer, 1907.

Erdmann, Johann Eduard. *Outlines of Logic and Metaphysics.* Translated by B. C. Burt. London: Sonnenschein, 1896.

Euclid. *Euclidis Opera Omnia.* Edited by J. L. Heiberg & H. Menge. 8 Volumes. Lipsiae: B. G. Teubneri, 1883–1916. [Peirce's reference is: "Heiberg admits 27 corollaries as genuine in the Elements" (LoF 1).]

Euler, Leonhard. *Lettres à une princesse d'Allemagne sur divers sujets de physique & de philosophie.* Saint-Pétersbourg: Imprimerie de l'Académie Impériale des Sciences, 1768–1772.

Girard, Albert. *Invention nouvelle en l'algèbre.* Amsterdam: W. J. Blaeuw, 1629.

Glanvill, Joseph. *Saducismus triumphatus: or, Full and plain evidence concerning witches and apparitions. In two parts. The first treating of their possibility. The second of their real existence.* London: Printed for J. Collins & S. Lownds, 1681.

Grassmann, Robert. *Die Bindelehre oder Combinationslehre. Drittes Buch der Formenlehre oder Mathematik.* Stettin, 1872.

Hamilton, William Rowan. "Recent Publications on Logical Science". *Edinburgh Review* 58(1833): 194–238.

Hamilton, William Rowan. *Lectures on Metaphysics and Logic. Volumes III and IV. Logic I and II.* London: William Blackwood, 1860.

Helmholtz, Hermann von. "On the Conservation of Forces". *Popular Lectures on Scientific Subjects*, (317–362). Translated by Edmund Atkinson. New York: D. Appleton & Co., 1885.

Hibben, John Grier. *Hegel's Logic. An Essay in Interpretation*. New York: Charles Scribner's Sons, 1902.

Hume, David. *A Treatise of Humane Nature*. London: Printed for John Noon, 1738.

Hume, David. *An Enquiry Concerning Human Understanding*. In volume 2 of *Essays and Treatises on several Subjects*. London: Printed for T. Cadell, 1788.

Isidorus Hispalensis (Isidorus of Sevilla). *Isidori Hispalensis episcopi Etymologiarum sive Originum*. In J.-P. Migne, *Sancti Isidori Hispalensis Episcopi: Opera Omnia*. Paris, 1830. [No information on the year or publisher of the edition that Peirce would have consulted in found in his text. References are to "Isodorus Hispalensis about A.D. 600 refers to [obelus] as an old sign" (LoF 1), "A.D. 600 by Isidorus Hispalensis (*Etymologiarum* lib.I.cap.xxi.3) as [obelus] being an old sign" (LoF 1) and to "his great work usually called his *Origines* (lib.XIII, cap.xi.tertus 2)" (LoF 1).]

James, William. "Experience of Activity". In: *Essays in Radical Empiricism*. Edited by Ralph Barton Perry, (155–190). New York: Longman Green & Co, 1912. [Mentioned in a letter to Josiah Royce in June 30, 1913, but may refer to an earlier edition from 1909 (LoF 3).]

Jevons, William Stanley. *Pure Logic or the Logic of Quality apart from Quantity: with Remarks on Boole's System and on the Relation of Logic and Mathematics*. London: Edward Stanford, 1864. (Peirce's Library, JHU)

Jevons, William Stanley. *The Principles of Science: a Treatise on Logic and Scientific Method*. London: Macmillan & Co., 1879. [Peirce makes multiple references e.g. to Jevon's ·|· , but no specific book or source is mentioned (LoF 1).]

Jordan, Camille. *Traité des substitutions et des équations algébriques*. Paris: Gauthier-Villars, 1870.

Kant, Immanuel. *Kritik der reinen Vernunft*. Part 2 of *Sämmtliche Werke*. Edited by K. Rosenkranz & F. W. Schubert. Leipzig: L. Voss, 1838.

Kant, Immanuel. *Disputatio de mundi sensibilis atque intelligibilis forma et principiis*. Part 1 of *Sämmtliche Werke*. Edited by K. Rosenkranz & F. W. Schubert. Leipzig: L. Voss, 1838.

Kant, Immanuel. *Critique of Pure Reason*. Translated from the German of Immanuel Kant by J. M. D. Meiklejohn. London, Henry G. Bohn, 1855. (Peirce's Library, Houghton) [Heavily annotated, virtually every page up to p. 160, including extensive corrections which bear mostly on the terminology of the translation, together with extensive marginal notes on the content. A separate leaf on Bacon is glued on p. 278. Very few annotations from the beginning the second division and virtually no annotations from p. 365 onwards (Div. II, Chap. III, Sect. IV).]

Kempe, Alfred Bray. "A memoir on the theory of mathematical form". *Philosophical Transactions of the Royal Society* 177(1887): 1–70.

Kepler, Johannes. *Astronomia Nova* αιτιολογητος *seu physica coelestis, tradita commentariis de motibus stellae Martis ex observationibus G. V. Tychonis Brahe*. Heidelberg: Vogelin, 1609. [Peirce refers to this as "De Motu stellas Marties", not *Astronomia Nova*, but this is the most likely source, as it contains *De Motibus Stellae Martis* (LoF 3).]

Ladd-Franklin, Christine 1883. On the Algebra of Logic. In: C. S. Peirce (ed.), *Studies in Logic, by Members of the Johns Hopkins University*. Boston: Little, Brown & Company, 17–71.

Lambert, Johann Heinrich. *Anlage zur Architektonik, oder Theorie des Einfachen und Ersten in der philosophischen und mathematischen Erkenntnis*. Riga: Hartknoch, 1771.

Lambert, Johann Heinrich. *Neues Organon oder Gedanken über die Erforschung und Bezeichnung des Wahren und dessen Unterscheidung vom Irrthum und Schein*. Two Volumes. Leipzig: Johann Wendler, 1764. (Peirce's Library, JHU) [No marginalia.]

Lange, Friedrich Albert. *Logische Studien: Ein Beitrag zur Neubegründung der formalen Logik und der Erkenntnistheorie*. Iserlohn: J. Baedeker, 1877.

Lange, Johann Christian. *Nucleus Logicae Weisianae*. H. Müller, 1712.

Laplace, Pierre-Simon. *Théorie analytique des probabilités*. Paris: Ve. Courcier, 1812.

Laurent, Hermann. *Traité du calcul des probabilités*. Paris: Gauthier-Villars, 1873.

Legendre, Adrien-Marie. *Éléments de géométrie*. Paris: F. Didot, 1794.

Leibniz, Gottfried (Godefridus Guilielmus Leibnitius). *Meditationes de Cognitione, Veritate et Ideis*. Acta eruditorum Lipsiensum, 1684. [Peirce's own copy at Houghton Library is Leibniz's *The Monadology and Other Philosophical Writings*, translated with introduction and notes by Robert Latta, London: Oxford at the Clarendon Press, 1898, with Peirce's marginalia. His Arnault & Nicole 1861 contains the translations of the *Meditationes*.]

Leibniz, Gottfried. *Nouveaux Essais sur l'entendement humain* (New Essays on Human Understanding). In *Oeuvres philosophiques latines & francoises de feu*, Amsterdam et Leipzig: Chez Jean Schreuder, 1765.

Listing, Johann Benedict. "Vorstudien zur Topologie". *Göttingen Studien* 2(1847): 811–875.

Listing, Johann Benedict. *Vorstudien zur Topologie*. Göttingen: Vandenhoeck und Ruprecht, 1848. [Peirce's reference is: "J. B. Listing, who was a colleague of Gauss in Göttingen. He published two papers on *Topologische Studien*. One of these in an octavo publication called as well as I remember *Göttingen Studien*, or something like that, the other later on in the quarto Vandenhoeck und Ruprecht" (LoF 1).]

Listing, Johann Benedict. "der Census räumlicher Complexe, oder Verallgemeinerung des Euler'schen Satzes von den Polyädern". *Abhandlungen der Königlichen Gesellschaft der Wissenschaften zu Göttingen* 10(1862): 97–182.

Locke, John. *An Essay concerning Humane Understanding*. London: Awnsham and John Churchill, 1694. (Peirce's Library, JHU) [Second edition.]

Lutosławski, Wincenty. *The Origin and Growth of Plato's Logic; with an account of Plato's style and of the chronology of his writings*. London, New York and Bombay: Longmans, Green, and Co., 1897. (Peirce's Library, Houghton).

MacColl, Hugh. "The calculus of equivalent statements". *Proceedings of the London Mathematical Society*, 9(1877): 9–22. [Peirce's citation is "McColl, (1877)" (LoF 1). Three out of the series of eight papers were published in 1877.]

Maxwell, James Clerk. *A Treatise on Electricity and Magnetism*. Two Volumes. Oxford: Clarendon Press, 1873.

Mill, John Stuart. *A System of Logic, Ratiocinative and Inductive*. New York, 1846. [Peirce mentions "the first edition of his *System of Logic, Ratiocinative and Inductive*, published in March, 1843" (LoF 3), and that "Mill's went through 9 editions (though with the advantage of containing no special novelty)" (LoF 3). Peirce's copy at Houghton is a heavily annotated *A System of Logic, Ratiocinative and Inductive: being a connected view of the principles of evidence and the methods of scientific investigation*. Longmans, Green, and co., 1886 edition (London), "People's edition".]

Mitchell, Oscar Howard. "On a New Algebra of Logic". In *Studies in Logic by Members of the Johns Hopkins University*. Charles S. Peirce, editor. Boston: Little Brown & Company, 1883, 72–106. (Peirce's Library, Houghton)

Müller, Max. *Three Introductory Lectures on the Science of Thought*. Chicago: Open Court, 1887. [Peirce's reference is "two little books by Max Müller published by the Open Court Co. at a quarter each" (LoF 1).]

Müller, Max. *Three Lectures on the Science of Language*. Chicago: Open Court, 1889. [Peirce's reference is "two little books by Max Müller published by the Open Court Co. at a quarter each" (LoF 1).]

Murphy, Joseph John. *Habit and Intelligence Vol. II*. London: Macmillan & Co., 1869. (Peirce's Library)

Newton, Isaac. *Philosophiæ naturalis principia mathematica*. London: Jussu Societatis Regiae ac typis Josephi Streater, 1687. Glasgow: G. Brookman; London: T. T. and J. Tegg, 1833.

Ockham, William. *Tractatus Logicae*. Paris: Johann Higman, 1488. [Peirce borrowed this incunabulum of his to a Harvard graduate student, with a contract; the item's provenance is now at Houghton Library. He refers to it as "The distinction [between *objectively general* and *subjectively general*], so far as I know, was first drawn, though not very accurately, by William Ockham, as is stated in his book variously called *Summa logices, Tractatus logicae* and *Logica aurea*, Pars 1ma, cap. xiiii, and in the two following chapters is made the basis of his variety of nominalism, which denies the reality of subjective generality" ("The First Part of an Apology for Pragmaticism", R 296; LoF 3).]

Pearson, Karl. *The Grammar of Science*. 2nd edition. London: Adam & Charles Black, 1900. (Peirce's Library)

Peirce, Benjamin. *An Elementary Treatise on Plane and Solid Geometry*. Boston: James Munroe, 1837. [Charles Peirce refers from memory to his father's "textbook of Elementary Geometry, 1832" (LoF 3).]

Peirce, Benjamin. *A System of Analytic Mechanics*. Boston: Little, Brown & Company, 1855. (Peirce's Library) [Peirce probably refers to this item from memory as "1852" (LoF 3).]

Peirce, Benjamin. *Linear Associative Algebra*. New York: Van Nostrand, 1882 (1870). (Peirce's Library)

Petrus Hispanus (Hispani, Petri/John XXI). *Summulae logicales (ff. 1 r. -84 v.) followed by a Propositio exponibilis (in a different hand) elucidating obscure points in the foregoing treatise*. de Ricci, Census, 753, no. 1. 15th Century. (Peirce's Library, JHU)

Philodemus. *On Signs and Semiotic Inferences* (Περὶ Σημείων καὶ Σημειώσεων/ Περὶ Φαινομένων καὶ Σημειώσεων). T. Gomperz. *Herkulanische Studien, i Philodem über Induktionslüsse*. Leipzig: Teubner, 1865.

Prantl, Karl von. *Geschichte der Logik im Abendlande*. Three volumes. Leipzig: S. Hirzel, 1855.

Priscianus Caesariensis. *Priscianus Caesariensis Grammatici Opera, ad vetustissimorum codicum, nunc primum collatorum, fidem recensuit, emaculavit, lectionum varietatem notavit et indices locupletissimos adiecit Augustus Krehl*. Two volumes. Edited by Krehl, August Ludwig Gottlieb. Lipsiae: Weidmann, 1819–1820.

Recorde, Robert. *The Whetstone of Witte*. London: Jhon Kyngstone, 1557.

Renouvier, Charles Bernard. *Essais de critique générale*. Four volumes. Paris: Bureau de la Critique Philosophique, 1854–1864. [Peirce's citation is "Essai de philosophie critique" (LoF 3).]

Royce, Josiah. *The World and the Individual*. New York: Macmillan, 1900.

Russell, Bertrand. *The Principles of Mathematics*. Vol. 1. Cambridge: Cambridge University Press, 1903. (Peirce's Library, Houghton) [Peirce's copy is lightly annotated, and includes two EGs in the margin (p. 18): "Carroll is not right. $\overline{(q\,\overline{r})}$ $\overline{(p\,q\,\overline{r})}$ for if q is absurd $q \prec r$ and $q \prec \bar{r}$ may both be true".]

Salmon, George. *A Treatise on the Higher Plane Curves.* Dublin: Hodges, Foster & Figgis, 1879.

Sayce, Archibald Henry. "Grammar". *Encyclopaedia Britannica.* 11th edition, 1911.

Schaff, Philip. *History of the Christian Church.* Translated by Edward D. Yeomans. New York: Scribner, Armstrong & Co., 1874.

Schönflies, Arthur. "Die Entwickelung der Lehre von den Punktmannigfaltigkeiten". *Jahresbericht der deutschen Mathematiker-Vereinigung* 8, part 2(1900): 1–250.

Schröder, Ernst. *Der Operationskreis des Logikkalküls.* Leipzig: B. G. Teubner, 1877.

Schröder, Ernst. *Vorlesungen über die Algebra der Logik.* Three volumes. Leipzig: B. G. Teubner, 1890–1895.

Schubert, Hermann. *Kalkül der abzählenden Geometrie.* Leipzig: B. G. Teubner, 1879.

Sigwart, Cristoph von. *Logic.* Second edition, enlarged and revised. Translated by Helen Dendy. London: Swan Sonnenschein & Co., 1895.

Smith, James & Smith, Horace. *Rejected Addresses: or, The new theatrum poetarum.* London: John Murray, 1879.

Southey, Robert. *The Doctor.* New York: Harper & Brothers, 1836.

Stout, George Frederick. *Analytic Psychology.* London: Swan Sonnenschein & Co., 1896.

Trendelenburg, Friedrich Adolph. *Logische Untersuchungen.* Berlin: S. Hirzel, 1840.

Tucker, Abraham. *The Light of Nature Pursued.* (Together with some account of the life of the author by John Mildmay). Cambridge: Hilliard and Brown, 1831.

Ueberweg, Friedrich. *System der Logik und Geschichte der Logischen Lehren.* Bonn: Bei Adolph Marcus, 1865. (Peirce's Library, JHU)

Ueberweg, Friedrich. *System of Logic, and History of Logical Doctrines.* Translated by T. M. Lindsay. London: Longmans, Green, & Co., 1871.

Venn, John. *The Logic of Chance. An Essay on the Foundations and Province of the Theory of Probability, with Especial Reference to Its Application to Moral and Social Science.* London: Macmillan & Co., 1876. (Peirce's Library)

Venn, John. *Symbolic Logic.* First edition. London: Macmillan & Co., 1881.

Venn, John. *The Principles of Empirical or Inductive Logic.* London and New York: Macmillan & Co., 1889.

Vives, Juan Luis. "De Censura Veri". In: *De disciplinis libri XX.* Antwerp: Michael Hillenius Hoochstratanus, 1531.

Wadding, Luke (ed.). *Scotus, Duns. Ioannis Duns Scoti Opera Omnia.* Twelve Volumes, 1639. (Peirce's Library, JHU) [Peirce owned Volumes 1–4 of Duns Scotus's *Opera Omnia*, together with several other 15th and 16th century works by Scotus. Thomas of Erfurt's *Tractatus de modis significandi sive Grammatica Speculativa* is included in Volume 1 of the Wadding edition.]

Watts, Isaac. *Logick, Or, the Right Use of Reason in the Inquiry After Truth. With a variety of rules to guard against error, in the affairs of religion and human life, as well as in the sciences*. London: Printed for J. Buckland, T. Caslon etc., 1772. (Peirce's Library, JHU)

Whately, Richard. *Elements of Logic*. 4th edition. London: B. Fellowes, 1831. (Peirce's Library)

Whitehead, Alfred North. "The logic of relations, logical substitution groups, and cardinal numbers". *American Journal of Mathematics* 25(1903): 157–178.

Wilkins, John. *An Essay towards a Real Character, And a Philosophical Language*. London: Printed for Sa. Gellibrand [etc.], 1668. (Peirce's Library, JHU)

Wilson, John Cook. *On the Traversing of Geometrical Figures*. Oxford: Clarendon Press, 1905. (Peirce's Library)

Wolff, Christian. *Vernünfftige Gedancken Von den Kräfften des menschlichen Verstandes Und ihrem Richtigen Gebrauche In Erkäntnißder Wahrheit*. Halle im Magdeburgischen Renger Halle, Saale Halle, 1713. [Peirce's citation is "*Vernünftige Gedanken von den Kräften des menschlichen Verstanden*, 1710" (LoF 1).]

Woods, Frederick Adams. *Mental and Moral Heredity in Royalty*. New York: Henry Holt & Co, 1906. (Peirce's Library)

Wundt, Wilhelm Max. *Logik, eine Untersuchung der Prinzipien der Erkenntnis und der Methoden Wissenschaftlicher Forschung*. 2nd edition. Stuttgart: Ferdinand Enke, 1893–1895.

Catalogue of Peirce's Writings

This list references Peirce's writings—manuscripts, letters, papers and pieces—that have been included in Volume 1 of *Logic of the Future*. Additions of alternatives, variants and pages from collateral sources are included but not listed as separate items. The details as well as references to sources from published papers of Charles S. Peirce are included in the individual selections.

R 595 Of Reasoning in General
  Summer 1895. *Selection 4.*
R 482 On Logical Graphs
  Summer 1896–March 1897. *Selection 5*
R 488 Positive Logical Graphs (PLG)
  October–November 1896. *Selection 6*
R 480 On Logical Graphs (Acad. Graphs)
  October–November 1896. *Selection 7*
  (Includes pages from R 14.)
R 481 On Logical Graphs [Euler and EGs]
  Late 1896. *Selection 8*
R 483 [Memoir for the National Academy of Sciences on Existential Graphs]
  December 21–29, 1896. *Selection 9*
R 497 Existential Graphs [Six Papers on Existential Graphs]
  June 15, 1897. *Selection 10.1*
R 486 Existential Graphs [Six Papers on Existential Graphs]
  1897–1898. *Selection 10.2*
R 438 The Logic of Relatives [Six Papers on Existential Graphs]
  February, 1898. *Selection 10.4*
R 513 Algebra and Existential Graphs (FL, Chapter XI)
  [Six Papers on Existential Graphs]
  May 1898. *Selection 10.5*
R 339 [Existential Graphs, from the *Logic Notebook*]
  June 1898–November 1909. *Selection 28*
  (Includes R 124, "The Calculus of Existential Graphs", February 7, 1909; R 1483, "Studies of the Eight Systems of Existential Graphs"; R 1601, "[Collections], from the *Family Record*", early 1909; R S-3, "The System of Existential Graphs applied to the Examination of Itself", February 15, 1909.)
R 484 On Existential Graphs (F4)
  July–August 1898. *Selection 11*

R 495 Logical Graphs [Six Papers on Existential Graphs]
  August 1898.   *Selection 10.6*
R 502 Peripatetic Talks. No. 2 [Peripatetic Talks]
  August 1898.   *Selection 12*
R 503 Peripatetic Talks. No. 4 [Peripatetic Talks]
  August 1898.   *Selection 12*
R 504 Peripatetic Talks. No. 6 [Peripatetic Talks]
  August 1898.   *Selection 12*
R 505 Peripatetic Talks. No. 7 [Peripatetic Talks]
  August 1898.   *Selection 12*
R 489 Investigation of the meaning of (It thunders) [Peripatetic Talks]
  August 1898.   *Selection 12*
R 485 On Existential Graphs [Six Papers on Existential Graphs]
  c.1898.   *Selection 10.3*
R 493 The Principles of Logical Graphics
  c.1899.   *Selection 13*
R 515 On the First Principles of Logical Algebra
  c.1901.   *Selection 14*
R 516 On the Basic Rules of Logical Transformation
  c.1901.   *Selection 15*
R 530 A Proposed Logical Notation
  c.1901.   *Selection 16*
R 430, R 431a The Simplest Possible Mathematical System
  January–March 1902.   *Selection 17*
R 316a(s) Multitude and Continuity
  May 1903.   *Selection 18*
  (Includes pages from R S-36 and R 1584.)
R 1132 [Intention, Resolution, and Determination]
  [Reasoning, Logic and Action]
  Late 1903.   *Selection 3.3*
R 515 [A System of Existential Graphs]
  1904.   *Selection 19*
R 693b Reason's Conscience
  A Practical Treatise on the Theory of Discovery; considered as Semeiotic
  Summer 1904.   *Selection 20*
  (Includes R S-26, "The Alpha Part of Existential Graphs".)
R 145, R 145(s) Topical Geometry
  April–May 1905.   *Selection 21*
  (Includes pages from R 507, R 839, R 1575 and R S-31.)

R 253 Logical Analysis of some Demonstrations in high Arithmetic
June 1905. *Selection 22*
R 70(s) A New Deduction of the Properties of Positive Integers
August 1906. *Selection 23*
(Includes material from R 1575.)
R 616 An Appraisal of the Faculty of Reasoning
[Reasoning, Logic and Action]
c.1906. *Selection 3.2*
R 277 [Logical Graphs, from the *Prescott Book*]
May 1907–September 1910. *Selection 27*
R 201 A Contribution to the Amazes of Mathematics
Summer 1907. *Selection 24*
R 678 The Art of Reasoning Elucidated [Essays on Reasoning]
1910. *Selection 1.2*
R 654 Preface, Essays on Reasoning
1910. *Selection 1.1*
R 680 Preface, Essays on Reasoning
1910. *Selection 1.1*
R 650 Diversions of Definitions
July 20–23, 1910. *Selection 2*
R 826 Some Reveries of a Dotard [Reasoning, Logic and Action]
Late 1910. *Selection 3.1*
R 669 Assurance through Reasoning
May 25 to June 2, 1911. *Selection 26*
R 670 Assurance through Reasoning
June 7–17, 1911. *Selection 26*
R 838 [Reasoning, Logic and Action]
April 10, 1911. *Selection 3.3*
R 855–856 Logical Critique of the Creed of Religion
April 1911. *Selection 25*
(Includes pages from R 514 and R 846.)
R 838 Notes for Essay on the Justification of Reasoning
[Reasoning, Logic and Action]
February 22, 1913. *Selection 3.3*
R 683 An Essay toward Improving Reasoning in Security and in Uberty
Essays on Reasoning.
1913. *Selection 1.1*

Name Index

Abbé Gratry 499
Abbot, Francis Ellingwood 111
Albertus Magnus 420
Ammonius, Saccas 443
Apuleius, Lucius Madaurensis 195, 421
Aristotle 142, 143, 200, 630, 631; *Nota notae* 361; on axioms 421; on fallacies 151; on indices 194; on logic 420, 631; on mathematics 443; on optics 443; on postulates 420
Arnauld, Antoine 136
Augustine of Hippo 559

Bain, Alexander 423
Baldwin, James Mark 2
Boethius 420, 421, 443; on mathematics 506
Boole, George 1, 23, 389, 390, 398, 402, 409–411, 423, 424, 426, 432, 463, 499, 509, 519
Brabant, Siger de 200
Bradley's regress 51
Buchanan, James 175
Buchler, Justus 52
Buckle, Henry Thomas 175
Butler, Joseph 559

Cantor, Georg 106, 470–472, 532
Cantor, Moritz 519; *Vorlesungen uber Geschichte der Mathematik* 509
Cardano, Gerolamo 519
Carroll, Lewis 51, 650
Carus, Paul 58, 64, 70–72, 74, 75, 83–85, 113, 116
Castrén, Matthias 197
Cayley, Arthur 507, 508
Chrysippus 631
Cicero 645
Clausius, Rudolf 175
Clifford, William Kingdon 54, 67, 73, 441, 507, 562, 579
Comte, Auguste 474
Cornelius, Hans 496

Davidson, Thomas 200

De Morgan, Augustus 1, 26, 57, 256, 361, 401, 422, 423, 426–428, 559; on collections 514, 547; on notation 410, 426, 427
Dedekind, Richard 106, 440, 445, 470, 517; *Was sind und was sollen die Zahlen* 472
Descartes, René 509; *Cogito* 189; on notation 432
Dugald, Steward 443

Euclid 184, 498, 501, 574, 630; *Elements* 501, 536, 631; *pons asinorum* 108, 489, 496; on axioms 421; on mathematics 442; on postulates 420; V proposition 108
Euler, Leonhard 149, 509

Faraday, Michael 176
Fechner, Gustave Theodor 139
Fermat, Pierre de 486, 517, 608
Franklin, Christine see Ladd-Franklin, Christine
Franklin, Fabian 543
Frege, Gottlob XIII, 2, 105

Gauss, Carl Friedrich 510
Girard, Albert 519
Grassmann, Robert 410, 423
Grove, W. B. 456

Hahnemann, Samuel 152
Halley, Edmund XV
Hamilton, William Rowan 471, 639
Hegel, G.W.F. 68, 409
Hegeler, Edward C. 64
Helmholtz, Hermann von 176
Hobbes, Thomas 170
Humboldt, Alexander von 153
Huntington, Edward V. 24, 28

Isidorus of Sevilla 162, 409, 432

James, William VIII, 2, 12, 88, 91, 111, 118, 630
Jevons, William Stanley 389, 398, 410, 411, 423, 425, 427, 431, 519

Kant, Immanuel; *Critic* 170 ; on continuity of time 574 ; on hypothetical propositions 422 ; on logic 174 ; on mathematics 443 ; on regulative and constitutive principles 514 ; on the ontological proof 394
Kempe, Alfred Bray 6, 54, 67, 70, 73, 509
Körös, Csoma de 197

Ladd-Franklin, Christine 100, 424, 426, 427, 430, 543 ; *Studies in Logic* 429, 431, 452
Lange, Friedrich Albert 74, 499, 562
Laplace, Pierre-Simon 560
Lathrop, Francis August 88
Legendre, Adrien-Marie 509
Leibniz, Gottfried 149, 170, 509 ; doctrine of infinity 561 ; notation of differential calculus 486
Lejeune Dirichlet, Peter Gustav 472, 557
Listing, Johann Benedict 506, 510
Locke, John 147
Lorentz, Hendrik 148, 176
Lutosławski, Wincenty 40

MacColl, Hugh 410, 423, 452
Malebranche, Nicolas 146
Marbais, Michel de 200
Mare, William de la 202
Michaelson, Albert 148
Mill, John Stuart 443, 499, 631
Mitchell, Oscar Howard 19, 58, 398, 426, 427, 521, 543
Morley, Edward 148
Müller, Max 169, 170, 173

Newcomb, Simon 59, 80, 518, 627
Newton, Isaac XV; notation of differential calculus 486
Nicole, Pierre 136

Ockham, William 420

Parmenides 631
Peirce, Benjamin 441; definition of mathematics 442, 444–446
Peirce, Juliette 111, 117
Petrus Hispanus 420

Philodemus 631
Plato 40, 260 ; on mathematics 443
Priscianus Caesariensis 162, 195, 196
Proclus, Diadochus Lycaeus 420, 421, 442
Pythagoras 442

Raleigh, Walter 501
Recorde, Robert 430, 432
Remsen, Ira 80
Riemann, Bernhard 446, 510
Robin, Richard S. XV, 18, 48, 76, 86
Rowland, Henry A. 79, 80
Royce, Josiah 471
Russell, Bertrand 25, 105, 117
Russell, Francis C. 64, 71, 113, 114

Saussure, Ferdinand De 42
Saxonia, Albertus de 200
Sayce, Archibald 190
Schröder, Ernst 25, 28, 316, 326, 358, 391, 402, 410, 412, 423, 424, 437, 499, 517, 569, 632 ; *Logik* 518
Schubert, Hermann 440, 509
Schönflies, Arthur 532
Scotus, Duns 146, 200, 202, 394, 420
Slaughter, John W. 117
Socrates 631
Stanley, Henry Morton 153
Stout, George Frederick 117
Sylvester, James Joseph 54, 67, 73

Tarski, Alfred 20, 23
Thomas Aquinas 162, 420

Valla, Lorenzo 427
Venn, John 410, 424, 425, 427, 452, 453, 562
Vives, Juan Luis 562

Weierstrass, Karl 557
Welby, Lady Victoria 116, 117
Williamson, Alexander William 67
Wilson, John 517
Wolff, Christian 142, 420
Woods, Frederick Adams 70, 116

Zeemann, Pieter 176

Keyword Index

a priori 443
Abduction see Retroduction
Abstraction 330, 427, 498, 513, 514, 603, 605, see also Hypostatic abstraction
Absurdity 78, 108, 330, 370, 454, 461, 477, 482, 571, 572
Action 171–173, 200 ; and conduct 258, 558 ; and diagrammatic thought 618 ; and Interpretant 636 ; and volition 173 ; of the Utterer 576 ; of the writer upon the reader of a graph 597
Adicity (of a graph) 268, 272, 293
Affirmation 40, 70, 145, 521, 564 ; and denial 145, 146, 158, 571, 580
Aggregation 370, 388–390, 396, 398, 410, 411, 423, 424, 521 ; and (mathematical) addition 519 ; sign of aggregation 389
Algebra 234, 248, 289, 423, 473 ; algebraic logic 440, 445, 603, 614 ; algebraic notation 185, 191, 303, 385, 396–398, 411, 426, 431–433, 463, 569, 570, 632 ; algebraic numbers 561 ; algebraic signs 191 ; Boole's algebra of logic 399, 410, 423, 509, 519 ; dichotomic algebra 440 ; linear Associative Algebra 441 ; of dual relatives 326 ; of dyadic relations 326, 434, 439, 518 ; of the copula 24–26, 33, 40, 59–61, 63–65, 100 ; pure algebra 441 ; universal algebra of logic 164, 289, 316, 518
Alio-relation 391, 392
Analytic–Synthetic distinction 443
Anaphora 105
Arithmetic 79, 82, 162, 268, 272, 520, 521, 574 ; and semi-logical relations 274 ; arithmetic propositions 443 ; arithmetic versus logic 424, 425 ; arithmetical dyad 225 ; arithmetical propositions 256 ; arithmetical relatives 223, 227, 231
Artiad 213, 332
Assertion; dual character of 201
Association 195; by contiguity 263, 333, 394 ; by resemblance 315, 333 ; by resemblance and contiguity 638 ; inward association 600 ; outward association 601
Associative Principle 31, 387, 411, 429, 521
Associativity 234, 235, 278, 390, 403, 463, 464
Atom 155, 176 ; atomic valencies 213, 217, 562 ; symbolical atom 490, 491, 502
Atom (graph) 567
Awareness 138, 139, 145 ; contrast-awareness 143 ; of two sensations at once 140
Axiom 379; and postulates 420

Belief 159, 187, 189, 203, 258, 328, 351, see also Religion ; as base for future conduct 189, 200, 350, 351, 520, 576
Brain 141, 157 ; and thinking 158 ; hemispheres of 172

Calculus 293, 434, 454, 561 ; barycentric calculus 509 ; calculus of geometry 440 ; calculus of probabilities 434, 632 ; differential calculus 434, 486, 551, 632 ; versus logical algebra 439, 440, 445
Cardinal numbers 161–164, 169, 556
Census Theorem 212, 213, 331, 332, 506, 509, 510, see also Listing number
Chemistry 470; chemical graphs 562, 579 ; double decomposition 175 ; progress in 470 ; reasoning in chemistry 173
Chorisy 212, 213, 293, 331, 332
christian-scientist 152
Cognition; and mathematics 443 ; cognitive possibility 159 ; of perception 557
Collateral experience 621
Colligation 203, 205, 207, 230, 426
Commands see Imperatives
Common experience 81, 82, 272, 297, 394, 572, 596–598, 620, 621
Common ground 45, 620
Common sense; and existential graphs 481, 577, 580 ; as propositions not in need of proof 421
Communication 137, 144, 487, 616
Commutative Principle 31, 386, 411, 521

658 — Keyword Index

Commutativity 234, 390, 403
Composition 386, 390, 401, 403, 411, 422, 424, 521; logical composition 519; relative composition 425, 441
Consciousness 41, 138, 599; act of 201; and reasoning 631; dyadic consciousness 140; immediate consciousness 171, 204; of contrast 140–142; relational form of 171
Continuity; and Beta Graphs 503; and identity 294, 298, 328, 356, 600; and moving pictures of thought 148; and topology 508; of time 574
Continuum 212, 507, 599; and universe 394; line continuum 513; of dyads of unity 273; of verbs 296, 300; peneperfect 590; perfect 590; pseudo continuum 590; quasi-pene 590; quasi-perfect 590
Copula 401, 422, 465; and Boole 402; and conjunction 426–428, 431; and negation as primitive 410; copulative conjunction 464; copulative proposition 223; transformations of graphs 230, 231, 423; transitiveness of 361
Corollarial; vs. theorematic reasoning 109, 501, 536
Critic 52, 188; logical critic 548, 563, 570; of deduction 568; of induction 551
Cyclic systems 532, 534, 536–546
Cyclosis 212, 213, 220–222, 241, 293, 331, 332

Deduction 549, 577, see also Reasoning, necessary; and apodicticity 561; and Existential Graphs 551; and mathematics 446; and real 551, 553, 564; probable and necessary 560, 565, 566, 577
Destiny; as a modality 89, 312
Diagram 137, 292, 351, 618; and icon 190, 347, 618; and maps 164; and mathematics 185, 489; diagrammatic syntax 312, 313, 566, 577; diagrammatic thought 444; Euclidean 631; Eulerian 74, 82–84, 86, 282, 283, 285, 427, 429, 431, 457, 519, 562

Diagrammatization; of assertions 562; perfection 229
Dialogue; dialogical thinking 40, 498
Dimensionality 260, 507; and moving pictures of thought 148; graph of lowest dimensionality 212, 292; of the Phemic Sheet 503; plane projection of graphs 137
Ding an sich 334
Disposition 146, 186, 636
Distributive principle 31, 403, 411
Doctrine of Chances see Probability
Doctrine of connectivity 510
Doubt 159, 446
Duplication 232, 235

Economy; scientific 49, 149, 155, 200
Ecthesis 536
Ego and non-ego 394
Electricity 138
Endoporeutic principle 20, 50, 79, 80, 168, 578
Ens Rationis 512
Entitative graphs 236, 249, 252, 312, 315–317, 333, 351, 397, 401, 567, 569, 579; ideal Graphs 249
Epicurean logic 631
Equiparance 449, 520, 521
Ethics; and logic 1, 557; of notation 100, 102, 411, 419, 426, 427, 519; of terminology 147, 389, 410, 419
Existential Graphs 236, 477, see also Endoporeutic principle, Grapheus, Graphist, Hook, Line of Identity, Nex, Replica, Rhema, Selective, Sheet, Spot; advantages 250; Alpha Graphs 490, 492, 502, 503, 505, 511; Alpha, Beta and Gamma Graphs 490, 511; Alpha, Beta and Gamma graphs 511; and everyday ideas 472; area 165–169, 174, 382, 383, 479, 481–483, 490–496, 503–505, 511, 519, 552, 564, 571–573, 575, 578–580, 582, 584, 616, 617, 628; as moving pictures of thought 148; Beta Graphs 503, 511; Beta graphs 58; constitutive conventions 328; evenly enclosed 167–169, 217, 230–233, 237, 241, 247–250, 275,

279, 280, 286, 287, 293, 317, 355, 357, 379, 451, 452, 466, 491, 519, 564, 571 ; Gamma Graphs 490, 511, 513 ; juxtaposition 289, 295, 300, 457, 464 ; nest 109, 167, 168, 492–495, 503, 504, 614 ; oddly enclosed 167, 168, 174, 230, 232, 233, 237, 241, 250, 275, 286–288, 290, 293, 317, 318, 335, 355, 357, 379, 451, 491, 495, 519, 564, 572, 575, 614 ; oppleted 109, 490, 492, 505 ; place of the cut 29, 168, 382, 479, 482, 492, 503, 504 ; Positive Logical Graphs 78 ; pseudograph 108, 477, 484 ; rules of 252 ; scroll 109, 169, 174, 404–406, 483, 484, 492, 494, 495, 503–505, 582, 583 ;
semi-significant 237 ; sheet of assertion 14, 165–167, 385, 386, 394, 395, 400, 401, 413, 490–496, 511, 615 ; tincture 21, 22, 90, 117, 565, 572, 629 ; to scribe 158, 165–168, 174, 178, 179, 382, 383, 477–479, 481–488, 490–492, 494–496, 503–505, 510, 520, 535, 545, 551–553, 564, 566, 567, 569, 570, 572, 573, 575, 579, 583, 584, 614–617, 628, 629 ; uncircled 221, 222 ; unenclosed 217, 218, 220, 237, 284, 287, 451

Experience 39, 89, 141, 172, 238, 258, 274, 298, 299, 312, 313, 315, 334, 349, 350, 370, 415, 497, 500, 503, 572, 576 ; of the hearer 193 ; possible 312 ; scientific 419 ; sense 334

Experimentation 298; and graphs 42, 598 ; and icons 205 ; and mathematics 463 ; and perception 142 ;
Michaelson–Morley experiment 148 ; results of ideal experimentation 260

Feeling 140, 157, 171 ; feeling-qualities 349 ; pure feeling 634 ; qualities of feeling 599, 634
Firstness 349, 599 ; as monadism 349
Free will 548, 558

Geometry 185, 440 ; and graphs 165, 462 ; axioms of Euclid 421 ; descriptive 507 ; enumerative 509 ; Euclidean 442, 498, 509 ; figure 190, 435 ; graphics 507, 509 ; postulates 420 ; projective 443, 507 ; pure 507
Gesture 194, 199
Graph; chemical graphs 213 ; imbalanced polar 217 ; polar 216, 217 ; versus Calculus 472
Graph-Instance 165, 478, <u>see also</u> Replica
Grapheus; as *advocatus diaboli* 295, 302
Graphist 22, 504
Graphist and Interpreter 158, 486
Graphs; and symbolical atom 491
Growth 559

Habit 147, 172, 186, 189, 350, 351, 457, 487, 496, 572, 576, 636 ; and belief 190, 350 ; and reasoning 184, 187 ; and sign 635 ; and symbol 313 ; as law 558 ; habit-representations 349 ; of mind 486 ; of reasoning 138, 315 ; of thinking 151 ; of thought 173
Holding 588
Homeopathy 152
Hook 486, 518
Hopkinsian <u>see</u> Quantifier
Human reason 152
Hypnotism 152, 172
Hypostatic abstraction 512–514 ; and gamma graphs 513

Icon 192, 202, 600 ; and assertion 360 ; and inference 205 ; and likeness 191 ; and potentials 194 ; composite 203 ; composite and complex 202 ; iconic index 638 ; iconicity of relations in EG 385, 387, 534, 618 ; index of an icon 196
Ideal Graphs <u>see</u> Entitative Graphs
Ideograph 196, 197, 269, 272, 273, 295, 296, 300, 302, 303, 370 ; direct 295 ; logical 240 ; simplified 240, 242
Idoseme (Eidoseme) 638
Illation 23, 25, 231, 234, 235, 243–245, 247, 278, 281 ; and inference 189 ; of index into an icon 315
Imperatives (exclamations, commands) 194, 485, 572, 576, 637
Inchoate proposition 315
Inchoateness of Being 589

Incompossibility 392
Indecomposable; transformations 385
Indefinite individual 393, 395–397, 435, 439, 581
Indefiniteness 145, 512, 520, 532, 578 ; and collection 514 ; qualitative 145 ; quantitative 145
Indesignate individual 300, 302, 303
Indeterminateness 296, 630 ; of interpretant 599
Index 191–194, 200–202, 334, 637 ; and brute force 313, 330, 333 ; and brute reaction 600 ; and inference 207 ; and reaction 313, 315 ; complex 202 ; composite 203 ; iconic index 638 ; indefinite 289, 372 ; index of an icon 196 ; pure 333
Individualism 631
Induction 260, 420, 549, 551, 560 ; Socratic 631
Inference; and Existential Graphs 173 ; and mathematics 149 ; and observation 205–207, 501 ; immediate 203 ; in Existential Graphs 289 ; modes of 148, 311, 449 ; rational 189, 205 ; theoric 533
Infimal graphs 331
Infinitesimals 49, 149
Infinity 440, 471, 561, 618 ; and chances 371, 560 ; infinite multitude 491 ; logarithmic 424
Instinct 183
Intention 186, 199, 572 ; intentional and unintentional attention 143
Interpretant 137, 190, 330, 514, 599, 634, 636 ; actual 515, 638 ; and diagram 618 ; dynamic 45, 618, 634, 638 ; eventual 618 ; genuine 634 ; immediate 634 ; individual 634 ; intended 633 ; middle 45 ; nature of 633 ; normal 633 ; passion of 633 ; representative 515, 516 ; trifissility of 515
Interpreter 158, 275, 298, 299, 572, 573, 576, 577, 617, see also Graphist and Interpreter ; and delineator 333 ; and deliverer 79, 81, 272, 275, 298, 370 ; and individual signs 435 ; and proper names 263, 415, 635 ; and sign 349, 576 ; and universals 393 ; as opponent of truth 80, 275 ; mental map of 299
Interpreter and Deliverer; common experience of 294, 298
Intuition 183, 326 ; and inference 189

Knowledge 206, 445 ; and observation 205, 207 ; and probability 560 ; apodictic 445 ; earliest conscious 548, 557, 563 ; knowing that one knows 639 ; lover of 153 ; uncriticizable 394 ; wide, deep & accurate 153, 154

Languages; and Existential Graphs 275, 336 ; and logic 354, 583 ; and rhema 414 ; and thought 137 ; and verb-substantive 196 ; Aryan 196, 414 ; Basque 198 ; Egyptian 194 ; gesture-language 194, 199 ; Greek 415, 420, 631 ; Indo-European 190 ; inflected 192 ; Inuktitut 190, 197 ; Irish 198 ; Latin 420 ; Native American 198 ; placing the subject before the predicate 520 ; Samoyedic 197 ; Semitic 415 ; Tibetan 197
Law 371, 548, 558, 559, 599 ; and habit 351 ; and uniformity 631 ; as mental 598 ; laws of dynamics 558 ; laws of nature 183, 497 ; laws of thought 144 ; of mind 191, 198
Leading principle; logical 27
Ligature 168, 484, 575, 580, 583
Line of Identity 473, 569, 573, 575, 578 ; and endoporeusis 578 ; and graphs 580 ; and Loose end 212, 217–219, 228, 229, 256, 289, 318, 331, 369 ; and teridentity 569, 583 ; furcation 583
Listing number 212, 213, 331, 332, 590
Logic; and science 188, 349 ; as a science of the security of thinking 147
Logica Utens 467
Logical breadth & depth 285, 286, 422, 436, 615
Logical equivalence 22, 26, 76, 78, 93, 94, 101, 195, 199, 202, 217, 267, 277, 279, 281, 294, 296, 300, 322, 353–356, 363–366, 421, 429, 430, 571

Logical Graphs see Entitative Graphs, see Existential Graphs, see Graphs
Logical machines 316, 440, 532

Map; and Diagrams 164
Map-coloring problem 502, 510
Mathematics 497–502 ; and logic 349, 433 ; and multiplication 425 ; and unmechanical theoric reasoning 533 ; as a branch of logic 440, 445 ; as science of quantity 442, 506 ; definition of 442 ; progress in 470 ; pure 170, 446, 632 ; reasoning in 147, 182, 184, 201, 232, 443, 471, 489, 512 ; simplest possible 452
Meaning; and Existential Graphs 168 ; as future conduct 258, 630 ; of Existential Graphs 313
Methodeutic XVI, 2, 49, 95, 118, 188 ; of theorematic reasoning 541
Mind 138, 184, 185, 190, 191, 313, 333, 486, 568, 570, 576, 636 ; and object 144, 192 ; mental icon 195, 201 ; nature's mind 205, 207 ; personal mind as egotistical anacoluthon 205 ; state of 351
Mind–Body distinction 138, 171, 204
Modality XVI, 89, 158, 159, 371, 589, 594 ; subjective possibility 22
Modus ponens 33, 60, 173
Modus tollens 174
Mood 178; declarative 194 ; imperative 195, 485 ; indicative 194 ; interrogative 195, 485 ; potential 194
Multitude 161, 402, 436, 471, 491 ; and dyadic relations 324 ; and plural 589 ; finiteness of 527 ; of whole and irrational numbers 574

Necessitarianism 631
Necessity 258, 512, 513 ; and Beta graphs 511 ; logical 264 ; real 159
Nex 236, 238, 239, 241, 331 ; nex-branch 238
Nota Notæ 361
Nominalism 631
Nonions 441
Novenions 440

Obelus 99, 387, 397, 409, 431, 432, 439, 519, 520, 646
Object (of a sign) 137, 514, 576, 633, 634, 636, 637 ; bifiss 515 ; dynamic 634 ; dynamical 638 ; immediate 634 ; quasi-real 514 ; real 634, 638
Omniscience 465
Onoma 611
Ontological proof 394
Ordinal numbers 149, 161, 532

Pasigraphy 561
Peg 544, 568, 583
Peirce's Puzzle 119
Peirce's Rule 25, 36, 40, 63
Peircian see Quantifier
Perception 183; and knowledge 548, 563 ; and mental constructions 557 ; and reasoning 557 ; objects of perceptual reaction 394
Perissid 213, 332, 508
Photograph; iconicity and indexicality of 190, 638
Physiology; and conduct 558 ; versus mental 138
Pons asinorum see Euclid
Port Royal Logic 136
Positive Graphs see Existential Graphs
Positivism 152
Possibilities 158, 400, 514, 552, 589, 617, 618 ; and Beta graphs 511 ; and icon 313 ; and tints 572 ; can-bes 171 ; logical 223 ; may-bes 144, 146, 566, 576 ; objective 512 ; rationally possible 159 ; subjective 511 ; would-bes 144, 146, 171, 576
Potentials 589
Pragmaticism XIII, XIV, 2, 38, 91, 96, 106, 107, 111, 118, 119, 121, 470, 472, 586, 595, 596 ; pseudo- 152
Predication 465, 512, 580 ; particular predicate 536
Prescissive abstraction 513
Principle of contradiction 142, 144, 145, 158–160, 178, 387, 388, 393, 395, 396, 512, 514, 611 ; and double encircling 242 ; and elimination 235, 249

Principle of contraposition 231, 251, 279, 341, 380, 382, 521
Principle of excluded contradiction 26
Principle of excluded middle 26, 82, 142, 144, 145, 158–160, 178, 387, 388, 393–395, 403, 413, 417, 423, 435, 512, 513, 611 ; and distribution 235, 249 ; and double encircling 242
Probability 402, 409, 423, 496 ; mathematical 560 ; numerical 149
Probable error 155
Proper names XIII, 82, 190, 238, 263, 268, 269, 272, 294, 298, 299, 313–315, 333, 370, 393, 395, 396, 413–416, 418, 428, 485, 488, 512, 520, 536, 540, 541, 613, 635
Proposition; ancipital 480 ; conditional 89, 387, 388, 421, 422, 569, 582 ; copulative 223, 248, 273, 386, 421, 422, 480, 549 ; definition of 263 ; general 45 ; indefinite 45 ; individual 297 ; singular 393
Proto-graphs 58, 84
Psychology 146, 157, 170, 203, 557, 563 ; and logic 137, 171, 510 ; psychophysical psychology 181
Psychophysical 139–141
Purpose; quasi-purpose 150

Qualia 597
Quality 292, 334, 464
Quantifier 99, 101, 260, 326, 398, 433, 439 ; non-standard 94
Quasi-mind 45, 616
Quasi-proposition 84
Quaternions 235, 551

Ramal (many-to-one) relation 324
Reaction; and existence 159, 394, 496 ; and Interpreter 596, 598 ; and proposition 335 ; between mind and body 204 ; perceptual reaction 394 ; sense-reaction 333 ; will-reaction 349
Real 146; absolute reality 393 ; modes of 178 ; real active force 297 ; real and ratiocinative modality 159 ; real fact 150 ; real necessity 159 ; realism 632 ; realism and nominalism 631 ; reality of possibilities 146 ; scholastic realism 170
Reasoning 41, 189, 283 ; and free will 558 ; and graphs 148, 378 ; and obligation 182 ; and ratiocination 189 ; as self-controlled thought 173, 205, 486, 548 ; demonstrative 206 ; dissection of 445 ; experimental 207 ; fourth form of 550, 560, 561, 563 ; good and bad 557 ; necessary 174, 500, 533, 536, 565 ; prerequisite of 152 ; probable 557 ; theoric 533, 536 ; three types of 548 ; utilitarian 419
Relation 311, 336, 412
Religion (theology) 549; faith 557, 563 ; virtues 162
Replica 490–492, 502–505, 520 ; entire 491, 504 ; graph-replica 519 ; instantaneous 491 ; partial 491, 504
Residuation see Peirce's Rule
Resistance and Effort 172, 173, 313, 315
Resolution 186, 187
Resolve 158, 200
Retroduction XVI, 330, 549, 551, 557, 572
Rhema 21, 59, 66, 79, 87, 94, 97, 348, 369, 413–415
Rhetoric; speculative 200

Science; and psychology 144 ; and religion 548, 549 ; nomological and normative sciences 497 ; scientific inquiry 206 ; scientific prejudice 559
Scriptibility 6, 60, 99, 100, 339, 340, 345–347, 399, 400, 402–407, 409, 410, 412, 413, 602, 608
Second intention; characters of 223, 253, 256 ; manipulation of 231 ; relatives of 223, 253 ; verbs of 274
Secondness 349; as brute reaction 599 ; as dyadism 349 ; degenerate and generous 599
Selective 518; particular 193 ; pronoun 193, 334, 354, 637 ; universal 193, 202
Self 258

Self-control 496, see also reasoning, as self-controlled thought ; and thought 173, 559
Semi-logical; medad and monad 273 ; triad 273 ; triad of duality 273 ; triad of triality 274 ; verb 272
Sensation 40, 135, 139–144, 157, 171, 556, 637
Set 238, 336, 379, 433, 436, 437, 441, 603
Sheet 284, 351, 490, 510 ; blank 304, 313, 400, 495 ; of affirmation 164 ; of assent 14 ; of assertion 28, 107, 164, 178, 385, 400, 491, 492, 511 ; of the graph 596 ; of truth 107, 478–484 ; Phemic 503, 553, 564, 566, 567, 570, 573, 579, 628 ; recto and verso 618 ; spread of 285
Sign 41, 638 ; and knowledge 190 ; and proposition 426 ; and representation 514 ; as a consciousness of a habit 616 ; collectional 570 ; complete 490, 636 ; dicisign 84, 515, 516 ; functional 569 ; incomplete 427 ; legisign 635 ; of identity 567 ; of negation 569 ; originals of 636 ; overtness of 636 ; primisign 84 ; qualisign 635 ; quasi-conventional 334 ; singular 533 ; sinsign 635 ; suadisign 84 ; sumisign 84 ; triadicity of 190, 313, 315, 333, 600, 636, 638 ; trifility of 514
Space and time 148
Spatial 135, 148, 194, 498, 630
Speculative Grammar 199
Speculative Rhetoric see Methodeutic
Spiritualistic 152
Spot 212, 217, 292, 485 ; ends of 213 ; of teridentity 568
Stereoscopy 49, 148
Stoics; and hypotheticals 421 ; and logic 631
Syllogism 173, 499, 522, 532, 562 ; and graphs 283 ; Barbara 501, 523 ; Celarent 523 ; Darii 347, 523 ; Ferio 523 ; Frisesomorum 499 ; rule of 346 ; spurious 256, 283 ; syllogistic principle 259
Symbol 191, 195, 200, 601, 617 ; and copula 201 ; term/proposition/argument 600

Telepathy 206

Teridentity; graph of 569 ; spot of 568
Terms; definite 512 ; individual 394, 395 ; singular 99, 395
Theorematic see Corollarial vs. theorematic reasoning
Thirdness 599; as mediation 349 ; degenerescent 599 ; generous 599 ; perdegenerate 599
Thought see also Dialogue, Dialogical thinking; and language 137 ; and signs 136 ; directed upon itself 204 ; grammatical analysis of 158 ; theoric 533 ; unit of 190
Token 43, 633, 634
Tone 633, 634
Topical Geometry see Topology
Topology 506–509
Transformability 6, 99–101, 289, 304, 306–308, 314, 328, 338, 339, 341, 344, 345, 347, 399, 400, 402–412, 416, 450, 452, 601, 602
Transformation rules; abstraction 231, 613 ; conjugation 240 ; contraposition 240 ; copulation 231 ; deiteration 495, 584 ; deletion 584 ; development 251 ; disjunction 230, 231, 422, 423 ; distribution 235, 249 ; diversification 230, 231, 233, 239 ; double encirclement 239 ; duplication 230, 232, 235 ; elimination 231, 235, 249, 251 ; erasure 492, 612 ; erasure and drawing 317 ; evolution 231, 235, 247, 248, 251 ; extraction 230 ; first illative 318 ; fusion 240, 248 ; generation 231 ; identification 239, 613 ; insertion 231, 232, 235, 239, 251, 473, 492, 494, 584 ; intraction 230 ; involution 231, 235, 247, 251 ; iteration 235, 239, 473, 495, 584, 613 ; mutual annulment 239, 248 ; omission 231, 235, 239, 248, 251, 473, 494 ; protraction 239 ; reassociation 240 ; second illative 318 ; segmentation 240, 248 ; severance 239 ; simple omission 380 ; unification 230, 232, 235
Transformations of graphs 382, 386, 394, 450, 458 ; basic formal rules 328, 337, 601 ; basic rules 304 ; basic rules of logi-

cal transformation 399 ; basic seven rules 602 ; derived illative 240 ; diversification 243 ; dozen basic formal rules 601 ; drawing conclusions automatically 584 ; elementary rules of illative transformation deduced from the basic rules 338 ; first illative permission 584 ; five rules 473 ; fundamental illative 239 ; hypothetical principle of graphical transformation 362 ; illative 231, 279, 311, 312, 361, 379, 583 ; indecomposable 385 ; inductive principle of graphical transformation 361 ; insertion 243 ; nine basic rules 313 ; omission 243 ; postulates of Alpha part 505 ; ratiocinative 230 ; second illative permission 584 ; six fundamental permissions 492 ; transformation of the Boolian 520

Triadic relations 311; and inference 174 ; and reasoning 173 ; intellectuality of 598 ; irreducibility of 214, 332, 513 ; of communication 137 ; of giving 218, 518 ; quale/relate/sign 597 ; sign/object/interpretant 634 ; triad of duality 273 ; triad of identity 278–280 ; triad of non-triality 274 ; triad of oddness 274 ; triad of severality 273 ; triad of triality 274 ; triad of unity 273 ; triadic verb 268

Truth 393

Tune see Tone

Tuone 634, see also Tone

Type; and graph 490 ; and signs 634 ; of meaningless proposition 263

Uberty 48, 135, 147, 490

Uniformity; and induction 631 ; of physical universe 559

Universe 444, 522 ; and propositions as signs of it 426 ; as common ground 351, 415 ; inwardly experiential 330 ; limit of 317 ; logical terms bound to 70 ; mathematical 500 ; of actuality 327 ; of discourse 238, 272, 275, 305, 370 ; of existence 360 ; of existents 512 ; of metaphysical possibility 572 ; real 297 ; total 393

Utterer; and particulars 393 ; and proper names 415

Utterer and Interpreter 145, 393, 520

Vagueness 205, 238, 295, 299, 300, 302, 303, 512, 548, 589, 597 ; of signs 334 ; of terms 334

Valental graphs 82, 212–217, 293, 312, 314, 331, 332

Verb 178, 195, 263, 268, 269, 275, 280, 281, 294, 311, 336, 352, 360, 369, 379, 414, 415, 577, 578 ; arithmetic 272 ; logical 272 ; meaningless 296 ; unanalyzed 302

Verification 151, 157, 205

Vexed questions of logic 3, 84, 85, 99, 111, 120, 517, 596

Vinculum 28, 57, 58, 62, 98, 385, 387, 388, 390, 519, 569, 632

Volition; and action 173 ; and assertion 201 ; and objects of mathematics 498 ; as action and reaction 201

Zeemann effect 176

www.ingramcontent.com/pod-product-compliance
Lightning Source LLC
Chambersburg PA
CBHW020601300426
44113CB00007B/467